The War on Sex

The War on Sex

Western Repression from the Torah to Victoria

Chad Denton

McFarland & Company, Inc., Publishers
Jefferson, North Carolina

LIBRARY OF CONGRESS CATALOGUING-IN-PUBLICATION DATA

Denton, Chad, 1981–
The war on sex : Western repression from the
Torah to Victoria / Chad Denton.
    p.   cm.
Includes bibliographical references and index.

ISBN 978-0-7864-9504-7 (softcover : acid free paper) ∞
ISBN 978-1-4766-1661-2 (ebook)

1. Sex—History. 2. Sex customs—History. 3. Sex—
Religious aspects—History.   I. Title.
HQ21.D44 2014   306.709—dc23   2014037030

BRITISH LIBRARY CATALOGUING DATA ARE AVAILABLE

© 2015 Chad Denton. All rights reserved

*No part of this book may be reproduced or transmitted in any form
or by any means, electronic or mechanical, including photocopying
or recording, or by any information storage and retrieval system,
without permission in writing from the publisher.*

Cover image © iStock/Thinkstock

Printed in the United States of America

*McFarland & Company, Inc., Publishers
Box 611, Jefferson, North Carolina 28640
www.mcfarlandpub.com*

For my idols,

Donald M. Nicol, Antonia Fraser,
and Louis Crompton,

who all taught me in their own ways
that history is about so much more than just
the victors and the "respectable."

Table of Contents

Acknowledgments xi
Preface 1
Introduction 3

I. The Torah 7

Sex and Purity 8
Leviticus 18:22 and 20:13 10
Female Sexuality and Its Male Victims 13

II. Ancient Greece and the First Sexologists 18

Old-Fashioned Greek Values 19
Homer and Hesiod, Sappho and Achilles 20
The Greeks Contemplate Pederasty 24
Sex, Honor and Hybris 30

III. The Decadent Past, from Alexander the Great to Antinuous 34

Sex in the Hellenistic World 34
When Romans Were Romans 37
Fornication, Marriage and Scandal under the Republic 39
Imperial Interventions 43
Perverts and Prostitutes 45
Celibacy and Sex for Pleasure 51
Punishing Desire in the Afterlife 53

IV. Rise of a New Order 56

When East Meets West 57
Sex and the New Testament 60
The Church Fathers versus Sex 64
Sex under the Late Roman Empire 69
Escaping the World 77

V. The War on Sin 80

Justinian I and the End of Antiquity 81
Sex under Irish and Welsh Law 84
Sex under Germanic Law 86
Choosing Holiness 89
Imposing Holiness 95
The Islamic Alternative 101

VI. Medieval Rigidness 107

Triumph of the Church 109
The Theology of Sex 114
Jews in a Christian World 117
On the Frontier: Scandinavia and Slavic Europe 119
Sex and (Imagined) Love 121
Civilization's Sewer 126
Invasion of the Sodomites 129
Sinners Defiant 134
Savonarola's Florence 137

VII. The Sensual Empire: Turkey, 1453–1800 139

Sharia Law, Civil Law and Sex 140
Beardless Youths 142
In the Harem 144
The War on Prostitution 147

VIII. Reforming and Reaffirming 149

The Reformers versus Sex 150
Sex in Protestant Europe 153

Table of Contents

Heaven on Earth: Calvin's
Geneva and Cromwell's England   159
Sex in Catholic and Orthodox Europe   162
The Radicals of the Reformation   170
The Erotic Side of the Printing Press   172
Deporting Morals   175
Rationalizing Sex   184

IX. Enlightened Bedrooms, 1700–1814   189

The Philosophes Debate Sex   191
The Age of Decadence   199
The Age of Reform   204
Tribads and Mollys   211
The Pornographic Underground   215
Sex under the First Republic and Napoleon   218

X. A Brave New World   222

A Bourgeois Mentality   224
Imposing Decency   230
Invasion of the Inverts   233
Indecency for Mass Consumption   237
The Science of Sex   239
Radicals versus (or for) Sex   240

Epilogue: The Thaw   243

Chapter Notes   249
Bibliography   267
Index   277

Acknowledgments

First I am grateful to all the dear friends, colleagues, and professors whom I coerced into commenting on drafts of my book as it took shape or who were captive audiences to some ideas related to the book as I was formulating them in my head. Many thanks must go to Linda Reeder, Ilyana Karthas, Elisa Glick, Lauren Martella, Chris Deutsch, Michelle Branco, Matt Stanley, Daniel Conner, Jennifer Wiard, Chuck Cottrell, Nathan Shumate, and Josh Rice. I cannot possibly name all the people who have given me support, sometimes without realizing it, but they too have my thanks.

Also I thank the librarians at George Mason University, the University of Virginia, Sweet Briar College, and the University of Missouri and offer my most sincere apologies for the countless overdue books resulting from this project.

Preface

The War on Sex was born, when I was still a master's student at George Mason, as a vague idea to write something about how societies tend to idealize the past and project their own anxieties about morality onto history as well as the present. At the same time, I was becoming interested in pursuing the history of sexuality, especially forbidden expressions of sexuality, in my academic work, so inevitably this project expanded into a general exploration of how sex was controlled, and how regulations on sex were defied, in European history. I could not help but see how the topic of sex and sexuality kept reappearing as the means by which individuals and societies defined what was good and ideal and what was corrupt and decadent. Still, I believe the original concept was not left that far behind, as if anything I acknowledge how sex, even if just between the lines, shapes how we view the past from "decadent" Rome to "prim" 1950s America.

Overall my goal has been to write a narrative about the political, legal, and cultural forces that tried to contain consensual sex and the individuals and movements that defied them in European history. Of course, this does mean I focus more on the illicit, especially prostitution and homosexuality, but I also explore topics dealing with marriage, contraception, and abortion. I do believe any discussion of sex and its regulation is incomplete without addressing access to contraception and the ability to form or end a social and legal relationship between spouses. When it comes to the different sexual topics and diverse cultures found in Europe, I have tried to cast as wide a net as possible, but like any historian I have been limited by the sources available to me—something that holds doubly true for a survey of this scale.

For the reader, I want this book to be many things, from a general reference for students of sexuality in history to an enjoyable introduction for a curious nonacademic reader to the sort of topics that are still usually not taught in high school or college introductory history courses, except maybe in fleeting naughty anecdotes to grab the attention of students. Most of all, I hope, like many writers do, that the obsession that inspired me to write this book and fueled my efforts in the first place will prove infectious.

Introduction

What's the problem with sex?

It was a question that the culture around me took for granted. I was born and grew up near Lynchburg, Virginia, the capital of the formidable media empire of the televangelist Jerry Falwell, who proclaimed, "Any sex outside of the marriage between a man and a woman is violating God's law,"[1] and, "AIDS is not just God's punishment for homosexuals; it is God's punishment for a society that tolerates homosexuals."[2] Falwell was also the founder of Liberty University, where students are trained to combat the United States' "secular liberalism" and learn in an environment that strives to be scrubbed clean of stereotyped campus hedonism. This is ensured through iron-clad rules ranging from those preventing students from spending the night with a significant other on or off campus down to those dictating how much physical contact is allowed on a date.

Even though I was not raised in an evangelical Christian household, Falwell's shadow still seeped into my adolescence. For starters, there was guilt by association. I was a high school student when the film *Escape from LA* was released, in which Lynchburg is named as the capital of a theocratic, near-future dystopian United States. Closer to home, when my high school's nurse had the audacity to begin teaching popular classes on birth control, a student Christian group prayed that "God would send the right person" to replace her. In spite of this environment and the advocacy of some of the school's Christian teens, I doubt my high school had fewer teenagers at least dipping their toes into the realm of sex than any other in the country.

To be fair, though, mixed messages about sex abounded everywhere for me, even far outside Lynchburg. One of the hit sitcom *Seinfeld*'s most famous and oft-quoted yet transgressive episodes was obviously all about masturbation, yet the word itself was not uttered once. President Bill Clinton was being simultaneously mocked and chastised by media pundits who obsessed over details like whether he received oral sex right in the Oval Office, how exactly a cigar came into play during their lovemaking, and Monica Lewinsky's semen-stained dress. Maybe the question should not be "What's the problem with sex?" but rather "Why is society repulsed and fascinated by sex in equal measures?"

The philosopher Michel Foucault, who would have gotten at least one entire book out of the Clinton sex scandal, opened his influential, multivolume study *The History of Sexuality* with the question, "Do we say, with so much passion and so much resentment against our most recent past, against our present, and against ourselves, that we are repressed?"[3] Today, depending completely on who is asked, Western society has either become too liberated or is still too repressed, and issues like the British tabloid press's focus on the various sexual peccadilloes of the British royal family seem to actually support both assertions at the same time. Celebrities, politicians, and even criminal suspects have their sexual sins, alleged or confessed, scrutinized on 24/7 news cycles, while "experts" pronounce judgment solemnly on whether they are worthy of redemption or are outright sociopaths to be scorned. Meanwhile an open fixation with—if not outright celebration of—lust and sex pervades the news, films, TV shows, and even fast-food commercials. Foucault himself argued that the Victorians, however much they tried to regulate sex and the body with the power of the bureaucrat and the doctor, also wrote and talked and thought about sex a great deal, perhaps with more candor and frankness than even we do today. Although in the post–Sexual Revolution age few people in Western countries think we are still trapped in the (allegedly) suffocating culture of Victorian Britain, something similar might be said about Western civilization at the dawn of the new millennium.

This book is an effort to untangle the various reasons underlying Western society's complex relationship with the biological realities of sex by looking at the history of how sex was controlled via society, culture, and law. Although I am not laying down any kind of grand theory of sex in Western history, I do emphasize continuity. The archeologist Timothy Taylor theorized, based on prehistoric artifacts, that the sexual landscape of Western people's distant ancestors would not be completely unrecognizable today, with knowledge of effective birth control and sadomasochistic ideas among other things, existing even among agricultural villages from before the dawn of written history.[4] My approach in his book asserts that historical evidence from antiquity to the early modern period similarly reveals more traits that are recognizable than are alien.

The other point that recurs here is that the history of sexuality in the West is much more complex than many people, even some academics, suggest. The traditional narrative is that Europe moved from a period of sexual freedom into an era of intense oppression. From the Enlightenment, Europe gradually discovered sexual liberation again, but not before it experienced a different and in some ways even more stifling form of oppression embodied in the Victorian period. As with all time-worn grand narratives, there is some truth here. For example, the type of sexual behavior that would have caused a man to be just mocked as an effeminate by a playwright like Aristophanes in ancient Athens would have gotten him burned alive in many places through much of the Later Middle Ages or forced into therapy, at best, in the 19th century.

At the same time, the actual story of how sex was regulated, and how people defied those regulations, is not nearly as clear cut. Rather than ancient Athens being a safe haven for same-sex desire, it was a place where the concept of pederasty was actually hotly debated and where the roots of modern homophobia may be discerned. Likewise, Europe in the Middle Ages was home to a surprisingly lewd literary culture and nuns and monks who felt free to prescribe recipes for contraceptives. Very few of the champions of the Enlightenment advocated anything resembling our idea of sexual freedom. Jean-Jacques Rousseau, often hailed as one of the architects of modern liberalism, railed against the expression of female sexuality and assumed masturbation was one of the greatest evils that could completely destroy a young man's life.

Theorists like David Halperin have suggested that the history of sexuality is actually best understood in terms of drastic shifts in mentality, so much so that one cannot even accurately use the word "sexuality" to describe the sexual attitudes and experiences of people living before the modern era. Halperin's view is of particular importance to homosexuality, which, according to him, has to be understood as a purely modern phenomenon.[5] I instead agree with the historian Helmut Puff, who, when discussing homosexuality in the premodern world, wrote, "Homosexuals ... are not absent from ancient texts, nor is the notion of the sexually fallen sodomite unknown in modernity."[6] The view that history is best understood as competing ideas and mentalities that fall in and out of favor but rarely if ever vanish without a trace, rather than shifts that all but erase old worldviews and bring in something mostly (if not entirely) new, is what informs this book. Even though the study of sexuality in history has been fraught with theoretical issues encompassing history, literary theory and criticism, psychology, philosophy, and biology, the purpose of this book is not to summarize or rehash these controversies. In fact, it is written just for any person who has wondered simply, "What's the problem with sex?"

I

The Torah

The first five books of the Hebrew Bible, the Torah, were completed sometime after the Diaspora, when the Assyrian and Babylonian empires dispersed conquered Jewish populations throughout the Middle East in the eighth and sixth centuries BCE. In the wake of the collapse of the kingdoms of Israel and Judah at the feet of foreign invaders and the razing of the First Temple of Jerusalem, the Hebrews made sure their religious traditions would survive. Instead of fatally disarming the Jewish faith, the incomprehensible shock of the Diaspora ignited the search for reaffirmation, a need fossilized in Lamentations: "Let us test and examine our ways, and return to the Lord."[1]

The books Genesis, Exodus, and Numbers establish the grand narrative of the creation of the universe by the one true god YHWH; humanity's banishment from paradise and into the horrors of uncertainty, mortality, and suffering; and the special place of the Jews as the chosen people of the Creator, who delivered them from slavery and promised them divine favor and a homeland, albeit one that was inconveniently already occupied. The other books of the Torah, Leviticus and Deuteronomy, are essentially law codes—albeit laws that may not have been put into actual practice in the days of ancient Israel before they were written down. Even so, they were—unlike the law codes of Mesopotamia—passed down by a king acting as the middleman between humanity and the divine. Instead, they came directly from Israel's sole God.

Just a brief skim of the Torah reveals the fastidious instructions for purity necessary for proving faithfulness. The lists of "clean" and "unclean" foods are meticulous in the extreme, marking out "what is detestable" and what is not in the categories of land animals, sea animals, birds, and insects.[2] Lepers were to be carefully examined with scientific exactness and, if decisive proof of illness was found, exiled from the community to prevent contamination.[3] Leviticus is exceptionally careful in its prescriptions for sin offerings, ordering different offerings based on the sinner's income.[4] The emission of semen and menstrual blood were both serious impurities, and the contaminated were liable to spread their impurity to anything or anyone they touched until they made themselves pure once again through bathing and offerings.[5] Even childbirth required rituals of purification from the woman; perhaps unsurprisingly, the length of the contamination period was longer if a female child was born.[6]

Such grueling commands were not at all unusual for priests in ancient Egypt, Mesopotamia, and Phoenicia, but the Torah took matters to a new extreme. Even though the Israelites had a distinct priesthood, according to the Torah the entire Jewish community was deemed sacred and held up to the same rigorous rules for preserving that sanctity: "You shall be holy to me; for I the Lord am holy, and I have separated you from the other peoples to be mine."[7] Comparing the Jewish community to Catholic monastic orders, Hyam Maccoby finds, "Israelites are required to regard themselves as a nation of priests, and therefore bound by a priestly code which is not binding on non-priests."[8]

While the Torah cast the ancient Hebrews as the leads in a grand cosmic drama, this added responsibility had its disturbing risks. A plot thread running through the book of Numbers features an angry YHWH, often on the verge of utterly annihilating the Israelites out of simple dissatisfaction. Toward the end of Leviticus, YHWH threatens a long series of escalating punishments for the entire community if the Levitical prohibitions and instructions are not observed properly and consistently. There are the expected divine threats of famine, plague, and military defeat, but there is also a sincere dread of social disorder and disharmony: the decay of cities and the abandonment of roads, anarchy, and even cannibalism.[9] Observance of law and ritual ensured not only the preservation of divine sanction, but also the very survival of the people. In the books of the prophets and in Lamentations, the invasions of Israel and Judah by the Assyrian and Babylonian empires are not blamed on Israel's enemies, on military failure, or even ultimately on the incompetence and squabbles of the kings of Judah and Israel, but rather on the Jewish people's failure to maintain the covenant with YHWH.

Sex and Purity

Even with the belief that semen defiled those who came in contact with it, the ancient Hebrews did not view sex as "wicked." One of the most celebrated and sacred texts in the Jewish canon remains the *Song of Solomon,* also known as the *Aisma Asmaton* ("Song of Songs"). Long interpreted by many Jewish and Christian authorities since antiquity as a religious allegory, the text is nonetheless explicitly erotic, bluntly yet artistically portraying the sexual desires of both a man and a woman for each other:

> My beloved is radiant and ruddy,
> outstanding among ten thousand.
> His head is purest gold;
> his hair is wavy
> and black as a raven.
> His eyes are like doves
> by the water streams,
> washed in milk,
> mounted like jewels.
> His cheeks are like beds of spice
> yielding perfume.
> His lips are like lilies
> dripping with myrrh.
> His arms are rods of gold
> set with topaz.

> His body is like polished ivory
> decorated with lapis lazuli.
> His legs are pillars of marble
> set on bases of pure gold.
> His appearance is like Lebanon,
> choice as its cedars.
> His mouth is sweetness itself;
> he is altogether lovely.
> This is my beloved, this is my friend,
> daughters of Jerusalem.[10]

Also, as critics of religiously motivated censorship love to point out, the Hebrew Bible has a number of sexual episodes that pass without comment or punishment, such as Lot's daughters getting their father drunk and raping him so that they can have children.[11] Tikva Frymer-Kensky asserts that sex "has not been demonized or condemned" in the Hebrew Bible. "On the contrary, it is not given sufficient status and importance to accord it a conscious valuation, even a negative one. It is talked about (or, most often, not talked about) as part of the social realm, as a question of societal regulation."[12]

Sex was meant to be enjoyed, but ideally only within marriage. In the Hebrew Bible, a husband and wife are meant to become "one flesh"[13] and men are urged to "find joy in the wife of your youth."[14] The double standard was in force, however: while women who strayed outside marital norms were brutally castigated, there were no punishments for men who had sex with unmarried women or prostitutes.

Laws dealing with family and marital relations were instead concerned with ensuring the smooth continuation of family lines, a priority most threatened by female infidelity. There were even laws that forced the man to remain married to a woman if he married her after impregnating her[15] or if he tried to get rid of his wife by claiming she was not a virgin when he married her.[16] Divorce was allowed in ancient Israel, although how it was instituted is far from certain.[17] A clue might lie in the fact that there is no surviving mention of a divorce begun by a wife.

Despite the strict enforcement of monogamy, men were allowed to take a concubine in cases where the wife was barren. This sort of arrangement was accepted in Genesis, where Abraham's wife Sarah offers her handmaiden Hagar as a substitute womb. The resulting child of Hagar and Abraham, Ishmael, is accepted as a legitimate heir without question. Men with a wife unable to bear children were apparently allowed to take a "second wife,"[18] a custom that also existed in Babylon and Assyria.

One of the most chilling episodes in the Hebrew Bible to a 21st-century reader is the episode in Numbers when YHWH sends a plague to punish the Israelites for finding wives among and worshiping the gods of the people of Moab:

> Just then one of the Israelites came and brought a Midianite woman into his family, in the sight of Moses and in the sight of the whole congregation of the Israelites, while they were weeping at the entrance of the tent of meeting. When Phinehas son of Eleazar, son of Aaron the priest, saw it, he got up and left the congregation. Taking a spear in his hand, he went after the Israelite man into the tent, and pierced the two of them, the Israelite and the woman, through the belly. So the plague was stopped among the people of Israel.[19]

YHWH praises Phinehas for his "zeal" and for making "atonement for the Israelites" and even offers to make Phinehas's descendants priests "for all time." Such a condemnation, although in a less dramatic light, appears again in Ezra: "Thus the holy seed has mixed itself with the peoples of the lands, and in this faithlessness the officials and leaders have led the way."[20] Again, in spite of some unfortunate modern interpretations, the prohibition is not against interracial marriage, but rather marriage with those who worshiped deities other than YHWH. However, it is very unlikely that this ban was observed or even existed before the Diaspora. The kings of Israel and Judah obviously married women from Phoenicia and elsewhere; likewise, worship of deities other than YHWH, particularly the Canaanite god Baal, was widely practiced during the histories of both kingdoms. After all, Deuteronomy and Ezra, along with much of the Torah, were written after the Diaspora, at a time when Jews felt every day an urgency to preserve their identity against the alien world they had been shoved into.

Leviticus 18:22 and 20:13

Where the Torah stands out from other ancient Middle East law codes is in its apparently stern and unforgiving attitude toward same-sex relations. Nothing recorded from Babylonian and Assyrian laws matches the thoroughness and clarity behind Leviticus 18:22, "You shall not lie with a male as with a woman; it is an abomination," and Leviticus 20:13, "If a man lies with a male as with a woman, both of them have committed an abomination; they shall be put to death; their blood is upon them." The question of origins is an enticing and tricky one. Any discussion of these two passages from Leviticus inevitably becomes as much about the present as about the Hebrew Bible and ancient Israel.

Interpretation itself poses a problem. For example, the word "abomination," *toevah*, seems to have a broader definition than its English translation, encompassing lying,[21] unclothing a woman while she is menstruating,[22] and using false weights and measures,[23] among other things. In his commentary on the Torah, Richard Elliot Friedman chooses to translate *toevah* as "offensive thing," implying the term's relative nature in Hebrew, and stresses the word's subjectivity by pointing to Genesis 46:34, where shepherds are said to be *toevah* to the Egyptians.[24]

Rabbi Steven Greenberg has suggested that the law was just meant for cases of same-sex rape, theorizing that the context and word choice in the original Hebrew of Leviticus 18:22 implies a sex act calculated to humiliate, a rape.[25] After all, the idea of anal penetration of one man by another as an exercise of power and degradation was widespread in the ancient Middle East, shown even in an Egyptian myth about the god Osiris and his eternal nemesis Seth. However, any ambiguity is erased in Leviticus 20:13. While appearing at first glance to be a redundancy, Leviticus 20:13 includes the active partner in the crime and sharpens the penalty and sense of abhorrence. Both active and passive partners are equally guilty of sin and are subscribed the same capital offense. Saul Olwyn helpfully points out a very practical reason for the similarity: the passage shows signs of being a later editorial reworking of Levitical 18:22, particularly thanks to the word play when the law abruptly shifts from condemning "a man" to "both of them."[26]

Seeking out references to same-sex intercourse or relationships elsewhere in the Hebrew Bible does nothing to help settle the issue. The most worn-out discussion of homosexuality in the Hebrew Bible, besides the prohibitions in Leviticus, revolves around the story of Sodom and Gomorrah in Genesis where YHWH, disturbed by a cry heard from Sodom, sends two angels to enter the city. In spite of the city's hostility toward foreigners, Lot invites the angels into his home and gives them a meal. A crowd gathers outside Lot's home and it is strongly implied that they are hellbent on assaulting and raping the guests. Wishing desperately to honor the laws of hospitality, Lot offers his daughters to the crowd, but they refuse. It is this outrage that finally provokes YHWH into destroying the two cities and all their inhabitants except Lot and his family.[27]

Nowadays biblical scholars agree that the sin of the two cities that infuriated YHWH was intended to be seen as inhospitality and violence toward foreigners. A story in Judges that parallels in almost every respect the fable of Sodom has Gibeah's house surrounded by an angry crowd, threatening to rape a male guest, but this time the mob accepts a woman as an alternative.[28] Also, according to rabbinic literature, the mysterious cry against the Sodomites referred to in Genesis 18:21 came from a young woman who was brutally executed for defying Sodom's law against feeding wandering beggars[29]—yet today the word "sodomite" almost never refers to someone who is selfish and xenophobic. In the context of the Hebrew Bible itself, there is very little to suggest that the destruction of Sodom and Gomorrah was motivated by divine disgust at sexual acts between men or women.

If the Hebrews were particularly revolted by all forms of same-sex intercourse, then the fact that female same-sex relationships are never explicitly mentioned in the Hebrew Bible is a serious omission. Both the Torah and Jewish religious authorities had little to say on the topic of lesbianism. It was discussed bluntly and condemned in later rabbinical literature,[30] but these prohibitions have only the loosest roots in the actual Torah. Also, opinions were not universally hostile. For instance, the second century CE rabbi Eleazer argued against barring women known to have indulged in sexual play with other women from marrying priests.[31]

Some scholars emphasize that there are actually positive views of general homosexual activity in the Hebrew Bible, although these are all controversial and open to interpretation. The story of David, the young warrior who would be king, and Jonathan, son of Saul, the first king of Israel, has been, wrongly or not, taken up as an ancient gay love story. In his book *Jonathan Loved David,* Tom Horner used the entire legend as a starting point for discussing homosexuality in Israel and the Bible.[32] In contrast, the tale of the intense friendship David shared with Saul's heir, who conveniently died before he could become an obstacle for David, might have proved very useful for defending David's reputation and dispelling any nasty rumors about how he treated Saul's family.[33] Whatever the truth, the legend of Jonathan and David, as well as the story of the extraordinary friendship of Ruth and Naomi in the Book of Ruth, showed that stories of heroic same-sex love, whether Platonic or erotic, could be worth preserving.

There may be no reason to believe in a more "gay friendly" ancient Israel, but still there are no recorded instances of the punishments outlined in Leviticus 20:13 being enforced.[34] Of course, records are thin at best and after the Diaspora Jewish communities were often forced to cope with the sensibilities of other cultures. Nevertheless, the lack of any record of punishment elsewhere in the Hebrew Bible or in any recorded Jewish history does hint that there was no big cultural push for such a punishment. This again begs the question of why it was put there in the first place.

Religious authorities and secular scholars alike have theorized that Leviticus 20:13 was scribbled down to help preserve the law of "Be fruitful and multiply,"[35] to keep "correct" gender roles from getting muddled,[36] or that it was meant to stamp out an ancient pagan ritual involving male prostitutes.[37] However, the real origin may not have been Judaism at all, but another monotheistic religion from next door, Zoroastrianism. Like Judaism, Zoroastrianism acknowledged only one god, Ahura Mazda. Growing from the teachings of Zoroaster, who may have lived in central Asia or what is now southern Russia sometime before 1200 BCE,[38] Zoroastrianism became the faith of an empire in 550 BCE when the Achaemenians, the Zoroastrian royal dynasty ruling over the Persians, overthrew and replaced the Emperor Astyages, whose Median Empire stretched from Central Asia to the Black Sea.

The first Persian Emperor, Cyrus the Great (r. 550–530), was determined to make an impression. Only 11 years after establishing the Persian Empire, Cyrus devastated the Babylonian armies and imprisoned or killed the last king of Babylon in history, Nabonidus. While one might think that they were simply exchanging one imperial boss for another, the Jews were exuberant, especially after Cyrus decreed that the Jews scattered by Babylon could return to Israel and commissioned the rebuilding of the Temple of Jerusalem. In Isaiah, Cyrus, despite being a Gentile, is proclaimed the Lord's anointed[39] and hailed as a liberator.

Cyrus's deliverance of the Jews might very well have just been good politics, especially since the Jews were not the only people who had been subjugated by the Babylonian Empire toward whom he showed generosity. Nevertheless, it is easy to see how a Zoroastrian Emperor could sympathize with a people who also worshiped one supreme creator. There were other matters a Jew and a Zoroastrian could bond over as well. While Zoroastrianism and Judaism were far from the only religions to adopt strict rules of observance and ritual, they were both armed with the sense that they were chosen peoples, ensuring divine benefits by obeying commandments revealed to them and them alone by prophets selected by the one true God. Like the Greeks and the Romans after them, however, the Persian Empire also usually preferred a policy of religious tolerance, so there was no temptation to substitute YHWH with Ahuramazda. In fact, like the Jews themselves, it seems that the ancient Zoroastrians (and their modern descendants) felt no compulsion to officially spread the good word, through force or otherwise.

Studying Isaiah, Alan Segal notes that the prophet, even in the midst of praising Cyrus, expressed uneasiness about the doctrine that Ahura mazda had two offspring, the good spirit Spenta Mainyu and the chaotic spirit Angra Mainyu.[40] It is unlikely that he was alone in this discomfort, but there are scraps of proof pointing toward the influence Zoroastrianism had over Judaism, including the topic of same-sex desire. Wasting no time with questions of sexual position, the foundational Zoroastrian gospel, the *Avestas*, explicitly singles out all male homosexual acts:

> Ahura mazda answered: "The man that lies with mankind as man lies with womankind, or as woman lies with mankind, is the man that is a *daeva* [demon or evil spirit]; this one is the man that is a worshiper of the *daevas*, that is a male paramour of the *daevas*, that is a female paramour of the *daevas*, that is a wife to the *daeva*; this is the man that is as bad as a *daeva*, that is in his whole being a *daeva*; this is the man that is a *daeva* before he dies, and becomes one of the unseen *daevas* after death: so is he, whether he has lain with mankind as mankind, or as womankind."[41]

Even a man who was anally raped can be cleansed in the *Avestas* only through a long series of beatings. It is even worse for men who consent; there is no hope of atonement.[42] A collection of Zoroastrian laws composed in the late ninth or early tenth century CE, *The Religious Explanation of Hemit, the Son of Aswahist,* is much more succinct: "The sin of sodomy deserves death. The worldly atonement for it would be killing [the sinner.]"[43] Even after the death penalty fell out of use in the medieval era, people found guilty of sodomy among Zoroastrian communities were made into pariahs and no prayers were to be said for them after their deaths.[44]

Christie Davis could be right that the venomous reaction against homosexuality in the *Avestas* and in Leviticus may be a coincidence emerging from similar circumstances. After all, the Zoroastrians and the Jews were both peoples that set themselves above and apart from other societies through religious law.[45] Still, Leviticus 20:13, like the Zoroastrian prohibitions, reveals similar wording and makes no fuss over position. Neither is lesbianism mentioned. Then there is the unequivocal demand for the death penalty, underscored by the sentence, "Their blood is upon them." Finally, this shared perspective fits into the history. Leviticus itself is believed by mainstream biblical scholars to have been composed, along with the rest of the Torah, after the Persian invasion of the Babylonian Empire.[46] Since Leviticus 20:13 appears to be a late addition, it could very well have come about at some point during or after the period when Zoroastrianism and Judaism came into close contact.

Whether the total absence of evidence of these laws ever being enforced speaks to a drought of sources, the laws' impracticality, or the laws historically never being considered an essential part of the holiness code, there is no way of knowing. What we do know is that these two short and otherwise marginal prohibitions in Leviticus are still cited from California to Uganda by lawmakers and religious authorities of different faiths, with dire consequences.

Female Sexuality and Its Male Victims

One does not have to go further than biblical Hebrew itself to find women's place in ancient Israelite society. While there was no word corresponding exactly with our word "husband," *ba'al* was used to denote the man in a marital relationship. In the Canaanite languages including Hebrew, *ba'al* was both an honorific and the name of the deity Baal (much the same way "Lord" is used as a name for God in the English Old Testament) and can be translated as "master." Likewise, instead of a word for wife, a married woman was called "the woman of [husband's name]." The mindset behind the language choices is not hard to see. Phyllis Bird notes, "It suggests why the marriage relationship was appropriated as a metaphor for the covenant relationship of Yahweh to Israel, a relationship characterized by intimacy—and subordination."[47]

For Hebrew society, the proper role of women is apparently spelled out in the epic of creation through Eve. There is, however, another account of the creation of mankind buried in Genesis that has gone more or less ignored in the West. Here "God created humankind in his image, in the image of God he created them; male and female he created them."[48] In the longer and much more well-known story of mankind's creation,[49] the first woman Eve is not only created after the first man Adam, but also comes about solely to "make him a helper as his partner."[50] Moreover, Eve is not entirely a creation in of herself, but is created from Adam's rib. On the face of it, this appears to be a small detail, but the metaphorical significance was not lost on later writers. Paul had it in mind when he wrote, "Woman is the reflection of man. Indeed, man was not made from woman, but woman from man. Neither was man created for the sake of woman, but woman for the sake of man."[51] To hammer home this point, after Adam and Eve eat the fruit from the tree of knowledge, YHWH curses Eve with the pain of childbirth and concludes, "Yet your desire shall be for your husband, and he shall rule over you."[52]

While the curse of Eve likely did not fully reflect social realities, it did at least reveal this society's ideals. The model wife of an affluent family, according to Proverbs, was one who spent her days weaving, worked from before dawn preparing food for the household, kept herself and her family well dressed with clothes she makes herself, and never left the house at night. She was also expected to be generous and charitable, as much a help to the larger community as to her own family.[53] In other words, the model wife was ruled over—if not entirely by men, then by a series of binding obligations that cut into her autonomy.

Of course, there were women who, willingly or not, lived outside the traditional Hebrew household and social networks, among them prostitutes. Contrary to popular belief, prostitution is never prohibited or even explicitly condemned in the Hebrew Bible. If anything, it is accepted as an essential aspect of society. Still, the reader of Proverbs is cautioned that a prostitute "is a deep pit."[54] Prostitutes are used to give an added dose of humiliation against King Ahab of Israel after he is killed in battle at Samaria: "They washed the chariot by the pool of Samaria; the dogs licked up his blood, and the prostitutes washed themselves in it, according to the word of the Lord that he had spoken."[55] In a calculated perversion of the metaphor of Israel as YHWH's daughter or wife, Israel is cast as a prostitute in the works of the prophets whenever they felt the urge to criticize Israel for its sins. The prophet Hosea is compelled to marry and have children with the prostitute Gomer, most likely the greatest single act of commitment to an allegory in recorded history.[56] Speaking through YHWH, Ezekiel growls, "But you [Israel] trusted in your beauty, and played the whore because of your fame, and lavished your whorings on any passer-by."[57]

Of course, there were also women who were not entirely "traditional," but were anything but resigned to the fringes of society. Deborah was both a female prophet and one of the 12 legendary "Judges" of Israel; she may have been based on a historical persona who was, if not a tribal leader, a prominent settler of disputes.[58] While neither leaders nor warriors, Naomi exemplifies care and attention for widows and Ruth demonstrates loyalty to one's family and friends. After marrying the Persian Emperor Artaxerxes, Esther risks her husband's displeasure—and her life—to save her people from a pogrom against the Persian Jews planned by his minister Haman.

Then there are slightly more complex female role models like Jochebed and Miriam, Moses's mother and sister, and the prostitute Rahab in the story of the fall of Jericho—women who are clearly meant to be seen as heroines, even when they act in naked defiance of male authority. The heroine Judith seduces and then beheads the Assyrian general Holofernes, bringing about a military reversal that saves her hometown from an invading army.[59] A similar story revolves around Jael, who gets the Canaanite general Sisera drunk and then murders him by driving a tent peg through his head.[60]

Miriam, Rahab, Jochebed, Judith, and Jael are saviors to the Jewish people, yet they also demonstrate how dangerous women, especially foreign women, may be. In fact, Judith and Jael save the Jews by securing men's trust sexually so as to render them vulnerable and murder them. Strangely, they share exactly the same *modus operandi* of the Hebrew Bible's female villains. For instance, Delilah is a Philistine woman who, for the sake of her people, becomes the judge Samson's lover, discovers that his hair is the source of his superhuman strength, and shears it. Jezebel, a Phoenician princess married to King Ahab of Israel (r. 869–850 BCE), infamously used her influence over her husband to spread worship of Baal.[61] The biblical narrative extends no sympathy to either woman, even though, like the biblical heroines, they are just promoting the interests of their people or deity with the only effective tool that a thoroughly masculine society allows them, their sexuality.

The Hebrew Bible gives us a small hole through which we can catch glimpses of a community where women were virtually the property of their fathers or husbands. This is not an exaggeration. After all, among the Ten Commandments men are ordered not to covet their neighbor's wives, along with their property, donkeys, oxen, or slaves.[62] Shockingly to our modern sensibilities, Lot is still considered a righteous man even after he offers his daughters, whose virginity (and thus their quality) is emphasized in the narrative, over to the mob in Sodom.[63] Nor is Gibeah condemned for offering his daughter and then the Levite's concubine to another deadly crowd.[64] In the laws of the Torah, which again may or may not have reflected everyday practice in ancient Israel, while a man who impregnated a woman still living with her family had an obligation to marry her, the father still had the right to refuse the man's offer, in which case the man was required to instead pay compensation for the would-have-been bride's virginity.[65]

A woman having illicit sex was serious business. In Genesis 34, Dinah, a daughter of Jacob, is raped, or more likely seduced,[66] by Shechem. As commanded in Exodus and most likely in compliance with custom in Canaan, Hamor, Shechem's father, offers to marry Shechem to Dinah. Hamor also urges that his and Jacob's children intermarry. However, the offense that Shechem committed when he slept with Dinah without her father's consent—"such a thing ought not to be done"[67]—remained and horrified Dinah's brothers. They demanded that Hamor and his sons become circumcised, a request that, while in the context of the story was only a pretext, must have conveyed a reminder to the reader that intermarriage was a threat to the Jews' unique status. Exploiting the fact that Hamor and his men were weak and in pain from the circumcisions, Jacob's sons attacked and slaughtered their town. After Jacob raises the perfectly valid point that this will mean they will be hounded by Shechem's neighbors, the brothers have the final word: "Should our sister be treated like a whore?"[68]

Deuteronomy goes far enough to prescribe death by stoning for the wife whose husband accuses her of not being a virgin before marriage.[69] Stoning is a particularly ritualistic form of execution, allowing the entire community to chip in, a fact brought to the fore by the law's concluding sentence, "So you shall purge the evil from your midst."[70] If the husband is found out to be lying after evidence provided by the parents, then he was simply fined and forbidden to divorce her. While impugning a wife's sexual integrity was clearly an offense for the husband and apparently a common enough tactic for getting out of marriage that it had to be addressed in the Torah, the father was apparently considered the wronged party, having had his authority over his daughter flaunted, since the stoning was to take place in front of her father's house.

Female adultery was considered an unforgivable offense. In Numbers, an elaborate and humiliating ritual before a priest is recommended for proving a wife's fidelity, reminiscent of the trials of ordeal in medieval Europe.[71] Leviticus and Deuteronomy both demand the death of the adulterous wife and her lover. Even a woman who claims to have been raped in a town was to be stoned along with the rapist, the presumption being that she actually consented since she was not heard crying out by the townspeople.[72] Outside the Torah, it seems adultery was at least seen as a problem that could easily lead to honor killings. A vivid, and probably realistic, depiction of adulterous encounters and their consequences is given in Proverbs:

> Do not desire her beauty in your heart,
> and do not let her capture you with her eyelashes;
> for a prostitute's fee is only a loaf of bread,
> but the wife of another stalks a man's very life.
> Can fire be carried in the bosom
> without burning one's clothes?
> Or can one walk on hot coals
> without scorching the feet?
> So is he who sleeps with his neighbor's wife;
> no one who touches her will go unpunished.
> Thieves are not despised who steal only
> to satisfy their appetite when they are hungry.
> Yet if they are caught, they will pay sevenfold;
> they will forfeit all the goods of their house.
> But he who commits adultery has no sense;
> he who does it destroys himself.
> He will get wounds and dishonor
> and his disgrace will not be wiped away.
> For jealousy arouses a husband's fury,
> and he shows no restraint when he takes revenge.
> He will accept no compensation,
> and refuses a bribe no matter how great.[73]

In this very pragmatic condemnation of adultery, no mention is made of the possibility of stoning, but rather of the perils of homicidal husbands.

However adultery was actually dealt with in ancient Israel, in the ideal society of the Torah adultery is the business of the people. The husband has no opportunity to pardon his wife or ask for a penalty other than death. The punishments, as well as the methods for ascertaining innocence or guilt, are laid down in holy writ, in total disregard to the sovereignty of the husband over the wife or the father over the daughter. After all, the community itself is put in danger of losing its own rights to the land—"But you shall keep my statutes and ordinances and commit none of these abominations, either the citizen or the alien who resides among you (for inhabitants of the land, who were before you, committed all of these abominations, and the land became defiled); otherwise the land will vomit you out for defiling it, as it vomited out the nation that was before you"[74]—so justice belongs to the people, not just to the wronged party.

There is no denying that the abuse of women is condoned by the Hebrew Bible, just as "Israel's best statements about woman recognize her as an equal to man, and with him jointly responsible to God and to cohumanity."[75] Delilah and Jezebel have become shorthand for the classic *femme fatale* in the Western imagination, but the resolute and courageous heroines Ruth, Naomi, Judith, and Esther loom just as large. The one consistent lesson in most of these stories, though, is that female sexuality is a profound force. Even when wielded for the benefit of the Hebrew people, it has the capacity to change the fate of peoples, corrupt kings, cripple or even kill determined warriors, and trigger the downfall of powerful ministers. On a more mundane level, prostitutes and adulteresses are predators, patiently lying in wait for the next reckless young man. For the sake of the individual man and the people at large, female sexuality is viewed as something to be distrusted and controlled, a lesson that was not at all lost to future generations in the West.

II

Ancient Greece and the First Sexologists

The film *Ghost World* shows a Greek American convenience store manager arguing with a man flagrantly stomping on the principle of "No Shirt, No Shoes, No Service." When the shirtless man appeals to American democracy, the clerk fires back, "Don't talk to me about democracy. We Greeks invented democracy." The man retorts, "Yeah? You also invented homos." A few modern Greeks seem to be sensitive about this reputation. On the one hand, in 2004, Greek lawyers threatened to sue those involved in the production of Oliver Stone's film about Alexander the Great over scenes that no more than imply that Alexander had a male lover, Hephaeston.[1] On the other hand, when the gay Catholic and British American pundit Andrew Sullivan married, the romantic myth of the origins of homosexuality from Plato's *Symposium* was read in the ceremony. Neither the positive nor negative view of Western antiquity's "gay heritage" exposes the whole picture. When thinking of homosexuality in antiquity, we usually remember only the homoerotic poems of Sappho or the fact that sodomy laws were unknown in classical Athens and pagan Rome, not the effeminate, "wide-assed" caricatures in Aristophanes's comedies who breathed political corruption and social decay, Plato's *Laws* where "the Athenian" yearns for a state where religious and cultural custom causes sex between men to be viewed with disgust, or the Stoic position that same-sex relations ran counter to nature.

The elite theories of academia have neatly dovetailed with the views of the general public. Using the ideas laid down by the philosopher Michel Foucault in his *History of Sexuality* as a beacon, scholars have portrayed classical Greece and ancient Rome as times and places where sex was conceived only in terms of dominance/submission and where same-sex relationships between men (and perhaps women as well) were "tolerated," but were still understood chiefly in the terms of pederastic relationships.[2] Other historians and classicists have argued that these positions sorely underestimate the diversity of historical evidence and the complexity of Athenian and Roman societies,[3] turning the study of sex in antiquity into something of a battleground.

Just as Athens and Rome have been portrayed as societies "tolerant" of homosexuality or where same-sex relationships were hammered into a socially acceptable construct, these same cultures have been condemned in recent decades for being misogynistic in root and branch and having a pathological need to curtail the sexual activities of the female sex. The historian Eva Klaus titled her study of sex and gender in classical Athens as *Reign of the Phallus* for a good reason. Female sexuality was indeed seen as a dangerous and even irresistible force, whether it manifested itself in the erotic power of Aphrodite–Venus or in the terrifying rage of Medea or Clytemnestra. Athenian politicians and philosophers alike discouraged "respectable" women from freely appearing in public except for chores or visits and Roman writers of the first century BCE listed the promiscuity of their women as one of the social ills of their time.

Even here, though, the portrait has more depth than it might seem at first glance. As far from modern feminist ideals as Hellenistic society was, it did produce intellectuals, such as the Cynics and Zeno of Citium, who were fully capable of imagining societies where women had as much freedom as men. At least the Athenians may have been at least an inch more progressive than often assumed, since there is proof that Athenian law actually included provisions that protected women, including slaves and noncitizens, from sexual exploitation by men, even ones in positions of power. According to Eva Cantarella, Roman women who lived in the time of Julius Caesar may have experienced something the vast majority of women in Europe did not see again until the 20th century: "sexual freedom."[4]

There has been a tendency to see the Greeks and Romans as existing on a plane utterly foreign to our own or as people trapped in a monolithic, pathological society, with a menu of options for conceiving and experiencing their external world and internal desires that were much more limited than what are available to modern industrialized cultures. Yet their intellectuals wrote extensively and insightfully about foreign societies, examined the underpinnings of their own civilization in sophisticated treatises that continue to spark intense debate and frustrate college students even today, and envisioned utopias radically different than anything that existed in their history. It is a form of bias against the people of ancient Greece and Rome to cling to the view that they also bound themselves to extremely narrow frameworks of sex and sexuality and to deny what Plato himself apparently noted: "I should point out, however, that although the customs regarding Love in most cities are simple and easy to understand, here in Athens (and in Sparta as well) they are remarkably complex."[5]

Old-Fashioned Greek Values

In Plato's *Republic,* Kephalos frets that he will be punished by the gods in the afterlife.[6] However, the philosopher Isokrates was more in line with the traditional Greek view, when he worried instead that any wicked man might die before he is punished.[7] For those of us acquainted with a God that actively hands out judgments and punishments on even the most private and victimless actions, the Greek deities seem curiously disinterested in personal conduct, especially sexual infractions.

Anyone who has read about the adventures and misadventures of the Greek gods would agree with Robert Garland: "The primary reason why the gods could not be the upholders of the moral order is that they simply were not qualified. Their track record was lousy."[8] There were, however, some arenas where the gods could intervene. In the persona of Zeus Xenios, for instance, Zeus upheld the fundamental laws of *xenia,* the mutual obligations between host and guest, while any of the gods could be invoked to enforce oaths.[9] The poet Hesiod personified Justice as a goddess and daughter of Zeus[10]; the Eurinyes, better known in English as the Furies, relentlessly tormented not only those who were guilty of matricide, but also anyone who broke oaths or committed "unnatural" crimes like the murder of a close relative; and the goddess Nemesis held the divine remit to punish anyone guilty of excessive pride.

However, in mythology the Olympian gods tended to punish only crimes that threatened their sanctity and to reward loyalty from a good, devoted follower, not anyone who ignored or sustained a prescription of personal conduct. Odysseus is confident he deserves the benevolence of the gods, but not because he is a virtuous person. Instead, he notes that he pays the gods their dues through rituals and sacrifices.[11] A much later tradition, dating at least to the Hellenistic era, has the Trojan princess Cassandra raped by the Greek warrior Ajax the Lesser in Athena's temple. The outrage of Athena is not over the rape itself, but rather the fact that the act desecrated her sanctuary.[12] Even the murder of a kinsman, such as Ixion's murder of his father-in-law Deionios, did not guarantee divine wrath. On the contrary, Zeus forgave Ixion, even after he failed to purify himself for his crime, and took him to Mount Olympus as a guest. It was only when Ixion lusted after Hera and Zeus tricked him into revealing his intentions that he was punished.[13]

Pythagoreanism, begun by the mathematician-mystic Pythagoras in the sixth century BCE, may have offered its followers the sexual regulations traditional religion lacked. Like the ancient Orphic sect, Pythagoras taught about the transmigration of the soul. He also encouraged his followers to follow a number of seemingly arbitrary rules, such as a requirement to always make one's bed, a mandate to avoid any clothing except white garments, and a prohibition against being buried in wool garments. Amidst all this there was at least one sexual law, a ban against adultery.[14] The philosopher Iamblichus, who wrote in the late third and early fourth centuries CE, claimed that there were also prohibitions against pederasty and all forms of intercourse "contrary to nature."[15] Iamblichus is rather unreliable, since several centuries separated him from Pythagoras and the first generations of his movement, but it is worth pointing out that one of the people deeply influenced by Pythagoras was Plato, who would eventually unequivocally condemn homosexuality in the *Laws*.

Homer and Hesiod, Sappho and Achilles

Desire and sex were collectively the cause of the most cataclysmic war in the Greeks' legendary history. Reflecting on the destruction of Troy, Helen in the *Odyssey* remembers being overjoyed while the Trojan women around her were lamenting: "Already my heart had been turned toward going back to my home, and I groaned for the madness that Aphrodite gave when she led me there from the much loved land of my fathers, leaving behind my child and my marriage chamber and husband, who lacked nothing at all in either his mind or his beauty."[16] Helen's own abductor and lover Paris is also described as mad, specifically "woman-crazy," by his brother Hector.[17] All readers of the *Iliad* knew from the start that Paris's love for Helen, sincere and deep as it might have been, would eventually lead to his death and the annihilation of his family and city.

Long before Plato and Aristotle cautioned their students about the dangers of immoderate emotions, the Greeks already thought of sexual passion, *eros*, as having a dangerous and profound potential. Even Zeus, king of the gods and all mankind, can be pushed and pulled by Aphrodite's powers. According to one of the Homeric hymns, only the virgin goddesses Athena, Artemis, and Hestia are immune.[18] At Zeus's contrivance, the same hymn goes, one day Aphrodite herself succumbs to *eros* and makes love to a mortal man, Anchises. Although the entire tryst ends with no ugly consequences for Anchises or Aphrodite, she admits, "A terrible grief possesses me since I fell into the bed of a mortal man."[19] *Eros* in the poetry and Orphic hymns of seventh and eighth century BCE Greece was seen as, Marilyn Skinner points out, "a violent and arbitrary force,"[20] one that could put into motion the fall of even a great city like Troy and the humiliation of the great Olympic deities.

An old legend had it that the seventh century BCE poet Stesikhoros was made blind via divine wrath when he wrote an epic about the Trojan War that put Helen in a bad light. To redeem himself, Stesikhoros wrote a poem claiming that Helen was stranded in Egypt while it was really a döppleganger identical to Helen who was at Troy throughout the war. The gods approved and Stesikhoros's vision was promptly restored. Euripides liked Stesichoros's editorial change enough to make it the plot of his play *Helen*. Yet even in Homer's original works, Helen was no *femme fatale*, but rather a victim of bad luck. In the *Iliad*, Helen rebukes Aphrodite herself, claiming that the goddess practically forced her to leave Sparta with Paris,[21] and later tells Paris flatly that she wished he had died fighting Menelaus for the sake of his own people.[22]

When Homer reintroduces Helen in the *Odyssey*, she takes an honored place as hostess at Menelaus's banquet. There is no real indication that she has been punished or even blamed, nor is a sharp line ever drawn between abduction and adultery. She certainly has not been forced into seclusion or stoned, as the Torah would have preferred it, or committed suicide, as would have been the Romans' wish. Perhaps Helen has been pardoned just because she is Zeus's daughter, but the narrative that runs through both the *Iliad* and the *Odyssey* wants the reader to see a Helen who is only barely accountable, if that. Paris was clearly the guilty party and he—and Troy—already suffered retribution.

Whether Helen's treatment is a reliable hint as to how adultery was usually viewed is an open question. Fortunately, Homer has left behind another clue. In the *Odyssey*, Odysseus hears a song by a bard about Aphrodite and Ares having an affair. While the two gods are in position, so to speak, Aphrodite's husband Hephaistos traps them with a net strong enough to hold divinity. Hephaistos lets them go only when he is satisfied that he will be paid the "adulterer's fine"[23] by Poseidon in Ares's name. Again, there is no mention that Hephaestus will seek some sort of retribution from his wife. Given that the story is comedic and part of the humor comes from seeing the gods act in a very down-to-earth manner, "adulterer's fines" may have been a fact of life in Homeric Greece. The idea that men, not women, were liable in cases of adultery was one that lasted, at least in Athens.

By the fifth century BCE, which forms a good slice of what is usually called ancient Greece's "classical period," the seclusion of women was something urged on by society's watchdogs. Back in Homer's Greece, even though women were thought vulnerable to abduction or seduction like Helen or the mythological heroines Medea and Ariadne, both of whom are sweet-talked into betraying their homelands and families by sly young heroes, women were allowed to attend banquets and acted as hostesses, like Helen and the princess Nausicaä in the *Odyssey*. When Odysseus's wife, Penelope, plays the role of hostess to her suitors, it is not a scandal for her to do so. Still, there is a hint of changing attitudes or some ambivalence about women mingling freely with men when Penelope's son Telemakhos tells her, "But go back to your room and devote more care to your own work, weaving and spinning, the loom and the distaff, bidding your handmaids to busy themselves with their labor. The men will attend to the talking, all of them, I above all, since mine is the rule of the household."[24] Penelope is amazed by her son's firmness, but defers without protest, believing that her son's statements were "thoughtful."[25]

As Robert Garland reminds us, Penelope and Helen are very different from certain other female models in the book. The sorceress Circe and the nymph Calliope exist outside settled society and impede, albeit in different ways, Odysseus's journey home to his wife and son: "The women whom Odysseus encounters exercise their power in ways that are usually indirect, sometimes magical, and often dangerous. They possess access to privileged information. They control hidden forces that can assist or impede him on the way. They counterfeit and deceive. And they can kill."[26] Calliope and Circe, as well as the Sirens, whose powers of seduction are so potent that Odysseus has to be tied to his ship's mast, can be seen as representing a wild feminine sexuality, erotically appealing but deadly to men and incompatible with civilized society.

The most hysterical warnings about the perils of female sexuality from preclassical Greek literature come from Hesiod. Any doubts about what Hesiod thinks about women and their sexual appeal are evaporated once a reader gets to his story about the first mortal woman, Pandora. Her creation was commissioned by Zeus to punish Prometheus and mankind for the theft of fire from the heavens and making a sacrifice of fat and bones look like quality meat: "And he bade famous Hephaestus make haste and mix earth with water and to put in it the voice and strength of human kind, and fashion a sweet, lovely maiden-shape, like to the immortal goddesses in face; and Athene to teach her needlework and the weaving of the varied web; and golden Aphrodite to shed grace upon her head and cruel longing and cares that weary the limbs. And he charged Hermes the guide, the Slayer of Argus, to put in her a shameless mind and a deceitful nature."[27] In the end, Pandora unseals a vase (commonly mistranslated in English as a box) and unleashes all the evil in the world. The metaphoric significance of a jar, in its resemblance to a vulva, was probably not an accident.

Hesiod elaborates:

> For from [Pandora] is the race of women and female kind: of her is the deadly race and tribe of women who live amongst mortal men to their great trouble, no helpmeets in hateful poverty, but only in wealth. And as in thatched hives bees feed the drones whose nature is to do mischief—by day and throughout the day until the sun goes down the bees are busy and lay the white combs, while the drones stay at home in the covered skeps and reap the toil of others with their own bellies—even so Zeus who thunders on high made women to be an evil to mortal men, with a nature to do evil.[28]

In his *Works and Days,* where the essentials of the Pandora myth reemerge with Pandora herself unnamed, women are not only inherently promiscuous, but also represent an almost intolerable economic burden. Unfortunately, they are necessary to produce the children required to support a man in his old age. Hesiod admits it is possible to marry a woman who is both honest and a hard worker, but even then she might give birth to children who will abandon both their parents.[29]

After reading his rendition of the Pandora legend, anyone could very well diagnose Hesiod as having "issues" with women.[30] There are other portrayals of women, such as Homer's complex heroines, including Penelope, who defends her own sexual integrity against an army of suitors. Where Hesiod and Homer meet is on the idea that marriage and domesticity represent the only proper arena for the honorable woman. Where women are powerful outside the home, their sexuality is nonexistent or they are placed in the world of the fantastic.

If sexuality was to be tamed for the sake of domesticity, where does that leave homosexual desire? The evidence surrounding same-sex love is much more sparse in preclassical Greece than it would be for Athens and Sparta later on. However, the era is still home to one of the most famous voices for same-sex erotica of all time, Sappho, who lived in the last decades of the 600s and died sometime around 570. Her reputation for same-sex love became so well known that the name of the island where she lived, Lesbos, stood for love between women in antiquity and even into the modern day. Whether Sappho had erotic feelings for her female students and other women or if the love between women expressed in her poetry is mainly a literary device is infinitely debatable, but it is difficult to deny that homoeroticism is there. For instance, there is this poem, dealing with Sappho's theme of the love between two women being disrupted by the inevitability of marriage, with one of the poem's speakers remembering the "sacred wreaths ... around your soft threat."[31] Tragically, little of Sappho's poetry survives in spite of her popularity in antiquity. This example shows, what bits there are usually survived only in fragments.

Despite the paucity of evidence, Sappho has received a lion's share of scholarly attention, in no small part because she is a rare example of a woman's voice from the era, much less a likely homosexual voice. Claude Calame envisioned Sappho presiding over a pederastic school of sorts where she had intimate and possibly sexual relationships with her young, aristocratic pupils, training them for married life.[32] Others have argued that Sappho's poetry was part of a "sensual education"[33] or that Sappho was, through her poetry, seeking to find expressions of feeling that she could not receive in the traditional life reserved for an aristocratic Greek woman.[34] That Sappho was popular enough to be praised as the tenth Muse during antiquity does not need to be explained by saying that readers understood that Sappho was not *really* desiring and making love to women; after all, her reputation for homoerotic desire began in antiquity. Looking past the lack of juicy details, Eva Stehle finds the emotional evidence compelling: "None of the major fragments, in which the persona is some manifestation of the poet, breathes a hint of sexual interest in a man."[35]

How Sappho's work was received by later generations of Greeks and Romans reveals quite a bit about what people thought about same-sex love. One example comes from a third or second century BCE anonymous biography of Sappho, which claimed that she had been accused, presumably falsely, of having sex with women.[36] The Latin poet Ovid wrote an imaginary letter between Sappho and Phaön, a man who, according to legend, rejected Sappho and drove her to suicide, where Sappho complains about all the rumors that have her sleeping with women.[37] His contemporary Horace explained that Sappho was described as *mascula* because she was a *tribas,* a Latin term that hints at lesbianism.[38] Another Latin poet, Catullus, imagined that he was Sappho, constantly lusting after women.[39] Then there is the name of Sappho's supposed husband, Kerkylas of Andros, innocently taken as a rare crumb of biographical information by scholars in the past. However, when translated from Greek, the name becomes a tad unlikely: "Dick All-Cock from Man."[40] Speculation on her sex life apparently did not defuse Sappho's popularity, but it seems it was taken as a bizarre bit of trivia at best or a scandalous detail at worst.

Another example is the love story of Achilles and Patroklos. As with Gilgamesh and Enkidu or Jonathan and David, it can be argued that their relationship was nothing more than a heroic friendship. However, even the Athenian elite wondered if Homer meant to imply something between the lines. Naturally the Athenians, through the haze of adult–adolescent male relationships that were the craze in their time, tended to assume that Achilles was Patroklos's teacher, elder, and lover. In a fragment from his lost play *Myrmidons,* Aeskhylos wrote of a grieved Achilles who "thought of Patroklos's thighs."[41] Pindar compared the pedaristic relationship of the adolescent boxer Hagesidamos and his trainer to that of Achilles and Patroklos.[42] In Plato's *Symposium,* Phaedros tells the story that Achilles was allowed to go to the Isles of the Blessed by the gods because he proved his heroism by loving Patroklos enough to avenge him, but points out (correctly) that Homer makes it clear that Achilles was actually younger than Patroklos.[43] Taking this track, Plato's peer and contemporary Xenophon, speaking through Socrates, denied that Patroklos's and Achilles's love ever drove them into the bedroom,[44] instead proposing it as a classic example of the chaste Platonic relationships that was the shining ideal of Athenian pederasty.

The Athenian fad for pederasty, Platonic and otherwise, has warped our perception of mythology. Bernard Sargent saw so many signs of pederasty in Greek mythology, from Ganymede to Heracles, that he was convinced pederasty had to have been an extremely old Indo-European ritual,[45] but actually stories that celebrated pederasty emerge no earlier than 630 BCE.[46] Even Ganymede, for so many centuries a symbol of same-sex love, was in Homer's stories taken away by the other gods simply because of his beauty—not because Zeus fell in love (or lust) with him, as later versions of the myth have it.[47] The Athenians were as stranded on the idea of pederasty as future generations of Europeans would be.

The Greeks Contemplate Pederasty

The Athenians thought and talked and argued about pederasty as much as, if not more than, present-day scholars of classical Greece. This has caused people of later generations to think of Athens as a lost homosexual Atlantis, giving punchlines to jokes, codewords for people looking for ways to navigate around societal disapproval and sodomy laws, and hope to generations of homosexuals looking for either tools for building an ancient historical identity or traces of a truly tolerant society. One writer, Robert Allen, went so far as to make the totally untenable but rather clever claim that the Athenian aristocracy might have seen a *heterosexual* underground.[48] As with so many things, the view that the Athenians had of pederasty—and male homosexuality in general—was not nearly so simple.

The geographer Strabo traced the origins of pederasty to Crete:

> They have a peculiar custom in regard to love-affairs, for they win the objects of their love, not by persuasion, but by abduction. The lover tells the friends of the boy three or four days beforehand that he is going to make the abduction, but for the friends to conceal the boy, or not to let him go forth by the appointed road, is indeed a most disgraceful thing, a confession, as it were, that the boy is unworthy to obtain such a lover. And when they meet, if the abductor is the boy's equal or superior in rank or other respects, the friends pursue him and lay hold of him, though only in a very gentle way, thus satisfying the custom, and after that they cheerfully turn the boy over to him to lead away. If, however, the abductor is unworthy,

they take the boy away from him. And the pursuit does not end until the boy is taken to the "Andreium" of his abductor. They regard as a worthy object of love, not the boy who is exceptionally handsome, but the boy who is exceptionally manly and decorous. After giving the boy presents, the abductor takes him away to any place in the country he wishes; and those who were present at the abduction follow after them, and after feasting and hunting with them for two months (for it is not permitted to detain the boy for a longer time), they return to the city.[49]

The point behind such an elaborate ritual is uncertain. Perhaps, for an island community sometimes hard pressed for resources, it was a way to address overpopulation[50] or a method for "domesticating" young men and inducting them into citizenship. The latter seems more likely, especially because the gifts were a military habit, an ox, and a drinking cup, which symbolized the young man's participation in the body politic and the founding of his own household (the drinking cup because it was used in religious rituals by the head of the household). At any rate, a much less formalized and (ideally) nonsexual version of this ritual seems to have spread through most of Greece over the course of the seventh century BCE.

The trend can be traced, at least somewhat, in Greek vase art. The popularity of depictions of pederasty in art peak by 550, but disappear almost entirely around 475.[51] However, not all erotic depictions of same-sex intimacy from this period were pederastic. One bowl dated to 430 BCE depicts two young men of the same age about to have sex while a man and a woman look on from behind a half-closed door.[52] Another shows two young, unbearded men embracing for a kiss while one has his hand over his comrade's genitals.[53] Other images are more subtle, showing male couples of the same age in intimate poses, but discreetly wrapped in a cloak. There are a few plausible depictions of female same-sex eroticism as well, but they are rather ambiguous, showing nothing more than female couples sharing a blanket.[54] While there are depictions of women being sexually degraded and women depicted as consenting partners in heterosexual couplings, there were also women who are entertained voyeurs.

The same haze surrounds the interesting bits of evidence that point toward female pederasty, at least in Sparta. In his biography of the foundational Spartan lawmaker Lykurgos, Plutarch mentions that there was a custom of aristocratic women taking female adolescents as lovers as initiation into adulthood.[55] The seventh century BCE poet Alkman described an annual Spartan ritual where a chorus of women express desire for their female chorus-leader, although the lack of context makes it difficult to know if this expressed some level of acceptance for same-sex female relationships or even if the feelings expressed were actually symbolic of opposite-sex pairings.[56] Any evidence is too rare, though, but perhaps female sexuality had more outlets in ancient Greece than typically believed.

What placed male pederasty so close to the heart of the Athenian aristocratic ethos was a small, failed conspiracy that nonetheless became the stuff of patriotic history. After 528 or 527, the brothers Hippias and Hipparkhos inherited the reins of their father Peisistratos's autocratic but popular regime over Athens. The sons failed to also inherit what made their father's regime digestible. Hipparkhos propositioned Harmodios, who was the younger lover or *euronomos* of Aristogeiton, twice, only to be rebuked. Perhaps further enraged by the fact that Harmodios was his social inferior, Hipparkhos retaliated by publicly calling Harmodios *malakon*, "soft" or "effeminate,"[57] and by revoking his invitation to Harmodios's sister to participate in a religious festival.[58]

Pushed over the brink by both events, Harmodios and Aristogeiton plotted to kill both

Hipparkhos and Hippias. In the middle of organizing the Panatheaean Festival in the Acropolis, Hipparkhos was stabbed to death by the two men. Hippias's bodyguard killed Harmodios, while Aristogeiton was detained and either tortured to death or personally killed by Hippias. Even though Hippias survived, Aristogeiton and Harmodios were celebrated as the *tyrannophonoi,* the Tyrannicides, and were honored by a pair of statues in the Agora, depicting a bearded Aristogeiton and a beardless Harmodios and holding the plaque, "They established the fatherland."[59]

The historian Thucydides is blunt in his version, inferring that Aristogeiton was Harmodios's lover and "possessed him."[60] In contrast, in his famous speech *Against Timarkhos,* the orator Aeschines takes a moment to instead call Harmodios's and Aristogeiton's friendship "chaste."[61] Such a model of pederasty was circulated among the elite, which had nothing to do with sex and everything to do with the inoculation of good old-fashioned democratic values into the next generation of men. Whether or not their love was "chaste," the Tyrannicides proved to posterity that the attachment between an older citizen and an adolescent was an antidote against tyranny, which is the reason why Phaedros in Plato's *Symposium* believes the Persians outlaw the practice.[62]

Even Socrates, who is said to be "crazy about beautiful boys" and "follows them about in a daze,"[63] was a true believer in chaste pederasty, at least according to Plato and Xenophon. True to his role as a philosopher who made a career out of endorsing philosophy and the self-examined life over carnal gratification, Socrates resisted the increasingly unsubtle flirtations of his handsome and athletic student, Alkibiades, even when he slept in bed with Alkibiades's arms around him.[64]

At least Plato had a sense of humor about sex, just before his attitude concerning same-sex love became more uncompromising, even venomous, in the *Laws*. He was willing to portray a Socrates who is mercilessly teased for spending so much time around Alkibiades[65] and who pushes his compatriots over in a gymnasium to make an empty seat right next to him for the intelligent, muscular young man Charmides.[66] Plato does not intend to portray Socrates as a hypocrite. If nothing else, Alkibiades's speech in the *Symposium* shows that Socrates's ability to overcome his own abundant lust, especially when he literally immerses himself in temptation, is part of what makes him an exceptional philosopher and citizen. Although the triumph of the mind over the loins was serious business for the Socratics, there is something playful in how Plato portrays his former teacher, as if his audience would appreciate the social and philosophical ideals of pederastic love as well as the open secret that physical attraction still had a role to play.

While the pre-*Laws* Plato occasionally wants his readers to chuckle politely over the steamy side of man-and-adolescent love, Aristophanes expects his audience to laugh long and maliciously. Writing to a broad audience, one that might have savored his ferocious satirical assault on Socrates in *Clouds,* Aristophanes presents pederasty as a transparent excuse for older men and particularly the leading citizens of Athens to make love to other men in their prime.

In Plato's *Symposium,* Aristophanes famously weaves a myth explaining that love and sexual attraction ultimately derive from the fact that all couples who fall in love were originally one being, cut apart into two separate individuals by Zeus.[67] In this story, Plato has Aristophanes teach that adolescents attracted to men are the ones who "grow up to be real men in politics" and "pay no attention to marriage or to making babies, except insofar as they are required by local custom."⁶⁸ There is some ambiguity cast around the question of how upfront Plato means for us to take Aristophanes, especially once, to prove his "point," he describes with apparently a straight face that the poet Agathon and his long-time lover Pausanias, who are present at the symposium, as "probably ... entirely masculine in nature."⁶⁹ Yet when the same Agathon makes a cameo in Aristophanes's play *Thesmophoriazusae,* it is as an effeminate and cowardly fop in drag addicted to anal sex. Rather than being an example of Aeschines's ideal manly citizen indoctrinated through pederastic love, Agathon is instead the specimen Aristophanes pins up in the *Symposium* to demonstrate that love between men does not really instill masculine virtues. Plato must have expected this point to ring true for his readers, who would have known Aristophanes's thoughts on the subject.

Where Aristophanes's real opinions on pederasty explode from the page is in *Clouds,* his grand sarcastic manifesto on the Socratics. The comic hero of *Clouds* is Strepsiades, a sort of everyman who is on the verge of bankruptcy because of the debts his son Pheidippides incurred by gambling on horse races. Hoping that Socrates can teach him how to talk himself out of debt using philosophical arguments, which can override the objective truths of reality, Strepsiades goes to the school, only to be thrown out after failing to appreciate Socrates's logic (especially his argument that there is no such thing as a god named Zeus but instead a giant vortex of air) and pass his tests (but not before Socrates manages to steal his clothes). Strepsiades then sends his son to the school, where he is treated to a debate between two characters representing "Just" and "Unjust Speech."

Just Speech, who personifies rhetoric drawn from proud Athenian tradition, promises Pheidippides that he will show him how to be "ashamed at shameful things" and to respect his elders.⁷⁰ As Just Speech goes on, although it is implied that "shameful things" are sexual, he gets increasingly excited at the thought of what the young Pheidippides could become: "You'll always have a gleaming chest, bright skin, / broad shoulders, tiny tongue, strong buttocks, and a little prick."⁷¹ If Pheidippides makes the mistake of following Unjust Speech, then, Just Speech promises, "he'll give you Antimakhos's disease [Antimakhos was another Athenian citizen satirized by Aristophanes as being effeminate], you'll be infected with his buggery."⁷²

The debate hits its crescendo when Just Speech asks Unjust Speech if rhetoric can save Pheidippides from accusations of being a "wide-assed bugger."⁷³ Unjust Speech shrugs off this insult, although Just Speech asks, "Can one suffer any greater harm / than having a loose asshole?"⁷⁴ However, Unjust Speech goes on to make Just Speech admit that all Athenian jurists, poets, politicians, and even the play's audience have all been buggered. Vanquished by the knowledge of the sex lives of Athenian men, Just Speech, while looking out at the audience, exclaims, "By all the gods, almost all of them are men who have spread their cheeks."⁷⁵ In front of an audience whose members would have all been raised with the intelligentsia's ideals of "chaste and lawful" pederasty, the personification of Athenian values admits that pederasty in practice is anything but chaste.

Aristophanes was apparently far from the only detractor of pederasty. Lawmakers from early in Greece's judicial history enacted legal bans geared toward limiting the practice. Xenophon claimed that while Sparta, much like the Athenian elite, encouraged pederasty between men and adolescents as a way to train future leaders and soldiers, Spartan law penalized any pederastic relationship that became sexual.⁷⁶ A relationship between an adolescent and a Spartan citizen that crossed into the bedroom was considered, Xenophon claimed, the "most shameful of all things."[77] Given Xenophon's extreme distaste for sexual pederasty, however, this claim should come packaged with a grain of salt.[78] Apollodoros mentions in Plato's *Symposium* that pederasty was outlawed in Ionia, although this is attributed to Persia's control of the city and to the fear of the democratic comradeship pederasty (hopefully) inspired.[79] Polykrates, the sixth-century tyrant of Samos, was said to have shut down the wrestling courts because they were popular meeting places between men and male adolescents (even though he had been a lover of young men himself).[80]

These laws did not just exist outside of Athens. In the late seventh century and early sixth century, the Athenian lawmaker Solon placed similar restrictions on pederasty by imposing strict opening and closing hours on *gymnasia* and banning unauthorized people from schools. Male slaves were also forbidden from starting sexual relations with free-born boys and entering a gymnasium, while a minimum age of 40 was required for men who taught adolescents choral music.[81] Although Solon was apparently a pederast himself, his laws reveal a fear that a pederastic relationship could just as easily become an invitation for sexual exploitation.

Contrary to popular (and sometimes academic) belief, there was no Greek consensus on same-sex love between men, much less pederasty. There were voices like the sixth-century poet Theognis, who celebrated the love between a fully grown man and an adolescent as well as the sexual passion that can be shared between two young men.[82] It was also taken as a fact of life that *gymnasia,* the banquets known as *symposia,* and certain hot-spots on the outskirts of Athens were all popular meeting places for men.[83] Like Plato, Xenophon has Socrates praise a pederastic relationship based on friendship and mutual respect,[84] but overall his Socrates warns his students not to get entangled with older men. Some orators and comic playwrights other than Aristophanes also painted men who were or had been involved in pederastic relationships as prostitutes and effeminates.[85] The orator Demosthenes's archenemy Aeschines labeled him as a *kinaidos*, a vague insult that has been interpreted as meaning for Athenians something like "anti-citizen"[86] but which is much better rendered in English as a broad insult with sexual connotations like "pervert."[87] Aeschines went further by claiming that there was a sleazy side to Demosthenes's relationship with an adolescent male, the specifics of which Aeschines maliciously left to his audience's imagination.[88]

Ironically, the most overt and uncompromising screed in classical Greece against not only pederasty, but same-sex love in general, comes from the same philosopher who gave us Aristophanes's sentimental myth for the origin of same-sex desire—Plato. The *Laws* was Plato's last known work and expands on the totalitarian undertones already cemented in his *Republic,* featuring an unnamed Athenian, a Spartan named Megillos, and a Cretan named Kleinias, who together map out a State that prevents its citizens from traveling abroad or operating businesses, mandates childbearing and marriage (and the age people can marry, at that), and regulates people's everyday activities down to where they can eat dinner and how often they can drink wine.

Compared to the multitude of other social, political, and judicial topics the Athenian dives into, the regulation of sex is only a momentary distraction, yet Plato's strong feelings on the subject are made plain. Here Plato declares that "the sexual act" should be reserved only for "its natural purpose, procreation" and denounces all same-sex relations (including sex between women[89]) as when "the human race is deliberately murdered."[90] Homosexual lust is called "one of the desires that dominate humankind so cruelly."[91] Plato's practical solution for dealing with such a nefarious inclination is to try to force homosexual lovers into hiding by making such pairings a social liability.[92] The most ambitious proposal is even more eerily prescient: reengineer culture, religion, and literature from the ground up so that homosexuality would automatically inspire the same revulsion that incest brings up among Plato's fellow Greeks. The Athenian may as well be foreseeing the future of sex in Europe when he adds, "[T]he fear that the act is a ghastly sin will, in the end, enable them to tame the passions that their inferiors have tamed before them."[93]

In spite of what seems to be a radical departure, the Plato of the *Symposium* and *Phaedrus* is still lurking in the margins. After all, the Athenian begins his discussion by praising the "calm and mutual affection that can last a lifetime" and "a mature and genuine desire of soul for soul" that two men may share while at the same time showing contempt for the purely physical relationship between men where the lover "hungry for his partner who is ripe to be enjoyed, like a luscious fruit, tells himself to have his fill, without showing any consideration for his beloved's character and disposition."[94] Nor is the demand for such intrusive legislation entirely unprecedented. It can be traced to Solon's laws on social and sexual matters and Sparta's own militaristic communal society. The stark and unmistakable emphasis on the unnaturalness of all forms of sexual intercourse that cannot result in a child is a fresh element in Plato's writings, but later became a favorite idea of the Roman Stoics.

Plato's star pupil, Aristotle, did not share his mentor's views on utopia-building through strict legislation and social engineering and, in fact, was mostly silent on the topic of pederasty. Presumably readers would have found out his opinions from a treatise he wrote titled *On Love,* but the entire text has been lost. Aristotle promises at one point in his *Politics* that he will discuss whether pederasty as practiced in Crete is socially beneficial,[95] but never does so, and gives only a brief and clinical description of male friendships based on either mutual lust or admiration.[96] The closest we come to an Aristotlean opinion on homosexual desire is his speculation on its causes. When discussing exceptions to bad moral states in the *Nicomachean Ethics,* Aristotle maintains that the sexual desire one man may feel for another or just the desire of one man to be sexually penetrated by another[97] is caused by external factors that play out in childhood: "For while some males are subject to this condition because of a natural deformity, others are subject to it as a result of habituation, as in the case of males who are sexually abused [that is, are victims of *hybris*] from childhood." Because it has a definite medical cause beyond the conscious control of the "victim," Aristotle continues, such an act should not be considered a vice.[98]

Basically Aristotle is, in a sophisticated and scientific way, suggesting what Aristophanes already took for granted: that adolescents in a pederastic relationship will have their sexual inclinations altered in some way. It should be noticed, too, that Aristotle makes this argument specifically to respond to those who *do* believe that consenting to same-sex male intercourse is a moral failing, suggesting the topic is and has been an open one. This explanation did not begin with Aristotle—a fifth-century philosopher Parmenides had a similar idea[99]—and it would become transfused to later Greek and Latin medical writers and astrologers, who wrote of sexual and gender deviance as defects that are inborn or inflicted during childhood. This strain of thought made it at least as far as the fifth-century Byzantine historian Procopius, who, while sympathetic to their agony, thought of the male homosexuals persecuted and butchered under Emperor Justinian I as suffering from a "malady."[100]

Just because we cannot find any laws (aside from those that existed only in one of Plato's phantom utopias) that expressly seek out and punish same-sex relations, it does not mean that we are viewing a society that was "accepting" in the modern sense or did not conceive that certain people had desires that inclined them to one sex or another. Nor should we think that there was any uniformity to Greek thought on any sexual matters, especially on pederasty and sex between people of the same gender and similar ages. The last word should come from historian Thomas Hubbard: "There is, in fact, no more consensus about homosexuality in ancient Greece and Rome than there is today."[101]

Sex, Honor and Hybris

Hybris was a vague legal concept that helped provide the Athenian government with an ax against sexual immorality. The best effort to pin down this slippery term comes, unsurprisingly, from Aristotle, who describes *hybris* as any action carried out by one individual that degrades another's honor.[102] Anyone could be a victim of *hybris*, even if they were a woman, a child, a noncitizen, or a slave.[103] Such an idea does seem to run against modern literary and cinematic portrayals of ancient slavery, but Demosthenes helpfully cites past legal cases where slaves were extended the full protection of the law from abuses by their masters, resulting in legal sanctions up to imprisonment until a fine could be assessed.[104] In one extreme instance, a man named Euthymakhos was said to have been brought up on charges by accusers, detained, and then executed for trying to force a female slave to work in a brothel.[105] Although *hybris* was often applied to the prosecution of rape cases,[106] consent did not matter and *hybris* could also easily apply to cases of adultery and seduction.[107]

Daniel Cohen has argued that, like many Mediterranean societies past and present, ancient Athens viewed sex as a matter of honor and disgrace.[108] Solon's restrictions on pederasty presumably existed to preemptively defend the honor of male adolescents. The Athenian regime also felt free to step in to protect respectable women's honor from seducers. A law again attributed to Solon existed to that end, including laws that barred women in mourning from leaving a tomb before the men[109] and that regulate women's clothing and jewelry.[110] Solon also made it legal for a father to sell an unchaste daughter into slavery[111] and turned female adultery into a capital offense for the woman.[112]

By the classical period, such laws, if they ever really existed outside legend, had fallen by the wayside. Still, the fear that women must be kept on a short leash to defend their sexual integrity, which had inspired the idea of such regulations in the first place, remained. Women caught committing adultery would be prevented from entering public temples and attending religious rites, a stricter punishment than it may seem at a glance given that religious life was more or less an Athenian woman's only vehicle for civic participation.[113] An adulterous wife's husband might also be required to divorce her or face losing his citizenship rights.[114]

Men who were implicated as seducers could be fined, a punishment also enforced in the Cretan city of Gortyn,[115] and prosecuted for *hybris*.[116] If they were particularly unlucky, the husband or the family could force them to pay compensation and publicly humiliate them in a degrading ritual. Aristophanes mentions one popular method that might have been used to humble a Don Juan: shoving a radish up his anus and singing off his body hair. There were state-imposed limits to how much revenge could be taken from a paramour, however. If the offended party killed the lover outside his home, he could still be prosecuted for murder.[117]

Orators and philosophers preached that women had to be secured against the pervasive threat of seduction and held up seclusion as a virtue. In one recorded speech the speaker brags that his sister and nieces "have been brought up so [respectably] that they are ashamed to be seen even by close relatives."[118] In fact, a male stranger coming across a respectable woman in her own home could be tantamount to *hybris*.[119] Comedy presents a somewhat less idealized view. Throughout the play *Assemblywomen,* when the wives of Athens' elite leave their homes to usurp the city government and end all war, the men instantly guess that their wives are really out having fun with their lovers.

Conventional Greek wisdom maintained that women were less rational and had less control over their emotions and, hence, their sexuality. The view was sardonically expressed by Xenophon when he wrote, "If there is a fault in a horse or a sheep, we blame the herdsman, but if there is a fault in a woman, perhaps it is right to hold her responsible, but there is no doubt about the responsibility of a man."[120] Xenophon was by Athenian standards something of a conservative, but his biases were shared by his government. Even though women could be citizens, the law limited the financial amount a woman could make in a contract.[121] In addition, throughout Greece, even in the more egalitarian Sparta, women had to have a male guardian, the *kyrios*.[122] Women technically had as much right to seek a divorce as a man, but they had to rely on a male relative or guardian to initiate proceedings. Still, we should take Daniel Cohen's warning to distinguish between ideology and reality and recognize that, just because the Athenian intellectual elite wrote at length that women should be isolated from men because of their vulnerability, it does not mean that they often were.

While the leaders of Athens fretted about seducers wanting their women and the horror of unrestrained feminine sexuality, ironically the toast of the city were still the *hetairai,* the rich and educated courtesans of high Greek society. The Athenian orators, as Alison Glazebook puts it, "present an image of the hetaira herself as extravagant, promiscuous, available to anyone, requiring payment, excessive in her behavior, scheming, and arrogant."[123] Yet the *hetairai* were also treated like Hollywood celebrities: they were invited to attend *symposia* (an honor not usually extended to women, even to wives), their witty quotations written down and published, and they had the freedom to accumulate wealth and property without ever needing a nod from a *kyrios*.[124] One particularly famous *hetaira* was the Athenian statesman Pericles's mistress, Aspasia, who casually debated with Socrates and his students as an acknowledged equal.[125] The other extreme was experienced by the *hetaira* Naerea, who was ruthlessly slandered in court, all for trying to pass off her daughter, who was born while she was a slave, as a free-born Athenian citizen with the help of her husband, an unpopular politician.[126]

Lower on the social ladder were the *pornai,* street and brothel prostitutes, and *pallake,* concubines who lived with men. The latter enjoyed the same rights as wives except that their children were considered illegitimate and thus were not eligible for citizenship.[127] Male prostitutes were just as accepted, with a special tax, the *pornikon telos*, being levied on their profits[128] (presumably a similar tax existed for female prostitutes). It was not a profession meant for respectable men. Prostitution was a common charge levied against politicians who had in the past been courted by older men in a pederastic relationship, something not helped by the custom of a younger lover accepting gifts from the man who pursued him. It was a nasty and disarming charge, because at least in several cases a male Athenian citizen thought to have prostituted himself for gifts and money had his rights to citizenship brought under scrutiny—the cool logic being that any man who had sold his body for money would also be capable of selling out the nation's interests.[129]

Besides the patriotic implications of male prostitution and the fear of seduction, another sexual boogeyman for ancient Athens was incest. The taboo against incest was yet another totem held up by the Athenians to prove their culture's superiority to that of the "barbarians." Yet according to Plato, there were no actual laws on the books against incest; the cultural drumbeat that hammered in the point that "these acts are absolutely unholy, an abomination in the sight of the gods, and that nothing is more revolting" was enough.[130] Given that a popular story for Greek playwrights was the tale of Oedipus, who accidentally marries his own mother, a crime deemed so hideous that a plague strikes his city of Thebes and he must blind himself and wander aimlessly to make penance, Plato might actually be understating the case.

Despite its militaristic culture, a government that was arguably a prototype for modern totalitarianism, and the ugly reality that it had the most brutal caste system in Greece, Sparta apparently had a more loose attitude toward women, marriage, and sex than Athens. Given an education and an exercise regimen as rigorous as that of men, Spartan women were well known across Greece for their fierce independence and their stern patriotic attitudes. A collection of sayings attributed to Spartan women by Plutarch includes coarse pronouncements like this one from a mother who had heard a rumor that her son had fled from a battle: "A bad rumor about you is circulating. Either absolve yourself at once, or cease to exist."[131]

There appears to have been no Spartan law against adultery in any form and no tradition of promiscuous men and women being prosecuted. This was perhaps because marriage in classical Sparta was semi-communal, with women taking sex partners outside their marriage whenever they saw fit. Plutarch even suggests that the purpose behind this custom was to increase the odds of women giving birth to strong future citizens and to circumvent the problem of male sterility. He also claims that women were allowed to freely choose their own lovers, with input from the husband as perhaps nothing more than a courtesy.[132]

It may have been this characteristically pragmatic Spartan approach to solving the age-old problem of how women and men should interact sexually and how procreation should be encouraged that was the main inspiration for the utopia in Plato's *Republic*, where Socrates argues that men and women should be considered equal in every respect except physical strength.[133] In Socrates's vision, the hypothetical Republic's highest class, the guardians, who comprised both women and men, would live communally with no private property while sexual relations and childrearing would no longer be the sole province of monogamous couples.[134] Here Plato was simply taking the Spartan approach to sex and children one step further.

Much less revolutionary was Plato's plan for women and sex in the *Laws*. Marriage would be mandatory for women after they turned 16 and before they became 20, just as it was for men between the ages of 30 and 35. Divorce would be imposed by the State if the marriage remained childless. Adultery would be punished for both wives and husbands, with husbands losing their citizenship rights and wives publicly shamed and barred from state ceremonies. Yet Plato was willing to extend to men the courtesy of withholding punishment if they made enough of an effort to keep the affair secret.[135] So much for the equality of sexes.

There are unfamiliar threads in the tangled mass that forms customs and ideas about sex in ancient Greece. But there is also a great deal that is very familiar, reflecting modern society's codes and mores—from assumptions that women have to be protected from seduction to Plato's notions that strict moral regulations enforced legally are desirable, if not necessary. Even in the midst of what has been thought of as a society with few sexual hang-ups, the seeds of future sex regulations in the West were planted in the soil. After all, the New Testament and the other writings of early Christianity were written in Greek and with Greek concepts and ideas.

III

The Decadent Past, from Alexander the Great to Antinuous

Alexander the Great's least recognized accomplishment, yet possibly his most impressive, is that he wiped out democracy in the eastern Mediterranean. After Alexander's death and the dissolution of his hastily built empire, the region was dominated by a clutch of hereditary monarchies, especially Ptolemaic Egypt, Antipatrid and Antigonid Macedon, and Seleucid Syria. Under them, the culture of Greece migrated into new climates, mixing with the mores of other societies and forming fresh ideas that would change how Europeans think about sex.

Sex in the Hellenistic World

Besides having a knack for finding new lands and conquering them, Alexander the Great draws attention for his rumored romances with men.[1] Theophratos, a student of Alexander's one-time tutor Aristotle, claimed that Alexander's parents, Olympias and King Philip II, were supposedly concerned about Alexander's sexual inclinations and hired a *hetaira* named Callixeina to sleep with Alexander, but he simply ignored her advances.[2] Alexander is more famous for his relationship with Hephaeston. Together they made a perhaps symbolic trip to the tomb of Achilles and Patroklos. Whether the reason, Alexander did not father an heir until late in his life, thus placing his infant empire into the hands of his very young son, Alexander IV (323–309), and his mentally handicapped half-brother, Philip III (323–317). Both of them were taken care of by Alexander's ambitious generals. Thus Alexander's inability—or refusal—to father an heir who would have been old enough to defend himself and his interests at the moment of Alexander's sudden death proved to have real consequences for not only Alexander's dynasty, but also his empire and, indeed, the future of the entire Greek-speaking world.

It is appropriate that a historical figure with a complicated sexuality like Alexander should open up the Hellenistic epoch, a time when more frank illustrations of sex would appear in literature, more refreshingly crude in its depiction of everyday life than the stylized literary styles of the classical epoch. This was also an era when women, long locked out of politics by the macho governments of the Greek city-states, would find ways to access power through the dynastic politics of the Hellenistic monarchies, as either wives, mothers, or courtesans.

The *hetairai* reached new rungs on the social and political ladder, achieving influential positions in court and occasionally even breaching the status of queen.[3] Although most were dependent on allowances and gifts from their kingly lovers, a few may have amassed their own private fortunes, like Ptolemy IV of Egypt's (r. 221–205) mistress Agathokleia, who owned a fleet of ships and had the resources to keep large retinues well funded.[4] There does not seem to have been much of an outcry against the visibility of the *hetairai* at the right hands of the kings. Likely enough such criticisms were never safe to make, at least not when the king was within earshot. Ptolemy VIII of Egypt (r. 182–116) had all the members of his bodyguard executed when they had the gall—and the lack of a survival instinct—to criticize his living openly with the famous *hetaira* Eirene.[5]

Art and literature became more infused with female eroticism, which is hardly surprising considering the queens, princesses, *hetairai,* and other rich, autonomous women who were out and about to act as audience and patrons. A trend in more frank, unrobed depictions of the female form in sculpture and art reflected, as Sarah Pomeroy describes it, "a more open acknowledgment of women's erotic impulses and their gratification."[6] This appeared in literature as well, manifesting in verses like this one from the poet Theokritos, which describes a woman falling in love with a young athlete named Delphis: "Tell, how Eros fell on me, Lady Moon! / The moment my eyes lit of them, madness lit on me, / and fire was laid to my heart, poor wretch that I am!"[7]

It is probably not surprising, then, that the Hellenistic era saw another potential voice of female same-sex attraction. What little remains of the work of the third-century epigrammist Nossis, who described herself as a friend of Sappho,[8] suggests that she took on female beauty as a major theme. As with Sappho, the surviving scraps of her writings show no erotic or romantic interest in men. Literary interest in male homoeroticism also blossomed. Poets like Kallimachos, Meleager, and Theokritos all claimed with literary flair that Heracles, Orpheus, and Plato had all been prodigious lovers of adolescent men.[9]

Although the evidence for a lesbian presence is scarce, there are traces of a satirical backlash. One third-century poem by Asclepiades named two *hetairai* with attachments to other women: "The Samian girls Bitto and Nannion are not of a mind / To meet with Aphrodite on her own terms / But desert to other practices, and not good ones. Lady Cyprus [Aphrodite], / Abhor these fugitives from your bed."[10] The poet Herodas, also writing in the third century, put together a scene where two wives excitedly talk about a brand-new red leather dildo. When talking about women who already had their fun with it, the names of Nossis and another female poet, Erinna, both spring up.[11] We can only guess if such comments were made out of stern disapproval inspired by actual gossip about their sexuality or if these women's new prominence ignited outright hostility.

Whereas Hellenistic literature and art honestly and bluntly explored sexuality, one of several new philosophical schools, Epicureanism, followed Plato's lead in arguing that sex ought to be treated like a dangerous force. Contrary to his modern reputation as a philosopher advertising a totally libertine lifestyle, Epicurus advised his followers on the perils of sexual pleasure. It is true that, while Plato and Aristotle thought some pleasures were "bad" because they do not and cannot contribute to one's long-term happiness, for Epicurus no pleasure was "bad" since pleasure is naturally the goal of any individual.[12] Still, the ultimate pleasure to be pursued is the contentment that can come only from the tranquility of the body and mind. Sex and other momentary pleasures endanger that desirable balance: "For it is not drinking and continuous parties nor sexual pleasures nor the enjoyment of fish and other delicacies of a wealthy table which produce the pleasant life, but sober reasoning which searches out the causes of every act of choice and refusal and which banishes the opinions that give rise to the greatest mental confusion."[13]

The Plato of the *Laws* wanted to make procreation mandatory for as many of his utopia's citizens as possible. The Stoic school, founded by Zeno of Citium around 300 BCE, did not quite go to those extremes, but did embrace the idea that marriage and parenting children was a necessary duty because it supplied the community with potential citizens.[14] Alongside this belief in the necessity of reproduction for the sake of the State was an embryonic idea of what might be termed as "natural law." Although earlier Greek intellectuals wrote about laws shared across cultures or of laws supported by divine sanction or by universal human tendencies, John Martens maintains that "[o]nly Stoicism claimed that nature supported justice and law in a systematic way [...] The Stoics alone depend on immutable nature as their guide."[15] This love affair between nature and law would make quite a lasting impression. The Stoic Chrysippos's statement, "Single people and states each have their law and customs, but they are all based on the universal law to which each adds something," would even be cited in the original Greek within the Emperor Justinian I's *Corpus Iuris*,[16] part of the most influential collection and reformation of law in medieval Europe.

Even so, like Plato, Zeno dreamed of utopias where the rules of gender and marriage were radically different from anything he knew in the real world. In his own *Republic,* which survives only in Diogenes Laertius's summary, Zeno envisions a society of communal marriage, unisex dress, pederasty, and nude exercise by both sexes in public places.[17] Another major school of the era, the Cynics, agreed with Zeno on communal marriage.[18] At least a few Cynics may have gone one step further by putting such radical principles into practice, at least to a degree. The Cynic Krates and his wife Hipparchia were said to have lived a completely egalitarian marriage.[19]

The founder of Cynicism, Diogenes, was alleged to have been a sexual radical, taking the philosophical idea of "Nature" to its logical but bizarre extreme. Believing that humans should live like dogs in a completely natural way without paying attention to extraneous and arbitrary social rules, Diogenes (or so Diogenes Laertius and his sources claim) masturbated in public.[20] Krates and Hipparchia took a cue from their teacher and supposedly had sex wherever and whenever the mood struck them.[21] Was this actually how Diogenes and his students lived, or was it just a sarcastic interpretation of their teachings that later generations confused for fact? If such accounts do have any truth to them, then later generations of Cynics toned down the antisocial overtones and did their best not to shock.[22] Also, as sexually free as he was in theory, Diogenes and his interpretation of nature had no kind words for gender-bending or homosexuality. In fact, the Christian writer Clement of Alexandria quoted Diogenes approvingly in a tirade against male effeminacy and homosexuality.[23]

For all the far-reaching intellectual breakthroughs in this era, it was, at least speaking in terms of the Hellenistic monarchies' lifespans, a flickering, going out forever in 31 BCE with the Battle of Actium and the suicides of Cleopatra VII and Marcus Antonius, less than three centuries after Alexander the Great's empire was first carved up. For generations the Greeks had anticipated with dread an invasion from Persia in the east. Instead, their Ragnarök finally came from the opposite direction, Italy, in the guise of Roman magistrates and soldiers, who cut the Greek city-states and the Hellenistic kingdoms down into imperial provinces. Although the Greeks lost their independence to a foreign empire, the philosophical schools and religious sects that blossomed under the shadow of the Hellenistic monarchies and were nourished by the fusion of Greek and other eastern Mediterranean cultures remained and prospered in a politically unified environment. The soul and mind of what would become the Roman Empire was in no small part Hellenistic.

When Romans Were Romans

In the first century CE, the unforgiving Roman moralist Valerius Maximus wrote approvingly of a man named Egnatius Mecennius who beat his wife to death when she came home drunk. A precedent for such violence could be dug up from Rome's legendary past—a decree by one of Rome's founders and first king Romulus, which forced the death penalty on not only the wife who became drunk, but also the family that raised her. The same extreme punishment could, after a decision handed down by a family council, be brandished in cases of a wife's adultery,[24] since apparently a wife's drunkenness merely indicated what the act of adultery made obvious: a total lack of sexual self-control. However, Plutarch disagreed, saying instead that Romulus made a woman's adultery nothing more than a legal cause for divorce,[25] which seems a more likely crumb of fact.

It is far from unusual for a culture to look backward to a golden age, where concepts like honor and morality had more substance and people simply acted the way they ought to as opposed to the denizens of the squandered, depraved present. Romans like Valerius Maximus, however, turned that age-old obsession into a literary genre. The bestselling historian Livy must have spoken right to his readers when he wrote that it would be a pleasure writing about Rome's distant past because in his time "excessive pleasures have led to a desire to ruin ourselves and destroy everything through excess and self-indulgence."[26] Considering the civil wars, political convulsions, and mob violence that became the exciting backdrop to everyday Roman life during the painful last decades of the Roman Republic and that justified the existence of the emperors for centuries to come, one can hardly blame them for believing with religious zeal that the best of times were well behind them, even though Rome seemed to be on the brink of controlling the entire known world.

The end of the second century BCE saw Rome's reach extend beyond Italy and encompass the entire Mediterranean, thanks to the obliteration of the mercantile empire of Carthage in North Africa. The only major player on the Mediterranean that seemed to keep a slipping grip on autonomy was Egypt, which was nonetheless a faint echo of what it had been at its apogee. That independence was finally revealed to be an illusion when King Ptolemy XII fled to Rome to escape the wrath of his estranged daughter Berenice IV. The exiled king had to bribe a Roman general into invading his own kingdom for him. Another daughter of Ptolemy, Cleopatra VII, felt obliged to tie herself in with Julius Caesar and Marcus Antonius in succession. She was simply trying to apply the Hellenistic dynastic approach to a republic the only way a daughter of the Ptolemies could.

This lack of real competitors and the flow of wealth pumping through Rome and its veins of patronage networks raised a disturbing question: What if the same strong and unique Roman virtues that made the Roman Republic not just a regional superpower, but the only superpower in Europe, North Africa, and Asia Minor, were also bringing about the soul-deep corruption of its ruling class and its very own institutional backbone? The first century BCE historian Sallust was convinced that the likes of Catiline, the blood-soaked King Mob intent on overturning the Roman Senate, were meant to be the natural leaders of Rome, but were instead turned rotten by excess. Tacitus, writing in a very different time, saw a once-vital Rome that had become so anemic from material wealth and moral corruption that it allowed itself to become enslaved to the Julio-Claudian family of emperors. No wonder modern historians have always been so obsessed with the idea of Roman decadence and decline; the Romans themselves believed in it.

Livy's obsession with the integrity of the earliest Romans reached a high point with the story of Lucretia, where an act of rape and an honorable suicide trigger the abolition of the monarchy headed by the Etruscan Tarquinii and the founding of the Roman Republic. In Livy's account, the royal princes were bragging about the chastity of their wives. Tarquinius Collatinus proudly claimed that his wife Lucretia exceeded all of theirs in virtue and challenged the men to come see what she would be doing when she did not expect a man to be present. While all the other wives were enjoying themselves at banquets, Lucretia was simply weaving with her servants. Embarrassed, a few nights later the prince Sextus Tarquinius raped Lucretia, forcing her to consent by threatening to kill her and a slave and to make it appear that they had been caught making love. Livy continues:

> After Sextus leaves, Lucretia sent out messages asking her husband and her father, Spurius Lucretius, to come with two trusted friends. A devastated Lucretia greeted them, saying, "The marks of another man are in your bed. But only my body has been violated; my mind is not guilty. Death will be my witness. But give me your right hands and your word that the adulterer will not go unpunished. Sextus Tarquinius is the man. Last night he repaid hospitality with hostility when he came, armed, and forcibly took his pleasure of me, an act that has destroyed me—and him too, if you are men." All duly gave her their pledge. They tried to console her distress by shifting the guilt from the woman who had been forced to the man who had done the wrong, saying that it is the mind that errs, not the body. For where there had been no intent, there is no blame. "You shall determine," she replied, "what is his due. Though I absolve myself of wrongdoing, I do not exempt myself from punishment. Nor henceforth shall any unchaste woman continue to live by citing the precedent of Lucretia." She took a knife that she had hidden in her garments and plunged it in her heart.[27]

Using Lucretia's suicide as a rallying point, Collatinus and his friend Lucius Junius Brutus, who was present, led a revolt against the monarchy, which soon drove the Tarquinii from Rome. Lucius Brutus and Collatinus, the only member of the royal family left, became the new republic's first consuls.

Every detail of the Lucretia legend drips with a fixation on honor and image. Collatinus holds up his wife's habits as a personal point of pride. Sextus threatens Lucretia by framing her for adultery with a slave (the class element must have given the threat an extra kick). Lucretia forces promises to avenge her on pain of the men no longer being seen as men. And, most of all, Lucretia kills herself not just out of her own disgrace, but to set a stern example to posterity.[28]

It may be that Livy was inspired not just by the supposed decadence of the late Republic or by the Emperor Augustus's program of changing morals with the law's hand—Lucretia's story was widely known and predated Livy by centuries. Livy may have added the not-so-subtle point about Lucretia setting herself up as a reference point for future generations of women, but the bare bones of the legend may have been very old indeed, especially if, as Valerie Warrior suggests, the contrast between the women at banquets and an industrious Lucretia came from a real culture clash between the Etruscan and indigenous Roman peoples over how women should spend their time.[29] Regardless, the point is bleak: honor—especially the honor of a woman who represents not just herself but the male members of her household—can be repaired through self-inflicted violence. It is not an easy mindset to understand in a time permeated by not only feminism but also very different notions of guilt and victimhood. Even the usually stern Saint Augustine of Hippo, writing in the fifth century CE, was appalled by the stories of Lucretia's suicide and struggled to understand why the victim Lucretia had to die while the rapist Sextus was merely banished.[30]

A more obscure but even darker legend is shared by Livy, and once more a woman and her sexual integrity become a focal point for tyranny. In 451 BCE, the consulship was abolished and a new executive body, a council of ten called the decemvirate, was established. In Livy's narrative, the decemvirate, invested with near-absolute power, becomes more and more arbitrary and bloodthirsty, but the proverbial straw occurs when the decemvir Appius Claudius attempts to seduce Verginia, the daughter of a plebian soldier who was already engaged to Lucius Icilius. Pulling the strings available to every patrician Roman, Appius has his client, Marcus Claudius, claim while Verginia's father is away on the field that Verginia is rightfully a slave of his who has been abducted and falsely raised as another family's freeborn daughter. Through a series of legal maneuvers, Appius manages to drag out a ruling in his favor. As Verginia and her father are cornered by soldiers sent by Appius to claim her, he stabs her to death, crying out, "Daughter, I am claiming your freedom in the only way I can."[31] Public outrage soon hits a crescendo and the decemvirate is trampled.

Ostensibly in Livy's version Verginia was killed to prevent her fall into slavery,[32] although any Roman reader would have known that, as a slave, Verginia would have had absolutely no recourse against Appius's sexual advances. Once again, we learn that death is a preferable—if not outright desirable—alternative to a drastic loss of honor and that sexual exploitation is a prime symptom of political evil. Although the Greeks had the same idea of "respectable" women as a sexual commodity to be protected, there is nothing quite like the stories of Lucretia or Verginia in Greek history or legend. This is because, while the Roman and Greek mindsets may have had similar concepts of honor, the Romans had a highly developed sense of suicide as a strong antidote to dishonor. Suicide as an acceptable solution to dishonor, rather than just an escape from suffering in life, is an event that happens again and again in Rome's history.[33]

Fornication, Marriage and Scandal under the Republic

The Roman Republic was about as far in conception and execution from modern Western governments as a political system can be. Public works projects and mass entertainments were undertaken by wealthy and well-connected citizens eager for a taste of the populace's fickle love, humdrum bureaucratic maintenance was entirely in the hands of local elites and their networks of clients, and elected officials paid out of pocket for the maintenance of roads, the city's upkeep, and distribution of bread and wine, among other day-to-day matters.

Quite a bit of authority was still in the hands of the male heads of households, the *paterfamilias,* at least in theory. On paper the *paterfamilias* still had the right of *ius vitae necisque,* the "power of life and death," over his children, both daughters and sons, who did not become full citizens until their father's death. Already by the time when most of our evidence from the Roman world survives, *ius vitae necisque* was seen as an extreme and outdated custom. Still, there are several examples of this being carried out and two cases involve daughters: Pontius Aufidianus and Atilius Philiscus were both said to have killed their daughters for promiscuity.[34]

In spite of such inhumane measures taken in the name of chastity, the Romans never picked up the Athenian obsession with encloistering women. Noting the cultural discrepancy, a first century BCE Roman, Cornelius Nepos, remarked:

> For what Roman man is ashamed to escort his wife to a dinner party? Or what lady of the manor does not sit in the forecourt of the house and venture out in public? In Greece it's very different, for a woman is not summoned to dinner unless it's with relatives, nor does she reside anywhere but in the interior part of the house, which is called the women's quarters, where no one goes except those connected by close ties of blood.[35]

Such freedom may have been an inheritance from the ancient Etruscans, who, judging from surviving artworks, saw nothing wrong with women and men dining together at banquets.[36] In spite of the relative freedom, there was still a strain of thought that led to private actions such as, at least according to Valerius Maximus, a man divorcing his wife simply because she was considered a respectable matron and she went out in public once with her head uncovered.[37]

Roman women were always expected, like poor Lucretia, to pay vigilant attention to their image. There was even a word specifically designated for this idea, *pudicitia*. Seneca describes in his *Controversies* what a wife with *pudicitia* exactly is:

> A matron who wants to oppose the lust of a seducer, let her come out of the house dressed up only just enough to avoid being scruffy. Let her have friends of such an age that the shameless, if nothing else, should be made to respect their years. Let her keep her eyes down; when people insist on greeting her she should prefer to seem rude rather than immodest. Even when she is returning the greeting of relatives she should be blushing greatly; thus she should pledge herself to modesty, so that her face should deny *impudicitia* sooner than her word. No lust should break through these defenses guarding her integrity.[38]

The underpinning idea—that women are always accountable for how men react to them sexually—should not seem too alien or barbaric, since it still has many adherents in modern society.

Although Maximus and like-minded commentators did indeed advertise an ideal where sexual integrity was preserved by vigilant patriarchs and matrons in their own homes, there was still an interest from on-high in imposing morality. Even during the early history of the Republic, the State was increasingly encroaching on the individual household's right to govern its own moral concerns. This intrusion was embodied in one elected office, the *censor.*

Every five years two *censors* would be elected; their primary responsibility was the management of the list of citizens—particularly the rolls of the top two classes, the senators and the *equites* (knights). Along with this duty came the power to strike off the names of any citizens who were judged unworthy of their rank, for any reason.

In a sense, the *censor* had the most powerful office in the Republic, since he had the means to threaten, humiliate, and "demote" any patrician who was guilty of a wide range of bad social and private decisions. In the recorded history of Rome, reasons that were used by the *censors* to chastise or punish their fellow citizens included an excessively luxurious lifestyle, failing to control the behavior of their children, and cruelty toward slaves and clients.[39] Naturally the sexual and matrimonial realms were not fenced off from the *censor*'s reach, and he could penalize citizens for a divorce that was improperly carried out or for never marrying in the first place.[40]

The earliest known move the Roman government made against a crisis in sexual morality came in 186 BCE, when the Republic persecuted a cult of the wine god Bacchus after accusations of nighttime orgies started circulating.[41] According to Livy:

> The joys of wine and food were added to those of the ritual, so that the souls of more people were seduced. When the wine, the darkness, and the fact that men mixed with women while the young joined with their elders had inflamed their souls and extinguished every sign of shame, corruptions of every kind first began to occur, since everyone had means of gratifying the desires that nature had inflicted on them.[42]

In spite of Livy's spicy account, the historian J.A. North argues that the suppression of the cult was not brought on by moral outrage, but by simple religious politics. The cult was nothing new and had a long history in Italy, yet the leaders of Rome distrusted it because it was a religion organized and promoted by its own adherents, not by the State or the *patresfamiliae*.[43] Of course, the alleged or actual sexual escapades of Bacchus's followers could still be a motive or exaggerated stories of the orgies might have been trumped up to help the State's case. Either way, the reaction from up high was a thorough one, and many of the cult's followers were massacred.

On a more everyday level, a man who sexually assaulted or harassed another person could be prosecuted under the legal principle of *iniuria*, which encompassed not only physical acts but also flirtatious speech. *Iniuria* made no distinction between the free and slaves, but female prostitutes, or even women who dressed in the typical fashions of the prostitute, had little recourse.[44] *Stuprum* was another broad principle that was used in cases of fornication. In 295 BCE, several noblewomen were charged with *stuprum* and exiled, but the actual charges were never spelled out.[45] For the most part, though, *stuprum* seems to have been the charge laid on men who had recurring sexual encounters or openly lived with an unmarried, free, and (of course) "respectable" woman.[46]

In spite of such a law, concubinage was quietly allowed, as long as class proprieties were observed. Eventually concubinage became legally defined as not falling under *stuprum*.[47] Concubines also enjoyed some of the rights given to wives, and in time concubinage was seen as a lesser form of marriage. The man who lived with both his wife and a concubine was at risk of becoming a social pariah, perhaps because such an arrangement looked too much like bigamy for comfort.[48]

Monogamy was so ingrained into the Roman concept of marriage that bigamy was not even addressed as a legal problem until arguably the reign of Justinian I.[49] Incestuous marriages were something that actually was dealt with thoroughly in Roman law, which carefully barred marriages between individuals who were too closely related by blood or by affinity. Around the end of the Republic, however, the law had softened and marriages between cousins had become allowed, but there were still limits. In 49 CE, the Emperor Claudius (r. 41–54) managed to marry his late brother Germanicus's daughter, Agrippina the Younger, but only after a cautious public relations campaign and an actual change in the law.[50] Agrippina and Claudius, who appear to have wed just for the sake of politics, failed to really push the envelope. Marriage between a man and his sister's daughter remained against the law. Also, from the time of the marriage to 342, when uncle–niece unions were banned once more, there were only two such marriages that are known and one of them was a centurion who lived in Claudius's time and simply wanted to show solidarity with the happy imperial couple.[51]

The right to a quick and painless divorce was an option ingrained in Roman law and culture. The oldest Roman divorce laws that historians can talk about with any confidence allowed only the husband to start a divorce, but even then he was fined if he divorced his wife without just cause. Things had become very different by at least the third or fourth centuries BCE, when all either the wife or the husband had to do to end a marriage was declare the intent to divorce in front of seven witnesses and send a letter or a messenger to the other spouse informing him or her of the decision.[52] The ease with which women could break off a marriage was a cause of some contention; Cicero shared a rumor that a husband had returned from a business trip only to find, to his surprise, that his wife had divorced him,[53] while the satirical poet Martial joked that the Augustinian legislation against adultery was pointless since divorce was so common that the typical woman younger than age 30 had ten marriages under her belt.[54]

Until Augustus came along, adultery was no crime. Ironically, it was the same Augustus, before he became Rome's first emperor, who helpfully demonstrated how far prominent adulterers might go without punishment or fatal stigmas. Augustus, then known as Octavian, had an affair with Livia, who was married to Tiberius the Elder. Either out of personal attraction, political motives, or both, Livia soon divorced Tiberius and married her clandestine lover. During the marriage rites she was even pregnant with a son, Drusus, and gossip claimed that Drusus was really Octavian's son.[55] Perhaps the future Augustus was simply a hypocrite or had a major change of mindset, but it seems just as likely that the episode was simply an extreme example of what Romans really thought about marriage and divorce, especially among those at the top, where the right or wrong marriage connections were a matter of political survival.

Scandals like the Octavian and Livia affair were the spice of Roman politics. True, the right and pleasure to scrutinize the private lives of the elite are perhaps as old as civilization itself. The Romans, however, went at it with gusto, especially in the ugly last years of the Republic. Cicero, the Roman Republic's undisputed champion of character assassination, portrayed Gaius Varres as an insatiable serial rapist,[56] Catiline as a seducer of young men in a figurative and literal sense,[57] Publius Clodius Pulcher as his sister's secret lover,[58] and Marcus Antonius as a veteran prostitute.[59] Julius Caesar was simultaneously smeared as the lover of King Nicomedes of Bithya—doggerel sung after his victory in the Gallic War went, "Caesar fucked all of Gaul, Nicomedes fucked Caesar / Now see Caesar ride in triumph after fucking Gaul. / Nicomedes gets no triumph, even though he fucked our Caesar"[60]—and as a Cassanova who specialized in married women. The senator Curio helpfully reconciled the two lines of attack by calling Caesar "every woman's man and every man's woman."[61] Marcus Antonius may have originally accused Octavian of not only forcing Livia to marry him, but also forcing her ex-husband to give away the bride during the ceremony.[62]

These outlandish efforts in defamation probably did have their purposes, and one of them may have been to make the labyrinthine politics of the first century BCE more interesting to the Roman public. For the elites themselves, transforming a rival into a creature driven by greed and lust was certainly easier than maintaining total honesty about one's own self-serving political motives and ambitions. This lesson that a good sex scandal is an excellent cover for a political power play was studied extensively by Rome's first imperial dynasty, the Julio-Claudians, who took scandalmongering to a new and often more dangerous level.

Imperial Interventions

In the year 2 BCE, the aged emperor Augustus was struck by a scandal whose epicenter was his daughter Julia from a previous marriage to Scribonia. Julia, then married to Augustus's stepson Tiberius the Younger, had been pursuing a number of affairs with men, motivated in no small part by her catastrophically miserable marriage with Tiberius. Eventually Julia's escapades reached the emperor's attention. The sting must have struck Augustus especially harshly because he had always presented himself as the restorer of old-fashioned Roman morals. After Augustus heard that one of Julia's friends, Phoebe, had hanged herself, he remarked, "I would rather have been her father." At Augustus's own prompting, the Senate exiled Julia to an island in the Mediterranean that was only two miles long, where she was denied wine and other luxuries, big and small, and was allowed only visitors who passed a rigorous screening process. Eventually her imprisonment was slackened and she returned to the Italian mainland (yet not to Rome). Augustus refused to ever visit her and, in his will, asked that she and her daughter, who was also named Julia and also infamous for promiscuity, never have their remains placed in the family mausoleum.[63]

All the ancient writers agree that Julia's crimes were sexual and Augustus's anger was moral. However, in dynastic monarchies (which the Roman government had become, although no one in Augustus's time was quite ready to admit as much), sex is always political, and it was probably no accident that Julia's sexual habits invoked retribution only after her hobby encompassed two prominent men: Sempronius Gracchus, a descendant of the famous second century BCE reformers the Gracchi brothers, and Jullus Antonius, a son of Augustus's old archenemy Marcus Antonius. It is unlikely Julia actively conspired to overthrow her own father—the sources, who mostly savored every detail of the Julio-Claudians' dysfunction, certainly would have made a note of it—but an illicit affair between the emperor's daughter and a man who, with the help of his family name alone, could attract public support had a treasonable edge to it. Tellingly, while almost all of Julia's lovers were simply banished, Jullus Antonius was either killed by decree or driven to suicide.[64]

Julia's banishment, and the more obscure sequel that ended with Julia's daughter and namesake also disgraced and banished, set a hideous precedent. This fact became very clear during the reign of Emperor Tiberius (r. 14–37), who was loathed by the public for encouraging informers and opening trails of *maiestas* (*lèse majesté*). When Claudia Pulchra, a distant relative of the imperial family and a supporter of Tiberius's political nemesis, Augustus's granddaughter Agrippina the Elder, was accused of *maiestas* by deploying witchcraft and poison to harm the emperor, an accusation of adultery was added to the charges for good measure.[65] Agrippina's son Nero (not to be confused with the emperor) was slandered on vague charges of sexual depravity before his arrest.[66] At the behest of his wife Messalina, Claudius put forward charges that his niece Livia, among other crimes, had an adulterous liaison with the philosopher Seneca.[67] Roman historians, too, got in on the fun and lobbed details of decadence and deviance at the memory of unpopular emperors. There is enough to say about the gruesome and below-the-belt way the Julio-Claudian emperors' sex lives were often depicted to fill another book, but for our purposes here it can all be summed up by pointing out that, in the main narrative sources for the early imperial period (Suetonius, Tacitus, and Cassius Dio), three of the five Julio-Claudian rulers are portrayed as pedophiles and two as bisexual nymphomaniacs with incestuous tendencies, with one empress, Messalina, cast as a woman who defeated a seasoned prostitute in a sex marathon.

It is impossible to say how much of a foothold in reality these and countless other vivid after-dark tales had to them, but they must have had their uses. The trend did not end with the Julio-Claudians either. In just one example, the widely reviled and deeply pious emperor of the Flavian dynasty, Domitian (81–96), was said to have had an affair with his niece Julia and accidentally killed her by forcing her to have an abortion.[68] The (in)famously unreliable *Augustan History* continues this tradition by accusing multiple emperors and their spouses of adultery and sexual excess. Throughout Roman history, sexual habits and general morality were closely intertwined, and it was taken for granted that proof of sexual extravagance and eccentricity was a sign that pointed toward other forms of very bad behavior, whether it was treason or tyranny.

Another motive for the reliance on sexual slander may have been that Augustus had enacted the most extensive and far-reaching morals legislation known to antiquity. The law, the *lex Julia de maritandis ordinibus,* was passed in 18 BCE with minor revisions under the *lex Papia-Poppaea* following nine years later. Of course, "Do as I say and not as I do" is the prerogative of both parents and politicians, so Augustus did not seem to have worried overmuch about the unpleasant contrast between how his marriage with Livia was started and what the laws he initiated demanded. Female adultery and *stuprum* could now be punished by heavy confiscations of property and exile to an island. The husband of a wife found guilty of adultery had to divorce her or face being labeled in the eyes of the law as a pimp. Almost overnight, adultery had been turned into a matter for private citizens and households into a public offense. In fact, the *lex Julia* also placed restrictions on the customary power of fathers to punish misbehavior of their children: fathers could now kill daughters they caught committing adultery only if the paramour could be killed as well.

Even more intrusive were the laws' mandates on marriage, remaining single, and procreation. Women who had more than a certain number of legitimate children were to be rewarded with certain rights and honors while their husbands would go to the top of the list for political appointments. Those unmarried by a certain age were punished by losing their right to receive inheritances from individuals outside the family. Divorced people faced a potentially unending series of fines until they remarried. Senators and their children and grandchildren were discouraged from marriages with emancipated slaves and actors, the dregs of Roman society, by fines and legal penalties.[69]

Naturally the laws were unpopular, especially the penalties slapped on the unmarried. An exasperated Augustus responded to a public protest by Rome's knights against the laws by appearing with his granddaughter Agrippina's children, pleading with the knights present to follow their father Germanicus's noble example.[70] No one really appreciated Augustus's logic, even in later centuries,[71] although the laws remained entirely in effect with relatively small tweaking[72] until the marriage law reforms of Constantine I. Later emperors may have been fully aware of the hatred stirred against the laws, but agreed with Augustus's basic premise: that the well-being of society—or more specifically society's natural elite—demanded official intervention in the bedroom.

Perverts and Prostitutes

> No one drives you away from there, nor yet forbids you, if you have the money, to buy what's openly on sale. No one forbids any person from going along the public road, so long as he doesn't make a path through the field that's fenced around; so long as you keep yourself away from the wife, the widow, the maiden, youthful age, and free-born children, love what you please.[73]

Here the comedic playwright Plautus crashes head-first into the beliefs of some scholars and laypeople, that ancient Rome was essentially one giant brothel where upper-class men had their pick of anyone who could be penetrated. Channeling the spirit of the philosopher Michel Foucault, the theorist David Halperin once claimed that sex in antiquity had "no moral value, positive or negative."[74] However, as Plautus helpfully points out, there were indeed codes—cultural, social, and even legal—that towered over sexual relations and determined who might be made an outcast for their sexual tastes.

The most shadowy species of Rome's sexual outcasts is the being some might call the "Roman homosexual." To be honest, any discussion of Roman homosexuality is bound to be rather headache inducing—partly because there is plenty of evidence to go around but plenty of frustrating gaps, and partly because modern-day historians, theorists, and classicists have burdened the poor Romans down with the weight of their own contemporary biases and expectations.[75] A case in point is the *Lex Scantinia,* a law obscure enough that no one alive knows exactly what it was for.

The law was either a blanket ban on all male same-sex intercourse between free Romans (or at least those who were "bottoms" in today's gay lingo)[76] or an attempt to criminalize pederasty.[77] It may have originated from a third century BCE case where a tribune named Scantinius Capitolinus was accused of attempting to seduce the son, a "young man," of Marcus Claudius Marcellus.[78] Roman laws were usually named after the people who proposed them, not the ones who were first prosecuted under them, however. Thus, given Rome's claustrophobic upper-class world, the name might just be a coincidence (at any rate, the source Valerius Maximus does not even mention a *lex Scantinia*). Also there is an even earlier account from the fourth century of a "very young man" who was forced by debt to sell himself as a bondsman to a man who ended up beating him for refusing to sleep with him. The scandal caused enough of a public outcry that the offender was arrested by senatorial decree and the practice of using indentured labor to pay off debts was abolished.[79]

Whatever the case, the law seems to have been invoked very rarely in the time of the late Republic and was used mainly as a weapon against political opponents in high offices.[80] In the late first century, Domitian revived the law and prosecuted a number of senators and knights under it as part of a big public morality campaign, but Suetonius disappoints by passing over the details of the accused's crimes.[81] Maybe it ended up being a core reason for Domitian's tremendous unpopularity.

Given how hostile the response to pederasty was in Rome, one wonders why any law would have been necessary. The distinction between pederasty involving a free-born adolescent or young man and prostitution and *stuprum* was a thin one. A distinguished war veteran, Gaius Cornelius, was arrested for having sex with a free-born adolescent (perhaps under the *lex Scantinia*?). His defense was that the young man was really a prostitute, which he must have thought would strike the right chord with the right people, but nonetheless Cornelius was left to die in prison.[82] Suetonius alleges, in a way that implies prostitution, that Domitian as a poverty-stricken young man had slept with an older man, Claudius Pollio, in exchange for gifts and favors.[83] This raises the interesting but unanswerable question of whether Domitian had found such experiences humiliating or even traumatic and had pushed the *lex Scantinia* as a way of rescuing other impoverished young men from the same fate. In his all-out assault on Marcus Antonius's character, Cicero describes what could be seen, from a much less rabid perspective, as a typical pederastic relationship:

> Then you began to wear the toga of manhood. How quickly you exchanged it for a womanly toga [female prostitutes were the only women that wore togas]. From the first you made yourself into a common whore; you fixed the fee for your debauchery, and it was not small! But Curio soon put an end to this when he seduced you away from your prostitute's trade and, just as though he had given you the gown of a wife, he settled you into a life of matrimonial stability. Never was there a boy, bought for the sole purpose of slaking another man's sexual thirst, who was so much under the power of his master as you were under Curio.[84]

The famous exception to the Roman distrust of pederasty is the love between the Emperor Hadrian (r. 117–138) and Antinous, who fell off a boat and drowned in the Nile at the age of 18 or 19. At Hadrian's insistence, Antinous was introduced as a new god in the empire's eastern provinces. Numerous images and postmortem honors were devoted to Antinous, culminating even in a new city, Antinoopolis, founded on the site of Antinous's death. There does seem to have been some disapproval of Antinous's exuberant promotion. The writer Celsus attacked Christianity by comparing the worship of Jesus to the way "Hadrian's boy-toy" was praised,[85] while Hadrian himself was criticized for crying "like a woman"[86] over Antinous's lifeless body. Yet Antinous's cult thrived well into the fourth century.[87] This might be a testimony to Hadrian's untarnished popularity as one of the best of the Roman emperors or to a cultural stew that nurtured new, esoteric cults, especially ones that, like Antinous's sect, held out a promise of rebirth after death. Perhaps it is enough to think that the romantic story of Hadrian and Antinous, a great ruler who loved a handsome young man who suffered an untimely death,[88] appealed to the masses.

Still, as Cicero was kind enough to remind us, the Romans still did have "issues" with sexual passivity, seeing it as something that dishonored and feminized a man. To sexually penetrate was to humiliate and degrade. After all, a very popular Roman icon was the dwarf god Priapeus, who boasted a massive phallus and whose image was decked on Roman yards, along with an inscription threatening the rape of any trespasser. One well-known example:

"Thief, for first time thieving you shall be buggered, / second time caught it's into the mouth; / And, should you attempt to plunder a third time, / This and that penalty you shall endure, / Back into the mouth and the ass."[89]

The ultimate effeminate in the Roman mind was the *cinaedus*, a word that was a borrowing from the Greek *kinaidos*. The ever uptight Scipio nearly foams at the mouth when talking about the *cinaedi*:

> A man who wears perfume every day and decks himself out in front of the mirror, who goes about with trimmed eyebrows, a plucked beard and hairless thighs, who, when he was a youth, attended parties in his long-sleeved tunic and bedded down with a lover on the corner of the couch, and who now unduly craves not only wine but men as well—would anyone doubt that such a man did the things that *cinaedi* usually do?[90]

What did a *cinaedus* usually do? Another verse attached to the god Priapeus is a clue:

> "This staff of office, which, cut from a tree, / Can now no longer show growth. / The staff horny women fondly loved, / Which even the kings delight to hold, / And by noble *cinaedi* kissed / This staff in robbers' vitals shall plunge / Up to its bushy base and bag of balls."[91]

Even slaves knew and happily slung the term around. One rude piece of graffiti, presumably written by a slave, exclaims, "Cosmus Equitias's [slave] is a big *cinaedus* and a cocksucker with his legs spread apart."[92] When the Latin poet Catullus called his contemporary Julius Caesar a *cinaedus*,[93] the stain was enough of a problem that Caesar demanded (and received) Catullus's apology.[94]

Craig Williams has argued extensively that *cinaedi* cannot be an euphemism with connotations of same-sex lust, since the insult has been applied to people like Julius Caesar and in the same breath as their heterosexual excesses.[95] In the seven samples from Roman literature that Williams cites, however, the word *cinaedus* is never actually used except in the aforementioned poem by Catullus. Besides, as James Butrica points out, "Of course the term is applied to men that we would not call homosexuals such as Julius Caesar, but that is because it could be used abusively as well as literally."[96] One might as well suggest that the insults "poofer" and "faggot" have no implication of homosexuality since they are and have been thrown about without regard to actual sexual orientation.

All this talk of manly men versus *cinaedi* and active versus passive roles obscures one simple but interesting question: was there any taboo against adult male same-sex relationships in ancient Rome? Gossip on the imperial court is, as always, useful for making this determination. With a disapproving tone, Suetonius writes that the emperor Galba (r. 68–69) enjoyed the company of "very muscular" adult men.[97] Far more notorious was the teenage emperor Elagabalus (r. 218–222), who handpicked his lovers, all exclusively male and all his age or older, based on their athletic bodies and penis sizes and, in the trashiest anecdotes, wanted to be the patient in history's first sex-change operation.[98]

Arguing against such a taboo, the poet Statius wrote a memorial poem commemorating the death of the 14-year-old slave Philetos, who was the lover of his older master, Flavius Ursus. The poem does not speak of the sort of boy-like and feminine qualities one would expect from a very young male slave, but rather emphasizes that he was physically and emotionally mature for his age, especially since he grew a beard.[99] Martial writes irreverently of a marriage between two fully grown men, Afer and Callistratus,[100] but is sympathetic when he describes two young men who were lovers and suddenly died.[101] The first century CE

"Warren Cup" depicts on one side a sexual encounter between a young male and a grown man; the other side depicts two adult men, possibly but not certainly both free born, having sex while a smiling male voyeur looks on.[102] John Clarke maintains that this side of the Warren Cup "breaks the rules" of Roman homosexuality by showing men of equal age and rank,[103] but perhaps the conclusion should be that, true to the nature of human societies, the "rules" were far more flexible than they appear at first glance.

Unfortunately but not too surprisingly, female homosexuality is harder to trace. Among Juvenal and Martial, who between them mention just about every sex act one can imagine (and would never imagine), only Martial mentions lesbians, and just a few times at that.[104] Scholars have argued that lesbians were seen as oddities in Roman culture, standing out through hypermasculine traits and actually possessing enlarged clitorises by which they could penetrate other women as well as men.[105] This conjuring up of a Roman lesbian nightmare, however, relies on proof that is as shaky as it is scarce.[106] Roman writers were perfectly well aware of methods for sexual pleasure that did not necessarily require men, such as dildos and cunnilingus,[107] so sex between two women was hardly something that had to be imagined through some sort of mutant sex organ.

There was no answer to the *lex Scantinia* for female same-sex relations, nor does it seem that a married woman's affair with another woman added up to adultery punishable under the *lex Julia*.[108] Martial has often been held up as demonstrating that there was a strong bias against lesbian love in imperial Roman culture. However, this viewpoint hinges on the belief that Martial was a fire-and-brimstone satirist, detailing sex acts he genuinely wanted to see shut down. In reality, his own words state that he writes to entertain and beg any "Catos" not to interfere with readers' simple enjoyment.[109]

Another piece of Latin literature cited as showing disapproval for lesbianism is a mythological story from Ovid's *Metamorphoses*. A girl living in a rustic region, Iphis, is disguised and raised as a boy to prevent her from being left in the wilderness to die by her father. After Iphis decides to marry "his" childhood friend Ianthe, "he" realizes the sex she was born into and declares that the desire she felt for another woman is something completely unheard of. The goddess Isis resolves the trouble by turning Iphis into a boy.[110] It may be that Ovid expected his readers to share in Iphis's revulsion, but in the overview she is presented as a victim of circumstances rather than a "pervert." Even today this story has a resonance for anyone who may have experienced growing up homosexual without any real reference point and seemingly overnight found themselves drawn to the same sex. In such a scenario, a *deus ex machina* sex change might indeed be welcomed as a happy ending.

More judgmental were two scattered references from the second century. The poet Lucian, in his *Dialogues of the Courtesans*, featured the adventures of Leaena, who meets a woman named Megilla who hails from Lesbos (to spell it out for slow readers, Leaena comments that she has heard that there are women from Lesbos who are "unwilling to consort with men, but only with women"). Megilla insists on being called "Megillus," has shaved her head, and calls another woman, Demonassa, her wife. Megillus tries to get Leaena in bed, but Leaena finds the idea "shameful."[111] Still, the tone is humorous, rather than inflammatory. Slightly more in spirit with the condemnations reserved for *cinaedi* is a third century CE Greek novel that mentions an Egyptian princess, Berenice, who goes through a marriage with another woman. Her actions are painted as "lawless."[112]

Thus there was some disapproving words against female love in the Roman Empire,

III The Decadent Past, from Alexander the Great to Antinuous

but none that match the harsh words kept in storage for the *cinaedi*. In fact, it does not appear that *tribas* was treated like an insulting piece of slang, at least not among an educated circle. None of this is to say that a woman attracted only to other women would find classical Rome a friendly environment; the custom of arranged marriages and the pressure to procreate if you were part of the elite during the imperial era alone would have made life difficult, to say the least. It is still tempting to speculate if, as with Martial's lesbian heroine Bassa, homosexual women's lack of interest in men was ever mistaken for a commitment to chastity.

While there are definitely observers like Martial who saw homosexuality as a fact of life that would entice readers, others were far more wary, and their objections went above and beyond any anxieties over gender-breaking or sexual position. For instance, Seneca the Younger invokes a philosophical idea of "Nature" in his condemnation of women who subvert sex and gender roles:

> But in lust they do not yield even to men. Though born to receive—may the gods and goddesses damn them!—they have contrived a kind of immodesty so perverse that they mount men. Is it any wonder then that the greatest of physicians and that the men most knowledgeable about nature is caught in a lie when so many women are gouty and bald? They lost the benefit of their sex through their vices, and were condemned in manly ailments because they had shucked off their womanhood.[113]

Seneca also gives male homosexuality his undivided attention in this passage:

> Don't those men who exchange their clothing with women's seem to you to live contrary to Nature? Don't those men who see to it that a boyish appearance shines at a different time of life also live contrary to Nature? What crueler or more wretched thing could happen? Will he never be allowed to become a man, just so he can continue to take the passive role with another man?[114]

While Seneca stresses passivity and the preference for feminine boys, the philosopher Epictetus condemns all participants: "What is lost by the man who endures the fate of the catamite? His manhood. And what is lost by the man who deals that fate? Among many other things, he loses his manhood no less than the other."[115] The Stoic Monsius Rufus extends the attack to all forms of nonprocreative sex by writing, "But of all sexual relations those involving adultery are most unlawful, and no more tolerable are those of men with men, because it is a monstrous thing and contrary to nature. But, furthermore, leaving out of consideration adultery, all intercourse with women which is without lawful character is shameful and is practiced from lack of self-restraint."[116] The Platonist Plotinus agreed, writing, "Those forms of love that do not serve the purposes of nature are accidents attending on perversion."[117]

Such concepts of "nature" and "law" were thoroughly Stoic, and it is difficult to get a sense of how widespread such an attitude might have been. Martial, who satirized not specific individuals but broad character types his audience would have chuckled over, mocks a Martinus for "being all for nature," yet whenever he bathes with Martial "his line of vision always goes beneath waist-level."[118] In an episode from his well-known yet difficult-to-interpret second Satire, Juvenal portrays a woman named Laronia being put on trial presumably for committing adultery. When her judges mention the *lex Julia,* she retorts, "If laws and statutes are being brought up, the *Scantinia* should be cited before the rest," and goes on to put her accusers on trial, claiming that they have all committed adultery with men, too. The episode concludes with the hypocritical "sons of the Stoics" literally running away from the "obvious truth."[119] Although the precise logic behind the Stoics' reactions to same-sex intercourse may not have been transfused down to the general public, Juvenal and Martial seem to have at least expected their readers to be familiar with them.

While the existence of something that might be even just loosely described as a "gay subculture" in ancient Rome is hotly and infinitely debatable, the Romans were clearly aware that there were people among them with inclinations toward one sex or the other. The fourth-century Latin medical writer Caelius Aurelianus, translating from a Greek source, wrote about men and women inherently attracted to their own sex,[120] while the astrologer Firmicus Maternus cautioned his readers that male children born under a certain alignment will "hate women and marriage."[121] A comedic story by the poet Phaedrus proposes that, when creating mankind, Prometheus must have gotten a little drunk and got the genitals of a few women and a few men mixed up, creating "tribads and soft men."[122] The existence of such individuals was not welcomed with anything we in the modern world would call "tolerance"—those slandered as *cinaedi* could testify to that—yet it also did not seem to spark the violent revulsion that would one day become an everyday reality in Europe.

Far less ambiguous is the status of prostitutes in the Roman world. Prostitutes as well as pimps were deemed to be *infames,* legally "persons of ill repute," and were second-class citizens. Along with gladiators and actors (two other professions that were perfectly legal and even celebrated by the general public yet considered disgraceful in the law's eyes), prostitutes and procurers lived under a number of civic and legal disabilities, such as never being allowed to hold any office or municipal honors, join the equestrian and senatorial classes, enter certain temples, and testify as a witness in a trial.[123] Under the *lex Julia,* prostitutes and procurers were barred from marriages with all *ingenui* (respectable free-born people) on penalty of suffering restrictions on inheritances and legacies.[124]

All prostitutes had to register with authorities, a requirement that caused a stir when a woman of senatorial rank, Vestillia, registered as a prostitute to take advantage of the female prostitutes' exemption from being prosecuted for female adultery under the *lex Julia*. This tempting loophole was quickly closed and female prostitutes who were married could still be prosecuted for adultery until Diocletian (r. 284–305) changed the law toward the end of the third century.[125] In any case, by law any upper-class woman who took up prostitution or even any artistic occupation that seemed a "gateway" to prostitution, such as music, dancing, or acting, was deprived of her status.[126] Men of standing who sold themselves do not seem to have been subjected to such scrutiny, although as in Marcus Antonius's case they could be attacked and slandered on suspicion of acts that amounted to prostitution.

There was no question that prostitution was dishonorable and people who were not technically prostitutes but were guilty by association were contaminated. Anyone who lived and worked in a brothel or had a job as a waitress in a tavern—notorious for being a place where prostitutes were readily available—was subjected to the same penalties as pimps and prostitutes.[127] It was illegal to compel anyone free born or freed to enter prostitution, since it was an occupation that was dangerous to one's physical and moral well-being.[128] Much more murky is whether slaves could be forced to prostitute themselves to profit their masters. The imperial government intervened to stop a female slave from being used as a sexual commodity by her master, establishing a precedent that any slave (or at least any female slave) who was abused in such a manner would be emancipated, but this did not take place until the third century CE.[129]

The laws indicate that at least female prostitutes were unable to bring charges against a man for sexual assault, although the reality on the ground seems to have been more complicated. A hypothetical case used in schools of rhetoric and cited by Seneca has a prostitute in a brothel completely exonerated after she kills a soldier who attempts to rape her.[130] A real-life, second century BCE case that has come down involved a prostitute named Manilla who was accused by a man named Hostilius Mancinus of throwing stones at him. Manilla appealed to the tribunes, who found that Manilla was acting in self-defense. This case is all the more impressive considering that Mancinus was at the time an *aedile,* one of the highest officials in the Roman government.[131] Although the evidence is not extensive, it does suggest that prostitutes were not completely legal nonentities and hints that at least a few of the men in power understood that prostitution was a dangerous business and were willing to give street and brothel prostitutes the benefits of legal protection.

Nonetheless the prostitute's standing in Roman culture was on shifting sands. On Rome's religious calendar there were feast days dedicated to the occupation: April 24 was marked out for female prostitutes, while the next day was dedicated to their male counterparts. During the *ludi Florales,* a religious festival held in the honor of the goddess Flora, prostitutes were gathered and stripped naked in front of an audience,[132] a gesture that simultaneously managed to acknowledge their essential contribution to the community and degrade them before the very same public.

Celibacy and Sex for Pleasure

Imagine a woman being carried through the streets of pagan Rome in a closed litter. Perhaps her family is waiting for her at her destination, the *Campus Sceleretus* ("the Field of Crime"), but more likely they are at home, hoping not to be contaminated by shame. There with all the solemnity of a marriage ritual, a priest says a prayer to Vesta, goddess of the hearth, and the woman is led to an open pit with a ladder leading down into the ground. Offering no resistance, she climbs to the bottom, where someone has placed a lighted lamp, a bed with a blanket, and enough bread, oil, milk, and water to last several days. As much resigned to the ceremony as the people above, she does not even scream as those people begin to seal the pit.

This was the proscribed punishment of any Vestal Virgin who broke her *castus,* "vow of chastity." Her paramour would not be let off the hook, but was instead tied to a cross and beaten to death with rods. Whatever justified such savagery was already long forgotten by the classical period. It was simply said that, like all the other rules behind the religious cults and rituals of Rome, the concept of the order of the Vestals was imparted to the legendary king Numa (r. 717–673) by the god Jupiter himself.[133] Certainly the order was older than the Republic itself. Among the Vestals' ceremonial responsibilities was to warn the king to be vigilant.

Selected between the ages of six and ten, the Vestals were consecrated to the virgin goddess Vesta and had the chief responsibility of attending to the sacred hearth of the city of Rome, ensuring that the fire burned perpetually. Eventually they were released from service, but not for at least 30 years. Given the extreme young age, it is unthinkable that there was anything voluntary about service to the goddess: Augustine, although as biased as one can possibly be, may have had a point when he wrote that the Vestals' task was more of a punishment than an honor.[134] If it was a prison, though, it was a gilded cage. The Vestals were given rights and privileges not usually extended to women and, under Augustus, enjoyed the same benefits given to women who married and bore children. They owed no accountability to the *paterfamilias* or a *tutor.* Only the *pontifex maximus,* Rome's top religious authority, had any real authority over them. Further, they provided an important civic function, handling the wills of Roman senators and knights.

Throughout their service, their persons were deemed sacrosanct. When in the second century BCE the unpopular general Appius Claudius Pulcher staged a triumph without the Senate's funding or permission, his sister Claudia, a Vestal Virgin, joined him in his chariot; both knew that even the tribunes of the Republic would be powerless to bar a Vestal's progress.[135] Custom also dictated that, if a condemned criminal happened to cross a Vestal's path, he was to be pardoned. The idea that abstinence from sex guaranteed a certain degree of sanctity was not unknown to the pagan Mediterranean, and virgin goddesses were well known to the Greeks and the Romans, but priestesses who lived a life of total chastity were rare in the territories of the Roman Empire.

Despite the benefits of having a relative in the order, by at least the imperial era the Vestals had become an unpopular institution. Without specifying why, Suetonius states that in Augustus's time leading citizens went out of their way to keep their daughters' names off the lists of potential candidates.[136] Domitian was said to have prosecuted a number of Vestals for breaking their vow of chastity; he allowed three to choose their own method of execution, but a fourth, Cornelia, he had killed in the traditional way along with her lovers, probably because she was a chief Vestal.[137] That Domitian went through the trouble suggests that scrutiny of the order had become very lax. Matters apparently did not improve by the late fourth century, when Ambrose of Milan noted with glee that while celibate Christian women thrived, Roman authorities were hard-pressed to keep the number of Vestals up to seven.[138]

Chastity had never been a popular concept in pagan Rome, where spiritual sentiment took a back seat to the social (and, after Augustus, legal) demand to produce new citizens. The Socratic idea that philosophy and a life devoted to contemplation was a higher calling than the demands of family and civic life had its adherents in Rome: even Cicero, who did marry and was as involved in politics as Roman ideals demanded, occasionally left the political arena for the sake of his intellectual pursuits.[139] Nevertheless, the influential philosophy of Stoicism also portrayed a world where civic participation, marriage, and children were moral duties—if not to the State, then to an abstract global community.[140] Musonius Rufus maintained that anything less than entering into marriage was to fail to live in accordance with nature,[141] a position taken up by other popular philosophers of early imperial Rome like Quintilian, Dio Chrysostom, and Hierocles.

However, the purebred Stoic Seneca still wondered numerous times if he would be better off giving up his wife and mistresses and dedicating himself solely to philosophy.[142] Given his personal life, which reached a nadir when he was exiled for sleeping with a married woman, no one can be blamed for doubting his sincerity. Perhaps he would have been interested in the advice from the second-century Cynic Sextus, who prescribed castration as the cure for uncontrollable lust.[143] Sextus's contemporary Epictetus also praised the Cynic who serves a valuable service by becoming a visionary illuminating the path to true happiness, unfettered by a wife or children.[144]

As for the Cynics, who advertised themselves as embodying the cutting edge of philosophical living, taking on a life of moderation and self-sufficiency was far more important than fulfilling any obligations to the city-state or the human community of the Stoics. Still, the Cynics did not put their sexuality on the shelf. Although an anonymous author of the *Cynic Epistles* urges the true Cynic to avoid sex altogether because it is a distraction away from true self-fulfillment, he prescribes masturbation as the antidote to pesky desires.[145]

The most extreme example of a religious revulsion to sex besides the Vestal Virgins was the cult of Cybele the Great Mother, which was imported into the Roman Empire from modern-day Turkey. According to myth, a young man named Attis had pledged his eternal devotion to the goddess Cybele, only to betray his vow. To punish himself for such adulterous blasphemy, Attis castrated himself. In a grim reiteration, during the goddess's rites particularly zealous men would make themselves sacred to the goddess by castrating themselves, becoming *galli*.[146] Less extreme was the practice of Greek devotees of Hippolytus, the legendary son of the hero Theseus who declared himself celibate in the name of the goddess Artemis. They took a holy oath not to marry until they personally dedicated clippings of their hair at Hippolytus's temple.[147]

If a strict commitment to chastity was rare, the idea that sex that did not result in procreation should have a strong cultural and religious stigma was practically unknown. Although Plato in the *Laws* had attacked homosexual intercourse for not serving the purpose of procreation and detailed measures designed to promote childbirths, he also viewed population control via contraception as a necessity for his hypothetical society.[148] Somewhat reliable contraceptives and abortifacients were not unknown to the ancient world, as the medical historian John Riddle has argued extensively[149] so Plato was being entirely theoretical. The Roman Stoics, for all their qualms about the necessary responsibility of family life, were mostly silent on the issue, although of course there is no inherent contradiction between approving of birth control and advocating procreation. Musonius Rufus, whose opinions on sex are as predictable as a watch, did make a strange statement, which seems to claim that the *lex Julia* outlawed contraception and abortion.[150] There is no indication elsewhere that such an outright ban, which would have certainly been referred to in the writings of Roman jurists at the very least, existed.[151] Instead, Musonius Rufus may have been suggesting that knowledge of birth control caused the low birth rates that led to such laws in the first place.

Punishing Desire in the Afterlife

As Virgil takes Dante into Hell, they witness the eternal and highly unpleasant punishment of adulterers, sodomites, pimps, and simply the all too lustful. In a literal sense, Virgil was the perfect guide for Dante, since in the first century CE he had also explored Hell in the *Aeneid* and envisioned sights not entirely dissimilar to what Dante saw in his *Inferno*. Did these similarities go so far that Virgil viewed sexual misbehavior as deserving stern retribution in the afterlife?

In Book VI of the *Aeneid,* the hero Aeneas, survivor of Troy's destruction and ancestor to Rome's founders, descends into the underworld, protected by the priestess, the Sybil, and divine approval. Aeneas discovers that there is a court in the afterlife, presided over by Minos as judge and with a jury stacked with the souls of the unjustly executed.[152] The passage is a little blurred, but presumably Minos and his court judged all the incoming dead, determining whether they belonged in a place of punishment, Tartarus; in a place of respite, the Elysian Fields; or with the morally neutral dead, which included Minos's jurors, deceased infants, suicides, and those who died from love (either of a person or the nation).[153] It does seem that Minos's role is very different from what it was in Homer's underworld. Instead of judging cases among the already dead, his duty is to judge the living transgressions of the newly dead.

Tartarus itself is still the home of mythological criminals such as the Titans, Tityos, and Ixion.[154] The inmate population has expanded greatly, now including average people who mistreated their clients, brothers, and fathers; refused to share money with their family; and exploited their masters' trust.[155] These lost souls all have something in common: they all appear to be male, and hence are full citizens, so they are all guilty of defiling the bonds that hold families and polities together. While Virgil precedes Dante in seeing categories of miscreants being punished in the afterlife, only behavior that overly kicks at the foundations of time-honored social institutions deserves such penalties.

We cannot say whether the image of a penal afterlife might have had some roots in indigenous Roman beliefs. Already by the third century BCE, when most of our Latin literary evidence begins to survive, the Roman cosmology had been thoroughly shaped by Hellenistic religion and philosophy. Virgil may have been inspired by Cicero's *Scipio's Dream,* where Scipio the Younger has a vision of the afterlife and his father who reveals, "For all who defend, aid, and expand the fatherland, there is a specific place set aside in heaven, where the blessed will enjoy an unending age of happiness."[156] Outside the musings of philosophers, postmortem justice may have had some appeal, although to others it may have seemed ludicrous. Cicero has a philosophy student blurt out that still believing in the traditional afterlife, with Cerebus, the River Styx, and all the rest, is unthinkable.[157] Grave markings—the closest thing available to an opinion poll on Roman ideas of the afterlife—do express denial of any afterlife, as shown by the popular Epicurean epitaph *Non fui, fui, non sum, non caro* ("I was not, I was, I am not, I care not"),as well as traditional views of Hades and Tartarus. Belief in not just an old-fashioned afterlife but one where certain spirits were punished was seemingly widespread enough at the first century CE that Seneca wrote, assuring a grieving woman, "Know that there are no ills to be suffered after death, that the reports that make the underworld terrible to us are only tales, that no darkness awaits the dead, no prison, no blazing streams of fire, no river of oblivion, that no judgment seats are there, nor culprits, nor in that lax freedom are there any tyrants."[158] Exactly what kind of crimes the average person would have to fear retribution for is left unstated, but presumably it was thought possible that the judges of the hereafter could punish even mundane sins.

A more detailed exploration of punishment beyond the grave comes from Plutarch. In his treatise *On the Delay of Divine Vengeance*, he takes up the vision of a harsh afterlife where wayward spirits are purged of their excessive desires. In the a vision had by a man named Aridaeus, the condemned dead fall into the hands of the goddess Dike (Justice), who painfully and surgically removes the soul's desires. If the patients relapse, then they are put through the wringer again, are forced to live once more and presumably suffer the consequences of their lusts again, or are left to stew in their own desires, which is perhaps the worst punishment of all since they lack a body with which to fulfill them. The totally incurable are imprisoned in nothingness.[159]

The nature of the crimes and even of the punishments is never spelled out, but uncontrolled emotions are clearly the core of the problem. Plutarch held the old Greek belief that lust was a typical characteristic of tyrants[160] and that bodily pleasure subverts reason.[161] Even here, the emphasis is on the relationship between unbridled thoughts and illicit actions, not on sex in and of itself. Of the two people whose crimes and punishments are actually revealed, Aridaeus's father is someone who killed his guests, and the Emperor Nero, despite his wide-ranging hedonism, is to be punished for killing his mother (at least until he benefits from divine mercy simply for granting Greece a degree of autonomy during his reign).[162]

Intellectuals like Plutarch worried about the corrosive effects of desire and connected it to the activities of criminals and tyrants. Still, in spite of ideas here and there claiming that abstinence was holiness and the philosophical urging that sex be considered only as a device to be used for the purposes of providing the city-state with citizens, sexual desire and the sex act itself were not considered corrupt in of themselves. Meanwhile, the founding thinkers of an infant religion, drawing from a fusion of Greek thought and Jewish religion, would have very different ideas and declare war on their own bodies for the sake of purity.

IV

Rise of a New Order

A very popular historical myth, which appears every now and then in Hollywood movies or in political editorials, is that Rome sunk under the weight of its own decadence and was literally paralyzed by uninhibited sexual freedom. However, the Rome of the late fourth and fifth centuries had nothing in common in its approach toward sex and legislation with the libertine Rome imagined by film executives and evangelical preachers alike. By the end of the fourth century, homosexuality was condemned in the harshest possible terms in the legal codes and divorce became far more restricted than it had been in the late Republic and early Empire. If critics really want to pursue the argument that the Roman Empire was undone by its sexual mores, then they will have to blind themselves to the unpleasant reality that history would instead endorse the verdict that the empire fell as a result of excessive prudishness, rather than hedonism.

It seems like common sense to suppose that Christianity was responsible for this metamorphosis in Roman law and the attitudes of the emperors. Yet some of these changes actually predate Constantine I's conversion and the growing Christian monopoly on the imperial government. The evolution of Christianity from just one of many cults competing in the Roman Empire's vast marketplace of religions to the state religion of the empire was not the only seismic change that overcame the Roman Empire in the same era. Power had slipped from the hands of the old Roman elites and was taken up by a new breed of "soldier-emperors," who came from the imperial provinces and achieved preeminence not through blue-blooded family connections or the traditional political offices, but through the military ranks. These men were likely to have a far less cosmopolitan outlook, especially when it came to bedroom matters.

Moreover, Christianity should not be seen as an alien force that infiltrated Greco-Roman morality, a view as old as the pagan criticisms rallied against Christians. As early as the epistles of Paul, Christianity expressed itself through language and rhetoric that would have been quite well known to the top philosophers of the day. The Church Fathers employed concepts of natural law and the dangers of sexual pleasure that would have been completely familiar, even welcome, to many Greek- and Latin-writing philosophers of different schools. All in all, even the most passionately isolationist Christian would have and did find much to agree with in the writings of non–Christians like Philo of Alexandria and Musonius Rufus.

Of course, Christianity also exhibited a distrust of the body and sexual pleasures that went above and beyond anything expressed in the dominant philosophies of the time. All sex outside monogamy and procreation was condemned in the strongest possible terms—arguments that had an impact totally unprecedented in the history of Mediterranean civilization. The raw power of belief motivated women and men into renouncing society and instead living in a self-imposed exile of discomfort and isolation that would protect them from the horrors of sexual temptation. By the end of antiquity, sexual purity was no longer something reserved for a priesthood or to a certain elite, but was strongly pushed on an entire community, "Christendom," where membership was no longer determined by voluntary conversion but by nothing more than birth.

When East Meets West

From where did orthodox Christianity inherit this strident view of sex? The answers lie in Christianity's birthplace, the eastern regions of the Roman Empire where Paul and his first converts became fluent in both Jewish theology and Greek philosophy. By Paul's time, Greek had surpassed Hebrew and rivaled Aramaic as a language of choice for the scattered enclaves of the Jewish Diaspora. Two centuries before Paul, King Ptolemy II of Egypt (r. 285–246 BCE) had sponsored a total translation of the Torah into Greek, the Septuagint. In the third century, a Jewish intellectual like the historian Demetrios of Alexandria would use the Septuagint for his quotations of Genesis and Exodus, instead of the Hebrew original.[1]

Whatever connections were being woven between Jewish and Greek cultures, the relationship had its ups and downs. A pro–Hellenization faction in second-century Palestine, then ruled by the Seleucids of Syria, had built a gymnasium in Jerusalem and actively encouraged people to adopt Greek customs. As the Hellenization program's message seeped into the younger generations, some young men began exercising and wrestling nude, a definite slap in the face of Jewish sensibilities; worst of all, these men took steps to disguise their circumcisions.[2] Inevitably the anger bloomed into rebellion, and Antiochos IV (r. 175–164) retaliated by revoking a number of rights that had been granted to the Jews by his predecessors; by dedicating the Temple to Zeus and forcing Jews by law to sacrifice to Greek gods; and outlawing Jewish rites, festivals, the practice of circumcision, and observation of the Sabbath.[3] Antiochos's persecution, the first systematic program of anti–Semitism in recorded history, would provoke one of the most devastating revolts of antiquity, which would end with the return of an independent Jewish kingdom for a time.

Although the policies of Antiochos IV seem to suggest otherwise, Greek writers did find much to admire in Jewish thought. At the end of the fourth century, the Alexandrian philosopher Hecataios apparently went so far as to propose that Plato's dream of a society where morality is governed by an unchangeable law came true in the form of the Jews and the Torah.[4] The admiration flowed both ways. The Jewish philosopher Aristobulos had attempted with unconvincing but interesting results to prove that Greek cultural giants like Orpheus, Homer, and Hesiod not only knew about Judaism but also gave it their seals of approval.[5]

The nexus of this cultural fusion was Alexandria, founded by Alexander the Great in 332 BCE. Nourished by its prime spot on the Egyptian coast, Alexandria grew like an organism, not only becoming the cosmopolitan capital of the Egyptian Ptolemies but also replacing Athens as the intellectual and artistic core of the vast Greek-speaking world. Besides being the home to both native Egyptians and imported Greeks, Alexandria was also, from at least the second century BCE on, the home of a rapidly growing Jewish community acclimated to Hellenistic culture.

The intellectual calling of one highly educated Alexandrian, Philo (ca. 20 BCE–50 CE), was to find the links between Greek philosophy and the Torah. Coming from what was most likely a well-connected family (at the least his brother had clout as a government official[6]), Philo had as much of an encyclopedic familiarity with Mosaic law and the lives of the Patriarchs as with classical Greek literature and philosophy. Philo saw enmity between the Greek and Jewish communities of Alexandria burst into outright brutality,[7] causing him to help lead an embassy to Rome to defend their people from accusations of sedition and ask (without much success) the Emperor Caligula (r. 37–41) to protect their rights and step in against persecution by the Alexandrian Greeks.

Whatever problems Philo had with his Greek neighbors, his faith that the Greek sages, whether Homer or Socrates, had tapped into the same divine truths as the Patriarchs was unshaken. Following the lead of the Stoics and their idea of humanity united as one community, Philo suggested there was little, if any, difference between divine law and natural law. The Torah was only the written reflection of an eternal and absolute unwritten law, which applied to the entire human race.[8] In Philo's words, "The law corresponds to the world and the world to the law" and "A man who is obedient to the law, being, by so doing, a citizen of the world, arranges his actions with reference to the intention of nature, in harmony with which the whole universal world is regulated."[9] In his view, the Torah, including its sexual regulations, is no longer simply a code meant to set the Jews apart as a chosen people, but a guidebook to the intrinsic designs of God and a universal moral ideal.

The Platonist distrust of bodily pleasure also inspired Philo. "God hates pleasure and the body without any especial cause," Philo succinctly claims.[10] In fact, God is so intuitively repulsed by the material realm, Philo argues, the word choice in Genesis reveals that even God had need of assistants to cope with the grit and grime of creating the world. Deploying an allegorical approach to the story of the Garden of Eden, Philo sees the account of the Fall as symbolizing humanity's inevitable submission to bodily desire.[11]

The sexual prohibitions of the Torah were made to protect the devout from the dangers of pleasure. Even so, Philo goes beyond the prescriptions of the Torah and urges that the penalty for adultery, stoning, should be extended to prostitutes. After recognizing that the prostitute has no special legal protections under Mosaic law, Philo justifies his bloody condemnation by appealing to both nature and the common good: "Let her, therefore, be stoned as an injury and mischief to, and a common pollution of, the whole state, having corrupted the graces of nature, which she ought to have adorned further by her own excellence."[12] Concubinage is seen as being on par with adultery and also demands stoning.[13] On the same note, Philo names adultery as "the greatest of all violations of the law" since it is a sin that derives from bodily pleasure, harms the adulterous parties as well as their spouses, and risks making children who are illegitimate.[14] Philo is more lenient toward premarital sex, but only as long as the male partner is willing to marry the woman.[15]

Throughout his writings on the sexual prohibitions in the Torah, Philo simultaneously confirms them, often favoring the strictest possible interpretation, and proposes that the laws have a purpose that conform to philosophical standards of logic and reason. For example, the Mosaic ban against sons marrying their stepmothers is explained as merited by the fact that such a union resembles something incestuous.[16] Likewise, he interprets the law against people marrying those who worship any other god as a bar against marriage with anyone from another "nation,"[17] a code that is necessary to preserve cultural cohesion for future generations, and reaffirms Moses's pronouncements against divorced spouses remarrying because for the wife it "[violates] former ties" and for the husband it reveals "a complete lack of manly courage and vigor."[18] The ban against intercourse with a menstruating woman is also justified on the grounds that, since the woman cannot conceive at that time, it would go against the natural purpose of intercourse, procreation.[19]

Even marriage between a man and a woman he knows is infertile excites Philo's disapproval. In Philo's eyes, the only reason for such marriages would be so that men could "gratify their excess in lust and incurable incontinence." These men "merely covet the carnal enjoyment like so many boars or goats, and deserve to be inscribed among the lists of impious men as enemies to God; for God, as being friendly to all the animals that exist, and especially to man, takes all imaginable care to secure preservation and duration to every kind of creature. But those who seek to waste all their power at the very moment of putting it forth are confessedly enemies of nature."[20]

Philo's strongest invective, however, is reserved for both pederasts and their lovers, an anger that was very likely sharpened by personal indignation at habits he observed among the more cosmopolitan Alexandrians. The lengthy passage is worth quoting for its enraged rhetoric:

> Moreover, another evil, much greater than that which we have already mentioned, has made its way among and been let loose upon cities, namely, the love of boys, which formerly was accounted a great infamy even to be spoken of, but which sin is a subject of boasting not only to those who practice it, but even to those who suffer it, and who, being accustomed to bearing the affliction of being treated like women, waste away as to both their souls and bodies, not bearing about them a single spark of a manly character to be kindled into a flame, but having eventhe hair of their heads conspicuously curled and adorned, and having their faces smeared with vermilion, and paint, and things of that kind, and having their eyes penciled beneath, and having their skins anointed with fragrant perfumes (for in such persons as these a sweet smell is a most seductive quality), and being well appointed in everything that tends to beauty or elegance, are not ashamed to devote their constant study and endeavors to the task of changing their manly character into an effeminate one. And it is natural for those who obey the law to consider such persons worthy of death, since the law commands that the man-woman who adulterates the precious coinage of his nature shall die without redemption, not allowing him to live a single day, or even a single hour, as he is a disgrace to himself, and to his family, and to his country, and to the whole race of mankind.[21]

Like the Torah itself, Philo seems to be silent on the topic of lesbianism, although he does write disapprovingly of "mannish women" and accuses female courtesans of corrupting women as much as they do men.[22] Otherwise, female same-sex intercourse does not sanction nearly as much revulsion, perhaps because the elements that torment Philo, the effeminacy of men and the waste of perfectly good semen, are not problems in that area.

In his analysis of the life of Abraham, Philo indulges in a digression about Sodom. Although the traditional view of Sodom as a place that exhibited the crimes of greed and inhospitality is still conjured up in Philo's writing, he suggests that "forbidden forms of intercourse" were a main symptom of the Sodomites' unrestrained luxury. In Sodom, Philo continues, "the men became accustomed to be treated like women, and in this way engendered among themselves the disease of females, and intolerable evil; for they not only, as to effeminacy and delicacy, became like women in their persons, but they made also their souls most ignoble, corrupting in this way the whole race of man, as far as depended on them." In the end, it is not the Sodomites' selfishness or even the threatened rape of guests that invokes divine revenge, but "unnatural and unlawful commerce" for which God "inflicted on them an astonishing novelty, and unheard of rarity of vengeance."[23]

As with Philo's analysis of the Mosaic law, male homosexuality defies nature not simply because it is a form of intercourse that cannot result in pregnancy, but also because it tears down even the strongest gender barriers. The stern lessons that can be learned from the destruction of Sodom seem to be that deviancy is a natural progression from luxury, and that sexual transgressions deserve a more drastic response from God than any other sins. This emphasis may have begun with Philo's own personal preoccupations. Surveying Jewish-Hellenistic writings that also mentioned the legend of Sodom from the same period, Derick Sherwin Bailey found that Philo was the first writer, or at least the first whose writings survive, to allege that Sodom was a Mecca for male homosexuality.[24]

Philo broke fresh soil in other ways. Much of his work was an extensive and unique effort to reconcile the Stoic vision of a global community and a natural law with the traditional ethics and monotheistic beliefs in Judaism. Further, in Philo's understanding of Mosaic law, prohibitions governing personal conduct are intended not just for a "chosen people" or a priestly elect, but for all people. The sophisticated, exhaustive writings of Philo and his mission to explain and justify Jewish law and theology to a Gentile audience attracted the fascination of early Christian theologians. In fact, Philo, although he gave no indication in his writings that he was even aware of Christianity's existence, would be deemed the father of the Church Fathers.

Sex and the New Testament

An irony in Christian theology is that Christianity's approach to sex has been formed more by the writings of the Apostle Paul than by the teachings of Jesus in the canonical Gospels. There is at least one good reason for this: the Gospels do not have much to report concerning Jesus's own thoughts on the subject. There is enough preserved, though, that it is easy enough to notice that the Gospels lack the stark fixations on bodily revulsion that appear in the works of later Christian writers.

Aside from several brief references to fornication,[25] Jesus seems mostly concerned with adultery and divorce. Taking a step beyond Mosaic law, Jesus urged that a man should only divorce his wife on grounds of adultery and that marriage with a divorced woman is tantamount to adultery.[26] What Jesus might have thought of a woman seeking divorce is not explained, since in the Gospels Jesus' opinions on divorce are prompted by a question specifically on divorce initiated by the husband, but a few later Christians filled the gap by recognizing the double standard on adultery and attacking it.

The idea that marriage should be bypassed entirely for a completely aesthetic life is something that is not exactly explicit in the Gospels. Still, a distrust of the body, or at least the material realm, is a theme that is not unknown to the Jesus of the Gospels. Matthew and Mark both report one of Jesus's sternest exhortations:

If your hand or your foot causes you to stumble, cut if off and throw it away; it is better for you to enter life maimed or lame than to have two hands or two feet and to be thrown into the eternal fire. And if your eye causes you to stumble, tear it out and throw it away; it is better for you to enter life with one eye than to have two eyes and to be thrown into the fire of hell.[27]

In a passage that appears only in the Gospel of Luke, Jesus states, in an apparent endorsement of celibacy, "Those who belong to this age marry and are given in marriage; but those who are considered worthy of a place in that age and in the resurrection from the dead neither marry nor are given in marriage."[28] The urge for an uncompromising rejection of the material is also driven home in the Gospel of John: "Those who love their life lose it, and those who hate their life in this world will keep it for eternal life."[29]

Although the sayings of Jesus as they are recorded in the New Testament do hint of a belief that material pleasures are a source of corruption, Jesus has no interest in lashing out against others for their attachment to pleasure, very unlike his contemporary Philo. The attention Jesus gives to people deemed pariahs by their communities and unsympathetic religious authorities is one of the overarching and most distinctive themes of all four canonical Gospels, culminating in Jesus declaring that prostitutes and tax collectors will enter heaven before the legalistic Pharisees.[30] For Jesus's understanding of personal morality, thought—hidden as it might be—is even more important than action and reputation. Hence the sin of a married man simply desiring another woman privately has the same magnitude as an act of adultery.[31]

When Jesus does mention Sodom, it is as a historical example of divine punishment for inhospitality,[32] not a moral lesson on sexual decadence. Also, during the Sermon on the Mount, Jesus warns his listeners not to use the Aramaic insult *raca*,[33] which has been translated as "fool" in the New Revised Standard English translation of the New Testament, but may have more specifically been slang for the passive partner in anal intercourse.[34] Of course, Jesus still considered adultery and prostitution to be sinful, and there is no indication one way or the other that his views on male homosexuality were any different; rather, what is strikingly unique is an attitude toward sexual stigmas proverbially summarized with, "Do not judge, so that you may not be judged."[35] Unfortunately, the lesson that no one is in a sanctified position to condemn others for their sexual indiscretions was one that would be tragically lost on more than a few Christian theologians and politicians throughout history.

One pivotal thinker far less inclined to reserve judgments was Paul. Before his revelation on the road to Damascus, Paul had been a zealous Pharisee persecutor of the nascent Christian movement, a career that peaked with his role in the stoning of Stephen, Christianity's first martyr. Conversion did nothing to quell Paul's rage against those who happened to not share his beliefs. In Paul's interpretation of history, all humanity once followed the God of the Hebrews, but turned away from God toward idol worship, provoking God into subsuming them in immorality. Paul's language makes it clear that he conceives such immorality as chiefly sexual:

Ever since the creation of the world his eternal power and divine nature, invisible though they are, have been understood and seen through the things he has made. So they are without excuse; for though they knew God, they did not honor him as God or give thanks to him, but they became futile in their thinking, and their senseless minds were darkened. Claiming to be wise, they became fools; and they exchanged the glory of the immortal God for images resembling a mortal human being or birds or four-footed animals or reptiles. Therefore God gave them up in the lusts of their hearts to impurity, to the degrading of their bodies among themselves, because they exchanged the truth about God for a lie and worshiped and served the creature rather than the Creator, who is blessed forever! Amen. For this reason God gave them up to degrading passions. Their women exchanged natural intercourse for unnatural, and in the same way also the men, giving up natural intercourse with women, were consumed with passion for one another. Men committed shameless acts with men and received in their own persons the due penalty for their error.[36]

For Paul, sexual behavior becomes a distinguishing mark between a follower of God and an idolater, with the Christians routinely displaying far greater sexual integrity than outsiders. This was the line of thinking that had been previously taken up by writers of the Jewish Diaspora, who increasingly saw their traditions in danger of being dissolved in an all-encroaching Gentile world.[37] Paul may very well have been acquainted with the *Wisdom of Solomon*'s statement that idolatry was the "beginning of fornication,"[38] the declaration in the *Book of Jubilees* that Gentile customs are "a pollution and an abomination and uncleanness,"[39] and an episode from the *Testament of Levi* where sex with prostitutes and adultery are plainly listed as standard Gentile behavior.[40] This was the sort of stark battle lines that Paul drew in the sand for his chosen ones.

What sort of depravities did Paul imagine that outsiders were enjoying? Paul's words on women exchanging "natural intercourse for unnatural" and men committing "shameless acts with men" have been interpreted as a straightforward condemnation of same-sex acts to church authorities up to modern times, who saw this passage in Romans as updating the Levitical ban on homosexual acts for the New Testament. Others have argued that Paul was attacking only same-sex rape or prostitution. Exactly what Paul meant by women "exchang[ing] natural intercourse for unnatural" also seems like a straightforward description of female same-sex intercourse, but it has been suggested that Paul might have been referring to noncoital methods of sex practiced between a man and a woman.[41] Such a reading is still controversial. The point is moot, in any event: as early as the medieval church Paul's words were seen as clearly condemnatory of female homosexuality as they were of male.

Much ink has been put to the purpose of tracing Paul's thoughts back to the Stoic and Cynic schools.[42] Still, there is more to Paul's words in Romans than him simply parroting philosophical rhetoric on the naturalness (or lack thereof) of certain methods of sex.[43] Within Plato's utopia, homosexuality is an intolerable aberration in need of harsh and immediate correction. For Paul, there is far more at stake than the disruption of the city-state and even a natural order. Unnatural sex exposes its participants as blacklisted by no lower authority than God and standing in absolute opposition to God's chosen. Along with thieves and idolaters, fornicators and both the active and passive partners in male same-sex intercourse are singled out as those who will never "inherit the kingdom of God."[44]

Although his vehemence is often poetically blunt, it should be remembered that sometimes Paul's thoughts on certain subjects can be difficult to pin down because his surviving writings are epistles written to specific people in response to specific circumstances, rather than broad treatises spelling out a comprehensive doctrine for posterity. As one example, Paul's words about marriage in his epistle to the Corinthians were composed in the shadow of the "impending crisis."[45]

Living as a celibate himself, Paul declared that "nothing good dwells within me, that is, in my flesh."⁴⁶ Submitting to "the flesh" entails death⁴⁷ and the genitals are cast among Paul's metaphors as the chief instruments for sin.⁴⁸ After urging the Corinthian congregation to remain loyal to their marriage partners, Paul admits that he would rather see them all celibate like himself, but concedes that it is better to find sexual satisfaction within a monogamous relationship than attempt abstinence and risk failing.⁴⁹

Perhaps Paul's words in these passages are not as radical a denouncement of sexuality as they might seem. There is a good argument that Paul's concept of celibacy is related far more strongly to the Cynics' ideal of a life without family commitments than to the later Christian aesthetic vision of an unending struggle between body and spirit.⁵⁰ After all, in spite of his anxieties about the allure of "the flesh," Paul objects to a doctrine spreading among the Corinthians that argues, "It is well for a wife not to touch her husband,"⁵¹ and instead proposes that "each man should have his own wife and each woman her own husband."⁵² It has been assumed (with reason) that Paul disapproved strongly of all forms of extramarital sex, although the Norwegian theologian Reidulf Molvaer argues that Paul actually did possibly approve of sex outside marriage, as long as it took place between two committed individuals and helped them with sexual self-control.⁵³ In any case, Paul sees sexual desire as something to be fought as an internal, pervasive threat to the elect. To succumb was to be no better than the idolaters.

If nothing else, Paul's views on sex tended to be more pragmatic than the arguments of more than a few of his successors. Paul opposes abstinence within marriage without the full consent of one's spouse on the grounds that doing otherwise will likely push a frustrated lover into adultery.⁵⁴ Divorce is off limits for both the wife and the husband.⁵⁵ Paul does not even mention Jesus's exemption that tolerates divorce to jettison an adulterous partner.⁵⁶

Paul did not go as far as some Jewish authorities, like Ezra or Philo, in condemning unions with outsiders. Divorcing a non–Christian was to Paul no more acceptable than divorcing a Christian spouse, although non–Christian partners were still free to do as they pleased.⁵⁷ He suggests there is nothing inherently wrong with such marriages and, in fact, even a non–Christian may be "sanctified" by marrying a believer.⁵⁸ This could very well be another instance of Paul's practical side, since he had to have been aware that a fragile, newborn movement cannot afford the luxury of total detachment. Paul does practically admit as much when he reminds his readers that the conversion of the spouse is always a possibility.⁵⁹ Curiously, Paul forbids widows to marry non–Christians.⁶⁰ Perhaps Paul thought of widows as more susceptible to apostasy,⁶¹ but more likely he had in mind the susceptibility of young Christian children to the beliefs of a fresh non–Christian stepfather.

As practical as Paul might be, he did not go to the lengths of Augustine of Hippo or Thomas Aquinas, who both suggested that prostitution might be necessary as a sexual outlet for men. Fornication in general is roundly condemned in Corinthians, but special attention is brought to the type of fornication that comes from soliciting prostitutes:

> Do you not know that your bodies are members of Christ? Should I therefore take the members of Christ and make them members of a prostitute? Never! Do you not know that whoever is united to a prostitute becomes one body with her? For it is said, "The two shall be one flesh." But anyone united to the Lord becomes one spirit with him. Shun fornication!⁶²

For Paul, it was probably unnecessary to lay down a detailed set of sexual regulations, since the old rules of Mosaic law still applied, at least to an extent. It is true that, while berating the Galatian congregation for practicing circumcision, Paul wrote, "No one will be justified through the works of the law."[63] However, the Mosaic law remained as a guide toward proper behavior (and, maybe more importantly, away from improper conduct); as Paul asserted in Romans, "if it had not been for the law, I would not have known sin."[64] The regulations of the Torah may have been rendered a dead letter as far as salvation was concerned, but this to me still had its uses as a handbook on sin.

Tradition is in all likelihood wrong in assuming that Paul was the actual author of the epistles to Timothy. Whoever the author was, he differed with Paul on points of Mosaic law, faith, and righteousness,[65] but not on sex. As with Paul's understanding that the law of Moses is an outline of what is sinful, the writer of Timothy argues that the law is "not laid down for the innocent" but exists to warn a number of sinners, including "fornicators" and "sodomites,"[66] who are categorized along with patricides, matricides, murderers, and slave traders. The writer goes on to urge that widowed women over 60 should be revered and receive the church's charity, while those younger should be allowed to remarry even though they "incur condemnation for having violated their first pledge" since "some have already turned away to follow Satan."[67]

If there is one theme that binds the rest of the New Testament together, it is the sense of an embattled enclave fighting a war of attrition against a seductive world. Addressing "adulterers," the author of the Letter of James warns, "Therefore whoever wishes to be a friend of the world becomes an enemy of God."[68] Sometimes this omnipresent corrupting power was expressed in terms of material wealth, but sexual desire remained as much of a menace. In the First Letter of John, "pride in riches" is ranked along with "the desire of the flesh" and "the desire of the eyes."[69] When Sodom and Gomorrah do reemerge in the Letter of Jude, they are not described as places condemned by their citizens' greed, as in rabbinic tradition, or as proverbial examples of inhospitality, as in the Gospels, but rather as the homes of people who "indulged in sexual immorality" and "pursued unnatural lust."[70]

The Church Fathers versus Sex

As odd as it might seem from our vantage point, there was not much of a Christian consensus on sex in the second century, when the Christian movement had grown large enough for ugly squabbles to erupt between believers clinging to different doctrines. In one corner, there was the *Acts of John,* a text apparently written by and for members of the esoteric Christian sects that usually fall under the umbrella term "Gnostic," where a young man guilty of killing for love castrates himself with a sickle, only for John to inform him that he still has to eradicate the "unseen spring through which every shameful emotion is stirred up and comes to light."[71] Tatian (ca. 120–ca. 180) and the Encartite sect also shared that corner, believing that Jesus endorsed the abolition of marriage and that salvation is meant only for the perfectly chaste.[72] In the other corner, the Nicolaitones and the followers of Basilides and Carpocrates either practiced plural marriages or lived in communities where everything was freely shared, even sex.[73]

Given that so much information about such groups come from unfriendly sources, partisans for the faction that would one day have the honor of being "Orthodox," it is reasonable to suppose that accusations of sexual license against "heretics" are just propaganda and hearsay. Nonetheless, given the near-perfect silence the Gospels maintain vis-à-vis the topic of sex, language about the abolition of the Law, the philosophical possibilities opened by belief in redemption by faith alone, and the extremely wide range of beliefs that are known to have been embraced by Christian groups in that time of the religion's history, it is not improbable that there really were sects like the Cainites, who allegedly believed that sin must be experienced for salvation to be effective.[74] Of course, certain allegations, like Epiphaneus's (ca. 310/320–403) disgusted claims that one Gnostic sect practiced ritualistic masturbation and consumption of semen while another taught its female followers that one can be a pure virgin and still practice oral sex, do invite some healthy skepticism.[75]

The radical aestheticism of Christian thinkers like Tatian was never pushed far from the mainstream and had great appeal to authors whose thinking would be embraced by later orthodox Christians. Origen (ca. 185–254), whose exegeses of the Hebrew Bible and New Testament would become deeply influential, saw sex as a primal source of corruption and believed that Adam and Eve experienced sexual desire only after the Fall.[76] Not one to shy away from putting principles into practice, Origen had himself castrated at the age of 20.[77] In blunt defiance of Paul's advice in 1 Corinthians, Origen's near-contemporary, the equally authoritative Tertullian (ca. 160–220), abruptly announced to his wife that he would cease sexual relations with her and wrote a treatise urging her to also become celibate.[78] Sadly, the feelings of Tertullian's wife on all this have not been recorded. Eventually Tertullian would join the Montanist Christians, who preached that all forms of sex and marriage were impediments to spirituality.

Tertullian does concede that the Gospels and Paul permit marriage, but he adds, "What is merely permitted is not good" and "[a] thing is not really good simply because it is not bad; nor is something not bad simply because it does no harm."[79] For Tertullian, women like his wife were the "Devil's gateway"[80] since through their attractiveness Satan could lure men away from salvation. Once in a while Tertullian hints that his revulsion was personal as well as intellectual. In his argument that virgin women should enter churches veiled, Tertullian denounces the unveiled woman who has the audacity to enter a church: "There she is patted all over by the roving eyes of total strangers, is tickled by the fingers of those who point her out, and, the darling of us all, she warms to it amid assiduous hugs and kisses."[81] This attire prohibition was, Tertullian argued, supported by both scripture and Nature.[82]

The most clear-cut early Christian treatise against sex is perhaps the early-third-century *Acts of Thomas*. The narrative follows the apostle Thomas to a kingdom in India, whose ruler is celebrating the marriage of his sole daughter. After blessing the happy couple at the king's forceful request, both of them have a vision of Jesus during their honeymoon, who makes a compelling if somewhat slippery argument on the dangers of childbearing:

> Know that if you refrain from this filthy intercourse, you will become holy temples, pure, free of trials and difficulties, known and unknown, and you will not be drowned in the cares of life and of children, who lead only to ruin. If you produce many children, you will become greedy and avaricious because of them, robbing orphans and defrauding widows, and by doing so you will render yourselves liable to the harshest punishments. For many children become a liability, being harassed by demons, some openly, others covertly. Some become lunatics, others are half-withered or lame or deaf or mute or paralytic or idiots. Even if they are in good health, they will be do-nothings, committing useless and disgusting deeds. They will be caught either in adultery or in murder or in theft or in fornication, and you will be afflicted in all these

cases. But if you are persuaded to keep your souls pure for God, living children will be born to you, who will suffer no harm. You will live an untroubled life, free from care and grief, while awaiting that true and incorruptible marriage. At that marriage you will be the attendants of the Bridegroom as you enter into that bridal chamber full of immortality and light.[83]

Instead of consummating their marriage, the young couple devote themselves to perpetual abstinence. Unsurprisingly the king proved not to be a supportive parent.

Other Christian writers were far less extreme and more in sync with traditional Greco-Roman and Stoic thoughts on sex and marriage. Clement of Alexandria (ca. 150–211/216) questioned the idea that lifelong abstinence was a good choice for every Christian and maintained that marriage could actually be beneficial to the Christian life.[84] Still, by no means was sex, even marital sex, appropriate unless it was for the sole purpose of having children.[85] Citing the Stoics, Clement proposes that sex not intended for procreation is irrational and unnatural. "Nature treats legitimate marriages as it does eating and drinking: it allows whatever is appropriate, useful and dignified, and it urges us to desire to produce children. But those who indulge in excess violate the laws of nature and harm themselves in illegitimate unions."[86] To keep lust at a minimum, Clement advised any wife to "devote herself to constant prayer and avoid leaving the house too often"[87] and any husband to "not feel lust for his wife"[88] and show "dignity during the pleasures of intercourse."[89] It is a bit disturbing to imagine what sex with Clement must have been like.

There is some evidence that not all Christians were quite as uptight as Clement would have wanted. Although the anonymous author of the third-century *Didascalia* shared Tertullian's and Clement's fears over well-dressed, attractive women, the writer also encouraged husbands not to treat their wives like servants and urged both partners to cultivate their mutual affection. Here the open expression of romantic feeling and desire is a help, not a hurdle, to the Christian life.[90]

Straight out of the gate Christian apologetics followed Paul's example and portrayed Christians as having more upright sexual and marital habits than their pagan neighbors. In his defense of Christianity to the emperor Antoninus Pius (r. 138–161), Justin Martyr (ca. 100–165) claimed that all Christians either married only to have children or stayed celibate for life.[91] Athenagoras (ca. 133–190), writing a treatise addressed to the co-emperors Marcus Aurelius (r. 161–180) and Lucius Verus (r. 161–169), also agreed that the only Christians who did not have sex just for the sake of impregnation were committed virgins, whereas all the Christians' pagan enemies were either adulterers, pederasts, or both.[92] Denouncing Greek culture itself, Tatian contrasted Sappho and her "lewdness" to Christian women who chatted about morally appropriate subjects over weaving.[93]

Likely enough the actual sex lives of Christians hardly lived up to the rhetoric, but from the beginning the community imposed high standards on itself. Even remarriage was, according to many authorities, off limits. Quoting 1 Corinthians 7:32–34, Tertullian bellowed, "Second marriage must be said to be nothing else than a kind of fornication."[94] After joining the Montanists, he raised his pitch even further, saying that the only conceivable motive for remarriage is lust and remarrying is every bit as immoral as murder.[95] The early-second-century author of *The Shepherd* was less severe: remarriage was not sin, but only in cases where the former spouse was safely dead.[96] Athenagoras, again bragging about the moral superiority of the Christians, disagreed: "For he who deprives himself of his first wife, even though she be dead, is a cloaked adulterer, resisting the hand of God."[97]

Becoming widowed was, under the morals endorsed by early Christian authorities, the only way a marriage could technically end. The only exception was when adultery took place. *The Shepherd* lays out a number of contingencies. If wives or husbands have a spouses who committed adultery, they must, if they know about the affair, divorce them. To do any less was to be complicit in adultery. If, however, the offending spouse sincerely repents, then the former partner is under a moral obligation to take that person back.[98]

Adulterers were not just to be excluded from their marriages, but from the church itself. Athenagoras implied that adulterers, apparently of either gender, were routinely excommunicated from the church, the harshest possible penalty.[99] How conscious early Christians were of the double standard involving male and female adultery is not absolutely certain, but Justin Martyr does praise a Christian woman for divorcing her husband who was "indulging in pleasure contrary to the laws of nature," since to do otherwise would have made her equally guilty of his sins.[100] For Tertullian, the composition of the Ten Commandments proves that adultery, no matter the sex of the offender, is equivalent to killing a human being.

Jesus and Paul had both provided unmistakable instructions on the topics of divorce and adultery, but thanks to certain precedents in the Hebrew Bible polygamy posed more of a challenge. Tertullian assumed that plural marriage was one of the practices abolished with the coming of Jesus.[101] Other church fathers agreed, adding that polygamy and the divine injunction "Be fruitful and multiply" were meant only for the time of the Patriarchs, when the Jews in particular and the human race in general were still relatively few in number. Now that humanity had populated the entire known world, having more than one wife, even in circumstances of infertility, was no longer needed.[102]

Even in the face of such hostility toward the sex drive, the idea that priests should be celibate was still centuries away from taking hold in the Christian mainstream. There were some uncertain steps that in hindsight seemed to lead in that direction. By the fourth century priests were barred from marrying after taking vows, and from then on priests were strongly discouraged from having intercourse with their wives, with chaste marriages promoted as the norm.[103] At the same time, however, the Council of Gangra in 345 excommunicated anyone who refused to take sacraments from a married priest and Pope Gregory I later forbade clerics to leave their wives before ordination.

There was no soothing of disgust toward sodomy, either. Clement of Alexandria, following Plato's *Laws* as much as the scriptures, decried sexual relationships between men, especially pederasty.[104] In a bitter digression against men who shave their faces and dye their gray hairs, Clement attaches effeminacy to homosexuality by adding, "If it is to attract men, [shaving and dying hair] is the act of an effeminate person; if to attract women, [it] is the act of an adulterer; and both must be driven as far as possible from our society."[105] The man who "in the light of day denies his manhood shall prove himself manifestly the woman at night."[106] Even Clement did not go quite as far as Tertullian, who bluntly approved of the Levitical death penalty for male homosexuality as "God's ordinance."[107]

The consequences threatened for stumbling into sexual sin could be dire—and everlasting. As early as the canonical Gospels, Christians took up Jewish concepts of a harsh hereafter for the sinful. Writers of the Jewish Diaspora such as the authors of the *Book of Daniel*[108] and the *First Book of Enoch*[109] had moved away from the gray, morally neutral afterlife of Sheol toward visions of postmortem judgment.[110] Ge-Hinnam, a ravine near Jerusalem associated with the worship of the gods Baal and Molech, became a byword for a place of punishment in the underworld.[111] For readers of the Septuagint, Ge-Hinnam was Gehenna, the place Jesus warns against in the Gospel of Mark.[112] Although with Matthew, Gehenna is the promised destination of those who fail to uphold Jesus's reinterpretation of the Law as banning lustful glances and the like,[113] the threat of such punishment seems to be aimed most at the uncharitable.[114] Luke, who shares the famous story of Lazarus and the rich man, refers instead to Hades, but carries the same implication that how one treats the disadvantaged, not sexual misbehavior, is the factor that determines the pleasantness of one's afterlife.[115]

This was not an idea that stuck. The *Epistle of Jude* and the *Second Epistle of Peter* threaten damnation not to the greedy, but to those who break away from church orthodoxy.[116] The *Apocalypse of Peter*, most likely dating from the middle of the second century, purports to be a vision of Hell given to the Apostles by Jesus and gives a special focus on sexual sins. The text paints a morbidly vivid Hell, becoming the first known work to reveal an afterlife where the condemned are punished according to their sins.[117] Female adulterers are suspended by their hair over a boiling lake of sewage while their lovers are dipped headfirst into the filth. No mention is made of male adulterers. Homosexuals of both sexes—"[men] that did defile their bodies behaving as women and the women that were with them were they that lay with one another as a man with a woman"—perpetually leap off a cliff, only to be flown back by demons to endlessly repeat the process. Women who had intercourse before marriage are shrouded in black clothes and have their bodies ripped apart.[118] Again, the anonymous author maintains the double standard, not mentioning any fate for men who have sex outside marriage.

We can only guess if such writings actually did help keep Christians in line. A somewhat similar text from the late third or early fourth century that is meant to be a record of Paul's tour of Heaven and Hell, the *Apocalypse of Paul*, was treated with skepticism by the Church and irritated Augustine but proved immensely popular throughout antiquity and into the Middle Ages.[119] As Paul is led through Hell by an angel, he witnesses people guilty of illicit sex withering in a river of fire. Women who lost their virginity before marriage receive special attention in the form of fiery chains that angels throw on their shoulders; female and male adulterers are hung by their hair or their eyebrows; and male homosexuals are consigned to a pit of brimstone and tar, their faces blood-red.[120]

However effective this belief in torments past the grave was in enforcing morals among believers, the manic diversity of second- and third- century Christianity did not leave theories on the afterlife uncontested. The third- century Platonic-Christian text *Zōstrianos* suggested reincarnation was the fate of the unenlightened and unsaved,[121] a belief apparently shared by some Gnostics.[122] Passages from the texts that would form the New Testament could be and were used as proof that unsaved sinners would either experience no afterlife at all or would someday join in universal salvation.[123] Using Paul's epistles and the Gospel of John as a guide, Origen also disputed the concept of an eternal, retributive Hell, instead arguing for an afterlife where souls are "corrected" by a demotion of sorts into becoming demons, yet it is always possible to move back up the celestial ladder to where they began and even toward angelic status.[124]

Sex was a rather important issue for the first generations of Christian writers. Even though many early Christian intellectuals relied on Platonic and Stoic language on natural and appropriate intercourse, it was through their sexual behavior (or more to the point, what they claimed were standard practices for their brethren) that the first Christians tried to prove the uniqueness and superiority of their way of life. These Christian bedroom morals were not simply a lifestyle for the spiritually ambitious or even just a set of rules from God. Instead, they aligned perfectly with natural law and intellectual reason; hence sexual deviance was not simply immoral, but irrational. As Clement of Alexandria sums up the point, "Everything that is contrary to right reason is sin."[125]

Sex under the Late Roman Empire

By the year 300, there may have been as many as 5 million Christians living within the borders of the Roman Empire.[126] As impressive as the frenzied growth of the new religion may have been, especially in the face of heavy competition from other religions such as the cults of Isis and Matthias as well as sporadic government persecutions and waves of popular hostility, the changes did not end there. The political structure Augustus built single-handedly was tottering as a brand-new species of emperors were beginning to leave their own fingerprints on Roman history.

After two very short-lived emperors and an outbreak of civil war, Septimus Severus (r. 193–211) took the imperial title by the sword. Augustus and his successors for the most part had previously presented themselves as senior statesmen (hence the title *princeps,* which carried the connotation of "first among equals") who drew their legitimacy from the ancient Republican institutions, but Severus, although of respectable senatorial rank like all past emperors, leaned on the strength of a massively expanded and overhauled military. However, the confidence of an army is not a reliable anchor even in the best of times—a lesson learned much too late by the last emperor of the Severan dynasty, Alexander Severus (r. 222–235), and his mother Julia Mamaea, who were both killed in a soldiers' revolt sparked by an unpopular truce with a German tribe.

After Alexander came Maximinus (r. 235–238), a Danubian peasant turned Roman soldier who did not last long as emperor but managed to prove once and for all that anyone could be emperor, even a nobody from the poorest, least "civilized" of the provinces. That was not exactly a positive precedent. In fact, Maximinus inaugurated what historians of ancient Rome call the Crisis of the Third Century, where from 235 to 284 about 19 of the 23 established emperors who ruled died fighting in civil wars, were assassinated by rivals, were murdered by their own soldiers, or were forced to commit suicide. In the midst of the madness there were attempts by the Senate and the old aristocracy of Rome to grab the wheel through their own candidates, but most of the emperors who tended to last were army officers from the provinces propped up by their comrades with the meek, petulant consent of the Senate. Real power no longer belonged to the senatorial Roman elite of the past or even to the historic imperial center of Italy, as the city of Rome itself lost its political significance piece by piece. The Emperor Diocletian (r. 284–305) did not find it necessary to visit Rome itself even once until the celebrations for the 20th year of his reign (and in the end he did not care for the experience).

Long before the conversion of Constantine and the Christianization of the Roman government, the attitudes of the emperors, who like Diocletian lived far away from cosmopolitan Rome, toward the sexual morals of their subjects had hardened. Septimius Severus, who came from North Africa, took a personal interest in the illicit marriage of a freedman to his female patron and demanded a strict punishment.[127] Apparently Alexander Severus pushed for the death penalty or exile with loss of citizenship in cases of female adultery,[128] although there is some debate over whether this decree is authentic.[129] Although a devout pagan who headed the most ruthless persecution of Christians in Roman history, Diocletian condemned incestuous marriages in terms strong enough even for Tertullian, complete with threats of divine wrath.[130]

There was also a slight shift in how the law dealt with homosexuality. Under Alexander Severus any attempt to seduce a free-born adolescent man, even if unsuccessful, could be punished with exile, imprisonment, or loss of citizenship.[131] The third-century jurist Ulpian argued that legally free-born men who were the passive partners in sexual intercourse should be labeled *infames* and thus subject to the same legal disabilities as actors, gladiators, prostitutes, and pimps.[132] Ulpian's colleague Paulus urged additional penalties for such men, including a ban keeping them from practicing law and restricting their inheritance rights.[133] A law against male prostitutes was, according to one source, put on the books by Philip the Arab (r. 244–249), but it apparently did not outlast him.[134]

The most drastic changes were brought on by Constantine I (r. 306–337), who not only was the first emperor to convert to Christianity but also carried out the most extensive revision of Roman marriage law since Augustus's *lex Julia*.[135] Most strikingly, in 320 Constantine abolished the law that dictated financial penalties and the loss of inheritance rights for the unmarried and the childless. In the suitably dramatic language of Constantine's decree, "[W]e release the commands of the law placed on their necks like yokes from everyone indiscriminately."[136] Scholars in the past have assumed that Constantine was following the lead of his Christian advisers by making life in the empire easier for Christian celibates. It is more likely, though, that Constantine was trying to appeal to the upper classes, who always had the most to lose under Augustus's legislation.[137]

In other ways, Constantine tightened the rules. By 326, there were barriers to a man being married and keeping a legal concubine at the same time.[138] There had always been a stigma in Roman society attached to living with both a concubine and a wife, but this was the first time a man having relationships with a wife as well as a concubine fell under legal scrutiny. Constantine also turned his attention to *raptus,* the custom of abduction marriages (which encompassed not only marriages where the would-be wife is taken by force, but also any marriage made without the consent and knowledge of the bride's parents), with severity.

If the complicity of the abducted bride could be proved, she would share the punishment of the abductor, which may have been either execution or exile and loss of citizenship.[139] Even daughters who *were* taken by force were not let off the hook. By Constantine's reasoning, "they too could have kept themselves at home until their marriage day and, if the doors were broken down by the abductor's audacity, they could have sought help from the neighbors by their cries and could have defended themselves with all their efforts." At least Constantine was magnanimous enough to give these "offenders" the lesser punishment of being denied their parental inheritance. No party in such a scenario was untouched. If the girl's governess was complicit in the crime, she would be killed by being forced to swallow molten lead; if the parents had eventually accepted the marriage, then they were to be deported.[140] The harshness of the law did not sit well with Constantine's successors and at least as early as 349 the prescribed punishments were eased, although slaves found guilty of assisting in an abduction (or, to make a distinction that would have been negligible to the Romans themselves, a seduction) were still to be burned alive.[141] Along the same lines a *tutor,* who by Constantine's time was a girl's guardian until she came of age at 12, will be exiled and his possessions confiscated by the imperial government.[142]

The adultery law from the *lex Julia* was not expanded, but it was refined. Women who owned taverns and inns, who were before unofficially kept under the radar, were now considered respectable enough to be liable to prosecution for adultery, along with their lovers, in contrast, tavern waitresses and other menial workers, whose job duties sometimes overlapped with those of prostitutes, were exempt.[143] Constantine did not institute the death penalty for female adultery.[144] His son Constans (r. 339–350) refers to punishing adulterers in the same way as parricides, being tied in a sack and burned alive, but nowhere is there proof that this punishment was ever put into practice.[145] In one proviso of Constantine's that must have come across as a blessing for the rich, accusations of adultery only could come from the husband, his father, or their relations[146] (the wife's family did not qualify), a sure move against blackmailers and informants.

Also extreme were Constantine's rulings on divorce, which brought an abrupt end to the traditional Roman view of marriage as a matter of ongoing consent. After Constantine stepped in, women could divorce their husbands only if they could prove that they were guilty of murder, sorcery, or robbing graves. Conversely, men could divorce their wives if it could be proved that they were guilty of adultery, procuring prostitutes, or sorcery (the similarity to what Plutarch claimed was Romulus's law on divorce cannot be a coincidence). Failure to have a good reason would cause the divorcing husband to lose all of his wife's dowry and, if he married again, the new bride would also have to surrender her dowry and any nuptial gifts to the ex-wife. A divorcing wife had it even worse: she would not only lose her dowry, but also be exiled to an island.[147]

It is entirely possible that Constantine was tilted toward these reforms by his newfound Christian beliefs and the urgings of his Christian entourage; all these changes in marriage law took place well after Constantine converted in 312. At the same time Constantine's reforms fit the pattern of emperors' escalating concern with the morality of their subjects, nor should the role of his ministers, who were not all Christians, be underestimated. If the laws were inspired by Christian ethics, then they were, at best, a half-hearted compromise. Exemptions to divorce other than adultery were still allowed while Christian objections to the double standard had no place in the laws.

Perhaps Constantine simply had a deeply personal interest in matters of sexual morality. In 326, Constantine had his wife, Fausta, and his son from a previous marriage, Crispus, killed; Crispus was poisoned while Fausta was locked in a hot bath (a humane method of execution, since the victim would have been painlessly smothered by the steam). Their crime is shrouded in mystery, but rumor had it Crispus engaged in an illicit affair with his stepmother. Whatever the connection between Constantine's severity and the origin of his laws, there is something of a tragic parallel between this and Augustus's efforts to become a great moralizer while having to treat his daughter's indiscretions with razor-sharp ruthlessness.

Future emperors tended to build on Constantine's example. While no one besides Fausta and Crispus were apparently executed for adultery during Constantine's reign, according to the late fourth-century Latin historian Ammianus Marcellinus, Valentinian I (r. 364–375) had one senator put to death for adultery and two others executed for fornication (*stuprum*). High-ranking women found guilty of adultery were likewise rounded up and executed, sometimes after being degraded and tortured. Even Marcellinus was appalled by how slaves were tortured to the brink of death to secure evidence for accusations of *stuprum*, which was not allowed under Augustan law.[148]

The one exception were the changes in divorce law, easily the most reviled of Constantine's reforms. Julian the Apostate (r. 361–363) and Theodosius II (r. 408–450) each rewrote the law back to the ancient *status quo*, although Theodosius II later amended his own revisions to require grounds that were in any case broader than what Constantine allowed, only to see both of their successors to reverse back to Constantine's divorce laws.[149] The double standard was eventually addressed in 449, when a joint decree by Theodosius II and Valentinian III (r. 425–455) made the husband's adultery grounds for divorce.[150] Along with restrictions on why one could divorce came restrictions on who one could marry. Constantine and his successors extended Augustus's ban on senators marrying women from lowly origins, such as actresses and the daughters of gladiators and tavern owners, to all imperial magistrates.[151] Under Valentinian II (r. 372–395), marriage between a Christian and a Jew made both parties, rather paradoxically, guilty of adultery.[152]

Even as the Church played more of a hand in drafting imperial policy, prostitution was never formally curtailed. Although Constantine had once sneered that prostitutes were too vile for even the law to bother with[153] and deprived notables who had children by prostitutes of their titles and public honors,[154] he still personally saw to it, when expanding the old Greek colony of Byzantion into his capital of Constantinople, that the city would have a clearly designated red-light district.[155] Even with drastically changing times, prostitution remained a fixed facet of Roman society and a profitable tax resource for the government. Still, Christian disapproval was not ignored entirely by the law. By the fifth century, bishops were empowered to step in when a prostitute petitioned to be released from service to a brothel.[156]

Male prostitution, and in fact male homosexuality in general, would enjoy less tolerance, however grudging. In 342, the emperors Constantius II (r. 337–361) and Constans had approved a strangely worded edict:

> When a man marries as a woman who offers herself to men, what does he wish, when sex has lost its significance; when the crime is one which it is not profitable to know; when Venus is changed into another form; when love is sought and not found? We order the statutes to arise, the laws to be armed with an avenging sword, and those infamous persons who are now, or who hereafter may be, guilty may be subjected to exquisite punishment.[157]

Despite the firmly worded references to "laws ... armed with an avenging sword" and "exquisite punishment, the actual penalty is not spelled out here. Neither does the law show obvious traces of Christian contributions, beyond the personal religious belief of the two emperors. The weight is on the passive partner, rather than on both partners according to Leviticus's and Paul's preferences; the language "when Venus is changed into another form" has no precedent in early Christian writings; and the concern that such sex acts are "not profitable" could very well have come from a Stoic writer or a commentary on the *Laws*.

True to form, Theodosius I (r. 379–395), the emperor who brought a violent end to Roman religious pluralism, clarified with appropriately biblical passion the empire's new approach to male homosexuality. After a preamble blasting the present generation of Roman men as "polluted ... by the poison of shameful effeminacy," the edict, also released in the names of co-emperors Valentinian II and Arcadius, starts with a loud attack against men who "condemn the male body to the submissiveness appropriate to the opposite sex"; specifying male prostitutes, Theodosius calls for them to be burned "with avenging flames in the sight of the people, so that they will understand that the lodging of the male soul must be sacrosanct nor without incurring the severest penalty shall they shamefully renounce their own sex."[158] Theodosius's rhetoric introduces a fresh reason to despise sex between men—it harms the masculine resolve of the body politic—and mandates the cruelest possible punishment with little precedent in Rome's classical history, although there is no proof that such extreme penalties were ever enacted. In fact, even after the edict was issued, a tax on male prostitutes continued to be collected until around the end of the fifth century.[159] Still, arrests were made, but the populace was apparently not on the side of the law. When a popular Greek charioteer was arrested for sodomy in 390, the official who ordered the arrest was lynched by a mob.

With the government taking more of a hard line against homosexuality, however far it actually went in practice, it is worth checking whether such measures went with the climate. Unfortunately, the proof is rare, although the fact that there are fewer references to homosexuality or pederasty in the Greek and Latin literature of late antiquity[160] than in early imperial literature may be in and of itself telling. The *Amores,* attributed to the second-century Latin poet Lucian but actually written by an unknown author sometime between the very end of the second century and the middle of the fourth century, is the only major work that deals at length with same-sex love, from a philosophical viewpoint or otherwise, from late antiquity. Composed in the classic Socratic style, the *Amores* pits Greek pederasty against the sort of militant heterosexuality promoted by the emperor Theodosius.

After detailing his sexual conquests, the bisexual libertine Theomnestus calls upon Lycinus, who is celibate to the point of being outright asexual, to apply his natural objectivity to the question of whether women or adolescent men are better lovers. Lycinus decides not to give a direct answer and recounts a debate between his two friends, Charicles and Callicratides, who were devoted to the love of women and men, respectively. The difference of opinion between the two men is severe enough that Lycinus had to suggest a debate to stop them from brawling. In an inversion of the sort of stereotypes that surface in Theodosius's rhetoric, Charicles wears cosmetics to maximize his appeal to women and is obsessed with sex. His opponent Callicratides is the ideal citizen in the old-fashioned Greek mold, involved in the politics of his home city Athens and an avid exerciser of his mind and body. Callicratides also surrounds himself with temptation, in the form of handsome adolescent slaves, but he practices moderation and sends them away once their beards begin to grow.

From the start of his argument, it is clear that Charicles is more concerned with attacking male same-sex love in general, not just Greek pederasty, than with defending the love of women. By Charicles's logic, heterosexuality was once universal, but at some point same-sex intercourse was invented. In addition to repeating the canard that sex between men is unnatural and effeminizing, Charicles echoes Aristophanes by accusing Callicratides of using the tradition of pederasty as an excuse to gratify his lust and suggests that, if sex between men is widely accepted, then sex between women must also be tolerated—and that, Charicles preaches, would be unthinkable. Lycinus notes that Charicles had a "wild, fierce glint in his eyes," a hint that the thinking behind Charicles's opinions is less than perfectly rational.

In response, Callicratides reveals himself as a misogynist, but is more concerned with answering Charicles than forming an argument of his own. Drawing largely from the pre-*Laws* Plato and other customary defenses of pederasty, Callicratides asserts instead that pederasty is the logical fulfillment of a masculine Greek tradition, where the lover is drawn not by crude physical attraction, but rather by the adolescent's skills as a soldier-in-training, his noble athleticism, and his studies of the ancient virtues. Lycinus, while declaring Callicratides the victor of the debate, makes something of a compromise declaration: "Marriage is a boon and a blessing to men when it meets with good fortune, while the love of adolescents, that pays court to the hallowed dues of friendship, I consider to be the privilege only of philosophy. Therefore all men should marry, but let only the wise be permitted to love boys, for perfect virtue grows least of all among women."[161]

Although Lycinus decides in favor of the pederast, Lycinus's conclusion is a conservative nod to Greek culture, especially when compared to the explicit omnisexual hedonism in early imperial literature such as the satires of Juvenal and Martial. Lesbianism appears only as a bogeyman invoked by Charides, while male homosexuality is acceptable only within the very narrow parameters of Greek pederasty, to be practiced just between grown men and adolescents as well as only by an intellectual and (by implication) aristocratic elite. Nonetheless the treatment of Charides is interesting, since in parts it seems like a mocking depiction of the sort of anti-male-love arguments that would be brewing among philosophical, Christian, and political circles in late antiquity. Callicratides is presented as a man's man, while Charides, the prodigious lover of women, is the one who is truly effeminate and lascivious. It is safe to say that Charides is a caricature, but considering the specific details of his blatant hypocrisy and his venomous arguments, it is perhaps not too much of an assumption to guess that the author pieced this character together from some real-life models, ones related to the voices that would soon come to dominate thoughts on homosexuality.

With Christianity—or at least Christians who toed what would become the official party line—free from persecution and orthodoxy finally being established with the Council of Nicaea, a comprehensive orthodox Christian doctrine on sexuality was beginning to be laid out. The Council of Elvira (early fourth century) released the strongest Christian statement against the double standard: men who cheated on their wives in one fling were given five years of penance, but habitual offenders had to perform penance for life and were denied communion until they were on their deathbed. Prostitutes and panderers were also excluded, along with non–Christian priests, gladiators, soldiers, and astrologers, from membership in the Church, with those who renounced their old occupations only to relapse being excommunicated. Men who were found to have had intercourse with their own sex were more harshly punished: they were denied communion even at death's door.[162]

The clergy were also to be put to higher standards than laypeople. The Council of Elvira made the first big step toward the modern Catholic Church's restrictions on the sexuality of their clergy by ordering married clerics to abstain from all intercourse, while the highest ranks were to divorce their wives.[163] This move, which incorporated aestheticism into church policy in a very tangible way, was just the beginning of a bitter controversy that would stay strong into the present day. In other ways, the early Church was opening marriage up to other parties. Pope Calixtus I (r. 217–222) ruled that the Church must acknowledge all marital unions otherwise deemed invalid under Roman law, which would include marriages between slaves and free individuals.[164] Respecting the fact that marriages between slaves by the third century were treated legally as simple cases of co-inhabitation and the only way a woman of high rank could be with a lower-class man and retain her status would be to register herself as that man's concubine, the Church was even prepared to respect concubinage.[165]

Meanwhile individual theologians continued to fine-tune the rules for personal conduct. Lactantius (ca. 240–ca. 320) had written the *Divinarum Institutionum Libri* (Divine Institutes), which was simultaneously a Christian apologia and an attack on Greco-Roman pagan religion. It may have been influential in reconciling Rome's elite attitudes to Christian opinions. Lactantius goes so far as to argue that Christians are much better at living out the Romans' own ideals toward marriage and family than most pagans.[166] At the same time Christian morals may be superior to the Romans' morals, since Christians do not expose their infants and are as intolerant of adultery in husbands as adultery in wives.[167]

Lactantius's view of sex in general is actually more restrained than what can usually be found among the early Church Fathers. Although he stands by the line that parenting children is the purpose of sex, he allows sex in circumstances where procreation will not happen (such as when the wife is pregnant), as long as sex still takes place within marriage.[168] When it comes to divorce (and how it should be allowed only in cases of adultery) and adultery, Lactantius's opinions are more predictable. Lactantius also accuses anyone who marries a divorced spouse whose ex is still alive of committing adultery.[169] On the hot-button issue of celibacy, he does not recommend it for everyone, but only for people who are well prepared to handle a lifelong war with their urges. Those who do will attain holiness,[170] the opinion that would eventually evolve into the official view of the Catholic Church.

Other Christian theologians writing at the end of the fourth century and the beginning of the fifth century stuck to the early distrust of sex that ran so strongly through the writings of Tertullian and Clement of Alexandria. Gregory of Nyssa (ca. 335–394) held that only lifelong virgins could be sure that they would be saved.[171] Jerome (ca. 347–420), whose enthusiasm for asceticism shocked even some of his fellow Christians and led him into a fierce debate with his peer Jovinian (d. ca. 405), preached that married Christians should refrain from intercourse as much as possible, even if they kept procreation in mind, and when they did engage in intercourse, they must at least refrain from getting any enjoyment out of it.[172] "Nothing is filthier than to have sex with your wife as you might do with another woman," Jerome famously decreed.[173] Ambrose of Milan (ca. 338–397), who was Theodosius I's chief mentor in all things spiritual and political, maintained that sex with a concubine was adultery. Sex with a wife was only somewhat better: it betrayed "just" a lack of moral resolve.[174]

John Chrysostom (ca. 347–407), who was Greek-speaking world's prototype of the fire-and-brimstone preacher in the late fourth century, is an ominous figure in the story of the development of both anti–Semitism and homophobia. For Chrysostom, homosexuality becomes the one and only sin of the men of Sodom and Gomorrah[175] and is described as a "new and lawless lust ... a terrible and incurable disease ... a plague more terrible than all plagues."[176] A historian of homosexuality, Louis Crompton, finds in Chrysostom's sermon on Romans 1:26 a condemnation of lesbianism as well as such colorful adjectives as "monstrous," "Satanical," "detestable," "execrable," and "pitiable," as well as an assurance that proper sexual intercourse is more pleasurable than buggery any day. As Crompton sardonically notes, "We are bemused to see this devout ascetic speak so knowledgeably."[177] For this sin greater than the sum of all other sins, Chrysostom prescribes the Levitical punishment of stoning.[178]

When it came to more conventional pairings, John Chrysostom was no less strict. Although he agreed that a life of abstinence was not for all Christians, he urged all widowers and widows to shun even the thought of remarriage and instead devote themselves to a life of self-mortification. After all, such persons should be wise enough to find atonement for their former enjoyment of the flesh.[179]

Among these usually austere men Augustine of Hippo (354–430), who as a sex-crazed adolescent once prayed, "Lord, grant me chastity and continence ... just not yet!," stands apart. His *Confessions* is a milestone in the history of autobiography and *De civitate dei* (City of God) is a work that manages to have equal weight in the realms of theology, philosophy, and history. Augustine's vast library of writings was founded on the painful tensions between his restless, piercing intellect and a belief system that demanded blind faith, but his words were also given form by a terror of his own libido. Into his teenage years, Augustine was, in his words, "controlled by the madness of sensuality."[180] Eventually he settled down with a mistress with whom he co-inhabited and had a son—an arrangement that would have met with some disapproval from Christian quarters, but which was hardly uncommon or socially inappropriate. After 14 years of this arrangement, he bowed to pressures from his devout Christian mother Monica and entered a betrothal at the age of 30, although such a commitment did not stop him from having an affair with another mistress. When Augustine converted to Christianity, he finally broke off the engagement and decided to become a lifelong celibate.

Oddly enough, the most influential theologian in the history of the Western Church not only converted late, but had pledged allegiance to another religion, Manichaeism. Founded by Mani, a native of Mesopotamia who lived under Persia's Sassanid Empire in the middle of the third century, Manichaeism became seen by Christians as a threatening heresy, yet also borrowed enough from polytheism, Platonism, and Zoroastrianism to qualify as its own religion. As a Manichaean Augustine would have learned that matter is synonymous with the Kingdom of Darkness while the spiritual comes only from the Kingdom of Light. Intercourse with Eve, for example, was a weapon used by the forces of Darkness to try to corrupt Adam. Sexual intercourse perpetuates matter, which in turn continues the enslavement of Light to Darkness. Because of this, the Elect, the intellectual and spiritual elite in Manichaenism, are called upon to abstain totally from sex.[181] How much Augustine the Manichaen may have inspired Augustine the Christian is a topic big enough for a book of its own, but the stern view of sex as the ultimate tool of cosmic evil and the idea of human nature as fundamentally and irreversibly infused with darkness cannot have failed to leave an impression.

At the very least, Augustine modified his Manichaean views to find some good in Adam and Eve's initial carnal knowledge. Augustine was willing to consider the possibility that Adam and Eve knew some form of sexuality in Eden, but it was free of corrosive passion.[182] Although in this primordial state sex brought on mutual happiness, in the post–Fall universe children are the "only worthy fruit" of sex.[183] Any form of sexual relationship outside a sanctified marriage is out of the question, with a homosexual relationship being at the top of the list. Although Augustine was not as concerned with homosexuality as he was with multiple other topics, he did take time to argue that homosexual intercourse is a violation of the innate contract between God and mankind.

Augustine declared that intercourse within marriage that takes place without the intent of procreation is a venial sin, one that can be easily redeemed. Adultery and fornication are, in contrast, mortal sins, which put the soul in peril. For spouses who had grown past the childbearing age, Augustine recommended abandoning sex to enter a union that is purely spiritual. Although Augustine was careful to defend marriage from Jerome and other radical aesthetics, celibacy was still in Augustine's opinion the superior option for the spiritually conscious, especially now that humanity was already so numerous: "Even they who wish to contract marriage only to have children are to be admonished that they practice the greater good of continence."[184]

Escaping the World

At this point in history, even moderates in the marriage-and-children-or-abstinence debate agreed that a lifetime of abstinence was the closest one could be to godliness on earth. Beyond the theoretical, however, what was taking place in the fourth and fifth centuries to drive so many people in the Roman Empire to abandon their families and communities and to adopt often isolated lives of complete chastity, particularly when there were so few precedents for such a movement and when most were not even aware of the debates going on between the likes of Jerome and Jovinian?

For this as well as any strange shift in social and cultural practice, there can be no easy answer—in fact, there probably cannot be even *one* answer. A good starting point is considering how different Christian celibacy was from most forms of pagan celibacy that had been practiced in the Mediterranean and the Middle East. Although pagan sects, while lacking Christianity's ideas on the dangers of the flesh and the importance to some significant degree of sexual forbearance for every living person, sometimes agreed that renunciation bestowed sanctity, abstinence was either imposed at an early age under harsh threats (as with the Vestal Virgins) or came along as just one of a number of responsibilities and requirements associated with joining a priesthood. For Christians, celibacy, and the spiritual fulfillment that accompanied it, did not require knowledge of ceremony or ritual or even dogma, only the most basic faith.

Still, this does not totally explain why so many people set themselves against the demands of their own bodies and their communities. In his study of the origins of Christian aestheticism, *The Body and Society,* Peter Brown put forward the theory that embracing the solitary life of an aesthetic was the individual's way of snatching control over his or her body away from a demanding society, and important changes in not only how the Roman government operated, but in how it presented itself, did happen to coincide with the explosion in the popularity of renunciation. Wishing to bring some stability in the wake of the Crisis of the Third Century, Diocletian finally tore away the last shrouds of republicanism from the imperial office, revealing it to be in full the monarchy it had been since it was founded by Augustus. Although Diocletian had established the Tetrarchy, where the empire was divided between two senior and two junior co-emperors, each emperor was now to be treated like the old Persian and Hellenistic autocrats. Diocletian's reforms required ministers and courtiers to bow in the imperial presence and for the first time established elaborate systems of ritual and etiquette that all but presented the emperor as a god on earth.

To accompany this ground-up ideological reconstruction, the reach of the government was drastically expanded and aspects of imperial government previously handled by regional authorities became the responsibility of armies of bureaucrats accountable only to a centralized imperial administration.[185] Taxation—and the government machinery used for collection—grew to unprecedented levels. Among Diocletian's other reforms, there were strict laws mandating that most occupations become hereditary. The State had become a presence in people's lives in a way that it had not been even under the first emperors.

Certainly for women, who had no path before them except that of an often prearranged marriage (one that would, likely enough, be to an overbearing or outright abusive husband), a quite possibly dangerous or fatal pregnancy, and the potential tragedies of family life, an existence as a Christian ascetic could be an appealing alternative. Although a man, Gregory of Nyssa is sympathetic to this motive:

> Assume that the moment of childbirth is at hand; it is not the birth of the child, but the presence of death that is thought of, and the death of the mother anticipated. Often, the sad prophecy is fulfilled before the birth is celebrated, before any of the anticipated goods are tasted, joy is exchanged for lamentation [...] But perhaps this is not the case. Let us assume that conditions are more favorable, that the child is born, the very image of the springtime of his parents; what then? Is the supposition of grief lessened because of this, or is it not rather increased? In addition to their earlier fears, they have added those in behalf of the child lest he encounter something unpleasant, lest some disagreeable chance befall him with regard to his upbringing, some unshared by both parents. But who could enumerate the special worries of the wife? I pass over the ordinary factors known to all, the discomfort of pregnancy, the risk of childbirth, the toil of education the child, and the special heartbreak caused by a child.[186]

In the end, Gregory sarcastically compares the "freedom of virginity" to married life and finds the latter lacking.[187]

The promise of autonomy must have been one of the celibate life's main selling points to women. Episodes in which women successfully defied their families and society, such as the story of the legendary virgin Thecla in the *Acts of Paul* and narratives like the *Acts of Xanthippe and Polyxena*, were popular among Christians in the second and third centuries, combining Christian conversion stories with lively sensationalist elements from Greek and Latin novels. For instance, after her conversion Polyxena escapes from several kidnappings, disguises herself as a man, and tames a lion through prayer, just for starters. Even the less adventurous stories at least depicted women proudly defying the demands of their families and the commands of their husbands, fiancées, or fathers to choose their own future in life, in spite of harassment and even threats of torture and death.

As attractive as the freedom to decide their own fates was, the role that Christian thoughts on the horrors of sex must have played in such choices for celibacy should not be forgotten. Speaking through Thecla, Methodius, writing sometime around the end of the third century, claimed that for the chaste bliss overcomes all pain while the worldly "will not see the end of their grief and sufferings until ... they satisfy the needs of their unspeakably great incontinence."[188] The anonymous biographer of the ascetic Olympias claims that she told her relative, the Emperor Theodosius I, after being brought before him on a charge of misusing her fortune, that she found her marriage, which was ended by the husband's unexpected death, to be a "very burdensome yoke" and chastity is instead a "very happy yoke."[189] Whatever the appeal, by the fourth century a new genre in Christian literature had arisen: biographies of ascetic women such as Macrina (ca. 270–ca. 340) and Olympias (d. 410) who went on to become influential Christians, sometimes establishing monasteries of their own.

The *Life of Anthony,* written by Athanasius between 356 and 358 and focusing on a wealthy Egyptian farmer who gave up his fortune and land to live as a hermit in a desert, has traditionally been seen as an account of the "first monk," but Athanasius already refers to a number of ascetics who often lived in the outskirts of cities and towns. What distinguished Anthony (ca. 251–356) was his total abandonment of not only civilized society but inhabitable land altogether. Living alone, Anthony took a minimum of sleep, food, and leisure time, sustaining himself on bread, salt, and water, which he savored only once a day, and spending his hours weaving baskets and engaging in other activities by which he could eke out a meager living. Like his fellow aesthetics, Anthony began at the fringe of his village, but eventually moved into the desert, taking up residence in an abandoned barracks. When Anthony first started his new career, his resolve was challenged by memories of his old life and the sister he had left after sending her to a convent. Next came the temptation of sex, which came in the form of images of a beautiful woman and a black boy.[190]

The fight with sexual urges was as much a part of the monk's inner turmoil as the pain of leaving behind family and society. The monk Arsenius (ca. 352–445), who like so many well-known aesthetics was constantly bothered by pilgrims (who apparently did not quite get the point of the monk's isolation), was horrified by a glimpse of an attractive female pilgrim and screamed, "I pray God to take the memory of you from my heart!"[191] Pachomius (ca. 292–348), another Egyptian who eventually founded the first known monastic rule, started his ascetic career with a group led by Palamon, who demanded that sexual thoughts be warded off through an intense regimen of manual labor all day and prayer all night.

Some couples, taking Joseph and the Virgin Mary as their models, adopted a practice called celibate marriage where men and women lived together, bound by a spiritual relationship. Augustine approvingly discusses one group, led by Paulinus of Nola (ca. 354–431), consisting entirely of couples who lived in celibate marriages. In the sixth century, Gregory of Tours (ca. 538–594) recounted a legend of a fourth-century aristocratic couple in Clermont-Ferrand who maintained a vow of celibacy they made on their wedding night.[192] However, Gregory also cited a case from the same region and an earlier period where a bishop tried to live chastely with his wife, but they lapsed and she became pregnant.[193] Other church intellectuals and authorities envisioned similar scenarios and condemned celibate marriages as reckless ventures that could easily collapse into sin. At least ten church councils and synods had denounced and attempted to ban the practice by 600.[194]

After the end of Constantine's century, the monastic communities had joined the ranks of the empire's richest landowners, bishops guided the course of imperial policy, and the most ancient and sacred rituals of the Roman State had been casually abolished. Rome's tolerance for a multitude of religious and philosophical beliefs, limited and flawed as it was in practice, was also entombed in the history books, as belief became, quite literally, a matter of life or death. However, this union between Christianity and the Roman State arguably did not become complete until Justinian I appeared on the stage. More so than even Theodosius I, Justinian did not hesitate to turn the full power of the State on his own subjects to impose orthodoxy, although, as we will see, his record as a secular enforcer of Christian morals was uneven at best.

V

The War on Sin

By the time Augustine of Hippo began work on the *City of God* in 413, Rome had been invaded and briefly occupied by the Goths, the first time the city had been captured by a foreign enemy since 389 BCE when the Gallic king Brennus rampaged through Italy. Augustine meant for his *magnum opus* to be a rebuttal to Roman traditionalists who were confident that the abolition of the city's sacred rituals and the neglect of the gods worshiped by past generations was exactly why Rome burned. One can sympathize with their point of view. In the years that followed Theodosius I and his persecution of pagans, the empire made what turned out to be a final split between west and east; the western half soon withered, with almost all of Gaul, Britain, North Africa, and the Iberian peninsula falling away.

The relative peace that the western empire enjoyed under Theodosius's dynasty came to a breakneck halt when, in 454, the last western emperor of the family, Valentinian III, was butchered in an old-fashioned German bloodfeud, killed by two Germans in retaliation for Valentinian's murder of his popular general, Aëtius (ca. 396–454). The subsequent emperors often found themselves, like poor Valentinian, on thin ice; the real power in the imperial court now belonged to the German majordomos, Ricimer (c. 405–472) and then Odoacer (435–493), who stopped short at claiming the imperial office for themselves but were not afraid to remove the emperor in power and replace him with their own candidate if the need arose. Eventually the charade became too tiresome: in 476 Odoacer had the adolescent emperor Romulus Augustulus shuffled off without even bothering to kill him and proclaimed himself ruler openly—not as the emperor in the West, but as king of Italy.

Odoacer's self-made promotion capped off a process that had started earlier in the fifth century, as former imperial provinces in Europe and North Africa were turned almost overnight into Germanic kingdoms, like the kingdoms of the Ostrogoths and then the Lombards in Italy, the Franks in Gaul, the Visigoths and the Suevi in Iberia, the Anglo-Saxons and the Jutes in Britain, and the Vandals in North Africa. They often received grudging acknowledgments from the emperors but were not willing to be mere extensions of the imperial governments in either Italy or Constantinople. Nonetheless, these kings were perfectly willing to allow their Roman subjects to continue to live under Roman law while the administrative machinery of the old Roman government was largely left intact.

However, the transition was not as easy for the Western Church, who lost their imperial sponsors. The new German rulers were either pagans or, perhaps even worse, Arian Christians, who went against established Catholic dogma by preaching that God was an entity separate from and superior to Jesus Christ. Nowadays historians inch away from the term "Dark Ages," which had traditionally been used to describe this period, preferring instead a less judgmental term such as "the early medieval era." Yet for the leaders of the Western Church it must have looked like a very Dark Age: after more than a century of being pampered by the Roman emperors, they once again found themselves on the defensive, facing a shadowy future.

In the east, where emperors could still claim an unbroken line of succession from Augustus, the Church continued to enjoy a good, if occasionally tense, relationship with the government. Following the precedent set by Constantine I, the Eastern Roman or Byzantine emperors felt free to call church councils and meddle in matters of doctrine. The distinction between what was the business of the Church and what was the business of the imperial office was a very thin one in Constantinople. By the time of the devout emperor Justinian I (r. 527–565), who did more than any other previous emperor (even Theodosius I) to "encourage" his subjects to become good Christians, the rulings of the first four canons of the Church were incorporated into the civil law.

Justinian I and the End of Antiquity

Like so many leaders who end up forcing change on their governments, Justinian came to Constantinople as an outsider. Starting out as a peasant, Justinian followed his uncle Justin, a farmer-turned-military-officer, to Constantinople, where he eventually earned enough credentials to join the imperial court. In spite of being elderly even by our standards, Justin became the appointed successor of Anastasius I (r. 491–518) and followed him as Justin I (r. 518–527). During his time serving in his uncle's court, Justinian met Theodora (ca. 500–548), who would become his wife and political partner. Like Justinian, Theodora had come from the bottom of the Byzantine Empire's caste system; her father was a bear-keeper and she had been an actress and a prostitute. Justinian overcame opposition to the love affair from Justin's wife, Euphemia, and after her death convinced his uncle to abolish the old ban on men of senatorial rank marrying actresses just so he could legally marry his lover.

Theodora and Justinian as well as the policies of the government they headed were roundly attacked by their contemporary Procopius. An educated member of the senatorial class who wrote a treatise praising Justinian and Theodora, *Peri Ktismaton (Buildings)*, Procopius also secretly put together a scathing philippic that he apparently hoped to publish after Justinian's death but never did, which became known as the *Anekdota (Secret History)*. Unable to get past the more surreal gossip in the book, including an assertion that when Theodora was a prostitute she wished that she had extra sexual orifices on her breasts and a report that a monk and various holy men were spreading rumors that Justinian was really a demon in disguise, some modern scholars have written off *Anekdota* as a "warped and fanciful attack"[1] despite its informed descriptions of even mundane imperial policies, right down to how the empire's postal service was being run.

If anything, Procopius composes a compelling description of a government that sees its central purpose as not protecting the public well-being, but rather imposing a specific way of thinking. Repulsed by the persecutions of pagans, Jews, Samaritans, and unorthodox

Christians that were validated by law or organized with Justinian's blessing, Procopius poignantly wrote, "For in his eagerness to gather all men into one belief as to Christ, he kept destroying the rest of mankind in senseless fashion, and that too while acting with a pretense of piety. For it did not seem to him murder if the victims chanced to not be of his own creed."[2] People who have lived under modern belief-obsessed governments might be able to relate personally to Procopius's horror.

However, it was not only those who did not agree with him on theology who died for Justinian's faith. The historian Malalas (ca. 491–578), writing in Justinian's time, describes one other group upon whom Justinian's full attention came crashing down:

> At this time, bishops of diverse provinces were prosecuted for the lustful act of sleeping with males. Among them were the bishops Isaiah of Rhodes, formerly the Nycteparchus of Constantinople, and Alexander of Diospolis in Thrace. After they were brought to Constantinople by an edict of the Emperor they were examined by the prefect of the city, stripped of their rank and punished. After he had suffered severe torture, Isaiah was sent into exile. Alexander, on the other hand, had his male organ cut off, and was placed in a litter and exposed as a spectacle to the people. Shortly after, the emperor passed a law that the crime of sex with males should be punished by castration. And at that time many men who slept with men [Malalas does not use any term that implies pederasty or a particular sexual position, but rather *androkoitai,* which does mean "men who have intercourse with men"] were seized and their genitals were cut off. And a great fear ensued among those who suffered from the evil desire for males.[3]

The historian Georgios Kedrenos, from his vantage point in the 11th century, adds the details that the persecution encompassed senators and people of lower rank. Some were tortured by having sharp reeds stabbed into their genitals, and after being castrated many were left to die in public view at the Forum of Constantinople.[4] It is the first time that historical sources attest to a pogrom targeted against men accused of having same-sex intercourse.[5]

Laws against male homosexuality became part of a massive reform of Roman law. This was carried out under the title of the *Corpus iuris civilis,* which was completed under a committee of jurists by 534. It included both the *Digest,* a collection of brief summaries of decisions made by earlier imperial jurists (and a blessing to modern legal historians of the Roman Empire), and the *Institutes,* a guide written specifically for law students. The *Institutes,* in a passage that claimed to be an extension on the *lex Julia,* recommended the death penalty for men who fornicated with other men.[6]

Why homosexuality should be such a sore spot for the State was made explicit in the *Novels,* a series of new laws enacted under Justinian's administration. Taking the tone of a concerned father, in Novel 77 Justinian warned his subjects to refrain from homosexual acts or the empire would be struck with earthquakes, plagues, and famine.[7] Novel 141, released 22 years later in 559, cites the legend of Sodom and urges latter-day sodomites to seek penance while ordering that laws against the "corruption of males" continue to be enforced, or else "we may provoke the good God to anger and bring ruin upon all—a fate which would be deserved."[8] That catastrophic earthquakes did strike Constantinople in 525 and 526, just before the persecution of 528, cannot be a coincidence.

In other ways Justinian's laws on sexual matters were less harsh than what came before. Changing the *lex Julia,* Justinian made it so that a husband who killed his wife in any circumstance after catching her in the act with a lover could be prosecuted for murder. A cuckolded husband still had the right to kill his wife's lover, but only if he caught them together in a tavern or in their own homes after giving both of them three written warnings, each attested to by three witnesses, which practically made killing the lover illegal.[9] However, a later law did allow a husband to confine an adulterous wife to a convent for life, if he decided not to forgive her within a two-year time frame. An adulterous husband, whose crime was not considered "adultery" but "fornication," was also to be punished, but just with the loss of any rights to the wife's dowry. Finally, the wife automatically had the right to initiate a divorce.[10]

Justinian did not follow scripture by making marriages virtually indissoluble. Instead Justinian, like a good Roman traditionalist, thought of marriage as a legal instead of a spiritual union.[11] In 533 he added more reasons that a man could legally divorce his wife: if she was repeatedly caught bathing in the presence of other men, was bigamous, or had an abortion. Still, the permission of the parents of both couples, if living, became a necessity.[12] Novel 22 went further by explicitly allowing divorce without cause if both parties were willing. In divorces that were contested, the lengthy list of approved causes included adultery of either wife and husband, impotence and infertility, the disappearance of the spouse in battle, one spouse putting the life and well-being of the other in jeopardy, and proof that either spouse was guilty of a number of civil crimes, like homicide, treason, witchcraft, grave-robbing, and aiding and abetting a robber. A husband could also justifiably divorce a wife for the horrific crimes of bathing in the presence of or dining with other men, going to the theater, or spending the night away from home without her husband's knowledge and permission.[13] Revisions under Novel 117 removed almost all the justified reasons for divorce that involved crimes committed against a third party, but also let a woman terminate her marriage if her husband tried to put her up on false charges of adultery or was enjoying "illicit" activities that hinted at adultery, including frequently visiting another woman or living with another woman who was neither his wife nor a relative. Failing to divorce for one of the officially approved reasons would result in losing the dowry and all nuptial gifts.

Toward the end of his life Justinian became far more reactionary. By 556 he changed his mind and made even divorce with mutual consent something that could be penalized by law unless one of the parties could present one of the prescribed reasons.[14] Tellingly, this was considered too much for the Byzantines. One of the first acts of Justinian's nephew and successor, Justin II (r. 565–578), was to acknowledge that the stricter divorce law was a disaster from the start, causing the courts to be flooded with angry spouses pleading that they all had a good case, and to abolish the penalties imposed on uncontested divorces.[15] Later emperors would return to placing unforgiving restrictions upon divorce, but by the ninth century Basil I (r. 867–886) had returned the laws on divorce to what they were under Novel 22.[16]

Forming marital unions received about as much scrutiny under Justinian as dissolving them. Even in the face of Church disapproval, Justinian gave concubines and their children virtually as many rights as "legitimate" families.[17] However, his laws explicitly made elopement illegal.[18] In fact, running off with a woman even with her consent could be punished with the death penalty, like rape or abduction, or with the confiscation of the perpetrator's property if the pair were of high rank.[19]

No doubt because of his wife's painful past, Justinian was also concerned about female prostitution. Theodora herself was involved in her husband's moral crusade and helped establish a convent just outside the city, on the cliffs overlooking the Marmara Sea, dedicated to repentant prostitutes. Procopius, usually keen to point out the hypocrisy or the dark side in Justinian and Theodora's morality program, alleges that not all the convent's inmates went there willingly. He even adds the scandalous detail that some despaired of their new lives and killed themselves by jumping over the walls and into the sea.[20]

Although he did not outright ban prostitution, Justinian did fine brothel owners, expel procurers from Constantinople, and pass a law forbidding anyone from accepting money from a prostitute.

> The name and calling of procurer was so odious both to the ancient laws and to those of the Empire that many legal enactments have been published against persons committing offenses of this description. We, Ourselves, have already promulgated a constitution increasing the penalties against those who are guilty of such wicked deeds, and We have, in addition, supplied by other laws what Our predecessors omitted, and have by no means lost sight of this matter, for We have very recently been informed of the evil consequences which such traffic has caused in this great city. We are also aware that certain persons are accustomed to employ cruel and odious means for the purpose of obtaining wealth; making a practice of traveling through the provinces and other places, in order to deceive young girls by promising them clothes, and, after having obtained possession of them, they bring them to this Most Fortunate City [Constantinople], place them in their houses, provide them with wretched food and clothing, and deliver them up to others for the purpose of debauchery, they themselves taking the entire profit of this wretched trade obtained from the bodies of their victims; and that they also draw up contracts by means of which the girls aforesaid are compelled to continue their wicked criminal life as long as those who have possession of them may desire.[21]

Justinian's less than objective wording, although standard rhetoric for him, does betray a genuine knowledge, no doubt gained from his wife, of the real-life conditions prostitutes suffered and the ways in which poor women were routinely exploited. He even saw to it that bishops had overreaching powers to investigate cases where women had been forced into prostitution and free them.

However pragmatic or ideological Justinian's laws are in the overview, he did manage to get in the final word on Roman law. Justinian's revisions more or less remained the basis of the Byzantine Empire's laws until Constantinople was taken by the Turks in 1453. However, their influence did not die there. In Western Europe by the 12th century, Roman law was rediscovered and revitalized, a process encouraged by scholars and monarchs alike. From there the criminalization of sexual nonconformity gained an even more concrete backing.

Sex under Irish and Welsh Law

On the other side of Europe from Constantinople were Ireland and Wales, home to societies that enthusiastically embraced Christianity early on despite being on and outside the margins of the Roman Empire. Cut off even more from the continent by the collapse of the Western Roman Empire, the "Celtic Church" that thrived there was largely free from Roman influences, as were the laws that regulated marriage and private behavior. These law codes eventually differed enough from those of the English that, according to historian Donnchadh Ó Corráin, 12th-century English jurists in Ireland found the native customs and laws to be "outlandish, barbaric, and utterly corrupt."

The craze for romanticizing the Celtic past has brought about some idealization of what these laws meant, especially for women, to the extent that ancient Celtic-speaking cultures have been more or less depicted as proto-feminist utopias. To be fair, on the whole it is true that Irish and Welsh laws regarding marriage and sexual practices tended to be more permissive than what developed in England and on the continent. In Ireland, *brehon* law, which was the law orally preserved by jurists since pre–Christian times, allowed concubinage, marriage between first cousins, and temporary marital contracts. However, distinctly Christian influences intervened when it came to those Irish society considered part of the "priestly" class, a motley group that included not only clerics but also teachers, tenants on church property, and poets. Those individuals could not remarry and were discouraged from marrying widows, prostitutes, and divorcées.

Polygamy was technically allowed, although given the complexities and nuances of dowries and spousal property in Irish marital law only wealthy men could afford to do so. Elopement was not harshly treated or even illegal, although couples who married without their families' consent had fewer inheritance rights. Nor was divorce forbidden or even limited; Irish law accepted divorce by mutual consent, in which event the spouses' property was divided evenly, but spouses found to be at fault had to surrender a third of the property to the other spouse. A wife could be found the aggrieved spouse if she could prove insanity, wife-beating (Irish law did explicitly allow a husband to strike his wife, as long as the blow was not hard enough to leave a bruise), impotence, sterility, severe and persistent illness, abandonment, the husband entering the priesthood or a monastery, the husband engaging in intercourse with a man, or even the husband talking publicly about their sex life! Only the husband had the right to divorce his wife for infidelity; on top of insanity, chronic illness, sterility, abandonment, or choosing the convent, a wife could be found at fault for infanticide, abortion without the consent of the husband, and running a household poorly.[22]

Welsh laws were first compiled and codified under Hywell Dda (r. 920–950), a king of Deheubarth who eventually united most of Wales under his rule. In spite of Wales being occupied by the Romans for centuries, the laws of Hywell Dda, which were pieced together from laws and traditions across the country, revealed similarities to Irish *brehon* laws. For instance, there was the recognition of couples who came together through elopement or extramarital intercourse. If a woman eloped she could be forced to return by her family unless she was no longer a virgin, in which case the pair's union would be recognized. A man who had intercourse with a woman who was a virgin could be liable to a special fine, the *amobr*, to be paid to her father or closest male relative, but this fine was also levied on any woman's new husband. Concubinage was tolerated just as it was in Ireland—in fact, the children of a mistress had inheritance rights equal to those of children from a marriage—but with the bizarre provision that the wife was allowed to strike a man's concubine without any legal consequences, even if she managed to kill her.

One way Welsh law was stricter than its Irish counterpart was that divorce by mutual consent was apparently not an option, at least not by Hywell Dda's day. Wives could end a marriage only if the husband was a leper, was impotent, committed adultery three times, or just had a recurring case of bad breath. Nowhere are the limitations for a husband seeking divorce stated, which may very well be because the husband had much greater legal freedom in seeking the termination of a marriage. A husband also had the right to "reclaim" his recently divorced wife; the law gave the husband this right up to the point where his ex-wife placed one foot in another man's bed.²³ Neither was a man allowed to have more than one wife, although it is possible that more antiquated Welsh customs did, like Irish laws, give room for polygamous arrangements.²⁴

As in Ireland, there are no indications that killing a wife and her lover in retaliation for infidelity was allowed by the law. Unlike men, women could be punished for adultery by losing their rights to the *agweddi,* their share of the common property between spouses. However, in stark contrast to the acceptance of honor killings in Roman and some Germanic law codes, a man was not allowed to kill a woman caught in the act of adultery. In fact, if he physically attacked her at all for infidelity, then he would lose any claims to her *agweddi.*

Even under pressure from England and the Church, such laws unique to Ireland and Wales persisted into the High Middle Ages, in spite of the outright revulsion they could inspire. In 1282, John Pickham, Archbishop of Canterbury, wrote a letter to the Welsh prince Llywelyn "the Last" (r. 1246–1282), condemning Welsh laws, especially the rights extended to illegitimate offspring, and thundered that Hywel Dda's mind must have been warped by the Devil. Nonetheless, even after the invasion of Wales by England in 1282, Welsh civil law endured for some legal matters until the 1530s. At that time, a series of acts by the Parliament of England, ironically carried out under a king with strong Welsh ancestry, Henry VIII, stamped out the last traces of Welsh legal autonomy and brought the entire country under English jurisdiction. Irish civil law remained strong for a little longer, at least outside the spheres of English influence on the island. Even so, by 1600 native law codes had been completely purged throughout the entire country by the English invaders.

Sex under Germanic Law

How much Germanic laws and customs in the sixth century owed to the actual tribal laws from ancient Germany is a matter for speculation, simply because we know so little about the German tribes before the fourth- and fifth-century migrations. Aside from archaeological findings, most of the evidence of ancient Germanic life depends on *Germania,* an essay written by the Roman historian Tacitus at the end of the first century, at least 150 years after the Romans may have first encountered the people they called *Germani.*²⁵ However, Tacitus's reliability as a narrator is suspect, partly because he seems to have picked up his information second-hand from soldiers and travelers²⁶ and partly because his idea of *Germani* does not match up with our concept of Germanic-speaking peoples. Also, in his upper-class Roman view, the Germans were noble savages, free from the corruption brought on by urbanization, wealth, and oppressive governments—a perception that peppered his account from the first to the last word.²⁷

So we should have our pinch of salt in hand when Tacitus, who obviously has his own complaints about the Roman women of his time in mind, writes that German women are "corrupted by none of the enticements of public performances, none of the temptations of banquets," and adds "no one there is amused at vice, nor calls the corruption of others and oneself 'modern life.'" In the same passage Tacitus claims that a wife found guilty of adultery is humiliated before her family with her hair cut short and is marched through the village, beaten with a whip the entire way.²⁸ Medieval Germanic law did in some cases allow men to punish and kill adulterous women, as we will see, so it seems likely enough that the death penalty for female adultery had origins in some tribal customs. Somewhat less plausible are Tacitus's claims that "only [female] virgins wed" and that there are "extremely few instances of adultery."[29]

Unsurprisingly, it does not occur to Tacitus to address the issue of whether men were punished for adultery, although he does imply that men adhered to a strict code of monogamy.[30] Yet he also admits that prominent men took multiple wives. This not only remained true for royal and noble families in early medieval Germanic societies, in some cases even after conversion to Christianity, but also coincides with practices in more recent bigamous cultures in imperial China, Africa, and the Middle East, where taking multiple wives is in and of itself an expression of a man's wealth and status.

In another passage, Tacitus maintains that, along with the "cowardly" and the "unwarlike," those who "disgrace their bodies" (*corpore infamis*), apparently meaning men who were sexually passive with other men, were drowned in bogs.[31] The grim existence of the famous "bog bodies" does show that people—women as well as men—were sometimes for whatever reason thrown into the bog by the ancient Germans, but evidence also reveals that they were killed beforehand. Were at least some of them sexual miscreants as in Tacitus's account? There are a few vague references in Latin writings: one claiming that homosexuality was unknown among the Germans, and others stating that sodomy was widely and openly practiced. However, these writers may be confusing the Germans with the natives of Gaul, who were widely believed as early as Aristotle in the fourth century BCE to have accepted, if not outright encouraged, sex between men.[32]

Among Germanic and Nordic people, there was a term, *arga* among the Germanic peoples or *argr* among the Norse, that had an ugly connotation of effeminacy and sexual submission. Calling a man an *arga* was quite serious business. It was even a punishable offense under Lombard law.[33] Medieval Scandinavian laws likewise punished anyone who used *argr* as an insult.[34] Still, except in Visigothic Iberia, which was under heavy Christian and Byzantine influences, sex between men as well as forms of noncoital intercourse were not punishable offenses.

Taken all together Visigothic law seemed to take a much more stern interest in sexual conduct. After the conversion of the Visigothic king Reccared (r. 586–601) from Arian to Catholic Christianity in 589, the king and the Catholic bishops at his court became close allies, with the former presiding over ecclesiastical councils and the latter involved in the election of kings, yet Rome had only a little input into the affairs of the church in Iberia.[35] About half a century after Reccared brought Iberia into the orthodox fold, King Kindasvinth (r. 642–653), perhaps inspired by the penalty Justinian preferred for male homosexuals, ordered that "those who lie with males, or consent to participate passively in such acts" be castrated.[36] Egica (r. 687–702), already infamous to historians for his decree that all Jews in his realm be stripped of their property and enslaved, also condemned "the detestable outrage of that lust by the filthy uncleanness of which men do not fear to defile other men in the unlawful act of fornication" and amended Kindasvinth's law to include punishments prescribed by the 16th council of Toledo in addition to castration: lashings, the shearing of hair, and exile.

The other Germanic law codes were strict in other ways, such as in their vigilance over nonmarital intercourse. Many codes fined the man who had sex with an unmarried woman,[37] with more severe punishments doled out to slaves caught with free women. Under Bavarian laws, the slave was handed over to his lover's family to be dealt with as they pleased, even to the point of killing him.[38] The Bavarian code also went to greater lengths to defend women's honor, making it illegal for anyone other than her husband to place a hand on a woman in an erotic gesture, lift her garments above the knees, and take off her head covering.[39] The only law against contraception was passed under the exceptionally devout Frankish king Guntram (r. 567–93), which fined women who took sterilizing herbs.[40]

Killing an adulterer was not a crime, as long as the offending wife was also killed by the husband in the act. Perhaps following the example of the *lex Julia*, Burgundian law added the stipulation that if only the wife or her lover was killed, then the *wergild*—a special fine paid to the victims of a crime or their relations by the perpetrator—would be paid to that person's family.[41] A slave caught with a wife in Bavaria was to be handed over to the tender mercies of the husband.[42] The Visigoths went a step further, allowing an adulterous woman's brothers and father to also kill her if she was found with a lover.[43] Besides the threat of sanctioned violence, the wife's lover could be fined at least or lose his property at most.[44] Evening the score to a small degree was a Lombard law that punished husbands who failed to prove their wife's guilt by dissolving their marriage[45] and Visigothic and Lombard regulations that fined an adulterous husband.[46]

Another type of illicit love affair that all Germanic codes condemned was incestuous union. Across the board Germanic laws threatened couples who were deemed too closely related with fines and the automatic annulment of their marriages. Under Alemanni law they could even be punished with the loss of all their property and enslavement.[47] In contrast to the Romans, the Germanic kingdoms were more tolerant of polygamy, at least among royal and aristocratic circles. Kings and noblemen were known to have kept multiple wives and concubines.[48] Gregory of Tours records one dramatic example where the Frankish king Clothar I (r. 511–561) is asked by his wife Ingund if he knew any nobleman who would be a good match for her sister Aregund. Gregory continues:

> On hearing this, the king, who was most amorous by temperament, began to desire Aregund, and betaking himself to the domain where she lived, he married her. When she was his, he returned to Ingund and spoke as follows: "I have done my best to procure for thee the reward thy sweetness asked of me. I sought a man wealthy and of good wit, whom I might give in marriage to thy sister, but I found none better than myself. Know therefore that I have taken her to wife, which I believe will not displease thee."[49]

Forming marriages was easy; breaking them not so much. If Gregory of Tours is right, even royalty suffered from such restrictions. According to him, another Frankish king, Chilperic I (r. 561–584), needed a pretext to annul his marriage to his wife Audovera. Like Constantine's laws, the Germanic kingdoms required some grounds for divorce from husbands and wives, such as adultery or evidence they committed some extraordinary crime, and penalized divorces that took place in spite of it. The harshest was the Burgundian law on divorce, which decreed that the wife who initiated an unlawful divorce be drowned in a bog.[50] A husband responsible for a divorce got off easy: he had to pay a fine and return his wife's dowry.[51]

Either reflecting the of influence of Justinian's reforms of Roman law or as a result of their peculiar fixation on morality by fiat, the Visigoths were the only ones to address prostitution extensively. A first offense by a free woman merited 300 lashes; a second offense meant that she would be forced to marry an impoverished man, who would vow to never allow her to ply her trade again. However, the laws did acknowledge the reality that a woman could be forced into prostitution. Someone who prostituted a slave could be punished with 50 to 300 lashes, while parents who exploited their child in such a way could be punished with 100 lashes.[52]

As the Roman law schools fell into disuse and the need and desire to keep separate descendants of German migrants and indigenous populations died out, the distinctions between Germanic and Roman laws thinned and fell away altogether. However, the differences were not as stark as some might assume. The civil law of the Germanic kingdoms was undeniably harsh by modern Western standards, but usually no more strict or brutal than what had existed under the rulers of the late empire. Also the legislation, while respecting to a great degree the age-old right of families to cope with private and sexual matters, still exhibited a degree of intervention for the sake of containing the destructive practice of bloodfeuds or honor killing by either limiting their acceptability or replacing them with fines. Like their Roman counterparts, German law codes were shaped by Christian morals, but they were just as often pragmatic. More radical and thorough experiments in sexual living would be left to the Mother Church.

Choosing Holiness

In defiance of the political earthquakes of the fifth and sixth centuries in Western Europe, the monastic houses continued to prosper. More than that, in fact, they became not only oases of education and welfare for the poor, the orphaned, and widows, but also entities that accumulated wealth and enjoyed local power like any rich landowner. Even very early in medieval history, they were an unavoidable fixture on the landscape, from the world of high politics down to everyday life.

Life in the monastic houses was organized to provide a shelter from as many worldly temptations as possible, chief among them the sexual. In the Church's hierarchy of purity, this placed monastics at an even higher keel than priests, who in the early Middle Ages were still allowed to keep their wives upon their induction or even marry after taking vows. To maintain this special promotion, monks and nuns were ideally to be kept separate from members of the opposite sex as much as possible, with their movements curtailed and visits to the monastery from representatives of the other sex strictly regulated, if not practically forbidden. Going well beyond the call of duty were the founders of the monastery of Mount Athos in Macedonia, where the presence of women and even most female animals were (and still are) strictly prohibited.

As might be expected, nuns were generally considered more vulnerable to the charms of the other sex and thus were often kept in check through stricter limits to their freedom (although the total exclusion of women from authority in the Church created something of a loophole that not merely allowed but actually mandated nuns to have regular contact with at least one man: their confessor). Remarking on the Rule of Caesarius of Arles (468/470–542), the first monastic rule written specifically for women, the historian Lisa Bitel noted, "For the sake of her soul and virtue, once a woman entered the walls of her new community, she was not even to advance as far as the basilica, where she could glimpse the door to the outside, so dangerous to her was the lure of the world left behind."[53]

Necessity is the omnipresent enemy of idealism, however, and nuns and monks often received visits from family members of either sex within the monastery, ran errands in the marketplace, and conducted other business with lay people from outside the walls. Monastics taking advantage of these opportunities and enjoying a bit too much liberty were a pesky concern for busybody clerics. In one instance a nun from Constantinople had to disguise herself as a man to travel to Palestine to see the holy sites. Even then she was uncovered and told by a monk, Lazarus Zographos (d. 867), to return herself to the cloister.[54] Female monastics were in this case not the only ones to receive such scrutiny. The Greek archbishop Eustathois of Thessalonike (ca. 1111–1198) complained that in his time monks could be found anywhere outside their monasteries: loitering on city streets and village roads, haggling at shops, and, most appalling of all, enjoying themselves in bathhouses![55]

Church authorities were even more anxious over male and female monastics associating with each other, which was seen as a sure ingredient for sin and scandal. Pope Gregory I (r. 590–604) completely believed a tale from the bishop of Fulda, who had heard that demons cavorting in a pagan temple were laughing with glee over the fact that the bishop had patted one of the nuns who lived with him on the back and were bragging that it was only a matter of time before friendly touching would blossom into sex. Without hesitation the bishop threw the nuns out of his house and sent them to a monastery.[56] With the same concerns, the Iberian bishop Isidore of Seville (ca. 560–636) ruled that monks and nuns must dwell in separate quarters regardless of the circumstances.[57] As for husbands and wives who joined a monastery together, the archbishop Fructuosus of Braga in seventh-century Iberia ordered that all spouses who joined a monastery together had to live apart and never even talk with each other without a third party present.[58] Later on, the eighth and ninth centuries in Western Europe saw a growing concern with the liberties, real and imagined, taken by monastics, with an increase in canonical laws restricting their movements, specifically those of nuns and abbesses.[59]

Even then, there were double monasteries, which housed monastics of both sexes, although they were strictly segregated to their own buildings. While the Church still fretted over the possibilities for lewdness, the arrangement was popular, especially in England and northern Europe.[60] In the Byzantine Empire, however, the story was quite different. By 787 the founding of any new double monasteries within the empire was banned. Less than 40 years later, even existing ones were shut down.[61] Eventually the concept also fell out of favor with the Western Church. Around the tenth century the practice of establishing double monasteries met with official disapproval and fell into sharp decline.[62]

In spite of the spiritual fulfillment and the assistance in containing the flesh offered by the monastery, and even in places where Christianity had long been widespread, the spiritually inclined had to overcome opposition from their families, motivated by more earthly considerations. The famous Irish saint Columban was said to have left his home in County Meath for a monastery over the desperate pleas of his mother, who threw herself at his feet. According to legend, a saint from Gaul, Genovefa, battled against an abusive mother to devote herself to prayer every day, although in her case she waited until after her mother's death to leave. The one account that has a depressing echo of reality, however, is the legend of the abbess Liliola of Arles, who, led by visions, discovered a wealthy heiress who had just inherited a fortune from her father. Wasting no time, Liliola worked hard to convince her to join her convent, so she and the sisters could make good use of the money. Her mother pitifully protested:

Give me hope for my child. Who now will care for my old age? She was the only one I had left. I seek my little sprout and cannot find her. Where can I run? Where to turn, I do not know! I pray grace and call on God to witness that you should have mercy on me, struck with such sorrow and order the restoration of my only child in my widowhood.[63]

As the parents of Columban and Liliola's meal ticket understood too well, the lure of the monastery was a disruption to the comforting and timeless cycle of domestic life. In fact, as had been the case with the earliest monastics, for some people of high rank that was the very thing that formed part of the appeal. Women of royal and noble birth in the Germanic kingdoms found the cloister to be an excellent alternative to the political marriages often forced on them by their families. After two marriages to two different kings, Ethelreda (ca. 636–679), a princess from East Anglia, fled the court of her current husband, King Egfrid of Northumbria (r. 670–685), to join a monastery at Ely.[64] Another Anglo-Saxon royal consort, Cuthberga (d. 718), who founded the monastery at Wimbourne, had left her husband King Aldfrith of Northumbria (r. 685–704/705).[65] Radegund (ca. 520–586), a princess from Thuringia who was forced to marry her homeland's conqueror, King Clothar I, escaped her naturally repugnant husband and convinced a reluctant bishop to consecrate her by telling him that God would punish him if he let one willing soul slip through his fingers. Unable to fight the Church, Clothar relented and with his funding Radegund went on to establish the first large-scale convent in Gaul, the convent at Poitiers.[66]

Even outside the royal courts, life as a nun had its appeal over a career as a nobleman's brood mare. A daughter of Frankish nobility, the saint Austrebertha (630–704) had joined a monastery chiefly to untangle herself from an arranged marriage, which was also the case with another seventh-century Frankish saint, Aldegonde (c. 639–680). At least one male monk, Saint Gal of Auvergne (ca. 489–ca. 533), was likewise said to have been escaping a marriage that was about to be forced on him.

What about people not lucky enough to have the benefit of royal or noble birth who also wanted to flee from family obligations and trade in the demands of everyday life for the solitude and comfort of the monastery? Again, church leaders' vision of communities just for those strongly inclined toward God faltered before the demands of reality: the harshest truth was that monasteries could not run on just some prayers and good will. As in a marriage, women were expected to bring a dowry with them when they entered a convent, while entering monks typically brought some sort of endowment.[67] Thus entry into a monastery was effectively limited to royalty, nobility, or the well-off mercantile and artisan classes, a trend that escalated as the newly Christianized kings and nobles of western and central Europe saw that a relative in a place of influence in the local monastery was a good political investment. This lesson was especially well understood in Anglo-Saxon England, where all the known abbesses of all the convents sprung from royal families. Likewise, the majority of monasteries in seventh- and eighth-century Italy were founded by aristocrats to mostly house their own relatives, such as the convent of St. Zaccaria in Venice, established by the Doge Giustiniano Participazio (r. 827–829) to serve as a place of saintly retirement for women in his family.[68]

None of this means that a life of self-imposed chastity was completely shut off to the less fortunate. Often escaped slaves, orphans, widows, abandoned children, abused wives, and simply the poor could find shelter and perhaps a permanent home at the monastery, but they could only aspire to become a lay sister or brother. To achieve more, it would have to be under the benevolence and at the expense of one of the monastery's wealthy inmates or the local bishop.[69]

While some may have been denied an opportunity to enter a life of church-sanctioned chastity, others found that lifestyle thrust upon them. The question of consent was old enough that, in his Rule, Caesarius of Arles specified that no one younger than the age of seven could join the community. Much later, however, the German nun and playwright Roswitha (ca. 935–ca. 975) ducked the problem of age and consent in her play *Abraham*. There the hermit Abraham and his friend Ephrem try to persuade Abraham's eight-year-old niece to join a convent. Although they worry if she will agree, there is no fretting over whether she is old enough to make a decision, in spite of her "childish heart" and "tender age."[70]

In a trend that might have horrified the pioneers of monasticism, it became perfectly normal to place women, men, and children in the monastery, in spite of any consent or lack thereof. Husbands could and did forcibly encloister their adulterous spouses. Even infants were sometimes pledged to a monastery as a tithe or as an act of thanksgiving by the parents. King Oswy (r. 642–670) of Bernicia dedicated his daughter Aelfflaed (654–713) to Hartlepool Abbey to give thanks for his victory over the kingdom of Mercia. The Byzantine saint Theodora of Thessalonika (d. 892) likewise donated her daughter to express gratitude, after the rest of her children were killed by a plague. One of the most famous monastic voices from the Middle Ages, the German abbess Hildegard of Birgen (1098–1179), was herself given to the Church as a tithe by her parents.

Noble families periodically paid off the monasteries to take in children who would be a burden or daughters who would be considered damaged goods when it came to the marriage market, including the blind, the malformed, the disabled, the mentally ill, and the extraneous son who stood to inherit little or nothing after his older brothers. This callous custom was practiced even at the top of the social pyramid. Despite being described by his friend and biographer Einhard as a caring father, Charlemagne (r. 768–814) apparently considered his eldest son, Pippin the Hunchback, unfit for any political or military responsibilities due to his deformity and had him tonsured. Resentment over this later drove Pippin, as an adult, to try to rebel against his father's reign. Charlemagne's grandson, Charles III (r. 893–922/923) of Western Francia, sentenced his youngest son Carloman at an early age to a lifetime in a monastery, simply because Charles III had enough sons to inherit his lands and titles and he anticipated that Carloman would pose a threat to his brothers. In the end, Charles III had only enacted a self-fulfilling prophecy.

Lower on the social ladder, a man named Eulalius gave his son John over to Innocent, bishop of Le Mans, to be consecrated as a priest in exchange for Innocent's help in returning some land to Eulalius's possession.[71] While the large number of people tonsured against their will did not seem to excite much negative comment from the Church, Gregory I did act to allow women encloistered against their will to leave, but only in extraordinary circumstances, such as a woman held on a false charge of adultery.[72]

One class of unwilling monastics that especially crowd the early medieval chronicles are political prisoners. The monastery was the fate of the deposed king Eadbert II of Kent (r. 796–798?). Audeca (r. 584–585), king of the Suevi, a Germanic tribe settled in what is roughly now northern Portugal and northwestern Spain, sentenced his predecessor Eboric (r. 583–584) to a monastery, but received his just desserts when the invading Visigoths also had him locked away in a house of God.[73] Louis the Pious's (r. 813–840) wife Judith was imprisoned in a convent by her rebellious stepsons. Another Carolingian, Lothar II (r. 855–869), got rid of his wife Theuberga by locking her up in a convent after slandering her with charges of sodomy, incest, and secretly having an abortion.

With so many unwilling nuns and monks, where did that leave sexual discipline in so many monasteries? In dire straits, apparently; as early as the sixth century the British saint Gildas felt obligated to advise in his letters that monks proven to have been fornicators should be kept from communion—as well as food—until they received penance.[74] An unamused Gregory I complained in his letters about monks who married out in the open[75]—whether they did so out of lust or because they were somewhat confused by the whole concept of being a monk is not mentioned—and angrily denounced a scandalous monastery where monks were "even allowed to cohabit with women without any fear."[76] Gregory also refers to the unnamed daughter of a Byzantine official in Italy, who was made to enter a convent and "debauched herself."[77]

Complaints of priests and monks fathering children spanned Western Europe from Gaul to Italy. The English missionary Boniface (d. 754) complained to Pope Zacharias (r. 741–752) that the priests he encountered kept four or five mistresses at once; far from being chastised a few of them had been promoted to bishop.[78] Hincmar of Rheims (806–882) relates a case where a priest separated from his wife, who joined a monastery, and vowed to refrain from their old marital schedule. After a few visits intended for religious instruction, she mysteriously became pregnant twice.[79] How easy it was to keep up secret visits with a lover in a monastery, or at least how credible accusations of such clandestine behavior could be, is shown at the convent of Poitiers. There, a Frankish princess-turned-nun, Clothild, accused the abbess Leubovera of various improprieties, including keeping an undercover lover around, always disguised as one of the nuns. The accusations were likely just a political power play, although the man defended Leubovera by claiming he dressed as a woman to show the world that he was completely impotent![80] Especially given how coy most chroniclers were, rarely going beyond vague accusations of debauchery and fornication against those who were in all likelihood their fellow clerics, it is impossible to get even a hint of how widespread sexual misbehavior were in the monasteries and cathedrals. An exception of sorts comes from 836 when the Council of Aachen thought it had a good sense of things and wearily declared that some of the convents within the Carolingian Empire had become like brothels.[81]

One of the most detailed descriptions of a monastery apparently converted into a pleasure pit comes from Bede and his history of the Anglo-Saxon Church. In his account the Irish missionary Adamnan lectures Aebbe, the abbess of the double monastery at Coldingham, on the routine behavior of most of the monastery's inmates:

> I have just visited every part of this monastery in turn: I have examined their cells and their beds, and I have found no one except you concerned with his soul's welfare; but all of them, men and women alike, are sunk in slothful slumbers or else they remain awake for the purposes of sin. And the cells that were built for praying and for reading have become haunts of feasting, drinking, gossip, and other delights; even the virgins who are dedicated to God put aside all respect for their profession and, whenever they have leisure, spend their time weaving elaborate garments with which to adorn themselves as if they were brides, so imperiling their virginity, or else to make friends with strange men [...] When this vision [of the monastery's destruction by fire] became known, those who lived in the monastery were some-

what afraid for a few days and began to give up their sins and do penance. But after the death of the abbess, they returned to their old defilement and committed even worse crimes.[82]

When, as Adamnan predicted, the monastery burned down, Bede declares that "all who knew the truth were easily able to judge that it had happened of the wickedness of those who dwelt there and especially of those who were supposed to be its leaders."[83]

Given the high degree of sex segregation in monasteries, though, were anxieties over same-sex encounters more justified than not? Homosexual mishaps seem to have been a cause for worry since the earliest days of monasticism. Basil of Caesarea (ca. 330–379), whose Rule was followed by all monasteries in the Byzantine Empire, was practically haunted by the idea. He warned young men in his order to avoid intimacy and even most contact with men their age: if they shared a bed with another young man, then they should have an elderly comrade sleep between them; if they were addressed in conversation, then they should avoid eye contact.[84] Maybe Basil was, as we would say today, projecting his own issues on his fellow monks.

On the other side of Europe, the Rule of St. Benedict stipulated that a candle had to be kept lit in the monks' dormitory, none of the young men were allowed to sleep side by side, and all of them had to sleep with their clothes on.[85] Augustine was also aware of the perils that can come from single-sex isolation, reminding the members of a convent that the "love between you, however, ought not to be earthly but spiritual."[86] He might have applauded the instructions given by Donatus of Besançon (d. ca. 660) in his rule for female monastic houses, *Regula ad Virginea* (*The Rule for the Virgins*), which ordained that nuns who held hands would be punished with 12 blows, and 40 blows if they were caught referring to each other with affectionate terms like "little girl."[87] Also, as in Benedict's rule for monks, nuns were forbidden to lie next to each other and had to leave candles burning as they slept fully clothed.[88]

Charlemagne was personally disturbed by the gossip he heard about what went on among monastics and threatened to legislate the problem away, but he never did so.[89] At any rate, it is uncertain how much of what Charlemagne and others heard sprang from reports of actual incidents and how much was just the sort of speculation that usually surrounds places where large numbers of the same sex are isolated together.

As the historian Vern Bullough pointed out, medieval clerical writers were usually brief and oblique in their references to homosexuality.[90] However, there is a great deal of candidness in the penitentials, guidebooks on the rules of penance that first appeared in Ireland and Wales and became widespread through Western Europe by the seventh century, as the private confession completely replaced the public statement of sins the earliest Christian communities preferred. In his own penitential, Bede prescribes seven years of penance to nuns who use a device, *machina,* on each other.[91] The Irish *Penitential of Cummean* has a series of penances against sodomy, which gives stricter punishments to the clergy and monastics than to the laity.[92] In what may have been an actual scandal from the late sixth century, a bishop named Parthenius in Gaul was accused of being "effeminate" and keeping male adolescents in "shame and debauchery." Still, Gregory of Tours, who describes the case, did not believe the charges himself and they apparently came to nothing.[93]

Battling sexual temptations in monastic houses was clearly an obsession for the Church from the very beginning. Unfortunately, we cannot know how much early medieval society added to these problems by making it acceptable to force political enemies and inconvenient relatives into monastic life, but certainly the ugly reality of the world outside the cloister did not help the mission of sexual denial. If the Church had so much trouble regulating its own house, then how well did it succeed with those people who lived outside the monastery's walls and the bishop's cathedral?

Imposing Holiness

When the ranks of Christianity were still thin and most Christians could be counted on to be sincere in their commitment, it was easy enough for Christian apologists to claim that all Christians were faithful to the rules of sexual restraint. With the successful expansion of the Christian community from a few huddled groups in cities around the Mediterranean to something that encompassed all the former territories of the old Roman Empire and beyond, this was a much harder line to maintain. However, that did not stop the medieval Church from trying to force the reality to align with old ideals.

A constant source of disappointment must have been the leaders of Christendom themselves. The Merovingian dynasty of the Frankish kingdoms showed themselves to be spectacularly bad role models with their armies of concubines and multiple wives. After the queen regent Brunhild invited Columban to baptize the children of her son Theuderic II (r. 596–613) and a concubine, Columban refused, blurting out, "Know that they shall never hold the royal scepter, for they were born into adultery."[94] The Merovingians rarely if ever distinguished between heirs born in or out of wedlock and Brunhild was infuriated enough by the challenge to protocol that Columban had to leave Gaul for Italy to save his life. Another wandering saint, Corbinian (ca. 670–730) was likewise driven out of Bavaria when he criticized its duke, Grimoald (r. 715–725), for marrying his brother's widow. Charlemagne allowed his unmarried daughters who lived at court to have their boyfriends around as much as they pleased, resulting in a few illegitimate children, and horrifying even faithful Einhard.

Despite being the representatives of Christ on earth, the Byzantine emperors were on the whole no better. Defying both Byzantine law and Church proclamations that barred a man from remarrying more than twice, Emperor Leo VI (r. 886–912) married four times in his quest to father an heir and eventually legitimized his son by a mistress, Zoë, while making her his wife as well. The Patriarch of Constantinople, Nicholas Mystikos, tried to punish the emperor by forbidding him from entering any consecrated building, but he was powerless to enforce the ruling. The chronicler Michael Psellus described the relationship of Constantine IX (r. 1042–1055) with a male court entertainer in terms that were not explicit, but did include a complaint about how the entertainer had the audacity to publicly kiss the emperor on his chest and face and speak to him before being acknowledged.[95]

Chroniclers from the time allege that even the popes came to fall below moral standards. During a period when the papacy was entirely under the thumb of Roman aristocrats, Pope Sergius III (r. 904–911) was said to have had a lover, Marozia, even after his pontificate began and allegedly had a child with her that grew up to be Pope John XI (r. 931–935). According to another rumor recorded by the very hostile Liutprand of Cremona, the young Pope John XII (r. 955–964) was beaten to death by a Roman senator whose wife was his lover, the perfect end to what was allegedly a lifetime of excess.

Unfortunately, medieval chroniclers were much less interested in highlighting the peccadilloes of the populace at large. Very little of the literature that survives from between 600 and 1000 deals explicitly with their authors' day-to-day lives. The plays of Roswitha, for instance, deal entirely with Christian legends and the lives of saints and convey the expected Christian line on the dangers of sexuality. Her play *Gallicanus* has the title character, a general under Emperor Constantine I who converts to Christianity, ask, "What temptation is to be feared more than the lust of the eyes?"[96] Sexual desire is the chief antagonist in many of Roswitha's dramas. The plot of *Abraham* has a nun who had a fling with a monk fall with depressing inevitability into the life of a prostitute, from which she has to be rescued by her uncle Abraham, who is forced to disguise himself as a john. The title character of *Callimachus* becomes obsessed with a Christian committed virgin, Drusiana, to the point that even after she (successfully) prays for death to save Callimachus's soul from his own desires, he attempts to defile her body. Before that can happen, he is killed by the bite of a poisonous snake. Still the play ends happily, thanks to Saint John, who miraculously resurrects Drusiana and Callimachus, who, like so many of Roswitha's characters, repents, converts, and takes a lifelong pledge of chastity.

It is hardly surprising to find such plot motifs or to glimpse a strange moral universe where all the players are either perfectly chaste or sex-crazed from a canoness most likely writing plays for an audience of clerics and to be performed by other nuns. The works of more worldly-minded authors tell a different story. Love poems and stories from Ireland in this era mostly drew from a legendary and mythical cast, yet they may have reflected a realistic understanding of sexuality's role in society in their authors' lifetimes.

At the least they reveal a frankness of language that has not been stamped out by the Church. An Irish love poem from the ninth or tenth century, *Tochmarc Becfola* (*Small Dowry*), features the legendary king of Temair, Diarmait mac Aeda Sláine, coming across a woman from a supernatural realm looking for wheat seed. When she approaches him for help, he replies, "If it be the seed of this territory that you desire, your destiny does not lie beyond me."

The Ulster Cycle, a collection of Irish legends that may date back at least to the seventh century, includes the sexual adventures of the heroes Cú Chulainn, whose sexual conquests were as detailed as his battles, and Queen Medb, who casually and without consequence had a number of adulterous escapades. A similar explicitness was shown in an epic poem from nearby Wales, *Canu Llywarch Hen* (*Song of Llywarch the Old*), in which the hero, Prince Llywarch, bemoans his old age. Among his many complaints are "ungreeted is my bedside" and "old age makes a muck of me from my hair to my teeth / And the shaft the women loved."

Given the paucity of written secular literature from the time, there can be no definite conclusions, but perhaps Wales and Ireland were culturally inclined to be blunter about the steamier aspects of human experience. If so, then the other side of the extreme was the Byzantine Empire, from which no erotic poems or epigrams have been found from between 870 and 1100.[97] The closest that exist were a few epigrams by the late ninth-century poet John Geometres, who wrote them only as a meditation on the evil of carnal desire and attached a prayer begging Christ to defend him from the dangers of lust.[98]

Regardless of such sentiments, a popular motif in the early medieval literature surrounding saints was the former prostitute or courtesan turned Christian heroine. There were plenty of prostitute and courtesan saints like Afra of Augsburg, Pelagia of Antioch, Thaïs of Alexandra, and, of course, Mary Magdalene, who was widely believed to have been a professional prostitute by the early Middle Ages (despite a lack of evidence in the Gospels themselves) and happened to be the most important female figure in the Gospels, second only to the Virgin Mary. The hagiographies about the prostitutes turned saints and martyrs invariably involved a male ascetic who braved the gauntlet of sexuality—specifically, untamed female sexuality—to win over a soul,[99] which may have been the appeal of the prostitute hagiographies, especially to the Church, in the first place.

What helped make this possible was the influence of Augustine, whose pessimistic view of the world led him to contemplate hypothetical laws against prostitution but conclude that prostitution was a necessary outlet keeping male lust in check. Indeed, Augustine concluded, a society that tried to repress prostitution would invite disorder and disaster.[100] The Church had early on rejected the Roman idea that prostitutes should be labeled as pariahs and instead turned the fury of canonical law against procurers.[101] None of this means, of course, that prostitutes were given a free pass. In her theatrical adaptation of the legend of Thaïs of Alexandria, Roswitha has the hermit Papnutius indict Thaïs, who was unusual in that she was a courtesan and already a Christian, by asking, "How ... can you destroy men in this manner and ruin so many souls, all precious and immortal?"[102]

A much wider view into the private lives of people in Western Europe from this time may come from an unexpected and accidental source, the penitentials, which as sexual crimes committed by clergy but were also largely concerned with the sins of the laity. Taken as a whole, the penitentials chronicle the struggle of ecclesiastics to restrict sexual expression to marriage and producing children. No doubt the penitentials advised penances for well-known and widespread sexual practices; in fact, many luridly describe the same sexual sins they prescribe punishment for, raising the question of whether the people who wrote them, who were likely enough aesthetics and monastics themselves, found a kind of release by caking on details of every sex act they could imagine. Two of the earliest penitentials, both from the sixth century, *The Synod of the Grove of Victory* and *Excerpts from the Book of St. David,* prescribe penances with bureaucratic detail for anal intercourse, for achieving orgasm by rubbing one's genitals against a thigh, and for masturbation.[103]

Even with the puritanical intent of the penitentials' authors, scholars from stuffier times were mortified by what they found. Charles Plummer, a Victorian scholar who translated and edited the works of Bede, had this to say on Bede's own penitential: "Penitential literature is in truth a deplorable feature of the medieval Church. Evil deeds, the imagination of which may perhaps have dimly floated through our minds in our darkest moments, are here tabulated and reduced to a system."[104] That the penitentials were advertising a similar (in many cases, even more prim) way of life to that proudly trumpeted by the likes of Queen Victoria made no difference.

Yet the penitentials, which had no centralized Church authority to cite from, were far from unanimous on even the most basic issues of sexual conduct. Columban's penitential prescribed only one year of penance for an unmarried couple who had intercourse,[105] while Bede insisted on four years, albeit with milder penance after the second year.[106] The abbot Regino of Prüm (d. 915) despaired that there was no consistency among penitential writers on what should be done about sodomy. According to him, the periods of penance demanded varied from ten years to seven years to one year.[107]

What the penitentials did agree on were that punishments for clerics should be more severe than those for the laity, with periods of penance rising with one's rank in the ecclesiastical hierarchy, and that even sex within marriage should be viewed with some revulsion. If a married couple set out to follow the rules on marital life demanded by all the various writers of the penitentials, then they would find that they could not have sex on Church holidays or on feast and fasting days; on Sunday, Saturday, Friday, or Wednesday; in daylight; within 30 days after marriage; while the wife was pregnant, nursing, or menstruating; and while either partner was completely naked. Also the sex act would be restricted within the parameters of what we would call the missionary position—intercourse that could not result in a pregnancy or having the woman on the top position were especially *verboten*—and was to be performed only once in a day. Above all, sex was not to be enjoyed if it could be helped.[108]

Adultery was always considered more of a sin than simple fornication,[109] with one authority recommending a five-year-long fasting—two of those years spent eating nothing but water and bread—for a husband.[110] Following Jesus's instructions, some penitentials advised that in cases of female adultery the husband should divorce her or do penance himself.[111] The *Penitential of Theodore* went further by recommending that the man who stayed with an adulterous wife should remain completely abstinent until she finished the period of penance (unsurprisingly a much longer timeframe than what Theodore demanded from an adulterous husband) required of her.[112]

The penitentials were just as careful in detail when it came to the issue of contraception. Unmarried women using herbs and potions to prevent a telltale pregnancy were specifically condemned in the *Irish Collection of Canons*.[113] As disgusted as they usually were with the idea of contraception providing an out for women, penitential writers were careful to distinguish whether a woman used contraception or abortion just to avoid pregnancy or because she was too poor to care for another child. In latter cases, the penances were drastically reduced.[114]

One topic that the penitential writers were fixated on that went largely unaddressed by the Church Fathers was a more solitary sin, masturbation. Although masturbation—or a "sexual experience while arousing the body," in the clinical words of the *Paris Penitential*[115]—appears with frequency in the penitentials, most likely because of the writers' monastic backgrounds,[116] they usually did not deal with it harshly. The longest penance for masturbation comes from the *Penitential of Theodore,* which prescribed three years for female masturbation, which is also his recommendation for lesbian intercourse (with time served increased if the woman was married, more or less placing a woman's affair with another woman on the same footing as adultery with a man). The same manual suggests only 30 days of fasting, but 40 days for young men.[117] Columban in his penitential is far less forgiving; seeing male masturbation as equivalent to bestiality, he insisted on two years of fasting for laymen and three for clerics.[118] Even those guilty of only a "wet dream" were not exempt. *Excerpts from the Book of David* suggests psalm singing and a short period of fasting for a man "who willfully has become polluted in sleep."[119] The *Penitential of Bobbio* agrees, asking the one who "sinned in sleep" to sing 25 psalms in the morning.[120] Theodore happens to make special mention of involuntary emission while a man is daydreaming or sleeping in church.[121]

Another particular gadfly for the penitential writers was what the *Penitential of Theodore* condemned as the activities of the "Sodomists" and the "effeminate"[122] and those an old Welsh penitential called "whoever commits the male crime as the Sodomists."[123] The *Penitential of Venina* condemns oral sex between men with penances for three years, and seven years for habitual offenders, while Columban prescribed ten years.[124] The *Penitential of Cumaean* goes into more detail by distinguishing between boys, adolescents, and men older than age 20. Boys imitating sex acts with each other are to do penance for 20 days, 40 days for habitual offenders. Mutual masturbation between young men merits 20 or 40 days of penances, with 100 days for femoral intercourse. Cumaean includes a provision where a boy "misused by an older one" must fast for a week. If he consented, then he should fast for more than twice that period.[125] Offensive to our modern sense of fairness, this dictate was also unusual for its time; it is very rare for the penitentials to punish someone who was deprived of consent.

Sometimes the writers of the penitentials seemed aware that boys and adolescents will experiment sexually and showed them more leniency. The *Penitential of Finnian* demanded seven years of penances from adult men guilty of anal intercourse and subtracted one year for boys.[126] Bede and Theodore did not even suggest long-term penance, but rather either whipping or a short time of fasting.[127] For sexual intercourse between women, the penitentials are less thorough and even less concerned.[128] However, female use of a *machina* in intercourse with another woman or in masturbation was judged more serious than the male equivalent.[129] Despite the general willingness of penitentials to treat homosexual acts with no more severity than other sexual mishaps, there is the attitude of the eighth-century *Bigotean Penitential* that homosexual intercourse should be considered an exceptional sin, one that "is not forgiven either in the present world or that which is to come."[130]

Although penitentials were often of dubious authority, at first they were widely recommended to priests. By the ninth century, as both the Church and the Carolingian emperors strove to bring the Church in the West into greater unity, there was a sea change. In 813, the Council of Châlons condemned all penitentials and called on secular authorities to outlaw their distribution. Sixteen years later, the Council of Paris went one step further and ordered them to be collected and burned.[131] The new penitentials that emerged throughout the rest of the century relied much more on papal decrees and church councils rather than simply the self-proclaimed theological knowledge of its writer (or, in the case of the many penitentials credited to a well-known saint or other ecclesiastic, the alleged writer). Even with uncompromising bans, the older penitentials continued to be widely copied, suggesting there was still a demand for them despite the best efforts of the Church.[132]

As haphazard as the penitentials were in the types of sexual offenses they detailed and the punishments they demanded, they shared a concern with fostering an all but ascetic lifestyle among the clergy as well as the laity. For the most part secular authorities in the West were not as committed, although this changed somewhat with the rise of Charlemagne's empire, which at its height stretched from the modern eastern Spanish provinces of Aragon and Catalonia to western Hungary and northern Italy. Charlemagne's brother, Carloman I (r. 768–771), granted bishops the right to charge and punish laypeople guilty of adultery and incest.[133] In spite of Charlemagne's own poor track record—he had his first marriage annulled on grounds of personal dislike and enjoyed relationships with a number of mistresses—it was Charlemagne who, in 802, adopted a policy that prevented even separated spouses from dissolving their marriage and legally remarrying as long as the other spouse lived.[134] This measure had far-reaching consequences; indissoluble marriage (at least in the eyes of the courts) remained a basis of civil law in most Catholic countries.

Charlemagne's son, Louis the Pious (r. 813–840), seemingly took another radical step in issuing a measure against prostitution by ordering that prostitutes and their customers be detained and whipped in public.[135] However, the law covered only the Carolingians' palace at Aachen and its environs, far from being enforced through the entire Carolingian Empire, and may have applied to all women accused of promiscuity.[136] This was in character for Louis, who, true to his sobriquet, was obsessed with morality, or at least the perception of morality, at the imperial court. One of his first acts upon becoming emperor was to banish his surviving sisters and other female relatives from Aachen. Louis's contemporary biographer, known only as "the Astronomer," claimed that Louis was motivated by his need to make a statement against the free lives Charlemagne allowed them all to lead and added that "they did not deserve of the emperor such treatment as they got."[137]

As for the Byzantine Empire, the zeal with which Justinian I once tried to reform society was not completely emulated, although the emperors occasionally did follow his example, at least with a few steps. Some brothels were seized by the government and turned into homes for the elderly, convents, and reformatories.[138] As mentioned before, remarriage, especially more than twice, was often discouraged by canonical and civil law, although the Church seems to have been more concerned with the matter than the State. More leeway was extended to the widowed,[139] while marriage among the lower ranks of the clergy was accepted.

Surprisingly, the brutality against male same-sex lovers that reached a fever pitch under Justinian eased later in Byzantine history. *Arrenomania*, "man-madness," and *gynaikomania*, "woman-madness," as they are at rare times termed in Byzantine Greek writings, seem to have been treated delicately after Justinian rather than with a sledgehammer. After the fifth century, records on homosexuality within the Byzantine Empire, much less its legal persecution, become very sparse, perhaps suggesting that there was a tacit tolerance as long as it was kept in the dark.[140]

Then there is the odd matter of the *adelphopoiia*, a Church ritual that sanctified the relationship between two individuals of either sex, similar to the rites for marriage, godparenthood, or adoption. The famous historian of homosexuality John Boswell presented the *adelphopoiia* as a culturally accepted way for same-sex couples to marry,[141] but despite the parallels to marriage, the purpose of the ritual seems to have been to acknowledge and formalize strong, lifelong friendships between two people. Still, *adelphopoiia* actually may have been exploited as a cover for same-sex love, which could explain why the Byzantine Church was determined at times to put an end to it.[142]

The early Middle Ages were a time when societies from the Visigothic kingdom to Constantinople made more strident, if more than slightly unfocused, efforts to impose an ideal of sexual conduct stricter than anything that was undertaken under the Greek city-states or pagan Rome except in the phantom utopias of Plato. The inevitable question is just how deeply into everyday life the campaign went so soon into the Christian era. Unfortunately, for this time and place there is no way of even making an educated guess on how many instances of adultery, premarital sex, "kinky" encounters between spouses, and so on there were. When it comes to the still somewhat appropriately termed "Dark Ages," glimpses into even the private lives of emperors, kings, nobles, and bishops are often fleeting and incomplete.

As with the penitentials, the most information on the sexual activities of the majority of the population may come from the institution that tried to tame such behavior: the Church. Of course, the Church, just as it is today, was in the business of perpetual outrage, so there is a good case that its proclamations on the state of morality in the Middle Ages may not be reliable. Still, it is interesting to see that the Third Council of Aachen in 862 wearily conceded that it was almost unheard of for men, free from the scrutiny women usually had to endure, to still be virgins by their wedding nights. Boniface was disturbed enough in the eighth century by the prevalence of adultery and marriages between close cousins among Frankish nobles that he asked for special instructions from the papacy.[143] In another letter to Cuthbert, Archbishop of Canterbury, he claimed with horror that nearly every town he visited in Gaul and northern Italy had English women who had set out to Rome on pilgrimage, but ended up becoming local prostitutes.[144]

In at least several instances, the Church seems to have accepted the state of things. Walrada, the mistress of the Carolingian royal Lothar II, was still welcomed warmly and without censure at the convent of Remiremont.[145] At an ecclesiastical court, a certain Count Stephen argued that his marriage should not be annulled on grounds of his impotence since he was recently able to have sex with a relative of his wife. The church authorities present did nothing to rebuke him.[146] Even in Visigothic Iberia, where, as we have seen, one act of adultery could lead to the death of a wife and her lover, Isidore of Seville remarked wryly, "It's hard to keep a pretty wife."[147]

Against one class of sinner, however, the Church was vehemently outspoken. In 829, the Council of Paris denounced sins "against nature." To prove how exceptionally repellent the sin of homosexuality was, the council not only cited Sodom and Gomorrah, but also claimed that homosexuality was responsible for the war against the Benjaminites described in Judges 20 (in reality the story is quite clear that the war was provoked by the rape and murder of the Levite's concubine) and even the Flood in Genesis.[148] Such a fantastic sin, the council concluded, could only be punished with death, although a capital offense against male homosexual acts never actually made it into the civil law books or the lists of edicts under the Carolingians.[149] For the time being, the Church was largely ineffective in enforcing such a punishment on its own.

Essentially a vital if poorly articulated sex-negative ideology was in place for both the Latin and Orthodox Churches by the early Middle Ages, but for what would become the Catholic Church the means of organized enforcement was lacking. While in Constantinople emperor and Church maintained a close, if often tense partnership, in Western Europe the papacy was often at the mercy of mob politics and warring factions in Rome while the efforts of Charlemagne and his successors to resurrect the Western Roman Empire, along with the supremacy of the imperial office, sputtered out. Later Charlemagne's nominal successors in the Holy Roman Empire (as it would become known, even though its *de facto* influence was limited to Germany and Austria, the modern-day "Benelux" countries, and parts of Italy and eastern France) would find themselves at odds with the papacy's vision of the proper state of affairs. After Europe entered the new millennium and as the papacy revitalized itself, it would be the Western Church, and not any lay government with imperial pretensions, that would establish a true supranational institution that would exercise extraordinary control over its own body as well as over the lives of those that lived in its shadow.

The Islamic Alternative

In the seventh century Christendom was placed in the awkward position of finding a rival religion and society right on its doorstep. Only one century after the death of the

Prophet Muhammad in 632, the Islamic Caliphate, which had found easy prey in the militarily exhausted and religiously divided Sassanid and Byzantine empires, stretched from the Atlantic Ocean to the Indus Valley. All of the Iberian peninsula except part of the mountainous north, which evolved from a guerrilla haven for those escaping from the collapse of the Visigothic kingdom into the Christian kingdom of Asturias, was eventually conquered by the Islamic Caliphate, forming a territory called al–Andalus in the language of the new rulers. The Umayyads—the dynasty that once ruled over the entire Caliphate but were scattered in the face of a violent uprising—founded a new dominion in al–Andalus by 747.

Although Islam shared the same roots in Judaism as Christianity, it was not exposed in its infancy to the anxieties over sex that haunted Greek and Latin philosophers. Also Muhammad was not a model for aestheticism like the Paul of the Gospels or the church fathers; he married 11 or 13 times, although at least some of these unions were forged for political reasons or to provide support for widowed women. In the Qur'an there is none of the ambivalence over marriage that was so characteristic of early Christianity:

> He created for you helpmeets from yourselves that ye might find rest in them, and He ordained between you love and mercy. Lo, herein indeed are portents for folk who reflect.[150]

The Qur'an also explicitly permitted polygamy.[151] In fact, monogamy is recommended only for husbands who worry that they "cannot do justice" to more than one wife.

All nonmarital and extramarital intercourse fell under the category of *zina,* a word usually translated into English as "fornication." The Qur'an ordered men to find women "in honest wedlock, not debauchery,"[152] although mistresses were not forbidden as long as they were unmarried and slaves,[153] and prescribed a punishment of 100 lashes to the man as well as the woman found guilty of nonmarital and adulterous sex. Also, those branded as fornicators were to be segregated by being allowed to marry only others like them or pagans.[154] Men did have one loophole: a *mut'a* contract, a practice under Shiite law that allowed a woman and a man to enter into what was essentially a marital contract with an expiration date.[155]

An additional punishment was meted out to women guilty of *zina*: being locked in their homes until they died. However, for any punishment for *zina* to be carried out, the accuser had to provide four male witnesses; failure to do so would result in them being whipped with 80 lashes.[156] It is possible that the provision of the four witnesses was tacked on to an existing pre–Islamic Arabic custom to severely limit its use, but it does call attention to the brutality the double standard over promiscuity could inspire. Even more harsh was the demand attributed to Muhammad that adulterous couples be stoned to death, but this comes from a *hadith,* an alleged saying of Muhammad which may or may not have been authentic, and the testimony of a former companion of Muhammad, the Caliph Umar (r. 634–644)[157] rather than the Qur'an itself.

Paying for the services of a prostitute of either sex also fell into the category of *zina* and prostitutes were routinely treated like pariahs. Although there were famous prostitutes and courtesans like Kharqa, who lived in Mecca and boasted that she was a "pilgrimage rite," female prostitutes were locked out of the social networks of their tribes[158] and male prostitutes were viewed with disgust for submitting to disgraceful sexual passivity for pay.[159] Like their Christian counterparts, however, medieval Islamic authorities recognized prostitution as an institution as unpleasant as it was necessary. Enforcement from the *muhtasib,* officials tasked with the responsibility to police moral breaches on the level of the street, seems to have usually just driven prostitution off the busiest public areas and into red-light districts.[160] At the same time medieval Islamic governments often collected taxes on prostitution, a practice recorded in the city of Valencia, one of the great urban centers of al–Andalus.[161]

As if adulterous wives and women deemed "promiscuous" did not have enough swords hanging over their head, Arabic custom dictated that a man who caught his wife and her lover in *flagrante delicto* could kill both without fear of punishment,[162] but only in that specific situation. The one route of escape for women in unhappy marriages was divorce, which appears to have been, as in much of the medieval Islamic world, quite common in al–Andalus.[163] Technically women could initiate a divorce, but while divorce was a very simple matter for any husband—under Sunni law a declaration by the husband to divorce does not even require witnesses—wives usually had to demonstrate cause to a judge or fulfill certain conditions. For example, one of the few documents dealing with marital matters that survives from Islamic Iberia, a 14th-century court record from the emirate of Granada in what is now southern Spain, relates the case of a woman who won a divorce in court, but at the cost of any claim to her dowry. Yet, as the historian Yossef Rapoport found in his study of medieval marriage records from Islamic countries, women could and very often did play the system to achieve easy and beneficial divorces.[164]

While in Islamic societies intimate and marital relations between the sexes were subjected to the sort of regulations and inequalities that might be expected from a patriarchal culture, the Qur'an lacked any marked hostility toward noncoital intercourse. The closest is a prohibition against having anal intercourse with one's wife without her consent.[165] Also the Qur'an was silent on contraception. One jurist from Iberia, Ibn Hazim, did argue that Muhammad eventually determined that *coitus interruptus* was "hidden infanticide," but the vast majority of jurists accepted contraception, not just *coitus interruptus,* as permissible.[166] The only major concern for jurists was that the practice of *coitus interruptus* denied a woman her right to both children and to sexual pleasure.[167] Jurists also accepted women's use of contraception, although they disagreed over whether it had to be done with the express permission of the husband.[168]

Islam still had its safeguards against *eros* and a suspicion that desire was something that could and must be contained. Muhammad advised women

> always to lower their gaze and be modest, and to display as their adornment only that which is apparent, and to draw their veils over their bosoms, and not to reveal their adornments save to their own husbands or fathers or husband's fathers, or their sons or their husband's sons, or their brothers or their brothers' sons or sisters' sons, or their women, or their slaves, or male attendants who lack vigor, or children who know naught of women's nakedness. And let them not stamp their feet so as to reveal what they hide of their adornment.[169]

The Qur'an also extended responsibility for the containment of desire to men, who were likewise advised to avoid eye contact and to keep their genitals—and presumably any telltale signs of sexual arousal—completely covered.[170] However, in the *fulfillment* of sexual desire within proper parameters, classical Islam was considerably lenient, finding even masturbation acceptable (but perhaps still problematic) as a remedy against overwhelming lust.[171]

Where, then, did this relative tolerance leave sexual relations between members of the same sex? Female homosexuality is never mentioned in the Qur'an. While medieval jurists insisted that sex between women should be denounced, the majority believed that there should be no punishment at all, with others prescribing only a discreet slap on the wrist.[172] There are seven references in the holy text to "the people of Lot," the Qur'an's version of "Sodomites." One such passage reads, "Lo! Ye come with lust unto men instead of women. Nay, but ye are wanton folk."[173] However, there is only one passage that prescribes punishment and it is more lenient and vague than the condemnations of *zina*: "As for the two of you [meaning the *umma*, the community of believers] who are guilty thereof, punish them both. And if they repent and improve, then let them be. Lo! Allah is relenting, merciful."[174] At the same time, the Qur'an claims that the faithful will be attended in *Jannah* (Heaven) not only by beautiful virgin women, but also by handsome adolescent men carrying cups of wine.[175] While some medieval Islamic jurists spoke about intimacy and sex between men in strong and venomous terms, many were uncommitted to any real form of reprisal.[176]

What Muhammad thought of homosexual relations outside the Qur'an is, as might be expected from any religious founder, open to endless debate, thanks in no small part to the proliferation of *hadiths* and other accounts over the centuries. On the one hand, one *hadith* urged the stoning of men caught having sex with each other and another claimed that Muhammad once openly cursed sodomites. On the other hand, the Arabic writer Ahmed al-Tifashi cited a legend that Muhammad had been friends with a man named Hayith, whom he tellingly allowed to sit and chat with his wives while they were unveiled.

Whatever Muhammad's own attitudes in his lifetime, there is no confusion over those of the first Caliphs. Abu Bakr (r. 632–634), the first Caliph and a companion of Muhammad, had a man accused of homosexual intercourse buried alive. Muhammad's son-in-law and the fourth Caliph, Ali (r. 656–661), ordered stoning as the preferred punishment on several occasions and had one accused man thrown off the top of a building.[177]

However, the cruelty of the early Caliphs was not the norm for medieval Islam, especially as Islam spread and mixed with new cultures in the Middle East, central Asia, and the Mediterranean. This seems to have been especially true for Islamic Iberia. Under the Umayyads, al-Andalus, and in particular its cosmopolitan capital of Córdoba, became part of the scientific and artistic outpouring that flooded across the Islamic world. Al-Andalus's own chief contribution was in the popularity of its poetry, especially the genres of love poetry and erotic verses. These poems were written not just in Arabic, but also in classical Hebrew by Jewish poets. Together these Arabic and Hebrew poems from present-day Portugal and Spain formed a collection of literature on love and sex that were generally more ribald and explicit than most of its contemporary Christian counterparts and could be read openly in what was largely a more relaxed climate.

The predominant attitude among the *literati* of al-Andalus may be best summed up by a poet and scholar from Córdoba, Muhammad ibn Hazm (994–1064). Despite his disapproval of certain sexual matters, he wrote, "It is sufficient for a good Muslim to abstain from those things which Allah has forbidden, and which, if he chose to do, he will find charged to his account on the Day of Resurrection. But to admire beauty, and to be mastered by love—that is a natural thing, and comes not within the range of divine commandment and prohibition." The same writer referred to numerous *imams* and jurists who wrote love poems.[178] There were some who disapproved, like the Sunni scholar Abu Hatim al-Razi (811–891), who bemoaned those "idle, effeminate men" who are too deeply influenced by "reading lovers' tales, reciting delicate amorous verses, and listening to sad music."[179] Yet love poetry in al-Andalus was a national pastime for the elite, written by people who also happened to be civil servants, scholars, philosophers, theologians, ministers, and even caliphs, emirs, and members of royal families.

Drenched in metaphor and playful language as the poems may be, they are still quite blunt. Pomegranates, an erotic metaphor for breasts, are in one verse said to be "tasty for those who pluck them."[180] Homoerotic sentiments were also far from uncommon. Samuel ibn Nagrilla (993–1056), the Jewish prime minister of the emirate of Granada, praised a saki, a young male cup-bearer, who invited him to drink wine from between his lips.[181] Yusuf ibn Harun al-Ramadi chose a black slave as the object of his desire, declaring that he was the slave and the slave was the lord.[182] Not all this poetry played on class hierarchies. Muhammad ibn Abd al-Malik ibn Quzman (1078–1160) wrote poems about a string of men whom he loved, many of whom were his social equals, and made it clear at least once that his love for them was more than fantasy.[183]

Like ibn Quzman, the poets of al-Andalus did not always restrict their passions to the realm of the imagination. One female poet, Wallada bint al-Mustakfi (994–1091), walked on the streets of Córdoba without being covered by a veil and had a number of open, non-marital relationships with high-ranking men. Muhammad ibn Abbad al-Mutamid (1040–1095), emir of Seville, had a romantic and sexual relationship with his vizier, ibn Ammar, but the relationship came to a violent end when politics soured their love and eventually led al-Mutamid to kill ibn Ammar with his own hands.

When homosexual anecdotes do appear in the history of al-Andalus, they do not seem meant to incite horror or indignation. There is the story of Caliph al-Hakam II (r. 961–976), who was said to have been so attached to other men that, to ensure that he produced an heir, his ministers set up his liaison with a woman dressed in men's clothes and named "Jafar."[184] One account claims that another caliph, Hisham II, had a harem of men.[185] Outside the royal court, ibn Hazm, at a banquet hosted by a merchant, was appalled at the sight of two male guests retiring to the same room together and recited a poem on the spot to express his indignation. The host simply ignored him.[186] It seems the worst that could happen to men who had open affairs with other men, at least according to ibn Hazm, was damage to one's career, which he claims is what happened to one famous theologian.[187]

If nothing else, the intellectual and cultural leaders of al-Andalus were not uncongenial to the idea of love between members of the same sex. Even love between women was the topic of Arabic erotic works and a lost treatise written sometime in the ninth century.[188] Far from an unnamable sin or a sexual crime, female mutual love seems, above all else, to have been treated as a curiosity. An Arabic medical treatise claimed to be derived from the Roman physician Galen recommends a recipe for a potion that would make women detest sex with other women "even if they madly lust for it." Also included was a recipe that would have the opposite result: "make lesbianism so desirable to women that they would keep busy with it and passionately lust for it forgetting all about their work."[189]

Even ibn Hazm, despite his outbursts of disapproval, wrote *Tawq al-hamama* ("The Ring of the Dove"), which approvingly tells six stories of people who died or nearly died from love: four involve men and women, while the other two feature male couples. Likewise, the theologian Abu Bakr Muhammad ibn Da'ud claimed in his *Kitab al-zara* ("Book of the Flower") that *ishq,* passionate love, could exist between men as easily as between a man and a woman.

This begs the question of how someone like ibn Hazm was able to reconcile his strong, moral disapproval of explicit, undisguised, and fulfilled lust between men at a banquet with the celebration of love across the boundaries of sex taken up by him and his contemporaries. The explanation is that in al–Andalus emotional attraction and the physical expression of desire were starkly differentiated. Such a seeming contradiction also appears in the *Muqaddimah,* a history composed by a native of al–Andalus who eventually relocated to Tunisia, Abu Zayd ibn Khaldun (1332–1406). The text carries the author's condemnation of male love as a threat to the cause of procreation and recommends that men who have had sex with men should be stoned, yet it also includes an anthology of Arabic Iberian poetry filled with overtly homoerotic verse.

A *hadith* widely known at the time reads, "He who loves and remains chaste and conceals his secret and dies, dies a martyr."[190] So we are left with no reason not to believe ibn Hazm, who did admit to being attracted to both women and men, when he swears "by Allah and by the most solemn oath that I have never taken off my underwear to have illicit sexual intercourse."[191] Consummation could meet with disapproval, but even moralists like ibn Hazm admired appropriately contained desire, expressed only through literature. As Jim Wafer described it, the "emphasis … is on feeling itself, which is regarded as especially privileged."[192]

Flawed as it may have been by modern Western standards of sexual liberty, al–Andalus was an oasis of permissiveness in an increasingly uptight Europe. However, its lifespan was relatively short. Crippled by civil war, the Umayyad Caliphate collapsed by 1031. What was the Caliphate shattered into the *taifas,* small states that were weak against the encroaching Christian kingdoms from the north and the invading Almoravid and Almohad dynasties from Morocco in the south. By the middle of the 13th century, all that remained of Islamic Iberia was the emirate of Granada, which eventually fell in 1492, completing the Christian *Reconquista.* Yet the influence of the scientific achievements and cultural movements in al–Andalus was hardly negligible, even to its Christian neighbors, and the Andalusian fascination with unrealized love that ran counter to convention ultimately provided the seed for the growth of the medieval *troubadours* and the genre of chivalric poetry.

VI

Medieval Rigidness

Arguably more than any other era in European history, the later Middle Ages, best known to medievalists as the High Middle Ages (1000–1300) and the Late Middle Ages (1300–1500), has been the victim of bad press. Generations of Protestant writers burned through pages painting the time before Martin Luther as the unchallenged reign of the papal Antichrist, and their work was taken up by the champions of the Enlightenment, who sold a concept of the Middle Ages as a time of root-deep ignorance, fanatical superstition, and omnipresent oppression. Even with romantic images of knights and courtly love kept fresh by films and novels, the popular imagination, when turning to thoughts of what everyday life in medieval Europe must have been like, usually conjures up phantoms of the Inquisition, bejeweled bishops, the Black Death, and burning heretics.

The professional reconstruction of the past by scholars has been, in some ways, nearly as bleak. Scholars specializing in sexuality, entranced by the idea that some point in the early modern era marked a very sharp and relatively sudden turn for European cultures and societies toward today's social landscape, have envisioned a place and an era where people lacked the very concept of individuality. Predictably, such opinions are often expressed by scholars who do not even specialize in the Middle Ages.[1] As the evidence comes together, however, the overview that emerges hints at something quite contrary to both popular and academic expectations—namely, an era when people managed to be quite diverse in their opinions and the ways they lived in spite of intense, occasionally murderous pressure from a Church and State invested in universal orthodoxy.

The beginning of the new millennium was the time the Western Church slowly began to claim more power over individual lives than was dreamed of by even the emperors of Rome, a process culminating in the decisive Lateran Council of 1215. For the first time ever, the Church had a simple guidebook to canon law in the *Decretum* of Gratian at the same time that it gradually devised efficient mechanisms for monitoring and punishing sexual offenses by not only clerics and monastics, but the laity and even nobles and monarchs. "Medieval churchmen claimed authority over virtually every aspect of human beliefs and actions," James Brundage writes, adding, "Church leaders claimed … that they must protect society and its individual members from immoral behavior as well as unorthodox thought, and so they claimed a broad jurisdiction over all varieties of sinful actions, commercial and non-commercial, sexual and non-sexual, civil and criminal, among the clergy and laity alike."[2]

Perhaps the Church's most far-reaching push into the bedroom was the campaign for clerical celibacy, which succeeded even in the face of intense opposition.

As the Western Church carved out a place for itself that transcended and even superseded secular governments, Christendom itself was hardly stagnant and expanded farther beyond the boundaries of the old Roman Empire. In eastern Europe, the Byzantine Empire demanded with success that Boris I, Czar of Bulgaria, convert to Orthodox Christianity, a cynical political move to preempt the possibility of Boris I aligning with the Latin Christian world. More peaceful and just as productive were missionary efforts among the Slavs of modern-day Russia and Eastern Europe over the course of the ninth and tenth centuries. Although the period did also see the grotesquely violent mass-forced conversion of the Slavs of the Baltic region during the Northern Crusades, King Mieszko I of Poland voluntarily joined the Latin Christian fold in 966. He was followed by the first king of Hungary, Stephen I, who was crowned by the Pope himself in 1000. The kings of Sweden, Denmark, and Norway also joined the flock in the 11th century, dragging their peoples with them.

The expansion of the Church also meant the expansion of the Church's rules on sexual conduct into these foreign climes. Unfortunately, we can only speculate how deeply the Church's prescriptions for a sin-free sex life seeped into the newly (and of course not entirely) Christianized countries. Even the native folklores and mythologies were interpreted and written down by Christians, in many cases monks and foreign missionaries, who were biased or at least filtered their accounts through a Christian mentality. Still, as we will see, customs, traditions, and even laws affecting the realm of sex that likely predated Christianity bubbled up through the morals legislation imposed by the Church.

The Church was not alone in managing a revival. The Carolingian Empire fell apart, the Byzantine Empire never fully recovered from the invasion of Constantinople by greedy and bigoted Latin Crusaders in 1204, and the Holy Roman Emperors eventually lost a war of wills first with the papacy and then with the rulers of the empire's German principalities. In hindsight, however, the smaller kingdoms and republics of Europe actually tended to gain ground, invigorated in no small part by the rediscovery of Roman law in Western and Central Europe during the 12th century. Like the Church, the governments of Catholic Europe, nurtured by a widespread economic recovery and the slow but steady growth of cities and towns, began to become more ambitious when it came to shaping day-to-day life, with strict secular laws against sodomy and prostitution appearing on the books, condemning sodomites to the death penalty and prostitutes to segregated areas.

In the face of the authorities' tremendous interest in stamping out unruly sexual behavior, anyone familiar with works of medieval literature, from the poems of the *troubadours* to the *Canterbury Tales* to the *Decameron*, will know that writers still talked frankly and often without moral condemnations about adultery, nonmarital sex, and the sex lives of priests and monastics—and expected their audience to find such stories amusing and understandable, rather than shocking and appalling. For medieval Europe, we lack statistics, but the existence of such literature alone suggests that a sizable proportion of the general populace did not accept, comprehend, or care that what the Church called fornication was a sin.

Triumph of the Church

The Eastern Orthodox Church never adopted Augustine's view of original sin, but nonetheless its view of sex could be relentlessly grim. Sex was the legacy of the Fall, devised by Satan himself.[3] Orthodox thinkers did not forget John Chysostom's claim that it was not really intercourse that caused reproduction, but rather the will of God.[4] In such a vein, devout Byzantines and Orthodox Slavs thrilled to stories of saintly couples who married, refrained completely from intercourse, and still pulled off the conception of a child.[5] The ambition here was to divorce the necessity of reproduction from the filthiness of sex altogether. If only those who followed John Chysostom's line of thinking could have foreseen the advent of artificial insemination.

Up until the end of their empire's history, the Byzantine authorities meddled in their Church matters and, as we have seen, passed and sustained laws enforcing sexual matters; they also did not shy away from engaging behavior conflicting with the canon laws that had been set down. The Slavic kingdoms that were in the Byzantine Empire's orbit but not under its thumb took a different tack, leaving (for the most part) sexual morality as the concern and responsibility of the Church. This was a double-edged sword: Orthodox clerics in the Slavic kingdoms often found to their chagrin that apathetic secular leaders were unwilling to lend a hand in ensuring proper enforcement of the rules.[6]

To the west, the Catholic Church sought to find a way to have it all. At first glance the mainstream medieval Western view might seem more restrained than the Orthodox alternative. As Pierre Payer explains, "Gender differentiation between male and female was considered to be natural and part of the initial creative intentions of God, not tailored to the state of fallen nature."[7] However, theologians added that the impact of the Fall did spoil the sex act, by introducing the sin of lust and making sex dangerously irrational. Further theologians like Peter Lombard (c. 1100–1160) argued that original sin was transmitted to the next generation through the lust inherent to sex. To seal the point, Peter drew on Psalms 50:7: "I was conceived in iniquities, and in sin my mother conceived me."[8]

Hand in hand with this fundamental suspicion of sexual pleasure was an ambitious reform movement that would culminate in the Western Church stretching its reach and freeing itself as much as possible from the grip of lay authorities. This was not just an ambitious push, but a matter of climbing out of the swamp. In the ninth and tenth centuries, kings, dukes, and sometimes just local strongmen typically called the shots over ecclesiastical matters, even placing members of their families in church offices.[9] The papacy itself was often at the disposal of the Roman aristocracy or the Holy Roman Emperors. Some kind of reform was perhaps inevitable. Although for the most part he owed his position as Pope to Emperor Heinrich III (r. 1039–1056), Leo IX (r. 1048–1054) insisted on having his election approved by the clergy and worked toward strengthening the Church's administration. Although worldly power politics was always at the forefront, sex was still very much on the reformers' minds. As James Brundage puts it, "Even more than the penitential authors and earlier patristic authorities, [Church reformers] were intent on limiting marital sex and on penalizing extramarital sex as severely as they could."[10]

A crucial part of this reform was to streamline canon law. Attempts to collect canon laws had been made by Regino of Prüm in the 10th century and Burchard of Worms (ca. 965–1025) in the 11th century, but it would take later writers like Ivo of Chartres (ca. 1040–

1115) to mine collections like Burchard's and package the information in a way that was easy to copy and distribute.[11] Like the penitentials before them, the canonical collections left no sexual topic unturned; in fact, they surpassed the penitential writers in their obsession with legal precision. The entire seventh book of Burchard of Worms' *Decretum* was dedicated to incest and marriages formed within the forbidden seven degrees of kinship, an especially sensitive topic among royalty and the nobility. Marrying even a relatively distant relative could result in any children being labeled *infames*, which stripped one of the right to hold office and testify in court.[12]

Sexual experimentation even within marriage, divorce and separation, adultery, bigamy, sodomy, masturbation, sex with Jews and Muslims, prostitution, and pandering were all to be punished with lengthy terms of penance, with, in extreme cases, the culprits being excommunicated; such a fate not only damned the soul, but also rendered its victim *persona non grata* among Christians.[13] Against what might be expected, the canonists tended to hold married couples to even higher standards than the unmarried. Burchard of Worms thought that a husband who had sex with his wife just for pleasure was four times worse than a bachelor who had sex with a prostitute.[14] Later the preacher Bernardino of Siena (1380–1444) went even further by maintaining that a man having sex with his wife in an "unnatural" position was worse than sleeping with a prostitute, incest, and even sex with a nun.[15]

Especially pivotal was the work of Gratian, a 12th-century canon lawyer from Bologna. Citing not only previous collections of canon law but also the writings of theologians, the letters and decrees of popes, and decisions made by synods and church councils, Gratian's *Decretum* was deemed so authoritative that it almost overnight became the standard textbook used by students of canon law across Catholic Europe. Like his predecessors, Gratian stuck to the official line that sex was acceptable only within a marital union (although he was accepting of concubinage, as long as the arrangement was still monogamous[16]) that was all but indissoluble. Gratian's interpretations allowed divorce in cases of impotence and where the spouse was a heretic, but even then only if the orthodox spouse had been unaware of the partner's heretical leanings before vows were said. In cases of adultery, both spouses would be considered merely separated, with remarriage forbidden as long as the other spouse lived.[17]

Nonmarital sex and adultery were to be considered crimes without question, but Gratian did conclude from his sources that adultery was equally serious with men as it was with women.[18] Like other writers on canon law, Gratian looked with extreme disfavor on killing the wife for adultery.[19] Another way Gratian saw some sort of equality between the sexes was in his promotion of conjugal debt, derived from Paul. The wife had as much right to demand sex from the husband as vice versa,[20] although of course "unnatural" and excessive sex between spouses was still out of the question.[21]

This more accessible legal understanding was soon followed by the Church finding ways to put these laws into practice. In the 13th century the Church, aided by the rediscovery of Roman law, spearheaded an effort to stamp out the custom of trial by ordeal, where questions of guilt or innocence were left up to divine intervention by subjecting the accused to some grueling challenge. Instead the Church advertised the idea that every step of the judicial process ought to be overseen by qualified officials, which took the process out of the hands of private parties and allowed for investigation and interrogation. In England and Scotland, juries would play a more significant role than they did on the Continent, but across continental Europe this new "officialized" system became the norm in both secular and ecclesiastical courts.[22]

As rational, humane, and "modern" as such judicial reforms may seem, they were also what later made the Inquisition, heresy trials, and witch hunts possible. A single accusation was still enough to bring a person to trial. An official, whether of the Church or the State, had the right to bring charges and conduct a case against a person based on hearsay alone, a tactic that can be traced as far back as the 9th century but became widespread by the late Middle Ages. In short, a bad reputation was grounds for being brought before a court and gossip was admissible evidence.[23] It was a perfect system for rounding up sexual miscreants, no matter how well they tried to hide their bedroom hobbies from their neighbors, but it was also ideal for anyone with a grudge and a colorful imagination.

To tighten the Church's grip on marriage, the Lateran Council of 1215 demanded that all marriages must be announced in churches, giving people who might know reasons why the marriage might be invalid the opportunity to speak out.[24] Determined to whittle down not only improper behavior between Christians, this landmark council also ordered that measures be taken to help ensure that Christians would not "accidentally" sleep with Jews and Muslims. Specifically, this would require Muslims and Jews in Christian towns to wear badges and distinctive clothing,[25] an ominous precedent. Civic authorities scrambled to either enforce this decree, beginning in England where Jews were ordered to wear two white tables (representing the Ten Commandments and hence the old law of the Torah) on their upper garments, or extort money in exchange for exemptions from Jews rightly terrified that wearing distinctive clothing would be an open invitation for violence.[26]

To make sure enforcement did not slacken, Church reformers initiated a number of measures to ensure that both the clergy and the community at large were kept in line. Before the end of the 11th century, it became common practice for bishops to regularly inspect every parish and monastic house in their jurisdiction and intervene in matters that called for correction. Because of the sheer amount of work this required, courts emerged under the bishops' authority that were run by subordinates, deacons and archpriests.[27] The Lateran Council of 1215 also asked that all priests instruct parishioners on their moral obligations and made confession mandatory for every parishioner once a year. The Council went even further by empowering the Inquisition to investigate moral offenses, not just suspicions of heresy, and giving ecclesiastical courts permission to hand offenders over to secular authorities for punishment.

Often with help from these officials, the ecclesiastical courts had options besides penance, fines, and excommunication. Clerics convicted of serious sexual crimes could be and were imprisoned in monasteries for life on top of losing their income, male and female adulterers were sometimes publicly humiliated by being marched down the street or village road while being whipped with their heads shaved, and the Church's courts could even order a man who abandoned his wife for another woman to return to his spouse.[28] It was, of course, a system that was begging for exploitation. In 14th-century England, the poet Geoffrey Chaucer (ca. 1343–1400); the author of *Piers Plowman,* William Langland (ca. 1332–ca. 1386); and the religious reformer John Wycliffe (d. 1384) all agreed that the summoner, a minor church official tasked with bringing offenders before the ecclesiastical courts, was a curse on society. All three authors showed that the summoner was susceptible to bribes, whether in the form of money, wine, or, ironically, sex; he made his living by exploiting the peccadilloes of the young and the poor; and, worst of all, he was often guilty of bringing people up on completely false charges to leech them of their money.[29]

For all this, the most ambitious war against sex waged by the Catholic Church was the movement to force celibacy on the priesthood. Although hard numbers are virtually nonexistent, it is very probable that a sizable portion of priests in both rural areas and towns and cities had wives and children as late as the turn of the millennium.[30] There was even a pope, Adrian II (r. 867–872), who had a wife not only before his election, but after he had entered the Church. However, there was one practical problem that priests with families created for reformers, who wanted above all else to ensure that church incomes and property were kept tightly in hand: these priests were spending church income on their families and passing church property on to the children. In fact, in some parts of Europe, church offices had practically become hereditary.[31]

Yet the push for celibacy was not all about money and politics. The reformers genuinely came to believe that priests should have an unsullied spiritual relationship with their parishioners, making a priestly marriage an act of adultery. Peter Damian (ca. 1007–1072), the rabid bulldog of the reform movement, preached that marriage dragged priests down to the dirt, making them vulnerable to impure thoughts,[32] and that being a husband and father rendered the priest too impure for his duties. The "hands that touch the body and blood of Christ must not have touched the genitals of a whore," Damian thundered.[33] For Damian and the growing numbers of reformers who agreed with him, support of priestly marriage was nothing less than a heresy.

The papacy was not hesitant to act, and clerical celibacy became a centerpiece of the reform movement from nearly the very beginning. Leo IX ordered all the wives and concubines of Roman priests to be seized and made servants in the Lateran Palace while issuing a decree ordering the laity not to go to any masses given by married priests. The most decisive measures were taken by Gregory VII (r. 1073–85), who at his first synod commanded that no one could be admitted to the priesthood without a vow of celibacy. When opposition arose, Gregory VII with calculating efficiency purged the Church's ranks of opponents and courted support from German nobles who were willing to back the papacy for any reason in exchange for papal actions against their detested overlord, Emperor Heinrich IV (r. 1084–1105).[34] The battle finally ended, at least as far as the papacy was concerned, when in 1139 canon law barred married priests from administering sacraments and Pope Innocent II (r. 1130–1143) declared that all priestly marriages were null and void.[35]

The rhetoric of reformers like Peter Damian and the drastic actions taken by the popes could not help but trickle down to the populace. In Milan, an armed mob rose up to drive out all priests known to have wives and mistresses.[36] Under the command of zealous bishops, wives were separated from their priest husbands across Europe, sometimes violently. A few separated wives committed suicide; others attacked the officials literally dragging them away from their spouses.[37] Once cut off from their husbands, they faced the tender mercies of a society that had viciously turned against them. Even the language describing them had changed from words like *uxor* (wife), *diaconissa* (female deacon), and *episcopissa* (female bishop) to *concubina, meretrix* (prostitute), and *scortum* (harlot).[38]

No mercy was given to the children of priests, either. Called the "cursed seed" by the Synod of Bourges in 1031, the same synod decided that such children should be labeled *infames* and barred from inheriting property from their parents, the right to testify in any court, or the ability to enter the priesthood—barriers that were eventually extended in the course of the Middle Ages to many illegitimate children. Pope Urban II (r. 1095–1099) went even further by ordering that any son of a priest who was currently ordained should be kicked out of office.

The backlash was brutal, in some cases literally. Gregory VII had been warned that an advocate for celibacy was burned alive by the priests of Cambrai in northern France, and in Italy a few bishops refused to distribute the celibacy orders, afraid for their lives.[39] The bishop of Paris had to run into the palace of the royal family to save himself from being ripped apart by his infuriated clerics.[40] Luckily other protests were not quite as harsh, except perhaps in tone. German clerics signed a letter to Gregory VII, demanding to know where he would find the angels to replace them.[41] An anonymous pamphlet from York passionately argued that not only did priests have the right to marry, but that it went against canon law and all sense of justice to strip priests' children of their rights and legitimacy.[42] A bishop Ulric from Bologna likewise denounced clerical celibacy as being against both scripture and natural law and made the stinging point that celibate priests may seek relief in "the embraces of other men."[43] Nonetheless, eventually the reformers won out.

If one takes the sardonic view, then it might be argued that all the reformers accomplished in the long run was to drive priests into the arms of lifelong mistresses or male lovers and expand the opportunities for hypocrisy. While the celibacy movement was still on the march, the English chronicler Henry of Huntingdon sarcastically observed that England's papal legate John of Crema "dealt with the wives of priests very severely, saying that it was the greatest sin to rise from the side of a whore and go to create the body of Christ. Yet having created the body of Christ that same day, he was caught after Vespers with a whore."[44] If a Flemish bishop, Enrik van Gelders, who still openly bragged that he fathered 14 children in 22 months,[45] is any indication, there must have been prominent ecclesiastics who thumbed their nose at the very idea of sanctified celibacy—and got away with it. The canonist Benenossa, writing after the pro-celibacy movement had for all intents and purposes won the day, bemoaned the fact that across Italy and Germany priests and clerics still kept all of their old mistresses and wives without any fear of reprisal.[46]

Yet in spite of the heckling, if not outright contempt, the new order inspired, it was still a lasting and far-reaching institutional change. Indeed, in spite of the massive social, cultural, and theological movements that have occurred between the present day and Gregory VII's lifetime, the celibacy mandate shows today almost no signs of being reversed. How did it come to pass, in spite of the odds?

The answer is inevitably complex, but part of it may have been just good timing. The movement for clerical celibacy coincided with—or resulted largely from—a hardening of the Church's attitudes toward sex, a strengthening of the papacy and the Church as an institution, and an escalating distrust of female involvement with the Church, including nuns and abbesses, let alone the wives and mistresses of priests. The rewards for (at least ostensibly) renouncing sex, not to mention the burden of family life, were also great: a guaranteed income, unparalleled opportunities for advancement, social influence, instant elite status, and membership in an organization that was already raising itself above all the governments of Catholic Europe, even the Holy Roman Emperors themselves. In short, for such a small price, you could join, as Anne Lewyllen Barstow put it, "one of the most powerful and enduring 'men's clubs' that history has recorded."[47] That alone might have been enough to make even a vow of chastity palpable.

The Theology of Sex

Catholic theologians and other writers after the dawn of the second millennium wrote about sexual sin in stark, even apocalyptic terms, stronger than even what existed for the penitentials. By the 12th century, only a small minority of Catholic theologians and canonists expressed the radical view that there was nothing evil about the desire to experience sexual pleasure. This disgust of sex was more than philosophical; it was quite personal. The abbot Guibert of Nogent (ca. 1064–ca.1125), who left behind one of the most detailed autobiographies of the Middle Ages, worshiped his beloved mother for her chastity and worried that if she had ever seen "the secret places of [his] heart" she would have been shocked to death.[48] On a similar melodramatic note, the bishop Anselm of Canterbury (1033/1034–1109) bemoaned his own helplessness before lust:

> There is one evil, an evil above all other evils, that I am aware is always with me, that grievously and piteously lacerates and afflicts my soul. It was with me from the cradle, it grew with me in childhood, in adolescence, in my youth it always stuck to me, and it does not desert me even now that my limbs are failing because of my old age. This evil is sexual desire, carnal delight, the storm of lust that has smashed and battered my unhappy soul, emptied it of all strength, and left it weak and empty.[49]

A much later German evangelical writer from the 15th century, Alexander Carpentarius, revealed a terror of women mixed with a revulsion of sex:

> And if some say that women decorating themselves exquisitely to improve their beauty do not have an evil intention in doing it. I respond, nor does the sword have an evil intention when someone is killed with it, but still he who turns the sword to unjust killing has an evil intention, thus the devil who uses women thus adorned like a sword has an evil intention.[50]

One sexual issue that went largely ignored by the church fathers and was treated with no special animus by the penitentials, but which became a special concern in this period, was masturbation. Curiously female masturbation was not always viewed with disgust; in fact, some writers, following as always the advice of Galen, saw medical benefits in at least a little genital stimulation. Medieval medical writers, starting with the German philosopher and theologian Albert the Great (d. 1280), actually thought that women after puberty, when there is no sexual outlet available, develop a physical illness and an overpowering urge to have sex, no matter the circumstances. So "rubbing" was actually a way for women to "cool off" their lust and become *more* chaste.[51]

Boys and men did not benefit from medieval medical thought the same way, since it was naturally assumed they would have more outlets to avoid "congestion" than girls and women would. Peter Damian, who chastised the Church for ignoring those who "sin alone," categorized masturbation as a sin against nature as bad as homosexual intercourse. In his penitential *Compilation,* Peter of Poitiers reasons that masturbation is even worse than sodomy, since the same person plays the role of man and woman in one act.[52] Robert of Flamborough's *Penitential Book,* written in the 12th century, says that masturbation is even more awful than sex with one's mother, since masturbation is the true ultimate case of incest.[53] The chancellor of the University of Paris, Jean de Gerson (1363–1429), maintained that masturbation counted as adultery, if it was not actually worse.[54]

With such hostility toward all forms of sex that cannot result in reproduction, then contraception should have been high on the list of medieval moralists. Contraceptive medicines did have bad associations for writers, even in the early Middle Ages. They were often referred to as *maleficium,* a term normally used in reference to witchcraft. Meanwhile the Church remained wary that contraception was just a tool for sinners to get around the earthly consequences of intercourse.[55]

However, the hard realities of medieval life for the vast majority were undeniable, even to those meant to follow the party line on sex. An archbishop of Florence, Antonio Pierozzi (1389–1459), explicitly sanctioned *coitus reservatus* (penetration without emission), explaining, "No one is obligated to have more children than one can support."[56] In fact, much of the medieval knowledge about herbal recipes that cause sterility or induce a miscarriage were shared in the writings of nuns and monks, some of whom included "disclaimers" arguing that they were only meticulously listing the ingredients one should *avoid,* so that they are not taken by "accident." Other writers outside the Church could afford to be more blunt. An Italian physician, Guglielmo de Saliceto (1210–1277), openly advised physically weak or ill women to use oils for contraception and, failing that, to try to induce a miscarriage through exhaustive jumping.[57]

Such compilations on contraception could be amazingly thorough. One such guide was *Thesaurus Pauperum (Treasury of the Poor),* ostensibly written to help poor families from having too many mouths to feed by a Portuguese doctor and prior Pedro Julião, who later became Pope John XXI (r. 1276–1277). The treatise included 26 recipes for contraceptive herbs and potions, many of which the medical historian John Riddle argues are more effective than people in our post–Pill era would guess. Monastic writers on medicine, like the famous Hildegard of Bingen (1098–1117), referred to abortifacients in discreet terms, such as menstrual stimulators or regulators, even though it was clear from the descriptions what such drugs could be used to accomplish.[58]

If nothing else, the story of how contraception was handled in medieval Catholic Europe shows that, on the institutional level, the medieval Catholic Church could be rigidly doctrinal, but on the ground where individual clerics and monastics lived, practical considerations were far from ignored. Nonetheless, such a discrepancy did not stop Catholic theologians from spinning absolutes out of sexual morality. Some respected voices like Albert the Great maintained that sex was not intrinsically sinful,[59] but most took it as a basic fact that sex was disruptive, a threat to not only persons' good standing with God and the Church but also their very ability to reason and even their health and lifespan. The theologian Giovanni di Fidanzi (1221–1274) was writing with the authority of common knowledge when he claimed that sex is "diseased" and "cannot be performed without disorder."[60] Drawing on what was believed to be cutting-edge medical knowledge, the English bishop and future Catholic martyr John Fisher (ca. 1459–1535) warned sternly in a sermon that sex weakened men both morally and physically,[61] a widespread belief that gives us the age-old French term for male orgasm, *le petite mort*—the "little death."

As for women specifically, medical theory at the time believed that they were naturally more vulnerable to seduction since they were less willful than men. Yet at the same time conventional wisdom taught that women had more insatiable sexual appetites than men, which made women who were "immodest" a *bona fide* social threat.[62] It was this attitude that was directly challenged by the indefatigable Christine de Pizan (1363–ca. 1434), the prolific poet and essayist and the first known woman in Europe to make a living exclusively by writing.

Writing sarcastically in *L'epistre au Dieu d'amours* (Letter to the God of Love), Christine asks why, if certain authorities in the Church are right that women are innately deceitful and gullible, then why do men have to resort to tricks to seduce them?[63]

The most systematic attempt in the Middle Ages to rationalize the Catholic Church's doctrine on sexuality was from Thomas Aquinas (ca. 1225–1274), whose intellectual contributions to Catholic thought were ultimately the most decisive since those of Augustine. Despite grunts of disapproval from hardliners who despised the very suggestion of consulting the works of a heathen philosopher, Aquinas was eventually celebrated for aligning Catholic theology with Aristotlean logic, a process that did not leave out sex. However, one suspects that Aquinas's biography reveals that his feelings on sex were more than just based on theory. After he was literally kidnapped and imprisoned by his Neapolitan aristocratic family for wanting to join the Dominicans rather than follow his uncle's footsteps by becoming a Benedictine abbot, Aquinas's brothers tried to change his career path by hiring a prostitute to seduce him. According to legend, Aquinas chased the prostitute out of his room with a burning stick.

Like Clement of Alexandria, Thomas Aquinas assumed that sin was more than simply actions that were displeasing to God, but was contrary to reason: "The more necessary a thing is, the more it behooves one to observe the order of reason in its regard; wherefore the more sinful it becomes if the order of reason be forsaken."[64] Hence sex is sinful when it is motivated by lust and concerns and desires other than having children. Even kissing and touching, when motivated by lust, can be classified as mortal sins under Aquinas's equations.[65] However, Aquinas was forgiving on the topic of nocturnal emissions, as long as the person experiencing them was not willfully indulging in dirty thoughts. After all, Aquinas believed, it is entirely possible that even someone talking or thinking about sex acts to condemn them may end up aroused in his sleep![66] We can only imagine if Aquinas was speaking from experience.

While Aquinas shared his peers' assumptions about the dangers of sex and female sexuality, his views on sex still stand out since he offered justifications outside pure theology. For example, when explaining why fornication should be treated as a mortal sin, Aquinas appeals to what we might today call "family values":

> This union with a certain definite woman is called matrimony; which for the above reason is said to belong to the natural law. Since, however, the union of the sexes is directed to the common good of the whole human race, and common goods depend on the law for their determination, as stated above, it follows that this union of man and woman, which is called matrimony, is determined by some law. What this determination is for us will be stated in the Third Part of this work, where we shall treat of the sacrament of matrimony. Wherefore, since fornication is an indeterminate union of the sexes, as something incompatible with matrimony, it is opposed to the good of the child's upbringing, and consequently it is a mortal sin.[67]

So adultery is damaging because it harms the well-being of children: in the wife's case, because it casts doubt on their legitimacy, and in the husband's case, by bringing disorder into the household.[68] In sum, Aquinas was trying to prove that the sexual ethics of the Christian religion could be compatible with, and even explained by, rationality.

When it came to sex that was nonprocreative, Aquinas's objections were even stronger. By his reasoning, "unnatural vice"—a class that explicitly includes masturbation, bestiality, nongenital sex, and homosexual intercourse—was not just "contrary to right reason" like adultery and nonmarital sex, but "contrary to the natural order."[69] For that reason, "since by the unnatural vices man transgresses that which has been determined by nature with regard to the use of venereal actions, it follows that in this matter this sin is gravest of all," making it worse than even incest.[70]

It is impossible to overestimate how much Thomas Aquinas shaped Catholic thought by the time of the Catholic Reformation. At the dawn of the 20th century, Pope Pius X (r. 1903–1914) decreed that the principles of Aquinas's philosophy "are to be considered as the foundations upon which the whole science of natural and divine things is based."[71] Meanwhile modern commentators supporting traditional sexual ethics have followed Aquinas's guideposts by mingling moral conviction with empirical arguments. A strong echo of this can be heard in Pope Benedict XVIII's comments that the Church exists not only to promote faith in the true God, but also, by endorsing traditional gender roles, to "protect human beings from self-destruction."[72]

Jews in a Christian World

What about those who did not believe—or for that matter just pretended to believe—in the resurrection of Jesus Christ? As one might expect, in the Middle Ages their opinions did not count for all that much. However, the walk to the expulsion and forced mass conversion of those who insisted on following the wrong religion was a slow one. Around the end of the first millennium, in modern-day Spain and Portugal, which held the largest Muslim and Jewish communities in Western Europe, there was a degree of mutual tolerance and cosmopolitanism that would surprise a modern time traveler raised on stereotypes of the Spanish Inquisition. As the Christian kingdoms of the Iberian peninsula pushed southward and as the murderously purist spirit of the Crusades made its rage known against Muslim rulers and powerless Jews alike, this already fragile harmony broke down even on the mundane level of day-to-day existence.

In spite of the growing hostility, Jews and Muslims were legally under the protection of the monarch throughout the Middle Ages, especially as the Reconquista resulted in Portugal and the Spanish kingdoms gaining large non–Christian populations. Although they paid a tribute to the monarch, Muslims and Jews in the kingdom were a people apart in almost every sense. Muslim and Jewish communities had their own judges and were allowed to follow their own laws, especially ones regulating marriage. Yet the consequences of their inferior status loomed just overhead. Their mosques and synagogues could be converted into Christian churches at any time their Christian overlords wished. Moreover, proselytizing a Christian would mean nothing less than death if caught.[73]

Conversely, if a Muslim or Jew chose to embrace Christianity, there were plenty of worldly incentives to do so. Among them were being freed from enslavement or from any binding marital arrangements with people from their native communities. There is one case of a Muslim woman who apparently converted just to get out of an arranged marriage: she converted just 15 days after the marriage took place and tried to get her dowry from her husband.[74]

Unlike medieval Muslims, European Jews were a stateless people who were also split along borders of language and culture. Nonetheless, there were aspects of Jewish family law and ideas about sex that were surprisingly constant. Divorce was allowed, although there are no known cases of a woman being allowed to initiate a divorce. The best women could do was "demand" a divorce from the Jewish court. While it was up to the court to act on their request, they could nonetheless make the "demand" on virtually any ground.

Contraception was, in stark contrast to the prevailing Christian attitudes, tolerated among Jews, at least in the form of the *mokh,* an absorbent used by women. Rabbis like Isaiah of Trani from Italy advised that the *mokh* was permitted, as long as the intent of the man and the woman was not to stop conception but to enjoy sex without fear of a pregnancy that might be too much of a burden at the time. It was a fine distinction that reflected the lack of medieval Jewish ambivalence over sex, at least as long as it was kept without the bounds of matrimony. After all, fulfilling a wife's sexual needs was widely considered a *mizvah,* a religious obligation.[75]

As always, Jewish communities were concerned about dissolving into a largely alien world. It was not only Christian law codes that forbade marriages between Christians and Jews, but Jewish communities across Europe as well. Because of this, clandestine marriages carried out without the knowledge of the bride's and groom's families were often punished. One of the harshest penalties came from the Jewish communities of Lithuania, which mandated that the groom and any witnesses would be excommunicated, ostracized, and even hung from a post and given 40 lashes.[76]

For all of these precautions, apparently there were Christian influences seeping in. Perhaps inspired by Christian efforts to make betrothals a verbal promise rather than a sexual fulfillment, authorities in medieval Jewish communities became concerned with keeping betrothed individuals from having sex with each other. In the 13th century, Meir of Rothenburg tried to put the ax to a common custom by ruling that a bride and groom are forbidden to move in together after they become engaged.[77] Even stipulations on divorce became stricter. Jewish laws began to insist that no divorce can take place without the consent of the wife or of community leaders. Still, this does not seem to have curtailed divorces significantly, enough so that a 15th-century German rabbi Seligmann of Bing tried unsuccessfully to forbid a couple planning a divorce to become engaged even before the divorce was finalized.[78]

However, where Jewish attitudes toward sexuality differed from Christianity was in permissiveness. Advice on sex encouraged wives to appear attractive and suggested the sex act ought to bring both partners to orgasm, since this was thought to help facilitate procreation. Further, a man should feel free to have sex in positions other than the missionary position, if only to keep him from thinking of other women. The law codes of the Jews are also quite explicit in saying that while men can do whatever they want in sexual relations with a wife, the wife should never be forced to engage in any act against her will. For the Jews, sex did not just exist for procreation, but for ensuring happiness between husband and wife.[79]

The Jewish philosopher Moses Maimonides (1135–1204) was born in Spain and lived most of his life in Morocco and Egypt, but his writings still managed to have a tremendous influence on the Jews of Spain and Portugal. On sexuality he took a somewhat reactionary tack, arguing that the laws against certain forms of sex were meant to keep people from becoming obsessed with their own lusts. Acknowledging the difficulty of monogamy, Maimonides argues that the Torah chiefly seeks to ease the desire that could lead to adultery. In fact, Maimonides claims that the Torah does not even have a vocabulary for intercourse or the genitals, describing them instead through euphemism. Even circumcision had the purpose of dealing with sex: it removed an all-too-tempting erogenous zone and thus discouraged lust.[80]

Other Jewish thinkers, however, rejected Maimonides's suspicion of the body and its desires. Abraham ben David of Posquières, who wrote under the acronym Rabad, maintained that sex and the body were not inherently corrupting. All that mattered was the motive behind the sex act. The desire to commit adultery or to just satisfy one's lust, for example, irredeemably corrupted the sex act, but if it was committed out of mutual love then it could not be immoral.[81] The sect of Jewish mystics, the Kabbalists, likewise usually supported a more positive assessment of sexuality. A nameless Kabbalist in Spain wrote *Iggeret ha–Kodesh* ("Letter of Holiness"), which asserted, "If we were to say that intercourse is repulsive, then we blaspheme God who made the genitals."[82]

On the Frontier: Scandinavia and Slavic Europe

We know a great deal—relatively speaking, of course—about the sexual habits and lives of the ancient Greeks and Romans. For most of the other pre–Christian cultures of Europe, much has been lost, or at least all but irrevocably buried under the gloss of Christian interpretations. In the end we should be careful not to fail to notice possible Christian influences dripping into the text from the pens of the monks and missionaries who recorded the histories and myths of these people once beyond the frontier of Christendom. At the same time we should dodge the opposite extreme by assuming that pagan societies naturally had a much more lenient view of sex.

For instance, there are no secular medieval laws against homosexuality before or after Christianization in any medieval Scandinavian country except for one 12th-century Norwegian law that mandated that two men who indulged in "the pleasures of the flesh together" should be branded outlaws and lose their property.[83] This law did not last, and other denouncements of homosexual activity existed only in Scandinavian canon law and penitentials. Even so, for medieval Scandinavia the idea of men submitting sexually to other men was a serious business.

Under Icelandic law, to simply insult another man by calling him a *ragr, strodinn,* or *sordinn*—all words that carried the connotation of effeminacy and having been penetrated sexually by another man—could lead to the insulter being branded an outlaw, one of the highest possible penalties. Even more dramatically, the insulted party had every right to kill the offender, a privilege that was usually granted only to the family of someone who was raped or murdered, or a husband whose wife had been seduced by another man. In a similar vein was a 13th-century Swedish law that ordered a man to fight any man who challenged his masculinity. If the insulted party backed down, then "he will become what he has been called" and lost the right to be a witness or swear an oath.[84] A Norwegian law punished with outlaw status anyone who accused a man of being "a woman every ninth night" or having given birth to a child. Also on the list of forbidden insults was "bitch," "mare," any other term for a female animal, and *sannsorğinn,* a succinct term that meant "demonstrably fucked."[85] Why these were fighting—killing, even—words is clear: medieval Scandinavian culture saw effeminacy and sexual passivity in men as inexorably linked.

Promiscuous couples, however, fell under legal scrutiny. Under the *Grágás,* an Icelandic law code compiled in 1117 and 1118 that stayed in force until the Icelandic Republic was annexed by Norway in 1264, a man who slept with any woman who was not his wife not only had to pay a fine to her "law-warden" but could wind up being branded a minor outlaw, a *fjorbaugsgaror.* This was his fate if he was lucky; any man had the right to kill a man caught in a compromising position with his wife, daughter, or any female relative.[86] If the man's lover happened to die giving birth to a love child, then the man became a full-fledged outlaw, meaning he was outside the protection of the law and anyone could harm or even kill him. A family even had every right to torture a pregnant relation who refused to surrender the identity of the father; even if she did comply, she might lose the right to inherit from her parents.[87] At least the killing of the wife for adultery was still forbidden.

In the Icelandic Republic, the concept of "for richer or for poorer" was worthless. Spousal poverty was one of the approved reasons for seeking a divorce, along with one spouse giving the other "large wounds," refusing to have sex, or allowing poor relations to sponge off the other spouse's money. Even with an approved divorce, however, at times a bishop's express permission was needed for another marriage. By the 13th century divorce was no longer legal in Scandinavia, which also became the case in Iceland once it fell under the jurisdiction of Norway.[88]

The rest of Scandinavia also tended to be harsher when it came to the matter of adultery. An adulterous wife's brother, father, son, stepson, and male in-laws all had the right to murder her lover in Norway.[89] Otherwise, a man guilty of sleeping with someone's wife was deemed an outlaw and denied Christian burial.[90] As for the unfaithful wives themselves, they could lose any property received in the marriage. Straying husbands, in contrast, simply had to pay a small fine to their wife for each offense (like a modern swear jar).[91] However, in Sweden and Denmark, a man could not even commit adultery, legally speaking; he could only be guilty of the minor crime of fornication and have to pay a fine to his mistress and her family. Also in those countries, adulterous women could be killed along with their lovers if caught in the act, exiled, mutilated, or have their property sequestered.[92]

How many of these laws were touched with heavy Christian influences is tricky, if not impossible, to determine. So is the case with the Slavic world since, as Eve Levin points out, "virtually all sources of information are of later Christian origin," causing past scholars to see the pagan Slavs as living in either a society of sexual anarchy or a veritable matriarchy.[93] While frank and open celebrations of sex and its role in life were part of Slavic pagan religion,[94] there are hints, albeit transmitted through Christian observers, that sexual misbehavior could be brutally punished. The German missionary Thietmar of Merseburg claimed that in recently Christianized Poland, men who even tried to seduce a married woman could have a nail driven through their scrotum and be given the choice of either being killed or cutting off that part of their body themselves.[95] This may be why at least one observer, a Spanish Jew named Ibrahim ibn Jakub sent to central Europe as an ambassador, claimed rather implausibly that wives never committed adultery. At the same time, he noted that it was acceptable for an unmarried woman to have a lover, and that a bride being a virgin was actually considered a *negative* sign, indicating to the groom that there was something wrong with his new wife.[96]

Violent retaliation for adultery was apparently not the norm among most Slavic societies, the exception being the kingdom of Serbia, where a husband had the right to cut off his wife's nose and one ear before throwing her out of the house.[97] Less gruesome was the solution in Russia under the 11th-century law code of Yaroslav, Grand Prince of Kiev: a woman could be exiled to a convent until her "clan redeem[ed] her."[98] Otherwise in the Orthodox Slavic kingdoms, a husband with an adulterous wife was encouraged, especially if he was a priest, to divorce her—an offer that was not extended to the wife with an adulterous husband.[99] However, the makers of canon law did give some thought to wives. For instance, one Slavic canon law tried to bar husbands from marrying their lovers after a divorce,[100] while others allowed a woman to seek a divorce if her husband was a persistent and unsubtle adulterer, if he was guilty of treason or another great crime, or if he was abusive.[101] On the other side of the coin, in Russia at least, canon law strongly discouraged divorced women from ever remarrying, a requirement that sprang from the assumption that any divorced woman must have been an adulterer.[102]

Remarriage was even more of an issue in Slavic canon law. Like the Byzantine Churches before them, the Slavic Orthodox Churches frowned on remarriage, especially fourth or fifth marriages. By the 16th century, the Russian Orthodox Church levied fines on people who remarried, which increased depending on how many marriages they had racked up.[103]

Divorce or the annulment of marriage does not seem to have been as simple a matter in Poland at the time. The priest and diplomat Jan Długosz (1415–1480), who is best known for his *Annales seu cronici incliti regni Poloniae* (Annals of the Kingdom of Poland), claimed that Gryfina, the wife of Leszek the Black, Duke of Sieradz (d. 1288), had declared her intent to dissolve her marriage by simply walking around with her head uncovered, although the dejected spouses were eventually reconciled.[104] All in all, though, Poland followed the standard Catholic attitude toward divorce and annulments: having none of it, unless someone happened to be wealthy and powerful enough to be able to bend the rules or was too poor and insignificant to appear on the radar.[105]

The Scandinavian and Slavic kingdoms provide interesting, if also occasionally frustrating due to the uncertain lines between pagan and Christian practice and custom, examples of societies that came to the party late. The way sex was controlled in both regions was, without a doubt, deeply influenced by Catholic and Orthodox models. At the same time, the diversity of the laws alone hints that native customs were far from obliterated by the Church.

Sex and (Imagined) Love

Perhaps the best proof we have that many people failed to follow the Church's prescriptions for correct and righteous living during the medieval era comes from the glimpses we have of what they wrote and read. Latin stayed strong as the language of philosophy, science, diplomacy, and the Church, but Latin's vernacular offspring began to surface, showing signs of becoming the national literatures of Europe. In the era of Geoffrey Chaucer, Petrarch, and Dante there are more works not dedicated to legendary battles or mythological and biblical episodes; instead, from Portugal to Germany, we find writers who are interested in their own times and places. Neither are they reluctant to portray cowardly, hypocritical noblemen and priests with ostentatious sex lives.

Even women and men getting away with egregious adultery—and sometimes being justified, or at least not having the righteous judgment of the author dumped on them—was an open subject for fun. The author of a popular 12th-century treatise on love, Andreas

Coppelinus, claimed that love was best enjoyed outside of marriage: "We declare and hold as firmly established that love cannot exert its powers between two people who are married to each other. For lovers give each other everything freely, under no compulsion of necessity, but married people are in duty bound to give in to each others' desires and deny themselves to each other in nothing."[106] It hardly needs explanation why such an attitude would be appealing among the aristocrats of Europe, whose marriages were usually arranged for them and who were taught that marriage was an inescapable institution.

The first *troubadour* was Duke William IX of Aquitaine (r. 1071–1086), who is probably better known as the grandfather of Eleanor of Aquitaine. Ruling over a region of southern France that was known for being more cultured than its northern neighbors, William IX easily cultivated the reputation of a learned *bon vivant* who wrote poems not only about the women he had seduced, but also the ideal woman whom he could only love from afar. But William IX should speak for himself:

> If she chooses to give her love to me
> I will take it with gratitude
> with discretion and with courtesy,
> to speak and act for her pleasure,
> to have her hold me dear
> and lift her praises high.
> I do not dare send a messenger,
> I fear she would hate to be revealed;
> nor can I go myself, to fail her,
> or declare my love,
> but she must decide what is best,
> since she knows by her I'm healed.[107]

In another poem, William IX sums up the new ethos of love declaring his love and devotion for a woman he had never seen.[108]

It was not long before new generations of poets writing in Occitan, the language of Provence, agreed enthusiastically with William IX. Jaufre Rubel (d. 1147) from Aquitaine found distant, idealized love comparable to an in-the-flesh lover: "I know no nobler or better love in any direction, either near nor afar."[109] However, courtly love was clearly not all fantasy. The poet Macabru in the 13th century alleged that adultery was rampant among the nobles of his day and thought courtly love a more wholesome alternative. Macabru went on to recommend courtly love not only for moral reasons but for the utilitarian reason that it really will make people happier.[110] In a class and society where marriages were usually arranged and where divorce was not an option, Macabru had a point.

The wildly popular and oft-repeated story of Tristan and Iseult exemplified the triumph of this form of love advertised by Macabru. The action of the classic version of the tale has Tristan run off with Iseult, the wife of his uncle, King Marc. Hiding in the woods, Tristan places a sword between the two of them as a symbolic guarantee that they will not have sex. Partially naked, they sleep together, kept apart only by the sword. When Marc finds them, he is persuaded that they are not really guilty of adultery, because they clearly did not have sex; thus, despite his original intent to kill them both he leaves them alone. When Tristan wakes up and realizes Marc was there, he is horrified and wakes up Iseult to flee. Marc still has the old idea that sex and love are inexorable, believing that the pair should be naked and have no sword between them if they were really lovers. However, for Iseut and Tristan, there can exist an erotic love between a man and a woman that is totally independent of sex. This particular conceit had such an appeal that it inspired a term, *épreuve,* for the wall of blankets and pillows that would be placed between a knight and his lady as a symbol of their chaste separation.

Literary idealism notwithstanding, physical consummation was not always, or maybe even often, precluded from a courtly relationship. Bernant de Ventadorn (ca. 1130–ca. 1190) was being one of the subtle ones when he wrote: "Noble lady, I ask of you nothing but that you should accept me as your servant, for I will serve you as I would a noble lord, whatever reward may come to me."[111] A female *troubadour,* Azalais de Porcairages, danced around the limits—and possibilities—of courtly love:

> Handsome friend, so kind,
> I will always pledge myself to you
> as long as you do not ask for something indecent.
> I put myself into your care.
> you swore to me an oath,
> now don't ask me to do a missdeed.[112]

In another anonymous poem written from the perspective of a woman, a lady chastises her knight for "Fretting more than I / about my reputation" and so curtailing his visits to her.[113] Maybe the lady is being too harsh on the knight, since the dangers of such a lifestyle were all too vividly illustrated by the legendary story of the Catalan *troubadour* Guillem de Cabestan, who is said to have joined the household of a Raimon de Rossillon and charmed his wife. Driven to a jealous rampage, Raimon kills Guillem, cuts his heart out, and roasts and feeds it to his wife before killing her, too.[114]

Dark warnings aside, it does seem as if *troubadour* poetry and the culture of courtly love provided an important pressure valve. Nathaniel Smith described chivalric poetry as the medieval prototype of modern role playing; it was a "word game" where the fun was in flouting social convention and going beyond the parameters of day-to-day life without consequences.[115] Female *troubadours* were not kept out of the game, nor were they reluctant to write in the explicit language of sexual attraction. One such woman from Provence, Tibors (b. ca. 1130), praises an attractive man who has freed her from desire since becoming her "courtly lover."[116] Another poem with female authorship by the Countess of Dia (b. ca. 1140) laments that her knightly lover has betrayed her because he refuses to lie down with her.[117]

The testimony given by a nobleman from Styria in modern-day Austria gives a rather disturbing perspective on the game. In the *Service of Ladies,* which may or may not have had at least a speck of truth in it, Ulrich von Liechtenstein describes his increasingly obsessive efforts to win some token of affection from an apathetic and unnamed noblewoman. When he injures his finger in a joust, he sends a messenger to tell her he suffered the wound in her name, but she later becomes upset and claims that she misunderstood the messenger. She thought that the finger was amputated, not just badly wounded. To make up for this appalling lack of commitment, Ulrich, in a van Gogh-esque gesture, lops off the offending finger and sends it to her. Since she is still nonplussed, Ulrich then tries to prove himself by riding around Bohemia dressed as a woman.

After that humiliating gender-bending gesture, the lady relents by agreeing to let him into her room with a warning: "If some people ever knew / of this, my honor would disappear." She then has her handmaidens drop the makeshift platform being used to raise him to her bedroom and forces him to sit outside in the freezing night dressed only in the rags of a leper. Something eventually happens that outrages Ulrich so much he finally breaks free from this abusive relationship, but unfortunately for us he refuses to relate what it was. True or not, Ulrich's story shows just how underscored with sexual tension courtly love could be.[118]

Next to the explosion of the popularity of courtly love were more cynical explorations, like medieval treatises that gave advice on how where, how, and when to seduce women. The anonymously written Le Clef du Amour ("Key to Love") talks about the merits of good hygiene, how to discreetly make oneself cry using an onion, and how to win at least one kiss. To encourage young noblemen who might be put off by blue-blooded beauties, it adds the more noble a woman the more likely she is to do "what you and Nature want her to,"[119] although the writer later goes on to warn men about the risks that come with trying to play footsie.[120] The equivalent for female readers, books like Robert de Blois's *Le Chastoiement des Dames* (*Advice for Ladies*), instead caution women to perpetually be on guard. They should never allow their breasts to be "felt, fondled, or caressed" and should always keep in mind "a kiss can lead to so much more."[121]

In the court of the English king Henry II (r. 1154–1189), Marie de France entertained her noble audience with poems about love and desire. Sometimes in Marie's poems adultery is ruthlessly punished. In her lay *Bisclavret,* the titular character is a werewolf who becomes trapped in his nonhuman form due to his wife's meddling. With her husband missing, she marries a knight. Later, when her path crosses with Bisclavret, he, still in wolf form, mutilates her face. In other lays, however, adultery is justified by a woman having a cruel husband who was forced on her, as in *Yonec,* or, as told in *Guigemar,* a marriage arranged to an elderly man.

Even the usually stodgy culture of the Byzantine Empire experienced a revival of interest in romantic and erotic literature.[122] A fad for novels based on the Greek and Latin novels of antiquity erupted in 12th-century Byzantium, but unfortunately only four such texts survive. All of them take place in a vague Greek past that is simultaneously historical and legendary, blurring the lines between the backdrops of classical mythology and the Hellenistic era, and are more explicit than the Byzantine writings that have come before. In the novels, characters in medieval Greek literature have sex outside of marriage for the very first time.[123] In one of them, the hero Kallimachos has kinky foreplay in a bath, leading up to full-on sex on the edge of the water.[124] Beyond the novels, mythological character studies by the Byzantine scholar Basilaces in the same era are explicitly erotic, choosing Danae, one of Zeus's lovers, and Pasiphae, who made love to a bull and gave birth to the Minotaur, as his subjects.[125]

An entire genre of medieval poetry written in northern Portugal using the Galician language was the *cantiga de amigo* ("song about a boyfriend"). Drawing on the timeless topic of a young woman meeting or waiting to meet with a young man, the *canitgas* danced around the uneasiness between love, lust, and social convention. One such poem, spoken in the voice of a concerned mother, reads:

> Lovely daughter, look what I'm telling you: / Do not talk with your boyfriend / Without me, o lovely daughter. / And, daughter, if you want

my love, / I ask you that you never talk with him / Without me, o lovely daughter.[126]

In the Spanish kingdom of Castile, King Alfonso X (r. 1252–1284) himself wrote or co-authored a number of spicy poems in Galician, belonging to a genre called the *cantigas d'escarnio e maldicer* ("songs of mockery and vilification"). Despite being written by a king who aspired to become the Holy Roman Emperor, this one poem mingles blasphemy with frank expressions of lust:

> The other day I went to lay a hand on a courtesan's cunt. She said to me: "Take that away, thief! This is not the [time to dirty me, during] Our Lord's passion. Let me be, sinner, as undeserving as I have been of him." [...] Lord, bless you, who make me suffer this martyrdom on your account![127]

One of the most explicit and thorough discussions of love and the sex drive to come out of the Iberian peninsula was Juan Ruiz's (1283–ca. 1350) *Libro de buen amor* ("Book of Good Love"). Possibly the work is semi-autobiographical, in which case the mostly mysterious author was an archbishop who was shipped off to prison because he had an affair with a woman. Even if the book's account was much more fictional than not, the author does seem to have some first-hand knowledge: "An incandescent coal indeed is passion's fierce desire; the more you try to blow it out the hotter burns its fire."[128]

First the book has an account of an unnamed archbishop (possibly but not certainly the author himself) who has had a number of encounters of women. Then there is the story of "Sir Melon," who works tirelessly to seduce "Lady Sloe." Within the book the goddess Venus herself tells Sir Melon that "Not modesty, but fear and shame, restrain her when she must" and to "live your little hour of life before you join the dust."[129] An old woman who helps Lady Sloe and Sir Melon finally meet to consummate their relationship also expresses a rationale that may have been very common in real life: "You burn for him, he burns for you, in that no sin appears"[130] since the church can pardon any wrongdoing and marry them afterwards. It does not seem that this sat well with everyone, realistic or not. In a crude display of medieval censorship, the episode where Lady Sloe and Sir Melon finally meet in private has been slashed out of every surviving manuscript of the book.

Still, probably nothing better reflects the blunt nature of medieval literature than the great anthologies of the era, Giovanni Boccaccio's (1313–1375) *Decameron* and Chaucer's *Canterbury Tales*.

In the "Fifth Day," Boccaccio's noble-born storytellers, hiding in a villa outside Florence from the Black Death, relate stories about lovers able to defy their families or arranged spouses, in several cases barely escaping death, but living happily and given the chance to sanctify their earlier premarital escapades by being allowed to marry. More bawdy is Chaucer, who in the *Miller's Tale* has a student getting away with sleeping with his landlord's sexy wife; two students who get revenge on a miller in the *Reeve's Tale* by seducing the miller's wife and daughter; and a woman who is granted the ability to convince her husband that she is not cheating on him, even when she is caught right in the act in the *Merchant's Tale*.

Most jarring to stereotypes about the medieval era is, years before printing presses across Europe were hot with attacks on the corruption of the papacy, how irreverent about religion this literature can be. To start with, an anonymous Welsh poem, "The Nun," has a speaker who tries, apparently with success, to seduce a nun, rationalizing that even God and the saints can "pardon love."[131]

The bawdy poets of Provence were every bit as willing to delve into the sex lives of clerics. The poem *De Bouener d' Abeville* ("Butcher of Abbeville") features as the butt of its joke a corrupt, selfish priest who has a live-in mistress. The titular butcher humiliates the priest by seducing her. Another Occitan poem, *Do Prestre ki Abevete* ("The Priest who Peaked"), offers an interesting twist on the proverbial Emperor's New Clothes tale by telling the story of a priest who has anal sex with a peasant's wife before the peasant's very eyes. He still manages to convince the none-too-bright fellow that he is not seeing any sex taking place at all.[132]

The most merciless critic of the clergy may very well be Boccaccio himself. The second story of the *Decameron* manages to be both a story of Christian conversion and an attack on the Church's hierarchy. A Jewish merchant discovers that the clergy at Rome is so mired in immorality and corruption that only divine favor could explain why Christianity continues to thrive. In the fourth story of the first day, a monk caught having sex escapes punishment by arranging to have his abbot seduced by the same woman. The second story of the ninth day echoes the same theme: a nun caught with her lover manages to preempt any action by the abbess when she accidentally discovers that the abbess herself has been having nightly trysts with a priest. The most potent combination of the erotic and anticlerical sentiment, though, must be the first story of the third day, where a man named Maesetto pretends to be deaf and dumb to secure work as a gardener in a convent, and ends up serving another job function as the nuns' chief source of recreation.

Of course, it should be added that not all medieval literature was so thoroughly infused with raunchy themes and that medieval writers often did censor themselves at times. Near the end of his life something compelled Chaucer to write a pious retraction, apologizing for the "enditynges of Worldly vanitees" in all his past work. By the same token, it should be remembered that these stories were read presumably by an audience interested in stories and jokes that reflected their lives and experiences, which were from most indications not dominated by the Church's prescriptions for proper living.

Civilization's Sewer

> Prostitutes were everywhere in the streets and neighborhoods of [Paris], seeking to drag passing clerics by force into their brothels. If the clerics refused to enter, they immediately shouted after them, "Sodomite!" In one and the same building, there might be a school upstairs and a brothel downstairs. While in the upper part, the masters taught their pupils, in the lower part the prostitutes plied their nefarious trade. In one part, the prostitutes quarreled with each other and their pimps; in the other part the scholars argued on scholarly matters.[133]

This was a snapshot of 13th-century Parisian life, provided by the bishop Jacques de Vitry. Even though by the 14th century many local authorities had segregated prostitutes to certain streets or outside the town or city walls, prostitution remained a mundane part of life throughout the Middle Ages. Market days and festivals in villages would be joined by bands of prostitutes who traveled the countryside,[134] while towns and cities across Europe provided municipal brothels to the public. The legacy left by such official sanctions of the world's oldest occupation lingers on from the blunt and unapologetic names once used; for example, Grape Street and Copice Alley in London were once Gropecunt Lane and Codpiece Alley.[135]

In the footsteps of Augustine, Thomas Aquinas described prostitution in practical terms: "The prostitute in society is like the sewer in a palace. If you take away the sewer, the whole palace will be contaminated."[136] This was not just philosophical rhetoric; public brothels were meant to be a check on rowdy, lustful young men. Ideally (but not often in reality), married men, as well as priests and Jews, were barred from entering a public brothel.[137] The laws in Munich spelled out why: the city's official brothel existed to prevent "evil to wives and virgins."[138] The municipal brothel in Florence had another but similar *raison d'etre:* to give bachelors an alternative to sodomy.[139]

Despite being defenders of social order, prostitutes were, like today, seen as a "nuisance" to their neighbors and magnets for sketchy activities. There are instances of prostitutes and brothel keepers being accused of running gambling rings or harboring thieves.[140] At the same time, in the Middle Ages there were no particular shame attached to being a john, as men from all walks of life often openly visited the local brothel. Jacques Rossiaud found in records that even 20 percent of the visitors to a brothel in Dijon in the 14th century were clerics.[141] Nor did the Dijon brothel usually turn them and married men away, in spite of regulations insisting that they do so, as long as they showed some discretion.[142]

Not only were clerics consumers, but they also did not shy away from dipping their toes in the business. Sometimes brothels were run on property rented out or subleased from bishops and monasteries. One blatant example were the "stewes" (bathhouses) owned by the Bishop of Winchester in Southwark, then London's red-light district. The bishop's stewes were such a fixture of London life that a series of city ordinances dealt with them specifically.[143] When Queen Giovanna I of Naples sold the city of Avignon to the papacy, the city brothel, known as "the Abbey," continued to be maintained. The only real change was that the prostitutes were required to become regular church-goers, keep up their prayer hours, and vow to kick out johns who were heretics.[144]

For all that, prostitution had become a tightly regulated business. The activities of prostitutes not working for an "official" brothel were severely curtailed, although judging from records this did not stop the spread of pimps, streetwalkers, women who prostituted themselves sporadically, and independent brothels.[145] Meanwhile the municipal brothels were closely supervised by officials tasked with the specific duty. Ordinances were designed to protect prostitutes from being abused or exploited by brothel owners and their clients, as well as to impose some sort of propriety. An example of the sorts of rules owners of brothels or "stewes" and prostitutes had to follow comes from 12th-century London: no brothels were to be open on holy days or during festivals; no pregnant women, married women, or nuns could be hired; no woman was to take money unless she had been with her client all night; no woman was to be kept from quitting; there was to be no open soliciting; no food or alcohol were to be served; and all prostitutes were to receive regular health checks.

By the same token, prostitutes by the 14th century were often required to wear distinctive clothing or emblems and were often barred from traveling to "respectable" areas.[146] The "Abbey" of Avignon required its employees to wear a red knot over the left shoulder; failure to do so would mean being marched through the streets and a public beating or exile for repeat offenders. Similarly, the prostitutes of Toulouse could be spotted wearing white cloaks. In Leipzig, they had to wear yellow cloaks trimmed with blue. The government of Vienna had the mandated fashion of a yellow handkerchief worn over the shoulder. Zurich and Bern demanded red caps and Milan insisted on clothing made from black wool.[147] Fifteenth-century Stockholm was content just barring prostitutes from wearing gold and silver jewelry or pricy furs, to keep them from being confused with "honorable" women.[148]

Even with these anxieties over prostitutes going about town unrecognized, medieval governments' attitudes toward prostitution were decidedly pragmatic, treating prostitutes like a civic resource. In 1414, after the King of Hungary and Holy Roman Emperor Sigismund (r. 1387–1437) stopped at Bern, the city authorities opened the brothels to the emperor's court free of charge.[149] However, it seems medieval prostitutes were far from a passive work force. When the city council of Toulouse changed the law to force prostitutes to wear a gaudy uniform made from a white scarf and ribbons, they petitioned King Charles VI (r. 1388–1420), who happened to be visiting the city, to veto the new law. The king did so, but bands of citizens, driven to rage at the idea that prostitutes might be going around without any telltale emblems, began to harass them. In retaliation, the prostitutes of the city organized a city-wide strike. Although the king placed the prostitutes of Toulouse under royal protection, the unrest eventually drove the prostitutes to move to a new quarter of the city. Luckily the local university agreed to donate a building to serve as a new brothel.[150]

As the angry citizens of Toulouse helpfully proved, not everyone was warm to the idea of having prostitutes around. A few towns outright exiled prostitutes and brothel keepers, often acting on pious fears excited by a bad harvest, a fire-breathing preacher, or a plague.[151] The first country-wide attempt to curb prostitution in the Middle Ages came from Alfonso IX of Castile (r. 1188–1230), whose law code sought to protect wives and slaves from being forced into prostitution, but the laws also confiscated the property of landlords who rented rooms to prostitutes. Pimps were flogged for a first offense or sent to the galleys for repeat offenses. Women assisting pimps were publicly whipped.[152] By far the most drastic measures, however, came from "Saint" Louis IX of France (r. 1226–1270), who in 1254 ordered that all prostitutes be expelled from France and all their property, even their clothing, confiscated. It was a step too far, and even the unusually pious Louis rescinded the order two years later, satisfying himself with commanding that prostitutes across the kingdom be kept out of good neighborhoods and as far away as possible from churches and monastic houses. However, a rush of righteousness from joining the Second Crusade in 1269 drove Louis to again exile prostitutes, as well as to lay down strict laws against blasphemy, gambling, and usury.[153] Needless to say, the ordinances proved almost impossible to enforce and apparently inspired more ridicule than action.[154]

As for male prostitution, there probably is no explanation needed as to why evidence of it becomes much more scarce after antiquity. John Boswell describes a medieval manuscript that mentions all-male brothels in Sens, Chartres, Orléans, and Paris and states that their number one employment requirement was large genitals, implying that not all men in the market for male prostitutes were after passive partners for other men.[155] Florence was home to a sizable number of young male prostitutes, some of whom had their own pimps.[156] Fourteenth-century trial records in London describe the case of John Rykener, a cross-dressing male prostitute picked up from the streets and accused of "detestable, unmentionable, and ignominious vice." Rykener confessed that he had both women and men as his customers, with priests as the most well paying.[157] Beyond being a medieval example of a transvestite, John Rykener is a bizarre case. If records of men soliciting male prostitutes from the Middle Ages are rare, known instances of women procuring sexual services from men, or from women for that matter, are more or less nonexistent.

While much is known about female prostitution in the Middle Ages, the references to male prostitution in literature and trial records are brief. Male brothels may have existed in France, Italy, and even elsewhere in Europe in the Later Middle Ages, but we do not really know how they operated or what dangers they faced. However, there is much that can be found in records and in between the lines about one of the most notorious renegades of the medieval world, the sodomites.

Invasion of the Sodomites

> Truly, this vice is never to be compared with any other vice because it surpasses the enormity of all vices. Indeed, this vice is the death of bodies, the destruction of souls. It pollutes the flesh; it extinguishes the light of the mind. It evicts the Holy Spirit from the temple of the human heart; it introduces the devil who incites to lust. It casts into error; it completely removes the truth from the mind that has been deceived. It prepares snares for those entering; it shuts up those who fall into the pit so they cannot get out. It opens hell; it closes the door of heaven. It makes a citizen of the heavenly Jerusalem into an heir of infernal Babylon. It makes of the star of heaven the stubble of eternal fire; it cuts off a member of the Church and casts it into the consuming fire of boiling Gehenna. This vice tries to overturn the walls of the heavenly homeland and is busy repairing the renewed bulwarks of Sodom. For it is this which violates sobriety, kills modesty, strangles chastity, and butchers irreparable virginity with the dagger of unclean contagion. It defiles everything, stains everything, pollutes everything. And as for itself, it permits nothing pure, nothing clean, nothing other than filth.[158]

This is just the opening salvo to one section of Peter Damian's *Book of Gomorrah,* a thunderous demand for action against homosexuality among the clergy. Damian was far from the only one in the High Middle Ages to find that sex between members of the same sex was an exceptionally nasty sin, too awful to even speak about except in the vaguest of terms. Like prostitutes, sodomites ran afoul of the push for conformity and sanctity in the High and Later Middle Ages.

Words like "sodomy" and "sodomite" did have multiple meanings to medieval writers and were used to refer to sex between a man and a woman that was not "natural," not just intercourse among the same sex.[159] Still, as Michael Rocke reminds us, that is no reason not to believe that medieval people "might well have recognized that a man's tastes or habits inclined him toward one sex or the other"[160] or to overlook how sodomy was used to refer specifically to same-sex relations. The philosopher Peter of Abano (1280–ca. 1320) said as much in his commentary to *Problemata,* a treatise wrongly attributed to Aristotle. Remarking on the author of *Problemata*'s assertion that a man's desire to have sex with other men is driven either by exposure to that kind of sex when young or by a bodily deformity, Peter adds his argument that both "active" and "passive" sodomites share the same "monstrosity and disorder happening by birth."

In a similar vein, the canonist Paul of Hungary wrote a guidebook on penance, the *Summa,* which, according to the theologian Mark Jordan, "gives the sin against nature more attention than the capital sins of vainglory, anger, envy, sloth, and gluttony combined."[161] Although generally he defines sodomy as any approach to sexual pleasure that defies procreation, Paul writes about a certain class of sodomites in medical terms. According to Jordan, "Sodomites seem to have a disordered reproductive desire, correlated with a dysfunction of the liver. They are 'enervated' because they exhibit a physiological susceptibility associated with women—here it becomes clear that Paul is thinking of male Sodomites."[162] Likewise, William of Saliceto thought that lesbianism was the result of uterine prolapse or an enlarged clitoris.[163] Yet even the idea that the desire to be intimate with one's own sex could be something innate or caused by illness hardly inspired compassion or even pity. Instead, to be a sodomite was more than just being like a habitual glutton and adulterer; it was something abnormal, deformed, and, above all, beyond redemption.

The danger of sodomy—including how it could be used to denote a very specific class of sinner and just how pervasive this particular sin could be—comes across in Robert of Flamborough's guidebook on hearing confessions. He warns priests to never talk openly about sodomy, unless they are speaking with someone they know has a track record of desiring and being with women. It was especially crucial not to discuss the ways sodomites seek each other out or mention that they have their own particular places to meet and their own methods for identifying each other.[164]

The city of Sodom was not the only reference point that could point toward what we now might call homosexuality. There was also one bit of slang lifted from Greek mythology. The poet Hildebert of Lavardin (ca. 1055–1133) denounced the "countless Ganymedes" who "tend countless hearths" while "Juno [goddess of marriage] grieves to have lost the duty she used to claim."[165] Another poem actually has Ganymede dive into a debate with Helen. The argument is launched when Helen tries to seduce Ganymede, whose total apathy toward her charms infuriates her. Helen lists a number of objections to sodomy that may have come from a Stoic philosopher in antiquity or a medieval canonist about the importance of procreation and the unnaturalness of any sex that does not take place between women and men. Ganymede calmly answers that he does not care about reproducing, only his pleasure, and asks why men should have to imitate animals (the idea that animals never act homosexually was still taken for granted). Nonetheless, Reason itself decides against Ganymede, who winds up repenting and marrying Helen.

Obeying the lessons from such writers, both religious and civil authorities had escalated the war against sodomy by the 12th century. The Council of Nalbus in the Kingdom of Jerusalem decreed that any man caught in the act of sodomy would be burned alive; so would his male partner, unless it could be shown he tried to fight off his would-be lover and was willing to repent. Synods across France and Germany clarified that homosexuality was a sin that must be dealt with harshly, culminating in 1279 with a statute among the Order of Cistercians to build prisons in abbeys to hold sodomites along with thieves, arsonists, forgers, and killers.[166] In sharp contrast to the relative leniency of earlier penitential writers, Paul of Hungary called for execution, exile, or lifelong penance and imprisonment in a monastery for these miscreants.[167]

Even in Scandinavia, where civil laws against sodomy were almost nonexistent, the rhetoric of the Church was vicious. The *Icelandic Homily Book* (ca. 1200) includes a sermon stating that among grave sins are "those appalling secret sins perpetrated by men who respect men no more than women." The penitential of the Icelandic bishop Thorlákr Thorhallson of Skaholt (ca. 1178–1193) demanded that women guilty of lesbian acts be flogged, the same punishment asked of men who confessed to adultery or bestiality. Another canonist in France,

VI Medieval Rigidness

William of Auvergne (ca. 1180–1249), described sodomy as the "unmentionable vice" which disgusts even Satan and linked it with sacrilege and murder.[168] Bernandino of Siena cut straight to the chase when he bellowed in a sermon, "To the fire! They are all sodomites! And you are in mortal sin if you seek to help them."[169]

Sodomy was such a strike against God's order that it became associated with heresy, even in everyday language. A heretical sect in northern Italy and southern France, known as the Cathars or the Bulgari (because the heresy was imported from Bulgaria), was often accused of needing to resort to homosexual sex because they rejected marriage and procreation as perpetuating a material world devised by Satan. Over time in Germany *Ketzer* became slang for both heretic and sodomite, while in French *bougre,* which eventually gave English the familiar term "bugger," could also refer to either.[170] One French man in the 18th century was burned alive on the basis of a regional law dating from 1272 condemning anyone of *bougrerie.* Ostensibly he was killed for sodomy, but the date of the law suggests that it was instead intended to persecute Cathars. Voltaire cynically mentioned the case in his *Dictionnaire philosophique* (1764), writing that a man was burned because of *une équivoque* (an ambiguity).[171] On the other side of the aisle, the heretical English sect, the Lollards, scored points by accusing orthodox priests of clandestine homosexuality.

Voices from the Middle Ages tended not to have much tolerance for sodomy, even when they were not explicitly calling for fires to be lit. Andreas Capellanus went out of his way to make the point that love can exist only between people of the opposite sexes: "Between two males or between two females it can claim no place, for two persons of the same sex are in no way fitted to reciprocate each other's love or to practice its natural acts. Love blushes to embrace what nature denies."[172] Hildegard of Bingen denounced sex between women in much stronger terms:

> And a woman who takes up devilish ways and plays a male role in coupling with another woman is most vile in my sight, and so is she who subjects herself to such a one in this evil deed. For they should have been ashamed of their passion, and instead they impudently usurped a right that was not theirs. And, having put themselves into alien ways, they are to me transformed and contemptible.[173]

The 13th-century philosopher Roger Bacon, offering a utilitarian objection to sodomy, argued that sodomites as well as "fornicators" should be exiled from towns and cities or else they would distract otherwise perfectly good men from getting married.[174]

Nonetheless, there were writers who did not treat homosexuality with total loathing. The tone of the bishop Etienne de Fougères, who wrote the *Livre de maniers* ("Book of Manners"), is just as dismissive as Hildegard of Bingen, but also more satirical:

> These ladies have made up a game: / with two bits of nonsense they make nothing; / they bang coffin against coffin, / without a poker stir up their fire. / They don't play at "poke in the paunch," / but join shield to shield without a lance. / They have no concern for a beam in their scales, / nor a handle in their mold. / Out of water they fish for turbot / and they have no need for a rod. / They don't bother with a pestle in their mortar / nor a fulcrum for their seesaw.[175]

It should be noted, though, that while the bishop was certainly aware of the existence of women who loved women, he was astonishingly unimaginative when it came to the logistics of lesbian sex.

As for sympathetic talk of sodomites, this is much more rare, but there is perhaps one unexpected medieval voice that defied the conventional wisdom in some ways: the poet Dante Aligheri (1265–1321). Even though in Dante's vision of Hell sodomites are guilty of "despising nature" and must forever travel a burning desert reminiscent of the final fate of Sodom and Gomorrah, Dante personally greets the suffering sodomites with understanding and respect, even admiration. Among their number is his mentor, the poet Brunetto Latini, whom Dante hails as "radiance among men." Brunetto introduces his fellow damned as "great men of letters, scholars of renown."[176] Next Dante and his guide Virgil are greeted by another group of sodomites, who are all celebrated Florentine statesmen and generals. Virgil tells Dante that they must be courteous and if it were not for the dangerous burning plain, then by rights they should be rushing toward them instead of the other way around. "The view would seem to be taken that most homosexuals are exceptional men rather than deranged or depraved," literary scholar Joseph Pequigney suggests.[177] The sodomites may still be condemned by divine law, but they are also not the reprehensible monsters of Peter Damian.

Curiously sodomites appear again in Dante's Purgatory, occupying the same terrace, that of the lustful, as those of opposite sexes who committed the sin of lust together. The sodomites clearly distinguish themselves by shouting, "Sodom and Gomorrah!"[178] There the lustful, including the sodomites, walk around the mountain of Purgatory through a perpetual wall of purifying fire. When one of the sodomites describes his sin, he associates it with no less a personage than Julius Caesar. Why were sodomites condemned to Hell in the *Inferno* but allowed a shot at salvation in the *Purgatorio*? Pequigney contends that Dante's beliefs simply changed, allowing for the idea that homosexual lust is no worse a spiritual threat than heterosexual lust: "The implication is clear and unmistakable that in some way it can be moderated and moral."[179]

Early commentators also sensed Dante's reticence about the horrors of sodomy and were puzzled or outraged by it.[180] One commentator on Dante from the 14th century, Benvenuto da Imola, admitted that he was "indignant" that Dante would associate great scholars and writers with the crime of sodomy, but he changed his tune about Dante and came to perhaps a slightly different conclusion than the one Dante may have intended:

> For in 1375, when I was at [the University of] Bologna and lectured upon this book, I found certain vermin bred of the cinders of Sodom who infected the whole of that University [...] I disclosed the matter, not without grievous peril to myself, to the Cardinal of Bourges, who was the [Papal] Legate at Bologna. He, as a man of great virtue and learning, who detested such abominable crimes, commanded an inquiry for the principal offenders, some of whom were caught while others fled in terror. And, but for the hindrances wrought by a certain traitorous priest to whom the commission had been entrusted and who was infected with that same disease, many would have been given over to the flames of fire.[181]

Another curious, if debatable, gesture of empathy toward same-sex love in the Middle Ages is a tomb slab decorating the resting place of two English knights who died at Constantinople in 1391. The inscription states they had been constant companions for 13 years. When one of them died, the other starved himself to death. Of course, none of this in of itself infers that the two knights were known for a romantic relationship that earned acceptance among whoever provided the grave markings. However, the slab also features a carving showing the two knights bearing the same shield, which has the arms of their two families mixed with each other, a very unusual feature.[182]

Another controversial but possible sign of love between the same sex is a poem by the thirteenth century female poet Bieris de Romans. Although classified as a troubadour poem, it does not contain any of the usual courtly love tropes or any indication that the poem's speaker is male. Yet the subject is a Lady Maria, who is told that "for in you lie my desire and my heart."[183] Scholars have argued that the poem's seeming romance between a woman and a woman might instead be a literary device or a religious allegory, given that the subject is a Maria.[184] As is usually the case with literature from another time and culture, definite conclusions remain elusive.

Whatever marginal acceptance of same-sex love existed in the Middle Ages, it did not surface among civil governments in Western and Central Europe anymore than it did in the mainstream of religious opinion. One of the earliest Western European laws harshly punishing sodomy in the later Middle Ages comes from the *Sendrecht,* the law code of the West Frisians from the modern-day Netherlands. Their law code, developed sometime in the 11th century, gives sodomites the macabre choice of being burned, buried alive, or castrating themselves.[185] Over the course of the 13th century secular authorities in Castile, Portugal, and parts of Italy and France began to actively impose the death penalty for sodomy.[186] Most laws prescribed burning, but the laws of Alfonso X of Castile punished sodomy with castration and stoning, which was later brought into line with the usual execution by fire under Isabel I (1474–1504) and Fernando II (1479–1516). English legal treatises written toward the end of the 13th century recommended live burial or burning as the proper penalty for sodomy, although one also suggested that judgment should be reserved only for the "notoriously guilty."[187]

While the majority of laws seemed directed at men, there were efforts to apply sodomy statutes to women. The strangest attempt comes from the Tuscan jurist Cino de Pistoia (1270–1336/1337), who interpreted a third-century Roman imperial edict that seemed designed to protect female victims of rape from legal stigma as a law denouncing lesbianism. His gloss reads, "This law can be understood in two ways: first, when a woman suffers defilement by surrendering to a male; the other way is when a woman suffers defilement in surrendering to another woman. For there are certain women, inclined to foul wickedness, who exercise their lust on other women and pursue them like men."[188]

While it is impossible to know how widely these and similar laws were enforced, there are recorded executions and imprisonments of both women and men. A woman named Katherina Hetzeldorfer was put to death in the German town of Speyer in 1477 for an unnamed crime. Witnesses testified that she "behaved exactly like a man with women" and she confessed that she had made a dildo out of leather, cotton, and a wooden stick.[189] Near Chartres a woman named Laurence Poitevin had been jailed for years for having a sexual relationship with a certain Jehanne, although their case came to the attention of authorities only when Laurence apparently tried to break things off and Jehanne attacked her in public.[190] Other women from Switzerland to Portugal were not only imprisoned and burned but also hanged, drowned, and beheaded for same-sex love.[191]

Men who were executed included nobles, like a Swiss nobleman executed for sodomy under the order of the Holy Roman Emperor Rudolf I, as well as commoners. The first such recorded case comes from the Flemish city of Ghent in 1292, when a knifemaker named Johann de Wettre was burned alive.[192] Tragically it was not uncommon for accused lovers to burn together, such as two Jews from the Pyrenees kingdom of Navarre, Juce Abolfaça and Simuel Nahamán, and two Venetians, Nicoleto Marmagna and Giovanni Braganza.[193]

There is even evidence of widespread persecutions, especially in Venice and Florence, where sodomy cases were specially handled by government departments called the *Signori di Notte* (Lords of the Night) in Venice and *Ufficiali di Notte* (Officers of the Night) in Florence. Florence was particularly notorious across Europe because of its citizens' reputation for sodomy (a German slang word for "sodomite" was *Florenzen*), perhaps inspiring the local authorities to act with a special ferocity. Registers in Florence record about 160 sodomy accusations a year between 1478 and 1502.[194] Although hefty fines, exile, beatings, imprisonment, public humiliation, and occasionally beheadings and burnings were usually the punishment of choice, once in a while authorities were creative. One 15-year-old Florentine, Giovanni di Giovanni, who was known to the government as a "public and notorious passive sodomite," was paraded through the city on a donkey, castrated in public, and then branded with a red-hot iron "in that part of his body where he allowed himself to be known in sodomitical practice."[195]

Sexual nonconformists were far from the only fiercely sought targets of this era in medieval history. Jews, heretics, lepers, and, as we have seen, prostitutes were also tracked down, forced to wear self-identifying marks, and isolated in unprecedented ways. The same mechanisms were unleashed with ferocity against "sodomites," who were also the favorite victims of a resurgent Church and increasingly assertive governments. Still, people high and low were far from cowed into chaste submission by either their kings or bishops.

Sinners Defiant

During this period in much of Europe, there was a good enough chance that having intercourse with someone of the same sex would result in a harsh, possibly gruesome punishment, no matter if one was a peasant, an artisan, a priest, or even a noble. Yet this was still not much of a deterrent, at least if several high-profile scandals are any indication. In his letters, Ivo of Chartres expressed total mortification when the Archbishop of Tours in 1097 pulled some strings to have a young man named Jean elected the bishop of Orléans. The new bishop's youth was the least of Ivo's concerns; he was also the lover of both the Archbishop and his brother. Ivo claimed that he was so enraged that he went straight to King Philippe I (r. 1052–1108), who allegedly just laughed and joked to Ivo that he had slept with Jean himself.[196]

The mores of the Church and the lifestyles of the rich and powerful clashed again in 11th-century England. The English chronicler William of Malmesbury was aghast at the fashions popular at the court of King William "Rufus" II: "[T]he model for young men was to rival women in delicacy of person, to mince their gait, to walk with loose gesture, and half naked."[197] The accusations of Anselm, Archbishop of Canterbury, who often butted heads with the hot-tempered king, maintained that "almost everyone in the whole kingdom daily talked about [the king]."[198] Spelling out these implications, another observer, Ordericus Vitalis, railed against the "filthy catamites" in the king's court.[199] A contemporary, Eadmer, added that Anselm had the audacity to approach the king, asking him to consent to and endorse a church council specifically called to denounce sodomy. William merely waved away Anselm and ordered him to "say no more about it."[200]

Another high-profile scandal involving medieval royalty was the relationship between

Charles VII of France and Agnès Sorel. Of course, French kings had many mistresses before, but Charles VII was shockingly open about his relationship and allowed her a preeminence in court traditionally reserved only for the queen. A contemporary, Georges Chastellain, huffed about the sway the king's mistress had over fashion, especially appalled by the new popularity of dresses that exposed women's nipples. Charles' and Agnès' daughter, Charlotte of France, happened to expose the horrific double standard over adultery when she and her lover were both caught *in flagrante delicto* by her husband Jacques de Brézé, who murdered them both. He lost favor with the still reigning Charles VII, but was quickly brought back into good graces by Charles VII's successor—and poor Charlotte's half-brother—Louis XI.

As much as medieval literature may have depicted adultery and nonmarital sex as commonplace, it also portrayed a world where families had the right, if not the duty, to punish any woman who acted to gain sex without marriage or any man accused of being a seducer. The Fourth Day of the *Decameron* tells the story of an Italian noblewoman tricked by a friar into believing that he is the angel Gabriel and making love with him. When she becomes pregnant she falls into danger of being killed by her family, who do not believe her miraculous story, but she is saved when instead the friar's family find out the truth and promptly have him imprisoned for life in a monastery. Another tale from the same day speaks sympathetically about a woman named Lisabetta whose brothers kill her lover. Outside the realm of fiction, in Spain, Portugal, and Italy judges actually were often forgiving toward men who killed their adulterous wives.[201] The law in Sicily, Hungary, and regions of France, and as mentioned before Sweden and Denmark, explicitly allowed a man to kill his wife if he could prove that she committed adultery. Elsewhere she could be humiliated ritually and publicly before the streets of her village or town or imprisoned, perhaps for life, in a convent.

This code of honor does not seem to have trickled down to the lower classes. From what little information can be pieced together, it seems that, in England at least, many peasant couples went to their weddings with their children or while the women were pregnant.[202] Despite this, theologians like Peter Paludanus in France and Johannes Nider in Bavaria found in their everyday experience that *coitus interruptus* was often used by men for birth control.[203] Looking at the demographics of 14th-century Tuscany, a historian of the medieval family, David Herlihy, noticed that women who married young curiously did not produce more children than women who married later. At the same time, the women of Florence, especially poorer women, stopped having children sooner than country women. Why? Bernardino of Siena offers a possible clue: "Oh, in how many unspeakable and unbelievable ways do husbands abuse their wives. Who could ever state them with decency?"[204] Apparently various contraceptive methods were widely known, or at least this was a fact of life Boccaccio expected his readers to recognize when he has a nun in one story assure another that there are ways to avoid getting pregnant: "[T]here will be a thousand ways of us of doing so that it shall never be known, provided we ourselves do not tell it."[205]

For all its regulatory power over laypeople, the Church still fretted that it was trying to hold back an ocean with its bare hands. The bishop Bartholomew of Exeter bemoaned that a majority of the people did not even believe that fornication was a sin.[206] The canonist Stephen of Tournai admitted in his collection of canon law that sex crimes were the most common type of crime clerics encountered.[207] In the early 13th century Johannes Teutonicus, a master general of the Dominicans, complained that nearly everybody was a fornicator under the Church's definitions.

Even within the Church's own walls, control was far from absolute. A French abbess, Huguette du Tamel, held a reign of hedonism over the convent at Saint-Royale alongside her lover, Baudes de Maître. Their idea of fun included coaxing nuns into bathing nude with both of them. When the authorities finally got around to intervening, Huguette ran off with her lover and most of the valuables in the convent's possession. Saint Brigit of Sweden complained that some of the convents in her homeland left their doors open at night for men. In France, Jean Gerson investigated similar allegations and claimed that he personally discovered convents that had become secret brothels.[208]

As spicy as these nun escapades are, the most famous sex scandal involving monastics was the 12th-century story of Peter Abelard and Heloise. A successful and well-liked teacher and theologian, Abelard nonetheless had a bad reputation as a dissenter against the medieval Catholic consensus on sex. "No natural pleasure of the flesh may be declared a sin," Abelard wrote, "nor may one impute guilt when someone is delighted by pleasure where he must necessarily feel it." Unfortunately, he handed his many critics a total public relations victory by having an affair with his student Heloise and, in his words, spending time with his hand "more searching in her bosom than in her book."[209] When Heloise became pregnant, her uncle, the canon Fulbert, had Abelard castrated and both lovers were forced into monastic life.

Later in life Abelard recanted his past transgressions and thanked God for using his castration to save his soul from damnation. Such pervasive belief in Hell may have had its use in keeping the people in line, but skepticism does bubble up here and there in the records. When the hero of the only 13th-century *chante-fable* ("sung story") to survive to the modern day, *Aucassin et Nicolette,* is threatened with eternal damnation, he is nonplussed:

> In Paradise what have I to do? I care not to enter, but to only have Nicolette, my very sweet friend, whom I love dearly so well. For into Paradise go none but such people as I will tell you of. There goes those aged priests, and old cripples, and the maimed, who all day and all night cough before the altars, and in the crypts below the churches [...] Such as these enter in Paradise, and with them have I nought to do. But in Hell will I go. For in Hell go the fair clerks and the fair knights who are slain in the tourney and the great wars, and the stout archer and the loyal man. With them will I go. And there go the fair and courteous ladies, who have friends, two or three, together with their wedded lords.[210]

The ultimate nonconformists were the heretics, who were constantly a thorn in the sides of both the Orthodox and Catholic Churches. One of the earliest pervasive medieval heresies were the Bogomils, who emerged in tenth-century Bulgaria shortly after the country had been Christianized. Following the path of dualists from antiquity such as the Gnostics and the Manicheans, the Bogomils believed in a God who held power only over the spiritual world while Satan ruled all that was material. Confident that the first duty of the believer was to prevent new souls from falling under Satan's sway, the Bogomils preached a radical program of abstaining completely from marriage and all sex acts. Even with such demands on the believer's resolve, the Bogomil doctrine spread from Bulgaria into Central Europe and the Byzantine Empire, breaching even the aristocratic circles of Constantinople.[211]

Similarly in Western Europe, there were the Cathars, who held a strongly dualist system and also shunned procreation. In Cathar doctrine, conception meant another human spirit would be imprisoned in a body and placed under the power of Satan. Cathar leaders actively taught that intercourse was as severe a sin as murder. Some went so far as to refuse to eat eggs or dairy foods since they represented the procreative force.[212]

Harder to trace were the sects that took the opposite extreme, because accusations of sexual excess were so often deployed by medieval writers against heretics, even ones who urged on universal celibacy like the Cathars, that it is difficult, if not impossible, to untangle slander from actual doctrine. There were heretics whose beliefs had the theoretical potential to justify libertine living, like the heretic Hugo Speroni from 12th-century Piacenza, who taught that there was no such thing as original sin and that a select group of souls predestined for salvation remained saved even after sinning.[213] Believers in the Free Spirit movement allegedly preached to their followers that sex was not sinful when both parties desired it.

The one sect that may have actually embraced free love was the Adamites. An outgrowth of the Hussite movement in early 15th-century Bohemia that demanded radical reforms of the Church, the Adamites tried to recreate the state of primeval innocence in the Garden of Eden, which for some of them may have meant going about nude and practicing free love. One group of Adamites, the Picards, set up an island community on the Nežárka River in what is now the Czech Republic, where accounts suggest that they did not enjoy nudity or hold constant orgies, but instead just held property and spouses in common. Still too extreme for the Hussites to stomach even without the casual nudity, they were massacred by a Hussite army in 1421.

The revitalized and ambitious Church of the Later Middle Ages was fond of labeling any deviation from the party line as heretical, but heretics like the Picards or the Cathars who attempted totally new ways of living seemed to inspire a spectacularly violent drive for extermination. So utopian efforts did exist in the Middle Ages; they just had a tendency not to last very long. There was a similar kind of experiment in Florence that succeeded for only a few years, but represented the other extreme—an attempt to use the hammer of secular law to mold a society that would actually conform to traditional morality.

Savonarola's Florence

For four brief years near the end of the 15th century, the firebrand preacher Girolamo Savonarola transformed the Republic of Florence into a kingdom where Jesus Christ was "King" and the "Captain, the One Who gives you a new reform of holy living." Shaken to the core by a French invasion in 1494, Florence had thrown out the Medici family that had unofficially ruled the city and gave the rare opportunity to fill the vacuum to Savonarola and his followers. Although known contemptuously as the *Piagnoni* ("wailers"), their ranks did include many of the *literati* who had thrived under the Medici.[214]

To be fair, the reform program pursued by Savonarola had more on its agenda than just banning dirty pictures. In fact, even the secular liberals of today might sympathize with several of his aims. Seeing poverty as incompatible with any true Christian society, Savonarola managed to convince the legislature to allocate state funds to fraternities providing poor relief; to establish the *Monte de Pietà*, a government-funded operation that offered loans at low rates[215]; to impose a 10 percent tax on all income from property; and to abolish all existing loans.[216] Savonarola even intervened to stop the government from selling off the Medicis' prodigious library and had the collection opened to the public.[217]

Savonarola was also not at all reluctant to direct the power of government to meddle in nearly every aspect of someone's day-to-day life. Little troops of boys called the *fanciulli* were even enlisted to go around to jeer at gamblers, drunkards, and lavishly dressed women.[218] Savonarola tried, but failed, to set up similar squads among Florence's women.[219] The government was far more enthusiastic over Savonarola's push against a certain reviled sex crime. In a sermon, Savonarola urged:

> It is necessary that the Signory pass laws against that accursed vice of sodomy, for which you know that Florence is infamous throughout the whole of Italy; this infamy arises perhaps from your talking and chattering about it so much, so that there is not so much in deeds, perhaps, as in words. Pass a law, I say, and let it be without mercy; that is, let these people be stoned and burned. On the other hand, it is necessary that you remove from among yourselves these poems and games and taverns and the evil fashion of women's clothes, and, likewise, we must throw out everything that is noxious to the health of the soul.[220]

A majority of legislators supported escalating the punishment for sodomy to strangulation, followed by the burning of the body, in all cases.[221]

Another type of righteous bonfire is what Savonarola is most famous for, the Bonfire of Vanities, which overshadowed the existence of the man himself. However, even the Bonfire was not entirely Savonarola's innovation. Similar mass burnings of cosmetics, secular paintings, and playing cards had been held before in regions of Italy, France, and Hungary, but they had been spontaneous events launched by charismatic preachers.[222] Florence had witnessed the first time someone in a preeminent, albeit unofficial, position in government encouraged such an event.

The proverbial Bonfire took place during Lent of 1497. As a chorus of children sang hymns on the topic of worldly vanity, books, portraits, sculptures, and songbooks with sexual and "pagan" content as well as wigs, dice, cards, mirrors, perfumes, dresses, musical instruments, and game tables were piled on a wooden pyramid 60 feet high and 230 feet in circumference constructed on the Piazza della Signoria. Every copy of a new edition of Boccaccio's *Decameron* and a statue carved by Donatello were among the art objects burned.[223] Even though there is no contemporary record of the artist Sandro Botticelli actually burning his own work as a follower of Savonarola,[224] there were explicitly erotic works consigned to the flames, out of fear from their influence on a susceptible populace. No wonder Savonarola, despite having a political career that flared out quickly, has become practically proverbial. The Bonfire still echoes, albeit with perhaps less extreme resonances, for modern readers.

Perhaps inevitably, Savonarola's reign of puritanism let loose a backlash, complete with revolts. Worse, Savonarola had earned no less a rival than the ruthless Pope Alexander VI (r. 1492–1503), who excommunicated him in 1497. Captured by a mob, Savonarola and two other ringleaders of his movement were put on trial by the Church for heresy, sedition, and a host of other religious and political crimes. They were burned, without the cruel mercy of strangulation, in the exact same spot the Bonfire of the Vanities took place. Like so many attempts at drastic social engineering in the Later Middle Ages, Savonarola's theocratic republic ended at the point of a sword. In a sense, however, Savonarola's execution was the perfect sign of the start of an era when neither Church nor State would be able to keep such highly ambitious reforming drives trapped in the bottle.

VII

The Sensual Empire: Turkey, 1453–1800

Admittedly with hindsight, the fall of the Byzantine Empire should have been the easiest, surest prophecy to make. By the start of the 15th century, all that was left of the "empire" was Constantinople and its environs along with a handful of cities and coastal areas around Greece. At all sides, the Byzantines were bordered by an Ottoman Empire that had spread rapidly across Anatolia and the Balkans. Yet after the Turks finally marched into Constantinople in 1453, a wave of horror broke across Christian Europe, over the very same countries that had done little if anything to stop Constantinople from becoming Istanbul.

Europeans actually had reason enough to be worried for themselves. Appropriately enough for the conqueror of the city that practically bridged Europe and Asia, Sultan Mehmed II styled himself as both the Caliph, the leader of the entire Islamic world, and the true heir to the Holy Roman Emperors. Neither was an empty claim. At its peak, the Ottoman Empire could feature as premier tourist destinations locales that had historical value to both Islamic and European civilizations, including Athens, Baghdad, Constantinople, and Mecca.

For Europeans, the Ottoman Empire not only remained a military threat, but also was a source of mixed messages about sex. European travelers and intellectuals saw a decadent society, where homosexuality and pederasty were not just tolerated but openly practiced, and where the Sultan and other elites had their pick of exotic women in the harems. Yet they also admired the Turks for how their society treated and contained the sexuality of women. In seeing Turkish women being kept in seclusion, some Europeans perceived the Turks as doing a better job upholding women's modesty than their own cultures.

As is often the case, the stereotypes had some grounding in truth, but did not match the complexity of the reality. A series of imperial edicts restricting women's travel and the places they could visit tellingly showed that women did not readily stay secluded in their homes under the watch of their male relatives. There were no homosexuals being stoned or burned alive in the Ottoman Empire and Turkish writers spoke more openly about same-sex erotica than most of their Western and Central European counterparts, but there was nonetheless a reticence, at least on the part of authorities, about homosexuality, particularly when it came to sexual acts between harem women. Pederasty was also treated as a pervasive threat, one that had to be addressed sternly through civil law, even though it had a long history within Islamic culture.

Contrary to modern stereotypes about Islamic societies, the Ottoman Empire made a firm distinction between civil and religious law. Further, the chief concern of the Ottoman laws dealing with sex was protecting paternal authority and defending females and male adolescents from what was seen as sexual exploitation. The Ottoman authorities had very little concern about protecting and nurturing any religious or social ideal about sexual behavior, but instead saw themselves as fighting an endless war against disorder in the family and in society at large.

Sharia Law, Civil Law and Sex

The Ottoman Empire did not put religious or *sharia* law on the same footing as civil or *kanun* law. By the end of the 15th century, the Ottoman government instead trained officers and judges who were familiar with both systems and were expected to rule according to both, depending on the situation. Eventually, even though the Ottoman Empire during the 17th century experienced a conservative era of religious revival and *sharia* law always remained an important source for Ottoman officials, it would become typical for *kanun* law to override *sharia* law.

At a glance *kanun* laws, when it came to sex, were usually much more lenient. Adulterers and people found guilty of having sex outside of marriage were fined based on their income. A cuckolded husband had to pay the fine for his cheating wife, if he decided not to divorce her. As Dror Ze'evi points out, this system of using progressive fines to punish misbehavior placed greater moral responsibility on the Empire's rich and powerful. It "declared that while the ruling elite was bound by moral responsibility, the lower classes were allowed a wider margin for illicit conduct."[1] Nor did the law punish the nonmarital sex of slaves, although they were allowed to marry only spouses chosen by their master. However, *sharia* law, for all its harsher punishments, demanded strict burdens of proof, including reliable and multiple witnesses. By comparison, *kanun* law sometimes found evidence produced by torture and hearsay to be perfectly admissible.[2]

The *sharia* prescription for dealing with a woman guilty of adultery, stoning, occurred only once on record, in 1680. Still, there were apparently customary punishments for an erring woman that were deployed with full force. In 1553, an Austrian ambassador reported that a wife deemed guilty of adultery in Amasya was led through the streets on a mule she had to pay for. She also had to pay a man who was ordered to hit her with a dogwood stick 100 times. After her beating was complete, she then had to kiss his hand and thank him.[3] While the law never required a man to divorce an adulterous spouse, it was officially encouraged. An edict made by Sultan Suleyman I (1520–1566) placed a special tax on any man who stayed married to a woman convicted of adultery.[4]

Relations between a married couple were usually not something the law bothered with. There were no laws limiting contraception or most forms of sexual intercourse. The exception was that a fine and an official rebuke awaited a married man who committed sodomy with his wife, although this was inspired by the Qur'an's concern for married women being forced to submit to sodomy and not any outrage over anal intercourse. Neither did the law concern itself with how many concubines or wives a man had, although polygamy remained rare because, as in so many societies elsewhere, it was an expensive lifestyle.[5]

One major worry for both *sharia* and *kanun* law was incest, including marriage between cousins. A husband was even barred from marrying a second wife who was related to the first. A man who had sex with his wife's slave could be fined and chastised by an official. Even two people who as infants shared the same nursemaid were prohibited from marriage for life.[6] Yet, as in Christian Europe, the realities of life in isolated rural villages trumped any official decrees against incest. Marriages between cousins in rural Turkey and the Balkans were still commonplace.[7]

While Turkish authorities may have in most cases refrained from intervening in sexual relations, the law was very much interested in curtailing relationships that are formed without the blessing of the family. A marriage between Muslims that was based on an elopement or abduction was automatically deemed null and void. A man's entry into a house with the intent to seduce a woman inside was legally equivalent to a fulfilled act of fornication. Kissing and romantic words between lovers could mean a fine for the man. An even more adventurous lover who took off a woman's clothing could be imprisoned. The most brutal retaliation, though, was reserved for a woman who willingly ran off with a lover. Her father would have to pay a fine while her vulva would be branded.[8]

Despite the distaste for marriages that took place without the consent of the family, divorce was a fairly simple procedure, as in most Islamic societies. The Turks adopted the Arabic concept of *talaq* divorce, where the husband had to notify neither his wife nor the courts. Still, the wife at least had the right to petition the courts to grant her alimony and her dowry. Women themselves could initiate a divorce, but they usually had to give up part or all of a dowry and the bridal gifts.[9]

That rowdy bachelors might go around seducing women was deemed a serious problem for Ottoman society at large. In some urban areas in the Empire, special bachelor residences or quarters were established to isolate single young men from neighborhoods where families lived. The authorities also went out of their way to promote men's organizations and fraternities to keep young unmarried men busy and distracted.[10] Communities were likewise vigilant to threats posed by miscreants, whether they were chronic liars or had a habit of putting women at risk of being seduced, and could petition courts to have them exiled.[11] In the summer of 1541, a judge at Aintab in southeastern Turkey sentenced a woman named Haciye Sabah to public humiliation and banishment because she not only allowed men to be present at the supposedly women-only religious classes she hosted in her home, but actually hired them as teaching assistants. The court records dramatically describe her choice in employees as "against the law and beyond all reason."[12]

The Ottoman Empire differed with its Christian neighbors on just how much both civil and religious authorities were willing to intervene in the sex lives of its people. For example, while Portugal and Spain were making a public spectacle out of burning alive men alleged to have had sex with other men, for the Ottoman authorities male homosexuality was a serious issue deserving of intervention only when minors were involved. Adultery seems to have been treated as a serious legal and social breach in just a few rare cases. However, the Ottoman government, on both national and local levels, did see sex as a potent danger to the sacred power of the family (especially over daughters) and to the general peace, one that had to be taken very seriously.

Beardless Youths

Legally speaking, once an adolescent man in the Ottoman Empire grew a beard, he was no longer considered *mushteha*, "sexually desirable."[13] This was an important milestone, since until then Ottoman society considered any adolescent man as highly sought after by roving older men. A 16th-century *fetwa*, or religious opinion, allowed any *imam* to keep a beardless 15- or 16-year-old from standing in the front row at prayer, so he would not be a pleasant distraction. To try to encourage the fathers of adolescent men to take their responsibilities seriously, Sultan Suleyman imposed legal penalties on fathers who failed to stop their sons from having sex with a pederast.[14]

While there were no laws brought to bear against sex between men considered full adults, pederasty was another matter completely. If a pederast had sex with an adolescent, he was fined and chastised—but that was only the beginning. His face would be blackened and his ears and nose cut off. Interestingly, Turkish law considered adolescent men as capable of also dangerously exploiting each other. If two adolescents had sex with each other, one or both of their fathers could be officially shamed and fined.

This does not seem to have really weakened the popularity of pederasty in certain circles. The Ottoman Empire inherited a cultural taste for pederasty from the Arabs, where it was a tradition for men to leap in water or cut their wrists to prove their devotion to some pretty young man.[15] While love for beardless adolescents was celebrated in Turkish poems, it was, as in the literature of Islamic Iberia, apparently meant to be understood as a chaste passion.[16] Still, among the Sufis, a mystic sect of Islam, the love between an older man and a younger man was seen as having profound spiritual meaning, and as a result accusations of and jokes about homosexuality concerning *dervishes*, Sufi ascetics, were frequent. At least a few men tried to put such ideas into practice. For one instance, records at the court of Aintab reported how a teenager named Davud Mahmud testified how he was harassed by an older man. "As I was on my way home, he said things to me like, 'My soul, my life.' When he said, 'I love you,' I said, 'Stop talking like you're out of your mind! Get away from me!' So he hit me and injured me."[17]

In spite of the legal efforts to restrain pederasty, the attractiveness of adolescent males was nonetheless kept on display as both advertising and simple showing off. Foreign visitors constantly noticed how the popular coffeehouses in Istanbul liked to employ handsome adolescents and young men.[18] The scholar Abu al–Wafa al–Urdi (d. 1660) praised a future Grand Mufti for going against what must have been a pervasive trend: "He likes neither pomp nor ostentatious clothes, nor does he employ beardless boys contrary to the practice of most *Mawali* [ministers]."[19] Likewise, an English traveler who accompanied an Ottoman army, Henry Blount, claimed, "Each Basha [Pasha] hath as many, or likely more Catamites [as wives] ... usually clad in Velvet, or Scarlet, with guilt Scymitars, and bravely mounted, with Sumptuous furniture."[20]

The tradition of pederasty also surfaced when it came to the notorious Ottoman "head tax." The Ottomans conscripted Christian boys from the Balkans who were physically and intellectually promising and had them educated in the palace schools, where most could hope for a position in the elite Janissery corps or a civil service position, but the best might actually become provincial governors or even Vizier. According to the British diplomat Paul Ricaut, individual beauty was a factor. They were selected for "bodily perfection, muscular strength and intellectual ability, so far as it could be judged without long testing."²¹ Still, Ricault adds that the boys were monitored by eunuchs, "to see or overhear if there be any wanton or lewd behavior or discourse among them."²² He goes on to try to describe, through the more than slightly biased perspective of a European coached in ideas of Turkish decadence, the tension between sexual ideas and practice:

> This is the colour of virtue, they paint over the deformity of their depraved inclinations; but in reality this love of theirs, is nothing but libidinous flames each to other, with which they burn so violently, that banishment and death have not been examples sufficient to deter them from making demonstrations for such like addresses; so that in their Chambers, though watched by their eunuchs, they learn a certain language with the motion of their eyes, their gestures and their fingers, to express their amours; and this passion hath boiled sometimes to that heat, that jealousies and rivalries have broken forth in their Chambers, without respect to the severity of their guardians, and good orders have been brought into confusion, and have not been again redressed, until some of them have been expelled from the seraglio with the Tippets of their vests cut off, banished into the Islands, and beaten almost to death.²³

Inside and outside the Sultan's court were the *koçekler* or the *yamakis,* young male dancers whose acts typically involved erotic dance and cross-dressing. A British tourist, John Hobhouse, painted the scene, or rather tried to avoid doing so: "That part of the entertainment which is most to the fancy of the company, and which no Englishman would patiently contemplate for a moment, is the exhibition of the *Yamakis,* or dancing-boys."²⁴ Beyond the fad for pederasty, love between adult men was also a known part of the Empire's urban culture. *Hammams* (bathhouses) were a by-word for clandestine sexual activity, and certain *hammams* became so well known for cruising between men that they were sometimes monitored by the Janissary corps, showing that, even though the authorities were typically more concerned about pederasty, there was some reticence over sex between adult men as well.²⁵

Still, at least in literature, homosexuality was acknowledged as a desire that was a fact of life, albeit sometimes irreverently. That one may desire a man who was old enough to grow a full beard was a recurring theme in Turkish erotic literature.²⁶ This body of erotica included pornographic prose and poems and guides on sexual techniques and how to choose partners. While many featured the sexual escapades of men and women as well as pederasts, some detailed the desire of women and men for adult members of their own sex.²⁷

An instance of lesbianism being treated as a joke appears in one shadow play from a wildly popular series, *Karagöz,* named for their scoundrel protagonist. In this play, titled *Buyük Evlenme* ("The Great Wedding"), Karagöz is desperately trying to stop a wedding he has been forced into by goading a group of female guests into protesting the nuptials. Not knowing that Karagöz is the groom, the women listen as he tells them that the would-be husband is a thief. "Well, so are we," they reply. Next he tells them that the groom goes out every night in search of sex; the women reply that they do the same thing. Then he states that the intended constantly frequents bathhouses, which were popular spots for sexual rendezvous. "Oh, so he must be very clean," they answer. Finally Karagöz exclaims that the groom is a serial pederast. "So what?" The women scoff. "We are women lovers, too."²⁸

There has been no real look yet at female same-sex love in the Ottoman Empire. Nonetheless, there are hints that it was practiced and perhaps even organized. Erotic female dancers, the *çenglier,* many of whom were Roma, were alleged to have had wealthy female lovers.²⁹ Outsiders to Ottoman society suspected that love between women was also rampant in the imperial harem. An Italian visitor, Luigi Bassano da Zara, remarked, "It is common knowledge that as a result of this familiarity in washing and massaging women fall very much in love with each other. And one often sees a woman in love with another one just like a man and a woman. And I have known Greek and Turkish women, on seeing a lovely young woman, seek occasion to bathe with her just to see her naked and handle her."[30] While certainly Europeans, fixated on the idea of the sensual harem, would be prone to exaggerating such things, but it does seem that the Ottomans themselves had exactly the same suspicions. Phallic vegetables like carrots were banned from being served inside the harem.[31]

However, while the women at the harem could be seen as engaging in sexual activity out of a lack of other sexual outlets, homosexual women, like their male counterparts, apparently had the option of the *hammams*. Of course, once again we have to rely on the claims of a European observer, the Austrian ambassador Ogier de Busbecq, who nonetheless spent lengthy amounts of time in Istanbul:

> The great masses of women use the public baths for females and assemble there in large numbers ... so cases occur of women falling in love with one another at these baths, in much the same fashion as young men fall in love with maidens in our own country. Thus you see a Turk's precautions are sometimes of no avail, and when he has succeeded in keeping his wives from a male lover, he is still in danger from a female rival! The women become deeply attached to each other, and the baths supply them with opportunities of meeting. Some therefore keep their wives away from them as much as possible, but they cannot do so altogether, as the laws allow them to go there.[32]

If the government's thoughts on pederasty, the need to keep soldiers stationed near bathhouses known to be hotspots for homosexuals, and the real fear that women in the imperial harem would exploit their dinner to pleasure each other are any indication, then the Ottoman Empire was far from ambivalent on the subject of same-sex love. Nonetheless, for the most part the Turks carried on with the medieval Islamic attitudes on sexuality. At the very least, homosexuality was something that could still be described in explicit and romantic terms, without blunt moral condemnation.

In the Harem

Nothing embodies the Western image of imperial Turkey quite like the harem of the Sultan. Representing both exquisite luxury and absolute decadence, the harem manages to embody everything that Westerners admire and disapprove of in the historic Islamic world. In reality, the Turkish imperial harem, like its precedents in ancient Egypt and Persia and the Byzantine Empire, was not a place for uninhibited sex, but was just where the women of the imperial household lived. Nonetheless, for the Ottoman Sultans the harem was a site thick with political intrigue, as concubines competed for the privilege of being among the Sultan's *kadins* (favorites) and the mother of the next Sultan.

Another misconception about the harem dear to Western writers is that it was only an imperial prerogative. In reality, harems existed in Muslim households, and even a few Christian and Jewish ones, throughout the Empire. They were used from the rich, who could have an entire wing of their homes dedicated to the purpose, to the poor, who would often have a curtain discreetly closing off one section of their small homes where the women slept and dressed. Geoffrey Godfrey describes the idea of the harem as "that of the privilege of privacy and the protection of women, whether in a modest home or the palace of the sultan."[33]

Turkish legend connected the idea of the harem directly to the Greek concept of the *gynaecium,* or women's quarters. According to this story, Sultan Mehmed II gave his mother Hüma Hatun, whose family may have been Greek, permission to model her private apartments after the tradition of the Byzantine emperors. Like them, she arranged to have rooms where her female servants and relatives would stay, segregated from the rest of the palace.[34] Following the footsteps of Hüma Hatun, the *valide sultan,* the Sultan's mother, was at the top of the harem hierarchy, overseeing the education and care of the women there.

After the lifetime of Suleyman, it became rare for a Sultan to have a wife. Instead the Sultan would select a favorite, an *ikbal.* If the *ikbal* became pregnant, then she would be promoted into the rank of *kadin.* Even then, however, the Sultans did not always treat the harem as a personal brothel. While there were indeed Sultans like Murad III (r. 1575–1594), who allegedly enjoyed the company of 40 *ikbals,* there were other Sultans who stayed faithful to only one *kadin.*[35] Heeding the Qur'an's insistence that a wife receive adequate care and attention from her husband, however, the Sultan himself followed the strict etiquette of the *nöbet gecesi* (night turn) of each of his lovers.[36] In a book published in 1844, the British observer Charles White described a system that had changed only a little by his own time:

> These ladies not being married, the designation commonly given to them, of the "Sultan's wives," is erroneous. Nor are they addressed by the title of Sultana, that being reserved for the Imperial children. *Kadins* cannot even sit upon divans [couch-like furniture] or chairs in the sultan's presence, although their daughters enjoy this privilege; their place is upon cushions, spread upon the floor. There is no such person officially as the *khasseky* (favourite), although former sultans permitted their first favourites to assume this appellation. Preferences naturally exist; but it is difficult for the Sultan to betray them in a marked manner without exciting dangerous jealousies and harassing clamours.[37]

Who were the women of the harem? Like the men who would become members of the Janissary corps, girls for the harem were selected out of the most attractive and most intelligent women from Christian villages. This spawned the irony that very few Ottoman Sultans could claim much Turkish ancestry; most had Greek, Slavic, or Caucasian mothers. The harem at the main imperial residence of Topkapi Palace encompassed approximately 400 rooms. According to Çağatay Uluçay, who was writing in the 18th century, there were 500 to 600 women in the imperial harem.[38]

The segregation of the harem women was enforced quite thoroughly. Eunuchs guarded the quarters of the harem, with the apartments of the chief eunuch, the *kizlar ağasi,* overlooking the entrance. Besides the Sultan and his family, the only people allowed to enter the harem were female Jewish or Christian merchants or married slaves. When the *kadins* left the environs of the Topkapi Palace, they left before sunrise, dressed in shawls and riding in curtained carriages or boats where they were seated in enclosures. This concern with keeping women secluded was not a uniquely imperial obsession. Until the 19th century it was taboo for women to walk on city streets unattended.[39]

As noted before, eroticism between women inside the harem was apparently enough of an occurrence that it prompted official pronouncements. Even if the men surrounding them exaggerated the lesbian peril, the women of the harem had no inhibitions among themselves. This was something an English visitor, Lady Mary Montagu, discovered when she toured the harem at Topkapi Palace and the women there invited her to bathe with them. Luckily Mary Montagu was narrowly able to avoid offending her hosts. "I was at last forced to open my shirt and show them my stays, which satisfied them very well, for I saw they believed that I was locked up in that machine, and that it was not in my power to open it, which contrivance they attributed to my husband," Mary writes.[40]

Of course, very few Turks could afford large homes to house their women, much less 400 women. However, the same principle—that women had to be protected from the gaze of men for their own sake—was pervasive. This attitude actually won admiration from Westerners such as Busbecq:

> The Turks set greater store than any other nation on the chastity of their wives. Hence they keep them shut up at home, and so hide them that they hardly see the light of day. If they are obliged to go out, they send them forth so covered and wrapped up that they seem to passers-by to be mere ghosts and specters. They themselves can look upon mankind through their linen or silken veils, but no part of their persons is exposed to man's gaze. The Turks are convinced that no woman who possesses the slightest attractions of beauty or youth can be seen by a man without exciting his desires and consequently being contaminated by his thoughts. Hence all women are kept in seclusion.[41]

As is usually the case, custom was not enough. In 1753, the following edict came down in response to the threat of women vacationing unescorted:

> Some women go to these places: Kısıklı, Bulgurlu, Çamlıca and Merdivenköy for the pursuit of pleasure. Some women even go as far as to travel in carriages to places on the Bosphorus such as Tokad, Akbaba, Dereseki and Uşâ with no shame. From now on, women are prohibited from commuting in carriages over a certain distance. If the carriage-driver accepts them, in spite of the prohibition, they will be exiled from Istanbul to the countryside.[42]

Another edict from the 16th century was issued to prevent women from sailing alone with sailors: "As was previously urged, it is imperative that you stop young ladies taking boat trips with sailors! Inform all boatmen of this situation."[43]

This was, of course, a culture that was not friendly to the concept of dating or casual romantic encounters. To make the necessary challenges of arranging marriages less onerous for families, Turkish culture had a special job, the *görücü,* for women to arrange marriages between two different families. The author Alev Lytle Croutier has left a vivid description of the age-old tradition, which lasted well into the 20th century:

> Unannounced the *görücü* appeared at a girl's house. Islamic custom not allowing one to turn away a guest, the girl's relatives would welcome the *görücü*—because that was their obligation. They served her coffee and sweets, acted polite, and made small talk. Meanwhile the young girl would be hiding in the kitchen or in another room, until her mother or aunts invited her in. She would be required to make and serve Turkish coffee since great importance was attached to her ability to brew this concoction. Her eyes cast down, she served the coffee to the *görücü* and her entourage, either leaving the room immediately after they had had sufficient opportunity to scrutinize her or sitting silently on the edge of her seat, listening to the other women carry on.[44]

Rather than being the exclusive playground of the Sultan, the harem was, in a sense, a society-wide institution. It was designed to preserve personal honor and civil peace by protecting all Muslim women from the gaze of strange men, or at least that was the ideal. In reality, many Turkish women, as Elsye Semerdjian argued, lived far more diverse lives than simply existing under the thumb of their fathers and husbands. They went out and held jobs as textile workers, managers of religious endowments, and even landlords and lenders.[45] As elsewhere, there were also those women who existed on the margins and flaunted their society's ideas of honor and sexual integrity, if only out of necessity.

The War on Prostitution

Even though prostitution was considered *zina* (fornication) under religious law, it was not an offense under the civil codes. As in the Christian West, prostitution was a reality that remained a reliable source of tension. Further, language itself blurred the line between any woman who stepped outside of notions of propriety and women who actually sold sexual services. The Turkish word, *sicils,* had roughly the same weight and breadth as the English word "whore," so it is difficult, if not impossible, to tell in records whether the term simply referred to women accused of having sex outside marriage and not those whom we would term "prostitutes."[46]

Whoever they actually were, the *sicils* since at least the 16th century were a problem for the government and for local communities. Prostitution was considered enough of a disgrace that the law explicitly protected slaves, who otherwise had few, if any, protections against being sexually exploited by their masters, from being forced into prostitution. Even the writers of court records, whenever an immoral woman was brought to the court's attention by the petitions of outraged neighbors, could not bring themselves to describe prostitution explicitly. One record from Aleppo discreetly describes one woman as a "mischievous" person who "brings strange men to her home."[47]

True to the Ottoman concern with defending the sexual integrity of women, procuring was considered a worse crime than prostitution. Again, though, the language used to portray brothels, madams, and pimps was subtle. The courts describe "mixings" of women and men who are "strangers"—that is, not related to each other by marriage or blood.[48] Even then, it seems clear when a professionally run brothel is being described. At least one brothel in the Empire was a family-run business. In the 17th century, an entire family was accused by their neighbors of letting "strangers mix" in their home.[49]

As with procurers, individual prostitutes were brought to the attention of courts by busybody neighbors distressed by their activities. In 1563, a neighborhood in Istanbul succeeded in petitioning a judge to exile five prostitutes, one of whom was a notorious madame. The practice of banishing prostitutes, especially at the request of horrified neighbors, may have been common in the Empire's urban areas. At the least it occurs multiple times in the court records of the Syrian city of Aleppo, one of the Ottoman Empire's major urban centers.[50]

The idea of community surveillance as a solution to the problem of prostitution proved popular enough that it was endorsed by Sultan Selim II (r. 1566–1574). The Sultan himself had enough of a bad reputation that posterity marked him as "Selim the Drunk," but that did not stop Selim from having a personal interest in his subjects' morals. In the second year of his reign, he urged people to keep watch over their neighbors and report any criminal activity, including prostitution. Any prostitutes that were found out would be detained and imprisoned.

However, it seems Selim's efforts were in vain. There were many places for prostitutes to ply their trade. Beyond having desirable male servers, there were coffeehouses known for offering male prostitutes on the side.[51] Laundrettes in the 16th century were especially a well-known front for prostitution, and they were not the only such places. Ice cream shops in Istanbul became a refuge for prostitutes trying to avoid the government crackdown, or otherwise became known as places where women tried to find ready and willing lovers, according to an edict issued in 1573:

> It has been noticed that that some women are going to ice cream shops with the intention of meeting men rather than how it appears, that is to eat ice cream. This situation cannot be overlooked. Women will be forbidden from going to ice cream shops in future. Shopkeepers are strongly urged not to allow women in their shops, if they do so, they will be subject to severe punishments.[52]

Far from leaving illicit sex as a private concern for families, the government of the Ottoman Empire had absolutely no hesitation over intervening to keep the sexuality of its subjects in the proper parameters. Ottoman sexual policy was designed to protect vulnerable women and male adolescents by encouraging paternal responsibility over susceptible members of the household and by discouraging, sometimes brutally, both would-be "exploiters" and those willing to be "exploited." However, by the 19th century this would change, as the Ottoman Empire, like the rest of the Middle East, began to feel the pressures of Westernization.

VIII

Reforming and Reaffirming

"Here I stand, I can do no other," Martin Luther allegedly said, in words that hint quite well that the Reformation was about more than just theology. It was a break from the pessimism of many intellectuals since the fall of the Western Roman Empire, asserting that society could be changed for the better from the ground up. Taking this optimism at face value, traditionally historians have claimed that the early modern era marked a tectonic shift from a rigidly hierarchical, communal, and oppressive society dominated by the Church to one that at least allowed room for individualism and pluralism and that saw the emergence of the State as a force to be reckoned with. More recently, historians have challenged the idea of such dramatic convulsions, either downplaying how much change actually was occurring or tracing these trends further back into the Middle Ages. Still, what happened in the 16th and 17th centuries—first and foremost the total demise of any concept of a unified Christendom—changed not just the structure of European society itself but the everyday experiences of Europeans, including their sex lives.

After all, sex was a favorite weapon in the war between Catholics and Protestants. Catholics accused their enemies of promoting a doctrine that permitted sexual anarchy; Protestants savored their images and descriptions of pleasure-loving priests and homosexual monks and nuns. Off the broadsheets and pamphlets, Protestants and Catholics, for all their serious divisions, tried to purify their own countries and cement their own moral superiority in surprisingly similar ways by cracking down on "deviant" sexuality, shutting down brothels, and promoting a sanctified and sanitized view of the world. Bawdy humor and irreverent behavior that would have been commonplace in the Middle Ages gradually became unthinkable, even blasphemous, in Catholic and Protestant circles alike.

Of course, happening alongside the Reformation and even helping it along was the spread of the printing press. The technology of printing was not yet as advanced as it would be even in the 17th century, but it did not take long after Johannes Gutenberg printed his first copies of the Bible for the press to become a weapon to be used and feared by all the various sects fighting for Europeans' minds and souls. While the first censors were largely concerned with heretical content, once the power of print to disseminate ideas far beyond the control of the elite became known, censors also began to wage war against sexual content that in an earlier time would have considered acceptable, if only among polite company.

The third great shock received by Europe in the era was the encounter with unfamiliar and even entirely new civilizations in the Americas and east Asia, which neither the Bible nor the just as sacred authorities of antiquity had prepared Europeans for. European scholars scrambled to explain how the existence of these new peoples in the Americas could still fit into the history of the world as presented by the Scriptures, leading to theories that Native Americans either were the descendants of another Adam and Eve or were actually not human at all (although one Jesuit writer, José de Acosta, did anticipate modern archeologists by theorizing that the natives' ancestors had crossed over from Asia). Wherever they came from, even the intellectuals who felt strongly that the way the natives were being treated by Europeans was immoral and barbaric could agree that the peoples of the Americas were mired in ignorance of proper morality. With the Chinese and the Japanese, who were admired for their populous cities and their wealth as well as for what Europeans perceived as the "Christian-like" characteristics of their cultures and philosophies, it was harder to come to term with these societies that went above and beyond in meeting Europeans' checklist for sophisticated civilizations, yet openly practiced polygamy and homosexuality.

From every angle, old certainties were being challenged in a way they had not been since the end of antiquity. Suddenly the 16th-century European had to face up to the reality that there were now many more "true Churches" than just the Catholic and Orthodox varieties, that a "heathen" empire had swallowed up most of Eastern Europe and was sitting right in the backyard of Austria and Germany, and that there were many books readily available about new ways of living and looking at the world, from recently unearthed works by Plato to the strange, far-off philosophy of Confucius. In light of all this, it should come as no surprise that the ways people thought about something as central to their lives as sex should change, too.

The Reformers versus Sex

The play and film *A Man for All Seasons* ends with the moral and loyal Thomas More being forced to choose between his conscience and his loyalty to his king. Refusing to accept Henry VIII's marriage to Anne Boleyn and his new rank as the Head of the Church in England cost Thomas More his triumphant political career and then his life. Outside the silver screen, More was made into a saint by the Catholic Church in 1935. Despite that, More was more a casualty of the ambitions of Henry VIII, who was no Protestant, than of religious persecution.

Nonetheless, in a way Thomas More was a victim of a movement he helped conjure into existence. While More and the other intellectuals historians call "humanists" for the most part had solid Catholic credentials, they inadvertently opened the gates for the Reformation by reviving interest in the philosophical writings of antiquity and by not just criticizing the present state of Church and society, but audaciously suggesting that something could and should be done about it. "Christian humanists saw social ills rooted in individual sin; however, their response did not stop at the sort of moralizing which had characterized medieval social criticism," Margo Todd explains. "Rather, they extended their critique from the individual to the larger society and demanded that the reformed individual reform the corruptions of his society."[1]

Specifically, leading humanists began to see social reform and moral guidance as the responsibility of not only the priest and bishop, but the magistrate as well. One well-known Spanish humanist, Juan Luis Vives, wrote a tract, *On Assistance to the Poor,* which urged secular officials to treat the indigent and insane humanely and laid out the earliest comprehensive plan in European history for a government to provide welfare and job training to the poor. However, to humanists like Thomas More, the government was also supposed to supply moral teachings. In his book *Utopia,* which was an international bestseller, More envisioned a compulsory educational system that would teach morals as well as facts.[2] Erasmus, a scholar who was born in Rotterdam but studied and taught across Western and Central Europe, urged authorities to attack bad sexual behavior at the source by discouraging dirty songs, stories, and dances. Inspired by what they read about the Roman Republic, both More and Erasmus agreed that governments of the day should create offices like the old Roman censor, empowered to single out and punish citizens guilty of poor moral behavior.[3] For them, both scripture and moralist writings from ancient Athens and Rome were helpful guides on how to improve Christian civilization by showing Christians just how to improve themselves (and, of course, push improvement on the ignorant populace).

Erasmus himself was a friend and admirer of a monk named Martin Luther, who after 1518 had been made into a celebrity when his *95 Theses* demanding reforms in the Church were published not in the Latin of the educated enclaves, but in everyday German. Their friendship fell apart when Luther and his allies turned their aim to the fundamentals of Catholic doctrine. After Erasmus refused to endorse their views, Luther, in his usual bombastic manner, denounced him as "the very mouth and organ of Satan."[4] Despite this falling out, Luther still agreed with Erasmus and other humanists that it was the responsibility of governments to deal with morals: "Let the government, if it wishes to be Christian, punish prostitution, rape, and adultery, at least when they openly occur; if they still occur in secret, the government is not at fault."[5] If the clergy was to have a role outside the church in dealing with moral infractions, it was to be only in urging officials to pass and enforce laws that defend society's moral well-being. After all, for Luther and his followers the Church should not exist as an institution, but rather as the community of the Christian "elect" with no leader except Jesus, who should have no intermediary.[6]

When it came to many sexual topics, Luther would not seem out of place next to most medieval moralists. Sex outside of marriage and contraception were explicitly denounced by Luther. He was particularly vehement when he meditated on the story of Sodom and the origins of male homosexual desire: "Whence comes this perversity? Undoubtedly from Satan, who, after people have once turned away from the fear of God, so powerfully suppresses nature that he beats out the natural desire and stirs up a desire that is contrary to nature."[7] One area where he did dramatically break with tradition was with the old idea of prostitution as an unpleasant social necessity. Luther blasted the Saxon town of Freiberg for reopening its municipal brothel in 1540 after previously closing it down. "Those who wish to reestablish such houses should first deny Christ's name, and recognize that, rather than Christians, they are heathens, who know nothing of God's name," Luther fumed.[8]

There were, though, areas where Luther's thoughts on marriage and sex were almost revolutionary. His most shocking declaration did not come from any of his fiery writings, however, but from what he did on a summer evening of 1523. That day Luther married, appalling a Europe that was already splitting at the seams. His bride was an ex-nun, Katharina von Bora, who met Luther through a sort of matchmaking service he was running for lapsed monastics.

From such blasphemous nuptials, Catholic propagandists prophesied that the happy couple would one day spawn the Antichrist. Meanwhile Luther's apostles, even after they were driven apart by squabbles over theology, continued to make the celibacy of priests their number one target.

The debate over priestly celibacy was not completely reopened by Luther. Early humanists like Coluccio Salutati (1331–1406) pointed out that priestly celibacy did not fit in at all with Nature as described by the philosophers of antiquity. Even Erasmus, despite his siding with Church doctrine, sardonically suggested that the Church punished priests taking lovers so rarely because even the Church realized that it had no choice but to allow priests to keep mistresses.[9] However, Luther went even further and saw celibacy as not only going against human nature, but also being a core explanation for the corruption of the Church. There is no mistaking Luther's thoughts on the sex lives of priests with quotes like "Now it is certainly obvious that these human laws forbidding the marriage of priests are really not the laws of man but of the Devil" and "If the pope had brought about no other calamity other than this prohibition of marriage, it would be sufficient to stamp him as the Antichrist, who is rightly called the man of sin and the son of perdition and the abomination, so much sin and perdition have come of this one prohibition."[10]

It is easy to overlook the fact that Luther's criticisms of celibacy were not simply an assault on the Catholic Church, but part of a serious reevaluation of sex and its role in life. A stable married life, not celibacy, was to Luther the sure key for godly living. In fact, for Luther sex was not inherently destructive; instead it was unhealthy *not* to have it.[11] "If a girl is not sustained by great and exceptional grace, she can live without a man as little as she can without eating, drinking, sleeping, and other natural necessities," Luther wrote. "Nor, on the other hand, can a man dispense with a wife. The reason for this is that procreating children is an urge planted as deeply in human nature as eating and drinking."[12] While Luther did emphasize the importance of procreation, sex also had the important role of fostering love between spouses. Summing up the views of Luther and other early Protestants, James Brundage claims, "It was the affectionate and loving relationship between married persons that constituted the good of marriage and lay at the heart of the marital state."[13]

Although he is remembered as the most stern and joyless product of the Reformation, Jean Calvin generally agreed with Luther. A French lawyer who was forced to flee his homeland after he broke from the Catholic Church, Calvin achieved fame when his book *Institutes of the Christian Religion* was spread across Europe by the printing presses. Calvin made a strong distinction between sex itself, which he saw as a God-given aspect of human experience and not a product of the Fall, and the addictive pleasures sex creates. Because of this, Calvin urges, a married couple should not be afraid of the act itself, but should still be on guard against too much lust untempered by love.[14]

One of the first reformers to propose a plan for merging these new morals with politics was Johannes Brenz, who argued for the replacement of the old ecclesiastical courts with synods run by citizens appointed by the government. For Brenz, dealing with the sexually deviant and their bad example was chiefly the duty of the secular ruler. The law did not have to try to reform the hopelessly depraved, but it did have to keep evil from corrupting and harming the saved.[15]

One of the first to help pressure governments into reshaping society as Luther and Brenz wanted was Huldrych Zwingli, a priest from Zurich whose attacks on clerical celibacy, the veneration of saints, and even some traditional ideas about Hell drew the backing of Martin Luther. Haunted by guilt over his one-time love affair with a prostitute and the fact that he was given only a slap on the wrist by the local bishop (who himself had a mistress), Zwingli made sexual excess a particular target of his sermons and urged the government of Zurich to crack down on sex crimes, including through a law mandating harsh fines for seduction. Like Brenz, Zwingli thought that because it was impossible to separate "true" Christians from the godless rabble, the government ought to act as if society was structured for Christians alone.[16]

Although it was only a matter of time before the reformers would split, they agreed on getting rid of the Church as an officialdom and shifting the responsibility for dealing with sex crimes over to secular magistrates and government-appointed ecclesiastical courts. This change should not be overstated; Europe's monarchies and republics were already taking on the responsibility of dealing with their peoples' sex lives long before Luther's words hit print. However, the reformers and the humanists did usher in a new understanding, where rulers, not priests, had the duty to keep the morals of the people in line, but this idea would not just be restricted to Protestant Europe.

Sex in Protestant Europe

In a phrase, what split the Protestants from the Catholics when it came to sex was the idea that it was marriage and family that were the higher calling and required the most work. Once more the trend had been set earlier by humanists like Erasmus, who in 1518 encouraged people to "leave celibacy for bishops" and advised that "the holiest kind of life is wedlock, purely and chastely observed."[17] Another humanist, Albrecht von Eyb, painted an idyllic image of family life, one that emphasized what it offered that lifelong abstinence could not:

> What could be happier and sweeter than the name of father, mother and children, where the children hang on their parents' arms and exchange many sweet kisses with them, and where husband and wife are so drawn to one another by love and choice, and experience such friendship between themselves that what one wants, the other also chooses, and what one says, the other maintains in silence as if he had said it himself; where all good and evil is held in common, the good all the happier, the adversity all the lighter, because shared by two.[18]

Promoting family life was intended for more than just a bit of happiness and good morals. In a time when populations were booming and towns and cities were growing with no end in sight, illegitimacy and women who were not financially supported by a husband or family became a natural target for overstretched communities. Simply put, both single women and illegitimate children were expensive.[19] Following the old double standard, Protestant courts would publicly admonish or fine men caught committing nonmarital sex, but women were beaten, imprisoned, or banished.[20] In Scotland, a session of the *kirk* (church) in a district of Edinburgh declared that fornication was not just a "scandal" but "hurtful to the commonwealth" because of the burden on the community unwanted children posed.[21] Early in the 17th century, the city council of Württemberg increased the period of imprisonment for having a child out of wedlock from a few days to four weeks for women and six weeks for men, while at the same time encouraging people in the community to keep a close watch on young unmarried women. On a similar note, in 1610 the Parliament of England passed a law sentencing any mother of an illegitimate child to a year in a workhouse.[22] Across Europe, ideas about legitimacy and the proper time for sex hardened accordingly. Sex during betrothal or as a way of marking one's engagement was soon no longer a commonly tolerated practice.[23]

Another Continent-wide social crisis coinciding with the Reformation was the debut of syphilis at the end of the 15th century. Originally called the "French pox" in most of Europe and the "Italian pox" in France because it was spread by French soldiers returning from a war in southern Italy, its very existence was at first denied by the doctors of the time, since no medical authority from ancient Greece and Rome had described its symptoms. Overnight syphilis became the topic of a large body of literature, as the disease showed a predilection for nobles and the clergy, and its unthinkable symptoms—disfigurement, blindness, and madness—became widely known. Although it was not the chief motive, syphilis did conveniently provide reformers with one more reason to shut down brothels and discourage prostitution. Still, in her study on prostitution in the German city of Ausburg, Lyndal Roper found no references to venereal disease in any anti-prostitution ordinance or campaign.[24]

All this said, the rise of Protestantism had its own influences, especially in the realm of marriage. Luther made his disagreement with the medieval Church clear when he declared, "Marriage is a civic matter. It is really not, together with all its circumstances, the business of the church."[25] Other Protestant reformers agreed, and Calvin himself sarcastically pointed out that the claim that marriage is a sacrament and the belief that even marital sex had the taint of sin was a contradiction.[26] The relationship of the Protestant pastor to the institution of marriage was to provide moral and spiritual guidance, but nothing more.

The Protestant reconstruction of marriage went deeper than its legal status. Reformers like Martin Bucer stressed the idea of woman as a caring companion, rather than a constant source of temptation to be endured. In the story of Adam and Eve, Bucer found evidence that God intended men and women to live in relationships that, while not equal (after all, Eve was created *for* Adam, not *with* him), were based on ideas of companionship. The implication was that human love was not just completely free of sin, but also reflected the divine.[27] It gave an important model for the wives of Protestant priests, who worked as mothers and wives as well as caring friends to their husbands' parishioners. While the pastor's wife, long demonized in European thought, slowly returned to the light, overall the Protestant Reformation diminished the role of women in religious life. Besides wiping out all trace of nuns and abbesses in Protestant countries, the father was expected to take full responsibility for religious education and leadership. Diarmaid MacCulloch explains, "No longer was it a matter of a mother teaching her child such formulas of the Church as the Hail Mary or Lord's Prayer. Now the ideal Protestant father would be expected to lead his family in prayer, and bring to that task the spontaneity or sense of particular occasion that characterized the minister's sermon in his pulpit."[28] In Protestant countries, women lost the option to choose celibacy instead of married life while spiritual and moral authority over the family was stripped from the Church and invested solely in the father.

Besides the matter of the role of women, the Protestant struggle with questions of marriage and family tore open very old debates about polygamy and divorce. When the Landgrave of Hesse, Philipp I, wrote to Luther for his opinion on whether it would be moral for him to marry his mistress without divorcing or annulling his marriage to his living wife, Luther ultimately decided to answer no, but added that bigamy might be permissible if the wife had leprosy. Bucer and the influential Protestant theologian Philipp Melanchton, also in contact with the Landgrave, reasoned that bigamy was much more preferable to adultery. Both Melanchton and Bucer offered similar advice to Henry VIII, advising that he should consider having Anne Boleyn as his second wife instead of annulling his marriage to Catherine of Aragon.[29]

Polygamy was too much for most other Protestant reformers, and in any case the reformers' marital advice for Henry VIII and Philipp of Hesse proved to be a public relations catastrophe happily exploited by Catholic opponents. More palpable to the reformers themselves and the populace were new ideas about divorce, which was the inevitable conclusion from the Protestants' treatment of marriage as little more than a civil contract. Furthermore, divorce was an easy way to resolve the problem of rescuing Protestants from marriages to unrepentant Catholics or to people who belonged to the wrong confessional tribe, whether they were Lutherans or Calvinists. Despite their own unwavering belief in the authority of the father and husband, early Protestants praised Anne Askew, an English woman who was tortured and burned at the stake for her religious views, even though she had refused to take her staunchly Catholic husband's surname and later left him. Significantly her admirers on the continent referred to her in their published editions of her writings by her maiden name, and not by her husband's surname, Kyme, which is also how history remembers her.[30]

Luther himself saw indissoluble marriage as another source of misery imposed by the Catholic Church and complained, "I would much prefer to ignore the whole problem and not to hear about it." Still, Luther advised that divorce should be acceptable only in times of impotence, adultery, or a spouse's refusal to have sex—restrictions that reveal just how integral Luther saw sex as being to a happy married life.[31] The other Protestant reformers shared Luther's reservations about condemning people to lifelong loveless (and sexless) marriages, but none really advocated for a return to the old Roman idea of marriage as a contract that can be dissolved at will. Calvin, for instance, thought people whose spouses deserted them or were adulterous were entitled to a divorce, but even then every possible effort should be made to force the pair to reconcile.[32]

The sort of mandatory marriage counseling Calvin had in mind was actually put into practice. The Protestant magistrates of Zurich granted divorces only in extreme situations. One court ordered an estranged wife and husband be put in a prison cell together with their meals served with one bowl and one spoon, reasoning that if they could not get along in such an extreme situation then it would really prove they could not stay married.[33] Swiss, German, Scottish, Scandinavian, and French Protestant courts did grant divorces for adultery and impotence, and sometimes for contracting a venereal disease, desertion, conviction for a capital crime, or assault. However, they differed over whether both spouses or just the wronged spouse could marry again.[34]

In spite of the old joke that the Church of England was founded just so Henry VIII could get rid of one wife for another, it was the sole Protestant church that completely rejected divorce and only allowed separations of room and board. It was not until 1670 that divorces could be granted by Acts of Parliament, but they were very rare and could be obtained only by the rich and influential. However, the 17th century also saw other Protestant governments expand their divorce laws. In that century, Sweden became the first Christian country to have laws allowing divorces for reasons other than those explicitly spelled out in the Bible—namely, alcoholism and physical abuse. Even then, divorces were effectively limited to just those privileged few who could afford the costly legal process. Just like in the Middle Ages, poor couples could and did break apart and their marriages were considered finished by their communities, but not the law.[35]

One rather bizarre practice carried out by villagers in lieu of a formal divorce in England and northern Ireland was the "wife sale." A ritual probably invented in the late 17th century, a man would lead his wife by a rope to a marketplace or a fair and sold her to the highest bidder, after the sale was advertised. However, the wife was a willing participant, the auction's winner was prearranged and was often the wife's lover, and the sale was purely symbolic, although real money and sometimes alcohol were traded. In isolated rural areas, the practice lasted as late as the early 20th century despite authorities imprisoning both the "buyers" and "sellers."[36] Before all their neighbors, the husband washed his hands of any obligations toward his wife, who gained the right to leave her husband and possibly start living with her lover, if she was not living with him already.

As Protestant governments were taking often hesitant and uneven steps toward making marriage secular and contractual, they also sought to remove prostitution as an acceptable option in society. Protestant reformers chiseled the very bedrock under the idea that prostitution was a necessary evil. One Protestant writer, Melchior Ambach, asked why, if women were more sensual and sex-crazed than men as the common medical theories of the time held, there were no brothels for women.[37] As for the rhetoric of Protestants themselves, the toleration of prostitution stood out against the fact that all women were expected to be chaste or married. Also, as Roper points out, efforts to shut down municipal brothels were "a recognition that men's sexual desires are not uncontrollable, and a faith that male lusts could be educated and redirected toward marriage."[38]

By the end of the 16th century, there were no municipal brothels left in Protestant Europe and laws that punished prostitutes and johns with jail and fines were commonplace.[39] The city government of London also made the effort to try to reform prostitutes, often seen as fallen women seduced into a life of uninhibited sex. The institution was Bridewell, a former royal residence that in 1553 was donated by King Edward VI to the city of London. From then on Bridewell had multiple functions, serving as a shelter for homeless children, a hospital for the poor, and a place where arrested prostitutes would receive both moral and job training. Less reform minded was the Danish king Fredrik II, who in 1574 made the town council of Helsingør arrest all the local prostitutes, had them beaten in public, and thrown out of town. If they returned, they would lose their ears. Anyone brave or foolish enough to return a third time would be drowned.[40]

Unsurprisingly, the laws and ordinances closing brothels and the would-be reformers of prostitutes did nothing to relieve the economic problems that drove many women into prostitution in the first place. Thus prostitutes who traveled from town to town, streetwalkers, and illegal brothels continued to function or popped up to replace their government-sanctioned competitors. There were also the so-called *amateurs,* female servants and laborers who sold sex in tough times or as another job.[41] Were there also prostitutes, male or female, who attempted to offer their services to wealthy women in this era? As absurd and grotesque as Melchior Ambach found the mere suggestion, an early 17th-century English play, *The True Tragi-Comedie Formerly Acted at Court,* has a reference to what might have been a real underground establishment in London that rented gigolos out to well-paying female customers. No other evidence of such a brothel exists.[42]

Now that there was no longer an institutional Church, moral reform in general became the growing concern and responsibility of Protestant governments. Consistories, which were government-appointed courts running traditional ecclesiastical matters, went after dancing, cosmetics, codpieces, low-cut dresses, carnival celebrations, and gambling in their communities.[43] Just as strict were state-run orphanages in the Netherlands. Not only were boys separated from girls, but young children were separated from their elders. Daily roll calls and barred windows were an everyday part of life. When the orphans were allowed to leave the building, they still had to wear uniforms and numbered armbands. At the Almsmen's Orphanage in Amsterdam, if a girl at the orphanage committed the worst crime of all by becoming pregnant, she was immediately sent to a workhouse.[44]

Although the Protestants rarely challenged the age-old double standard, most Protestant authorities did not give pleasure-seeking men a break. Calvinist elders in the French village of Ganges kept tabs on a local man suspected of having an affair.[45] Another Frenchman, Vidal du Vray, may have regretted his decision to convert to Protestantism in 1562 when a consistory at Nîmes ordered him to marry the female servant he had children with and had been living with for many years.[46] Outside of Calvin's own courts in Geneva, the title of strictest Protestant consistories should go to the Calvinist *kirks* of Scotland, where 2,523 out of 4,594 *kirk* sessions involved sex. Typically people charged with fornication were required to do penance by sitting on a stool in front of the entire congregation during Sunday services. Unfazed by social prominence, one *kirk* excommunicated a noble couple after they were charged with "whoredom" and refused to perform an act of public penance. In extreme cases, the *kirks* would gain the cooperation of secular magistrates in having sinners fined, imprisoned, or, in the case of sodomites, put to death.[47]

Although the most infamous persecutions of sodomites from the era were carried out under the Inquisition, Protestant countries were not at all reluctant to attempt to purge "unnatural acts" from their people. As we will see, Calvin's Geneva was especially vigilant on this front. In fact, Protestants, when faced with both the Catholic and Muslim "other," used accusations of sodomy and same-sex lust to prove their enemies' depravity. The English Protestant scholar and writer John Bale (1493–1563), who was a former friar, wrote an allegorical play, *The Three Laws of Nature, Moses, and Christ, Corrupted by the Sodomites, the Pharisees, and Papists,* where "Sodomismus" appears in robes, dressed like a monk.

In Protestant Europe, the number of laws and persecutions against sodomy actually increased, in some cases encouraged by regimes like that of Henry VIII seeking to take over matters once dealt with by the Church.[48] It took until 1683 for Denmark and Norway, then ruled by the same monarchy, to see a sodomy law, but even before that in 1613 a Norwegian man named Peter Johannes was burned alive for "sodomitical intercourse with males."[49] Sweden introduced its first sodomy law in 1608, although only 20 trials for sodomy ever took place.[50] By the close of the 1500s, most German cities and principalities had laws harshly punishing sodomy and specifically same-sex acts. The legal punishments were morbidly diverse. Some laws demanded burning, but others asked for drowning, starvation, and decapitation or nonfatal but still draconian punishments such as banishment, forced service on galleys, and indefinite confinement to an insane asylum.[51] The Parliament of Scotland tried to stop local courts from carrying out the death penalty for sodomy as the *kirks* demanded, but a few courts did so anyway.[52]

Other parts of Protestant Europe were slower in embracing strict sodomy laws. Most districts in the Dutch Republic—even Amsterdam, the most populated city in the Netherlands—had no laws against sodomy. The rare persecutions of both women and men accused of same-sex love that did take place in the 1500s and 1600s were justified based on vague accusations of violating "natural and divine laws." Records show that in the 17th century several women who lived together like married couples were persecuted. One of them was Hendrikje Vershuur: disguised as a man, she served in the Dutch army until she was discovered and then allegedly lived with and tried to marry a woman. Vershuur, like the other women on record, was exiled.[53]

England's law against "buggery" was first put on the books in 1533 (with the Parliament of Ireland following suit late in 1634), but even then—unlike many sodomy laws on the Continent—there was no provision for the "unnatural" acts of women.[54] After becoming one of the laws abolished during the reign of Mary I, who tried to return authority over morality to the Catholic Church, a new sodomy law was enacted under the Protestant Elizabeth I, which remained unchanged until 1861. Even then, people were rarely convicted under the law in the 16th and 17th centuries, although there were a few high-profile cases. Undoubtedly the most scandalous was the trial of the Earl of Castlehaven, who was beheaded in 1631 for sodomy. However, his crimes exceeded just having two of his male servants as lovers, allegedly including having his lovers rape his wife in hopes that one of them would father a child he could pass off as his heir. Then there was John Atherton, an Anglican bishop in Ireland who was hanged in 1640 for allegations that he had sex with a man named John Child, who was also hanged one year later. It is worth pointing out, though, that both cases were exacerbated by circumstances outside same-sex love. Atherton was closely linked to the Earl of Strafford, a detested enemy of the Parliamentarians who would soon win the English Civil War, and Castlehaven's crimes struck at the very core of the nobility's anxieties about lineage and household order.[55]

In a time of increased religious tension and when the printing press made hysteria about sodomites easier to spread than ever before, how did people on the ground react to the sodomite threat in their midst? One telling case involved a pastry chef from Frankfurt, Ludwig Boudin, who was put on trial for sodomy in 1598. For the most part, the numerous male witnesses of various ages nonchalantly described Boudin attempting to fondle them or declaring his love for them. One witness admitted that he and Boudin touched each other sexually and that Boudin exclaimed that he better go to bed with him or "he would go crazy." Another witness, who shared a bed with Boudin, said he was appalled when Boudin began caressing him, but simply told him that he should be ashamed and that "such things belonged to women." Other men Boudin allegedly tried to seduce just reminded him that he had a wife. Still, even though rumors about his tastes spread, Boudin seems to have been well liked in his neighborhood, rather than treated like a pariah, and went about his business for many years. When Boudin was finally bought up on charges, it was because of an accusation from Thomas de Fuhr, who had never been solicited by Boudin but instead was a rival pastry chief who had once tried unsuccessfully to have Boudin arrested for unfair business practices. Nonetheless, the courts had Boudin tortured and accused him of not only sodomy in general but also raping adolescents. The gulf between the attitudes of the authorities and those of Boudin's neighbors, even the ones he had tried to seduce, is striking.[56]

Nonetheless, average people were expected to do their part in keeping up society's morals. In the Middle Ages, household heads had some responsibility over making sure their servants, apprentices, and employees stayed in line, but it was also expected that the men could find an outlet at the municipal brothel. Now, however, older men and women had the duty to make sure both younger men and women working in their households or workplaces stayed not only sexually pure until marriage but also respectable. "Mistresses and masters were to keep servants from idleness, teach them good manners, make sure they attended church and correct their faults, firmly but gently ... as a parent would!" Susan Dwyer Anssen explains.[57] Naturally, Protestants were also encouraged by their pastors to be sure to control themselves, but the Calvinists made an art out of self-monitoring, perfecting techniques like regular Bible reading, moral log books, and daily journals.[58] It simply is not true that Calvinists, even the infamous Puritans, did not value individualism, as long as the individual in question kept in mind that she or he was utterly depraved.

There was an entire industry in manuals dedicated to teaching readers about their moral and family duties, made possible by the increasingly cheap and widespread technology of the printing press. Many books were devoted to instructing fathers on how to lead their families in prayer and Bible readings. There were also books written for girls and women, who throughout the era were more likely to be well educated, with titles like *The Mirror of Virtue for Christian Maidens* and which encouraged both spiritual devotion and total sexual self-control. These books were found both in the home and in Protestant schools.[59] The Protestants understood quite well and quickly how to spread not only their theology, but also the values they saw as essential to good living.

Heaven on Earth: Calvin's Geneva and Cromwell's England

Jean Calvin's well-known relationship with the Swiss city of Geneva did not start out well. The first time he lived in the city, he was politely but firmly asked to leave after his preaching caused a riot. Once the Grand Council of Geneva decided to embrace Calvin's theology to the point of giving it the force of law in 1541, Calvin practically ran the Council. He had gone from being a pariah to having the means to mold Geneva into one of the most morally strict and demanding governments in world history.

Even before Calvin was invited back to Geneva, the Council was already punishing unrepentant fornicators and adulterers with public whipping and banishment.[60] However, under Calvin's influence Geneva's intervention in its citizens' sex lives became stricter and more organized through the consistory. This body was composed of secular officials who were elected annually, along with magistrates and ordained ministers. Most minor indiscretions were just punished with a reprimand, but repeat sinners or ones whose crimes were too public to ignore would be put on trial. Also anyone could be brought before the Grand Council or any official committee based on hearsay alone. If found guilty, they would be sternly lectured, "of which Calvin was particularly adept,"[61] but if their crimes were especially heinous they could end up in prison, publicly degraded, excommunicated, or executed through a myriad of methods, as if the magistrates of Geneva could not settle for one: burning, strangling, hanging, burning, or decapitation. Using the Old Testament as its inspiration, the government deemed almost any moral offense could be purged through blood. Even a young child who struck his mother was executed in 1568.

Even in Geneva, there was resistance against Calvin's moralistic regime. One delegation of Genevan citizens dared to appear before the Council to argue that the moral laws demanded by the consistory were impossible to put up with. If the consistory continued to insist on such pure behavior, they declared, all their wives might as well be tied into weighted sacks and thrown into the river. The delegation was lambasted and the leader imprisoned. Others who spoke out against the government and its brutal moralizing ended up either imprisoned, exiled, or killed.[62]

Then there were those who seemingly agreed with Calvin and his allies in the government, but found that even they fell on the wrong side of the new moral line. Pierre Ameaux, hoping for favoritism since he was an early supporter of Calvin, went to the consistory asking for permission to divorce his wife Benoite, who had the shocking, not to mention heretical, belief that "she can associate with all men and all men are her husbands."[63] It was the first divorce case brought before the Genevan government, but Ameaux must have expected a favorable verdict. When interrogated by the consistory, Benoite gave a long, barely coherent speech where she claimed that since everyone belonged to the body of Christ, any woman could sleep with anyone. Her answer exposed her not only as a heretic, but also as mentally ill or, in the words of court documents, "monstrous and famous, against God and reason."[64] After a short stint in jail, Benoite was released once she admitted that she had been "transported in spirit"—that is, was out of her mind—and made a public apology. What followed was not marital bliss, but a long series of countersuits between husband and wife: Ameaux swearing that his wife had slipped back to her old views about adultery and even put them into practice, Benoite arguing that her husband had been abusing her. Eventually the consistory ordered Benoite imprisoned until death or sincere repentance, whichever came first, for adultery. Only then did the consistory grant Ameaux a formal, permanent divorce and permission to remarry.[65]

Adultery was a crime that particularly incensed Calvin, who demanded that adultery of either the husband or the wife be punished with death regardless of the circumstances. In fact, the only thing that saved Benoite Ameaux's life was the fact that even the stern moralists on the consistory could agree that she was unbalanced. Less lucky were Anne Le Moine and her lover Antoine Cossonex. Within just a week of being arrested, they were both put to death. Antoine was decapitated, while Anne was drowned.[66]

Like other authorities in Europe, the sexual sin that most distressed the Genevan authorities was sodomy, especially because sodomy appeared to them to be an imported sin. Almost 80 people were tried for sodomy from 1544 to 1789, and fewer than half of them were natives.[67] One sensational catch made by authorities was when the Genevans got their hands on a group of Turkish galley slaves in the middle of a war with the Duke of Savoy. Three confessed that they had sex with two French Catholics. All five were promptly burned alive.[68] One case that struck close to home was that of Pierre Canal, a Genevan official charged with treason. Perhaps to save his skin, under torture Canal also admitted to having sex with over 20 men. After being broken on the wheel, Canal was burned alive. Using names beaten out of Canal, the authorities made 11 arrests, with three drowned and seven banished (after refusing to confess under torture). One got off with a fine and the loss of political privileges, no doubt because he happened to be a high-ranking politician.[69]

Like some medieval commentators, Genevan jurists saw sodomy not just as an act, but as a diabolical predisposition that drove the accused to crave the sin. As such, jurists and magistrates looked for telltale signs of a "true compulsive sodomite." One woman was put on trial for fornication and committing a sex act with another woman. Since she was charged with blasphemy, because she had sworn under oath that she was a virgin when a physical examination proved she was not, jurists concluded that if she was capable of blasphemy then it was likely she was also a sodomite. In the end, she was drowned. Likewise Genevan jurists had a young French printer executed for trying to rape his male roommate. One of the jurists thought he should have a lesser punishment because he did not succeed, but the others countered that desiring to commit sodomy was surely as bad as actually doing it.[70]

A group of Calvinists made a second, but much less successful, attempt at social engineering in England. The vocal minority of Puritans, motivated by a volatile mix of hardline Calvinist theology and suspicion of lingering traces of Catholicism within the Church of England, had long been at odds with the monarchy. However, the powder keg exploded under the amazingly inept leadership of King Charles I, who aggravated the Puritans with unnecessary Church reforms that seemed designed to slice at the very roots of their theology. Unfortunately for Charles I, the Puritans found common cause with those infuriated by the king's knack for reviving obscure medieval taxes and his refusal to call the English Parliament for 11 years. These disputes snowballed into civil war, and from there the totally unprecedented trial and beheading of the king himself.

In the monarchy's place, the victors of the civil war took the step of creating a new form of government, the English Commonwealth. Theoretically the Commonwealth was meant to be a republic with the Parliament at the top. In practice it became a military dictatorship controlled by the general Oliver Cromwell, who as "Lord Protector of England" exercised more power than Charles I ever did as king. To this day Cromwell remains an enigma to historians. On the one hand, he massacred and persecuted Ireland's Catholic population to such an extent that dominance of Ireland shifted unquestionably to the minority of Protestant landowners. On the other hand, he ended the centuries-old expulsion of Jews from England. One thing is certain: Cromwell and his supporters, like their coreligionists in Geneva, wanted a government that would regulate both actions and minds. Even though they shut down the old ecclesiastical courts that fined people for moral misdemeanors, it was only because they saw such institutions as a relic of the Catholic Church. Instead the government would fully take on the responsibility of keeping the masses respectable.

First the Puritans in power tried to stamp out the causes of decadence. A favorite target was holidays, even Christmas, which were seen as occasions when people justified immoral behavior and which were the fossilized remains of pagan worship. By 1642, theaters were also shut down, being seen without question as promoters of idleness and sexual sin. Beyond dealing with the sources of illicit behavior, the Puritans sought to "cure" the symptoms as well. Swearing could be fined, with the fines based on a sliding scale, and fornicators could be imprisoned for three months at most. As in Geneva, adultery by either the woman or the man was made into a capital offense. Prostitutes and brothel owners were to be whipped, branded, and imprisoned for first offenses; any subsequent offense would mean the death penalty. Cromwell personally appointed a number of old army colleagues as major-generals and gave them broad instructions to "encourage and promote godliness, and discourage and discountenace all profaneness and ungodliness."[71]

This Puritan revolution never caught on for a variety of reasons. Chief among them was that the Puritans were never seen by the rest of the English populace as anything but an annoying minority trying to push their morality on the country by force. Only two people were ever put to death for adultery, and Christmas celebrations for the most part went on as normal every winter under the Commonwealth.[72] Many local officials were unsympathetic, to say the least, and often ignored the new moralistic legislation, if they did not go out of their way to undermine it.

Another problem that irritated Cromwell was that his attempt to change moral thinking in England worked too well, with far too many people feeling as if they had a voice in what England should be like. Even beyond radical groups like the Ranters, there were more moderate but nonetheless daring voices like that of the poet John Milton, who was a tireless advocate for legalizing divorce, no doubt because of his miserable marriage to Mary Powell. Powell had left Milton, but he had to remain legally married to her. One anonymous pamphlet, *A Remedy for Uncleanliness,* was dedicated to Oliver Cromwell and argued that polygamy should be legalized, since it would reduce promiscuity, spousal abuse, and even infanticide. The Quakers were inspired enough by the radical air to openly urge people to adopt truly egalitarian marriages and to let women have an equal voice in church and public affairs.[73]

The most telling sign of failure was that the Puritans' efforts to build a truly godly society came to nothing in the end. The Commonwealth lasted just a few years after Oliver Cromwell's death until the restoration of the monarchy in 1660. The new king, Charles II, presided over a boisterous court that could very well have sprung out of a Puritan's darkest nightmares, full of elegant royal mistresses and young male rakes who dedicated their lives to good drink, fine food, and sexual conquests. In the meantime, traces of the Commonwealth—and Puritanism itself—faded so completely from history outside the fame and notoriety of Oliver Cromwell that the English Commonwealth may as well have never existed.

Sex in Catholic and Orthodox Europe

As Russia fully recovered from the Mongolian invasions of the 13th century that swept away the wealthy and influential state of Kievan Rus and then gave way to the rise of the powerful imperial monarchy devised by Ivan IV "the Terrible" (r. 1533–1584), Western European countries and Russia reestablished diplomatic and trade contacts. For the first time, Russia even became the destination of English traders and diplomats, some of whom claimed to be shocked by the casual sexual activities indulged in by the Russian people.

Some commented on how widespread—and unremarkable—homosexual acts appeared to be among Russians.[74] The poet George Turberville, who visited Russia on official business for Elizabeth I in 1568, was disgusted by the open homosexual acts enjoyed by Russian peasants, even those, he remarked with astonishment, who were married to women.[75] Sir Jerome Horsey, an English commercial agent who carried out diplomatic chores for the Russian government, righteously declared that the bloodshed carried on under Ivan the Terrible was just punishment for the "lust and wickedness of the crying sodomitical sins" of the Russian people.[76]

Lesbianism in Russia seems to have been somewhat controversial, especially if the women threatened to fully usurp the role of the man in sex. Lesbianism was also vaguely associated with witchcraft and blasphemy, with women accused of same-sex relations sometimes being

VIII Reforming and Reaffirming

labeled as "God-insulting grannies."[77] There are reports of a traditional game where two young, unmarried women would pretend to be a newly married couple and were put to bed together, apparently to enjoy sexual play that provided an audition for the wedding night.[78]

The Western view of Russia was of a society that treated its women like chattel and where beating wives was absolutely rampant. The late 15th/early 16th-century Austrian ambassador Sigmund von Herberstein, in his *Notes upon Russia,* claimed with austere authority, "The condition of the women is most miserable; for they consider no women virtuous unless she live shut up at home, and be so closely guarded that she go out nowhere" and "Russian women consider beating a sign of love."[79] Vindicating such a view was the fact that, as part of the traditional Russian wedding ceremony, fathers handed a ceremonial whip to the new husbands, while aristocratic and royal women were strictly segregated and made to live in their own quarters, the *terem*. While spousal abuse was undoubtedly common, Russian canon law did allow women to seek a divorce on grounds of cruelty and abuse. Certainly as early as the 13th century, canon law allowed a woman to seek a divorce if her husband falsely accused her of a serious crime, including adultery,[80] which was crucial since false charges of adultery must have been widely used by unhappy husbands wanting a divorce.

Although Russian noblewomen were kept secluded in the *terem* to help defend their modesty, it was apparently expected among Russian peasants that some women would indulge long before their wedding nights. A folklorist in the 18th century collected a number of sayings from villages in the northwestern Russian province of Vologda like "Of ten marriages, only one involves a pure maiden." As late as the dawn of the 20th century, peasant villages followed the custom of *skakaniya,* "galloping," which took place on the eve of the wedding ceremony in the groom's house where all the young guests would stand in a circle, resting their arms on each others' shoulders and galloping, kicking their legs up high, the maidens lifting up their skirts, and all of them singing erotic songs. This would end with all the partiers falling asleep side by side. Then there was the *yarovukha,* named for the Slavic god of fertility Yarilo, which was a pre-marriage gathering of young people at the bride's home for a party, after which they would sleep side by side with anything short of sex being permitted. None of this is to say that Russian villages were hotbeds of sexual anarchy. Village councils could and did dissolve marriages where the wife—and sometimes the husband— was known to be excessively adulterous.[81]

As for Catholic Europe, it was not a passive victim of the unfolding Reformation, but rather launched its own reevaluation, the Counter-Reformation or Catholic Reformation. Starting in 1545 and ending in 1563, the landmark Council of Trent convened 25 sessions in what is now the Italian city of Trento. While the Council of Trent left no topic of theology and church politics untouched, one of the most controversial topics was that of the sex lives (or lack thereof) of priests. By no means did the papacy's insistence on preserving clerical celibacy go unchallenged. One heated anonymous pamphlet, distributed during the Council's first sessions, urged the Council to let priests marry or else they would just depend on the caresses of concubines.[82] A delegate representing Duke Albrecht V of Bavaria went so far as to argue, "Chaste marriage would be preferable to sullied celibacy."[83] Nonetheless, there was no serious push to end mandatory celibacy. The Council ultimately declared, "If any one saith, that the marriage state is to be placed above the state of virginity, or of celibacy, and that it is not better and more blessed to remain in virginity, or in celibacy, than to be united in matrimony; let him be anathema."[84] The Jesuit Robert Bellartine concentrated on this stress on the importance of celibacy in 1598 when he wrote, "Marriage is a thing human, virginity is angelical. Marriage is according to nature, virginity is a thing above nature."[85]

Although ultimately its confidence in celibacy was unshaken, the Catholic Church turned its attention to accusations of sexual corruption among the clergy and monastics. The Council wanted to make sure that leniency toward priests who had sex would be a thing of the past. For the first time it set definitive, church-wide rules on how to proceed against priests who had less than appropriate relationships with women. After being warned and given a punishment deemed fit by their superiors, relapses would mean being stripped of more of their income and offices until finally they lost everything and even faced excommunication. Low-level clerics who had no church income had it worse; they could be suspended or even imprisoned.[86] This crackdown had mixed successes. In Würzburg, 45 percent of rural priests were suspected of having mistresses just before the Council of Trent, but by the middle of the 17th century the total number had been reduced to four.[87] By comparison, in 1581 a papal nuncio was less than pleased to find that in Salzburg fewer than 10 out of 220 parish clergy did not have a mistress or were not married. Of course, this statistic might not be shocking considering that they had role models like Salzburg's prince-archbishop, Wolf Dietrich von Raittenau, who lived with a woman who bore him 15 children. While he was deposed and imprisoned for life in 1613, he suffered this fate not because of his lifestyle, but because he led Salzburg into a disastrous war with Bavaria.[88]

The Council also tried to stop the flow of unwilling women into the convents, although it was a move fought by nobles across Europe who did not want to lose their convenient dumping ground for unmarriageable daughters. Eventually the Church settled for trying to keep convents under even tighter administrative control and for encloistering nuns, forcing them to contribute to Christianity through quiet lives of seclusion and prayer, and preventing independent Catholic women who claimed spiritual sanctity from inspiring unpleasant rumors.[89] For instance, in Spain the Inquisition began targeting the *beatas,* women mystics, and sentencing some of them to house imprisonment where they would be constantly supervised by a priest. One *beata* from Seville, Catalina de Jesús, drew both friendly and hostile attention because she raised a following that numbered more than 700 people and was the subject of saintly stories such as one where a young rake dedicated his life to God after just touching the hem of her robe. When Catalina was brought before the Inquisition, her judges mocked her for daring to claim that she remained chaste and pure while she was out in the world.[90]

At the same time, at least a few theologians writing in the shadow of the Catholic Reformation reassessed the sinfulness of sex. While sex was not at all split off from sin, the points of emphasis were changing. The Jesuit Tomás Sanchez wrote that even oral sex and fondling were just trifling sins or perfectly acceptable as long as they led up to "actual" sex, with both partners in their right positions (although Sanchez was far from a sexual free thinker; for instance, he suggested that sex with the woman on top was a reason God unleashed the Flood in Genesis).[91] Penitential writers began to emphasize the state of one's conscience and the interior self more than the acts themselves. For example, in his penitential the future French saint Francis de Sales urged priests not to focus on the penitent's actions, but instead try to get at their "purely interior desires and urges."[92]

Alongside this trend toward looking at the purpose and thinking behind sinful acts, the Church and Catholic governments, like their Protestant counterparts, became more vigilant and were obsessed with stemming the surge in illegitimate births. It became common in Italy for both local governments and the Church to forbid single mothers from raising their own children and instead require them to leave their offspring in orphanages (*ospizi*). Law or not, the mothers still had to pay a mandatory fee. If they could not afford it, they were arrested, placed in prison, and had to work as a wet nurse in the same *ospizo* where their child was placed. Most children placed in the overcrowded and poorly funded *ospizi* did not live long.[93] In much of Catholic Europe, the Magdalene Houses or conversion houses were ideally reformatories for "loose" women, who were barely distinguished from prostitutes. In practice, they were prisons where women could be imprisoned indefinitely for any act outside the bounds of good society.[94]

Like Protestant magistrates, the Council of Trent tried to end the old and widespread tradition of marriages being consummated through sex. A far-reaching decree, Tametsi, formalized marriage by asserting that marriages were valid only when the promise was publicly announced on three occasions at the parish church and officially contracted in the presence of a priest. This was to stress the strength of the verbal promise over physical consummation.[95] The Council wanted to make sure that sex was restricted to a sharply defined marital sphere, a move backed by governments. The laws of France went beyond even the call of the Council by classifying all marriages entered into without parental consent as *rapt*, "abduction." Another weapon in the French monarchy's arsenal were the *lettres de cachet*, decrees from the king of France himself that ordered the indefinite imprisonment of anyone whose family petitioned to have them incarcerated because their lifestyle posed an economic burden or a threat to family honor. Anyone with out-of-control gambling habits or a history of sexual excess could suddenly find themselves victims of a *lettre de cachet*. Also, despite the Council of Trent's interest in curtailing the practice of forcing women to enter convents, it became customary for people who had female relations who indulged in scandalous behavior or refused to marry their family's choice of husband to be placed in a convent.[96]

Under the Holy Roman Emperor Charles V, the first law code that attempted to cover all of Germany and Austria, the *Constitutio Carolina Criminalis,* was published in 1532 and included new laws on sex. It punished sodomy by both women and men as well as adultery by husbands and wives, citing "public opinion" as the damaged party in any adultery case. French law could also punish both partners in the marriage, although women unsurprisingly often received the worst punishment: publicly whipped and sentenced to a convent for at least a couple of years. A case where an adulterous man was punished took place in 1552 when Verier de Monbrison was convicted of adultery with a married woman, Martine Galliot. While wearing nothing but a shirt with a cord around his neck and holding a candle, he had to beg for forgiveness from God, the king, and Martine's husband before all his neighbors. Verier was fined and banished, while Martine was whipped and imprisoned in a convent for two years, with her husband given her dowry and the option of leaving her. Martine's punishment was typical, but a commentator did note that Verier's punishment was unusually strict.[97]

Violence against adulterous wives and their lovers did take place, although the historian Scott Taylor noticed that at least in one region of Spain it was far more common for wronged husbands to resort to legal complaints against their wives' lovers instead of a vendetta.[98] Still, the vendetta was a recurring theme in literature, which allowed a few writers to scrutinize their societies' attitudes toward honor and sex. One such author was the 17th-century Spanish playwright Pedro Calderón de la Barca, who wrote a series of plays remembered as his "honor plays." One play, *El pintor de su deshonra* (*The Artist of His Own Dishonor*), is about two cousins, the painter Don Juan and Serafina, who have been pressured by their family into marrying. Even though Don Juan wanted to be a lifelong bachelor, he eventually enjoys married life. Serafina is far less satisfied because she had previously promised to marry Don Alvaro, a sailor who was thought to have drowned at sea. When Don Alvaro returns alive, Serafina refuses to run away with him. Unsatisfied, Alvaro abducts and rapes Serafina. She realizes that, even though she was taken against her will, she has been disgraced and will have to either join a convent or die. Under pressure from all sides, Don Juan reluctantly kills Serafina and Alvaro. After the murders, he wants to commit suicide, but his own father and Serafina's father pardon him, recognizing that his hand was forced by society's code of honor.[99]

Prostitutes were one alternative to faithful married life that governments were targeting. Municipal brothels also began to vanish from Catholic Europe during the 1500s, although most countries from Portugal to Poland allowed independent brothels to continue to operate freely, albeit under restrictions such as workers having to live and ply their trade in designated red-light districts. Other countries took more drastic measures. King Felipe IV (r. 1621–1640) of Spain did not just shut down municipal brothels, but outlawed brothels altogether in 1623. The popes had to make two attempts in 1555 and 1566 before they could finally shut down all of Rome's brothels. One of the many obsessions of King Louis XIV (r. 1643–1715) of France was ridding Paris of all prostitution. To that end, in 1658 he established the Salpêtriere, a reformatory (or prison, depending on one's point of view) for women found guilty of not just prostitution but also fornication and adultery.[100]

As governments moved more into bedrooms, so did the Church. The combative atmosphere of the Catholic Reformation encouraged a few hardliners such as Pope Sixtus V. The son of poor Croatian Christians fleeing a Turkish invasion, the future Sixtus V rose through the Church's ranks with a reputation for strictness and butting heads. Once he became pope, Sixtus V decreed that all forms of contraception and abortion held at any stage of the pregnancy were murder and anyone committing those sins could be excommunicated. This was a break from the traditional belief that the fetus was "ensouled" when it started showing signs of movement, and indeed was a prelude to the contemporary Church's stance on abortion. Nonetheless, after Sixtus V died a reviled man in 1591, Gregory XIV altered his decree, making abortion only an excommunicable offense after the ensouling of the fetus.[101]

Beyond Rome itself, the Catholic Church was careful to combat the widespread belief that there was nothing wrong with casual sex. In fact the Inquisition was far more interested in making sure people had the right ideas about sex than in punishing sex crimes themselves. The records of the Inquisition reveal cases like that of a widow in 17th-century Spain who had several children with a married man, insisting, "It is not a sin. God ordered us to multiply and fill the Earth and have children."[102] Some apparently even believed that it was *not* having sex at the slightest opportunity that was the sin. A Portuguese sailor who tried to sleep with a Brazilian slave woman retorted to the man that stopped him "that whomever does not sleep with women in this world will sleep with the Devil in the other."[103]

Sodomy was still in this time an umbrella term that covered any type of "unnatural" intercourse. Nonetheless the Catholic Church, governments, and the populace were united by a special ferocity against same-sex acts, which was usually reserved only for heretics. This was especially true for Spain, which Garza Carvajal writes "emerged as a bastion of Catholic conservatism […] sternly fixated on the suppression of heresy and sexual desires."[104] In the

Spanish province of Valencia, after a Franciscan friar in the summer of 1519 preached a sermon blaming a recent plague on unchecked sodomy, a mob tracked down five suspected sodomites and handed them to the authorities, who promptly had four of them burned. When the fifth, who was a minor cleric, was given a light sentence by the ecclesiastical court, he was grabbed by the mob again and strangled to death, and his corpse burned.[105]

In 1524, Pope Clement VII had given the Inquisition in the Spanish regions of Aragon, Valencia, and Catalonia special permission to try sodomites. In Castile and Seville, with the blessing of the Church, secular courts also worked hard to condemn sodomites. The populace's support for the executions manifested in the popularity of the *auto de fé*, a public festival arranged by the Church and the monarchy where heretics, lapsed *conversos* (Jews and Muslims who converted to Christianity), and sodomites were burned after a lengthy sermon. William Monter paints the scene: "Crowds of familiars [secular officers] gathered from all over the district, dressed in the uniform of the Holy Office. Solemn processions with gigantic crosses and green candles advertised the main event. Specially dressed prisoners, sometimes with their crimes identified by placards around their necks, prostrated themselves before the Inquisitors in order to receive absolution."[106] From 1570 to 1630, more people were executed for sodomy in Aragon, 70 in all, than for heresy. Although Spain's neighbor Portugal was relatively more lenient, 30 men were burned alive for sodomy by the Portuguese Inquisition.[107] The fact that other forms of sodomy did not attract the same official revulsion as same-sex love was revealed by cases like that of Juan de Buendia, a cleric from Seville who in 1612 confessed to the Inquisition that he had anal sex with a woman three times. Instead of being burned, he was imprisoned in a monastery for a year, exiled, and deprived of the right to hear confessions.[108]

Even in Spain at the height of sodomy persecutions, female homosexuality was not seen as a threat. The Inquisition in Seville recorded only two convictions of lesbian acts. In the first case, a group of women convicted of having intercourse with each other were whipped and exiled, but not burned. In the second case, a woman charged with using a false penis was hanged on vague charges of robbery, murder, and "audacity."[109] The Inquisition in Aragon had even ruled that it was impossible for a woman to commit sodomy unless she used a dildo.[110] In the entire history of the Portuguese Inquisition, no women were ever arrested, much less burned, for same-sex acts.[111] Generally, then, lesbianism was deemed a threat only when women tried to usurp the man's role by inverting their "natural" role in sex and reproduction.

That lesbian sex was not taken seriously was best shown by what the writers of erotica, despite living in a completely different world than the Inquisitors, were saying. The seigneur de Brantôme, whose bestselling *Lives of Fair and Gallant Ladies* was purported to be a steamy exposé of noblewomen at the French court, praised sex *donna con donna* as something husbands should not discourage, since it gave wives a safe and acceptable alternative to adultery with men. Many husbands, Brantôme claimed, "were right glad their wives did follow after this sort of affection rather than that of men, deeming them to be thus less wild."[112] Other authors of erotica acknowledged the enticement of lesbian love for women as well as men, but also made sure it was clear that lesbian love was just a warm-up to "proper" sex with men. "There is a tacit understanding that the women will soon escape from their frustrations to the arms of men, where they will finally find real sexual pleasure," Lillian Faderman writes. The most blatant example of this was in Nicolas Chorier's *Satyra Sotadica*. In it two women discuss lesbian sex, act out the theories from their discussion, and then are joined by men who fully satisfy their sexual needs.[113]

In spite of this double standard, there were still male sodomites who were unapologetically flagrant. In Seville, a sheriff was caught keeping male prostitutes in the gambling house he ran, while an African named Mayuca, who went about the city dressed in cosmetics and a wig, was a well-known procurer of male prostitutes for an aristocratic clientele.[114] In Venice, the priest Alessandro Rubilio was charged with running a small brothel of women out of his house, allegedly to attract men who would have sex with him.[115] Others simply defied the law and social disapproval to pursue relationships. The Brazilian scholars Luiz Mott and Aroldo Assunção discovered letters in the archives of the Portuguese Inquisition written from Francisco Correa Netto, who had a job managing relics for the cathedral of Silves, to Manuel Viegas, a guitarist and maker of musical instruments. For whatever reason, Viegas handed the letters over to a vicar, who eventually gave them to the Portuguese Inquisition. The Inquisition charged him not only with sodomy but also with being part Jewish, since he could not produce papers demonstrating good Christian blood. He was never put on trial, because even with the letters the court needed proof of more than one consummated act of sodomy. One poignant letter reads:

> Mirror of my sight and joy, if I have any right to you, bring peace to my heart and confirm the news I received this evening, that you were betrothed to a niece of Francisco Luiz last Monday. I would have said that by Easter you would be betrothed to me. You implied that often, and you gave your word on it. But do as you please: in spite of this I shall not stop doing what I can to be at your service. And remembering your arms and the kisses you gave me, that is what torments me most! And you know this subject well, in that heart of your loins, it was that which desired me, with its craving to fly up. There was no Lent for that heart in your loins, when I touched it with my fingers, and instantly it sprang up! And you, so evil, who did not want to do what comes so naturally!
>
> Goodbye, my darling, my happiness, my true love!
>
> My idea is that, even though you may be married, you do not have to break your promise to be the betrothed of your devoted Francisquinha [a feminine diminutive of Francisco]. It seems to me you told Manuel da Costa that if I complied with your whims, even then you would come to me, because you do not care, and it was all sham.
>
> Here is paper to answer: Now you have no excuse not to write for lack of paper.[116]

In certain intellectual and artistic circles, it appears being known as a sodomite gave one a certain notoriety that was treated as a joke or even as a homage to the classical tradition. As Italian humanists explored and promoted the culture and literature of antiquity including its poetic and heroic descriptions of pederasty, defenses of love (and lust) between men emerged, if only on the margins. A Franciscan monk, Antonio Rocco, wrote *L'Alcibiade fanciullo a scola* ("Alcibiades the Schoolboy"), a book about the seduction of the titular schoolboy by his teacher Filotimo. Over the course of the seduction Filotimo makes a case for homosexual desire, stating that the idea that sodomy is unnatural is absurd, since "actions are natural when nature inclines us to them." The book was actually published anonymously, but Rocco's authorship of the book was an open secret. The Inquisition made several accusations against him, yet he died a free man. A similar book from Italy that raised eyebrows was *La Cazzaria* ("Discourse of Pricks"), published in 1530. Written by a nobleman from Siena, Antonio Vignali, the book was a dialogue between Arsiccio and his friend Sodo, the nicknames Vignali himself and his friend Marcantonio Piccolomini were known by in the Academy of Siena. In the book Arsiccio argues, "If nature had wanted men not to engage in buggery, she would not have made the experience so enjoyable; or she would have it physiologically impossible."[117]

The most flamboyant male lover of men in Renaissance Italy, however, had to have been Giovanni Antonio Bazzi (1477–1549), who was widely known as *il Sodoma,* a nickname he even used as his signature. A married man, il Sodoma was said to have been literally surrounded by male lovers.[118] In spite of his reputation, which caused him (and his pet baboon) to once be stoned by a mob of boys in Florence, he was made a Cavalier of Christ by Pope Leo X. Afterward Bazzi began proudly employing the signature "Antonio Sodoma, Knight of Siena." Perhaps *il Sodoma* was not quite as notorious as he might have been, arguably because his public persona was treated as something of a joke, but accounts show that he at least occasionally suffered harassment that required the intervention of some powerful friends.[119]

Even at the height of hysteria over sodomy in Europe, it appears that elite status might have protected one from persecution and even the very worst of public scorn. This was more or less true for royalty. Queen Christina of Sweden (1626–1689) was dogged by rumors that she had sexual relations with women—most famously Ebba Sparre, who according to a Danish ambassador "associated with [Christina] in a special way."[120] Neither the widely circulated rumors of her affairs with both women and men, nor her habit of dressing in eclectic combinations of male and female fashion items, stopped Christina from being warmly welcomed in Rome as a celebrity convert from Protestantism to Catholicism by the pope himself.

Not as lucky, and perhaps the best proof that men who were suspected sodomites were harder to stomach than their female counterparts, was King Henri III of France (r. 1574–1589). Deemed by his own secretary Pierre de L'Éstoile as a "buggerer, son of a whore, tyrant,"[121] Henri III, who unfortunately reigned during the destructive Wars of Religion that shredded France in the later 1500s, is easily one of the most reviled French kings. According to contemporaries and historians, Henri III was alleged to have dressed in effeminate clothes that verged on transvestism and to have made lovers out of his *mignons,* male hangers-on collected from the lowest ranks of the nobility. Either Henri did frequently commit the unmentionable sin or, as Katharine B. Crawford suggests, he was the victim of propaganda warping his favoritism toward lesser nobles and his attempts to associate service to the king with Renaissance notions of love and devotion.[122] The author of one pamphlet alleged that one of Henri's *mignons* won his honors through his ass rather than his sword; prominent notables like the ambassador from Savoy claimed, "I will say only that [Henri's] cabinet has been a real harem of all lubricity and lewdness, a school of sodomy, where filthy revels have occurred which all the world has known about."[123]

Christina of Sweden and Henri III were never deposed for sodomy (although Henri III was assassinated in 1589 by a fanatical Catholic friar). Even if the allegations had any truth to them, these monarchs were—like their near-contemporary James VI/I of Scotland and England, who was known for his relationship with his "favorite" the Earl of Buckingham—able to conduct their same-sex affairs despite living in a public, crowded realm like a royal court. Likewise, intellectual celebrities like *il Sodoma*, even in a climate where burning sodomites alive was a perfectly acceptable judicial option, were defended and even acknowledged and respected. However, only the elite, whether royal or social, enjoyed such protection (limited as it was)—though in Henri III's case sometimes even power and privilege were no guarantee against the savaging of a reputation.

Although there were enclaves within the culture where even sodomites might be seen as eccentrics at worst, they raised no challenge to the *status quo* on sexual ethics, at least not yet. The real threat in this era did not come from royals known across Europe for their alleged romances with members of the same sex or from books offering updated celebrations of classical homoerotic ideals. Instead it came from religious dissidents whose conclusions about theology led them to question old notions about marriage and the family.

The Radicals of the Reformation

Since the lifetime of Charlemagne, the northern German city of Münster had been ruled by bishops. Like so many Catholic institutions in much of Germany, that legacy faced its first serious threat in the Reformation, as Münster's city council turned against its newly appointed prince-bishop, Franz von Waldeck, and sided with the followers of Melchior Hoffman, who had prophesied that the Second Coming of Christ would happen any day now. Hoffman had joined with the Anabaptists, a radical Protestant sect named for their claims that only adult baptisms were valid. After Hoffman ended up in a Strasbourg prison, his followers rallied around the charismatic prophet Jan Matthijszoon, a baker from the Netherlands who predicted that Münster would be ground zero for the Second Coming. What made Matthijszoon dangerous was not just that he picked up his mentor's knack for apocalyptic prophecy, but that he totally rejected Hoffman's pacifism. Unlike mainstream Reformation leaders, Matthijszoon preached that violence and open rebellion against civil governments were completely and always justified in the name of true religion.

Driven by bitter disappointment that the spread of Protestantism had not brought with it real social change, thousands from the Netherlands and northern Germany heard Matthijszoon's call and congregated in Münster to be baptized and to hear promises of an approaching paradise. By February 1534, the Anabaptists fully took over Münster, a triumph which fueled their own apocalyptic fervor. The exiled Waldeck raised an army supported by his scandalized Lutheran neighbors, who were horrified enough by the Münster Anabaptists to put aside their own anti–Catholic feelings. After Matthijszoon found out the hard way that God was not willing to protect him from a violent death in battle as he had naturally assumed, leadership passed to a Dutch tailor who went by the title "John of Leiden." Not satisfied with simply waiting for the Second Coming, especially since the deadline given by Hoffman had passed, John of Leiden presented himself as a new King David and as the messianic king of the world whose reign would usher the world into the End Times.

The new Anabaptist regime legalized polygamy, in spite of some resistance. The rationale was that polygamous marriage paralleled Christ's many marriages with his followers. This was not the only radical reform the Anabaptists forced on Münster. When the Anabaptists first took over, most of the Catholic, Calvinist, and Lutheran men left, in many cases leaving behind their wives to keep watch over their homes. Allegedly the Anabaptist leaders ordered that all women's marriages to Catholics, Calvinists, and Lutherans were null and void and they had to remarry immediately to fulfill the divine command, "Be fruitful and multiply." Naturally, their new husbands had to be Anabaptists. Most who resisted were imprisoned; a few were executed. There was also an Anabaptist woman who took the rhetoric on polygamy at face value and married multiple husbands. She was executed for her presumption.[124]

John of Lieden's kingdom did not last for two years, much less until the end of the world. Franz von Waldeck retook the city in June 1535 and John of Lieden's reign ended that January with his body being torn apart with iron tongs. The cages where John of Lieden's remains and those of other Münster Anabaptists were held still hang from St. Lambert's Cathedral in Münster, a silent testimony to the futility of radicalism in the 16th century. Still, the Anabaptists were not the only ones who found that the Reformation provided the perfect opportunity to devise new ideas about Christianity as well as to experiment with new ways of living.

Unfortunately, it is difficult to know how far some Reformation radicals went. Few left many traces, and even records of the persecutions against them by authorities are usually vague and filled with stock accusations. Like medieval heretics, Reformation radicals were usually accused of sexual deviance, often obscuring what the actual sexual practices and beliefs of these fringe groups were. Still, the new print technology gave many nonconformists the opportunity to truly speak for themselves. One such figure was Giorgio Siculo, who was executed by the Inquisition in 1551. In his writings, Siculo taught that the truly redeemed cannot be led astray by the flesh.[125] More explicitly, a small sect composed mainly of illiterate peasants in Germany, the Dreamers, preached that even sex could be a spiritual and sanctified act, dictated not by lust but by the Holy Spirit.[126]

The most hospitable environment to religious radicals of the era was perhaps England. Henry VIII's plan to break away from the papacy while preserving for the most part Catholic theology and hierarchy in the form of the Anglican Church made England more of a theological war zone, with a three-way struggle between Anglicans, Protestants, and traditional Catholics. The social and legal controls against radicalism, already under strain, broke when King Charles I was beheaded in 1649 and a republic dominated by the staunchly Protestant Puritans, the English Commonwealth, took the monarchy's place. In the wake of the Commonwealth's founding, small but vocal groups emerged out of the woodwork to seize a rare opportunity by crying out for a total reconstruction of society.

One of the most notorious groups was the Ranters, whose philosophy allegedly centered on the message, "No matter what Scripture, saints, or churches say, if that within thee do not condemn thee, thou shalt not be condemned."[127] One Ranter who left behind a body of work was Laurence Clarkson, whose 1650 tract *A Single Eye, All Light, No Darkness, or Light and Darkness One* was published under the sponsorship of the wealthy William Rainsborowe, himself a sympathizer of a radical utopian sect called the Levellers. Known for his own sexually liberated lifestyle, Clarkson argued that the concepts of sin and Hell were invented by the powerful to control the masses and that only intent, not the action itself, mattered to God.[128]

There were probably many more Laurence Clarksons forgotten by history who did not benefit from a publisher. However, as with so many revolutions, the Reformation was quick to moderate itself and squelch extremism and utopianism. As happened in Münster, Lutherans and Calvinists were prepared to close ranks, even if it meant aligning with Catholics, against radicals. Unfortunately, there was another revolutionary force unleashed in this era that was much harder to contain: the printing press.

The Erotic Side of the Printing Press

In his famous diary, the Londoner Samuel Pepys gave eyewitness accounts of events like the Great Plague of London and the Great Fire of 1666, but he offered interesting glimpses into his own day-to-day life, including an encounter with pornography:

> Thence away to the Strand, to my bookseller's, and there staid an hour, and bought the idle, rogueish book, *L'escholle des filles* ["The School of Girls"] which I have bought in plain binding, avoiding the buying of it better bound, because I resolve, as soon as I have read it, to burn it, that it may not stand in the list of books, nor among them, to disgrace them if it should be found.[129]

Of course, the history of erotica is as old as that of recorded civilization (if not older, depending on the real purpose of certain prehistoric artifacts uncovered by archeologists), but by Samuel Pepys's time the printing press made possible a vast international market of erotica. In fact, one of the earliest bestsellers spread by the printing press was 1527's *I Modi* ("The Ways"), a series of mythological engravings depicting different sexual positions between men and women accompanied by illuminating sonnets by the poet Pietro Aretino (1492–1556) and published by Marcantonio Raimondi. In spite of attempts by the papacy in Rome to have copies of it destroyed, it sold well and became something of a classic.[130] Remarking on the episode later, Giorgio Vasari, the author of a biography of Raimondi, complained, "One should not employ God-given things (as so often happens) for disgraceful purposes and in completely detestable things."[131]

Such reactions to this book's success reveal a concern about the corrupting power of words, a power made all the more dangerous by the growing availability of books and the challenge of controlling their circulation. "*I Modi*'s unique threat was that, printed in bulk, its distribution could reach a more or less indiscriminate readership and, thanks to its illustrations, its message did not require literacy skills for its interpretation," Benjamin Jacob explains.[132] There are hints here and there that even before the printing press there was a concept that the influence of written and visual materials could ruin morals. In a curious plea that would not be completely out of place in modern times, a notorious 15th-century mass murderer of children, Gilles de Rais, defended himself before the Duke of Brittany's court by saying that as a child he had been allowed to read his grandfather's copy of Suetonius' *Twelve Caesars,* which had included graphic descriptions and illustrations of rape and torture.[133] However, the 16th and 17th centuries experienced a sea change, where ribald literature that would not have been disturbing to medieval ears could no longer be tolerated. It was a change that transcended cultures and denominations. When founding their schools, the Jesuits took the ancient Roman playwright Terence off their curriculum, citing Terence's frank descriptions of sex. At the same time, 17th-century schools in England used a heavily censored copy of Terence with all sexual content removed.[134] This was in sharp contrast to Erasmus, who, writing just in the early 1500s, saw nothing wrong with a textbook designed for children frankly discussing prostitution.[135]

The change did not happen overnight. The explosive early growth of the printing press—print runs of 1,000 began to appear as early as the 1470s—demanded a response from the overwrought governments of the late 15th century. Already by 1475, a number of books that offered controversial ideas, whether promoting the study of Hebrew or denying the immortality of the soul, were subjected to censorship by the Church or secular authorities. The spread of Protestantism naturally escalated the process. In 1521, the Holy Roman Emperor, Charles V, banned the printing, sale, law, possession, reading, or copying of any of Martin Luther's works within the Empire. France, Spain, and many Italian regimes followed suit over the next couple of decades. Of course, Protestants retaliated, and went after heretical and Catholic writings on their own. Right after the city of Strasbourg sided with Protestantism, it confiscated the entire press run of an anti–Luther tract. Zwingli and Zurich's city council appointed a committee of pastors and laymen to investigate all manuscripts before publication for Catholic and heretical ideas. In turn Luther urged his patron, the Elector of Saxony, to outlaw all the writings of Zwingli and the Anabaptists.

Outside the occasional burning of "decadent" literature in the Middle Ages, the first documented censorship of books for reasons of sexual language came with the reactionary Pope Paul IV, under whom the first version of the Index of Prohibited Books was devised in 1557. Besides Protestant writings, the Index covered "immoral" books like all the works of Rabelais and the *Decameron*. Censorship under the Index became thorough enough that publishers of later editions of the *Decameron* changed horny nuns into noblewomen and blasphemous monks into wizards. The Index would remain a facet of Catholic life until 1966. Naturally, Protestant and Catholic governments were both quick to assert their own right to judge which books were fit to print, and the Spanish monarchy went so far as to draft its own version of the Index of Forbidden Books. Unsurprisingly the uptight city of Geneva went the furthest, outlawing the printing of and destroying existing copies of not only blatant erotica but also chivalric romances and the love poems of Ovid.[136]

Images, not just literature, became suspect. In no small part this trend was a backlash against the Renaissance fad for the idealized, muscular human body even in religious art, but it also revealed the growing concern with the influence of sexualized images on the masses. The Council of Trent had issued a vague condemnation of nudity in art, but the campaign against arousing images in religious art was taken up by Clement VII, who took a personal inspection of Rome in 1592 for that purpose. Under his orders crucifixes displaying Christ's nearly nude and buff body were draped and a provocative wooden statue was clothed. More explosive was the controversy surrounding Michelangelo's *The Last Judgment* in the Sistine Chapel. Pietro Aretino, despite being the author of erotic works himself, blasted what would be deemed one of the most stunning achievements of artistic talent in history as "obscene and lascivious" while the cleric Scipione Saurolo bemoaned "the indecency of the nudity."[137] In what might be the most famous case of sanctioned artistic vandalism, the artist Daniele da Volterra was hired after Michelangelo's death to cover the genitals of the figures in *The Last Judgment* with clothing and fig leaves, giving him the epithet "il Breghettone" (the "breeches maker"). These "improvements" were removed only when *The Last Judgment* was restored in the 1980s.

Such visuals, even when employed in erotica like *I Modi* to an extent, were still drawing on a respected classical legacy. More dangerous was another legacy of the Renaissance, the association between cutting-edge knowledge and taboo sex. Although cultures and attitudes had drastically changed, classical writings about pederasty kept offering a compelling connection between sex, pleasure, and learning. This theme was strengthened by new ideas about education that spread in the 17th century and argued for, James Turner writes, "direct, sensuous knowledge as the basis for acquiring complex ideas."[138] In fact, much erotica written since the Renaissance and into the Enlightenment came in the form of dialogues or discourses, a classical genre that was also usually the preferred mode of philosophical and educational tracts. Finally, this erotica, while clearly written by and for men, depicted women enjoying, savoring, and discussing their own sexual desires. Perhaps ironically, works written just for the titillation of men was also putting forward to audiences the uncomfortable idea that women, too, could want and know about sex.

A prime example of the genre and its classical and philosophical roots is another work by Aretino, *Dialogues*. A Roman courtesan named Nanna talks with her friend Antonia and tells her that she does not know if her daughter Pippa should be a nun, a wife, or a courtesan. Nanna talks with authority about each of those occupations since she herself has been all three. She dismisses the idea that being a nun is no fun, since she was able to watch orgies between women and men going on in other cells and spy on the Abbess having sex with her confessor. She takes her own lover, known only as the Bachelor; while he fondles her, she is "inwardly blessing the hour and minute I had become a nun and thinking that the sisters lived in a true paradise."[139]

Next Nanna discusses wives who have affairs, especially wealthy women who sleep with servants, something Nanna herself did. Nanna gave up married life when her husband discovered her own affair and she stabbed him in self-defense, leading her into life as a courtesan. In the end, Antonia advises, "My opinion is that you should make a whore of your Pippa. The nun betrays her sacred vows and the married woman murders the holy bond of matrimony, but the whore violates neither her monastery nor her husband."[140]

Whatever the text says about the author's own misogyny, it does depict a world where women struggle (rather successfully) against socially mandated restraints on their sexuality. Another popular Italian work of erotica that became an international hit and was attributed (probably falsely) to Aretino, *La Puttana Errante* ("The Errant Whore"), is basically the sexual biography of a woman named Maddalena. At the age of 11, Maddalena first discovers sex when she spies on her 15-year-old cousin Federico masturbating. She excitedly shares this revelation with her sister, who proceeds to use her finger to show how women can do the same. Later, Maddalena stumbles across Federico having anal sex with his friend Roberto. That night, her aunt teaches her how women may also pleasure each other. However, Maddalena's education is considered complete only when she watches Federico have sex with his virgin bride and she repeats the same act with Roberto. She goes on to become a courtesan, a career that kicks off with a *menage à trois* between her, a handsome young man, and a church canon. Of the canon, Maddalena scornfully notes, "Never did that traitor of a canon want to put it in my cunt."[141]

Similar disappointment waited for the heroine of the poem *The Choice of Valentines*, by English writer Thomas Nashe (1567–ca. 1601). A prostitute named Frances (who goes by Frankie), she meets with her boyfriend Tomalin. Unfortunately, Tomalin is unable to arouse her, forcing her to use a dildo. Another erotic anecdote from Brantôme describes a nobleman coming across two women having sex via a strap-on dildo. Hopelessly naive about the possibilities for sexual fulfillment between two women, the nobleman is incredulous rather than disgusted.[142]

Although women were the stars of this erotica, were they ever actually readers? Specific numbers are completely unknown, but there are examples of erotica being found in the libraries of women and even examples of female writers who wrote pornographic verses in manuscripts.[143] Female writers of published erotica are also very rare, but a well-known figure is Aphra Behn (1640–1689), one of the first English women known to have made a career out of writing. Best known for the novel *Oroonoko,* a love story involving an African slave, Behn also wrote a poem titled "The Disappointment," which was published in a poetry collection composed by Behn's friend, the libertine Earl of Rochester. Like *The Choice of Valentines,* the poem is about two lovers, Lysander and Cloris, and describes how Cloris's beauty actually leaves Lysander impotent. In 1671, Aphra Behn's play *The Amorous Prince* disgusted audiences by opening with a man and a woman rising from bed after sex.

The constant theme in this genre of early modern pornography is the notion that sexual desire is natural and that it always triumphs over the institutions that seek to control it. Perhaps this message was why the French writer Rabelais's novel *Gargantua and Pantagruel,* despite its lack of much explicit pornographic content, was targeted by the Index of Forbidden Books and other censorship lists. Toward the end of the novel, Gargantua builds the Monastery of Thelema. This new monastery's rule condemns hypocrites, the greedy, and religious fanatics, and then it moves on to sexuality: "Keep out, you husbands sour and warped and jealous, / Imprisoning desire in chains and locks." Rabelais goes on to describe this utopian project:

> Their whole life was lived, not in accordance with laws, statutes or rules, but by their own choosing and free will. They got up when they felt like it; they drank, ate, worked and slept when they so desired. Nobody woke them up, nobody forced them either to drink, or to eat, or to do anything else at all. This is how Gargantua had laid it down. In their rule, there was only one clause: DO WHATEVER YOU WANT. This is because free, well-born, well-educated people, thoroughly at home in decent company, by nature have an instinct and goad which always impel them to carry out virtuous deeds, and hold them back from vice: this they call "honor." These people, when by vile subjection and constraint they are oppressed and enslaved, call on the noble feelings by which they freely tend towards virtue, and throw off and set aside this yoke of servitude. We always try to do things that have been forbidden to us and desire whatever has been denied us.[144]

Future generations would pick up on the Monastery of Thelema and what it represented. Sir Francis Dashwood would place the words "DO WHAT THOU WILT" over the door to the abbey where meetings of the Hell-Fire Club were held. In the 19th century, the occultist Alistair Crowley would even name his radical mystic philosophy "Thelema." Likewise, to Rabelais's contemporaries, Thelema and other ideas carried by these erotic and radical works were a threat, one that chipped away at the authority of political and social structures to dictate how people should express and satisfy their desires. If sexual desire was natural and transcended gender and social roles, then its suppression must be counterproductive. This became a more tempting conclusion as Europeans were being forced to confront alien societies that played by very different rules.

Deporting Morals

On travel, the conservative essayist Jean de la Bruyère warned that people who set out to see new lands complete the corruption of their minds by going on too long voyages, during which they lose what remnants of religious belief they had. In the end, la Bruyère solemnly warns, all religious beliefs and cultural practices appear interchangeable.[145] The same essential point, although from a more radical position, was made in Pierre Charron's *De la sagesse* ("On Wisdom"):

> If we had to say how many laws of nature there are, and what they ordain, we would be at a loss. The sign of a natural law must be the universal respect in which it is held, for if there was anything that nature had truly commanded us to do, we would undoubtedly obey it universally: not only would every nation respect it, but every individual. Instead there is nothing in the world that is not subject to contradiction and dispute, nothing that is not rejected, not just by one nation, but by many; equally, there is nothing that is strange and (in the opinion of many) unnatural that is not approved in many countries, and authorized by their countries.[146]

These pronouncements were likely no more true by the 16th century than they were in the Middle Ages, but the very notion of natural, universal laws was coming under added pressure after Europeans' encounters with completely new societies in the Americas. Even how to incorporate these peoples into their mental landscape baffled Europeans and led them to very opposed conclusions. On the one hand, in his *Chronicles of Peru,* Pedro Cieza de León portrayed Native Americans as compulsive cannibals and sodomites. On the other hand, Peter Martyr, the author of one of the first bestselling books describing the Americas, *Decades of the New World,* claimed that the Native Americans lived an innocent and pristine existence like Adam and Eve in the Garden of Eden.[147] The Americas were simultaneously an uncorrupted paradise and a hellish pit of violence and unnatural sex.

At first, Catholic explorers and missionaries in South and Central America were impressed by the cultures they encountered. Among the peoples of Mesoamerica, they especially held high hopes for the Nahua peoples of modern-day Mexico, of whom the Aztecs were only one group. They originally praised the Nahuas for their exquisite cites and temples, their laws that strictly kept jewelry and other luxuries out of the hands of the majority of the population, and their cool tempers. Their religious practices also drew some respect, despite the Spanish believing that their gods were really demons. Much to the delight of ambitious missionaries, Nahua religion had a concept that could be reasonably translated as "sin" and its own confessional rite.

Unfortunately, as they often did with other peoples they encountered, the Spanish missionaries were too quick to see parallels. The Nahua notion of "sin" did not emphasize purity and uncleanliness, but order and chaos. "Sin" in Nahua terms was associated with recklessness and stupidity, not European ideas of evil and excess. There were restrictions on sexual activity, but again unlike in Christianity these were not expected to be followed by everyone. The nobility, who were obliged to practice self-control, were as a matter of course expected to follow more chaste lives than their inferiors. These differences and more made the conversion of the Nahuas more difficult than the Spanish Christians anticipated, which soon enough in their eyes turned the Nahuas from confused and misguided but ripe for conversion to willful and sexually depraved liars.[148]

From Mexico to Brazil to Peru, missionaries were similarly disappointed with the prospects of their would-be converts, a disillusionment that helpfully coincided with the *conquistadors'* lust for land and gold. Pedro de Villagómez, the archbishop of Lima, explained why the natives of South America were so vulnerable to sin—and so richly deserving of slaughter and conquest: "[The Devil] deceives them with the greatest of ease, for [the natives] are childish, slow in understanding, clumsy in reasoning, and lacking in knowledge of the secrets of the natural world. And since they lack the necessary Christian doctrine, these *miserables* have no capacity to see through the tricks of the Devil."[149] However, spreading beliefs about the inferiority of the natives did not stop Spanish and Portuguese colonists from finding native mistresses and wives. The notorious Hernán Cortés took a Nahua mistress known to history as "La Malinche." In modern Mexico, *malinchista* is still a term that means someone who prefers foreigners over their own people to the point of treason. Another *conquistador*, Francisco de Aguirre, whose career saw him both imprisoned and made a governor over a province of Peru, boasted about fathering 50 illegitimate children on native women. Even clerics in Spain's and Portugal's colonies were known to have native lovers, prompting the Catholic Church to urge priests in the colonies to employ only old women as their servants.

Yet for the most part it was accepted, even expected, that in the colonies where European women were few, men would mingle with the natives, who likewise saw in such relationships a shot at improving their ever-worsening lot. In 1606, one native woman testified to a church court that she agreed to become the concubine of Sebastian Moreno because "she was getting along very well with this man and furthermore wanted to be with him, but she didn't want to marry because when he became her husband he might make her life very difficult." It was not until the 1700s, when the gender ratio of European colonists balanced out more, that the governments of Portugal and Spain began to officially frown on interracial mixing.[150]

Strict laws against adultery and a firm preference for monogamy among the Incans and Aztecs did not stop Europeans from spreading rumors about native promiscuity. Likewise, European stereotypes held that sodomy was rampant among the natives of South and Central America, even though attitudes toward homosexuality among the Incans and Nahuas may have been outright inimical and it is still debated among historians exactly how Mayan culture addressed homosexual love.[151] Along with human sacrifice and cannibalism, sodomy was one of the crimes seen as endemic among native societies. As early as 1495, a member of Columbus's crew claimed in a letter that the Caribs and Awawaks they encountered on Hispaniola were "largely sodomites."[152] Fernandez de Oviedo repeated an anecdote about a Yucatan island where there was a Mayan temple with a large wooden statue depicting men engaged in sex. About his travels in Panama in 1515, Oviedo wrote, "In some part of these Indies [an early Spanish term for the Americas], they carry as a jewel a man mounted upon another in that diabolic and nefarious act of Sodom, made in gold relief."[153] Oviedo proceeded to smash the priceless jewel with a hammer.

The reports of sodomy were about more than asserting native immorality: they sought to legitimize European sovereignty over the Americas. In a treatise filled with accounts of native sodomy, Bishop Tomás Ortiz urged Emperor Charles V, who was also king of Spain, to consider that enslaving the natives was justified because they were irrational.[154] These assertions justified both policies in Europe and brutality in the Americas. Peter Martyr relates how Vasco Nuñez de Balboa was shocked to see the brother of a king in Panama engaged in sodomy with a group of men and had 40 of the men torn apart by his dogs. A rector in Peru, Antonio de la Calancha, called the massacre a "fine action of an honorable and Catholic Spaniard."[155]

Sodomy was so much a part of the conversation about the natives that defenders of native rights were forced to downplay such anecdotes. One such advocate was the Dominican friar, Bartolomé de las Casas (ca. 1484–1566), who was once a soldier who fought against natives in Hispaniola and Cuba. Worn down by the atrocities he both witnessed and participated in, las Casas finally freed his native slaves, sold his lands, and became a monk. Returning to Spain after he found that his fellow colonists were deaf to his humanitarian pleas, las Casas worked hard to convince Charles V that the Americans were rational beings deserving protection from enslavement and mass murder.

Las Casas's needling eventually led Charles V to host a debate in Valladolid between the determined friar and his greatest rival, the philosopher Juan Ginés de Sepúlveda (1489–1573). He lacked las Casas's experiences in the New World, but drew on Aristotle to assert that the natives were barbarians and hence "natural" slaves. Both men addressed the rampant reports of native sodomy. Las Casas dismissed these stories, but Sepúlveda instead insisted that the stories proved that war was necessary not just because the Spanish had the God-imposed obligation to root out the unnatural crime of sodomy wherever and whenever they found it, but because natives could not be trusted to become civilized and Christian unless at swordpoint. In the end, as with so many debates throughout all of human history, both sides announced they were victorious but neither officially won. While some laws were enacted that limited the ability of landowners in the colonies to exploit Native Americans, massacres and forced servitude continued.

In North America, the French and English were similarly horrified when they came across what the French called the *berdache* (essentially "male prostitutes," which helps explain why today the term "Two-Spirit" is preferred among Native Americans). With varieties documented as far south as the Incan Empire and as far north as Canada, the so-called *berdache* blended the society's gender roles within his own person, forming a "third sex," and sometimes took lovers and even spouses of either sex. What exactly the *berdache* meant has naturally been debated by archeologists and historians. Perhaps for at least some societies they were shamans filling a sacred niche, or maybe it was a socially accepted refuge for those dissatisfied with their culture's gender roles or for people with same-sex desire. Whatever the case, Europeans were not sympathetic and simply saw cultures that scandalously tolerated the effeminate sodomites in their midst. The sight of a cross-dressing man who not only perhaps had sex with other men but also performed women's work was, to Europeans, "a corruption of morals past all expression."[156]

Just as Peter Martyr proposed that the Americas were an earthly Eden, however, some Europeans found in the Americas the promise of liberation from their own society's strict codes. The baron de Lahontan (1666–1716), who traveled extensively in modern-day Wisconsin and Minnesota, published his travel journals. In them, he suggested that the Native Americans he encountered were actually closer to God and Nature than Europeans themselves, since they left their daughters free to marry and make love with whomever they wished.[157] Another such person was Thomas Morton, an English lawyer who founded the colony of Merrymount in Massachusetts. Morton's neighbors in Plymouth were horrified that Morton erected a maypole in the middle of the colony and danced around it with native women. Convinced that Morton had not just "gone native" but was introducing the natives to European styles of sinful fun, Morton's Puritan neighbors successfully schemed to get him deported back to England. Even more unlucky than Morton was an English trader who married the daughter of a Creek chief. Probably assuming that he could get away with cheating on a native woman, the trader slept with the wife of another chief. The trader was beaten and barely escaped having his ears cut off.[158]

Stories of native promiscuity evoked both disapproval and enticement among European settlers. Seventeenth-century English visitors to Virginia and the Carolinas wrote alluringly for readers back home about the beautiful bodies of native women and the physical strength of the men. Meanwhile French Jesuit missionaries among the Huron and Montagnais tribes of modern-day Canada decried how their "lewdness and licentiousness hinders them from finding God."[159] As with many stereotypes, there was some basis in fact. As Richard Godbeer writes, "Many Indian nations condoned sexual experimentation among young people prior to marriage; they also sanctioned polygamy within their elites, usually in the service of political and diplomatic goals; and those Indians who were not allowed to take more than one spouse at a time could nonetheless enjoy several relationships during the course of their adult lives, since marriage was not perceived as necessarily permanent."[160] Still, very few Europeans in the 16th and 17th centuries were prepared to view these customs as evidence of different but equally valid cultural values, but instead as absolute proof of an innate inferiority.

Yet to their credit, some Europeans testified to the existence of native modesty. A visitor to New England in 1602, Gabriel Archer, claimed that native women would not tolerate "any immodest touch."[161] Others who had first-hand experience of native cultures attacked rumors of rampant sin. One such defender was the Virginian planter Robert Beverley, who wrote:

> Tho the young Indian Women are said to prostitute their bodies for Wampom Peak, Runtees, Beads, and other such like fineries; yet I never could find any ground for the accusation, and believe it only to be an unjust scandal upon them. This I know, that if ever they have a Child while they are single, it is such a disgrace to them, that they never after get Husbands. Besides, I must do 'em the justice to say, I never heard of a Child any of them had before Marriage, and the Indians themselves disown any such custom; tho they acknowledge at the same time, that the Maidens are entirely at their own disposal, and may manage their persons as they think fit.[162]

Whether or not native women and men were superb and willing lovers, the English who made new homes and towns around the Chesapeake Bay, along the coasts of North and South Carolina, and in New England were much more reluctant than Portuguese and Spanish men to mingle with the natives. Fear of racial contamination was not yet part of the equation. When James Rolfe famously married Pocahontas, the concern of King James I was not the mixing of European and American blood but rather that a commoner like Rolfe was wedding the daughter of a king, "savage" or not.[163] Part of the explanation was certainly that the settlers of New England, unlike their neighbors to the south, had a more equal gender ratio, but even that does not fully explain the hostility inspired by unions with even Native Americans who converted to Christianity. One notorious case among the Puritans was that of Eunice Williams from Massachusetts, who was taken prisoner in a raid by the Caughnawaga, a tribe allied with the French. Even after peace negotiations made it possible for Eunice to return to Massachusetts, she chose to stay in Canada with her Caughnawaga husband, who, much to the horror of Eunice's friends and family, was not only an Indian but had converted to Catholicism.[164] Less fortunate was Mary Mendame from Plymouth, who was arrested for having an ongoing affair with a native man named Tinsin. For her crime, she was whipped in public and forced to wear a badge identifying her as a woman who fornicated with native men.[165] Even without modern ideas about racial purity, Europeans still saw, as Richard Godbeer describes, sex with the natives as an "agent of cultural apostasy."[166]

Fears about what romantic and sexual *mésalliances* with natives might lead to were justified by William Baker. Pursued by authorities in Hartford, Connecticut, because of charges that he had intercourse with a native woman, Baker was taken in by a group of Mashantucket Pequots and "turned Indian in nakedness and cutting of hair, and after many whoredoms, [was] there married." Eventually Baker was captured and forced to return to Hartford, where he was publicly beaten.[167] Elsewhere, accusations of sex with natives was serious business. The wealthy trader Jacob Young was accused of conspiring with the Susquehannah Nation against the governor of Maryland. A key piece of evidence used was the allegation that Young had secretly married a Susquehannah woman and had children with her.[168]

The societies of East Asia were also home to cultures whose customs were at odds with European notions of proper living and natural law, but it was harder to dismiss these societies that seemed to better match Europeans' own ideals of civilization and even Christian-like behavior. Matteo Ricci (1552–1610), the first Christian missionary allowed into mainland China under the Ming dynasty as well as the first to become fully literate in Chinese, gave a powerful compliment:

> Of all the pagan nations that are known to our Europe, I know of none which has made fewer errors contrary to the things of Religion than the nation of China in its early Antiquity. Indeed, in their books I find that they have always worshiped a supreme deity which call the King of Heaven or of Heaven and Earth…. When we examine these books closely, we discover in them very few things which are contrary to the light of reason and many which are in conformity with it, and their natural philosophers are second to none.[169]

In fact, Ricci and other Jesuits came to believe that in China belief in the true God was once widespread. That faith had been twisted by the spread of the mysticism and idolatry of Taoism and the atheism of Buddhism. Yet the old understanding of God and natural law were preserved in the writings of Confucius and other Chinese classics, with their references to the *shangdi* ("Sovereign on High") and invocations to "serve Heaven" (*shi tian*), "to respect" and "to fear Heaven" (*jing tian, wei tian*). If only so many works had not been lost during the First Emperor's burning of countless Confucian texts in the third century BC, the Jesuits believed, then it would be plain that ancient Chinese thought was almost identical to that of the Hebrew Bible. One Jesuit, Joachim Bouvet, even formed the ambitious theory that classic Chinese historical texts were in reality allegories about Genesis and the Jewish patriarchs.[170] Unfortunately, as happened with the Nahuas, cultural misunderstandings led to the Jesuits misplacing their optimism. For instance, the Jesuits were thrilled when they saw Chinese villagers publicly dragging through the dirt and smashing idols of gods, not understanding that this was routine practice when the local gods failed their worshippers and needed to be "fired."[171]

Although Ricci became the first European invited into the imperial court at the Forbidden Palace, the Wanli Emperor was interested in Ricci's knowledge of astronomy and mechanical clocks, not his religion. At least Ricci did gain permission to establish a church in Beijing, which still exists today. In spite of Ricci's hard work and successes, after his death the missionary effort became more strained as more Jesuits questioned Ricci's acceptance of Chinese culture. One insurmountable barrier came from sexual customs. Even Ricci, for all his confidence in the Chinese being naturally close to true religion, was outraged by what he saw around him and claimed that most Chinese men lost their virginity at the age of 14 or 15 before they even married. Worse, prostitution and adultery were rampant. Buddhist monks, always the target of special contempt from missionaries, were the worst. Despite their own laws, they lived all but openly with women and, to protect themselves, forced their lovers to take drugs that induced miscarriages.[172]

However, it was an apparent acceptance of homosexuality that proved the most jarring to even Jesuits prepared to admire Chinese civilization. While reports of Chinese decadence were certainly exaggerated, there may have been something to one Jesuit claim that "the greatest fault we do find in them is sodomy, a vice very common in the meaner sort, and nothing strange among the best."[173] Although there were Indian and Chinese Buddhist writings that denounced homosexuality and a law against male prostitution in China from the tenth century, a romantic legend provided some popular legitimacy for male same-sex love, the tale of Duke Ling of Wei (534–493 BC) and Mizi Xia. According to the story, Mizi Xia broke the law by using the duke's carriage to visit his sick mother, but the duke pardoned him and praised his filial devotion. Later Mizi Xia ate half a peach and gave it to the duke, who saw it as a sign of affection and selflessness. However, once Mizi Xia aged and became less attractive, the duke then angrily accused him of using his chariot without permission and of giving him half-eaten food. Regardless of the cynical postscript, the peach among the Chinese *literati* became a widespread symbol of love between men. Another and even more famous emblem was the cut sleeve. One night the lover of the Emperor Ai of the Han dynasty (6 BC–1 AD), Dong Xian, had fallen asleep with his head resting on the emperor's sleeve. Ai cut his sleeve rather than disturb his lover, even though it meant humiliating himself before his court. From then on, young men at the Han court wore cut sleeves to publicly show their love for a male beloved.[174]

Eventually the relationship between the Jesuits and the Chinese began cooling on both sides. Although there were Chinese who were genuinely interested in Christianity—the Shunzhi Emperor of the Qing dynasty (r. 1644–1661) may have come close to conversion when he fell to his knees while hearing the story of the Crucifixion—others, especially among the *literati,* saw Christianity as a possible source for sedition among the masses. One of Christianity's most vehement critics, Zu Dashou, was appalled at the presumption the Jesuits showed toward the Creator, which bordered on earthly treason:

> Recently, when I had set up a family temple to worship my ancestors, the Western men of letters found fault with me, saying: "These are your family masters. But there must also be a greater master. Do you not recognize him?" To which I scoffingly replied: "That greater master is the Sovereign on High and in our China only the Son of Heaven [the Emperor] may sacrifice to him. Nobody else would dare to do so."[175]

There was more than just religious and political misunderstandings at play. Just as Europeans saw China as rife with sodomy, so the Chinese suspected Christians of libidinous behavior toward women. Since in Chinese society girls and boys were sharply segregated from the age of seven on, the mere sight of priests baptizing women was scandalous. When missionaries went to see aristocratic women, rumors spread that they were using the sacraments as an excuse to fondle their breasts.[176] While the Jesuits criticized the Chinese for practicing concubinage and polygamy and tolerating sodomy, Chinese writers like Zu Dashou retorted that Christian priests were guilty of shameless hypocrisy:

> They would like all kings and sovereigns to adhere to their vicious doctrine, expel all their concubines from their women's quarters and live like common people with but a single wife.

But in their residences they themselves invite ignorant women at nightfall to enter a room draped with red hangings, where they close the doors and practice unction with holy oil, give them holy water and place their hands on five places of their bodies: these are impure and secret rituals. How could one possibly contravene the rule on the separation of the sexes any more seriously than that?[177]

Ironically, the Chinese also gossiped about sodomy among the Jesuits. Even a harsh critic of sodomy like Matteo Ricci was suspected of kidnapping a Chinese adolescent and keeping him drugged in his quarters. According to the rumor, which reached the ears of Ricci himself, Ricci raped him repeatedly for three days before selling him to Portuguese sailors.[178]

Japan inspired similar hopes and disappointments. Until the 16th century, Japan was for Europeans only a legendary far-off land barely mentioned in accounts of China. The first Europeans to reach Japan were shipwrecked Portuguese merchants who arrived in 1542 or 1543. By the end of the decade, a Jesuit mission headed by Francisco Xavier reached the Japanese archipelago. The land Xavier visited was still in the midst of wars that had lasted for about a century, but it was slowly being reunified under the military dictatorship of the Tokugawa shogunate. In spite of the unrest, and the rise of a regime that would one day outlaw Christianity, Xavier was deeply impressed, declaring that the Japanese were "the best who have as yet been discovered, and it seems to me that we shall never find among heathens another race to equal the Japanese."[179]

In his letters, Xavier reveals a sincere admiration for Japanese manners and the code of honor that existed among the samurai. Like the Jesuits in China, however, Xavier had nothing good to say about the Buddhist monks, *bonzes*. Besides Buddhists encouraging idolatry among the Japanese, the *bonzes* were social parasites, taking alms but never distributing them to the poor. Worse, they had sex with nuns and coerced them into getting abortions if they became pregnant. Most shocking of all, though, was their predilection for sodomy. It was the Buddhist influence, Xavier argued, that caused sodomy to become so common among the Japanese, who were a rational and ordered people in spite of having never experienced Christian revelation. Xavier writes, "The people thus do it, taking from them example, saying that if the *bonzes* do it, they will do it as well."[180] Even though a group of Zen Buddhists offered Xavier hospitality, Xavier angrily left them when he caught two of the monks being intimate. In another letter written soon after he arrived, Xavier warned, "The evil is simply become a habit among the Buddhist clergy. This evil, moreover, is so public, so clear to all, men and women, young and old, and they are so used to seeing it, that they are neither depressed nor horrified."[181]

As much as Xavier wanted the monks to be responsible for all the sins he saw in Japan, he found that the samurai he admired also practiced *nanshoku*, "the love of males." At Yamaguchi, a feudal lord or *daimyo*, Ouchi Yoshitaki, became curious about who exactly the *kirishitans* were and warmly welcomed Xavier and his entourage. Xavier's translator read aloud a Japanese translation of the Ten Commandments along with an appendage lambasting sodomy as the filthiest of all sins. This alone turned Ouchi's mood completely, and the Jesuits found themselves so abruptly dismissed they were afraid for their lives.[182]

As in China, Xavier's outrage was somewhat justified: Japan had a long and rich tradition vindicating same-sex homoeroticism between men. The notion among a few Buddhist texts from continental Asia that same-sex love was a sin had apparently never reached Japan. On the contrary, Japanese Buddhist monks, who lived in strict gender segregation, adopted a tradition not unlike Greek pederasty. Love between a monk and a young acolyte became celebrated to the point that an entire genre of monastic literature, *chigo monogatari* ("tales of acolytes"), told of monks being led to enlightenment by their love for a handsome acolyte, who was always a Buddhist *bodhisattva*, "enlightened one," in disguise. In one such tale, a monk mourns the death of his acolyte-lover, only to be visited by the *bodhisattva* Guanyin, who reveals that she had taken the physical form of the acolyte and reminds him of the impermanence of all things, even love.[183]

However, love between men was not just the province of monks. Samurai also idealized the love between a warrior and a younger page or apprentice, with published stories describing samurai choosing between love and duty.[184] In 1482, the scholar Ijiri Chusuke praised such love as something that could transcend even hierarchy and class:

> [I]n the world of the nobles and warriors, lovers would swear perfect and eternal love, relying on no more than their mutual goodwill. Whether their partners were noble or common, rich or poor, was absolutely of no importance. Consequently, some abandoned their property or lost rank as a result of their passion, while others gained a fine position or acquired a name thanks to their love.... This was must be truly respected and it must never be allowed to disappear.[185]

In everyday life, male brothels were common in both cities and rural areas, although once the Tokugawa clan took power and established what was essentially a police state, all brothels had to be registered or risk being shut down. People also spoke of the *nanshoku-zuki* ("man-love-enthusiast"), who eschewed sex with any woman. A popular stereotype was that the *nanshoku-zuki* hated sex with women so much that he despised all women. One tale describes an elderly male couple who, whenever women passed their house, one of them would rush out with a broom and chase them away while shouting, "Such filth! Disgusting! Get out of here!" Even then, however, the *nanshoku-zuki* was held as a figure of interest and parody, not moral outrage.[186]

Other Japanese notions about sexuality proved at odds with mainstream European notions of the time. Shinto—indigenous Japanese beliefs organized around the sacred figure of the emperor—taught that sex was a holy practice passed down to every living being by the divine couple Izanagi and Izanami.[187] Wooden phalli in Shinto temples were a common sight, and in modern times the phalli are still taken out of the temples and into the fields to ensure good crops. European observers were surprised that the virginity of brides was not a particular concern.[188] Also, in the words of a Dutch East India Tea Company official who married a Japanese woman, "One Man hath but one Wife, though as many Concubines as he can keep; and if that Wife do not please him, he may put her away, provided he dismiss her in a civil and honorable way."[189]

If Europeans found Japanese sexual customs decadent, then the Japanese found the values Christian missionaries attempted to push on them perplexing. Fabian Fucan, a Japanese convert who later renounced the religion, complained, "Jesus was born from a couple who had sworn chastity. What kind of a virtuous ideal is that? ... The universal norm is that every man and every woman should marry. To go against that natural law is evil."[190] Later Fucan attacks the alleged celibacy of priests, alleging that he had heard reports of them keeping wives and children in Europe and in the colonies.[191]

However, it was not these discrepancies between European and Japanese culture that stopped Christianity from ever making serious, long-term inroads into Japan. Instead reports of how Catholic missionaries preceded Spanish conquest in the Philippines and a major uprising by Christian Japanese peasants brought down the boot of the Tokugawa regime. Christians were violently persecuted and tortured and barred from most professions, even prostitution, while Japan closed itself off from Western contact for centuries.

Despite such precautions, Western sexual attitudes would ultimately make their mark on both Japan and China. When the American commodore Matthew Perry used the force of the United States navy to bully Japan into reopening regular trade with the West in 1854, the Japanese responded by turning their country into an industrialized, colonizing power, striking an effective balance between native and Western models. Imitating the German law code, in 1873 the reforming Japanese government passed a law making sex between men punishable with 90 days' imprisonment. However, the law lasted only ten years before it was repealed. In modern Japan, however, both female and male homosexuality were forced into the shadows through social stigma and the tradition of same-sex love in Japanese culture being allowed to fade into obscurity. Only relatively recently has the facade shown signs of slipping, with the first Tokyo gay pride parade being hosted in 1994.

A similar, if harsher, veil of shame and secrecy fell over homosexuality in Communist China. No formal sodomy law exists in modern China; instead, the Communist regime has taken the novel approach of denying the existence of gay people in China, ignoring China's homoerotic literary past and decrying homosexuality as purely a Western and *bourgeois* phenomenon. A Chinese textbook for university students speculates, "One reason for this may be despair in marriage or love affairs. Some people fail in marriage and become disappointed with it so they decide no longer to love the opposite sex, but instead begin to love a person of the same sex. Another reason may be that some people want to find and do something 'new' and 'curious.' ... Through this we can see clearly the spiritual hollowness of these people and distortion of the social order."[192]

Europe's encounter with the rest of the world was a turning point, so much so that the shape of a world where European colonization did not happen as it did is virtually unthinkable. However, as Europeans altered much of the rest of the world—sometimes traumatically—Europe itself was not untouched. Colonization brought with it unprecedented wealth and trade and completely new categories of knowledge. By at least the end of the 17th century, Europe would have no choice but to change under the weight of capital and unfamiliar ideas.

Rationalizing Sex

Luther's act of hammering his theses onto the cathedral doors had another unexpected effect: it triggered almost a century of the worst warfare Europe had ever experienced. The flood of violence hit a crest with the Thirty Years War, which roped in nearly all the nations of Europe and blazed on from 1618 to 1648, making it still the longest sustained military conflict in world history. Worst hit was Germany, the main battleground, which lost at least one fourth of its population. Although Catholic France fought on the side of the Protestants for the sake of undermining Spain and Protestant Denmark allied itself with the Catholic powers against its own enemy Sweden, for the most part the combatants in the war were split down denominational lines, urged on by ministers on both sides who claimed divine sanction and demanded the obliteration of their heretic opponents. The fabled unity of Christendom had simultaneously become tragedy and farce.

VIII Reforming and Reaffirming

The horror and disillusionment in the wake of the war were not lost on many people, including one French soldier, René Descartes (1596–1650). Looking at a Europe where different parties asserted different truths about God and Christianity and were willing to have countless people persecuted, executed, and slaughtered in battle to vindicate their own "truth," Descartes as a philosopher attempted to learn about reality and God not through faith in a doctrine, but through pure reason alone. In his *First Meditations on Philosophy,* Descartes dispensed with any and all assumptions and began to reconstruct his knowledge about himself and the universe with the fateful words, "I think, therefore I am." The potential in such an extreme deconstruction, even from someone who remained a devout Catholic until his death, was recognized in a fashion by the Catholic Church, which condemned his works. That did not stop Descartes from becoming one of the most celebrated and controversial thinkers of his time across both Protestant and Catholic Europe. In countless European universities, traditionalists accused the "Cartesians" of trying to subject the Bible itself to reason—and, although Cartesians denied it, their critics had a point.[193]

An even more bold advocate of pure reason was Baruch Spinoza (1632–1677), a citizen of Amsterdam with Portuguese Jewish ancestry. Spinoza was part of a despised minority barred from any university education and was excommunicated from his Jewish congregation for his ideas, with his works outlawed even in the more tolerant Dutch Republic. In the end, however, he had such a tremendous hold over Western thought that the philosopher Hegel could safely pronounce in the early 19th century that a modern philosopher was either a Spinozist or not a real philosopher at all. The two works that earned Spinoza both his infamy and intellectual sainthood were *Ethics,* which etched out a concept of God that was indistinguishable from Nature, and *Tractatus Theologico-Politicus,* which promoted the hot-button idea that the Bible can and must be read critically like any other text. In life Spinoza was likely a pantheist, one who believes the divine exists within and not apart from the universe; nevertheless, later generations—both enemies and supporters of his philosophy—would cite his name as the emblem for total unbelief in the spiritual and supernatural.

Descartes spent much of his life in, and Spinoza always lived in, the Dutch Republic—and not just because they liked the climate. Descartes's and Spinoza's lifetimes luckily coincided with the golden age of the Dutch Republic, which had gained independence from the Spanish monarchy in 1581. Lax censorship laws, (relative) religious tolerance, and large communities of exiles from other countries like Protestants from France and Jews from Spain and Portugal such as Spinoza's family made the Dutch Republic a comfortable environment for cutting-edge intellectuals and the publishers, whether legal or illicit, that spread their ideas across the continent. The fact that across Western and Central Europe the international language of scholars was changing from Latin to vernacular French helped place those debates in reach of a much wider audience of readers, including women.

The implications of this revolution in thought for sexuality—and the authority of churches and governments to define what was proper and natural as well as what was immoral and illegal—were not immediately obvious. Spinoza did not directly address matters of sex and marriage at length; Descartes even less so. Yet Spinoza did lay down some thoughts on the subject that were taken up by later writers. To begin with, Spinoza took on the old notion that the sole purpose of sex is procreation, an idea taken for granted by the Catholic Church for centuries but traceable all the way back to at least the Stoics, and turned it on its head. Sex does not exist because of procreation; instead, procreation exists *because of* sex, a minute yet important distinction that reduced reproduction from the sacred purpose of intercourse to its by-product.

Even more audaciously, Spinoza defined sex as not only a source of corruption or pleasure, but also an aspect of the self. The historian Alexandre Matheron explains, "Sexuality is a necessary moment of this self-deployment of our individuality and, because joyful, is good in itself."[194] In spite of this, Spinoza was no sexual anarchist. In fact, he came to the conclusion that monogamous marriage is the best way to organize people's sexual relationships. However, he did so through entirely pragmatic and secular reasoning. Monogamy reduces the conflicts that emerge out of matters of the heart and genitals. Not only that, but monogamy and fidelity should be promoted through cultural and social training, never by the force of law. Making adultery and fornication illegal, especially without sharing the knowledge why these acts should be taboo, merely makes them more exotic and attractive. In the end, Spinoza dismissed the entire premise that certain sexual acts or relationships should be judged morally "right" or "wrong." No matter what laws or threats of divine punishment are brought to bear, Spinoza concluded, human beings will adopt whatever relationships and arrangements suit them best. Society's obligation, in turn, is to educate, not regulate.[195]

Meanwhile Descartes's arguments were quickly seen as demolishing age-old distinctions between male and female, even the commonly accepted "fact" that women were more sexually promiscuous than men. If the mind and the body were separate, as Descartes asserted, then there was no reason to deny women an equal place in society. One of the most vocal proponents of the view was a French priest turned Protestant exile in Geneva, François Poullain de la Barre (1647–1725). De la Barre wrote a number of anonymous pamphlets on the subject, the most explicit of which was *De l'Égalité des deux sexes* ("On the Equality of the Two Sexes"). Using Descartes's logic, he concluded that the mind "has no sex"[196] and theorized that women's subordinate status in society is simply the product of historical circumstances, beginning with men exploiting the physical disadvantage women have from pregnancy. In reality, de la Barre argued, women are in every respect men's equals, hobbled only if they fully believe society's message that they are inferior.[197]

De la Barre was not alone: some female intellectuals were also arguing that women's "natural" subordination was not natural. The daughter of an English coalmine manager, Mary Astell (1666–1731) became an advocate for women's education, the lack of which she blamed for allowing ideas like women being less sexually moral to endure. In her pamphlet *A Serious Proposal to the Ladies,* Astell wrote, "The Cause therefore of the defects we labour under, is, if not wholly, yet at least in the first place, to be ascribed to the mistakes of our Education; which like an Error in the first Concoction, spreads its ill Influence through all our Lives."[198] The marquise de Lambert agreed, describing men's power over women as oppressive and maintained "by force rather than natural right."[199] Lambert was among the first in a growing number of aristocratic and wealthy middle-class women—many in France— who organized *salons,* home-run "academies" where the best and brightest were invited to debate the intellectual and social issues of the day in a casual and free environment. Through these *salons,* the question of women's education, a fiercely debated topic since at least the days of the medieval writer Christine de Pizan, became wrapped up with more daring questions of women's social and even sexual emancipation.

Some writers merely hinted at the implications the writings of Spinoza and Descartes had for sexual and family relations; others dreaded such issues altogether. Yet there were a few who tackled the subject with glee. The French Protestant philosopher Pierre Bayle (1647–1706) bluntly stated that only fear of social punishment, not religious morality or any physiological differences, restrained female sexuality.[200] The Dutch philosopher Adriaan Beverland (1650–1716) went directly against the medical common sense of his day by asserting that women's sexual desire was really no different than men's and that female modesty had nothing to do with a natural morality, but everything to do with the whims of a male-dominated society. More infamous was Beverland's pamphlet, *De Peccato Originali* ("On the Original Error"), which deployed without remorse the biblical criticism advocated by Spinoza and others. Beverland argued that the Scriptures had been corrupted by Christians taking them out of their historical context and attempting to interpret them in contemporary ways. For instance, the story of the Fall in Genesis had no messages about original sin or the evils of sex, but was simply an allegory about the development of sexual knowledge. Therefore, if one followed Beverland's reasoning, a large basis for Christianity's teachings about sin and sexual morality was based on a clumsy interpretation. Unsurprisingly, *De Peccato Originali* remained difficult to obtain due to censorship laws until late in the 18th century.[201]

The ties between sexual liberation and cutting-edge intellectualism were embodied in the libertines. Aristocratic, highly educated, often witty and sophisticated, and mostly male (with spectacular exceptions like Aphra Behn), the libertine came in many forms, but they were united under the tendency to flaunt religious and traditional morality, if they did not explicitly jettison belief in anything divine or supernatural altogether, and celebrate lives of easy sex and extravagant spending on paper and ink. "Libertine" and "libertinism" had long been insults; Calvin was fond of slapping the label on his opponents, and Milton's critics named him a libertine just for advocating no-fault divorce. Even if they did not identify as such, writers and intellectuals like Théophile de Viau (1590–1626) stepped into the devilish cutout by publishing poems that boasted of their own dalliances with prostitutes, sodomy, and heresy. For his poems that celebrated the many ways to say "fuck" and had the author himself declare that catching syphilis from a prostitute made him vow to God that he would become a sodomite, de Viau became, in the words of literary historian Joan de Jean, "the first writer to undergo a thoroughly modern writer's trial."[202] French authorities burned him in effigy, but in the flesh de Viau spent two years in prison and died in exile at Chantilly.

John Wilmot, Earl of Rochester (1647–1680), similarly gained a name for himself through his dirty writings, but also made it clear that he wrote what he knew. Even in the English court of King Charles II, which was infested with young rakes driven by wit and testosterone, Rochester stood out, punished with exile from court and even imprisonment. The original rebel without a cause, Rochester abducted an heiress, Elizabeth Malet, and pressured her into marrying him—an act that earned him a stay in the Tower of London. Then there was a long list of petty crimes he and his circle of friends indulged in, including throwing bottles filled with urine into a London crowd and beating up the poet John Dryden for insulting them in his writing.[203]

Although Rochester may not have been the real author of the play *Sodom, or the Quintessence of Sodomy,* which likened Charles II's court to that of the King of Sodom, he had plenty of incendiary writings of his own. In them he celebrated both his belief that the afterlife was nothing but a fairy tale and the fact that he "swived more whores, more ways than Sodom's walls."[204] None of his poems was published in his lifetime, but they were widely shared in the royal court and among fashionable Londoners. In the end, Rochester would vindicate the way of life he spent so much effort and energy trying to sabotage. Prematurely aged at 33 by venereal disease, he spent his last months alive in 1680 recanting his old views and trying to become the model Christian. The man responsible for Rochester's change of heart, Bishop Gilbert Burnet, bragged about Rochester's conversion in a poem, "The Rake, or The Libertine's Religion," and in his own biography of Rochester, which overnight became a bestseller.

Whether or not there were any female Rochesters, ideas that might be seen as "libertine" were expressed by women as well. One such writer was Margaret Cavendish, Duchess of Newcastle-upon-Tyne (1623–1673), through her play *The Convent of Pleasure*. The heroine, Lady Happy, is troubled by the problems facing any wealthy woman in a Protestant country, since her options are strictly either get married, stay single and risk having her reputation destroyed by seeing lovers, or become a courtesan. Lady Happy decides to make her own option: use her fortune to establish a secular convent of pleasure, where women can live pleasurable lives without the burden of husbands and lovers. In deciding this, Lady Happy comes to a distinctively libertine conclusion: "Can any Rational Creature think or believe, the gods take delight in the Creature's uneasie life? or, Did they command or give leave to Nature to make Senses for no use; or to cross, vex, and pain them?"[205]

Unfortunately, Lady Happy's faith in pleasure is put to the test when the convent accepts a foreign princess who dresses in men's clothing. Obviously the princess of the play is modeled after Queen Christina of Sweden, and Lady Happy is distressed when she finds herself attracted to the princess. In one scene Lady Happy wonders, "But why may not I love a Woman with the same affection I could a Man," although she immediately answers herself: "Nature is Nature, and still will be the same she was from all Eternity."[206] The play dismisses the slightest possibility of homosexual love, but, even though the princess turns out to be a prince who went undercover to find his bride, the questions the play raises about the pursuit of pleasure and how women's sexuality is repressed in a society that gives them almost no safe options for pursuing a sex life remain standing.

The "rakes" of late 17th-century Europe like Rochester were not much different from the profligate and hypermasculine aristocrats of the past, nor was there much new in Margaret Cavendish's endorsement of pleasure over self-denial. By the end of the century, however, the libertine was becoming more refined, more polished, and more presentable, and the idea of "rational pleasure" was launching more of a serious assault on Christianity's traditional teachings about the flesh. With the tide of the Enlightenment overtaking Europe, the libertine became a symbol for a potent combination of skepticism, intellectualism, and the search for individual freedom that was becoming more mainstream.

IX

Enlightened Bedrooms, 1700–1814

"Pleasure is now, and ought to be, your business," the Earl of Chesterfield wrote to his young son, encouraging him to seek out the intimate company of women as part of his "education."[1] Innovations such as Johannes Kepler's laws of planetary motion and Isaac Newton's theory of gravity encouraged those in the know to view the universe as a well-ordered machine—hence the 18th-century image of God as a watchmaker—but the human body itself was also sometimes conceived as a machine. As such, the human machine could not be blamed for being drawn to pleasant sensations. In fact, while excess of food, drink, and sex could ruin an otherwise perfectly good human machine, some degree of pleasure was actually necessary for the body's proper functioning.

That this human machine could be trained and conditioned was a cornerstone of 18th-century thought. Plato's belief that human knowledge is based on ideas innate to the mind from birth had been challenged and eventually made obsolete. According to the new model, all minds instead began as a blank slate, molded by their environment and experiences. And if individuals can be shaped, then so could societies, and it ought to be seen whether old and sacred traditions actually provided the optimal conditioning or instead held back human potential. It was a tempting outlook for a Europe where some certainties had been shaken down to the roots by new scientific discoveries, contact with many new societies across the globe, and the Protestant–Catholic schism and the hellish and seemingly unending warfare it unleashed.

Historians have questioned, as historians often do with all-too-convenient labels, the idea of the 18th century being an "Enlightenment." After all, the *philosophes* were in some ways building on scientific work and intellectual conversations that could be traced back centuries. At the same time, it is undeniable that for many "enlightened" thinkers the 18th century was both an exciting era and a disturbing time. In 1784, the German philosopher Immanuel Kant expressed these feelings in an essay asking, *"Was ist Aufklärung?"* ("What is Enlightenment?"). "Have courage to use your own reason! That is the motto of Enlightenment," Kant answered himself. The opponents of this "Enlightenment" likewise saw themselves as living in interesting times. Just one year after Kant wrote his epoch-defining essay, the French theologian and future martyr of the French Revolution Charles-Louis Richard proclaimed in a pamphlet, "Read, if you can, the innumerable writings to which modern philosophy has given birth. You will see that the great motor of human action is love of the self, of this *me* that constitutes the center and final end of everything. All is related to the self and to one's well being, one's interests, one's pleasures."[2]

In fact, when it came to sexuality, the Enlightenment birthed an entire generation of aggressively intellectual libertines. Although few libertines were as openly criminal as the "rakes" of late 17th-century England, the libertines did to an extent personify the fears reactionaries had, as they combined religious skepticism, fascination with the newest intellectual controversies, and seemingly unrestrained sexuality in their lifestyles and their writings. Whether or not they were complete egotists the way Charles-Louis Richard meant, the libertines lived and advertised the idea that the life worth living was one unrestricted by rules that did not stand up to rational scrutiny—and that included needlessly denying oneself pleasure. It was better to live in accordance with Nature and Reason, the two twin poles by which the *philosophes* defined their ethics, than according to dusty aesthetic rules better suited for a monk. There were areas where even the more radical *philosophes* did not stray from age-old teachings—very few *philosophes* were willing to entertain the slightest possibility that sodomy could be moral, for example—but nonetheless they were offering an entirely secular and utilitarian way of thinking and talking about sex that threatened the mainstream Christian view of sexuality that had dominated for more than a thousand years.

Of course, even long before the American War of Independence and the French Revolution, the Enlightenment was not limited to aristocratic mansions or to the occasional political pamphlet. Coffee houses and *salons* hosted by affluent women broke down class and gender barriers, uniting the increasingly literate and educated middle- and upper-class people of Europe through ideas and debate in what was deemed a "Republic of Letters." Also, from Stockholm to Naples, monarchs and ministers put the concepts of the Enlightenment into practice, by banning torture and capital punishment, extending freedom of religion and speech, placing restrictions on the powers of churches, and funding public education, among other measures. Part of this was, as the theorist Michel Foucault observed, a consequence of governments becoming stronger and more centralized, but it also represented the optimism of the age. Society and the lives of the people, it was thought, could be made better through careful but long-reaching reforms.

While discussions and debates about sex were being secularized, new "rational" reasons for regulating sex rose up to replace the religious reasons. Medical professionals denounced masturbation increasingly less as a sin and more as a health risk, while libertines were warned off excess by not threats of eternal damnation but rather warnings of physical decline. So it is far from accurate to say that the Enlightenment unconditionally brought with it greater sexual liberty. One can see images of the depraved fornicator or the sinful sodomite gradually disappear from laws and police records and the like as the century goes on, but by the end of the 18th century sexual deviants began to be labeled as mentally ill and condemned to sanitariums. Such was the fate of arch-pornographer and radical sexual anarchist the Marquis de Sade, who spent most of the end of his life in forced therapy.

The Enlightenment left an untidy legacy, as much for sex as for politics and society. Of course, the 18th century produced nothing resembling a gay rights movement, but at the same time Enlightenment thinkers articulated ideas about liberty and every individual's right to self-fulfillment that give a basis to conversations about human rights and sexual liberation held even today. Simultaneously, the Enlightenment defined the human body as a thing that could become broken and needed to be kept functioning well for the sake of the state and the country. As Foucault puts it, beginning in the 1700s the body was "being taken over by another mode of analysis and management of the body, by a different, secular, and medical power."[3] In other words, moral sin was beginning to be replaced by medical dysfunction.

The Philosophes Debate Sex

An English physician, John Locke (1632–1704), would change what Europeans thought they knew about thinking. Every scholar had known from Plato that the mind contained ideas from the moment of birth. Even that revolutionary deconstructionist Descartes agreed, assuming at the very least that every mind already knows some basic logical and mathematical concepts. In *An Essay on Human Understanding,* however, Locke argued that the mind began as a completely blank slate and learned only through experience, by what it perceived in its environment through the body's senses.

According to Locke, humans are not born with a grasp of even mathematics or logic, as philosophers in the Christian world had assumed since antiquity. Instead, Locke suggested, the only true guiding principle in the developing human mind is to search for pleasure and avoid pain. This natural pursuit of pleasure was a—if not *the*—key part of how an individual learns. It was an unparalleled lesson for Enlightenment intellectuals. As the historian Roy Porter writes, "The pursuit of pleasure, leading to happiness, became seen in Enlightenment writers ... as the behavior dictated by Nature to man."[4] Locke made it perfectly clear in his writings that he still strongly supported the power of the law and Scripture to define what is right or wrong morally, but he could not stop what later, more radical philosophers would do with his ideas.

Locke's concept of the pursuit of pleasure was an idea tailor-made for a society that was seeing unprecedented wealth and opportunities for leisure. The ideal of the Enlightenment became the men (and, increasingly, the women) who devoted themselves to a moderate consumption of luxury goods and pleasure in general. There was even a word for this model: "sensibility," perhaps best described as the state where one can express inner virtue and intelligence through refinement and good taste. Luxury itself was no longer a dirty word in most mainstream circles. Instead asceticism and self-denial came to be seen as unhealthy and dangerous as deranged excess.

Sensibility was even a way to ensure sexual morality. This point was taken up by the Italian philosopher Paolo Mattia Doria (1667–1746) in his 1726 work *Lettere e Ragionamenti* ("Letters on Reasoning"). Looking at how men and women across Europe were more freely speaking with each other, Doria admitted that this was eroding traditional ideas about chastity, male authority, and sexual morality and that women might become more prone to adultery and amorous encounters. However, the solution was not to lock women up behind closed doors and punish them sternly when they stepped out of line. Instead women should be allowed, even encouraged, to learn and make contacts with men of learning. Education and philosophy would make women more moral and virtuous.[5]

Besides changing ideas about how people learned and about luxury, the *philosophes* were excited by what they were seeing from foreign civilizations. For example, the pioneering mathematician and philosopher Gottfried Wilhelm Liebniz (1646–1716) saw vindication of his theories in traditional Chinese philosophy and science.[6] Likewise, Henri de Boulainvilliers's biography *Vie de Mahomed,* which was unfinished at the time of his death in 1722, unabashedly interpreted the Prophet Muhammad as a proponent of Enlightenment "natural religion" since he crafted a religious system free from superstition and schisms springing from disputes over obscure metaphysical details.[7] If foreign societies vindicated some of the *philosophes'* ideas, they also demonstrated that there was not much to the traditional concepts of natural or universal laws. In his article on "Natural Law" in the *Dictionairre philosophique,* Voltaire raises the objection that "it was forbidden to marry one's sister in Rome. It was allowed among the Egyptians, the Athenians and even among the Jews, to marry one's sister on the father's side" (although he does add that, while there may be such a thing as natural law at least when it comes to justice, "it is also natural to forget it").[8]

How could education help promote traditional morals, even if educated people were aware that the world was full of radically different cultures and values? The baron de Montesquieu (1689–1754) was confident that reason and "Nature" would vindicate most age-old sexual norms. Based on his theory about how governments develop, Montesquieu argued in his grand work of political and social theory, *L'esprit des lois* ("The Spirit of Laws"), that sexual norms vary according to different countries' geography and climate, but generally for their own good and the good of their people governments should intervene through law to promote population growth. For that reason, Montesquieu believed monogamous love should be a social ideal:

> It is a rule drawn from nature that, the more one diminishes the number of marriages which can be made, the more one corrupts those which are made; the fewer married men and women, the more infidelity in the marriages; just as when there are more robbers, there are more robberies.[9]

In spite of the emphasis on monogamous love that Montesquieu showed in his philosophy, he also attacked the idea of indissoluble marriage in his *Persian Letters,* a social critique written through fictional letters between two Persians traveling through France. One of the Persians, Usbec, remarks that since the Christians banned divorce in ancient times their marriages have been plagued by hatred and fighting between unhappy spouses, as it is easier to handle marital discord when both spouses know escape is an option. Usbec—and Montesquieu—concludes that all indissoluble divorce does is ensure, once the spouses do inevitably begin living separately, that the husband takes up with some pretty young alternative and produces illegitimate children.

Back in the *Spirit of Laws,* Montesquieu constantly questioned the effectiveness of harsh laws against sexual crimes and suggested instead that punishments should never be out of proportion to the actual crime. Addressing lawmakers who like to think they are avenging offenses against Christian morality, he noted, "The mischief arises from a notion which some people have entertained of revenging the cause of the Deity. But we must honor the Deity and leave him to avenge his own cause."[10] When Montesquieu got to the touchy issue of that worst of moral crimes, sodomy, he exclaimed, "God forbid that I should have the least inclination to diminish the public horror against a crime which religion, morality, and civil government equally condemn."[11] The concern came out of his own assertion that sodomy should be treated like any other moral offense, since social disapproval should be sufficient and, without customs that encouraged homosexuality like Greek pederasty or polygamy which in Montesquieu's mind caused an unequal distribution of wives in a society, "nature will soon defend or resume her rights."[12] Despite his misgivings and reluctance, Montesquieu did make an extreme claim about sodomy, simply by never citing religious morality as a reason to continue sodomy laws, only "Nature" and the fear that sex with other men makes men more effeminate.

Frequent appeals to Nature were also made by the more radical Denis Diderot (1713–1784), a would-have-been priest and lawyer who was disowned by his father because he decided to be a professional writer instead. Diderot was more outspokenly atheistic than most of his fellow *philosophes* and dabbled in writing satirical erotica, one of which was the descriptively titled *The Indiscreet Jewels,* which mocked the court of the French king Louis XV by describing an imaginary Islamic royal court where the Sultan had a magic ring that made the genitals of his mistresses talk. Both habits would land him in prison. For Diderot, the natural urge to have sex was about pleasure, not reproduction. When faced with moral objections to masturbation, Diderot complained, "Nature tolerates nothing useless, so how am I to blame for helping her when called to do so by unmistakable promptings?"[13] In fact, he said, masturbation is always the best option, since unlike adultery or prostitution it solves the problem of lust without any risk of venereal disease.[14]

Diderot not only saw pleasure as the purpose behind the sex drive, but also accused Christianity of defying the dictates of Nature and forcing unnatural behaviors on humanity. The ultimate gag of *The Indiscreet Jewels* is that no woman is faithful, but neither is any man, so fidelity is an illusion that simply creates hypocrisy and unhappiness. Many sexual morals and social conventions are not just opposed to Nature, but Nature will win every time. This war was most obvious in the institution of religious chastity, which Diderot ruthlessly attacked in his novel *The Nun.*

The novel began as a hoax Diderot played on a friend by sending him letters purportedly from a nun who needed help in breaking her vows. Suzanne, the titular nun of the novel, is forced into convent life by her aristocratic family. She ends up under the authority of a sadistic mother superior who nearly has her starved in a cell. Although she does encounter kind authorities in the Church who are aghast at her treatment, it takes a lawyer from outside the Church to rescue her and have her transferred to another convent. There Suzanne finds a much kinder mother superior, who falls in love with Suzanne and becomes obsessed with her. Hopelessly naive because she has never been taught about the ways of the world, Suzanne is completely helpless. Although a priest warns her about the mother superior, Suzanne cannot understand why she should avoid one of the few people who has been kind to her. When Suzanne finally overhears the mother superior, who has gone insane, admit that she loves her, Suzanne flees the convent with a priest, who takes advantage of the situation by raping Suzanne. In the end, a victim of both the Church and her total ignorance of sex, she dies poor and alone on the streets of Paris.

Interpretations vary over whether Diderot's view of love between women in the novel is at all sympathetic.[15] Elsewhere Diderot did try to reconcile a distaste for same-sex love with his view that sex should be enjoyed. The solution comes from a dialogue appended to one of his works, *D'Alembert's Dream,* in which d'Alembert's mistress, Julie d'Espinasse, talks about the relativity of sexual customs with Dr. Bordeu, Diderot's real-life doctor. When the topic of sodomy comes up, Bordeu rejects the entire expression "contrary to nature," since by definition it is impossible for any sex act to exist outside of nature. Even if there were sexual acts against nature, then celibacy really should by rights be counted as "contrary to nature" as much as sodomy. When Julie asks why some desire love with the same sex, Bordeau theorizes, "Invariably they can be traced to a weakness in the nervous organizations of young people or the decay of the brain in elderly people. In Athens they were brought about by the seductive power of beauty, in Rome [the Vatican] by the scarcity of women, and in Paris they are caused by fear of the pox."[16]

Another popular French writer and philosopher, François-Marie Arouet, far better known by his pen name Voltaire, was also perplexed by this dilemma. He asked, "How can it be that a vice, one which would destroy the human race if it became general, an infamous assault upon Nature, can nevertheless be so Natural?"[17] In a 1764 essay titled "On the Love Called 'Socratic'" written for the *Dictionare philosophique*, Voltaire asserted that since logically no society would ever approve of same-sex acts, then accounts of pederasty in ancient Greece must really refer to completely innocent and chaste relationships. When same-sex love did happen, it must have been the result of warmer climates, all because people there wear less clothing! In fact, "this vice unworthy of mankind is unknown in our harsh climate."[18] Yet in life Voltaire was a friend of King Friedrich II of Prussia and the marquis de Villette, both of whom were widely suspected of carrying on with men; indeed, Voltaire hinted at and joked about their preferences in his correspondences with them.[19] Why Voltaire venomously and publicly denounced a "vice" he teased friends about in private, and what this means for Voltaire's real views, can only be left to speculation.

Voltaire was a bit less traditional when it came to other sexual matters, especially when it came to the insistence on celibacy. "In some provinces of Europe the girls make love, without their afterwards becoming less prudent wives," Voltaire writes in the *Dictionaire philosophique*. "In France it is quite the contrary; the girls are shut up in convents, where, hitherto, they have received a most ridiculous education." For Voltaire, this was even worse than the shutting up of married women practiced in other countries: "We pity the great ladies of Turkey, Persia and India; but they are a thousand times happier in their seraglios than our young women in their convents."[20]

As was true of other Enlightenment thinkers, in Voltaire's view denial of sexual urges had the potential to be more unhealthy than any kind of sexual expression. As Diderot implied frequently in *The Nun* and Voltaire openly asserted, celibacy is the only true "unnatural" act, because it causes a person to force the body to act against its instincts and needs. In a 1771 revision to his essay on "Socratic love," Voltaire added an anecdote about a priest in his own neighborhood who had been caught seducing the adolescent men in his charge. From here he added, "The monks responsible for educating the young have always been somewhat addicted to pederasty. This is the necessary consequence of the celibacy to which these poor men are condemned."[21]

Although many of the *philosophes* wrestled with the moral question of sexuality, even if sexuality was not a central concern for them, none was as audaciously contradictory or as flamboyantly hypocritical as Jean-Jacques Rousseau (1712–1778). In his fiction and writings on education, marriage, and family life, Rousseau attempted to rescue the "natural" human from the corruptions of modern civilization, a mission that led him to endorse family values not unlike those held dear by the Victorian middle class or the conservative nuclear family of the 20th century. Yet, in his own life as revealed in his autobiographical *Confessions*,

Rousseau did not marry his lover until late in life and gave up to adoption all five children whom he fathered with her.

In his treatise *Discours sur l'origine et les fondements de l'inégalité parmi les hommes* ("Discourse on the Origin and Foundations of Inequality Among Man," 1754), Rousseau hypothesized that in the beginning, before organized society, the family simply did not exist. Men and women had intercourse but no monogamy, and women raised children on their own. Once people started claiming land as their own property and began living in permanent homes, this changed, as women and men needed each other and more children for the purposes of agricultural labor. Although Rousseau did concede that the family is not the primal state of humanity, he considered it an ideal stage, since it created family relationships that produce the "sweetest feelings known to humanity."[22]

For the human being who must exist in civilized society, Rousseau made his recommendations in his educational tract, *Émile*. Throughout most of the book, Rousseau described in detail the ideal way in which his hypothetical pupil Émile is raised by his tutor, who must make Émile into a "natural man" who can nonetheless exist in society. In the last chapter, Rousseau described the education and upbringing of Émile's future wife, Sophie. There Rousseau revealed his belief that men and women, while both victims of their natural desires, are fundamentally different and must be raised in different ways to function optimally in civilization. Men can tame their sexuality through reason, while women like Sophie must be conditioned to control themselves with modesty. In words that disgusted Rousseau's contemporary, Mary Wollstonecraft, Rousseau described women as "passive and weak," their only real strength coming out of their sexual influence over men. "Women are wrong when complaining about the inequality of man-made laws," Rousseau wrote. "This inequality is not of man's making, or anyway it is not the result of mere bias, but of reason. She whom nature has entrusted the nurturing of children must herself be responsible to their father for them."[23]

This is not to say that men should be left completely to their own devices. Émile's tutor is warned: "Do not leave him alone day or night. At least sleep in his room. Beware of the sexual impulse as soon as you are not watching."[24] Rousseau knew exactly what he was warning his pupil's teacher about. In his *Confessions*, he described how he was spanked at the age of eight by his surrogate mother, Mademoiselle de Lambercier. When Lambercier noticed that little Rousseau was sexually aroused by the experience, afterward he slept in his own room and was treated like a "big boy." Impressed by how this one incident shaped the rest of his life, Rousseau wrote:

> Who would have believed that this childhood punishment, received at age eight by the hand of a girl of thirty, would determine my tastes, my desires, my passions, my very self for the rest of my life, and furthermore quite contrary to the sense that naturally should have ensued? At the same moment that my senses were set afire, my desires took a turn that, confined to what I had experienced, they never decided to seek anything else.... To be at the knees of an imperious mistress, obey her orders, beg her forgiveness, were the sweetest pleasures, and the more my lively imagination inflamed my blood, the more I seemed a transfixed lover. One can imagine that this fashion of making love does not get one very far.... Therefore, I have possessed few, but nonetheless I have enjoyed great pleasure in my own fashion; that is, by the imagination.[25]

Rousseau and other intellectuals of the time were convinced that the mind itself, whether described as the "nerves" or the "imagination," could be permanently twisted out of shape.

In this light, one actually could commit sexual acts "against nature," if by nature one meant the "healthy functioning of the body."[26]

The *philosophes* of France did the most to steer the conversation, but the Enlightenment was not confined to France's borders. As just one example, the German Immanuel Kant tackled a wide variety of subjects—and sexuality was just one of them. Through entirely rationalistic means, Kant devised an ethics of sex as pessimistic as anything to come out of Thomas Aquinas. For Kant, the mere act of sex was inherently degrading because it "makes of the loved person an Object of appetite."[27] Kant drew stark lines between sex and love, defining sexuality as only the desire for sex, and not for a person. At the other extreme was the English social reformer Jeremy Bentham (1748–1832), whose philosophy of utilitarianism urged that societies and individuals seek the greater good, which Bentham defined as what produces the most happiness. If a sex act does no harm but instead provides pleasure to all parties involved, then there is simply no reason to forbid that act, either legally or socially. Bentham scoffed at the idea that sex without procreation is "unnatural," since if "unnatural" pleasures should be forbidden then music would also qualify. Further, if God created humans to desire pleasure but forbade them most ways of achieving pleasure, then God must be a petty tyrant. Bentham was even one of the few voices of the Enlightenment to explicitly call for the end of any regulation, social or legal, against same-sex acts, but as a sign of the times he never dared publish such writings.[28]

As the gap between Kant and Bentham shows, there was no Enlightenment consensus on sex. The one thing the champions of Enlightenment often agreed about was that it was no longer adequate to consult either the Scriptures or ancient writers about matters of morality or sexuality. Also they often agreed that pleasure was healthy and natural, or at least healthier and more natural than the option of self-denial. This was in itself revolutionary, but it did not quite go that far by modern standards. Nearly all mainstream Enlightenment writers still went off on their own line of reasoning, sometimes with bizarre results, to explain away why homosexuality should be tolerated. In fact, for the most part no Enlightenment writers truly treated sexuality as its own subject; almost always it was a subtopic filed under ethics, social and legal reform, or anthropology. The one famous exception is the Enlightenment's most radical, disturbing, and still controversial voice—that of Donatien Alphonse François, Marquis de Sade (1740–1814).

Born from one of the oldest living aristocratic families in Provence, after his death Sade made his prestigious family name famous for being the basis for the word "sadism." A libertine from the start, Sade was arrested for alleged abusive and blasphemous acts with prostitutes, including an incident on Easter of 1768 where Sade placed a holy wafer in a woman's vagina before intercourse and began exclaiming, "Lord, avenge thyself!" The scandals triggered a mostly unbroken stint of imprisonment that would eat up much of Sade's life, totaling 32 years in various prisons (including the notorious Bastille, albeit only briefly) and insane asylums.

In confinement, Sade channeled much of his libido and his rage into writing, turning someone who would have just been another young rake into an immortal voice for sexual anarchy. How much Sade was genuinely laying down the groundwork for a radical ethical system and how much he was just raging against what he saw as a hypocritical society that had wrongly stolen his freedom is up to debate. In his fiction Sade depicted monarchs who savored orgies and murders in equal measure and nobles who imprisoned, tortured, and raped those below their rank, yet he was a tireless supporter of traditional monarchy and aristocracy, even when publicly he had to denounce both to survive the French Revolution. His scenes frequently mingled bloodlust and sexuality to the point that the two instincts are indistinguishable, but he passionately advocated against the death penalty during the French Revolution's Reign of Terror even though it nearly brought his own neck under the guillotine.

Sade's first work, composed within the walls of the Bastille, was the novel *Justine* (1787). Savagely and ruthlessly the novel mocks the genre of "sentimental novels" like Rousseau's *Julie* and Samuel Richardson's *Pamela,* which were highly popular in the later 18th century and typically portrayed a heroine surviving adversity (although not always) through the power of her own virtue, a virtue that was often expressed in sexual terms. Justine clings to her chastity and plays strictly by the rules her society has written for women, and she suffers for it at every turn: she is harassed by a woman in charge of a gang of outlaws, imprisoned and repeatedly raped in a corrupt monastery, forced to participate in a sadomasochist's games, and sentenced to die for crimes she did not commit because she refuses to join an orgy involving the judge presiding over her trial. Justine does at first get the standard happy ending, rescued by her long-lost sister Juliette, who has by sharp contrast become independently wealthy through a life of prostitution, theft, and murder. Then, just when she is secure and happy for the first time in her life, Justine is killed by a random lightning bolt.

Years later, Sade revised *Justine* to make it much more graphic, and published it alongside a new sequel, *Juliette* (1797–1801). Detailing Juliette's adventures, the narration begins with Juliette being forced to move into a convent. The abbess, madame Delbène, another woman made to choose convent life, indoctrinates young Juliette into lesbianism and atheism. Thrown out of the convent when her family's money runs out, Juliette becomes a successful prostitute and thief, but her career does not really take off until she becomes the lover of the powerful government minister Norceuil. Even Norceuil's confession that he murdered her father hardly undoes her attraction to him. If anything, the connection thrills her. Norceuil instructs the eager pupil Juliette on his conception of Nature:

> Instead of taking pity on his sufferings, of mitigating them and turning them ridiculously into a burden to be borne by your own sympathies, be sensible, my dear, and view him merely as a creature Nature has designed for your entertainment, as one she offers for whatever use you deign to put him to; rather than wipe his tears, redouble the cause of his weepings, if you like, if it amuses you: lo! here are human beings Nature's readied for the scythe of your passions; reap a goodly harvest, dear Juliette, Nature is bountiful; emulate the spider, spin your webs, and mercilessly devour everything that Nature's wise and liberal hand casts into the meshes.

Hearing Noirceuil's philosophy of violent hedonism, Juliette is overjoyed. "'My beloved!' I cried, hugging Noirceuil to me, 'how enormous is my debt to you for dissipating the miasmas of ignorance childhood instruction and prejudice brewed in my spirit! Your sublime lessons are unto my heart what the healing dew is to scorched vegetation!'"[29]

Over the course of the novel Juliette becomes the ultimate libertine. She is privileged, enlightened, skeptical, ravenously sexual, and aware of the arbitrariness and relativity of the rules regulating sex and everything else. In an extreme interpretation of the meaning of libertine, Juliette even liberates herself from both family ties and the biological consequences of sex by burning her own daughter to death in the middle of an orgy. Juliette's enlightenment, which is as every bit sexual as it is intellectual, allows her to join the ranks of Europe's ruling elite, all of whom revel in violence and torture. The King and Queen of Naples, for example, have sex while an adolescent is decapitated in their presence. Juliette ends her sprawling tale rich, happy, and surrounded by friends and lovers, the type of ending otherwise reserved for virtuous and virginal heroines like Justine.

Sade had told an earlier tale of power, sex, and privilege in *120 Days of Sodom* (1785), an epic where a group of noblemen in the middle of the Thirty Years War imprison peasants and, taking inspiration from stories told by veteran prostitutes, engage in elaborate acts of sexualized torture and murder against their captives. However, perhaps his most succinct comments on sex and morality were in *Philosophy in the Bedroom* (1795). There, in the tradition of Renaissance erotic tracts, intellectual debate and education are inseparable from sexual experience. A naive young woman, Eugénie, who has been raised in strict isolation by her religiously devout mother, Madame de Mistival, is sent by her father to be educated in libertine ways by the incestuous madame de Saint-Ange and the homosexual Dolmancé. In a mockery of Rousseau's own theories on education, the project here is, in the words of Angela Carter, "to strip [her] of all her socialized virtues and to restore her to the primal and vicious state of nature."[30] Their mission is proven to have succeeded once madame de Mistival intervenes, frantically trying to save her daughter's morality and religious faith. Instead Eugénie proves herself a full-fledged Sadeian heroine by having her mother raped by a servant with syphilis and her vagina and anus sewn up. Also deep in the book is a political pamphlet titled "Yet Another Effort, Frenchmen, If You Are to Be Republicans." Allegedly in support of the social engineering launched by France's revolutionaries, the pamphlet includes a stirring exhortation for women to free their sexuality:

> Charming sex, you will be free; just as men do, you shall enjoy all the pleasures that Nature makes your duty, do not withhold yourselves from one. Must the diviner part of mankind be kept in chains by the other? Ah, break those bonds; nature wills it. Have no other curb than your tastes, no other laws than those of your own desires, no more morality than that of Nature herself. Languish no more under those barbarous prejudices that wither your charms and imprison the divine impulses of your heart; you are as free as we are and the career of the battles of Venus as open to you as to us.[31]

Sade remains as controversial in modern times as he was when he was alive. In the 20th century, Andrea Dworkin held up Sade as proof that pornographers never fail to preach violence against women. Angela Carter and Simone de Beauvoir defended him as a prophet, albeit perhaps a flawed and difficult one, of sexual freedom and gender transcendence. In the terms of the Enlightenment itself, Sade completely and satirically perverted Rousseau's worship of Nature. For Sade, civilization and all of its trappings, from the Church to the State, were just a machine built and designed to preserve entrenched elites. However, Nature was viewed as no more or less cruel; the key difference is that the hypocrisies of civilization are washed away while cruelty and dominance remain. In the end, Sade agreed with Kant that sex carries with it the power to dominate and degrade, but this is a fact that should be fully acknowledged, if not embraced with gusto. "Sade has a curious ability to render every aspect of sexuality suspect, so that we see how the chaste kiss of the sentimental lover differs only in degree from the vampirish love-bite that draws blood, we understand that a disinterested caress is only quantitatively different from a disinterested flogging," Angela Carter writes. "For Sade, all tenderness is false, a deceit, a trap; all pleasure contains within itself the seeds of atrocities; all beds are minefields."[32] Sex is exciting and dangerous, Sade warned, but not because it is right or wrong, healthy or unhealthy, rather, it is because it is irrevocably linked to power and privilege. It is up to the individual to decide how he or she will cope with this truth, and in deciding become either a Juliette or a Justine.

The Age of Decadence

Of course, Sade has given us a rather distorted view of the 18th century, unless the pope really was in the habit of presiding over blasphemous orgies where he loudly announced his secret atheism as he does in *Juliette*. Still, there was a pervasive sense among 18th-century conservatives that something was driving society into the abyss. Jean-Antoine Rigoley de Juvigny protested in 1787, "*Philosophisme* has penetrated everywhere, has corrupted everything.... The outcome of this distressing revolution has been the general deprivation of morals."[33] Naturally, libertines and radicals like Sade were not invented by the 18th century, but they did prosper in a world where luxuries were spreading and where cities were refuges for markets in pleasure.

If 18th-century Europe had its own sin city, it was London. The capital of England was easily Europe's fastest-growing city in the 17th and 18th centuries. It entered the 1700s with a population of 630,000 and ended the century with over 1 million. In his 1728 pamphlet *Augusta Triumphans,* the pioneering journalist and novelist Daniel DeFoe blasted this latter-day Babylon: "Go all the world over, and you'll see no such impudence as in the streets of London, which makes many foreigners give our women in general a bad character, from the vile specimens they meet with from one of the town to the other." In fact, DeFoe explored the debilitating effects of urban life on one such woman in his novel *Moll Flanders,* where the titular heroine, born from a prison inmate, finds herself having to steal, cheat, and prostitute herself to survive, until she finds happiness and redemption by fleeing metropolitan England altogether for the pristine land of Virginia.

Foreign visitors came to London not only to experience the capital of an empire on the rise, but apparently also to enjoy themselves. An anonymous German tourist in 1725 estimated that there were 107 brothels just in the area of Drury Lane.[34] Visitors to London from elsewhere in Britain or abroad could consult a number of guides to help them manage all the delightful options, such as *The London Belles or, A Description of the Most Celebrated Beauties in the City of London* (1707) or *Kitty's Atlantis for the Year 1766,* which not only provided the addresses of brothels but also gave reviews of their piano playing, singing, ability to handle booze, and specialties in bed.[35] If you happened to enjoy a bit of a beating, there was Theresa Berkeley's brothel at No. 28 Charlotte Street. She even had a special mechanized "flogging machine" called the Berkeley horse, which allowed a man of any size to be restrained while being whipped.

The sex trade existed in less obvious locales. Just as in the past, taverns and inns remained hotspots for prostitution, serving alcoholic drinks to protect themselves from even the spottily enforced British laws against "houses of ill repute." By the 18th century, there were also coffee houses, a Turkish innovation that spread across Europe over the course of the 17th century, where one could also meet a paid lover on the side. The most famous for offering more than coffee and conversation was Tom King's Coffee House. After midnight, one could have his pick of the "Women of the Town, the most celebrated, and dressed as elegant as if to sit in the stage box at an opera."[36]

Even this did not inspire too much of a public outcry. What did was the hard-to-deny existence of the "molly houses," male brothels, which became the center of an urban subculture as London continued to expand. Detailed in historian Rictor Norton's book *Mother Clap's Molly House,* "molly houses" were brothels and taverns where men could not just solicit services from other men, but the patrons dressed in drag, took on female mannerisms, and occasionally entered into "marriages" with each other that did symbolize a commitment.[37] One of the most vivid and condemnatory descriptions came from the journalist Ned Ward's *History of the London Clubs* (1709). After indulging in funny details about clubs like the Surly Club and the Farting Club, his tone reaches a hysterical pitch with the "mollies":

> There are a particular Gang of Sodomitical Wretches in this Town, who call themselves Mollies, and are so degenerated from all masculine Deportment, or manly Exercises, that they rather fancy themselves Women, imitating all the little Vanities that custom has reconcil'd to the female Sex, affecting to speak, walk, talk, tattle, courtesy, cry, scold, and to mimick all manner of Effeminacy that has ever fallen within their several Observations, not omitting the Indecencies of lewd Women, that they may tempt one another, by such immodest Freedoms, to commit those odious Bestialities, that ought forever to be without a Name.[38]

Sodomy trial records detail the existence of numerous such "molly houses." The most famous, thanks to Rictor Norton, is Mother Clap's Molly House in central London, but there was also the "Sodomite's Walk" in Moorfields and, worst of all, several places near St. Paul's Cathedral. The government never stopped trying to shut down the molly houses. The situation was somewhat different in France. Although sodomy remained a crime, by the 1770s authorities settled for forcing male prostitutes to register as they did with women.[39]

Prostitution had always been by its very nature a commercial activity, but it was also responding to a culture that openly valued consumerism and respectable consumption. There is no better example of this than the *sérails* of Paris. Named for its inspiration, the harems or *sarays* of the Ottoman Empire, the *sérail* was designed to offer the discerning client a more romantic and respectable experience. The women were chosen for their beauty as well as their skills in the bedroom, could hold a decent conversation, and had skills in music or dancing. Meanwhile the decor of the rooms was kept up to aristocratic standards. Most important of all, the women were kept strictly in line, forbidden from rowdy behavior, too much fattening food, or strong alcohol.[40]

Alongside such illicit and yet respectable options for a respectable clientele, there was a surprising candidness about enjoying such venues in 18th-century culture. Erotica was nothing new, but the 18th century saw the emergence of a new enticing genre: the courtesan and libertine memoir, which was in some ways the "reality television" of the 1700s. By far the most famous example today was the autobiography of Giarcomo Casanova (1725–1798). The son of Venetian actors, Casanova experimented with a number of failed careers—soldier, musician, lawyer, even cleric—while traveling across Europe, where his real mission in life became charming the rich and powerful. Even the pope was impressed enough by the young Casanova that he gave him a gift of several books, including erotica and volumes banned under the Index of Forbidden Books. The draw of Casanova's memoirs for readers were his numerous adventures, including an escape from prison and a duel with a Polish count, but it was his skill at womanizing that made his name proverbial. Just as lustful but not nearly as charming was the Scottish lawyer and writer James Boswell (1740-1795). In his own memoirs, Boswell recounted a number of passionate affairs he had across Scotland and England. His memoirs left few details behind in the bedroom:

> I picked up a girl in the Strand; went into a court with the intention to enjoy her in armor [wearing a condom]. But she had none. I toyed with her. She wondered at my size, and said if I ever took a girl's maidenhead, I would make her squeak. I gave her a shilling, and had command enough of myself to go without touching her. I afterwards trembled at the danger I had escaped.[41]

While libertine memoirs were the majority, there were a few bestselling courtesan memoirs. One such was written by the Irish woman Margaret Leeson (1727-1797), who went by the alias Peg Plunkett. At the start Leeson revealed an understanding of her target audience, vowing that while she would "not ... excite a blush on the most refined and delicate cheek," somehow she could offer up "some nice tit bits, and delicious morsels of scandal."[42] Once her brother squandered her family's finances and she was abandoned by her lover after becoming pregnant, Leeson became a professional courtesan established in Dublin. Leeson's memoirs portrayed a world where a woman in poverty who fails in her duty to be chaste just once would be dragged into the gutter, but where the same "fallen" woman could nonetheless survive and even thrive through toughness, ingenuity, and a willingness to challenge genteel society's rules. She would have to work much harder and be subjected to harassment from countless sources, but the moral of Leeson's tale was that a woman could be as financially—and sexually—independent as any man.

The fact that women, while still subjected to double standards, were becoming more literate and increasingly asserting themselves as part of Europe's intellectual networks seems to have been reflected in fashion, where barriers between genders were also falling down. Remarking on the pink waistcoats and silver coats of several English noblemen, Sarah Osborne joked, "I believe the gentlemen will wear petticoats very soon for many of their coats were like our mantuas."[43] On a more serious note, Rousseau infamously complained in a letter that "unable to make themselves into men, the women seek to make us into women."[44] On the other side of the aisle, it became acceptable, even fashionable, for women to wear masculine horse riding gear, even pants. Female monarchs like Empress Elizabeth of Russia (r. 1741-1762), who needed to project the idea of a warring Amazon, even if it meant looking a little butch, naturally had themselves painted this way. However, such portraits were also commissioned for women like princesses and noblewomen who did not have such a need. In fact, the mad King Christian VII of Denmark (r. 1766-1808), who had very strange issues with masculinity, was said to have been aroused whenever his wife Caroline Matilda of Hanover (1751-1775) dressed in her manly riding clothes.

Not helping the fears of men like Rousseau was the fact that the elites did not rush to pass laws to prop up gender roles; instead they reveled in this new ambiguity. The medieval tradition of the *carnivale* was resuscitated in Venice, which was reinventing itself as the Las Vegas of early modern Europe to make up for its lost trade empire. Carnivals' allowance for controlled chaos and assumed identities was especially popular, and across Europe royal courts and cities hosted masquerade balls where people could dress as they pleased, even as the opposite gender. Cross-dressing was a particularly key and mandatory element to the balls hosted by the Empress Elizabeth in St. Petersburg. When Catherine II ("Catherine the Great") came to the Russian throne, she also hosted masquerades, but did not require the partygoers to go drag, although she did enjoy coming disguised as a man herself.[45] It is understandable why a powerful female monarch in a patriarchal society might enjoy a bit of gender-bending, but cross-dressing masquerades were not just for the imperial palaces in Russia. Britain's first prime minister, Horace Walpole, casually mentioned in one letter that he did have a "large trunk full of dresses" at hand in case he was invited to a masquerade ball.[46]

Fashion and parties proved not to be a threat in demolishing gender barriers in the long run. Over the course of the final decades of the 18th century, men's fashions became more distinct from women's with the disappearance of large wigs, lace, and frock coats that could sometimes resemble skirts.[47] Also even the suggestion of cross-dressing for fun became more infinitely unacceptable in the more militaristic and humorless royal courts of the 19th century. A more lasting legacy came from the libertine intellectuals, who became in the 18th century more organized and in some cases more respectable.

Not so respectable was the infamous Hell-Fire Club or the Medmenham Friars, the more tame title they were known by in their own time. The group was established by the English nobleman Francis Dashwood at an old Cistercian monastery in 1751. Dashwood and his friends probably met just for rounds of alcohol, conversation, and sex, but nasty rumors quickly claimed that they were also enjoying Satanic rites. Likely Dashwood did name himself as "abbot," his friends as "friars," and the women who serviced them as "nuns." Still, that was probably as far as their blasphemy went, even though other branches surfaced across England and Ireland. It is yet another case where the myth became much stronger and more enduring than the reality. In modern times, the Hell-Fire Club, even though harmless by 18th-century standards, has been the subject of a horror novel and a model for a supervillain team in comics.

The Scottish answer to the Hell-Fire Club was the Beggar's Benison club. While the men did do perfectly respectable things like discuss their business and economic interests (less respectable was the fact that a significant number of businessmen in the club were involved in smuggling goods into Scotland), they also partied on holidays by hiring young local women to dance nude or just show off their genitals. Among the collection of items surviving from the Beggar's Benison club, and its offshoot the Wig Club, are three phallic drinking cups, complete with testicles.[48]

Threats to sexual norms were not limited to the secular realm. A Polish Jew, Jacob Frank (1726–1791), went about proclaiming himself to be the reincarnation of Sabbatai Zevi, a 17th-century religious leader whose followers named him the Messiah. Even though Sabbatai Zevi eventually converted to Islam, which one imagines disqualified him from being the Messiah, the movement he began was still going strong. The Sabbataians went against Jewish views of pleasure by embracing some degree of asceticism, although their opponents accused Jacob Frank and others of performing ritualistic dances around naked women. Before a court of rabbis, Frank's followers confessed to preaching adultery and promiscuity, but likely enough they may have been under pressure to do so.[49]

Among Christians there was Swedenborgianism or the New Church, which spun out of the writings of the Swedish theologian Emanuel Swedenborg (1688–1772). If Swedenborg had been born just a century or two earlier, he would have been burned alive. Instead, his bold claims—that angels and demons were once human spirits and that the Second Coming occurred in a purely spiritual dimension sometime in 1757—helped make him a wildly popular thinker. Some of Swedenborg's ideas about sex were in a firmly rooted Protestant mainstream. For instance, for Swedenborg celibacy went against not just nature but the eternal plan, since marriages last forever beyond even death.[50] More striking was how central sexuality was to Swedenborg's concept of spirituality. Sex was even how a woman and a man could reunify the parts of divinity within humanity shattered by the Fall, and as such it was even permissible for men in the Church to have mistresses in certain situations.[51]

Enthusiasts for Swedenborg went further. August Nordenskjöld and C.B. Wadström from Finland and Sweden, respectively, spearheaded an international scheme to found a colony on the coast of Sierra Leone, then under the control of Britain. This colony would be completely governed according to Swedenborgian principles and would strive for both spiritual and political liberty. The project never got off the ground, but the two did publish a pamphlet in 1792, written in English and titled *The Plan for a Free Community upon the Coast of Africa under the Protection of Great Britain; but Intirely* [sic] *Independent of All European Laws and Governments*. Even in the age of the American War of Independence and the French Revolution, it was an extreme document, simply by proposing a society where Africans and Europeans would live together as complete equals. In the pamphlet, sex and love are presented as the very basis of society, and marriage as practiced today is an instrument of oppression. Unfortunately, we do not know how far a Swedenborgian nation would have gone in pursuit of these ideas. Swedenborg's ideas still had a long reach after his death, helping to inspire liberal Christians, utopia planners, occultists, and New Agers in the centuries to come.

Swedenborg wanted to steer Christian sexual ethics away from self-denial toward union and love achieved through sexuality; the English scholar Richard Payne Knight (1750–1824) more or less wanted to revive the classical pagan morality of sex that Christianity had once displaced. To put it bluntly, Knight was fixated on the penis, finding it the symbol of the sexual freedom Christianity had repressed for many centuries. Published as *The Discourse on the Worship of Priapus, and Its Connexion with the Mystic Theology of the Ancients* (1786–1787), Knight's first work made a splash young academics can only dream of. There he maintained that archeological discoveries in Naples and elsewhere showed that worship of phallic symbols was widespread in ancient times. Further, the Christian Church adopted these phallic emblems as its own, even Christianity's most important and sacred symbol: "One of the most remarkable of [the symbols of male reproduction] is a cross, in the form of the letter T, which thus served as the emblem of creation and generation, before the church adopted it as the sign of salvation; a lucky coincidence of ideas, which, without doubt, facilitated the reception of it among the faithful."[52]

The book was not well received, to put it mildly. Horace Walpole himself, even though he knew about Knight's research and offered to loan him an ancient idol of the Roman goddess Ceres with a phallic bull on it to help him, recanted his earlier favor as soon as he read the book. The scholar Thomas James Mathias blasted it, accusing Knight of promoting debauchery and, worst of all, sexually arousing him personally with some of the dirty scholarly pictures he included! Matthias also prophesied that if the book, especially the 20 obscene illustrations of different phalli he found horrifically enticing, made it to Britain's young male students, the entire country would face an apocalyptic wave of sodomy that would destroy the nation.[53]

Of course, such a sexual Armageddon never happened, and reactionary commentators like Matthias were apt to completely forget the long history of erotica and sexual renegades that stretched back long before the 18th century. This is not to say there were not valid reasons to see the 18th century as an "age of decadence"; after all, the same factors that historians cite to explain the Enlightenment and the path to the French Revolution also shaped sex in this era. The rise of newspapers meant brothels could widely advertise (even if discreetly); a more affluent middle class meant more of what we would today call "sex tourism," especially in cities like Venice and London; and the triple punches of a rapidly developing print industry, the logistical problems of effective censorship, and an increasingly more literate and educated populace meant steamy works like *Discourse on the Worship of Priapus* would reach larger and wider audiences. Still, it would be a mistake to think, like reactionaries often do, that the forces of progress and change are only on the side of radicals. On the contrary, people in the 18th century were also harnessing the powers of print, the city, and Enlightenment to rein in deviance or discover new healthy and moral ways of living.

The Age of Reform

Sickened by the growing urban populaces that seemed completely out of anyone's control and by the licentious culture of Restoration England, the first organized and politically active group of middle-class busybodies was born in the 1690s: the Society for the Reformation of Manners. They were helped by a nascent journalism industry that also stoked their paranoia by reporting on sensational sodomy trials and famous adultery cases. There were sympathetic actions from above, such as Queen Anne (r. 1702–1714) making stern proclamations against public drunkenness, fornication, and swearing. However, the Society for the Reformation of Manners was a true grassroots movement, formed by business owners and professionals and acting with only the vaguest of government sanctions.

The Society targeted anything that it saw as undermining traditional morality. There were the more obvious targets—sodomy, prostitution, and drunkenness—but the group also took the time to fight shopkeepers selling on Sundays and cursing. Early on, the Society adapted aggressive tactics, handing out blank arrest warrants to magistrates and bribing or bullying people into becoming informants. Every year the Society published a list of people they successfully convicted that averaged 2,000 names and became known as the "black list" because it was printed with Gothic black letters, giving the English language an ominous new term.

The Society's golden age was at the turn of the century. Although the first Society was founded in London, it spread to other major urban centers across England. In 1699, the same decade it was founded, the Society and its offshoots claimed to have shut down about 500 brothels through ordinances against lewd behavior. In another wave of activity in 1726, the Society claimed it had broken up more than 20 molly houses, thanks to reports from members who volunteered to go disguised as clients. Two such spies, afraid that they were in for more than they could handle, pretended to be a homosexual couple to ward off any flirting.[54] However, 1726 proved to be the Society's last grand venture. From the start, the Society had been criticized from all sides. The Anglo-Dutch satirist Bernard de Mandeville cruelly but truthfully pointed out that the Society's campaigning tended to promote the very same crimes it was trying to stamp out, especially since the group very helpfully gave the addresses of brothels in its literature.[55] He also complained that if people like the Society's members had their way they would "break down the Printing-Presses, melt the Founts and burn all the Books on the Island, except those at Universities ... and suffer no volume in private Hands but the Bible."[56] Worst of all, the general public resented the Society's omnipresent informers, and the magistrates the Society had on their side tended to be corrupt. Over the course of the 1730s the Societies declined into nothing.[57]

Nonetheless, the simple idea of mixing modern social reform with Christianity did not die with the Society, but thrived through a new movement in Protestant Christianity, evangelicalism. Beginning with the Pietists of Germany, the Netherlands, and Scandinavia and continuing on with the Methodists of England and Wales, evangelical Christianity promoted individual transformation, a state of being "born again," over abstract theology and orthodox ritual. For quite a few 18th-century evangelicals, encouraging a personal metamorphosis into a true follower of Jesus Christ naturally proceeded moral reform on the social scale. Although most evangelicals would not have seen themselves on the same side as the *philosophes* on most issues, they did share an assumption that through educating the populace and grassroots action, society might be pulled in better directions.

Working with the governments of Prussia and Denmark, officials with evangelical and Pietist leanings established compulsory school and national poor relief systems.[58] Evangelicals also had a hand in the very earliest stirrings of temperance movements and teaching literacy to the poor. One of the most effective and persistent moral reformers was William Wilberforce (1759–1833) in Britain, who advocated with tremendous success laws against the slave trade. Less of a triumph was one group Wilberforce founded, the Proclamation Society, which among other moral crusades specialized in shutting down publishers of pornography. Like the old Society for the Reformation of Manners, the Proclamation Society was widely bashed. The most stinging critique came from the Anglican cleric Sydney Smith, who accused the Proclamation Society of focusing so much on the sins of the poor that it should rename itself the Society "suppressing the vices of persons whose income does not exceed £500 per annum."[59] Whatever the reason, the Proclamation Society never recreated the successes of the original Society for the Reformation of Manners, but the 19th century would nonetheless belong to the likes of Wilberforce.

Although not "evangelical" by most definitions, some Catholic reformers also railed against the consequences of the untempered expansion of commerce and urbanization while also capitalizing on the Enlightenment thirst for social change. In Spain, a new breed of missionary priests, such as Miguel de Satander and Pedro de Catalayud, who all specialized in reaching out to the rural masses and the urban poor while preaching that luxury spawned all evils and warning against the libertine attitudes being spread by supporters of the *philosophes*.[60] Seminaries in Portugal, like Varatojo near Torres Vedras, were known for churning out popular, charismatic preachers who made their warnings of fiery punishments for their sinful deviance from morality more palpable by also railing against corruption and ignorance.[61]

On the other side, a new generation of medical writers and doctors tackled the problem of sex with an approach that was less moral and more clinical. By the end of the 17th century, across Western Europe there was an explosion of medical books about sex: how to court women or attract men; almanacs providing advice on the best times to conceive; folk secrets on sex and fertility; and increasingly newspapers and magazines providing articles on the same sensitive topics. An especially popular topic for advertisements was cures for venereal disease, especially alternatives to ineffective mercury treatments. Open up any periodical or newspaper in 18th-century Edinburgh, Barcelona, Vienna, Munich, or Lyon and you might find ads for anti-venereal treatments like vegetable soups, teas, surgeries, diets, and pills. Undoubtedly the most market-savvy doctor of all was Le Fébure de Saint-Ildephont, who sold chocolates injected with mercury (a commonly used treatment for syphilis) on the premise that wives could treat their Lothario husbands or, conversely, husbands could help their wives without having to awkwardly confess their affairs.[62]

In the growing industry of sex advice for sale, the biggest bestseller, bar none, was Nicolas Venette's *Tableau de l'amour conjugal.* Originally published in 1686, *Tableau de l'amour conjugal* was translated into Dutch, German, Spanish, and English. Like the *philosophes,* Venette paid heed to Nature, and advised his readers to consider love and desire to be Nature's way of communicating with mortals. Too much sex was something to be avoided, but so was refusing the call of Nature. The "unnatural" desires like sodomy were to be shunned—not because of fear of God's wrath or moral failing, but because they would lead to pain, premature aging, and even senility.[63]

Just as popular in Britain was the anonymously written *Aristotle's Master-Piece,* which appeared in 1684 and remained a bestseller through most of the 18th century, and presumably not just because of people who erroneously thought the book was really a heretofore lost work by Aristotle. Of course, the main concern of *Aristotle's Master-Piece* was not really sex, but pregnancy and birth. The book offered advice on how to conceive, remedies for infertility (which was almost entirely blamed on the woman), and ways to tell the sex of the future child. There were also a variety of pregnancy tests, including one that involved placing the woman's urine in a glass for three days, plunging a needle into it, and checking the needle for either red specks or rust. The entire book is underwritten with a sense that sex is healthy, and in fact the author warns against the common practice of letting young people marry relatively late because forced chastity is what makes young people promiscuous.[64]

Aristotle's Master-Piece set a trend of medical advice that assumed the point of sex is reproduction, but also encouraged a frank and joyful outlook. This was the approach of Dr. James Graham (1745–1794), a physician from Scotland whose perspective on medicine was changed forever when he learned about the experiments with electricity by Benjamin Franklin. Graham set about claiming that his electrical treatments could cure infertility and waning libidos. His popularity hit a peak with his Temple of Health, where patients were treated with chairs infused with magnetic fields and electric currents alongside techniques that today hold more respect, like music therapy. What Graham is most known for, however, is the Celestial Bed. For £50 a night, a couple could sleep on an extravagant bed placed under a dome filled with self-playing musical devices, fresh flowers, and perfumes. Magnetic fields and electrical currents were part of the experience, but there was also a clockwork representation of Hymen, the Greek god of marriage.

History has written off Dr. James Graham as a charlatan, but his recommendations of a balanced diet, fresh air, and frequent bathing would be considered common sense today. In his own way, he also represented where the science of sex was going. In his public lectures at the Temple of Health, Graham urged listeners to treat themselves well and try to enjoy sex—not just for self-fulfillment, but so that they could produce more children for the good of the nation. Ahead of his time in at least a couple of ways, Graham nonetheless faced increasing criticism and a sharp drop of financial support—not so much as a result of his medical theories, but because such open discussion of sex was slowly becoming less tolerated. In the end, Graham went bankrupt, was forced to return to Edinburgh where his practice started, and became an evangelical Christian who recanted much of his life's work. It was as if his life itself became an allegory for Britain's transition from the rowdy Hanoveran era to the more prim Victorian age.[65]

The main sexual threat that 18th-century doctors had to wage war against was Onanism. Even though the sin of Onan in Scripture had more to do with disobedience than with touching one's own genitals, nonetheless "Onanism" in the 1700s became the official medical term for masturbation. The threat of Onanism was first given a name in a small pamphlet with a pompous title: *Onania; or, The Heinous Sin of Self Pollution, and all its Frightful Consequences, in both SEXES Considered, with Spiritual and Physical Advice to those who have already injured themselves by this abominable practice. And seasonable Admonition to the Youth of the nation of Both SEXES*. Written in or around 1712, the pamphlet warns about how this particular sin is worse than even sodomy, because it is so easy to indulge in: "Whilst yielding to filthy imagination, they endeavor to imitate and procure for themselves that Sensation, which God has ordered to attend the Carnal Commerce of the two sexes for the Continuance of our Species." The tract had such a meteoric impact that as early as 1726 "Onanism" became a word in the English dictionary. Despite the moral tones of the pamphlet, ultimately the remedies offered were not just prayer. Instead the author, after consulting an unnamed religious physician, suggested buying a "Strenghtening Tincture" and a "Prolific Powder" to the victims of the disease of Onanism. It was, the historian Thomas Laqueur writes, a "shameless effort to invent a new disease and at the same time offer its cure."[66]

In spite of its shady beginnings, the hysteria over Onanism took an unstoppable life of its own. A German schoolmaster, C.G. Salzmann, wrote an entire book on how the male students in his charge succumbed to the horrors of masturbation. One letter written to Salzmann from a 13-year-old boy confesses, "I did it without any sense of it being bad."[67] Bernard de Mandeville, who was no prude, wrote in his pamphlet, *A Modest Defence of Publick Stewes*, that one of the benefits of keeping brothels around was that it would discourage young men from masturbation. Prostitution could at least be watched and controlled; masturbation, since it was free and easy to do and could always be done in private, could not.[68]

One of the most celebrated voices on the Onanism menace was the Swiss physician, Samuel-August Tissot (1728–1797). A true medical celebrity, his work on masturbation, *Avis au peuple sur sa santé* ("Advice to the People on Their Health"), was translated into almost every European language. Alongside the latest medical theories, Tissot offered heartbreaking accounts of patients who had their lives shattered beyond repair by their addiction to masturbation. Many were young men who did not stop their ugly habits until it was too late and found themselves now suffering blindness, fatigue, memory loss, and even paralysis. One patient from 1755 wrote, "I certainly feel that this evil action has diminished the strength of my faculties, especially that of my memory." The next year another patient claimed, "If religion did not restrain me, I would already have put an end to my life, cruelly ravaged as it is though my own fault." Tissot was especially inspired by the case of a young watchmaker, whom he referred to as L.D***:

> L.D***, watchmaker, had been good, and had enjoyed good health, up until the age of seventeen; at this period, he began to masturbate, an act which he reiterated daily, and often as many three times a day.... Before a year had passed, he began to notice a great weakness after

each act; this warning was not sufficient to pull him from the mire; his soul, already given over to this filth was no longer capable of other ideas, and the repetitions of his crime became daily more frequent, until he found himself in a state where he feared death was imminent.[69]

While the likes of Tissot and Graham worked hard to improve people's bodies, monarchs and politicians were likewise attempting to apply the Enlightenment's doctrines toward improving their societies. The first of the so-called enlightened despots, who combined absolute power with social reforms, was undoubtedly Tsar Peter I "the Great" of Russia (r. 1689–1729). The fact that Peter was nearly the victim of a coup masterminded by his half-sister Sophia helped make keeping himself on top of the mountain an all-consuming obsession, but Peter was also driven by the need to transform Russia into a modern European country. To that end, he introduced Russia's first newspapers; simplified the Cyrillic alphabet; imported the newest Western ideas about education, administration, and military technology; gave Russia its first real navy; and even built a new capital, St. Petersburg, that could boast extensive street lighting and a logical grid plan.

However, Peter's reforms reached right into his subjects' personal lives. Painfully aware of how Westerners saw the Russian penchant for long beards and heavy robes as proof of the country still being locked in the Middle Ages, Peter passed laws that fined anyone who had a beard, with exceptions only for Russian Orthodox priests. In general men were to adopt Western European fashions as their own, even if such styles clashed with Russia's brutal winters. Women, especially women from the aristocracy, were expected to change both their fashions and their lifestyles. For example, one Russian noblewoman, Daria Golitsyna, was accustomed to leaving her home only two or three times a year—and even then only in a closed carriage—and dressing in a way that left most of her body covered. In 1700, after Peter's reforms on Russians' dress took full effect and women on the pain of a fine were required to wear French and German dresses and petticoats that revealed much more of the woman's form than traditional Russian attire, the 31-year-old Golitsyna in 1700 complained in a letter: "In my old age I was reduced to showing my hair, arms and uncovered bosom to all of Moscow."[70] In another strike against noble traditions, Peter made it more difficult for parents to force their children into arranged marriages, while at the same time creating more hurdles to thwart the spouse who wanted to leave their marriage to enter a monastery.[71]

Peter's schemes ultimately worked. While there were many like Golitsyna who were appalled and scandalized, other Russian women, according to foreign observers, took to the new way of living with gusto, trying to outdo each other with Western makeup and with jewels. Still, even after the reforms, Friedrich Christian Weber, the ambassador from Hanover, remarked that "Russian Wives and Daughters are extremely retired, and never go abroad, unless it be to the Church, or to see their nearest Relations." Significantly, though, Peter's reforms seem to have deliberately tried to curtail Russian notions of female chastity, by forcing women to reveal the bosoms, arms, and heads that had previously been covered and by encouraging them to drink and dance with men other than their husbands.[72]

Ever concerned about the effectiveness of his army, Peter, in addition to barring brothels and taverns from St. Petersburg, forbade prostitutes from soliciting near army barracks.[73] Imitating Swedish army regulations, in 1706 he adopted execution by burning at the stake for "unnatural lechery" among soldiers. Even then, Peter, who may have engaged in sexual encounters with men himself, eventually altered the punishment to lifelong exile.[74] This would be the closest thing Russia would have to a sodomy law until the 19th century.

IX Enlightened Bedrooms, 1700–1814

Although Peter's "liberation" of Russian women was not welcomed from every quarter—and in fact seems like a far-off prototype of France's recent law against the wearing of *burqas*—it did signal a trend of laws regulating personal lives becoming less restrictive. Grand Duke Leopold II (r. 1765–1790) made his country of Tuscany the first in Europe to abolish capital punishment for all crimes, including sodomy. His brother Emperor Joseph II (r. 1765–1790) likewise ended the death penalty for almost all crimes and reduced the penalty for sodomy from death to life imprisonment. One unlikely reformer was Dr. Johann Struensee, a middle-class doctor from Saxony who became the court physician to the schizophrenic King of Denmark, Christian VII. His affair with the king's miserable queen, Caroline Mathilda, a sister of King George III of Britain, made him a minister of state and finally the *de facto* ruler of Denmark once the king slid further into insanity. Among Struesnee's reforms was the removal of legal handicaps placed on children born out of wedlock. After a coup by Christian's stepmother and half-brother, Struesnee was executed and Caroline Mathilda exiled to her family's ancestral domains in Hanover, but the new regime proved unpopular enough that even though most of Struesnee's reforms were abolished, many of them were eventually restored.

In Germany, Bavaria actually *increased* penalties against nobles convicted of sex crimes. A few German states like Baden continued to cite religious justifications for sex laws as late as 1760 and tried to change the punishment for adultery from fines to public humiliation, a decision that was definitely the reverse of overall 18th-century tendencies. These were exceptions, however. The margrave of Baden-Durlach, Karl Friedrich (r. 1738–1811), was an eager pupil of the Enlightenment and had the law codes revised to remove biblical justifications in favor of the public good as the basis of all laws.[75] Prussia saw the punishment for sodomy reduced from burning to a year's imprisonment, whipping, and exile. However, although this reform was recommended by a committee formed by King Frederick II, Prussia did not make this change until eight years after his death.[76] In a 1791 commentary on Denmark's sodomy law, the jurist Christian Brorson remarked that sodomy was a crime not against God, but rather against society. Another young jurist, Anders Ørsted, who was assigned the job to reform the law code, argued that the purpose of the law was not to impose morality, but to ensure equal freedom and security for all. For that reason, he argued that sex outside of marriage should no longer be illegal. However, he balked at making sodomy legal, finding that sodomy nonetheless was against "reason" and threatened the "highest moral good."[77]

While it is true that laws punishing sexual transgressions were slowly becoming somewhat more lax, in the latter part of the century governments were becoming more interested in their own human resources—what Foucault creatively termed "biopower" and "biopolitics." Both the marquis de Pombal (1699–1782), a Portuguese minister who became so powerful he was the *de facto* ruler of the country, and Emperor Joseph II risked the wrath of the Catholic Church by shutting down hundreds of contemplative monasteries, forcing thousands of monks and nuns into either more active forms of monasticism or another line of work entirely. In Bavaria, the government under the advice of Dr. Johann von Wolter (1711–1787) founded a number of midwifery schools; by the end of the century it was illegal to practice midwifery without being licensed by any of the schools.[78] Finding his beloved Poland threatened by its more powerful neighbors Austria and Russia, the reformer Adam Czartoryski (1734–1823) advocated the value of women and female sexuality as important for the nation's cause. Polish women needed to be educated, he said, so they could promote and preserve Polish culture and, of course, raise an educated and patriotic generation.[79] Enlightenment ideas did help make all this fashionable—for instance, the pioneering historian Edward Gibbon blamed the fall of the Roman Empire in part on Christianity for inspiring men to drop out of society and the army—but governments facing more complex problems and needs were becoming more interested in keeping their populations mobilized.

As sometimes happens, what really affected change was not extensive acts by a reforming ruler, but rather the direction in which the culture moved. Indissoluble marriage increasingly came under question, and not just from the *philosophes*. A legal challenge of sorts came from a Jewish convert to Catholicism, Joseph-Jean-François Elie Lévi, who sued for the right to divorce his wife whom he had married based on Jewish law. The case hinged on the argument that since the principle of indissolubility did not exist in Jewish law, Lévi had a right to divorce his wife based on the same law under which he married her. Lévi's lawyers also argued that Scripture allowed a convert to divorce a non–Christian, but their key point was a secular and far-reaching one: that the rule of indissolubility placed unrealistic expectations on human nature. On January 2, 1758, however, the *parlement* of Paris, then the highest court of the land, declared that Lévi could not appeal the earlier church court's refusal to grant a divorce. The decision justified indissolubility not only on religious grounds, but also by appealing to natural law and civil law. Nonetheless, it was an unpopular decision and exposed a growing gap between the law and social attitudes. When the Academy of Châlons-sur-Marne offered a prize essay question, "What would be the best means of perfecting the upbringing of women?" one of the answers came from Choderlos de Lacos, author of the novel *Les liaisons dangereuses* ("Dangerous Liaisons"). In his essay, Lacos asserted that more educational opportunities for women would have little impact as long as marriage laws and customs treated them like property. Only legalizing divorce could even begin to fix this massive cause of inequality.[80]

With the sharp decline of the ecclesiastical courts in Britain, fornication and adultery by the 18th century had become completely decriminalized, although the new legal concept of "criminal conversation" did allow a husband to sue his wife's lover. Much of Europe was going in the same direction, albeit more gradually. Laws punishing adultery often stayed on the books, but they were being enforced less and less, until by the end of the century such laws may as well have no longer existed. This was brought about by an all but universal change of attitudes. Especially among the middle classes, adultery went from being an assault on the community and morality to a private, tragic matter, a change reflected in—and even promoted by—novels.[81]

Two hugely popular novels from the century both presented readers with the painful conflict between individual desire and the institution of marriage. Rousseau's novel *Julie*, which was so popular bookstores were forced to rent instead of sell copies, had its titular heroine tormented by having to choose between her love for her young tutor and her obligation to marry the husband her father chose for her. Readers were so emotionally invested in Julie's inner torment that they flooded Rousseau with gushing fan mail, like this letter from the Protestant minister Paul-Claude Moultou:

> No, Monsieur, I can no longer keep quiet. You have overwhelmed my soul. It is full to bursting, and it must share its torment with you.... Oh Julie! Oh Saint-Preux! Oh Claire! Oh Edouard! What planet do your souls inhabit, and how can I unite mine with yours? They are the offspring of your heart, Monsieur; your mind alone could not have made them as they

are. Open that heart to me so that I can contemplate the living models of the characters whose virtues made me weep such sweet tears.[82]

Johann Wolfgang von Goethe's 1774 novel, *Die Leiden des jungen Werthers* ("The Sorrows of Young Werther"), was about a young man who shoots himself over grief that his love, Lotte, had become married to another man. *Die Leiden des jungen Werthers* was in a sense an even bigger phenomenon than *Julie*. It inspired depressed young men across Europe to dress like Werther himself and commit suicide with a pistol. From Rousseau's fans to the dozens of young suicides, there was just something about the idea of a sensitive person being tormented or destroyed by the conflict between desire and individuality that had unimaginable appeal to the people of the 18th century.

Tribads and Mollys

In 1700, a neighborhood in Paris was under its own private horrific reign of terror, from one Madame de Murat. "The crimes that are attributed to [the countess] Madame de Murat are not of a kind that can be easily proved by means of making inquiries, since it is a matter of domestic wickedness and a monstrous attachment for persons of her own sex," the lieutenant-general of the Paris police, the Marquis d'Argenson, writes. She was also guilty of singing "[l]ewd songs during the night and at all hours," "audacious conversation ... as far from modesty as from religion" with a curé of Saint-Côme, and, in perhaps the biggest *faux paux* of all, the "insolence of pissing out the window after prolonged debauchery." Argenson balked at the usual punishment for such renegade women, locking her up in a convent, because "no religious community will be found bold enough to take her in." In the end, the countess was imprisoned in a chateau in the Loire valley for seven years, with one female attendant the Marquis d'Argenson made sure would be elderly.[83]

On the other side of the spectrum was King Friedrich II of Prussia, one of Europe's most celebrated generals and cultural patrons. Although modern biographers of Fredriech II went so far as to guess that his apathy toward sex with women, including his queen, was the result of either a philosophical chastity or a botched operation to cure a venereal disease, Frederich II was surprisingly flagrant. In his library at Potsdam, Friedrich had a bronze statue of Ganymede that had been made in the Hellenistic era, which was carefully placed under his library window at his palace of Sanssouci. He purchased the statue from the estate of Prince Eugene of Savoy, who was also suspected of enjoying same-sex love. Another Ganymede image was in the central fresco at Frederich's New Palace in Potsdam. Near there he erected a Friendship Temple decorated with portraits of classical pederastic lovers, like Euryalus and Nisus, Orestes and Pylades, Heracles and Philoctetis, and Peirithous and Theseus.[84]

Here is a third famous case from the 18th century: two daughters of aristocratic Anglo-Irish families, Eleanor Butler and Sara Ponsoby, left Ireland together in 1778 for Wales. They lived together as a couple for 50 years and became known across Britain as the Ladies of Llangollen. Whatever the real nature of their relationship, they were held up as examples of "romantic friendship" and were visited at their Welsh cottage by celebrities such as Edmund Burke, Charles Darwin, Sir Walter Scott, Richard Sheridan, William Wordsworth, and the Duke of Wellington. Even Hannah More, an evangelical Christian who angrily denounced the depravity of "tribads," a classical term for women in sexual relationships, happily took time to meet with them.

A 1790 article in the *General Evening Post* was cruel enough to imply that the Ladies were *tribads*. Conjuring up the specter of their sexuality by questioning their femininity, the article says, "Miss Butler is tall and masculine, she wears always a riding habit, hangs her hat with the air of a sportsman in the hall, and appears in all respects as young man.... Miss Ponsonby, on the contrary, is polite and effeminate. Fair and beautiful."[85] The insinuation was enough of a threat that the Ladies looked into suing the newspaper for libel, but they were advised by their friend, politician and writer Edmund Burke, not to pursue the matter at risk of spreading rumors. Other than that, they remained public darlings. When both the Ladies died in 1831, they were even buried together.

The Ladies of Llangollen and Fredriech II were protected (for the most part) from negative suspicion by a widespread cultural admiration of romantic friendship and by the respectable classical veneer over same-sex love. Yet even in the homeland of the Ladies of Llangollen there was no defense for tribads who showed signs of cross-dressing and sexual experimentation. The pioneering novelist and founder of the first modern police force, Henry Fielding (1707–1754), wrote a pamphlet about Mary Hamilton, a woman arrested on allegations that she had 14 marriages to women. She was sentenced to be publicly whipped and imprisoned for six months—but for fraud, not for sodomy. Naturally, the British public could not get enough of the scandal, and Fielding's pamphlet, while moralizing in tone, was obviously designed to capitalize on the scandal by serving up the most tantalizing details.

When looking for someone to blame for Mary Hamilton's career as a cross-dressing polygamist, Fielding turned toward a terrifying new religious movement: Methodism. Mary's neighbor, Anne Johnson, befriended her and converted her to Methodism and eventually they "became now inseparable companions, and at length bed-fellows."[86] Needing money, Mary married an Irish widow and deceived her sexually "by means which decency forbids me to mention."[87] Fielding alleged that when Mary was inevitably found out, she fled in the middle of the night and, pretending to be a doctor in Dartmouth, married one of her patients. Once more she had to flee when her real anatomy was uncovered. Like any good scandalmonger throughout history, Fielding simultaneously makes his subject out to be a sad victim and a depraved monster. He makes it clear that she was seduced into sin, claiming that when Mary was in prison Anne Johnson wrote a letter to her pleading, "I was indeed the first seducer of your innocence, for which I ask GOD's pardon and yours," but shortly afterward Fielding also alleges that Mary paid the man hired to whip her to procure a woman for her.

Even Mary Hamilton was lucky compared to Catherina Linck, a Prussian woman who dressed as a man and went so far as to marry a woman named Catherina Mühlhahn. Her marriage came to the law's attention when she was accused of beating up her wife and stealing her clothes and linen. Her mother-in-law accused Catherina Linck of tricking her daughter into the marriage; Catherina Linck countered that her wife knew all along that she was secretly a woman. No matter the truth, Linck was inspected by the authorities and found to have had used a leather dildo attached to a pig's bladder and two stuffed testicles as a makeshift penis. After some debate the court decided she did not "really" commit sodomy since her device could not emit semen, but testimony that she had oral sex with Mühlhahn sealed her fate. She was beheaded for "unnatural acts" in 1721, while Catherina Mühlhahn was imprisoned for three years.

IX Enlightened Bedrooms, 1700–1814

The Linck case was something of an exception, as law enforcement across Europe, as always, was more concerned with male same-sex acts. Authorities over the course of the century made more of a distinction between "sin" and "crime," but policing pickup spots became even more of a priority in the increasingly crowded cities of Europe. One of the best records of such enforcement comes from the police records in Paris, where undercover enforcers went after the "pederasts" (by then a French term that referred to men who sought sex with other men, no matter their age) who haunted the public gardens, even and especially the ones near the royal residences. One record reports that in January 1750:

> Bruno Lenoir, journeyman shoemaker, 21 years of old, native of Douai in Flanders, in Paris for three years, living on the rue des Cordiers at the home of Lepy, master shoemaker, stated today, 9 January 1750, that … he, the deponent, going along the rue Montorgueil at 9 o'clock in the evening, he was met there by an individual unknown to him and whom he has since learned to be named Jean Diot, a runner of errands, 40 years old [...] said Jean Diot accosted him and proposed infamy to him, that he even asked him, the deponent, to put it in him from behind, that to this end Jean Diot undid his pants and that he, the deponent, put it in him from behind, without, however, being able to finish the business, given that they were surprised by the watch, who arrested them.[88]

Another police report recorded a mason who was accosted by a cleric, who asked him, "My friend, would you be willing to lodge me tonight? I will give you twelve francs?" After the mason took the cleric up on his offer, the encounter quickly grew stranger: "[The cleric] asked him, the deponent, if he liked women, which he, the deponent, answered yes, that he then asked if he liked men, that he, the deponent, answered 'I do not hate them. Why would you want me to hate them? They've never done me harm.' That then said abbé said, 'Well, kiss me, then,' presented himself to kiss him, the deponent, and put his hand on his private parts on top of his breeches, while saying to him, 'Do you like to f___ in the ass?'"[89]

There were even subcultures of same-sex love safely tucked away in the halls of power. At the court of Louis XIV, who was believed to have had a particular antipathy toward sodomy, the Chevalier de Mailly, the Prince de Conti, and one of Louis XIV's illegitimate sons, the Comte de Vermandois, organized a "brotherhood" centered on same-sex love, called the *confrére italienne* ("Italian brotherhood") based on stereotypes that still associated sodomy between men with Italy. They even drew up a constitution: "They must observe chastity in regard to women, and if anyone breaks the rule, he will be driven out of the company without the ability to return later under any pretext" and "If any of the brothers marry, he would be obliged to prove that it was only for money, because he was forced by his parents, or because he needed an heir."[90] This "brotherhood" was uncovered, and a particularly enraged Louis XIV had his son beaten before the court. Much later, on an April night in 1722, 17 young noblemen from the royal court had intercourse in the gardens of the Tuilieries Palace, allegedly right outside the apartments of the 12-year-old King Louis XV. Their ringleader, the Marquis de Rambure, was imprisoned in the Bastille, while many of the others were exiled into the provinces. When Louis XV asked what happened to the ones who were exiled, he was told that they had been caught digging up fences in the gardens. After that, the journal writer Matthieu Marais writes, "fence-diggers" became "another name given to these young gentlemen."[91]

The real sites of 18th-century anti-sodomite hysteria, however, were the Netherlands and England. For the Dutch Republic, old anti–Catholic hysteria, especially after facing French invasion and occupation in the later 17th century, drove much of this paranoia about sodomite conspiracies. One Dutch pamphlet claimed that no less than Pope Sixtus VI gave cardinals permission to commit sodomy during hot weather.[92] Old prejudices and fears were brought to a fever pitch by the 1730s, when the Dutch Republic had already lost its place as one of Europe's leading economic powers. After a number of men were arrested for sodomy in Utrecht in April 1730, the government had placards posted in every city and major town, urging local magistrates to punish sodomy with death, not to spare those who allowed sodomy to happen under their own roofs, and to burn the remains of executed sodomites and throw the ashes into the sea. More than 60 men would be executed in the years to come, all of them either strangled or burned and many of their remains thrown into the ocean. Persecutions came to a trickle toward the end of the century, but executions continued until 1803, when the Netherlands saw what was possibly the last execution for sodomy in continental Europe. How many of these men were actually guilty remains something of a mystery, although guilty or innocent there are cases of victims facing their accusers and killers with pride. One victim, the 18-year-old Jan Ides, was reported to have said, "I forgive you for the sin which you have committed against me."[93]

The persecutions in the Netherlands were a frequent topic for the press in Britain, which was in the throes of its own anti-sodomy frenzy. Much of this attitude was whipped up by a news media that encouraged readers to denounce a crime that was both socially dangerous and distinctly "un-English." The *London Journal* published a letter in 1726 from a "Philogynus" (women-lover) that decried the men who "despised the fair sex" and were spawned from modern "effeminacy."[94] Another letter published in a 1728 edition of *The Weekly Journal* offered a solution to the plague: "'Tis humbly propos'd that the following Method may not only destroy the Practice, but blot out the Names of the monstrous Wretches from under Heaven, viz. when any are Detected, Prosecuted and Convicted, that after Sentence Pronounc'd, the Common Hangman tie him Hand and Foot before the Judge's Face in open Court, that a Skilful Surgeon be provided immediately to take out his Testicles, and that then the Hangman sear up his Scrotum with an hot Iron, as in Cases of burning in the Hand."[95]

Although this "modest proposal" was never put into practice, the courts themselves gave sodomy special attention. There were very few executions for sodomy before the 1700s, but by the start of the century the number increased exponentially. The best a man convicted of sodomy could hope for was time in the pillory, a crippling fine, and a prison sentence of a year or two. Sometimes the pillory *was* the death sentence; in 1762, a 60-year-old man sentenced to a stint in the stocks for attempted buggery was attacked by a mob that stripped him naked, covered him with mud, and lynched him.[96] Like in the Netherlands, the number of executions declined over the course of the later 1700s, but the last recorded execution for sodomy in Britain was not until 1835.

Executions and persecutions for sodomy were in steep decline elsewhere, even in Spain and Portugal, where sodomy executions were once most common. So why did they flourish again in the Netherlands and Britain? The common denominator was that both countries were home to Europe's most urbanized areas, which were nourishing environments for subcultures of same-sex love, whether they were the molly houses of London or certain public toilets in Amsterdam that had telling names like the Long Lady or the Old Lady. These metropolitan zones also harbored sleazy yet moralistic journalists, the direct ancestors of today's tabloids, who in these Protestant countries gave old stereotypes about sodomy being a uniquely foreign and Catholic sin new and powerful life. Just as the 18th-century press kept the public well aware of the evil deviants in their midst, so they also addressed the compelling social and intellectual issues of the day through an unexpected medium: pornography.

The Pornographic Underground

The new and rapidly growing international press of 18th-century Europe quickly found that sex was a powerful weapon, as it allows writers and artists to depict offending public figures as morally depraved while at the same time titillating readers and viewers. This network of libelous and often graphic literature had many centers: the scandalous Grub Street in London, which was the home of legions of hack writers; the seedy journalistic and intellectual underground of Paris; and publishers in Amsterdam, Switzerland, and the Rhineland who spread their quasi-legal publications across Europe. These writers and publishers were not in the slightest unified by any kind of radical politics or social agenda, but only by their appetite for profit. This realization was especially painful for the many writers who were sure they would be the next Diderot or Voltaire, but instead found themselves barely able to eke out a living.

Some countries were able (with mixed successes) to hold back the tide. Under the enlightened regime of Catherine II of Russia, who was herself an avid reader of books by the likes of Voltaire and Diderot that rankled conservatives across Europe, the censorship of books was actually tightened. Meanwhile the Inquisition in Spain continued to work hard to make sure all published novels and sermon collections were licensed, although the sheer volume of materials produced by the printing presses left the censors scrambling, especially by the end of the 17th century, and most of their efforts by necessity had to focus on religious literature.[97]

In Britain, the government had even less control over the printing presses. One man who took advantage of this freedom was John Wilkes (1725–1797), a radical Member of Parliament who pioneered the use of sleaze to bind together journalism and radical politics. Wilkes very well understood how sex could be used to distill down for a wide audience otherwise complex and dull ideas about politics and society. Through graphic caricatures that were published and widely distributed for the public's eyes, Wilkes attacked King George III (r. 1760–1820) for being a despot whose mother, Princess Augusta, exploited the government to dispense personal favors. A favorite target was George III's Scottish prime minister, the Earl of Bute, whom Wilkes accused of gaining his post simply because he was Princess Augusta's lover. One particular pamphlet, *The Scotch Broom Stick,* made the point crystal clear. In it, a group of Scottish courtiers look up and see Princess Augusta and the Earl of Bute. One looking up into the princess' skirts remarks, "I see the road to Preferment; 'tis well fenced and water'd"; another agrees, "There's the road, thro bushy park," a rather vivid sexual pun on the royal garden "Bushey Park."[98] Wilkes was eventually brought up on charges of libel for other publications of his, although his political and journalistic career endured.

Wilkes's contributions were tame compared to the products of the underground press in France, which managed to spawn an entire genre best described as "political pornography." Unlike Britain, the French government did not rely on libel laws and tried to maintain a strong system where only books explicitly approved by officials would hit the streets. Between

1771 and 1789 alone, 3,544 books were classified for various reasons as illicit, with the underground book industry still thriving.[99]

The most dangerous books and the most sought after by both government censors and certain clientele were those books deemed "philosophical." This language was in vogue for book publishers across France. One publisher in Lyon wrote to his supplier, "My line is all philosophical, so I want almost nothing except that kind."[100] More than a few books from this genre blurred the lines of what readers today would consider philosophy and pornography. Like the Renaissance contemplations expressing pederasty or the instruction of sexuality, these examples of "philosophical pornography" took the format of the educational tract or the Socratic dialogue and interspersed them with sex scenes.

The mother of the genre of "philosophical pornography" was *Thérèse philosophe,* a book by the Marquis d'Argens that was first published anonymously in 1743.[101] Argens was inspired by a real court case, where a young woman from Toulon, Catherine Cadière, accused a Jesuit priest, Father Girard, of taking advantage of his position to seduce her. Girard was acquitted, but that did not stop others like Argens from exploiting the anti–Jesuit sentiments the case invoked. In fact, the book opens with Thérèse, the daughter of a *bourgeois* family, telling the story—with proper erotic relish—of Catherine and Father Girard, or as their names were clumsily disguised in the literature surrounding the trial, "Eradice" and "Dirrag."

Thérèse is intrigued and aroused by "Dirrag," who serves as her confessor, but she is wasting away. Two family friends, Mme C and Abbé T, convince her that it is because she is being kept as a virgin in her mother's house. Her body, a "machine," is severely out of sorts because it is being denied the necessary outlet of pleasure. Since women had to fear pregnancy and damage to their reputations, Thérèse must master the art of masturbation. Thérèse's new confessor, Abbé T, assures her, "How could we fear that we offend God in relieving our needs by the means He has afforded us, the objects of His creation, especially when these means in no way disturb the social order?"[102] The education of Thérèse under her new confessor goes even further when she eavesdrops on him confiding to his lover, Mme C, that he believes God is simply part of nature and that morality amounts to, in the words of Robert Darnton, "a utilitarian calculus based on pleasure and pain."[103]

Later Thérèse becomes the lover of Madame Bois-Laurier, a former prostitute, who further instructs Thérèse on the ways of sex. Eventually she moves on to the count. The two become infatuated with each other, but the count refuses to marry her given their difference in rank; besides, the count has a strong distaste for matrimony. Thérèse devours his library of erotic and philosophical books, and he challenges her to make it through two weeks of reading his collection without masturbating. If she wins, the collection will be hers; if he wins, she will be his.

Thérèse succumbs under the desire stoked by her reading and the pornographic portraits around the room. The count, who has been spying on her, swoops in, begins to make love to her, and withdraws just in time to avert pregnancy. From then on, assured by the count's mastery of the delicate art of *coitus interruptus,* Thérèse and the count live as a philosophical couple, enjoying each others' minds and bodies while Thérèse lives without fear of pregnancy. Happily still living with the count ten years later, Thérèse recounts her experiences in the very book in the reader's hands. On a truly philosophical note, she concludes:

> Yes, you know-nothings! Nature is an illusion, everything is the work of God. It is from Him that we take our needs: eating, drinking, and sensual enjoyment. Why then blush when we

fulfill His designs? Why fear to contribute to the happiness of men by preparing for them different dishes which are apt to satisfy sensually their different appetites? Could I worry about displeasing God and men when I assert truths which can cause no harm, only enlighten?[104]

Other erotic works had motives less benevolent than enlightening readers. One of the more popular was the *Anecdotes sur Mme la comtesse du Barry,* an "unauthorized" biography of Madame du Barry, the last "official mistress" of King Louis XV (1715–1774).[105] Despised because she was the only royal mistress to have come from the lowest ranks of society, du Barry is presented in this professionally historical narrative as a low-class waif who enjoyed a life of sexual promiscuity and prostitution until she caught the king's attention. Once ensconced in Versailles, Barry kept the king addicted to a steady diet of sex and booze, all the while living extravagantly off of state coffers. Although a string of tantalizing anecdotes very thinly disguised as a serious biography, the book had much more of an explosive impact. As Robert Darnton explains, "The anecdotes reinforced one another by working over the same themes: the vulgarity of du Barry, the feebleness of the king, the triviality of court intrigues, the baseness of everyone's behavior, and the arbitrary power abused through the whole system. By their cumulative effect, they made the monarchy look decadent as well as despotic, and they did so without a great deal of commentary, in a manner typical of libel literature."[106]

While a few members of the royal family and even many ministers were attacked by the libelous underground press, the worst target was Louis XVI's queen, Marie Antoinette (1755–1793). Even in the niche genre of French political and philosophical pornography, libel against Marie Antoinette constituted a genre in of itself. Even before the French Revolution, the number of titles were steadily growing from 1774 to 1788.[107] Even Madame du Barry, often presented as the lowly mistress of a corrupt and senile king, did not inspire so much concentrated venom. For pamphleteers, Marie Antoinette embodied all that was secretive and arbitrary about the French monarchy. Combining erotic scenes with denouncements of Marie Antoinette's insatiable decadence, the reader of such pamphlets "is made into voyeur and moral judge at the same time."[108]

The various authors of the pamphlets savored portraying Marie Antoinette as a nymphomaniac, who had sex with men and women, Louis XV, her father and her son, guards, her female servants, her brother-in-law the Comte d'Artois, and other well-known members of the royal court. One pamphlet, *The Austrian Woman on a Spree,* details Marie Antoinette's amorous encounters with her brothers-in-law and countless servants. Not only is Marie Antoinette completely uninhibited in her sexual desires, but she wallows in her notoriety. 1789's *Essai historique sur vie de Marie Antoinette* ("Historical Essay on the Life of Marie Antoinette") has Marie Antoinette introduce herself as "barbaric Queen, adulterous wife, woman without morals, soiled with crime and debauchery."[109]

Tragically, these fantasies about Marie Antoinette's perversions had very real consequences. When the French Revolution spiraled out of everyone's control and resulted in the abolition of the monarchy and the execution of Louis XVI, the new Republic of France made the trial of Marie Antoinette one of its first priorities. In the bill of indictment brought against the former queen in the fall of 1793, Marie Antoinette is accused of various political crimes: secretly sending French funds to her brother, the Holy Roman Emperor; teaching Louis XVI how to lie to his own people; using her influence to appoint corrupt ministers; and embezzling state money to spend on her own personal pleasures. However, the bill also declares the widow Capet, immoral in every way, the new Agrippina, is so perverse and so familiar with all crimes that, forgetting her quality of mother and the demarcation prescribed by the laws of nature, she has not stopped short of indulging herself with Louis-Charles Capet, her son—and on the confession of the latter—in indecencies whose idea and name make us shudder with horror.[110]

In fact, Louis-Charles, who had been long isolated from his family, had been thoroughly coached by his guardians and made to sign a statement, accusing his own mother of committing incest with him and forcing him to have sex with a prostitute infected with syphilis. Such accusations, seriously placed in court, may as well have been taken straight from the pamphlets. At the trial itself, when the prosecutor pointed out that Marie Antoinette did not immediately respond to these charges, she replied in a tense voice, "If I have not replied, it is because Nature itself refuses to respond to such a charge laid against a mother." Although even some of the women in the otherwise hostile jury vocally sympathized with their former queen, she was still found guilty and sent to her death.

With Marie Antoinette's execution, the First Republic had, in its own eyes, finished its destruction of all the decadence Versailles represented. However, the First Republic found itself with a mixed and even contradictory legacy. Its war against royalty and aristocracy had often been couched in sexual terms, but the radical Jacobin faction of the new republic also promised liberation from the archaic moral rules of the old order. It was a tension that the revolutionaries had to break.

Sex under the First Republic and Napoleon

Although there was a widespread feeling that there had to be some serious reforms of the government, no voices in France by the start of the fateful summer of 1789 were raised to demand anything close to an overturning of the entire system. Yet at the end of January 1793, France's ancient monarchy had been torn down and replaced with a republic explicitly based on Enlightenment ideas, King Louis XVI had been beheaded, and the leaders of the new republic had vowed to liberate the rest of Europe from the twin dragons of royal tyranny and religious superstition. Even the old Gregorian calendar was completely tossed out, replaced with a new calendar devoid of pagan and Christian references that presented 1792, when the republic was born, as Year I. Maximilien Robespierre (1754–1794), a provincial lawyer who ended up as the leader of the extremist Jacobin party, declared in a newsletter to his constituents, "It is not enough to have overturned the throne: our concern is to erect upon its remains holy equality and the imprescriptible Rights of Man."[111] In the end, the French Revolution was about much more than even a violent change in government; it represented an attempt to erect a new civilization over the ashes of the old.

The potential for creating a new secular morality in law and society was glimpsed even before the revolution fully took root. Sometime around 1790, the National Assembly, which had just declared itself the voice of the nation and was hearing ideas for real change across all sectors of French society, received a pamphlet by Albert-Joseph Hennett titled *Du divorce*. Hennett asserted that it was pointless to expect any guidance whatsoever from Christianity on whether divorce was right or wrong, since there were so many inconsistencies and disagreements among the writings of the Church Fathers, the pronouncements of church councils through history, and the New Testament itself. Instead, according to *Du divorce,* divorce should be based on reason and pragmatism, especially on people's needs for happiness and to raise their children well in an environment unsullied by adultery or the misery of their parents. Another pamphlet that took a more entertaining approach was presented to its readers as the actual letters of a nobleman who married a young heiress for her fortune and was sleeping with other women on the side. He fretted over the mere chance of legalized divorce, which would let his wife leave him with her own money in tow and send him spiraling back to poverty.[112]

The National Assembly heeded these pleas. In a flurry of reforms and new laws, the National Assembly rejected centuries of church tradition and fully instituted no-fault divorce and the ability to divorce based on grounds ranging from abuse to incompatibility. There was a restriction of remarriage, but only in the form of a one-year waiting period.[113] Thousands did not hesitate to take advantage of the new laws. Anywhere from 38,000 to 50,000 divorces took place between 1792 and 1803.[114] In 1794, when the divorce law was further liberalized, the legal declaration read: "Divorce is a consequence of the first of the rights of man; it is incontestable that one may not constrain any individual to remain attached in his destiny to another, and that the will of one of the spouses is sufficient to break their ties; however, marriage is too important an institution for the happiness of families and the maintenance of morals to permit one to dissolve it without formalities."[115]

The revolutionaries were more uncertain about what to do with prostitution. For them, the prostitute was a living, breathing symbol of the corruption France experienced under the monarchy. She was a woman driven to desperation by poverty and exploited by aristocrats. The Society of Revolutionary Republican Women formally proposed to the legislature that "prostitutes be moved to state-run houses in order to occupy them with useful work and, if possible, return these victims of libertine behavior, whose hearts were often good, and whom poverty alone almost always reduced them to this deplorable state."[116] Legislators were divided between this cry for educating prostitutes and ensuring that they receive good jobs, and a desire to return the old medieval trend of making sure prostitutes went about the streets wearing badges.[117]

The debate was sharpened by an alleged upswing in Parisian prostitution, inspired by the chaos of the time. The gardens of the Palais Royale became even more of a hotbed for sex sales than they were under the monarchy, and were known for the prostitutes who daylighted as singers and actresses and at night dressed up like nationally known women. The women even fulfilled their patriotic duty by offering discounts to members of the National Assembly and wearing bonnets in the patriotic colors of red, white, and blue.[118]

However, despite the feelings of some that prostitution had to be strictly policed, if not stamped out entirely, by the First Republic, no law was ever passed that even explicitly addressed prostitution. The closest was a vague statute against "encouraging lewdness." Even if the Republic had attempted a crackdown, it is unlikely that it would have been successful. Although it is unclear if the number of prostitutes was increasing, at the end of the 18th century they were becoming younger and fewer had even the pretense of other employment.[119]

The laws of the First Republic also made no mention of sodomy, save by abolishing sodomy laws altogether. While the revolutionaries had erased the laws, they did not erase the attitudes. In the spring of 1794, a young soldier and a 50-year-old stove-setter were arrested after being caught with their clothes disheveled and in a compromising position. They were sentenced to one year in prison for encouraging lewdness, the corruption of a youth, and a public offense against morality. When the case was put to an appeal, however, the judges were reluctant to make a verdict without a sodomy law to cite. We do not know what happened in that particular case, but by the early 1800s French courts had gotten into the habit of sentencing sodomites based on the charge of public offenses against decency. Still, in 1798, one police official decried the fact that the laws were "inadequate" for dealing with an apparently rising tide of sodomy.[120]

The French Revolution dramatically changed gears again in December 1799, when Napoleon Bonaparte (1769–1821), a general who began his political life as a Corsican nationalist, made himself the head of the Republic in a bloodless coup. In a bizarre reversal of the earlier revolution's political aims, Napoleon established himself as the First Consul of the Republic and, by 1804, was crowned the Emperor of the French in a new imperial monarchy. Today Napoleon is most remembered for the stunning series of military victories that left him in control of much of Western and Central Europe, but he also left behind a law code that moderated the extremes taken by the First Republic while retaining the influence of the Enlightenment. Long after Napoleon's short-lived empire fell apart, the Napoleonic Code remained one of the most influential law codes in history, being instituted in Belgium, Luxembourg, Switzerland, and parts of Germany and Italy and imitated in such diverse places as Portugal, the Netherlands, Romania, the Dominican Republic, and Louisiana.

Although Napoleon brought monarchy back to France, the last thing he wanted was to turn the clock back to 1788. Napoleon certainly declared as much when, during his coronation as emperor, he crowned himself instead of letting the pope do so. The Catholic Church would not have the same input over how France would govern itself that it had under the old monarchy. Moral and sex crimes would be judged entirely under secular and rationalistic criteria.

Napoleon did nothing to change the lack of sodomy laws in France, and the very few sodomy trials to take place under his rule involved defendants accused of exploiting adolescents.[121] However, men "guilty" of same-sex love who happened to fall into the hands of the police could find themselves punished, law or no. In Paris, police searching for stolen items stumbled across love letters between two servants, 28-year-old Philippe Jacques Bergerat and 35-year-old Henri Duhem. Notes from the police prefect state with disgust that "these two individuals engage together in *Pederasty*." Even though they broke no laws, they were imprisoned separately for a month and a half and then exiled from Paris, Jacques to his hometown of Etampes and Henri to his homeland of Belgium.[122]

The most notorious case involving sodomy in Paris, and one that drew the attention of the Emperor of the French himself, began in Chartres. By 1800, Chartres was home to a thriving subculture of male same-sex love, a "sect of pederasts" in contemporary language. These men referred to each other with female pronouns and used female nicknames like *Mimi Fluet* ("Slender Mimi"), while men interested only in women were said to be "a pain in the side." In 1805, an army tailor, Louis Fonteneau, had his buttocks caressed by a stranger. When he told someone about the incident, he learned about the city's "clique" of sodomites. With the help of soldiers from his regiment, Fonteneau lured two men, a pharmacist Louis Nicolas Millet and a printer Lubin Cassegrain, to an inn and attacked them. The local magistrates were willing to charge the men with assault, but after further investigation they instead accused the two victims of an offense against morals and of attempted corruption of young people.

All the legal officials involved shared the assumption that sodomy, even if it was not outlawed in the code, was still, at best, an act of rebellion against society and morality. The debate reached as high up as Napoleon himself, who came to this conclusion during one of his weekly meetings with the minister of justice:

> We are not in a country where the law should concern itself with these offenses. Nature has seen to it that they are not frequent. The scandal of legal proceedings would only tend to multiply them. It would be better to give the proceedings another direction.

Millet and Cassegrain were let off the hook, but so was Fonteneau. In the end, the case established the precedent that only the most publicly known cases of sodomy should be prosecuted under the excuse of punishing an offense against public morals; otherwise, by making such crimes widely known, more harm was done than good.[123]

The pragmatic stance of Napoleon's government was also turned toward the unending question of prostitution. Rather than outlawing prostitution or allowing prostitutes to ply their trade with little oversight, Napoleon and his ministers founded the *maisons de tolerance,* also known as the *maisons closes,* because their window shutters, which advertised the purpose of the house by always being painted green, were closed tight during the day. There the prostitutes were registered and given medical inspections twice a week. This tightly regulated system, probably the ultimate expression of the Enlightenment's rational solutions to easing the tension between sex and society, would become an inspiration throughout Europe in the 19th century, and a popular target for the first wave of feminist activists.

Still, there were areas where the Napoleonic government was more prudish than the republic it replaced. Even though Napoleon had divorced his own first wife, Joséphine de Beauharnais, on grounds of adultery, in 1803 he implemented new laws that made divorce more restrictive than they had been. Divorce by mutual consent was still allowed, but now the couples had to be a certain age, had to be married between 2 and 20 years, and needed the permission of both parents if still living. The restrictions on contested divorces were even harsher. Only three grounds for such divorces were now allowed: adultery (male or female), criminal proceedings against one spouse, and abuse. Finally, the old practice of separation of room and board was brought back.[124] France would not see the level of freedom surrounding divorce under the First Republic again until the late 20th century.

While Napoleon was defeated once and for all and the royal family of France was restored to their throne (although in one concession to the reality of the French Revolution, they were forced to live with a constitution that formally limited the king's powers), the ghosts of the French Revolution and Napoleon could not be exorcised. It was no longer taken for granted that the Catholic Church and tradition would set the rules of society. Instead, the idea of natural rights, as developed by thinkers like Locke and Rousseau, opened the question of whether a right to sexual pleasure was part of people's right to liberty and the pursuit of happiness, a debate that carries on to this day.

X

A Brave New World

Historians write of a "Long Nineteenth Century" that began with the French Revolution in 1792, which toppled one of the preeminent monarchies in Europe, and ended with the start of World War I in 1914, which decisively dismantled the legacy of faith in human progress left behind by the Enlightenment. Before the "Great War," however, the potential to improve the individual and society seemed limitless. To many Europeans the unprecedented series of technological and scientific breakthroughs, the spread of representative government and democratic reforms, and European domination over much of the globe (for example, Europeans went from controlling only 10 percent of Africa in 1870 to the entire continent except Liberia and Ethiopia in 1914) all pointed toward the ability of their civilization to finally transcend the problems that had plagued human societies throughout recorded history. There were still those like Fredriech Nietzsche, who proclaimed that humanity had murdered God and had not yet devised an order and purpose to replace Him, but both Karl Marx and Sigmund Freud helpfully suggested new struggles and discoveries that were yet to be made in politics and the human mind, respectively.

Beneath the grand narratives and theories about the inevitability of progress and the triumph of reason, there were more bleak and uncertain realities. For the first time in human history since hunter-gatherers somewhere had the idea to settle down in one place to grow crops, the nature of everyday life was fundamentally changing, an event heralded by the birth of the world's first industrial economy in Britain. As increasingly more people relied on their employers' wages, rather than the food and products they made at home, they were likewise liberated from the age-old restrictions enforced by their families and communities. On a darker note, the gaps between those who profited from and those who are abandoned by the new economy were becoming incomprehensibly vast, especially in the proverbially dire industrial cities of Victorian Britain. So great was the poverty and desperation in these new industrial centers, in fact, that both Karl Marx and Fredriech Engels were certain that their promised worldwide communist revolution would begin among the overworked and starving workers of England.

Just as the Industrial Revolution was shaking up traditional certainties about community, work, and class, so the French Revolution had already made politics even more divisive. Serious disagreements over politics were anything but new, of course, but now there were larger and more vocal factions questioning the very nature and structure of their governments.

The political spectrum in many nations was fractured between not only a Right and a Left (both terms that originated from the French Revolution), but between republicans, traditionalist and liberal monarchists, anarchists, and conservatives, liberals, and socialists of various beliefs and affiliations. The history of France itself shows the combustibility of politics in the era, as from 1789 to 1870 the country lurched from being a traditional monarchy to a constitutional monarchy to a radical republic to a liberal imperialist monarchy to a constitutional monarchy again to a liberal monarchy to a moderate republic to a liberal imperialist monarchy again to (after a socialist regime seized power in Paris for a couple of months), finally, a moderate republic. Out of such a volatile mixture emerged novel reactionary and leftist movements, which proposed various means for liberating or regulating individual lives.

Often the political and economic changes of the 1800s are described as all being part of the "rise of the middle class." This is easy to exaggerate, especially since even in Britain, which had one of the largest and most diverse middle classes in Europe, landowning nobles still held sway over national politics. Yet among Europe's intellectuals and artists there was a sense that there was such a tangible thing as bourgeois values, and that they had been allowed to take over society and culture. Among the liberal bourgeoisie themselves, this meant that they could stand as a vanguard against the decadence of the aristocracy and the sexual experimentalism of radicals and socialists, while serving as a moral example for the working classes. As Frederic Morton summarizes the middle-class liberals' hopes for the 19th century, "The liberal intelligence had dreamed the great nineteenth century dream of equality and riches. There would be greater abundance for all through greater production; there would be freedom perfected through democracy; through science there would be new technology and greater knowledge. That was the promise. This was the delivery: new rootless poverty and new excessive wealth equally rootless; new forms of inner and outer want; new envy, new doubt, and an entirely new furious bewilderment."[1]

The Victorian middle class, from London to Madrid and Budapest, is often blamed for turning its reformist drive toward sex. In fact, there were both government and grassroots campaigns against pornography, abortion, prostitution, homosexuality, and the sexual freedom that middle-class reformers obsessively thought the working classes were unfairly burdened with. Reformers especially fretted over the massive market specializing in literature, from tawdry erotica to sophisticated novels nonetheless offering explicit scenes of passion, catering to populations whose literacy and access to education were growing rapidly.

However, it was the bourgeoisie's own push for reform that, however hopelessly prudish it might look to 21st-century eyes, helped the cause of greater sexual liberation. Middle-class women fighting for the "domestication" of poor city workers inspired 19th-century feminists struggling against laws and customs surrounding marriage. Medical professionals advocating for more humane and rational treatment of criminals and the mentally ill created a medical language that could also be used to argue against laws punishing same-sex love, even while they denounced homosexuality as an obvious symptom of generational decadence. Activists and politicians extended debates about the rights of ethnic and religious minorities into the sexual realm. Even outside respectable bourgeois politics, socialism was seized upon by homosexuals and women as the ultimate key to full sexual liberation. By the end of the 19th century, modern feminism and the gay rights movement had been born out of both the liberal middle-class and radical politics made possible by the chaotic yet optimistic developments of the century. Rather than simply being an era of prudish oppression, the 19th century bestowed the very language of modern sexual rights on the West.

A Bourgeois Mentality

The ever irascible Nietzsche condemned the whole middle class as *Bildungsphilister*—"cultivated Philistines." They cared about art and literature only as hollow commodities. The great French novelist Gustave Flaubert loathed the bourgeoisie with a pathological passion for much the same reason. However, the bourgeoisie were not just the professionals, shopkeepers, and bureaucrats whose income was at the middle of the economic spectrum. It was an entire state of mind, which had infected all of France by the middle of the 1800s. In 1871, nearing the end of his life, Flaubert wrote to fellow writer George Sand, declaring, "I put *messieurs* the working people all in the same bag as the bourgeoisie. One should chuck them all in the river together." Flaubert also declared that the bourgeoisie found novels to be too long, no matter what they were about, and were interested in literature only if it threatened to "corrupt" people's minds.[2]

Flaubert's real denouncement of the bourgeoisie came in the form of a novel, *Madame Bovary,* which was published in serial form in 1856. The titular character, Emma Bovary, is the wife of a doctor in a small market town who constantly fantasizes about a life of romance and wealth. After she gives birth to a daughter, Bovary tries to find satisfaction in the exalted middle-class virtue of being a wife and mother, but the emptiness and boredom of her life drive her to have affairs with a rich landowner, Rudolphe, and a law student, Léon. Both men eventually abandon her. In the meantime, a local merchant named Lheureux encourages her to go into debt in a vain attempt to live the lifestyle she wanted. When Lheureux calls in his debts, Bovary commits a slow and painful suicide through arsenic. Her husband, impoverished by his wife's debts, dies soon afterward, and their daughter, who is given no support from the government, is forced to work as a child laborer in a mill. At the same time, Lheureux prospers and is even awarded a Medal of Honor.

Emma Bovary's desires and ambitions are inflamed by the romantic novels she read, which were written for bourgeois consumption, but she is nonetheless expected to become an "angel in the home," where she would devote herself entirely to pleasing her husband and raising her children to be good, moral citizens. The conventional wisdom about women in the Victorian era was that their sexuality was "cooler" than that of men, so it was the duty of a good wife to domesticate her husband and tame his lusts. If Emma Bovary had an opposite number, she was Amparo from the Spanish novelist Benito Pérez Galdós's 1884 novel *Tormento,* who was sexually attractive but modest, pious, submissive, and chaste. These were traditional Western values to be found in a wife, to be sure, but what middle-class Victorians now stressed was how such women's purpose in life was to provide a domestic refuge for their husbands, who were themselves under strain from a world that was increasingly pushing them out of their farms or home workshops and offices and into the uncertain, cutthroat dystopia of wage labor. Over the course of the novel, Amparo, who comes from a poor family, wins the heart of the young businessman Augustín Cabarello, who decides he wants to build a stable family life with Amparo as the skilled and devoted homemaker.[3] As Peter Gay describes the trend, "Man stands in the grinding, ugly world of business and politics; gratifying ambitions and searching out profits are as imperative for him as satisfying the tender passion. Woman, for her part, guardian of the hearth and of familial purity, has the time, the duty, nothing less than the sacred mission to put love first."[4]

The model for the entire British nation, if not much of Europe, was Queen Victoria (r. 1837–1901). Ascending to a monarchy that had been sullied by her free-living uncles George IV and William IV, who were a foppish spendthrift with a long history of mistresses and a foul-mouthed sailor with ten illegitimate children, respectively, Victoria established a model family with her beloved and uptight husband Albert of Saxe-Coburg-Gotha. Even though the crown belonged to Victoria, she played the part of the submissive wife, dutifully raising her children and following her husband's guidance even in her country's politics.[5] That none of her sons—especially the future Edward VII, who became something of an international playboy—lived up to her expectations caused Victoria nearly as much grief as her beloved Albert's death. Other monarchs followed suit, and exchanged lavish robes and their isolated, semi-divine portraits for bland upper-middle-class clothing or military uniforms and serene family portraits and photographs.

While Victoria's name has become shorthand for timeless family values or destructive yet ineffective oppression (depending, of course, on the point of view), Victoria herself had a definite sexuality. Her attraction to Prince Albert was certainly physical, and her diary still gushes with her feelings from after her wedding night: "I NEVER, NEVER spent such an evening!!! My DEAREST DEAREST DEAR Albert ... his excessive love and affection gave me feelings of heavenly love and happiness I never could have hoped to have felt before! He clasped me in his arms, and we kissed each other again and again!"[6] However, with this simple declaration, Victoria was going against the medical doctrine that was defining the era to which she gave her name.

The idea that women were less "sexual" than men had been accepted as medical orthodoxy. The British doctor and bestselling writer William Acton (1813–1875) and his near-French-contemporary and prolific medical writer Louis Fiaux (1847–1936) both agreed that the blame for men constantly resorting to adultery and prostitution was women's sexual coolness.[7] Acton once authoritatively decreed, "Women (happily for them) are not very much troubled with any sexual feelings of any kind."[8] Those women who were promiscuous were often deemed as fallen, if not outright pathological, according to medical science. To want instead to be a wife and mother was not just socially correct, but good mental health. According to one marriage manual, *The Physiology of Marriage,* "Woman, as is well known, in natural state—unperverted, unseduced, and healthy—seldom, if ever makes any of those advances, which clearly indicate sexual desire; and for this very plain reason that she does not feel them."[9]

For working-class women, the problem was somewhat different. Middle-class reformers strove to tame the working class by establishing museums and concert halls, reading rooms, reform societies, and temperance societies that crusaded for laws enforcing Sunday bans on the sale of alcohol and even tougher restrictions.[10] Reformers feverishly imagined that working-class men went straight to the bar or to a prostitute instead of home from work. When they did finally see their wife and children after work, they battered them out of rage or drunkenness. Women who worked wage jobs—and there were more of them over the course of the 19th century, as factories tapped into both women and children as cheap labor— were not much more trusted. Working women in Paris were thought to be spending their hard-earned money and precious few leisure hours in wine bars, where it was feared women, married or not, could meet their lovers. It did not help that wine bars often were staffed by prostitutes, who acted as barmaids and went from bar to bar whenever the owner felt that their novelty had worn off with the bar's regulars.[11]

Despite the best efforts of reformers and our own ideas about the effectiveness of Victorian morality, rates of illegitimacy and premarital sex stayed high. In much of Germany and France, the average was that one fourth of women were pregnant at the time of marriage. Rural communities and working-class families had their own ways of supporting single mothers and handling commitment between couples. Also, poor families had neither the means nor the time to try to imitate the mores that had become fashionable among the middle classes. Surveys of couples living in slums did find that most couples were monogamous, but they rarely bothered formalizing their relationships with the sanctity of marriage. G.R. Sims, in *How the Poor Live*, recorded how one English female activist who worked with a young working couple was shocked to discover that, although they fit her criteria for a sober, hardworking family, they were unmarried. She offered to pay for the marriage, but was disappointed when the husband called off the wedding for the trivial reason that he wanted to take up a well-paying job for two days.[12]

Even for the "respectable" classes, the old ideal where women were to be kept in check by their families and communities was being challenged, as more women entered the work force and were freed by the power of their wages, albeit only to a small extent. More change was needed before today's culture of dating could replace the ritual of courtship. Still, there was something new in the air. Commentators noted with mixed feelings how women flocked to the new department stores like Bainbridge's in Newcastle or the Bon Marché in Paris, unattended by men and free to browse stores or sit and drink coffee while chatting with their friends at their leisure. Places like the Bon Marché still went far out of their way to assure their customers and investors that their female employees were kept pure, by being segregated from their male co-workers in the dining areas and even in their work stations,[13] but at the same time their services were offering women spaces where they could enjoy the very same freedom often denied to the stores' workers.

Visible cracks were forming in the middle class's vision of utopia. About the same time the first department stores opened (i.e., the 1860s) journalists in Britain were writing about girls from "respectable" families who were "fast." They walked on city streets without any male companion, addressed young men by their first names, smoked cigarettes, and talked openly about their boyfriends and when they would "spoon" with them.[14] In 1905, Moscow University conducted one of the most thorough surveys of the sexual thoughts and behaviors of university students carried out in any country of the time. All the participants in the survey were male and from middle- and upper-class backgrounds. Out of 2,150 respondents, 67 percent admitted they had lost their virginity before enrolling at the university and 16 percent claimed to be avid readers of pornography.[15] A similar 1910 survey conducted in Germany discovered that 20 percent of boys about to finish their secondary education had already paid for sex at least once.[16] The fear that such young men could not control themselves was always a painful thorn on the side of middle-class reformers. The vice president of France's Anatomical Society, Dr. Demeaux, earnestly proposed creating trained brigades of masturbation investigators to spring surprise inspections on young people from the ages of 10 to 20.[17]

Educators, reformers, and doctors such as Demeaux believed that with the proper education and the right amount of surveillance, the sex instinct could be tamed and channeled toward socially beneficial ends. Such efforts mixed old-fashioned religious morality with the latest scientific arguments and social theories. One of the most successful (and, depending on one's perspective, notorious) was the pioneering feminist Josephine Butler (1828–1906). The child of respectable middle-class parents and the wife of a scholar and pastor, Josephine was drawn to the plight of British prostitutes. She and her followers succeeded in getting the British Parliament to repeal the Contagious Diseases Act, which allowed authorities to investigate prostitutes for contagious diseases; if found to be infected, the women were forced to enter hospitals that were widely known to be completely inadequate. Not content with her victories in her homeland, Butler became a spokesperson for the international abolitionist movement, which campaigned to end the government-regulated systems of prostitution common in Europe and would have prostitution outlawed altogether. Arguing that even regulated prostitution brought about the exploitation of women and encouraged the immorality of men, Butler took her message to France, Switzerland, and Italy in 1877.[18]

Although the abolitionist campaign attracted prominent supporters and firebrand activists like Butler, it mostly failed to make lasting impacts, outside shutting down Norway's brothels in 1895. Yet it did demonstrate the power and mass appeal such crusades could muster, uniting medical experts, evangelical Christians, feminists, and even conservatives and liberals. Among the organizations linked to this movement were young men's associations, designed to counteract the effects of an increasingly mechanized and secular world, leaving young men effete and godless. The first were Scotland's Young Men's Society for Religious Improvement, founded in 1824, and the Jünglingsverein ("Youth Club"), established at Bremen in 1834. They opposed feminism in even its more moderate forms, what was seen as the rampant egotism inherent to the intellectual thought of the day, the slow but sure assertion of homosexual rights, and the countless temptations of modern consumer society. For the leaders of these men's clubs, self-control, most especially abstinence from nonmarital sex, ensured their status as both Christian men and members of the middle class.[19]

This spread of values was not limited to Christians. Confronted with the sobering facts of brutal pogroms in Eastern Europe and the spread of a less direct but still dangerous secular anti–Semitism in Western and Central Europe, a new group of Jewish intellectuals, the *maskilim* ("learned men"), urged on the assimilation of Jews into 19th-century European society. In particular, they denounced traditional marital practices as both archaic and psychologically harmful. For example, the continued practice of marriages arranged in early adolescence was seen as damaging children's minds by causing them to be separated from their parents and brought about sexual dysfunction. Nearly as damaging was the power women wielded in traditional Jewish families, which, some *maskilim* argued, were in dire need of stronger male presences.

Jewish sexual life itself needed to be reformed; in particular, traditional celebrations of erotic desire had to be curbed and brought in line with modern notions of decency and discretion. "The solution to what they saw as the promiscuity and sexual dysfunction of traditional society was the imposition of bourgeois constraints upon desire," David Biale writes. Of course, they did not want to abandon their Jewish identity altogether, but there was a feeling that some aspects of the Jewish way of life were woefully out of tune with the newest social and medical developments.[20]

A similar inferiority complex infected the Ottoman Empire. Once a seemingly all-powerful force that seemed on the cusp of adding all of Europe to its provinces, the Ottoman Empire in the 19th century had been dubbed the "sick man of Europe," its armies excruciatingly out of date and its economy saddled with debts to the European powers. Rather than choosing complacency, Sultan Mahmud II (r. 1809–1839) ushered in the Tanzimât ("Reform") era. Besides modernizing the administration of the empire (by, for example, opening the first imperial postal service), the Ottoman law code was completely overhauled, following French, Belgian, and Swiss models.

The Ottoman legal system was made more secular, with *zina* ("fornication"), which was once both a state and a religious crime, exorcised from the law codes, as were most legal distinctions between Muslims, Jews, and Christians. The laws also no longer assumed the responsibility of the clan to protect its own. Instead, the existence of something like the close-knit middle-class family was sanctioned, whose protection was guaranteed not by an extended kin group but by the state. Further, following the example of the French, the Ottoman laws rejected any regulation of sexuality. In fact, as far as sex was concerned, the law codes were concerned with only the protection of minors from sexual abuse.[21]

In conjunction with this trend, Ottoman elites became more painfully conscious of how Europeans looked at their society through the lens of "Turkish sensuality." The power of state censorship was turned on old Sufi books that praised young beardless men and even just used such beauty as a metaphor for the spiritual. The Sufis were persecuted into near extinction by the end of the 19th century, and what remained of them could no longer be so open about their admiration for the male form.[22] The self-consciousness of the Turks over love between men was clear. In his widely read memoirs about his trip to Turkey, the British admiral Adolphus Slade (1804–1877) noted with contempt a party where distinguished government ministers seduced young men: "One grey-beard actually seized a handsome lad belonging to the *cadi* [local official] with felonious intent. The struggle was sharp between them, and the company stifled with laughter at beholding the grimaces of the drunken old satyr." The *bey* (governor) in attendance apologized to Slade, tried to convince him that such behavior was rare nowadays, and pleaded with him—obviously to no avail—not to include the episode in his writings.[23]

Despite the *bey*'s efforts, Slade and other European observers were convinced that Turkey was infected with sodomy. Polygamy was another sore spot. The Qur'an was clear that polygamy was permissible, but reformers began to debate if it was acceptable in modern Turkey. A contemporary, Osman Bey, records a meeting between government officials where one declares that that polygamy is an incurable cancer in Ottoman society. According to some reports, Ottoman officials kept a "diplomatic" wife who would meet with European diplomats, while their other wives remained at home. Regardless, there was no attempt to even really remove the tumor, although polygamy was becoming more rare—especially arrangements with more than two wives—and emerged as a favorite complaint of Turkey's social activists. The journalist and politician Celâl Nuri (1882–1938) wrote with authority, "The needs of today make monogamy a necessity."[24] Polygamy was eventually purged from Turkish society, but only later, at the moment the Ottoman Empire was in its twilight.[25]

The Victorian middle-class ethos hailed marital monogamy as far away as Istanbul, but it never imagined that the blissful state of matrimony had no room for acknowledging sex. In fact, most of Europe in the 19th century saw a boom in guides on how to be an attractive and healthy wife or husband, and an interest in how sex was necessary for a healthy marriage.

Carmen Burgos's *Arte de saber vivir* ("The Art of Knowing How to Live"), first published in Spain at the dawn of the 20th century, urged wives and mothers to keep up their physical attractiveness by remaining physically active, and had an entire chapter discussing how wives and husbands could go about swimming, playing tennis, skating, and even car racing.[26] Sexual attraction and love were the necessary cornerstones of a successful marriage. No less an authority than a 1817 German encyclopedia defined marriage as a lifelong relationship "which in its perfection is based on love."[27] Despite the social and often legal inequalities in marriage, the bourgeois ideal still insisted on the sanctity of mutual companionship and women's special role as homemakers and mothers. The French novelist Honoré de Balzac (1799–1855) paid heed to the contradiction when he wrote, "The married woman is a slave whom one must know how to put on a throne."[28]

The popular fiction of the day abounded with stories of couples who fell in love and married, or were prevented from marrying due to outdated class prejudices or social barriers. Of course, in real life and even among the middle classes, marriage "out of one's rank" could still be difficult, if not impossible. One German novelist, Louise Aston (1814–1871), made her own unhappy marriage, begun largely for financial reasons when she was not even out of her teens, the subject of her bestselling 1847 novel *Aus dem Leben einer Frau* ("From the Life of a Woman").[29] While not specifically tackling the issue of arranged marriages or "marriages of convenience," the Portuguese novel *O Primo Bazillo* ("Cousin Bazillo") depicts a young, urban, and upper-middle-class couple, Jorge and Luiza. They enter marriage convinced they love each other, but their love is actually shallow and their marriage is essentially based on their mutual lust for each other. As such, their marriage is under threat once Luiza's cousin and one-time lover Bazillo appears on the scene while Jorge is away on a business trip. In spite of Jorge being so old-fashioned that he admits he believes a husband should murder his wife when she commits adultery, Luiza succumbs to Bazillo's seductions. Rather than being murdered by Jorge, however, Luiza finds herself abandoned by Bazillo the instant he becomes bored with her. Afterward, Luiza goes the way of many tragic Victorian heroines: she falls into a deep depression, sickens, and dies.[30]

What if a couple like Luiza had lived, and she and Jorge eventually realized their own lack of compatibility? In Catholic countries like Portugal, the strict taboos against divorce stayed strong. Despite relatively persistent and victorious republican and anticlerical movements in countries like Spain, where a republic was (temporarily) established, divorce stayed out of the question for Catholic countries from the Republic of Ireland to Italy. The exception was France, where the Third Republic established in 1870 was eager to cut loose from the influence of the Catholic Church, but even then divorce was far more limited than it had been in revolutionary France. In Protestant countries, in the early 19th century divorce remained a fairly rare and costly process, and governments across Europe still thought of marriage as a public affair and not just an individual contract.[31]

The later 19th century did see divorce become more accessible for those without fortunes or political connections to call upon in Protestant countries, as happened with the Matrimonial Causes Act of 1857 in Britain. Behind the trend was a humanitarian concern, fostered by liberal and moderate politicians and feminist activists, for the well-being of wives suffering bad marriages or financial and emotional neglect by their husbands. The legal fad for divorce did benefit women, especially those who had been abandoned or were being abused by their husbands.[32]

The lessons of the middle class, which slowly began to inspire both the old aristocracies and the working classes, were deeper and more positive than they might seem from our perspective. Anything that deviated from sex between a wife and a husband was discouraged in forums ranging from churches to doctors' offices, but genuine feeling was valued, help for women and children trapped in shoddy family situations was codified into law, and the once timeless idea of marriage as first and foremost a financial and social arrangement withered. While the values of the middle class were largely promoted through a wide range of instruments such as cheesy romance novels and flawed medical advice, they were also taken up by the governments of 19th-century Europe, which became obsessed with being able to prepare and tap into the needs of their populations in a world where economies and warfare were becoming more and more complex.

Imposing Decency

If any intimate topic concerned the regimes of Europe, it was the question of population control. On the one hand, these governments wanted to keep their urban populations in check, especially keeping down the number of children who might prove to be a burden on state coffers. On the other hand, they felt pressure to keep crops of healthy young men at hand in case of war. The scientific theories about racial purity that were currently in circulation, and the fact that the populations of most European countries had increased dramatically through the early 19th century only to suddenly plummet toward the century's end, stressed the necessity for the careful gardening of one's national population. This fear was felt most of all by the French, whose catastrophic defeat at the end of the Franco-Prussian War was all but universally blamed on the fact that France had the lowest national birth rate in Europe at the time.

Technological innovations made the issue even more pressing. Condoms made from rubber, rather than from the traditional linen or sheep bladders, became commercially available, as did contraceptive sponges, spermicides, diaphragms, and pessaries. Although folk remedies and outright snake oil contraceptives were still sold everywhere, more modern and reliable contraceptives were by the middle of the century widely available, if discreetly sold, through pharmacies and mail-order catalogs. The majority of doctors tended to condemn such "artificial" aids, except in special cases such as when a female patient's health was endangered from a pregnancy, and instead promoted ancient methods like keeping a fertility calendar or practicing *coitus interruptus*. In spite of such campaigns, popular demand for modern contraceptive tools was loud enough that they were widely advertised in newspapers and journals, sometimes delicately as "hygienic aids" but sometimes not.[33] At the start of the 20th century, governments began acting with a heavy hand. The French government in 1909 was contemplating the criminalization of most forms of artificial birth control, all pessaries on the market were confiscated by police in Vienna, and the Dutch outlawed the advertisement of all birth control products.[34] Such bans had the pragmatic purpose of trying to reverse declining birth rates (although historians still debate how much of a factor the spread of effective birth control technologies really was), but were also carried out in the name of "decency."

Anything that seemed to have the goal of making sex less risky provoked the ire and suspicion of churches and conservative activists. "Condoms … did not only protect both men and women from diseases, but also prevented pregnancy, and that is precisely why the churches and morally purity organizations, relentlessly opposed making access to condoms easier," Dagmar Herzog comments.[35] However, opposition to contraception was not exclusive to conservatives and staunchly traditionalist institutions like the Catholic Church and the Anglican Church. At least in France, some secular liberals were skeptical about claims that there was a population crisis, but were concerned as much as religious conservatives about women forfeiting their duty to become mothers and anxious that the whole issue was designed to distract from reforms to benefit the poor.[36]

In a complete reversal from today's reproductive politics, abortion was, according to Herzog, "popularly considered far *less* immoral than mechanical or chemical contraception."[37] In the 19th century and early 20th century, Europe had a number of colorful euphemisms for the restoration of menstrual flow, from Italy's "going in reverse gear" to Hungary's "wash bed linens rather than babies' diapers."[38] Drawing on new medical knowledge about conception and the continued debates over population decline, both the medical community and the Catholic Church were united in taking a harder line against abortion, whether conducted using modern surgical techniques or through the long list of folk remedies designed to induce miscarriage, but even after the end of the 19th century the general public did not fall in line.[39] These abortion foes had an unlikely (from our modern perspective, at any rate) ally in the form of some feminists, who opposed abortion on the basis that it was a violent denial of motherhood and helped men exploit women by enabling them to take their sexual fill from their girlfriends and wives without consequence. While some early feminists supported access to abortion, others referred to the reasoning first articulated by Mary Wollstonecraft, which decried women who induced a miscarriage for the sake of their male lovers.[40] That until the 1930s medical abortion even by a professional was often a more dangerous procedure for the mother than childbirth was a widely known fact often cited by disapproving feminists.

To answer such calls for reform, laws were made, albeit usually not until near the end of the 19h century. One of the first anti-abortion laws was passed by the British Parliament in 1861. While these laws were often enforced, the proliferation of home methods and the profits that could be made from providing abortion services made such laws somewhat ineffective. A woman from England, Louisa Fenn, was put on trial for selling abortifacients under the alias of "Madame Douglas." The trial may have given the public the message that providing abortion services could land one in prison, but it also revealed just how much money could be raked in for anyone willing to take the risk. During the trial it came out that "Madame Douglas" spent 600 pounds (about 12 times a working-class man's annual wage) in six months just on advertising.[41] The impact of the laws was also dampened by how easy and relatively cheap it was to travel in the age of the railroad and steamboat. After 1861, middle- and upper-class British and Irish women who found themselves unexpectedly pregnant would secretly vacation in Paris and return home with their problem resolved. In Switzerland, where abortion was illegal in most of the country except Geneva, there was an entire network, tactfully ignored by the police, that helped women coming in to Geneva by train from elsewhere in Switzerland or from neighboring countries meet helpful midwives or doctors.[42]

Efforts by activists to rid Europe of legalized prostitution were much less successful in winning the support of politicians than the crusade against abortion. Even at the end of the 19th century, most countries in Europe had some form of government-regulated prostitution that required registration with the state and regular health checks. Many systems were modeled after the institution of state-monitored brothels, *maisons de tolérance,* that developed in Napoleonic France—thus the nickname "the French system." Still, there were significant numbers of unregistered prostitutes who walked the streets or doubled as barmaids and waitresses. Although the system did extend to prostitutes some protection from exploitation by pimps and clients, there were abuses. In Russia-controlled Warsaw, one could find on the gateways of apartment buildings a list of the residents and their occupations. Having a blank instead of the name of an occupation was a telltale sign of a prostitute. Because of this lack of transparency, it was easy for apartment owners to milk high rents out of prostitutes, who in the Russian Empire were allowed to live in only certain—and always impoverished—neighborhoods.[43]

There were concentrated attempts to keep women from falling into prostitution, funded either by the state or by wealthy benefactors, such as the Russian Society for the Protection of Women and the London Mission Society. The most famous—and infamous—were the Magdalen houses of Ireland, 11 of which were established in Dublin alone by the 1830s. Through strict supervision and religious doctrine, women, who either entered voluntarily or were forced to enter by their families as a result of "promiscuous" behavior, were trained to be good workers. Typically women stayed on a few years until they could be found jobs, usually as servants. The majority were free to come or go as they pleased. Over the course of the 20th century the reputation of the houses worsened, as more women were committed to them unwillingly and were forced into the physically demanding and sometimes skin-burning task of doing mass laundry.[44]

The real sexual menace that threatened to forever destroy European civilization was still masturbation. "In my opinion, neither the plague, nor war, nor smallpox, nor innumerable other such evils produce as disastrous results for humanity as this fatal habit," wrote the French doctor Joseph Henri Reveillé-Parise. "It is the destroyer of civilized societies, and all the more active since it operates continually and saps the generations."[45] Even a forward-thinking sexologist like Richard Krafft-Ebing claimed, "Nothing is so prone to contaminate—under certain circumstances, even to exhaust—the source of all noble and ideal sentiments, which arise of themselves from a normally developing sexual instinct, as the practice of masturbation in early years."[46] Masturbation was seen as a sign of primitive, antisocial behavior that if left unchecked in children and youths could lead to homosexuality. It was even a profound threat to the survival of the nation. "Men would be too feeble to defend or serve their country," Herzog writes. "Women would be incapable of being effective mothers."[47] Of course, all this did nothing to hinder the invention of modern sex toys—the origins of the electric dildo and the anal plug are both in the Long Nineteenth Century—and their advertisement, as massagers or medical aids, in newspapers. Although there is no proof that doctors massaged women's genitals as a treatment for what doctors at the time termed "hysteria," vibrators were openly sold as a medical aid for women, much like how anal plugs were advertised as treatment for male problems with ejaculation.

Keeping up decency was a concern for both doctors and politicians, but it was becoming more difficult to prevent the public from becoming educated about new methods of contraception and about medical and technological advancements that had the power to change their sex lives. Near the end of the 19th century, nations' literacy rates were nearing 100 percent and writings about medicine and sex were no longer limited to educated enclaves. This would have myriad consequences, perhaps the foremost being the first stirrings of the first major change in how same-sex love was thought and talked about since antiquity.

Invasion of the Inverts

On August 29, 1867, a one-time legal adviser, Karl Heinrich Ulrichs, presented himself before the Congress of German Jurists at Munich. For years Ulrichs had tried with mixed results to explain to his family and friends that he was a *Urning,* a man born with no sexual or romantic interest in women whatsoever, only men. He could prove by pointing to countless examples from literature, philosophy, and history that *Urnings* had always existed and that, not only had they loved other men, but "nature developed the physical male germ in us, yet mentally, the feminine one."[48] Since they were born with not only a different sex drive but unique gendered characteristics, *Urnings* and *Urningins,* women who likewise had a sex drive tuned toward other women, were a separate class of humans, who deserved the freedom to love who they wish. Because of religious persecution and "scientific error,"[49] however, they were viewed as sinners, criminals, and insane by the *Dionings* and *Dioningins,* "heterosexuals." Ulrichs urged the Congress to act against sodomy laws across Germany, but his speech was shouted down before he came even close to finishing. In spite of that, it was in many ways the "coming out" of the modern gay rights movement.

Drawing on classical metaphors (in English *Urnings* and *Urningins* mean "Uranians," referring to Plato's *Symposium,* where male same-sex love is associated with the Greek myth of the sky god Uranus giving birth to Aphrodite without any female part), Ulrichs devised an elaborate naming system that encompassed heterosexual women or men whose behavior was like that of the other gender, heterosexuals who have strong feelings for the same gender but are sexually attracted only to the opposite sex, bisexuals, pederasts, pedophiles, intersex, and heterosexuals who engage in "situational homosexuality." Sexual desires, he thought, cannot be either sin or illness because they are inborn, which can be demonstrated through unbiased scientific research (although at the time of his writing Ulrichs thought such research did not yet exist) or through earnest explorations of history and classical philosophy. This system, and his argument for why Uranians deserved to have both the law and medicine off their backs, was carefully laid out in a series of essays, *Forschungen über das Rätsel der mannmännlichen Liebe* ("The Riddle of Man-Manly Love"), which he first published under an alias but later published and promoted under his real name.

It was not enough for Ulrichs to prove the existence of Uranians; instead, using ideas about rights inherited from the Enlightenment, he sought to demonstrate how and why they deserve freedom from persecution. Ulrichs declared defiantly, "When I love the person I am naturally attracted to, I am not acting contrary to nature,"[50] and asserted that the right to sexual intimacy is an "inalienable right."[51] "We *Urnings* form a small minority," Ulrichs argued. "But, by God, we have the same rights as you, who are a powerful majority. You have no authority to take away or encroach upon our equal rights."[52] Nearly as much as his confidence that Uranians were a class of people with a presence across the world and throughout history, Ulrichs's assertions were shaped by his belief in love and sexual pleasure as innate rights. That principle even formed the basis of what is perhaps his most devastating critique of his German Protestant enemies. "It sounds particularly touching when a Protestant minister preaches that we should practice mortification for life, while he is in no way especially hard on himself, as is evident by the fertility of his wife, which almost reminds us of the times of the patriarchs. These gentlemen, who deny themselves nothing, can easily give speeches."[53]

As groundbreaking as Ulrichs's writings undoubtedly were, ultimately Uranian and Dionian lost to two terms coined only a few years after the initial publication of *The Riddle of Man-Manly Love* by the Hungarian journalist Károly Kertbeny (1824–1882): "heterosexual" and "homosexual." Kertbeny had seen a close friend driven to suicide after he was blackmailed for his homosexuality and, like Ulrichs, he argued that sodomy laws represented a violation of natural rights. However, in the late 19th century another term gained wide currency, "invert." So named because doctors saw same-sex desire as an "inversion" of the sex instinct onto the individual's own sex, inversion became one of the most hotly debated topics among the growing number of professional sexologists, especially in Britain, France, and Germany.

Even in the middle of the 19th century, there were professional doctors who still condemned homosexuality as a vice, but a growing number were condemning sodomy laws on the basis that "inversion" was a medical condition. Richard Krafft-Ebing was hardly sympathetic to people with same-sex desire, but, attributing their inclinations to their heredity or to "injurious influences" in childhood,[54] he urged that inverts be committed to hospitals rather than imprisoned. This was the consensus of Krafft-Ebing's French colleagues, who found homosexuality to be at best a psychological reversion to a primitive state of humanity's evolution or at worst an unmistakable sign of hereditary decay that was just one small step above mental retardation.[55]

At first very few medical writers were willing to go so far as to suggest that same-sex desire was not unhealthy or a symptom of an unhinged mental state, but that, too, was beginning to change in the late 19th century. One of the most decisive of these voices was the English sexologist Havelock Ellis (1859–1939), who in a way lived out his research. He married a lesbian, Edith, and together the two had an open marriage. Ellis, who was accustomed to thinking of himself as asexual, had been pleasantly surprised to discover that he was sexually attracted to women in the act of urinating. With the English literary critic and homosexual John Addington Symonds, Ellis wrote *Sexual Inversion* (1896), although the fact that Germany dominated the field of sexology led them to first write their book in German. The reception to Ellis and Symonds' morally neutral treatment of homosexuality was less than warm. One review published in the newspaper *The Lancet* reads:

> It must be pointed out ... that a more than ordinary danger is attached to Mr. Havelock Ellis's work as a book for laymen in that the author's views happen to be that sexual inversion is far more prevalent than we believe it to be and that the legislature does injustice to many by regarding as crimes the practices with which it is abound up. He has failed to convince us on these points; and his historical references and the "human documents" with which he has been furnished will, we think, fail equally to convince medical men that homo-sexuality is anything else than an acquired and depraved manifestation of the sexual passion but, be that as it may, it is especially important that such matters should not be discussed by the man in the street, not to mention the boy and the girl the street.[56]

An Austrian neurologist who was at the time developing a small but devoted group of admirers, Sigmund Freud (1856–1939) was starting to draw a firm dividing line between the individual and his or her sexual activity. In his 1905 essay collection *Drei Abhandlungen zur Sexualtheorie* ("Three Essays on the Theory of Sexuality"), Freud asserted that inverts could not be considered "degenerate" because inversion is found in people who display "no other serious deviations from the normal" and whose "efficiency is unimpaired."[57] His contemporary the sexologist Magnus Hirschfield (1868–1935) in 1897 had founded the Scientific-Humanitarian Committee, which was dedicated to using scientific research not for the "treatment" of homosexuality but for rebutting political and social prejudice. Although the organization failed completely in its initial goal of decriminalizing sodomy in Germany, it attracted hundreds of members across Central Europe and prestigious supporters like Albert Einstein and Leo Tolstoy. In his own writings, Hirschfield went so far as to establish a biological justification for homosexuality, which would have been virtually unthinkable to the earliest sexologists: "[Same-sex desire] binds us to life by means of feelings of desire; second, it bonds individuals to one another, producing the cohesion between them, from which humanity develops as a higher organism; and third, it allows men and women to thrive and excel mentally and physically. One could say in summary that the sex-love drive is not reproductive but rather the drive for the enhancement of desire and life."[58]

Writings by sexologists like Magnus Hirschfield attracted a wide readership, but medical professionals were not alone in debating what same-sex desire meant in modern society. In the 1880s, the French novelist Emile Zola received a strange invitation from an anonymous Italian nobleman, who sent him a series of letters and postcards detailing his struggle with his "illness." Eventually the letters were published as *Le roman d'un inverti* ("Novel of an Invert"). Attracted to Zola's interest in medical issues and to the taboo and sensual, the Italian candidly told Zola the tale of his sexual awakening, his attraction to a handsome male servant at the age of 13, and having fantasies of being Andromache in *The Iliad* and experiencing the caresses of her muscular husband Hector. Zola himself, who was intrigued by the Italian's earnestness and tragic introspection, hoped that the publication of the Italian's letters would "inspire some pity and a modicum of equity for these wretches."[59]

Despite growing sympathy among the medical and intellectual communities, homosexual acts were still against the law in many countries. Under the influence of French-style divisions between sin and crime, and church and state, many Catholic countries, including Belgium, Italy, and Spain, no longer had sodomy laws on the books. An exception was Austria-Hungary, which still punished same-sex acts between men with jail time. The countries that did maintain such laws or even passed new sodomy laws tended to have a solid Protestant heritage, including the Scandinavian countries, the Netherlands, Britain, and Germany. A series of acts by the British Parliament made any sexual acts between men illegal and punishable by prison or hard labor. When Germany was cobbled together into the German Empire in 1870 under Prussia's monarchy, the new imperial government took Prussia's sodomy law and made it the basis for Paragraph 175, outlawing male same-sex acts. Paragraph 175 inspired much campaigning by the likes of Karl Heinrich Ulrichs, and it is an irony of history (although not a coincidence) that imperial Germany was home simultaneously to one of the most clearly defined and often enforced sodomy laws as well as the earliest gay rights movement. At the personal wish of the reactionary Tsar Nicholas I, Russia in 1845 passed its first sodomy law, punishing anal sex between men with confiscation of property and at least four years of exile in Siberia.[60]

While the legal enemies of homosexuality were digging in their heels, discussions of "deviant" sex in literature were still being held. Themes of same-sex love did exist in Victorian novels, but if such lovers were not condemned as perverts, then their love was described in veiled language or between the lines. One late work resulting from 19th-century ideas about homosexuality that dared to be outspoken was the English novel *The Well of Loneliness,* which was published in 1928 but almost immediately banned and subjected to an obscenity trial, even though it had no sexually explicit scenes. A young girl, named "Stephen" because her parents were expecting a boy, grows up somewhat boyish, but is treated sympathetically by her father, who has been enlightened by reading Karl Heinrich Ulrichs. The novel details Stephen's attempts to find love. Hurt by a hostile society, she can find comfort only by reading the writings of prominent sexologists and seeking out other inverts. For its totally unambiguous discussion of what it meant to be attracted to the same sex at the end of the Long Nineteenth Century, *The Well of Loneliness* rose above attempts to censor it and became an inspiration for an entire generation. One woman who read a Polish translation of the book would claim that the only way she survived her imprisonment in a Nazi concentration camp was by clinging to the hope that someday she, too, would experience what it was like to kiss another woman.[61]

Other tantalizing sources of stories about same-sex love were the real-life scandals gleefully reported on by the international press. In 1890, a routine theft investigation led police to discover that 19 Cleveland Street in London was a brothel offering young men doubling as telegraph boys to a high-class and largely aristocratic clientele. At the time, it was suspected one of the clients was "Eddy," Prince Albert Victor, who was Victoria's grandson and second in line to the throne. Historians still debate whether "Eddy" narrowly avoided exposure or was guilty only of associating with one of the brothel's actual clients, Lord Somerset.[62]

The Cleveland Street scandal validated suspicions that the aristocracy was plagued with homosexuality, and prepped the public for the trials of the playwright Oscar Wilde (1854–1900) several years later. Throughout his career Wilde was known for his foppish personality and had admirers who identified themselves as Uranians. In fact, Oscar himself became familiar with and enamored of the term by reading Joris-Karl Huysman's novel *A Rebours* ("Against Nature").[63] Yet Wilde did try, perhaps half-heartedly at times, to play at the role of the happily married upper-class man. Unfortunately, the father of one of his lovers, Lord "Bosie" Alfred Douglas, was the coarse and temperamental Marquess of Queensberry, who in February 1895 left a card declaring, "For Oscar Wilde, posing as a somdomite" [*sic*], with the porter at the Albermarle Club. Wilde went against the advice of his friends and sued the marquess for libel. The libel trial was decided in the marquess's favor, and the controversy stirred up in the trial gave the government the ammunition to accuse Wilde of sodomy and gross indecency, a vague criminal category that could encompass just about any form of same-sex intimacy.

When Wilde was put on trial, one of the charges against him ended in a verdict of "not guilty" and the other three charges ended in an undecided verdict. Unfortunately, it was decided that Wilde would be tried again, along with his friend Alfred Taylor. Wilde denied everything, but the government brought before the court a series of witnesses who could attest to Wilde and Taylor referring to young men as "darling" or "the boy for me." The trial ended with a guilty verdict, in the eyes of both the court and the public, which had turned from adoring Wilde to loathing him. The judge, Justice Alfred Wills, was echoing the sentiments of many when he stated before sentencing:

> Oscar Wilde and Alfred Taylor, it has never been my lot to try a case of this kind before which has been so bad. One has to put a stern constraint upon oneself to prevent oneself

from describing in language I ought not to use the sentiments which must arise in the breast of every man who has a spark of decent feeling in him, and who has heard of details of these two terrible trials. That the jury have arrived at a correct verdict I cannot persuade myself to entertain the shadow of a doubt.... I shall, under the circumstances, be expected to pass the severest sentence that the law allows. In my judgment, it is utterly inadequate for such cases.

Both Wilde and Taylor were condemned to two years of hard labor, which for a man of Wilde's age amounted to a slower and less direct death sentence.[64] While the verdict did vindicate British hatred of homosexuality, and was even treated as a kind of patriotic victory (that the day of the verdict coincided with Queen Victoria's birthday helped the media make the connection), Havelock Ellis observed that the trials also "aroused inverts to take up a definite stand."[65]

Yet Britain did not monopolize all the fun. In 1907, the German and international press hinted that the eccentric Kaiser Wilhelm II was surrounded by a cabal of homosexual aristocrats, who accompanied him on yacht rides and vacations to his forest retreat. Like all good scandals, there was a grain of truth, in the form of the liaisons the Kaiser's close friend, Philipp Eulenburg, had with several other men in the Kaiser's entourage. Eulenburg's libel suit against one journalist, Maximilian Harden, and the anti–Semitic insinuations made over Harden being Jewish merely inflamed the wags who claimed that Germany's government and army were being run by effeminates and perverts. The scandals were even hinted at in language justifying why Paragraph 175 needed to be kept in place.[66]

The specters of Oscar Wilde, Lord Somerset, and Philipp Eulenburg vindicated fears that there was an infiltration of homosexuals among the aristocracy, who exploited and perverted the young men of the nation and stood opposed to all the values cherished by the bourgeois family. At the same time, an organized, international campaign was fighting to prove that homosexuals were also included in the Enlightenment concept of the natural right to pursue happiness, by combining the ancient ideas about love inherited from classical philosophy with the rapidly evolving language of medical professionals. The question remains: was the idea of homosexuals as a distinct group with its own history and identity the creation, however accidental, of 19th-century doctors, or did such a concept exist before that, only in ways different from those espoused by 19th-century science? It is still hotly argued among today's scholars in different fields, and will likely never receive a definite answer. What is sure is that the 19th century, for all its associations today with oppression, was also the era that shaped gay rights in ways that continue to endure.

Indecency for Mass Consumption

With illiteracy vanishing near the end of the century, the Long Nineteenth Century is a good candidate for the birth of a true mass media, especially in Britain with its massive print industry. On one side, classic works of literature from Shakespeare to Jane Austen was being made affordable to even members of the working class in the form of cheap, mass-produced novels. On the other side, there were the "penny dreadfuls," which titillated readers—often the young and women—with lurid stories of sex and violence. One particularly popular novel was *Varney the Vampire*. Published in 1847, decades before Bram Stoker's *Dracula* saw print, *Varney* in text and image shows the tormented, tragic vampire feeding on a young woman's neck while one clawed hand clutches her breast. Another popular penny dreadful, George W.M. Reynolds's *Wagner, the Wehr-Wolf,* depicts a convent of nuns whose favorite pasttime is stripping to the waist and turning a whip on one another's bare breasts.[67]

It had also become cheaper to print more explicit pornography, although these works were still pushed to the underground. Some of these publications presented themselves as being in the same spirit as popular adventure novels, although their titles alone were revealing, such as *The Lustful Turk* (1828) and *Rosa Fielding, or, A Victim of Lust* (1876). While their plots may be sanitized, their use of sex is clearly one of the main appeals. For example, *The Lustful Turk* intimately details the adventures of an English woman, Emily, who survives a shipwreck only to end up a slave in the Ottoman Empire. After describing how she is raped by a Turkish official—"my cries seemed only to excite him to the finishing of my ruin, and sucking my lips and breasts with fury, he unrelentingly rooted up all obstacles my virginity offered"—Emily is, as summarized by Steven Marcus, "made to love her master and his 'grand master-piece.'"[68]

Even pornography was a topic of interest to sexologists, even if sometimes they were reluctant to admit it. One sexologist Henry Spencer Ashbee exhaustively catalogued every English, French, German, and American work of pornography. In the introduction of his own catalog, *Index Librorum Prohibitorum* (which he significantly named after the Catholic Church's own list of forbidden books), he wrote, "Improper books, however useful to the student, or dear to the collector, are not 'virginibus puerisque'; they should, I consider, be used with caution even by the mature; they should be looked upon as poisons, and treated as such; should be (so to say) distinctly labeled, and only confided to those who understand their potency, and are capable of rightly using them."[69] In an age where printed books could be cheap and even many of the poor could read, Ashbee was not entirely wrong to fear corruption.

While the British in the 19th century did have a fairly well-deserved reputation for sadomasochism and flagellation, illicit erotica was hardly just a British prerogative. One international bestseller, published in Berlin in 1851, were the *Memoirs of Lola Montez.* As the title promised, the book was purported to collect the diaries of the Irish dancer (who nonetheless pretended to be Spanish) Lola Montez, who managed to become the mistress of King Ludwig I of Bavaria until both she and the king were ousted by the 1848 revolutions. The edition even promised to give readers "intimate letters" written by the king himself to Lola. While not all that explicit, even by the standards of its own era, the *Memoirs of Lola Montez* offers the adventures of a sexy young woman who loses her virginity at an early age and runs off with a handsome young Irish officer. While she marries him, she continues to explore her desires through experiments in adultery, leading up to her first rendezvous with the Bavarian king, to whom she does not remain loyal.[70]

The Memoirs of Lola Montez was banned in Prussia, and later imperial Germany, with the police authorized to confiscate copies. In 1851, the Prussian government had passed the so-called laws of *unzüchtige Schriften* (literally "lewd writings") that allowed the police to confiscate "immodest" writings and persecute offenders. The wording behind the law was vague, allowing prosecution for any publications that "injured modesty or morals." Such vagueness facilitated the banning of any literature that not just had sexually explicit material, but could be argued to undermine the public's faith in traditional marriages and families.[71]

A similar fear about the influence of not only pornography but also risque books was behind the Obscene Publications Act passed by the British Parliament. During a parliamentary debate, one member of the House of Lords, Lord Lyndhurst, asked if the act would also cause copies of a classic like *The Decameron* to be removed from bookshelves. Lord Campbell replied that "the keeping or the reading, or the delighting in such things must be left to taste, and was not a subject for legal interference; but when there were people who designedly and industriously manufactured books and prints with the intention of corrupting the public morals, and when they succeeded in their infamous purpose, he thought it was necessary for the Legislature to interpose and to save the public from the contamination to which they would otherwise be exposed."[72] Such was the reasoning that justified banning books that ranged the spectrum from obvious and blatant pornography to what is now considered classic literature such as D.H. Lawrence's 1928 novel *Lady Chatterley's Lover*. When it comes to taboo topics that touch on intimacy, desire, and sex, often even clumsy censors can appreciate that the ideas are even more dangerous than the images.

The Science of Sex

In a time of unprecedented technological innovations and scientific discoveries and profound social change, it was not unexpected that scientists had grand hopes for the future, including the total elimination of crime through psychological research and completely mastering with clockwork precision the social training of children. Unfortunately, this "rational" push for social and national improvement was completely mixed in with the racist beliefs in fashion among even the intellectual elites. In fact, eugenics was very much considered "progressive" thought by the first years of the 20th century, and was the unquestioned assumption of many conservatives, liberals, feminists, and socialists. Catholics were the only fairly consistent opponents of eugenics, yet even then their opposition was usually not so much based on humanitarianism as it was on moral opposition to any "unnatural" meddling with fertility.[73] Still, there were popular and influential eugenic organizations and activists even in Catholic countries, such as the Spanish League for Scientifically Based Sex Reform.

Adding urgency to schemes for improving Europe through eugenics were the fears in the late 19th century that the nations of Europe were spiraling into decline. From the 1860s and well into the 1880s, the argument that some mental illnesses were inheritable, the theory of degeneracy, was extremely popular in French medical circles. Bad habits by one's ancestors, such as excessive drinking, poor diet, and breeding with the wrong stock were thought to cause deformities and even mental illnesses that could be passed on to future generations, including tendencies toward depression, hysteria, criminal behavior, and homosexuality.[74] Supporters of degeneracy theory also believed that inherited mental illnesses worsened generation by generation.[75] Eugenics was the clear solution, whether it was practiced "positively" (incentives for people of "good stock" to have children or bans on contraception) or "negatively" (promotion of contraception and abortion among those of "bad stock" or sterilization of people with mental illness or mental retardation).

In the words of one of Britain's most well-known eugenicists, Francis Galton: "Many who are familiar with the habits of [the lowest eugenic "class"] do not hesitate to say that it would be an economy and a great benefit to the country if all habitual criminals were resolutely segregated under merciful surveillance and peremptorily denied opportunities for producing offspring. It would abolish a source of suffering and misery to a future generation, and would cause no unwarrantable hardship in this."[76] Even doctors with strongly held Christian convictions, like Wilhelm Mensinga, the German inventor of the diaphragm, would endorse contraception if it served their just as strongly held eugenicist beliefs in limiting the procreation of the poor, the chronically ill, racial minorities, and the "criminal classes." "The sick, the incapable, the mentally deficient, the bad ones, the inferior races must be systematically educated to birth control," the Swiss doctor Auguste Forel wrote. "The robust, good, healthy and mentally higher standing ones, however, must be, as I have repeatedly argued here, encouraged to multiply strongly."[77]

Improving one's society and race was not the sole goal of scientists. They also wanted to perfect ways to purge the human sexual instinct of perversity. Homosexuality and masturbation were the obvious targets, but fetishism in all forms was found an unbearable deviation from the norm that was a symptom of wider psychological problems. In contrast to "morbid love," where someone fetishizes an object like shoes or urine, the French doctor Gabriel Tarde (1843–1904) described "normal love" as "that through which are pursued jointly not only the vital ends of generation and the purity of races, but also the social goals of patriotic greatness, family preservation, and the purity of manners."[78]

As psychology developed as a science in its own right, there was more pessimism about how much strict lines could be drawn between the normal and the pathological. Sigmund Freud did more for the modern study of the human mind than simply explore the topic of sex and the mind in a morally neutral fashion. The shocking yet unavoidable implication of Freud's theories was that *everyone* was pathological. There was no "normal" when it came to human sexuality. "No healthy person, it appears, can fail to make some addition that might be called perverse to the normal sexual aim," Freud writes in his *Three Essays*. "[A]nd the universality of this finding is in itself enough to show how inappropriate it is to use the word perversion as a term of reproach."[79] This would soon become the mainstream of psychological thought, although it would take the horrors of Nazi eugenics to, more or less, purge the yearning for a perfectly engineered genetic community from scientific thought.

Radicals versus (or for) Sex

"Home is the eternal prison-house of the wife," the Irish reformers William Thompson and Anna Wheeler declared in their 1825 pamphlet, *An Appeal of One Half of the Human Race*.[80] Decades before Karl Marx and Friedrich Engels addressed the world with *The Communist Manifesto*, people already dissatisfied with rapid industrialization, the destabilization of old ways of life, and the ever-widening gap between rich and poor in Western and Central Europe were embracing utopian ideas. Lacking a loud-enough political voice, they often found the best way to experiment with their ideas was to begin with the home. Marriage and the family were for them a microcosm of a flawed and corrupt society. The patriarchal stranglehold kept by the father embodied the unquestioned, undemocratic, and arbitrary authority of the ruling classes. The exploitation and abuse of the wife was itself a parallel to the perpetually disadvantaged position of workers in society. Thus the best way to improve society was by restructuring the family itself.

X A Brave New World

Charles Fourier (1772–1837) was a French utopian thinker who had the opportunity to try to make his ideals a reality. In his writings, he called his plan for a new society the Phalanx. Polygamy, which Fourier considered more natural than strict monogamy, would be not only allowed but actually encouraged. All adults would form stronger ties with their neighbors by taking several lovers, and just as they were entitled to a minimum income, all adults needed a sexual minimum. If women and men were not attractive enough to fulfill their sexual needs on their own, a special squad of reasonably attractive men and women happy to volunteer their services would be on hand. Fourier's ideas were appealing enough (and hopefully not simply for his proposal on sex volunteers) that he attracted enough followers to establish real phalanxes. One of his most successful groups was in Ohio, although it endured for only a few years before it was abandoned.[81]

During the tumultuous 1830s and 1840s, another communal group was founded in France by Claude-Henri de Saint-Simon (1760–1825). Named after their founder, the Saint-Simonians put into practice their ideals of communal living and freeing women from oppression, although allowing women into positions of authority and the extent to which women's roles should be defined by motherhood were still contentious questions. Part of the Saint-Simonian program was "free love," or at least more freedom for both women and men to choose sexual partners and end their relationships, and a suspicion of traditional monogamy.[82]

The largest such communal-socialist movement was Owenism in Britain, which propagated itself through its own newspapers and speakers. Like the Saint-Simonians who influenced them, the Owenites attacked marriage as an oppressive system, especially when the husband was the sole wage earner and the wife was expected to do all the housework and provide child care with no pay. They also preached the virtues of egalitarian love and the freedom to choose one's sexual and romantic partners. Sadly, the Owenite message was not as well received among Britain's working-class women as was hoped. They saw in the Owenite program of "free love" an excuse for men to use women for sex and abandon them. One female Owenite lecturer in Scotland was met with such hostility that a crowd of women threw stones at her.[83]

Where the Owenites and the Saint-Simonians failed to truly change the face of Europe, two young German journalists did in the long run. Appalled at the conditions created by industrialization but enthusiastic about the political potential heralded by the new masses of urban industrial workers, Karl Marx (1818–1883) and Friedrich Engels (1820–1895) collaborated on a short political treatise, *The Communist Manifesto,* which decisively decreed, "The history of all hitherto existing society is the history of class struggles." In the years to come, communism would promise an end to the sexual exploitation of women and attract homosexual members who glimpsed hope for a future of total social acceptance in the international movement's rejection of both religious authority and middle class values. Sex to Marx and the early communists was purely an economic and social issue; the moral and medical concerns that haunted most 19th-century intellectuals were at best a smokescreen in their view. Further, unlike some religious leaders and medical doctors, they completely rejected any notion that there was anything timeless in family and sexual experience, instead seeing both as elements of society that could—in fact, *must*—be rebuilt in the coming global revolution.

The influence of the free-spirited Friedrich Engels on the nascent movement helped, too. In his 1884 publication *Origin of the Family, Private Property, and the State,* Engels prophesied that with the fall of capitalist production, prostitution, loveless marriages, and oppressive social regulations would also disappear. Engels even deemed some of his fellow socialists too prudish. After reading some uptight German socialist writings, Engels exclaimed, "You'd think people had no sexual organs at all."[84] By the 1900s, Engels and Marx had brought inspiration to outspoken feminists like Alexandra Kollontai, who declared, "Sexuality is a human instinct as natural as hunger or thirst,"[85] and looked forward with joy to the dissolution of the family once the communist revolution continued to unfold.

Once the Bolshevik party achieved power in what had become the Soviet Union, those who wanted a more ascetic communist revolution won out. Vladimir Lenin (1870–1924) had no patience for those who advanced plans for heavy-handed social engineering, but he was also contemptuous of all young, hot-blooded libertines who treated *The Communist Manifesto* like a passport for free love. Lenin was one of the first to judge that it was not sexual oppression that was in the spirit of the bourgeois; instead, "[l]ack of restraint in sexual life is bourgeois: it is a sign of decadence."[86]

Before the emergence of the Soviet Union, none of the socialist utopias of the 19th century lasted long, much less completely changed the way of life for their compatriots. Nonetheless, they pointed toward what would become one of the defining traits of the 20th century: the idea that the personal and the political are completely interconnected. However, if it was in the best interests of governments and nations to strictly police their people's sexuality, those on the ground were motivated to reach out and try to change not just the political actions of governments, but the attitudes and cultures of entire nations. History after the Long Nineteenth Century has seen totalitarian attempts to reengineer everyday life, including sex, for entire populations in ways only Plato or the most ambitious 19th-century sexologist could have imagined. Yet it has also seen people acting in concert to change laws as well as minds.

Epilogue: The Thaw

In 2005, a Danish man with cerebral palsy, Torben Hansen, petitioned his government to have state benefits directed toward providing him with a prostitute. Hansen argued that his disability kept him from traveling to brothels, and the added expense of having prostitutes come to his home should be covered by local funds used to compensate the disabled for day-to-day expenses related to their disability. In Hansen's words, "It's unfair to deny people with disabilities the right to a sex life." Hansen's case drew criticism even from national Danish politicians like Kristen Brosboel, who countered, "Obviously I recognize that he has a problem that people without a disability may not have—but I disagree with the fact that we should support his visits with a prostitute with tax money." This scenario reveals much about sex in the West at the dawn of the new millennium. In his petition, Hansen echoed Enlightenment notions of rights and the ancient assumption that access to sex through prostitution is a necessary facet of society, but opposition to his arguments is not being voiced in the form of traditional religious moral objections.[1] So the history of sex in the West from the end of the Long Nineteenth Century to the 2000s is hardly the simple story of sexual liberation.

One of the more grim stories about the promise of radical sexual freedom becoming something else entirely involves of how the communist revolution unfolded in the Soviet Union. Although once upon a time communism drew homosexual and feminist members by promising to completely revolutionize the family and sexual morality, under Stalin such notions were tossed aside. Homosexuality became a symptom of bourgeois corruption, of the degenerate state of the aristocracy, or the warped psychology of the Fascist—or all of the above, depending on the writer. The Soviet writer and passionate communist Maxim Gorky went so far as to declare, "Destroy the homosexuals—Fascism will disappear."[2] Russia after the Bolshevik Revolution had legalized both homosexuality and abortion. With Stalin in charge, the Soviet Union passed a law punishing male homosexuality with prison time and the Soviet medical establishment officially proclaimed that homosexuality was caused by the "moral decadence of the bourgeoisie," not any biological factors. Abortion was outlawed in 1936, ostensibly because the Soviet Union's birth rate was falling, yet the new law did nothing to reverse the trend.[3] The same year, divorce, which was made a simple procedure after the Bolshevik Revolution, was made much more complicated.

Ironically, even though they were rabid ideological enemies, fascism took a similar path to Stalinist communism in regulating sex, even if the aims and the language were vastly different. Fascism was often advertised as a "third way" between capitalist parliamentary democracy and communism. It promised to harness capitalism to the goals of the State instead of leaving the nation at the mercy of self-interested plutocrats, while defending workers without demanding that they sacrifice all their earnings for the good of the community. Fascists also promised salvation from the damage done by radical socialists and the women's rights movements, in the form of a return to a world where gender roles were obvious and plainly defined; loyalty to family, nation, and race were respected and rewarded; and the streets were purged of smut and perversion. Benito Mussolini steered the Italian government to discourage women's work, especially in offices, and to outlaw homosexuality, abortion, and contraception. A reactionary French politician before World War II who refused to join a Fascist party nonetheless praised Adolf Hitler and Mussolini, explaining, "One day Hitler and Mussolini woke up and said, 'Honestly, the scandal has gone on long enough; the streets are dirty and smell bad; we need a radical cleansing'"[4]

Whether they demanded their people follow strict sexual rules for the revolution or for nation and race, the underlying thesis of fascism was not all that different from Stalin's Soviet Union. Still, no regime has gone to quite the same extremes as the Nazis in regulating bodies for the sake of their ideals. The Nazis were the first to put eugenics extensively into practice. Every German doctor was expected to report patients who were "ideal" for sterilization. The Law for the Prevention of Hereditarily Diseased Offspring led to the sterilization of 400,000 individuals, mostly those diagnosed as "feebleminded," between 1934 and 1939. Also the Nazis offered loans to married men if their wives would agree to stop working outside the home, and as an added incentive the loan principal was to be reduced by 25 percent for each child born. By the spring of 1936, over 500,000 loans had been granted.[5] Like other fascists, the Nazis were also determined to purge Germany and Austria of smut. An early victim of this campaign was Magnus Hirschfeld, whose library at the Institute for Sexual Research was ransacked and its books and collection of sexual curios burned. Hirschfeld would die in exile in Paris by 1935.

Race was more of an obsession among the Nazis than in any other fascist country. The Nuremberg Laws, passed in 1935 just two years after the Nazi Party came to power, prohibited not only marriage between Jews and Germans, but sexual relations, and barred Jews from employing German women under the age of 45. That Germany became the cradle of both the gay rights movement and one of the most repressive regimes in history is a warning for those who would place faith in any kind of progress. Nazi science theorized that homosexuality was caused by a biological flaw—Himmler had even commissioned a Danish SS doctor, Carl Vaernet, to research a cure for homosexuality[6]—but Nazi policy still targeted both female and male homosexuality with venom. Lesbians could be arrested and sent to concentration camps, although they were relatively few in number. Overall homosexuals were still a minority in concentration camps compared to "race enemies," but an estimated 15,000 homosexuals may have died in the camps.[7]

Outside fascist and communist Europe, parliamentary democracies—including those that kept a monarch as a figurehead, like Britain and the Scandinavian countries—had sprung up or had been cemented in the wake of World War I. While these countries had their share of reactionary politicians, their governments were too weak and divided to even begin to enforce the kind of unrelenting control over their people's private lives that the fascist countries and the Soviet Union took for granted, whether or not they felt the urge. Instead of attempting to control sex through the brute force of law, these countries in the main attempted control through knowledge. In Sweden, Britain, and elsewhere, the government established institutions for the research of sexual issues and funded the development of educational materials on sex, fertility, and birth control that were distributed to the general public.

The Bolsheviks were not totally off-base when they accused these capitalist countries of letting "decadence" thrive. As always, vice is profitable, and urban centers like Paris, London, and, most famously, Berlin under the Weimar Republic during the 1920s were laboratories for daring innovations in pornographic literature and films, activist organizations and publications for sexual minorities, and bars, nightclubs, theaters, and brothels catering to countless sexual preferences and fetishes.[8] A brand-new media for offering erotic images was also coming into its own. In 1896, just two years after the appearance of the first motion pictures, the very first pornographic film known to history, *Le Bain* ("The Bath"), had been screened. To be sure, there were attempts to shut down these experiments in selling sex or offering personal freedom, but the vague laws against obscenity and gross indecency were usually not up for the job.

Sometimes the public was, for all that. A play by the Austrian Arthur Schnitzler, *Reigen*, consisted of ten dialogues where various couples were featured chatting before and after the sexual act, which was simply represented by drawing down the curtain for six seconds, during which the audience was exposed to a brief waltz or the sound of a train. Despite the discretion surrounding the sex act itself, the play instantly became controversial. In Vienna, a mob greeted the performance by using fire hydrants to flood the theater. In Berlin, anti–Semitic thugs, denouncing the play as yet another Jewish plot to subvert German morals, threw stink bombs on the stage.[9] Nonetheless, the cities offered a refuge from the more conservative rural areas. A lesbian who lived in Paris as an artist in the 1930s claims, "It wasn't easy to live freely as a homosexual at that time, the way I did, because I was in an artistic world where it was very common. The artists really didn't give a damn about it and in fact considered it a sign of originality."[10]

The future of sex in Europe was pushed toward liberation by the conclusion of World War II. Nazi Germany was not only defeated in war, but the detailed news of the staggering horrors that Hitler's regime committed in its quest for national and racial purity drove its ideology underground and completely blackened the very word "eugenics." The totalitarian answer to sexuality persisted in the Soviet Union and the last outposts of fascism such as Francisco Franco's Spain, but the most notorious and catastrophic was the regime of the communist dictator Nicolae Ceaușescu. Deciding that his country needed to increase its population by millions, Ceaușescu outlawed abortion and all modern forms of contraception while offering the title of "Heroine Mother" to any woman who bore ten or more children. Romanian women, who were aware that the quality of life in Romania was falling, had other ideas. Although 1967 saw a massive population boom as a result of Ceaușescu's policies—a boom that would push Romania's resources to the limit—Romania would also experience a wave of deaths caused by illegal abortions.

In a sharp contrast, for much of Europe the appearance of the birth control pill on the market heralded a new era, when heterosexual sex was finally and truly divorced from reproduction. Whether or not this alone triggered a change, the 1960s and early 1970s did see a series of events suggesting that the tide had in some way turned. The obscenity trial over the publication of *Lady Chatterley's Lover* in 1959 greatly expanded notions of what was legally fit to print in Britain. Denmark became the first country to completely decriminalize pornography and was the host country for the first porn fair. Lesbian activists in France burst from the studio audience at a radio station and disrupted a talk show where the theme was "That Painful Problem, Homosexuality." Even the Communist government of West Germany, although it had inherited the Stalinist distrust of sex, repealed its sodomy law in 1969.

The decades since the "wild '60s" have seen a backlash against such efforts, or perhaps more accurately a complex dance with seemingly countless steps forward and steps back. The spread of HIV/AIDS did much to damper optimism that some magnificent utopia of free love was in the making. Also, beginning in the 1970s feminists began to look back and ask how much the sexual liberation movements of the later 20th century had really been for women's benefit. A resurgence in conservatism sought to target the "permissive society," encompassing Margaret Thatcher and her government's paranoia over sleazy B-movies and homosexual infiltration of the educational system in Britain. Since then, there has been a revival of religious fundamentalism in locales from Israel to the American Midwest and the more sex-obsessed Vatican of Pope Benedict XVI. In Eastern Europe, the former countries of the Soviet Union have become more openly opposed to the influences of international feminism and gay rights, glimpsing in both the sinister shadows of threatening Westernization and economic domination by the United States and the European Union.

Naturally, it is easy for advocates of sexual freedom to be gloomy, but here and there are reasons for them to remain hopeful. The end of the 20th century also saw the liberalization of laws regulating divorce and abortion. Even the Republic of Ireland, which long resisted legalized divorce, repealed its own constitutional amendment forbidding divorce under any circumstances in 1995. While in 2007 two gay rights activists were savagely attacked during a march in Moscow and were arrested by the same police who willfully overlooked their attackers, Turkey in 2003 became the first Muslim majority country to host a gay pride march. However, there is the nagging question of what "sexual progress" or "sexual freedom" *is*. By 2009, Sweden, Norway, and Iceland had all outlawed prostitution, albeit by criminalizing the johns without punishing the prostitutes themselves. The move's supporters praised it as ensuring true sexual freedom for women, who are coerced at least by circumstance into sex work. At the same time, its critics have suggested that such laws merely marked a return to older forms of intrusive (and ultimately ineffective and counterproductive) moral control, only this time justified with the latest humanitarian and feminist rhetoric.

The war on sex does not always have clear battle lines, as in Scandinavia's case, and there are no signs of a permanent treaty, especially as long as a tremendous gap remains between the ideals of intellectuals, religious leaders, and politicians and the actual practices and behaviors of the great mass of human beings. The ascension of a politicized Christian and Islamic authoritarianism that is able to effectively engage with modern technology and ideas even as it rejects modernity, the ability of the Internet to bring together entire communities based around sexual identities or just preferences, the creeping revival of fascism in Eastern Europe, and the revolutionary spread of same-sex marriage on a global scale all suggest, at the least, that the story told in this book has no clear ending—and almost certainly never will.

With nearly 4,000 years of the history of sex in the West to look back on, can we answer the question, "What is the problem with sex?" Well, maybe not to everyone's satisfaction. To a strong believer in sexual freedom, the mentality of those who want society and the government to keep watch over the bedroom may seem completely alien (although, to be fair, some loud advocates of legalized prostitution, nonmarital sex, and kinky intercourse might seem like savage anarchists to the more conservative). Still, both sides can agree that the problem is that sex, like it or not, overshadows seemingly all aspects of human experience—not simply the personal and moral, but the political, the economic, and the spiritual. It is too ensnared in questions of biological reproduction, social order, and, as both the Marquis de Sade and Andrea Dworkin realized in their own ways, power to be treated lightly as a purely private affair. What does all of this mean for the future? The only sure thing is that history is not kind enough to allow us confidence in any kind of march toward perfect freedom or any lasting break in the war.

Chapter Notes

Introduction

1. Jerry Falwell, Interview, Public Broadcasting Station, "Assault on Gay America: The Life and Death of Billy Jack Gaither," http://www.pbs.org/wgbh/pages/frontline/shows/assault/interviews/falwell.html, accessed May 20, 2011.
2. Quoted in Robert S. McElvaine, *Grand Theft Jesus: The Hijacking of Religion in America,* 2nd ed. (New York: Three Rivers Press, 2009), 35.
3. Michel Foucault, *History of Sexuality, Vol. 1: An Introduction,* trans. Robert Hurley (New York: Pantheon, 1978), 8–9.
4. Timothy Taylor, *The Prehistory of Sexuality: Four Million Years of Human Sexual Culture* (New York: Bantam, 1997).
5. See, for example, Mark Halperin, *How to Do the History of Homosexuality* (Chicago: University of Chicago Press, 2004).
6. Helmut Puff, *Sodomy in Reformation Germany and Switzerland, 1400–1600* (Chicago: University of Chicago Press, 2003), 7.

Chapter I

1. Lamentations 3:40.
2. Leviticus 11; Deuteronomy 14: 3–21.
3. Leviticus 12–14.
4. *Ibid.*, 5:1–13.
5. *Ibid.*, 15.
6. *Ibid.*, 20.
7. *Ibid.*, 20:26.
8. Hyam Maccoby, *Ritual and Morality* (Cambridge: Cambridge University Press, 1999), 194.
9. Leviticus 26.
10. Song of Songs 5:5–9.
11. Genesis 19:8.
12. Tikva Frymer-Kensky, "Law and Philosophy: The Case of Sex in the Bible," in *Women in the Hebrew Bible,* ed. Alice Bach (New York: Routledge, 1999), 295.
13. Genesis 2:24.
14. Proverbs 5:17.
15. Deuteronomy 22:28–29.
16. *Ibid.*, 22:21.
17. Phyllis A. Bird, *Missing Persons and Mistaken Identities: Women and Gender in Ancient Israel* (Minneapolis: Fortress Press, 1997), 23–24.
18. 1 Samuel 1:2.
19. Numbers 25:6.
20. Ezra 9:2–3.
21. Proverbs 6:17–18.
22. Leviticus 18:19, 18:26.
23. Deuteronomy 13:16.
24. Richard Elliot Friedman, *Commentary on the Torah,* Vol. 2 (San Francisco: HarperCollins, 2001), 377; Leviticus 18:22n.
25. Steven Greenberg, *Wrestling with God and Men: Homosexuality in the Jewish Tradition* (Madison: University of Wisconsin Press, 2005), 205–9.
26. Saul M. Olwyn, "'And with a Male You Shall Not Lie the Lying down of a Woman': On the Meaning and Significance of Leviticus 18:22 and 20:13," *Journal of the History of Sexuality* 5 (1994): 187–90.
27. Genesis 18:16–19:29.
28. Judges 19:22–30.
29. Greenberg, 65, n7.
30. *Ibid.*, 68–90.
31. Babylonian Talmud, Sukkah 6:130.
32. Tom Horner, *Jonathan Loved David: Homosexuality in Biblical Times* (Philadelphia: Westminster Press, 1978).
33. Steven L. McKenzie, *King David* (Oxford: Oxford University Press, 2000), 85–86.
34. Greenberg, 82.
35. Chaim Rapaport, *Judaism and Homosexuality, An Authentic Orthodox View* (Portland, OR: Valentine Mitchell, 2004), 16.
36. Martii Nissinen, *Homoeroticism in the Biblical World: A Historical Perspective* (Minneapolis: Fortress Press, 1998), 53.
37. For this argument, see, for example, Louis Crompton, *Homosexuality and Civilization* (Cambridge: Harvard University Press, 2003), 39–43; Bruce Gerig, "The Levitical Ban: The Final Verdict," http://epistle.us/hbarticles/leviticus6.html, accessed December 5, 2013; and John Boswell, *Christianity, Social Tolerance and Homosexuality: Gay People in Western Europe from the Beginning of the Christian Era to the Fourteenth Century* (Chicago: Chicago University Press, 1980), 89–103.
38. Mary Boyce, *A History of Zoroastrianism,* Vol. 2 (Leiden: E.J. Brill, 1982), 1–3.
39. Isaiah 45:1.
40. Segal, 198–199.
41. Avestas, Vendidad, 8.5.32.
42. *Ibid.*, 8.5.26–27.
43. Richard N. Frye, ed., *Rivayat-i Hemit-i Ašawahistan, A Study in Zoroastrian Law,* trans. Nezhat Safa-Isfehani (Cambridge: Harvard University Press, 1980).
44. Jamsheed K. Choksy, *Purity and Pollution in Zoroastrianism, Triumph over Evil* (Austin: University of Texas Press, 1989), 92–93.
45. Christie Davies, "Sexual Taboos and Social Boundaries," *American Journal of Sociology* 87, 5 (1982): 1037–39.
46. "But virtually all 'mainline' scholars date the finalization of the Torah, prophets, and historical books no earlier than the Persian period..."; quoted from John Joseph Collins, *The*

Bible after Babel: Historical Criticism in a Postmodern Age (Grand Rapids: Eerdmans, 2005), 33.
47. Bird, *Missing Persons*, 37.
48. Genesis 1:27.
49. Ibid., 2–3.
50. Ibid., 3:18.
51. 1 Corinthians 11:7–9.
52. Genesis 3:16.
53. Proverbs 31:10–31.
54. Ibid., 23:27.
55. 1 Kings 22:38.
56. Hosea 1:2.
57. Ezekiel 16:15.
58. James Maxwell Miller, *A History of Ancient Israel and Judah* (Philadelphia: Westminster Press, 1986), 93.
59. Judith.
60. Judges 4:18–22.
61. 1 Kings 17:31–33.
62. Exodus 20:17.
63. Genesis 19.
64. Judges 19.
65. Exodus 22:15–16.
66. Tikva Frymer-Kensky, 298.
67. Genesis 34:7.
68. Ibid., 34:31.
69. Deuteronomy 22:13–21.
70. Ibid., 22:21.
71. Numbers 5:11–29.
72. Leviticus 20:10; Deuteronomy 22:23–27.
73. Proverbs 6:23–35.
74. Leviticus 18:26–28.
75. Bird 1997, 51.

Chapter II

1. BBC News, "Bisexual Alexander Angers Greeks," November 22, 2004.
2. This interpretation, called the "constructionist" view, has been utilized by a large number of scholars, but is probably best laid out in David M. Halperin, *One Hundred Years of Homosexuality and Other Essays on Greek Love* (New York: Routledge, 1990) and Jack Winkler, *The Constraints of Desire: The Anthropology of Sex and Gender in Ancient Greece* (New York: Routledge, 1990). Michael Dover, *Greek Homosexuality* (Cambridge: Harvard University Press, 1978); Craig A. Williams, *Roman Homosexuality: Ideologies of Masculinity in Classical Antiquity* (Oxford: Oxford University Press, 1999); and Marilyn B. Skinner, *Sexuality in Greek and Roman Culture* (Malden, MA: Blackwell, 2005) are also useful for understanding "constructionist" arguments as they connect to classical history, but are easier on the eyes of non-academic readers than Halperin and Winkler.
3. Again, the literature is too vast to do justice here. However, for good starting points, see the introduction to Thomas Hubbard, ed., *Homosexuality in Greece and Rome: A Sourcebook* (Berkeley: University of California Press, 2003); Thomas Hubbard, "Popular Perceptions of Elite Homosexuality in Classical Athens," *Arion* 6 (1991): 48–78; Amy Richlin, "Not Before Homosexuality: The Materiality of the Cinaedus and the Roman Law against Love between Men" *Journal of the History of Sexuality* 3, no. 4 (1993): 523–73; Daniel Cohen, *Law, Sexuality, and Society* (Cambridge: Cambridge University Press, 1991); and Edward E. Cohen, *The Athenian Nation* (Princeton: Princeton University Press, 2000), 155–91.
4. Eva Cantarella, *Pandora's Daughters: The Role and Status of Women in Greek and Roman Antiquity* (Baltimore: John Hopkins University, 1987), 141.
5. Plato, *Symposium,* 182a.
6. Plato, *Republic,* 1.330D–331B.
7. Isokrates, 8.120.
8. Robert Garland, *Religion and the Greeks* (Boston: Duckworth Publishers, 2001), 4.
9. Jon D. Mikelson, *Athenian Popular Religion* (Chapel Hill: University of North Carolina Press, 1983), 18–26.
10. Hesiod, *Works and Days,* 248–62.
11. Homer, *Odyssey,* 1.65–67.
12. Lycophron, *Alexandria,* 360.
13. Pindar, *Pythian Odes,* 2.
14. Garland, 2001, 88–91.
15. Iamblichus, *On The Pythagorean Life,* 209–10.
16. *Odyssey,* trans. Rodney Merrill (Ann Arbor: University of Michigan Press, 2002), 4.260–264.
17. *Iliad,* 3.39.
18. *Homeric Hymns,* 5.6–43.
19. Ibid., trans. Diane J. Rayor (Berkeley: University of California Press, 2004), 5.45–201.
20. Skinner, 29.
21. *Iliad,* 3.395–412.
22. Ibid., 3.428–29.
23. *Odyssey,* 8.266–366.
24. Ibid., l.356–59.
25. Ibid., 1.360–61.
26. Robert Garland, *Daily Life in Ancient Greece* (New York: Greenwood Press), 47.
27. Hesiod, *Works and Days,* trans. Hugh Evelyn-White (Mineola, NY: Dover, 2006), 60–68.
28. Hesiod, *Theogony,* trans. Hugh Evelyn-White (Mineola, NY: Dover, 2006), 589–602.
29. Hesiod, *Works and Days,* 608–12.
30. For a detailed discussion of the Pandora myth and what it may reveal about Hesiod's attitudes, see Patricia Marquardt, "Hesiod's Ambiguous View of Woman," *Classical Philology* 77, no. 4 (1982): 283–91.
31. Sappho, *A Garland: The Poems and Fragments of Sappho,* trans. Jim Powell (New York: Ferrar, Straus, Giroux, 1993), fr. 94.
32. Claude Calame, "Sappho's Group: An Initiation into Womanhood," in *Reading Sappho: Classics and Contemporary Thought,* ed. Ellen Greene (Berkeley: University of California, 1995), 113–24.
33. Judith P. Hallett, "Sappho and Her Social Context: Sense and Sensuality," *Signs* 4 (1979): 447–64.
34. Eva Stehle, "Emotional Sensuality, Poetic Sense: A Response to Hallett on Sappho," *Signs* 4 (1979): 464–71.
35. Ibid., 466.
36. Quoted in Dover, 174.
37. Ovid, *Tristia,* 2.365.
38. Horace, *Epistles,* 1.19.28. This interpretation is controversial, especially among historians who argue that the Romans possessed no concepts—indeed, *could* not conceive any concepts—that even remotely paralleled modern identities such as "gay" or "lesbian." However, for me the likely etymology of *tribas,* which may have been derived from *terere,* meaning "to rub," along with the clear application of the term to Sappho, reveals a Latin terminology of sexual identity. See James L. Butrica "Some Myths and Anomalies in the Study of Roman Sexuality," in *Same-Sex Desire and Love in Greco-Roman Antiquity,* eds. Beert C. Verstraete and Vernon Provencal (London: Routledge, 2006), 239–40.
39. Catullus, 51.
40. For a brief discussion of the translation and the joke's origins, see Holt N. Parker, "Sappho Schoolmistress," *Transactions of the American Philological Foundation* 123 (1993): 309–10.
41. *Aeschylus*, trans. Alan H. Sommerstein (Cambridge: Harvard University Press, 2008), fr. 228.
42. Pindar, *Olympians,* 10.
43. Plato, *Symposium,* 180b.
44. Xenophon, *Symposium,* 8.31.
45. Bernard Sargent, *Homosexuality in Greek Myth* (Boston: Beacon Press, 1984).
46. See William Armstrong Percy, "Reconsiderations about Greek Homosexualities," in *Same-Sex Desire and Love in Greco-Roman Antiquity and in the Classical Tradition of the West,* eds. Beert C. Verstraete, Vernon Provenca, et al. (New York: Harrington Park Press, 2005) and William Armstrong Percy, *Pederasty and Pedagogy in Archaic Greece* (Urbana: University of Illinois Press, 1995).

47. *Iliad,* 20.230–35.
48. Robert Allen, *Classical Origins of Modern Homophobia* (Jefferson, NC: McFarland, 2006), 12.
49. *Strabo,* trans. Horace Leonard Jones (Cambridge: Harvard University Press, 1966–1970), 10.4.21.
50. Aristotle thought so (*Politics,* 1272a12). See also Percy, 69–72.
51. Skinner, 89.
52. *Ibid.,* 93.
53. J. Paul Getty Museum, Malibu, California, 82.AE.53.
54. See Dover, 101–9.
55. Plutarch, *Lycurgus,* 18.2.
56. Alcuin, fr. 1, 64–77.
57. Aristotle, *Athenian Constitution,* 17.2.
58. Thucydides, *History of the Peloponnesian War,* 6.56. Aristotle (*Athenian Constitution*) claims that Harmodios's sister was barred from the festival *because* Harmodios had been labeled as *malakon.* However, it appears that Aristotle confused Thucydides's account with another tradition, especially because a question of the sister's sexual integrity seems much more likely a cause for the revocation of her invitation than a slur against her brother, regardless of how effective an insult it was.
59. The story of Harmodios and Aristogeiton is mentioned throughout Greek history and literature, but the main accounts come from Herodotus, 5.62–65; Theucydides, *History of the Peloponnesian War,* 6.54–59; and Aristotle, *Athenian Constitution,* 17.
60. Thucydides, 6.56.
61. Aeschines, *Against Timarchus,* 40.
62. Plato, *Symposium,* 182d.
63. *Ibid.,* 216d.
64. *Ibid.,* 216–221.
65. Plato, *Protagoras,* 309a.
66. Plato, *Charmides,* 155c.
67. Plato, *Symposium,* 189c–195b.
68. *Ibid.,* 192b.
69. *Ibid.,* 193c.
70. *Aristophanes,* trans. Jeffrey Henderson (Cambridge: Harvard University Press, 1999–2000), *Clouds,* 989–99.
71. *Ibid.,* 1011–13.
72. *Ibid.,* 1020–22.
73. *Ibid.,* 1385.
74. *Ibid.,* 1392.
75. *Ibid.,* 1100–103.
76. Xenophon, *Spartan Constitution,* 2.12–14.
77. *Ibid.,* 2.12.
78. It is worth pointing out, though, that Plato in the *Laws* (837e) does briefly suggest that such a law did exist in Sparta.
79. Plato, *Symposium,* 182b.
80. Athaeneus, *Diapnosophists,* 13.

81. Aeschines, 1.9–11.
82. Theognis, 1063–64.
83. Hubbard, 2003, 3–4.
84. Xenophon, *Memorabilia,* 8.7–11.
85. *Ibid.,* 7–9. Hubbard also makes the suggestion that such hostility may have been motivated in part by the fact that pederasty was, at its core, an aristocratic pastime.
86. Victoria Wohl, *Love among the Ruins: The Erotics of Democracy in Classical Athens* (Princeton: Princeton University Press, 2002), 56.
87. Hubbard, 2003, 21.
88. Aeschines, 1.13.
89. Plato, *Laws,* 636c.
90. Plato, *Laws,* 838e.
91. *Ibid.,* 838d.
92. *Ibid.,* 841c–e.
93. *Ibid.,* 840c.
94. *Ibid.,* 837c.
95. Aristotle, *Politics,* 1272a12.
96. Aristotle, *Nicomachean Ethics,* 8.4.1–2.
97. Hubbard, 2003, 260 152n.
98. Aristotle, *Nicomachean Ethics,* 7.5.3–5, trans. Thomas Hubbard in *Homosexuality in Greece and Rome: A Sourcebook* (Berkeley: University of California Press, 2003).
99. Caelius Aurelianus, *On Chronic Disorders,* 4.9.
100. Procopius, *Secret History,* 16.
101. Hubbard, 2003, 7–8.
102. Aristotle, *Rhetoric,* 1378b.
103. Aeschines, 1.15; Demosthenes, 21.47. See also Daniel Cohen, *Law, Sexuality, and Morality: The Enforcement of Morals in Classical Athens* (Cambridge: Cambridge University Press, 1991), 160–67.
104. Demosthenes, 21.48–9.
105. Deinarkhos, *Demosthenes,* 23.
106. Daniel Cohen, "Sexuality, Violence, and the Law of Hybris," *Greece & Rome* 38 (1991): 171–88.
107. Daniel Cohen, "Law, Society, and Homosexuality in Classical Athens," *Past & Present* 117 (1993).
108. *Ibid.,* 10–12.
109. *Sylloge Inscriptionum Graecorum,* 1218.
110. Plutarch, *Solon,* 8.21.
111. *Ibid.,* 23.1–2.
112. Lysias, 1.33.
113. Demosthenes, 59.85–86; Aeschines, 1.183.
114. Demosthenes, 59.87.
115. *Gortyn Law Code,* 2.3.
116. Aristotle, *Atheninian Pol.,* 59.3.
117. Lysias, 1.
118. Lysias, 3.6; quoted in Michael Gagarin, "Women's Voices in Attic Oratory," in *Making Silence Speak: Women's Voices in Greek Literature and Society,* eds. A.P.M.H. Lardinois and Laura McClure (Princeton: Princeton University Press, 2001), 161–76.
119. Lysias, 3.6–7; Demosthenes, 47.53.
120. Xenophon, *Oeconomicon,* 3.11; quoted in Kenneth James Dover, *Greek Popular Morality in the Time of Plato and Aristotle* (Berkeley: University of California Press, 1974), 96.
121. Isaeus, 10.10.
122. Stephen Hodkinson, "Female Property Ownership and Empowerment in Classical and Hellenistic Sparta," in *Spartan Society,* ed. Thomas Figuiera (Swansea: Classical Press of Wales, 2002), 105; Sarah Pomeroy, *Goddesses, Whores, Wives, and Slaves,* 2nd ed. (New York: Schocken, 1995), 66–67.
123. Allison Glazebrook, "The Bad Girls of Athens: The Image and Function of Hetairai in Judicial Oratory Prostitutes and Courtesans in the Ancient World," in *Prostitutes & Courtesans in the Ancient World,* eds. Christopher A. Faraone and Laura K. McClure (Madison: University of Wisconsin Press, 2006), 128.
124. Skinner, 99–100.
125. Plutarch, *Pericles,* 31.4.
126. Demosthenes, 59.
127. Pomeroy, 91.
128. Aeschines, 1.119.
129. Aeschines, 1.19–21, 29, 32, 40, 73, 193; Demosthenes, 22.21–32, 73.
130. Plato, *Laws,* 8.838a–b.
131. Plutarch, *Sayings of Spartan Women,* 241.3.
132. Plutarch, *Lycurgus,* 15.3–7.
133. Plato, *Republic,* 5.451c–452d, 454d–e, 455c–456b.
134. *Ibid.,* 457c–d.
135. Plato, *Laws,* 6.784e, 8.841d.

Chapter III

1. For a general look at the questions surrounding Alexander the Great's sexuality, see Daniel Ogden, "Alexander's Sex Life," in *Alexander the Great: A New History,* eds. Waldemar Heckel and Lawrence A. Trittle (Chichester: Wiley-Blackwell, 2009) and John Maxwell O'Brien, *Alexander the Great: The Invisible Enemy* (London: Routledge, 2001), 56–59. A more irreverent analysis, but one that does give an overview of the sources, is in *Alexander the Fabulous: The Man Who Brought the World to Its Knees* (New York: Advocate Books, 2004).
2. Athenaeus, 10.435a.
3. Daniel Ogden, *Polygamy, Prostitutes, and Death* (Aberystwyth: Classical Press of Wales, 2000), 231–35.

4. *Ibid.*, 238.
5. Diodorus Siculus, 33.13.
6. Sarah Pomeroy, *Goddesses, Whores, Wives, and Slaves: Women in Classical Antiquity* (New York: Schocken Books, 1975), 146.
7. *Theocritus*, trans. Anna Rist (Chapel Hill: University of North Carolina Press, 1978), 2.81–84.
8. Nossis, 7.718.
9. Theocritus, *Idyll*, 13; Phanocles, *Fragment 1*; Pseudo-Plato, 5.78, 7.99, 7.100, 7.669.
10. *Asclepiades*, 5.207, translated in Hubbard, 2003.
11. Herodas, *Mime*, 6.
12. Paul Oskar Kristeller, *Greek Philosophers of the Hellenistic Age*, trans. Gregory Woods (New York: Columbia University Press, 1991), 62.
13. Epicurus, *The Philosophy of Epicurus: Letters, Doctrines, and Parallel Passages from Lucretius,* trans. George Kleppinger Strodach (Evanston: Northwestern University Press, 1963), 131–32.
14. Will Deming, *Paul on Marriage and Celibacy* (Cambridge: Cambridge University Press, 1995), 50–89.
15. John W. Martens, *One God, One Law: Philo of Alexandria and Greco-Roman Law* (Boston: Brill Academic, 2003), 16.
16. *Digest*, 1.3.2.
17. Diogenes Laertius, *Lives of the Eminent Philosophers*, 32–33, 129–31.
18. *Ibid.*, 6.72.
19. *Ibid.*, 6.94–97.
20. *Ibid.*, 6.69.
21. *Ibid.*, 6.97.
22. F. Gerald Downing, *The Cynics and Christian Origins* (Edinburgh: T&T Clark, 1992), 51–52.
23. Clement of Alexandria, *Paidagogos*, 3.3.
24. Valerius Maximus, *Memorable Deeds and Sayings*, 6.3.9. The claim about Romulus's laws is made in Dionysius of Helicarnassius, 2.25.6. Another reference to the ancient penalty for female adultery is in Aulus Gellius, *Attic Nights*, 10.23.
25. Plutarch, *Romulus*, 22.
26. *Livy*, trans. B.O. Foster (Cambridge: Harvard University Press, 1964), 1.1.
27. Livy, 1.58.
28. Livy's Lucretia specifically uses the Latin *exemplum,* which can be translated into English as "example" or "lesson."
29. Valerie M. Warrior, *The History of Rome, Books 1–5* (Indianapolis: Hackett, 2004), 161n.
30. Augustine, *The City of God*, 1.19.
31. Livy, 3.48.
32. This was, however, probably not even the predominant interpretation of the story. For example, Valerius Maximus finds only the moral of chastity important (6.1.2).
33. Valerie M. Hope, *Roman Death: Death and Dying in Ancient Rome* (London: Continuum, 2009), 57–60.
34. Valerius Maximus, 6.1.3, 6.
35. Cornelus Nepos, 6–7, translated in Robert W. Cape, "Roman Women in the History of Rhetoric and Oratory," in *Listening to Their Voices: The Rhetorical Activities of Historical Women,* ed. Molly Meijer Wertheimer, 127n4.
36. Ellen Macnama, *Everyday Life of the Etruscans* (New York: Putnam's Sons, 1973), 168–69.
37. Valerius Maximus, 6.3.10.
38. Seneca, *Controversies*, 2.7.3, translated in Rebecca Langlands, *Sexual Morality in Ancient Rome* (Cambridge: Cambridge University Press, 2006), 71.
39. Aulius Gellius, 4.12; Livy, *Periochiae,* 14.38.4, Plutarch, *Cato the Elder,* 18; Valerius Maximus, 2.9.4; Plutarch, *Cato the Elder,* 17; and Dionysus, 20.3.
40. Valerius Maximus, 2.9.1–2.
41. The main accounts are in Cicero, *Legates,* 2.3.7; Livy, 39.8–18; and Valerius Maximus, 1.3.1.
42. Livy, 39.8.5–6.
43. J.A. North, *Roman Religion* (Oxford: Oxford University Press, 2000), 63–66.
44. Ulpian, 47.10.15.15. For a discussion, see Thomas A.J. McGinn, *Prostitution, Sexuality, and the Law in Ancient Rome* (Oxford: Oxford University Press, 1998), 331–37, and Jane Gardner, *Women in Roman Law and Society* (Bloomington: Indiana University Press, 1989), 118–19.
45. Gardner, 122–23.
46. Papinian, 48.5.6.1, 48.5.35. Confusingly, the latter excludes male homosexual relationships from the definition from *stuprum*, only to immediately claim the opposite.
47. Ulpian, 25.7.1; Modestinus, 48.5.35.
48. Gardner, 54.
49. Eduardo Volterra, "Per la storia del reato di bigamia in diritto romano," in *Studi in memoria di Umberto Ratti* (Milan: A. Guiffré, 1934), 420.
50. Anthony A. Barrett, *Agrippina: Sex, Power, and Politics in the Early Empire* (New Haven: Yale University Press, 1998), 101–2.
51. Dio Cassius, *History of Rome,* 68.2.4; Suetonius, *Domitian,* 22.
52. Gardner, 83–84.
53. Quoted in Gardner, 58.
54. Martial, 6.7.
55. Anthony Barrett, *Livia* (Boston: Yale University Press, 2002), 21–27.
56. Cicero, *Varretine Orations,* 2.1.24.62.
57. Cicero, *Contra Catalina,* 2.23–4.
58. Cicero, *Pro Caelo,* 13–6.
59. Cicero, *Philippics,* 2.45.
60. Suetonius, *Julius Caesar,* 73.
61. *Ibid.*, 52.
62. Barrett, 24–25.
63. The most detailed but undoubtedly the most exaggerated account of Julia's fall from grace and exile comes from Seneca, *On Kindness,* 6.32.1–2. More grounded accounts are in Suetonius, *Augustus,* 65.2 and 101.3; *Tiberius,* 50.1; and Tacitus, *Annals,* 1.53.1–4. See also Dio Cassius, 55.10.12–14, 13.1, 56.32.4, and Pliny, *Natural History,* 21.9.
64. Which was it? Vellius Patronicus, 2.100.4, claims suicide, while Tacitus, *Annals,* 4.44.3, believes it was an official execution.
65. Suetonius, *Tiberius,* 53; Tacitus, *Annals,* 4.52.
66. Tacitus, *Annals,* 12.26.2.
67. Dio Cassius, 60.8.5.
68. Suetonius, *Domitian,* 17.3.
69. Gardner, 121–31; Treggiari, 37–80.
70. Suetonius, *Augustus,* 34; Dio Cassius, 56.1.2.
71. Dio Cassius, 76.16.4; Tertullian, *Apology,* 4.8.
72. Judith Evans-Grubbs, *Law and Family in Late Antiquity: The Emperor Constantine's Marriage Legislation* (Oxford: Clarendon Press, 1995), 108–12.
73. Plautus, *Curculio*, 1, translated by Henry Thomas Riley in *The Comedies of Plautus* (London: H.G. Bohn, 1852).
74. Halperin, 68.
75. James L. Butrica, "Some Myths and Anomalies in the Study of Roman Homosexuality," in *Same-Sex Desire and Love in Greco-Roman Antiquity,* eds. Beert C. Verstraete and Vernon Provencal (New York: Routledge, 2006), 209–69, is both a good summary and a rebuttal of a number of prevailing scholarly assumptions about female and male homosexuality in late republican and early imperial Rome. See also Amy Richlin's brief critique of Halperin, Winkler, and James Boswell in "Not Before Homosexuality: The Material Reality of the Cinaedus and the Roman Law against Love between Men," *Journal of the History of Sexuality* 3, no. 4 (1993): 528–30.
76. Richlin, 569–71.
77. Craig A. Williams, *Roman Homosexuality* (Oxford: Oxford University Press, 1995), 119–24; Saara Lilja, *Homosexuality in Republican and Augustan Rome* (Helsinki: Societas Scientiarum Fennica, 1983), 112–21.

78. Valerius Maximus, 6.1.7.
79. Livy, 8.28; Dionysius, 16.5; Valerius Maximus, 6.l.9. Although all three accounts share most of the basic details, they differ drastically in the names of the two men involved.
80. F.X. Ryan "The *Lex Scantinia* and the Prosecution of Censors and Aediles," *Classical Philology* 89, no. 2 (1994): 159–62.
81. Suetonius, *Domitian* 8.
82. Valerius Maximus, 6.1.10.
83. Suetonius, *Domitian,* 1.
84. Cicero, *Philippics,* 2.45, translated in Hibbert, 1997.
85. Celsus, *On the True Doctrine: A Discourse against the Christians,* trans. R. Joseph Hoffmann (Oxford: Oxford University Press, 1987), 3.36.
86. Scriptores Historiae Augustae, 14.6.
87. Royston Lambert, *Beloved and God: The Story of Hadrian and Antinous* (New York: Viking, 1984).
88. It should be noted, though, that there were rumors that Antinous had actually sacrificed himself as part of a ritual to secure his lover's well-being. Such tales are strangely reminiscent of the most bizarre conspiratorial speculations surrounding Princess Diana's death. See Dio Cassius, 69.11.2–4.
89. Priapea, 35, trans. and ed. Leonard C. Smithers and Richard Burton (Athens: Erotika Biblion Society, 1890). The language has been slightly modernized by the author.
90. Aulus Gellius, 6.12.4–5, translated in Hubbard, 2003.
91. Priapea, 25, trans. and ed. Leonard C. Smithers and Richard Burton (Athens: Erotika Biblion Society, 1890). The language has been slightly modernized by the author.
92. Quoted in Richlin, 549.
93. Catullus, 29, 57.
94. Suetonius, *Julius Caesar,* 73.
95. Williams, 206–9.
96. Butrica, 223.
97. Suetonius, *Galba,* 22. For a discussion of *exoletus,* a complicated term that appears in Suetonius's description of Galba's sexual tastes, see Butrica, 223–36.
98. The central accounts about Elagabalus are in *Scriptores Historiae Augustae,* 15.1–35; Dio Cassius, 79–80; and Herodian, 5.
99. Statius, *Silvae* 2.6. For a discussion, see Butrica, 231–36.
100. Martial, 12.42.
101. Martial, 6.68.
102. For a description, see John Clarke, *Roman Sex* (London: Harry N. Abrams, 2003), 78–91. For an alternative "reading" of the cup than Clarke's and what is presented here, which argues that the two adult men were not equal in status, see Butrica, 237.
103. *Ibid.,* 79.
104. Martial, 1.90, 7.67, 7.70.
105. Winkler, 39; Judith Hallett, "Female Homoeroticism and the Denial of Roman Reality in Latin Literature," in *Roman Sexualities,* eds. James Hallett and Marilyn Skinner (Princeton, NJ: Princeton University, 1997), 255–73.
106. For a full rebuttal of this scholarly view of Roman lesbianism, see Butrica, 238–61.
107. See, for example, Martial, 7.67; Ovid, *The Art of Love,* 2.707–16; pseudo-Lucian, *Amores,* 28; and Seneca, *Controversies,* 1.2.23.
108. One case—the only one in classical Latin literature as far as I know—is mentioned in Seneca, *Controversies,* 1.2.23. Weirdly enough, it is brought up in a roundabout way, in the context of advice on how to discuss obscene topics, not as part of an argument concerning adultery or homosexuality. At any rate, the description does treat a married woman having intercourse with another woman as something other than "true" adultery. This may not have been because same-sex female intercourse did not "count" (especially because in the passage it is suggested that penetration through a dildo was actually involved) but because the real danger of adultery, illegitimate offspring, was not a concern.
109. Martial, 1.1.
110. Ovid, *Metamorphosis,* 9.666–789.
111. Lucian, *Dialogue of the Courtesans,* 7.381.
112. Crompton, 99.
113. Seneca the Younger, *Moral Epistles,* 95.21. Quoted in Budrica, 257, who also suggests that Seneca was describing women penetrating men with dildos.
114. *Ibid.,* 122.7.
115. Epictetus, *Discourses,* 2.10.14–20, translated in Hibbert, 2007.
116. Monsius Rufus, 23, quoted in Niko Huttunen, *Paul and Epictetus on Law: A Comparison* (London: T&T Clark, 2009), 76.
117. Plotinus, *Enneads,* trans. Stephen A. McKenna and B.S. Page (London: Faber, 1957), 3.5.7.
118. Martial, *Epigrams,* trans. James Michie (New York: Random House, 1978), 1.96.
119. Juvenal, 2.36–65. Quoted in Budrica, 265.
120. Caelius Aurelianus, *On Chronic Disorders,* 4.8–9.
121. Firmicus Maternus, *Mathesis,* 5.2.11, quoted in Budrica, 244.
122. Phaedrus, *Fables,* 4.16. For the view that the story has a sympathetic tone, see Budrica, 244–45.
123. Thomas A.J. McGinn, *Prostitution, Sexuality, and the Law in Ancient Rome* (Oxford: Oxford University Press, 1998), 23–64.
124. Painian, *Digest,* 23.2.43–4.
125. Papinian, *Digest,* 48.5.11.
126. Paulus, *Digest,* 23.2.47.
127. Marcellus, *Digest,* 23.2.41.
128. Gaius, *Institutes,* 37.14.7.1, 38.1.38.
129. Alexander Severus, *Codex,* 4.56.1-3.
130. Seneca, *Controversies,* 1.2.
131. Gellius, 4.14.
132. Valerius Maximus, 2.10.8.
133. Plutarch, *Numa,* 10.
134. Augustine, *City of God,* 3.18.
135. Aullus Gellius, *Attican Nights,* 10.6; Livy, *Periochae,* 19; Suetonius, *Tiberius,* 2; Valerius Maximus, 8.1.4.
136. Suetonius, *Augustus,* 31.
137. Suetonius, *Domitian,* 8.
138. Ambrose, *Letters,* 18.11–12.
139. Neal Wood, *Cicero's Social and Political Thought* (Berkeley: University of California Press, 1988), 122–23.
140. Deming, 70–93.
141. Musonius, fr. 14.92.6–9, 94.32–96.8.
142. Seneca, *De Brevitate Vitae,* 3.2, 7.2, 14.2.
143. Sextus, 5.4.
144. Epictetus, *Discourses,* 3.22.67–74.
145. Pseudo-Diogenes, *Cynic Epistles,* 44.
146. A negative but detailed description of the *galli* is in Apulleius, *The Golden Ass,* 8.21–31. A more neutral portrayal is in Lucian, *The Syrian Goddess,* 50–54.
147. Lucian, *The Syrian Goddess,* 60.
148. Plato, *Laws,* 5.740.
149. John M. Riddle, *Contraception and Abortion from the Ancient World to the Renaissance* (Cambridge: Harvard University Press, 1992) and John M. Riddle, *Eve's Herbs: A History of Contraception and Abortion in the West* (Cambridge: Harvard University Press, 1997).
150. Musonius Rufus, fr. 15a. For a discussion, see Keith Hopkins, "A Textual Emendation in a Fragment of Musonius Rufus," *Classical Quarterly* 15 (1965): 72–74.
151. Keith Hopkins, "Contraception in the Roman Empire," *Comparative Studies in Society and History* 8 (1965–1966): 141.
152. Virgil, *Aeneid,* 6.430–49.
153. Alan Bernstein, *The Formation of Hell* (Ithaca: Cornell University Press, 1993), 65–68.
154. Virgil, *Aeneid,* 601–7.

155. Ibid., 607–13.
156. Cicero, *The Republic*, 6.13.
157. Cicero, *Tusculan Disputations*, 1.5.9.
158. Seneca, *Consolation to Marcia*, 19.4–5, translated in *Death in Ancient Rome: A Sourcebook,* ed. Valerie Hope (New York: Routledge, 2007).
159. Plutarch, *On the Delays of Divine Vengeance*, 25–26.
160. Tim Duff, *Plutarch's Lives: Exploring Virtue and Vice* (Oxford: Clarendon University Press, 1999), 95.
161. Bernstein, 79.
162. Plutarch, *On the Delays of Divine Vengeance*, 30–32.

Chapter IV

1. Elias J. Bickerman *The Jews in the Greek World* (Cambridge: Harvard University Press, 1988), 101.
2. 1 Maccabees 1:11–5; 2 Maccabees 4:7–19. All translations of Bible verses are from the New Revised Standard Version.
3. 2 Maccabees 6:1–11.
4. Josephus, *Against Apionem*, 1.22.
5. Bickerman, 225–28.
6. Josephus, *Antiquities of the Jews*, 18.8.29.
7. Philo himself (*Embassy to Gaius*, 28–31) claims that the Jews were brutally prosecuted without provocation by the Greeks. However, Josephus (*Antiquities of the Jews*, 18.8.28) implies that the violence was mutual.
8. Markus Bockmuel, "Natural Law in Second Temple Judaism," *Vetus Testamentum* 45, no. 1 (1995): 39–42.
9. Philo, *On Creation*, 3. All translations of Philo are from Philo Judaeus, *Works,* trans. C.D. Yonge (London: H.G. Bohne, 1854–1890).
10. Philo, *On Allegorical Interpretation*, 3.77.
11. Philo, *On Creation*, 151.
12. Ibid., 50–51.
13. Ibid., 71–73.
14. Philo, *Decalogue*, 121.
15. Philo, *Special Laws*, 3.65–71.
16. Ibid., 3.20.
17. Ibid., 3.29.
18. Ibid., 3.30–31.
19. Ibid., 3.32–33.
20. Ibid., 3.34–36.
21. Ibid., 3.37–42.
22. For a discussion of lesbianism in Philo, see Roy B. Ward, "Why Unnatural? The Traditions behind Romans 1:26–7," *Harvard Theological Review* 90, no. 3 (1997): 263–84, and Holger Szesnat, "Philo and Female Homoeroticism: Philo's Use of *Gunandros* and Recent Work on *Tribades*," *Journal for the Study of Judaism* 30, no. 2 (1999): 140–47.
23. Philo, *On Abraham,* 133–37.
24. Derrick Sherwin Bailey, *Homosexuality and the Western Christian Tradition* (London: Longmans, 1955), 9–28.
25. Mark 7:21.
26. Matthew 5.31–32, 19:9, Mark 10:10–12, Luke 16:18.
27. Matthew 18.8–9. See also Mark 9:42–48.
28. Luke 20:34–36.
29. John 20:25.
30. Matthew 21:31–33.
31. Matthew 5:21–28.
32. Matthew 10:15, Luke 10:12.
33. Matthew 5:22.
34. *Encyclopedia of Homosexuality,* ed. Wayne R. Dynes (New York: Garland, 1990), 2:1093.
35. Matthew 7:1.
36. Romans 1:18–27.
37. Jennifer Knust, *Abandoned to Lust: Sexual Slander and Ancient Christianity* (New York: Columbia University Press, 2006), 56–64.
38. Wisdom of Solomon 14.12.
39. Jubilees 22:20.
40. Testament of Levi 14.1–8.
41. James E. Miller, "The Practices of Romans 1:26: Homosexual or Heterosexual?" *Novum Testamentum* 37, no. 1 (1997): 1–11.
42. See, for example, David L. Balich, "1 Corinthians 7:32–5 and Stoic Debates about Marriage Anxiety and Distraction," *Journal of Biblical Literature* 102, no. 3 (1983): 429–39; F. Gerald Downing, *Cynics, Paul, and the Pauline Churches* (London: Routledge, 1998); Deming, 2004, 105–206.
43. Ward, 263–84.
44. 1 Corinthians 6:9–10.
45. 1 Corinthians 7:25.
46. Romans 7:19.
47. Romans 8:12.
48. Romans 6:13, 19.
49. 1 Corinthians 7:7–9.
50. Deming 2004, 207–19.
51. 1 Corinthians 7:1.
52. 1 Corinthians 7:2.
53. Reidulf K. Molvaer, "St. Paul's Views on Sex According to 1 Corinthians 7:9 and 36–39," *Studia Theologica* 58 (2004): 45–59.
54. 1 Corinthians 7:5–7.
55. 1 Corinthians 7:10–11, 39.
56. 1 Corinthians 7:10–11.
57. 1 Corinthians 7:12–15.
58. 1 Corinthians 7:14.
59. 1 Corinthians 7:16.
60. 1 Corinthians 7:39.
61. Margaret Y. Macdonald, "Early Christian Women Married to Non-Believers," *Sciences religieuses* 19 (1990): 221–34.
62. 1 Corinthians 6.15–18.
63. Galatians 2:16.
64. Romans 7:7.
65. Jouette M. Bassler, "Introduction to 1 Timothy," in *The Harper Collins Study Bible* (1993), 2229.
66. 1 Timothy 1:9–11.
67. 1 Timothy 4:9–16.
68. James 4:4.
69. 1 John 2:15–7.
70. Jude 7.
71. Acts of John 2:241, quoted in Peter Brown, *The Body and Society: Men, Women, and Sexual Renunciation in Early Christianity* (New York: Columbia University Press, 1988), 117.
72. Iranaeus, *Against the Heresies*, 1.28.1.
73. Ibid., 1.24.6, 1.25.4, 1.26.3.
74. Ibid., 1.31.1.
75. Epiphaneus, 26.11.10.
76. Origen, *Commentary on Genesis*.
77. Eusebius, 6.8.2–3.
78. Tertullian, *To My Wife*.
79. Ibid., 1.3.
80. Tertullian, *On The Dress of Women*, 1.1.2.
81. Tertullian, *On The Veiling of Virgins,* 1.2. The translations of Tertullian are from *The Anti-Nicene Fathers,* Vol. 3, eds. Alexander Roberts and James Donaldson (Edinburgh: T&T Clarke, 1873).
82. Ibid., 2.16.
83. *Act of Thomas,* 12, translated by David G. Hunter in *Religions in Late Antiquity in Practice,* ed. Richard Valantasis (Princeton, NJ: Princeton University Press, 2000).
84. Clement of Alexandria, *Miscellanies,* 3.6.45, 3.12.80–81, 3.17.102–3.18.110. All translations of Clement of Alexandria are from Clement of Alexandria, *Works* (Cambridge: Harvard University Press, 1919).
85. Clement of Alexandria, *The Instructor,* 2.10.83.
86. Ibid., 2.90. See also *Miscellanies*, 2.95 and 3.28.
87. Clement of Alexandria, *Miscellanies*, 2.146.
88. Ibid., 3.7.58.
89. Clement of Alexandria, *The Instructor*, 2.10.97.
90. Didascalia, 1:20–21.
91. Justin Martyr, *Apologia*, 1.29.
92. Athenagoras, *Embassy*, 33–34.
93. Tatian, *Oration to the Greeks*, 22.
94. Tertullian, *Exhortation to Chastity*, 9.
95. Tertullian, *On Monogamy*, 1.1, 15.1.
96. The Shepherd, 32.4.
97. Athenagoras, *Embassy*, 33.
98. The Shepherd, 29.1.
99. Athenagoras, *Embassy*, 34.
100. Justin Martyr, *Apologia*, 2.2.

101. Tertullian, *Exhortation of Chastity*, 6.
102. Clement of Alexandria, *Miscellanies*, 2.99.1 and 3.82.3; Justin Martyr, *Dialogue*, 141.4; Tertullian, *To My Wife*, 1.2.2.
103. Anne Llewylyn Barstow, *Married Priests and the Reforming Papacy* (Lewiston, NY: E. Mellen Press, 1983), 21–25.
104. Clement of Alexandria, *The Instructor*, 2.10.86.
105. *Ibid.*, 3.3.3.
106. *Ibid.*, 3.3.20.
107. Tertullian, *Against Marcion*, 1.29.4.
108. Book of Daniel 12.1–10.
109. Book of Enoch 18:10–27:3, 83–90.
110. For a discussion, see Bernstein, 154–78.
111. *Ibid.*, 167–69, 171–72, 185–86.
112. Mark 9:43–48.
113. Matthew 5:21–28.
114. Bernstein, 231–38.
115. Luke 16:19–31.
116. Jude 1:6–7, 2 Peter 2.4.
117. Bernstein, 284.
118. *The Apocryphal New Testament*, ed. and trans. M.R. James (Oxford: Clarendon Press, 1924). There are two extant versions of the *Apocalypse of Peter* that differ significantly, the Ethiopic and Akhmim texts, although the punishments listed remain the same for both versions.
119. Bernstein, 292–93.
120. Apocalypse of Paul, 32, 37–39.
121. *Zōstrianos* in *The Gnostic Scriptures*, ed. Bentley Layton (New York: Anchor Bible Reference Library, 1995), 45–46.
122. Clement of Alexandria, *Miscellanies*, 4.81.2–83.2, Epiphaneus, 26.10.7.
123. Bernstein, 205–27.
124. Origen, *On First Principles*, 1–3.
125. Clement of Alexandria, *The Instructor*, 1.13.
126. Ramsey MacMullen, *Christianizing the Roman Empire* (New Haven: Yale University Press, 1986), 135–36.
127. *Corpus Iuris Civilis*, 5.4.3.
128. *Corpus*, 2.4.18, 9.9.9.
129. For the debate, see Antii Arjivi, *Women and Law in Late Antiquity* (Oxford: Oxford University Press, 1996), 195; Judith Evans-Grubbs, *Law and Family in Late Antiquity: The Emperor Constantine's Marriage Legislation* (Oxford: Oxford University Press, 1995), 102; Joëlle Beaucamp, *Le Statut de la femme á Byzance (4e–7e siècle)*, 1.
130. *Corpus*, 9.9.27.
131. *Sentences*, 5.4.14.
132. *Scriptures*, 4.5, 14.9–10.
133. *Sentences*, 2.26.13.
134. Aurelius Victor, *The Book of the Caesars*, 28.6–7.
135. Evans-Grubbs, 333–6.
136. *Codex Theodosius*, 8.16.1., quoted in Evans-Grubbs, 103.
137. Evans-Grubbs, 123–39.
138. *Codex Theodosius*, 5.26.1.
139. Evans-Grubbs, 186.
140. *Codex Theodosius*, 9.7.2.
141. *Codex Theodosius*, 9.24.2.
142. *Codex Theodosius*, 9.8.1, 4.
143. *Codex Theodosius*, 9.7.1, 9.9.28.
144. Evans-Grubbs, 215–18.
145. Arjava, 196–97.
146. *Codex Theodosius* 9.7.2.
147. *Codex Theodosius*, 3.16.1.
148. Ammianus Marcellinus, 28.1. 30–35, 49–56.
149. Brundage, 1987, 94–96.
150. *Codex Theodosius*, 5.17.8.
151. Evans-Grubbs, 1995, 287–8.
152. *Codex Theodosius*, 1.9.6.
153. *Codex Theodosius*, 9.9.23.
154. *Codex Theodosius*, 15.8.1.
155. Brundage, 1987, 105.
156. *Novels*, 18.1.
157. Bailey, 70.
158. *Codex Theodosius*, 9.7.6.
159. Evagrius, *Historia Ecclesiastica*, 3.39–41.
160. Crompton, 127–29.
161. Pseudo-Lucian, *Affairs of the Heart*, trans. M.D. McLeod (Cambridge: Harvard University Press, 1967).
162. Council of Elvira, 44.
163. Council of Elvira, 18, 27, 33, 65.
164. Brundage, 1987, 99.
165. *Ibid.*, 71.
166. Lactantius, *Divine Institutes*, trans. Mary F. McDonald (Washington, D.C.: Catholic University of America, 1964), 5.19.5–8.
167. *Ibid.*, 6.23.23–30.
168. *Ibid.*, 6.23.26.
169. *Ibid.*, 6.23.33–36.
170. *Ibid.*, 6.23.37–40.
171. Gregory of Nyssa, *On Virginity*, 2.
172. Jerome, *Against Jovinian*, 1.13, 1.26.
173. *Ibid.*, 1.49; quoted in James A. Brundage, *Law, Sex, and Christian Society in Medieval Europe* (Chicago: University of Chicago Press, 1987), 90–91.
174. Ambrose, *On Abraham*, 1.4.25.
175. John Chrysostom, *Homily VIII on Thessalonians*. All translations of John Chrysostom are from Chrysostom, trans. Henry Lamar Crosby (Cambridge: Harvard University Press, 1946–1951).
176. John Chrysostom, *Against the Opponents of Monastic Life*, 3.8.
177. Crompton, 141–42.
178. Chrysostom, *Homily IV on Romans*.
179. Chrysostom, *On Not Marrying Again*.
180. Augustine, *Confessions*, 2.2. All translations of Augustine are from *The Fathers of the Church: Augustine*, trans. Vernon J. Bourke (Washington, D.C.: Catholic University of America Press, 2010).
181. Samuel N.C. Lieu, *Manichaeism in the Later Roman Empire and Medieval China* (Tübingen: Gulde-Druck, 1992), 151–90.
182. Augustine, *City of God*, 14.10.
183. Augustine, *On the Good of Marriage*, 1.
184. Augustine, *Confessions*, 3.8.
185. Stephen Williams, *Diocletian and the Roman Recovery* (Boston: Belknap Press, 1985), 102–14.
186. Gregory of Nyssa, *On Virginity*; quoted in *The Fathers of the Church: Gregory of Nyssa*, trans. Virginia Woods Callahan (Washington, D.C.: Catholic University Press, 2010), 3.3–6.
187. *Ibid.*, 3.6.
188. Methodius, *Symposium*, 8.2; quoted in *Women in Early Christianity: Translations from Greek Texts*, ed. and trans. Patricia Cox Miller (Washington, D.C.: Catholic University of America Press, 2005).
189. *Life of Olympias*, 3, translated in *Pagans and Christians in Late Antiquity: A Sourcebook*, ed. and trans. A.D. Lee (New York: Routledge, 2000).
190. *Ibid*.
191. Arsenius, 28.65.96.
192. Gregory of Tours, *History of the Franks*, trans. Lewis Thrope (New York: Penguin, 1976), 47.
193. *Ibid.*, 44.
194. Rosemary Rader, *Breaking the Boundaries: Male/Female Friendship in Early Christian Communities* (Mahwah, NJ: Paulist Press, 1983), 65.

Chapter V

1. Roger D. Scott, "Malalas, the Secret History, and Justinian's Propaganda," *Dumbarton Oaks Papers* 39 (1985): 104.
2. Procopius, *The Anecdota or Secret History*, trans. H.B. Dewing (Cambridge: Harvard University Press, 1935), 13.8.
3. Malalas, 86.868, quoted and translated in Crompton, 143–44.
4. Georgius Cedrenus, 1:645–46.
5. Crompton, 142–49.
6. *Institutes*, 4.18.4. All translations of Justinian's law codes are translated in *The Civil Law*, trans. S.P. Scott (Cincinnati: Central Trust, 1932).

7. *Novels*, 77.
8. *Novels*, 141.
9. *Novels*, 117.
10. *Novels*, 134.
11. *Novels*, 22.
12. *Codex Justinianus*, 5.17.11–12.
13. *Novels*, 22.
14. *Novels*, 122.
15. *Novels*, 140.
16. Vern Bullough, *Sexual Variance in Society and History* (New York: John Wiley, 1976), 322–23.
17. Brundage, 117–18.
18. *Codex Justinianus*, 9.13.2.
19. *Codex Justinianus*, 9.13.1.
20. *Secret History,* 17.5–6. See also *Buildings,* 1.9.5–10.
21. *Novels,* 14, translated in *The Civil Law, Including the Twelve Tables,* trans. Samuel Parsons Scott (New York: AMS Press, 1973).
22. Donnchadh O'Corráin, *Marriage in Early Ireland* (Dublin: A. Cosgrove, 1985), 24.
23. Huw Price, *Native Law and the Church in Medieval Wales* (London: Clarendon Press, 1993), 89–95.
24. *Ibid.,* 91–92.
25. J.B. Rives, "Introduction" to Tacitus, *Germania,* 21–27.
26. Clarence W. Mendell, *Tacitus: The Man and His Work* (New Haven: Yale University Press, 1957), 216.
27. Rives, 61–62.
28. *Germania,* 19.1.
29. *Ibid.,* 19.1–2.
30. *Ibid.,* 18.1,19.2.
31. *Ibid.,* 12.1.
32. Rives, 174.
33. *Leges Rothair,* 381.
34. Jenny Jochens, *Women in Old Norse Society* (Ithaca: Cornell University Press, 1998), 74–75.
35. P.D. King, *Law and Society in the Visigothic Kingdom* (Cambridge: Cambridge University Press, 1972), 122–58.
36. *Lex Visigothicorum,* 3.5.4.
37. Leges Langobard, *Rothair,* 189; Leges Baiwar, 8.8; *Lex Salicae* 36.1–4; Lex Ribuaria, 39.2–3.R.
38. *Leges Baiwar,* 8.9.
39. *Ibid.,* 8.1–5.
40. *Lex Salicae,* 19.4.
41. *Leges Burgundionum* ,68.1–2.
42. *Leges Baiwarr,* 8.2.3.
43. *Leges Visigothicorum,* 3.4.10–1.
44. *Leges Visigothicorum,* 3.4.12; *Leges Burgundionum,* 44.1.
45. *Leges Rothair,* 196.
46. *Leges Visigothicorum,* 3.4.2; *Leges Rothair,* 196.
47. *Leges Alemanni,* 10.
48. Brundrage 1986, 130–31.
49. Gregory of Tours, 197.
50. *Leges Burgundionum,* 34.1.
51. *Ibid.,* 34.2.
52. *Leges Visigothicorum,* 3.4.17.
53. Lisa Bitel, *Women in Early Medieval Europe, 400–1000* (Cambridge: Cambridge University Press, 2002), 137.
54. *Vita Lazari,* 3.538A–C.
55. Eutathios, *Opusculia,* 245.7–30; 250.22–24, 29–32; 255.30–40.
56. Gregory I, *Dialogues,* 54.3.7.
57. Jo Ann McNamara, *Sisters in Arms* (Cambridge: Harvard University Press, 1996), 151.
58. *Regula Communis,* 1:208–19.
59. McNamara, 148–59.
60. George Cyprian Iston, "Double Monasteries," in *The Catholic Encyclopedia,* Vol. 10 (New York: Robert Appleton, 1911).
61. Carolyn Connor, *Women of Byzantium* (New Haven: Yale University Press, 2004), 167.
62. Iston.
63. Florintinus, *Vita Rusticiculae,* 3.
64. Bede, 4.19.
65. Aldhelm, *On Virginity,* 151–53.
66. Gregory of Tours, 168.
67. C.H. Lawrence, *Medieval Monasticism* (London: Longman, 1984), 110.
68. Patricia Skinner, *Women in Medieval Italian Society* (Upper Saddle River, NJ: Prentice Hall, 1998), 81–82.
69. McNamara, 108.
70. Roswitha, *Abraham,* 74, translation in *The Plays of Roswitha,* ed. and trans. Israel Gollancz (London: Chatto & Windus, 1923).
71. Gregory of Tours, 340.
72. Gregory I, *Dialogues,* 9.3.
73. *History of the Goths,* 92.
74. Gildas, *Letters,* 7.
75. Gregory to Anthelm, April 591, from *The Letters of Gregory the Great,* trans. John R.C. Martin (Toronto: Pontifical Institute of Medieval Studies, 2004).
76. Gregory to Leo of Catana, March 604.
77. Gregory, *Dialogues,* 4.6.
78. Bonface, *Epistles,* 50.
79. Vita Regimii, 42–3.
80. Gregory of Tours, 567–83.
81. Council of Aachen, 2.12.
82. Bede, *Historia Ecclesiastica Anglorum,* 4.25, translated in Bede, *The Ecclesiastical History of the English People,* trans. Bertram Colgrave (Oxford: Oxford University Press, 1999), 220.
83. *Ibid.*
84. Basil of Caesarea, *De renuntiatione saeculi,* 23–24.
85. Rule of Saint Benedict, 22, 29–30.
86. Augustine, *Epistles,* 116.
87. *Regula ad Virginea,* 32.
88. *Ibid.,* 65.
89. *Capitulate missorun generale,* sec. 17.
90. Bullough, 1976, 195.
91. Bede, 223.
92. Cummean, 3.19–21.
93. Gregory of Tours, 4.39.
94. Fredegar Chronici, 4.36.
95. Michael Psellus, *Chronographia,* trans. E.R.A. Sewter (New Haven: Yale University Press, 1953), 6.139.
96. Roswitha, *Gallicanus.*
97. Marc Lauxtermann, "The Erotic Muse," in *Desire and Denial in Byzantium,* ed. Liz James (London: Ashgate, 1999), 169.
98. Hans Georg Beck, *Byzantinishes Erotikon* (n.p., 1986), 120.
99. Bullough, 1994, 62–4.
100. De Ordine, 2.4.12.
101. Leah Lydia Otis, *Prostitution in Medieval Society* (Chicago: University of Chicago Press, 2009), 12–13.
102. Roswitha, *Papnutius,* 102–3.
103. Bullough, 1976, 358.
104. Charles Plummer, *Historia Ecclesiastica gentis Anglorum* (Oxford, 1896), cclvii f.
105. Columban, 16.
106. Bede, 3.1–6.
107. *Of Synodical Cases and Ecclesiastical Discipline,* 2.254.
108. Brundage, 154–63.
109. *Ibid.,* 164–5.
110. Theodore, 1.14.9.
111. Brundage, 165.
112. Theodore, 1.14.4, 2.12.5.
113. John Thomas Noonan, *Contraception: A History of Its Treatment by the Catholic Theologians and Canonists* (Cambridge, MA: Belknap Press, 1986), 159.
114. *Ibid.,* 158–60.
115. *Paris Penitential,* 42.2.
116. Brundage, 165.
117. Theodore, 1.2.9.
118. Columban, B10.
119. *Excerpts,* 8.
120. Bobbio, 39.
121. Theodore, 1.8.3.
122. Theodore, 28.
123. Pierre Payer, *Sex and the Penitentials: The Development of a Sexual Code, 550—1150* (Toronto: University of Toronto Press, 1984), 41.
124. Columban, B3.
125. 10.4, 10.6–7, 10.9.
126. Finnian, 2.
127. Theodore, 1.2.11; Bede, 3.30–32.
128. See, for instance, Bede, 3.23; Theodore, 1.2.12–13; and Decretum, 19.5.
129. Brundage, 167 193f.
130. Quoted in Payer, 20–23.
131. *Ibid.,* 58–59.
132. *Ibid.,* 62–63.
133. *MGH Leges,* 255.
134. *Capitularia,* 1:103.
135. *Capitularia,* 1.298.
136. Otis, 15–6.

137. Astronomer, *Life of Louis*, 2.6., translated in *Charlemagne and Louis the Pious: The Lives by Einhard, Notker, Ermoldus, Thegan, and the Astronomer*, trans. Thomas F.X. Noble (University Park: University of Pennsylvania Press, 2009).

138. Demetrios J. Constantelos, *Byzantine Philanthropy and Social Welfare* (New Brunswick: Rutgers University Press, 1968), 185–221.

139. Brundage, 323.

140. Dion C. Smythe, "Same-Sex Desire," in *Desire and Denial in Byzantium*, ed. Liz James (Aldershot: Ashgate, 1999), 144. See also A.E. Laiou, *Mariage, Amour et Parenté à Byzance aux Xie–XIII3 Siècles*, Travaux et Mémoires Monographies 7 (Paris, 1992), 71–78.

141. John Boswell, *Marriage of Likeness: Same-Sex Unions in Pre-Modern Europe* (London: Fontana, 1995).

142. Smythe, 147.

143. Suzanne Wemple, *Women in Frankish Society: Marriage and the Cloister* (Philadelphia: University of Pennsylvania Press, 1981), 76.

144. Boniface and Lullus, *Briefe*, 169.

145. Wemple, 99.

146. Hincmar, *Epistles*, 22.

147. Isidore of Sevile, *De eccl. Off.*, 2.20.9.

148. Council of Paris, Canon 34.

149. A decree seemingly from Charlemagne and ordering the death penalty for sodomites was a ninth-century forgery by Benedict the Deacon. See Crompton, 159–61.

150. 30.12. All translations of the Qur'an are from the M.M. Pickthall translation (Hyderabad: Government Central Press, 1938).

151. 4.3.

152. 4.24.

153. 70.29–31; 13.5–7; 3.24f.

154. 24.2.

155. Bullough, 1976, 217–18.

156. 24.4.

157. Muhammad ibn Idris al-Shafti'i, *Risala*, 6.122–27, 137–40l, 9.230–32, 197–99.

158. *Ibid.*, 9/70.

159. Everett K. Rowson, "The Categorization of Gender and Sexual Irregularity in Medieval Arabic Vice Lists," in *Body Guards: The Cultural Politics of Ambiguity*, eds. Julia Epstein and Kristina Straub (New York: Routledge, 1991), 66–67.

160. Vern Bullough and Bonne Bullough, *Women and Prostitution* (New York: Prometheus Books, 1987), 71.

161. R.I. Burns, "Socio-economic Structure and Continuity: Medieval Spanish Islam in the Tax Records of Crusader Valencia," in *The Islamic Middle East, 700–1900: Studies in Economic and Social History* (Princeton: Darwin Press, 1981), 268.

162. Bullough, 1987, 216.

163. D. Powers, "Women and Divorce in the Islamic West: Three Cases," *Hawwa* 1 (2003): 29–45.

164. Yossef Rapoport, *Marriage, Money, and Divorce in Medieval Islamic Society* (Cambridge: Cambridge University Press, 2005), 69–89.

165. 14.5–6.

166. B.F. Mussallam, *Sex and Society in Islam: Birth Control before the Nineteenth Century* (Cambridge: Cambridge University Press, 1983), 14–19.

167. *Ibid.*, 30.

168. *Ibid.*, 37–38.

169. 20.4.

170. 24.30.

171. Bullough, 1976, 220–21.

172. Dror Ze'Vi, *Producing Desire: Changing Sexual Discourse in the Ottoman Middle East, 1500–1900* (Berkeley: University of California Press, 2006), 55.

173. 7.81.

174. 4.16.

175. 56.17–18.

176. Ze'vi, 55.

177. Louis Crompton, "Male Love and Islamic Law in Arab Spain," in *Islamic Homosexualities: Culture, History, and Literature*, eds. Stephen O. Murray and Will Roscoe (New York: New York University Press, 1997), 143.

178. Ibn Hazm, *The Ring of the Dove: A Treatise on the Art and Practice of Arab Love*, trans. A.J. Arberry (London: Luzac, 1953), 23, 76.

179. Quoted in Roth, 96.

180. Quoted in Samuel Miklos Stern, *Hispano-Arabic Strophic Poetry* (Oxford: Oxford University Press, 1974), 84.

181. *Divan*, ed. Dov Jaren (Jerusalem, 1966), 305.183.

182. Quoted in Alois Richard Nykl, *Hispano-Arabic Poetry and Its Relations with the Old Provençal Troubadours* (New York: Hispanic Society of America, 1970), 59.

183. Crompton, 1997, 168.

184. *Ibid.*, 151.

185. Michael Gerli, *Medieval Iberia: An Encyclopaedia* (London: Routledge University Press, 2003), 398–99.

186. Ibn Hazm, 229.

187. *Ibid.*, 243.

188. *Encyclopedia of Islam* (Leiden: Brill, 2005), 5:777b.

189. Martin Levey and Safwat S. Souryal, "Galen's *On the Secrets of Women* and *On the Secrets of Men*: A Contribution to the History of Arabic Pharmacology," *Janus* 55 (1968): 210–11.

190. Lois Griffen, *Theory of Profane Love among the Arabs: The Development of the Genre* (New York: New York University Press, 1971), 99.

191. Crompton, 1997, 147–49.

192. Jim Wafer, "Muhammad and Male Homosexuality," in Murray and Roscoe, 156.

Chapter VI

1. See Jacqueline Murray, "Introduction" in *Desire and Discipline*, eds. Jacqueline Murray and Konred Eisenbacher (Toronto: Toronto University Press, 1996).

2. James Brundage, *Medieval Canon Law* (London: Longman, 1995), 70–71.

3. Eve Levin, *Sex and Society in the World of the Orthodox Slavs* (Ithaca: Cornell University Press, 1989), 56–62.

4. Bullough, 1976, 321.

5. Levin, 61–65.

6. *Ibid.*, 297–98.

7. Pierre Payer, *Bridling Desire: Views of Sex in the Later Middle Ages* (Toronto: University of Toronto Press, 1993), 40.

8. Peter Lombard, *Liber Quattuor Sententiarum*, 2.13.7.1.

9. Brundage, 1995, 30–31.

10. *Ibid.*, 182–83.

11. Brundage, 1987, 181–82.

12. *Ibid.*, 191–92.

13. *Ibid.*, 199–214.

14. Jacques Rossiaud, *Medieval Prostitution* (London: Blackwell, 1988), 75–76.

15. Henry Ansgar Kelly, "Bishop, Prioress, and Bawd in the Stews of Southwark," *Speculum* 75 (2000): 344.

16. *Ibid.*, 245.

17. Gratian 27 q. 2 d.p.c. 23; 30 q. 5 c. 4; 32 q. 7 c. 1–10, d.p.c. 16 and 18.

18. Gratian 3 q. 11 d.p.c. 3, 32 q. 5 d.p.c. 22 and q. 6 pr.

19. Gratian 23 q. 5 c. 40; 33 q. 2 c. 9; Brundage, 1987, 248.

20. Gratian 27 q. 2 d.p.c. 26 and 28.

21. Brundage, 1987, 235–42.

22. L.W. Levy, "Accusatorial and Inquisitorial Systems of Criminal Procedure: The Beginnings," in *Freedom and Reform*, eds. H. Hyman and L. Levy (New York: Harper and Row, 1967), 16–54.

23. Brian P. Levack, *The Witch-Hunt in Early Modern Europe*, 2nd ed. (Harlow: Pearson, 1985), 72.

24. Lateran Council of 1215, 51.

25. Lateran Council of 1215, Canon 68.

26. Mark R. Cohen, *Under Crescent and Cross: Jews in the Middle Ages*

(Princeton, NJ: Princeton University Press, 1995), 42.
27. Brundage, 1995, 42–43.
28. James Brundage, "The Church Judges Sexual Crimes," in *The Medieval World* (London: Routledge, 2002), 296–97.
29. William Langland, *Piers Plowman,* A-text, ii. 1.46, B-text, ii, 59, 168–76, iii, 1.129, 34; iv, 167, xv, 129–132, xix, 373; "The Grete Sentence of Curs Expounded," in *Select English Works of John Wyclif,* ed. Arnold, III, 320; Geoffrey Chaucer, *Canterbury Tales,* "The Summoner's Tale."
30. Anne Llewylyn Barstow, *Married Priests and the Reforming Papacy* (Lewiston, NY: E. Mellen Press, 1983), 37.
31. Brundage, 1987, 215.
32. Peter Damian, *Against Intemperate Clerics,* 7.
33. Peter Damian, *Book of Gomorrah,* 145.149.
34. Barstow, 71–76.
35. *Ibid.*, 1, 103.
36. Brundage, 1987, 216.
37. *Ibid.*, 82–83.
38. *Ibid.*, 43.
39. Orderic Vitalis, *Historia Ecclesiastica,* 4.
40. Brundage, 1987, 221.
41. Lambert of Hersfeld, *Annals,* 218.
42. Anonymous of York, 1–2.
43. Quoted in William E. Phipps, *Clerical Celibacy: The Heritage* (New York: Continuum, 2004), 131.
44. Henry of Huntingdon, *Historia Anglorum,* 250–51.
45. James Brundage, "Sin, Crime, and the Pleasures of the Flesh," in *The Medieval World,* eds. Janet Nelson and Peter Linehan (London: Routledge, 2004), 299.
46. Gabriel Le Bras, "Canon Law," in *The Legacy of the Middle Ages,* eds. G.C. Crump and E.F. Jacob (Oxford: Oxford University Press, 1959), 168.
47. Barstow, 181.
48. Guibert of Nogent, *Self and Society in Medieval France,* ed. John F. Benton (Toronto: University of Toronto Press, 1994), 63–68.
49. Anselm, *Oratio,* 4., quoted in Brundage, 1987, 186.
50. Alexander Carpentarius/Angelicus, *Destructorium victorium,* 6.69, quoted in Ruth Mazo Karras, *Common Women: Prostitution and Sexuality in Medieval England* (Oxford: Oxford University Press, 1996), 110.
51. Thomas Laqueur, *Solitary Sex: A Cultural History of Masturbation* (New York: Zone Books, 2003), 93–94.
52. Peter of Poitiers, 18–19.
53. Robert, *Liber poenitentialis,* 55.27–8.
54. Jean Gerson, *Early Works,* ed. and trans. Brian Patrick McGuire, (New York: Paulist Press, 1998), 188.
55. Brundage, 1987, 358.
56. Danielle Jacquart and Claude Alexandre Thomasset, *Sexuality and Medicine in the Middle Ages* (New York: Polity Press, 1988), 218.
57. Helen Rodnite Lemay, "Human Sexuality in 12th to 15th Century Scientific Writings," in *Sexual Practices and the Medieval Church* (New York: Prometheus Books, 1982), 200.
58. John M. Riddle. "Contraception and Early Abortion in the Middle Ages," in *A Handbook to Medieval Sexuality,* eds. James Brundage and Vern Bullough (New York: Garland, 1996), 268–70.
59. Brundage, 1987, 421.
60. Saint Bonaventure, *Commentarium in quattuor libros Sententiarum,* 4.31.2.1, quoted in Brundage, 1987, 424.
61. John Fisher, "Sermon on Psalm 38," in *English Works* (Oxford: Oxford University Press, 2002), 64.
62. Brundage, 1987, 427–28.
63. "The Letter to the God of Love," trans. Thelma S. Fenster in *The Writings of Christine de Pizan,* ed. Charity Cannon Willard (New York: Persea Books, 1994).
64. Thomas Aquinas, *Summa Theologiae,* II–II, 153.2–3. All translations of Aquinas are from Thomas Gilby et al., *Summa theologiae* (New York: McGraw-Hill, 1964–1973).
65. *Ibid.*, II, 154.4.
66. *Ibid.*, II–II, 154.5.
67. *Ibid.*, II–II, 154.2.
68. *Ibid.*, II–II, 154.8.
69. *Ibid.*, II–II, 154.11
70. *Ibid.*, II–II, 154.12.
71. Pius X, *Doctoris Angelici* (29th June 1914).
72. Hada Messia and Alessio Vinci, "Pope's Message Angers Gay Rights Activists," *CNN,* December 23, 2008.
73. Joseph F. O'Callaghan, "Mudejars of Castile and Portugal," in *Muslims Under Christian Rule, 1100–1500,* ed. James M. Powell (Princeton, NJ: Princeton University Press, 1990), 31–32.
74. Mark D. Meyerson, *The Muslims of Valencia in the Age of Fernando and Isabel: Between Coexistence and Crusade* (Berkeley: University of California Press, 1991), 232.
75. Kenneth Stow, *Alienated Minority: The Jews of Medieval Latin Europe* (Cambridge: Harvard University Press, 1998), 206.
76. David Biale, *Eros and the Jews* (Berkeley: University of California Press, 1997), 64.
77. Meir of Rothenburg, *Responsa* (Lemberg, 1860), no. 141.
78. Biale, 74–75.
79. *Ibid.*, 78–80.
80. Maimonides, *Guide,* 3.49, 3.8.
81. *Ibid.*, 93–95.
82. Quoted in *Ibid.*, 101.
83. Gulathingslong, 32.
84. Jan Löfström, *Scandinavian Homosexualities: Essays on Gay and Lesbian Studies* (New York: Psychology Press, 1998),42.
85. O.M. Nøttveit, "The Kidney Dagger as a Symbol of Masculine Identity," *Norwegian Archaeological Review* 39, no. 2 (2006): 146.
86. Gragas, 1:47, 2:17
87. Gragas, 74.
88. Birgit Sawyer and B.T. Sawyer, *Medieval Scandinavia: From Conversion to Reformation, 800–1500* (Minneapolis: University of Minnesota Press, 1993), 173–74.
89. Frostaping, 4.39.
90. Frostaping, 1.10.
91. Frostaping, 11.13–14.
92. Skanske lov, 215–16.
93. Levin, 38.
94. *Ibid.*, 39–41.
95. Kronika Thietmar, 582, 584.
96. Norman Davies, *God's Playground: A History of Poland,* Vol. 1 (New York: Columbia University Press, 1982), 3.
97. Levin, 184.
98. Quoted in Levin, 183.
99. Levin, 182–84.
100. *Ibid.*, 115.
101. *Ibid.*, 117.
102. Natalia Pushkareva, *Women in Russian History*, trans. Eve Levin (Armonk, NY: M.E. Sharpe, 1997), 103.
103. Levin, 108–11.
104. Jan Długosz, *Annals of the Kingdom of Poland,* trans. Martha A. Brozyna in *Gender and Sexuality in the Middle Ages* (Jefferson, NC: McFarland, 2005), 96.
105. Maria Bugocka, *Women in Early Modern Polish Society* (London: Ashgate, 2004), 17.
106. Quoted in Irving Singer, *The Nature of Love* (Cambridge, MA: MIT Press, 1980), 80.
107. William IX, "I Set Myself to Love…," trans. James H. Donalson, colecizj.easyvserver.com/virbooks.htm, accessed November 7, 2011.
108. Quoted in L.T. Topsfield, *Troubadours and Love* (Cambridge: Cambridge University Press, 1975), 22.
109. Quoted in *Ibid.*, 8–13.
110. Quoted in *Ibid.*, 70–71, 104.
111. Quoted in *Ibid.*, 49–52.
112. Quoted in Magda Bogin, *Women Troubadours* (New York: Norton, 1980), 97.
113. Quoted in *Ibid.*, 141.
114. Jean Boutière and Alexander

Schutz, *Biographes des Troubadours* (Paris: Nizet, 1964), 530-35.

115. Nathaniel Smith, "Games Troubadours Play," in *Poetics of Love in the Middle Ages,* eds. Moshé Lazar and Norris J. Lacy (Fairfax, VA: George Mason University Press, 1989), 3-12.

116. Quoted in Bogin, 89.

117. *Ibid.*, 85.

118. Ulrich von Lichtenstein, *Service of Ladies,* trans. J.W. Thomas (Chapel Hill: University of North Carolina Press, 1969).

119. Quoted in *The Comedy of Eros: Medieval French Guides to the Art of Love,* eds. Norman R. Shapiro, James B. Vadsworth, and Betsy Bowden (Urbana-Champaign: University of Illinois Press, 1971), 15.

120. Quoted in *Ibid.*, 32.

121. Quoted in *Ibid.*, 68, 70.

122. Roderick Beaton, *The Medieval Greek Romance* (London: Routledge, 1996), 12.

123. *Ibid.*, 109.

124. Panagiotis A. Agapitos, "The Erotic Bath in the Byzantine Vernacular Romance *Kallimachos and Chysorrhoe,*" *Classica et mediaevalia* 41 (1990): 257-73.

125. Beaton, 26.

126. Bernal de Bonaval, 8, translated in Rip Cohen, *500 Cantigas d'amigo: A Critical Edition* (Porto: Campo das Letras, 2003).

127. Quoted in Benjamin Liu, *Medieval Joke Poetry* (Cambridge: Harvard University Press, 2004), 71.

128. Juan Ruiz, *Book of Good Love,* trans. Elisha Kent Kane (Chapel Hill: University of North Carolina Press, 1968), 75-76.

129. *Ibid.*, 89.

130. *Ibid.*, 840.

131. *Medieval Welsh Poems,* ed. and trans. Joseph Clancy (Dublin: Four Courts, 2002), 281.

132. *Cuckolds, Clerics, and Countrymen: Medieval French Fabliaux,* eds. and trans. John DuVall and Raymond Eichmann (Fayetteville: University of Arkansas Press, 1982), 43-47.

133. Quoted in Jeffrey Richards, *Sex, Dissidence, and Damnation: Minority Groups in the Middle Ages* (London: Psychology Press, 1994), 116.

134. Rossiaud, 3.

135. Andrew McCall, *The Medieval Underworld,* 2nd ed. (New York: Barnes & Noble, 1993), 191.

136. Thomas Aquinas, *Summa Theologia,* 2-2.10.11.

137. Ruth Karras, "Prostitution," in *Handbook to Medieval Sexuality,* eds. Vern L. Bullough and James Brundage (New York: Routledge, 1999), 253.

138. Quoted in Karras 1996, 37-38.

139. Philippe Ariès and Georges Duby, *History of Private Life, Vol. 2: Revelations of the Medieval World,* trans. Arthur Goldhammer (Cambridge, MA: Belknap Press, 1993), 307.

140. Karras, 1996, 95-100.

141. Rossiaud, 41.

142. *Ibid.*, 40-2.

143. Bodleian Library MS. e MUS 229, Oxford.

144. Vern Bullough, *The History of Prostitution* (New Hyde Park, NY: University Books, 1964), 114.

145. Buirlough, 1987, 528.

146. Karras, 1999, 245.

147. Bullough, 1964, 121-22.

148. Dahlbäck, 123-24.

149. Bullough, 527.

150. Fernando Henriques, *Prostitution in Europe and the New World* (London: MacGibbon and Kee, 1968), 48-49.

151. Rossiaud, 44.

152. Vern Bullough and Bonnie Bullough, *Prostitution: An Illustrated Social History* (New York: Crown, 1978), 118.

153. *Ordinaces des rois de France,* 1.65.34, 77, 104.

154. Rossiaud, 56.

155. John Boswell, *Christianity, Social Tolerance, and Homosexuality* (Chicago: University of Chicago, 1980), 255. Boswell's source is translated in 262-64. Interestingly, as Boswell points out, the manuscript adds a contrarian poem that declares, "Nothing is more certain than this, that Venus would / Be devoid of every sweetness if she lacked Ganymede."

156. Michael Rocke, *Forbidden Friendships* (Oxford: Oxford University Press, 1996), 106-7, 165.

157. David Lorenzo Boyd and Ruth Karras, "The Interrogation of a Male Transvestite Prostitute in Fourteenth Century London," *GLQ: A Journal of Lesbian and Gay Studies* 1 (1995): 459-65. The essay includes not only a discussion of the case, but also a translation of the entire transcript.

158. Peter Damian, *Book of Gomorrah,* trans. Pierre J. Payer (Waterloo: Wilfrid Laurier University Press, 1982), 16.

159. For a detailed discussion of how the term "sodomy" evolved in the Middle Ages, see Mark Jordan, *The Invention of Sodomy in Christian Theology* (Chicago: University of Chicago Press, 1998).

160. Michael Rocke, *Forbidden Friendships* (Oxford: Oxford University Press, 1998), 11.

161. Jordan, 95.

162. *Ibid.*, 100.

163. Helen Lemay, "William of Salisbury on Human Sexuality," *Viator* 12 (1981): 178-80.

164. Robert of Flamborough, *Book of Penance,* prologue.

165. Thomas Stehling, *Medieval Latin Poems of Love and Friendship* (New York: Garland, 1984), 57.

166. Michael Goodlich, *The Unmentionable Vice* (Santa Barbara, CA: ABC-CLIO), 46.

167. Paul of Hungary, 209a.

168. Goodlich, 59-60.

169. Quoted in Rocke, 147.

170. Crompton, 2006, 190.

171. Voltaire, *Dictionnaire philosophique,* 79.

172. Quoted in Leila J. Rupp, *Sapphistries: A Global History of Love Between Women* (New York: New York University Press, 1999), 74.

173. Hildegard of Bingen, *Scivias,* trans. Columba Hart and Jane Bishop (Mahwah, NJ: Paulist Press, 1990), 279.

174. Roger Bacon, *Opus maius,* 7.2.1.1.

175. Etienne de Fougères, *Livre de maniers,* 275-81.

176. Dante, *Inferno,* Cantos 15-16.

177. Joseph Pequigney, "Sodomy in Dante's *Inferno* and *Purgatorio,*" *Representations* 36 (1991): 26.

178. Dante, *Purgatorio,* 26.40.

179. Pequigney, 36.

180. Crompton, 210-11.

181. Coulton, 4:700.

182. Ruth Mezo Karras, *Sexuality in Medieval Europe: Do onto Others* (London: Routledge, 2005), 145.

183. Bogin, 137.

184. *Ibid.*, 66-67.

185. Gade, 129.

186. Karras, 2005, 136. For details on the various local laws against sodomy in medieval France, see Crompton, 2006, 197-99.

187. Crompton, 199.

188. Cino de Pistoia, *In Codicum Commentaria,* 1578, 2:546A.

189. Helmut Puff, "Female Sodomy: The Trial of Katherina Herzeldorfer (1477)," *Journal of Medieval and Early Modern Studies* 30 (2000): 59-61.

190. Discussed in Judith Bennett, "'Lesbian-Like' and the Social History of Lesbianisms," *Journal of the History of Sexuality* 9, nos. 1/2 (2000): 18-19.

191. Crompton, 2006, 204.

192. Goodlich, 35.

193. These and other cases are discussed in Crompton, 2006, 201-4.

194. Rocke, 53.

195. *Ibid.*, 24.

196. Crompton, 2006, 183-4.

197. William of Malmesbury, 337.

198. Eadmer of Canterbury, *Life of Anselm,* 64.

199. *Ordericus Vitalis,* 4:189.

200. Eadmer, *History of Recent Events*, 50.
201. Sandy Bardsley, *Women's Roles in the Middle Ages* (Westport, CT: Greenwood Press, 2007), 144.
202. Barbara Hanawalt, *The Ties That Bound: Peasant Families in Medieval England* (Oxford: Oxford University Press, 1986), 194–97.
203. *Hostiensis Golden Summa*, 4; *Palude Sentences*, 4.31.3; Nider, *De Morali lepra*.
204. David Herlihy, *Medieval Households* (Cambridge: Harvard University Press, 1985), 146.
205. Third Day, First Story, *Decameron*.
206. Bartholomew of Exeter, *Penitentiale*, 69.
207. Stephen of Tornai, *Summa*, D. 89 d.p.c. 5 v.
208. Bullough, 1964, 129–30.
209. Quoted in David M. Friedman, *A Mind of Its Own: A Cultural History of the Penis* (New York: Simon & Schuster, 2008), 44.
210. *Aucassin et Nicolette*, trans. Eugene Mason (Cambridge, Ontario: In Paranthesis, 2001).
211. Michael Lambert, *Medieval Heresy* (New York: Holmes and Meier, 1977), 12–23.
212. *Ibid.*, 106–8.
213. *Ibid.*, 81–82.
214. Desmond Sewart, *The Burning of the Vanities, Savonarola and the Borgia Pope* (Phoenix Mill: Sutton, 2006), 116.
215. Lorenzo Polizzoto, *The Elect Nation: The Savonarolan Movement in Florence, 1494–1545* (Oxford: Clarendon, 1994), 31–2.
216. Seward, 124.
217. *Ibid.*, 123–24.
218. *Ibid.*, 122.
219. Polizzoto, 41–42.
220. Girolamo Savonarola, *Selected Writings,* trans. Anne Borelli (New Haven: Yale University Press, 2006), 157–58.
221. Polizzoto, 31.
222. Seward, 171.
223. *Ibid.*, 167–68.
224. *Ibid.*, 174.

Chapter VII

1. Ze'evi, 67.
2. *Ibid.*, 65.
3. Cemal Kafadar, *Between Two Worlds: The Construction of the Ottoman State* (Berkeley, University of California Press, 1995), 202; Ogier Ghislain de Busbecq, *Turkish Letters,* trans. E.M. Forster (Oxford: Oxford University Press, 1968), 203.
4. Uriel Heyd, *Studies in Old Ottoman Criminal Law* (Oxford: Oxford University Press, 1973), 57–58, 63.
5. Madeline C. Zilfi, "'We Don't Get Along': Women and Hul Divorce in the Eighteenth Century," in *Women in the Ottoman Empire,* ed. Madeline C. Zifi (Leiden: Brill, 1997), 269.
6. Majid Khadduri, *Law in the Middle East,* Vol. 1 (Middle East Institute, 1955), 104.
7. Godfrey Goodwin, *The Private World of Ottoman Women* (London: Saqi Books, 1997), 69.
8. Ze'evi, 61.
9. Zilfi, 1997, 273.
10. Leslie Pierce, "Seniority, Sexuality, and Social Order," in Zifi, 1997, 181.
11. Leslie Pierce, *Morality Tales: Law and Gender in the Ottoman Court of Aintab* (Berkeley: University of California Press, 1995), 179.
12. *Ibid.*, 251.
13. Pierce, 1997, 178.
14. Heyd, 57–58, 63, 96–97, 102.
15. Khaled El-Rouayheb, *Before Homosexuality in the Arab-Islamic World 1500–1800* (Chicago: University of Chicago Press, 2005), 26–27.
16. Khaled El-Rouayheb, "The Love of Boys in Arabic Poetry of the Early Ottoman Period, 1500–1800," *Middle Easten Literatures* 8, no. 1 (2005): 3–23.
17. Quoted in Pierce, 1995, 195.
18. Ralph S. Hattox, *Coffee and Coffeehouses: The Origins of a Social Beverage in the Near Middle East* (Seattle: University of Washington Press, 1985), 105.
19. Quoted and translated in El-Rouayheb, 2005, 40.
20. Henry Blount, *A Voyage into the Lavant,* 14.
21. Paul Ricaut, *The Present State of the Ottoman Empire* (New York: Arno Press, 1971), 11–12.
22. *Ibid.*, 27.
23. Ricault, 33.
24. John Cam Hobhouse, *A Journey through Albania and Other Provinces of Turkey in Europe and Asia, to Constantinople* (London, 1817), 262.
25. Arsian Yuzgan, "Homosexuality and Police Terror in Turkey," *Journal of Homosexuality* 24, nos. 3–4 (1993): 160.
26. Pierce, 1997, 177–78.
27. Dr'or Ze'evi, "Hiding Sexuality: The Disappearance of Sexual Discourse in the Late Ottoman Middle East," *Social Analysis* 49, no. 2 (2005): 42–53.
28. Quoted and translated in Ze'evi, 2005, 41.
29. Sema Nilgün Erdoğan, *Sexual Life in Ottoman Society* (Istanbul: Dönence, 1996), 69.
30. Quoted in Leslie Pierce, *The Imperial Harem: Women and Sovereignty in the Ottoman Empire* (Oxford: Oxford University Press, 1993), 91.
31. Goodwin, 131.
32. Busbecq, 231–32.
33. Goodwin, 121.
34. Alev Lytle Croutier, *The Harem: The World Behind the Veil* (New York: Abbeville Press, 1989), 24.
35. *Ibid.*, 103–4.
36. Fanny Davis, *The Ottoman Lady* (Westport, CT: Greenwood Press, 1986), 2.
37. Charles White, *Three Years in Constantinople* , 3.10.
38. M. Çağatay Uluçay, "The Harem in the XVIIIth Century," Akten des Vierundzwanzigsten Internationalen Orientalisten–Kongress, München, 28 August Bis 4 September 1957, 397.
39. Goodwin, 104–5.
40. Lady Mary Montagu, *Turkish Embassy Letters* (Athens, GA: Broadview Press, 1993), 59–60.
41. Busbecq, 117.
42. *Documents and Information about Ottoman Life Woman—I*, 192.
43. *Ibid.*
44. Croutier, 146–47.
45. Elsye Semerdjian, "Sinful Professions: Illegal Occupations of Women in Ottoman Aleppo, Syria," *Hawwa* 1 (2003): 60–85.
46. Marinos Sariyannis, "Prostitution in Ottoman Istanbul Late Sixteenth–Early Eighteenth Century," *Turcica* 40 (2008): 37–39.
47. Quoted in Semerdjan, 72.
48. *Ibid.*, 73.
49. *Ibid.*, 74.
50. *Ibid.*, 71.
51. *Ibid.*, 75.
52. Quoted in Aytu Çakici, "Immoral Earnings: Portraying Prostitutes in Ottoman Turkey," *Illuminating the Dark Side: Evil, Women and the Feminine,* eds. Andrea Ruthven and Gabriela Mádlo (Witney, UK: Interdisciplinary Press, 2010), 279.

Chapter VIII

1. Margo Todd, *Christian Humanism and the Puritan Social Order* (Cambridge: Cambridge University Press, 1987), 22.
2. *Ibid.*, 37–38.
3. *Ibid.*, 36, 38.
4. Martin Luther, *Werke: Kritische Gesamtausgabe. Briefwechsel* (Weimar: Böhlau), 7.40.
5. Martin Luther, *Letters of Spiritual Counsel,* 293. Unless otherwise

noted, all translations of Martin Luther are from *Works,* ed. Jaroslav Pelikan (St. Louis: Concordia, 1955–1986).
6. Johannes Brenz, *Godly Magistrates and Church Order,* trans. and ed. James Estes (Toronto: University of Toronto Press, 2001), 48.
7. Luther, "Lectures on Genesis," in *Works,* 3.255.
8. Quoted in Leah Lydia Otis, *Prostitution in Medieval Society* (Chicago: University of Chicago Press, 1985), 43.
9. Katherine Crawford, *European Sexualities, 1400–1800* (Cambridge: Cambridge University Press, 2007), 86.
10. Quoted and translated in *What Luther Said,* 890.
11. Luther, "On Conjugal Life," 2.276–301.
12. Quoted in *What Luther Says* (St. Louis: Concordia Press, 1959), 889.
13. Brundage, 1986, 556.
14. Jean Calvin, *Institutes,* 2.8.44.
15. Johannes Brenz, *Godly Magistrates and Church Order,* trans. and ed. James Estes (Toronto: University of Toronto Press, 2001).
16. Bruce Gordon, *The Swiss Reformation* (Manchester: Manchester University Press, 2002), 49–59.
17. Erasmus, *Complete Works,* ed. J.K. Sowards (Toronto: University of Toronto Press, 1985), 25.130, 137.
18. Quoted in Steven Ozment, *When Fathers Ruled: Family Life in Reformation Europe* (Cambridge: Harvard University Press, 1983), 7–8.
19. Carlo Cippola, *Before the Industrial Revolution,* 2nd ed. (New York: Norton, 1980), 150; Gordon, 264.
20. Weisner-Hanks, 81.
21. Michael F. Graham, *The Uses of Reform: "Godly Discipline" and Popular Behavior in Scotland and Beyond* (New York: E.J. Brill, 1996), 282–83.
22. Katherine Crawford, *European Sexualities, 1400–1600* (Cambridge: Cambridge University Press, 2007), 169–70.
23. Weisner-Hanks, 74.
24. MacCulloch, 608–11; Weisner-Hanks, 86; Lyndal Roper, "Discipline and Responsibility: Prostitution and the Reformation in Augsburg," *History Workshop* 19 (1985): 15.
25. Quoted in *What Luther Says,* 885.
26. Brundage, 552–53.
27. MacCulloch, 626–27.
28. *Ibid.,* 627.
29. *Ibid.,* 222–23.
30. *Ibid.,* 633.
31. Quoted in *What Luther Said,* 558.
32. Weisner-Hanks, 65.
33. Gordon, 263–64.
34. Weisner-Hanks, 78.
35. *Ibid.,* 79–80.
36. E.P. Thompson, "The Selling of Wives" in *Customs in Common* (London: New Press, 1993).
37. Ozment, 55–56.
38. Roper, 21.
39. Weisner-Hanks, 86.
40. Nils Johan Ringdal, *Love for Sale: A World History of Prostitution* (New York: Grove Press, 1985).
41. Cissie Fairchilds, *Women in Early Modern Europe* (London: Longman, 2007), 167.
42. Alan Haynes, *Sex in Elizabethan England* (Sutton: History Press, 1999), 70.
43. Weisner-Hanks, 85–86.
44. Philip S. Gorski, *The Disciplinary Revolution: Calvinism and the Rise of the State in Early Modern Europe* (Chicago: University of Chicago Press, 2003), 65.
45. Oudot de Dainville, "La Consistoire de Ganges a la Fin du XVIe Siecle," *Revue de L'Eglise de France* 18 (1932): 466.
46. Raymond A. Menzer, *Sin and the Calvinists: Morals Control and the Consistory in the Reformed Tradition* (Kirksville, MO: Truman State University Press, 2002), 72.
47. Graham, 283–84.
48. Crompton, 2006, 363.
49. Wilhelm von Rossen, "Denmark" in *Queer Masculinities, 1550–1800* (New York: Palgrave Macmillan, 2006), 178.
50. Jonas Liliequist, "State Policy, Popular Discourse, and the Silence on Homosexual Acts in Early Modern Sweden," in *Scandinavian Homosexualities: Essays on Gay and Lesbian Studies,* ed. Jan Löfström (New York: Haworth Press, 1998), 16–17.
51. Crawford, 158.
52. Weisner-Hanks, 87.
53. Dirk Jaap Nordam, "Sodomy in the Dutch Republic, 1600–1725," in *The Pursuit of Sodomy: Male Homosexuality in Renaissance and Enlightenment Europe,* eds. Kurt Gerard and Gert Hekma (New York: Routledge, 1989), 209–12.
54. Crompton, 2006, 362.
55. For a brief survey of both cases, see Crompton, 2006, 392–94.
56. Maria R. Boes, "On Trial in Early Modern German," in *Sodomy in Early Modern Europe,* ed. Tom Betteridge (London: Routledge, 2002), 30–34.
57. Susan Dwyer Amussen, *An Ordered Society: Gender and Class in Early Modern England* (London: Basil Blackwell, 1988), 40.
58. Gorski, 20.
59. Weisner-Hanks, 71–72.
60. Robert M. Kingdom, "The Control of Morals in Calvin's Geneva," in *The Social History of the Reformation,* eds. Lawrence P. Buck and Jonathan W. Zophy (Columbus: Ohio State University, 1972), 5–6.
61. *Ibid.,* 10.
62. *Ibid.,* 12.
63. Quoted in Robert M. Kingdom, *Adultery and Divorce in Calvin's Geneva* (Cambridge: Harvard University Press, 1995), 33–34.
64. *Ibid.,* 36.
65. For a description of the case, see *Ibid.,* 31–70.
66. *Ibid.,* 121–23.
67. E. William Monter, "Sodomy and Heresy in Early Modern Switzerland," in *The Gay Past,* eds. Salvatore J. Licata and Robert P. Peterson (Binghamton, NY: Harrington Park Press, 1985), 41–53.
68. Crompton, 326.
69. Bryne Fone, *Homophobia: A History* (New York: Metropolitan Press, 2000), 211–12.
70. *Ibid.,* 213; Crompton, 2006, 324.
71. Christopher Durnston, "Puritan Rule and the Failure of Cultural Revolution, 1645–1660," in *The Culture of English Puritanism, 1560–1700,* eds. Christopher Durston and Jacqueline Eales (New York: Macmillan, 1996), 217.
72. *Ibid.,* 223.
73. Christopher Durnston, *The Family in the English Revolution* (New York: Basil Blackwell, 1989), 12–32.
74. Igor S. Kon, *The Sexual Revolution in Russia,* trans. James Riordan (New York: Free Press, 1995), 16.
75. George Tuberville, *Rude and Barborous Kingdom,* 76.
76. *Ibid.,* 271.
77. Quoted in Paul Bushkovitch, *Religion and Society in Russia: The Sixteenth and Seventeenth Centuries* (New York: Oxford University Press, 1992), 55–56.
78. Levin, 203–4.
79. Sigmund von Herberstein, *Notes upon Russia,* 73–74, 93–95
80. Pushkareva, 34–35.
81. Kon, 17–18.
82. Ozmet, 5.
83. Quoted in Weisner-Hanks, 105.
84. Council of Trent, Session XXIV, Canon X, ed. and trans. J. Waterworth (London: Dolman, 1848).
85. Quoted in MacCulloch, 588.
86. Council of Trent, Decree on Reformation XIV.
87. Weisner-Hanks, 116.
88. MacCulloch, 433, 442.
89. Weisner-Hanks, 106; MacCulloch, 620–21.

90. Mary Elizabeth Perry, *Gender and Disorder in Early Modern Seville* (Princeton, NJ: Princeton University Press, 1990), 109–16.
91. Tomás Sanchez, *On Sacred Marriage*, 9.44.2.8–11.
92. Quoted in James F. Farr, *Authority and Sexuality in Early Modern Burgundy (1550–1730)* (Oxford: Oxford University Press, 1995), 44.
93. Weisner-Hanks, 122.
94. Lisa Vollendorf, *The Lives of Women: A New History of Inquisitional Spain* (Nashville: Vanderbilt University Press, 2005), 93.
95. Allyson M. Poska, *Regulating the People: The Catholic Reformation in Seventeenth Century Spain* (Leiden: Brill, 1998), 101.
96. Weisner-Hanks, 116, 121.
97. Crawford, 148.
98. Scott K. Taylor, *Honor and Violence in Golden Age Spain* (New Haven: Yale University Press, 2008), 196–97.
99. For a description of the play, see Darci L. Strother, *Family Matters: A Study of On- and Off-Stage Marriage and Family Relations in Seventeenth-Century Spain* (New York: Peter Lang, 1999), 68–75.
100. Weisner-Hanks, 124–26.
101. *Ibid.*, 109.
102. Quoted in Alain Saint-Saëns, "'It Is Not A Sin!': Making Love According to the Spaniards in Early Modern Spain," in *Sex and Love in Golden Age Spain* (New York: University Press of the South, 1996),15.
103. Quoted in Luiz Mott, "Crypto-Sodomites in Seventeenth Century Brazil," from *Infamous Desire: Male Homosexuality in Colonial Latin America*, ed. Pete Sigal (Chicago: University of Chicago Press, 2003), 178.
104. Garza Carvajal, *Butterflies Will Burn: Persecuting Sodomites in Early Modern Spain and Mexico* (Austin: University of Texas Press, 2010), 72.
105. Crompton, 2006, 293.
106. E. William Monter, *Frontiers of Heresy: The Spanish Inquisition from the Basque Lands to Sicily* (Cambridge: Cambridge University Press, 1990), 53.
107. Crompton, 2006, 296, 312.
108. Mary Elizabeth Perry, "The Nefarious Sin in Early Modern Seville," in *The Pursuit of Sodomy: Male Homosexuality in Renaissance and Enlightenment Europe,* eds. Kent Gerard and Gert Hekma (New York: Harrington Park Press, 1989), 79.
109. Perry, 1990, 125.
110. Weisner-Hanks, 127.
111. Crompton, 2006, 312.
112. Pierre de Bourdeille de Brantôme, *Lives of Fair and Gallant Ladies,* trans. A.R. Allinson (New York: Liveright, 1933), 33.
113. Faderman, 25–26.
114. Perry, 1990, 126.
115. N.S. Davis, "Sodomy in Early Modern Venice," in Gerard and Hekma, 70.
116. Quoted in Luiz Mott and Aroldo Assunção, "Love's Labors Lost: Five Letters from a Seventeenth-Century Portuguese Sodomite" in Gerard and Hekma, 97.
117. Tom Bettridge, *Sodomy in Early Modern Europe* (Manchester: Manchester University Press, 2002), 72–74.
118. Bullough, 1978, 420.
119. Crompton, 2006, 278–81.
120. Quoted in Georgia Masson, *Queen Christina* (New York: Farrar, Straus, and Giroux, 1968), 186.
121. Pierre de L'Éstoile, *Mémoires-Journaux,* ed. G. Bruner et al. (Paris, 1888), 2:241–42.
122. Katharine B. Crawford, "Love, Sodomy, and Scandal: Controlling the Sexual Reputation of Henri III," *Journal of the History of Sexuality* 12, no. 4 (2003): 513–42.
123. Pierre Chevallier, *Henri III, Roi Shakespearien* (Paris: Fayard, 1985), 433.
124. George Huntston Williams, *The Radical Reformation* (Kirksville, MO: Sixteenth Century Journal Publishers, 1992), 66.
125. Nicholas Davidson, "Atheism in Italy, 1500–1700," in Michael Hunter and David Wootton, *Atheism from the Reformation to the Enlightenment* (Oxford: Clarendon Press, 1992), 69.
126. Lyndal Roper, "Sexual Utopianism in the German Reformation" *Journal of Ecclesiastical History* 42, no. 3 (1991): 399–403.
127. Quoted in Christopher Hill, *The World Turned Upside Down: Radical Ideas during the English Revolution* (London: Penguin, 1972), 190.
128. Christopher Hill, *Milton and the English Revolution* (New York: Penguin, 1979), 313.
129. Samuel Pepys, *Diary,* February 8, 1668.
130. Walter Kendrick, *The Secret Museum: Pornography in Modern Culture* (Berkeley: University of California Press, 1987), 96.
131. Quoted in Bette Talvacchia, *Taking Positions: On the Erotic in Renaissance Culture* (Princeton, NJ: Princeton University Press, 1999), 6.
132. Benjamin Jacob, "Whore, Court, Church, and the Origins of Modern Obscenity," in *Papers Presented at the Third Global Conference on Sex and Sexuality* , 37.
133. P.L. Jacob, *Curiosites de l'Histoire de France: IIe Serie: Proces Celebres* (Paris: Paul Lacroix, 1848), 94.
134. Philippe Ariès, *Centuries of Childhood: A Social History of Family Life*, trans. Robert Baldick (New York: Alfred A. Knopf, 1962), 109–10.
135. Norbert Elias, *The Civilizing Process,* rev. ed. (London: Blackwell, 2000), 142–49.
136. Paul F. Grendler "Printing and Censorship," in *The Cambridge History of Renaissance Philosophy,* eds. Charles Schmitt and Quentin Skinner (Cambridge: Cambridge University Press, 1988), 28, 43–49.
137. Quoted in Cynthia Stollhans, "Michelangelo's Nude Saint Catherine of Alexandria," *Women's Art Journal* 19, no. 1 (1998): 27.
138. James Turner, *Schooling Sex* (Oxford: Oxford University Press, 2003), 20.
139. Aretino, *Dialogues,* trans. Raymond Rosenthal (New York: Ballantine, 1973), 37–38.
140. *Ibid.*, 175.
141. Quoted in David O. Frantz, *Festum Voluptatis: A Study of Renaissance Erotica* (Columbus: Ohio State University Press, 1989), 99.
142. Brantône, 1.14.
143. Ian Frederick Moulton, *Before Pornography: Erotic Writing in Early Modern England* (Oxford: Oxford University Press, 2005), 55.
144. *Gargantua and Pentegruel*, from François Rabelais, *Complete Works*, trans. Donald M. Frame (Berkeley: University of California Press, 1999), 137.
145. Quoted in Tullio Gregory, "Charron's 'Scandalous Book,'" in M. Hunter and D. Wooton, *Atheism from the Reformation to the Enlightenment* (Oxford: Oxford University Press, 1992), 91.
146. Quoted in *Ibid.*, 92.
147. Roger Schlesinger, *The Impact of the New World, 1492–1650* (Wheeling, IL: Harlan Davidson, 1996), 53–54; Walter L. Williams, *Sexual Diversity in Native American Culture* (Boston: Beacon Press, 1986), 135.
148. Louise M. Burkhart, *The Slippery Earth: Nahua–Christian Moral Dialogue in Sixteenth-Century Mexico* (Tucson: University of Arizona Press, 1989), 18, 34–35, 92–131.
149. Quoted in Jorge Cañizares-Esguerra, *Puritan Conquistadors: Iberianizing the Atlantic, 1550–1700* (Stanford: Stanford University Press, 2006), 97.
150. Susan Migden Socolow, *The Women of Colonial Latin America* (Cambridge: Cambridge University Press, 2000), 72–74.

151. Crompton, 2006, 317; Pete Sigal, *Infamous Desire* (Chicago: University of Chicago Press, 2003), 122–23.
152. Quoted in Richard C. Trexler, *Sex and Conquest* (Ithaca: Cornell University Press, 1995), 65.
153. Quoted in Walter L. Williams, *Sexual Diversity in Native American Culture* (Boston: Beacon Press, 1986), 135.
154. Guerra, 53.
155. Quoted in Crompton, 2006, 319.
156. John D'Emilio and Estelle B. Freedman, *Intimate Matters,* 2nd ed. (Chicago: University of Chicago Press, 1997), 7.
157. Baron de Lahontan, *Nouveux Voyages,* 2.143.
158. Richard Bodbeer, *Sexual Revolution in Early America* (Baltimore: John Hopkins University Press, 2002), 164–65, 182–83.
159. Quoted in Karen Anderson, *Chain Her by One Foot* (London: Routledge, 1991), 77.
160. Godbeer, 155–56.
161. Quoted in *Ibid.,* 157.
162. Robert Beverley, *The History and Present State of Virginia,* 3.7.
163. Gary B. Nash, "The Hidden History of Mestizo America," in *Sex, Love, Race: Crossing Boundaries in North American History,* ed. Martha Hodes (New York: New York University Press, 1999), 10.
164. June Namias, *White Captives: Gender and Ethnicity on the American Frontier* (Chapel Hill: University of North Carolina Press, 1993), 91.
165. Godbeer, 167.
166. *Ibid.,* 164.
167. *Complete Writings of Roger Williams,* 6:67, 85.
168. Godbeer, 164.
169. Quoted in D. Chidester, *Christianity: A Global History* (San Francisco: Harper, 2000), 435.
170. D.E. Mungello, *The Great Encounter of China and the West, 1500–1800* (Lanham, MD: Rowman & Littlefield, 1999), 68.
171. Jacques Gernet, *China and the Christian Impact* (Cambridge: Cambridge University Press, 1985), 25–29.
172. Jonathan Spence, *The Memory Palace of Matteo Ricci* (New York: Viking, 1984), 220, 224.
173. Quoted in *Ibid.,* 221.
174. Bret Hinsch, *Passions of the Cut Sleeve: The Male Homosexual Tradition in China* (Berkeley: University of California Press, 1990), 20–22.
175. Quoted in Gernet, 106.
176. Mungello, 41–2.
177. Quoted in Gernet, 191.
178. Spence, 228.
179. C.R. Boser, *The Christian Century in Japan, 1549–1650* (Berkeley: University of California Press, 1967), 11.
180. Quoted in Robert Richard Ellis, "'The Best Thus Far Discovered': The Japanese in the Letters of Francisco Xavier," *Hispanic Review* 71, no. 2 (2003): 162–63.
181. Quoted in Gary Leupp, *Male Colors: The Construction of Homosexuality in Tokugawa Japan* (Berkeley: University of California Press, 1997), 42.
182. Crompton, 2006, 412.
183. Margaret Childs, "Cigo Monogatari: Love Stories or Buddhist Sermons?" *Monumenta Nipponica: Studies in Japanese Culture* 35 (1980): 127–51.
184. Crompton, 421.
185. Tsuneo Watanabe and Jun'ichi Iwata, *The Love of the Samurai: A Thousand Years of Japanese Homosexuality,* trans. D.R. Roberts (London: GMP, 1990), 109.
186. Luepp, 100–4.
187. H.D. Harootunian, *Things Seen and Unseen: Discourse and Ideology in Tokugawa Japan* (Chicago: University of Chicago Press, 1988), 298.
188. Weisner-Hanks, 61.
189. Michael Cooper, ed., *They Came to Japan: An Anthology of European Reports on Japan, 1543–1640* (Berkeley: University of California Press, 1965), 61–62.
190. Translated in George Elison, *Deus Destroyed: The Image of Christianity in Early Modern Japan* (Cambridge: Harvard University Press, 1973), 279.
191. Elison, 305.
192. *Survey of Britain and America,* 1994.
193. Jonathan I. Israel, *Radical Enlightenment* (Oxford: Oxford University Press, 2001), 26.
194. Alexandre Matheron, "Spinoza and Sexuality," in *Feminist Interpretations of Spinoza,* ed. Moira Gatens (University Park: Pennsylvania State University Press, 2009), 91.
195. See *Ibid.,* 87–107.
196. François de la Barre, "On the Equality of the Two Sexes" in *Three Cartesian Feminist Treatises,* trans. Vivian Bosley (Chicago: Chicago University Press, 2002), 82.
197. See *Ibid.,* 26–83.
198. Mary Astell, *A Serious Proposal to the Ladies,* 3.
199. Marquis de Lambert, *Reflexions nouvelles,* 9.
200. Bayle, *Pensées diverses,* 2.25–26.
201. Israel, 2001, 87–90.
202. Joan de Jean, *The Reinvention of Obscenity* (Chicago: University of Chicago Press, 2002), 29.
203. Evelyn Lord, *The Hell-Fire Clubs* (New Haven: Yale University Press, 2008), 9–12.
204. Quoted in *Ibid.,* 7.
205. Margaret Cavendish, *The Convent of Pleasure,* 220.
206. *Ibid.,* 234.

Chapter IX

1. C. Strachey, *The Letters of the Earl of Chesterfield to His Son,* 2.133.
2. Charles-Louis Richard, *Exposition de la doctrine des philosophes modernes* (Lille, 1785), vii.
3. Michel Foucault, *Abnormal: Lectures at the Collège de France, 1974–1975,* eds. Valerio Marchetti and Antonella Salomoni and trans. Graham Burchell (London: Picador, 2004), 222.
4. Roy Porter, "Mixed Feelings: The Enlightenment and Sexuality in Eighteenth-Century Britain," in *Sexuality in Eighteenth-Century Britain,* ed. Paul-Gabriel Boucé (Manchester: Manchester University Press, 1982), 4.
5. Paolo Mattia Doria, *Lettere e ragionamenti,* 2.346.
6. David E. Mungello, "Leibniz's Interpretation of Neo-Confucianism," *Philosophy East and West* 20, no. 1 (1971): 3–22.
7. For a discussion, see Israel, 572.
8. Voltaire, "Natural Law," *Dictionaire philosophique.*
9. Montesquieu, *Spirit of the Laws,* 23.22. Quotations are from Thomas Nugent's 1752 translation.
10. *Ibid.,* 12.4.
11. *Ibid.,* 12.6.
12. *Ibid.*
13. Diderot, *Ouvres philosophiques,* 377. Unless otherwise noted, all translations into English from French are mine.
14. Diderot, *Rameau's Nephew,* 176–77.
15. Crompton, 2006, 491.
16. Diderot, *Rameau's Nephew,* 179–82.
17. Quoted in David West, *Reason and Sexuality in Western Thought* (Cambridge: Polity Press, 2005), 66.
18. Voltaire, *Ouvres,* 30:569–70.
19. Crompton, 514–19.
20. Voltaire, "Adultery," *Dictionaire philosophique.*
21. Quoted in Crompton, 2006, 519.
22. Rousseau, *Discourse,* 150.
23. Rousseau, *Émile,* 358–61.
24. Jean-Jacques Rousseau, *Emile,* 663.
25. Jean-Jacques Rousseau, *Confes-*

sions, 15–17; quoted in Vernon A. Rosario, *The Erotic Imagination: French Histories of Perversity* (Oxford: Oxford University Press, 1997), 32.

26. Rosario, 32–34.

27. Immanuel Kant, *Lectures on Ethics,* 163.

28. For a summary of Bentham's views on sexuality, see Crompton, 2006, 530–33.

29. *Ibid.*, 180.

30. Angela Carter, *The Sadeian Woman and the Ideology of Pornography,* rev. ed. (New York: Penguin, 2001), 101.

31. Quoted in Carter, 119.

32. Carter, 25.

33. Quoted in Darrin M. McMahon, *Enemies of the Enlightenment* (Oxford: Oxford University Press, 2001), 41.

34. Julie Peakman, *Lascivious Bodies: A Sexual History of the Eighteenth Century* (London: Atlantis Books, 2004), 10.

35. *Ibid.*, 12–4.

36. Quoted in Dan Cruickshank, *London's Sinful Secrets* (New York: St. Martin's Press, 2009).

37. Rictor Norton, *Mother Clap's Molly House* (London: Gay Men's Press, 1992).

38. Ned Ward, *Columbia Anthology,* 209.

39. Ringdal, 212.

40. For a description of how these were adopted in London, see Cruickshank, 207–8.

41. Boswell, *London Journal,* November 25, 1762.

42. Quoted in Peakman, 75.

43. Quoted in Anne Buck, *Dress in Eighteenth-Century England* (New York: Holmes & Meier, 1979), 20.

44. Jean-Jacques Rousseau, *Politics and the Arts: Letter to M. d'Alembert on the Theatre,* trans. Allan Bloom (Ithaca: Cornell University Press, 1968), 100–1.

45. Gary Kates, *Monsieur d'Eon Is a Woman,* rev. ed. (Baltimore: John Hopkins University Press, 2001), 75–76.

46. Quoted in *Ibid.*, 180.

47. *Ibid.*, 179.

48. Peakman, 133–40.

49. *Ibid.*, 123–24.

50. Swedenborg, *The True Christian Religion,* 156.

51. Robert W. Rix, "William Blake and the Radical Swedenborgians," 2002, 115.

52. Richard Knight, *Discourse on Priapus,* 21.

53. G.S. Rousseau, "The Sorrows of Priapus," in *Sexual Underworlds of the Enlightenment,* eds. G.S. Rousseau and Roy Porter (Chapel Hill: University of North Carolina Press, 1988), 123.

54. Edward J. Bristow, *Vice and Vigilance: Purity Movements in Britain since 1700* (London: Rowman and Littlefield, 1977), 23–30.

55. Peakman, 15–16.

56. Bernard Mandeville, *The Fable of the Bees: Or, Private Vices, Publick Benefits,* 2 vols. (Oxford: Clarendon Press, 1924), 1:232.

57. Netta Murray Goldsmith, *The Worst of Crimes* (Aldershot: Ashgate, 1998), 9.

58. Aage B. Sørenson, "On Kings, Pietism, and Rent-Seeking in Scandinavian Welfare States," *Arts Sociologica* 41, no. 4 (1998): 367–70.

59. Stephen Tomkins, *William Wilberforce: A Biography* (Oxford: Lion, 2007), 55.

60. Charles C. Noel, "Missionary Preachers in Spain: Teaching Social Virtue in the Eighteenth Century," *American Historical Review* 90, no. 4 (1985): 866–92.

61. David Higgs, "The Portuguese Church," in *Church and Society in Catholic Europe of the Eighteenth Century,* eds. William J. Callahan and David Higgs (Cambridge: Cambridge University Press, 1979), 86.

62. Katherine Crawford, *European Sexualities, 1400–1800* (Cambridge: Cambridge University Press, 2007), 137–38.

63. For a summary of the book, see Roy Porter and Lesley Hall, *The Facts of Life: The Creation of Sexual Knowledge in Britain, 1650–1950* (New Haven: Yale University Press, 1995), 65–90.

64. For a summary, see *Ibid.*, 33–64.

65. Lydia Sison, *Doctor of Love: James Graham and His Celestial Bed* (London: Alma Books, 2008).

66. Thomas Laqueur, *Solitary Sex: A Cultural History of Masturbation* (New York: Zone Books, 2003), 16. For a summary of Onanism, see Laqueur, 2003, 13–16, 25–37.

67. Quoted in *Ibid.*, 56.

68. Jean Stengers, *Masturbation: History of a Great Terror,* trans. Kathryn A. Hoffman (New York: Palgrave, 2001), 55; Laqueur, 283–90.

69. Quoted in Laqueur, 64–65.

70. Quoted in Barbara Alpern Engel, *Women in Russia, 1700–2000* (Cambridge: Cambridge University Press, 2000), 14.

71. *Ibid.*, 12–13.

72. Lindsey Hughes, "From Caftans into Corsets: The Sartorial Transformation of Women during the Reign of Peter the Great," *Gender and Sexuality in Russian Civilization* 5 (2001): 17, 23–28.

73. Laurie Bernstein, *Sonia's Daughters: Prostitutes and Their Regulation in Imperial Russia* (Berkeley: University of California Press, 1995), 13–14.

74. Kon, 16.

75. Isabel Hull, *Sex and Law in Early Modern Germany,* 107–10.

76. Crompton, 2006, 511–12.

77. Wilhelm von Rosen, "Sodomy in Early Modern Denmark: A Crime without Victims," in Gerard and Hekma, 190–200.

78. Claudia Stein, "The Birth of Biopower in Eighteenth-Century Germany," *Medical History* 55, no. 3 (2011): 331–37.

79. Karen Offen, *European Feminisms, 1700–2000* (Stanford: Stanford University Press, 2000), 47.

80. James F. Traer, *Marriage and the Family in Eighteenth-Century France* (Ithaca: Cornell University Press, 1980), 62–63, 77.

81. David Turner, "Adultery: Comparative History," in *The Oxford Encyclopedia of Women in World History,* Vol. 1 (Oxford: Oxford University Press, 2008), 32.

82. Quoted in Robert Darnton, *The Great Cat Massacre and Other Episodes in French Cultural History* (New York: Basic Books, 1984), 245.

83. Marquis d'Argenson, *Papers,* 24 February 1700–30 April 1702; quoted in Jeffrey Merrick and Bryant T. Regan, *Homosexuality in Early Modern France* (Oxford: Oxford University Press, 2001), 68.

84. James D. Steakley, "Sodomy in Enlightenment Prussia: From Execution to Suicide," in Gerard and Hekma, 168.

85. "Extraordinary Female Friendship," *General Evening Post,* July 24, 1790.

86. Henry Fielding, *The Female Husband, or The Surprising History of Mrs. Mary...* (London, 1746), 31.

87. *Ibid.*, 37.

88. Argenson, "Interrogation, 9 January 1750," *Homosexuality in Early Modern France: A Documentary Collection,* eds. Jeffrey Merrick and Bryant Regan (Oxford: Oxford University Press, 2000).

89. Argenson, "Arrests, 22 February 1785," from *Ibid.*

90. Lever, 158–60.

91. Armand de Vignerot du Plessis, Duc de Richelieu, *Mémoires,* Vol. 3, ed. J.L. Giraud Solaire (Paris: Joseph de Boffe et al., 1790), 178–80.

92. Crompton, 463.

93. Rictor Norton and Louis Crompton, "Gay Genocide from Leviticus to Hitler," *Gay Academic* 7 (1978): 73–77, 85–91.

94. Quoted in Peakman, 150.

95. *Weekly Standard*, May 14, 1728.
96. Peakman, 151–52.
97. Patricia W. Manning, *Voicing Dissent in Seventeenth-Century Spain: Inquisition, Social Criticism and Theology in the Case of El Criticón* (Leiden: Brill, 2009), 21–31.
98. For a description of the caricature and the context, see Anna Clark, *Scandal: The Sexual Politics of the British Constitution* (Princeton, NJ: Princeton University Press, 2004), 19–34.
99. Robert Darnton, *The Forbidden Best-Sellers of Pre-Revolutionary France* (New York: W.W. Norton, 1996), 4.
100. *Ibid.*, 8.
101. For a summary and discussion, see *Ibid.*, 85–114.
102. *Thérèse philosophe*, 85.
103. Darnton, 1996, 97.
104. Quoted in Darnton, 1996, 298–99.
105. For a discussion of the book, see Robert Darnton, *The Devil in the Holy Water, or the Art of Slander from Louis XIV to Napoleon* (University Park: University of Pennsylvania Press, 2010), 379–83.
106. Darnton, 2010, 383.
107. Lynn Hunt, *The Family Romance of the French Revolution* (Berkeley: University of California Press, 1992), 105.
108. *Ibid.*, 107.
109. Quoted in Simon Schama, *Citizens: A Chronicle of the French Revolution* (New York: Vintage, 1989), 225.
110. Quoted in Hunt, 93.
111. Quoted in Ruth Scarr, *Fatal Purity: Robespierre and the French Revolution* (New York: Henry Holt, 2006), 230.
112. James F. Traer, *Marriage and the Family in Eighteenth-Century France* (Ithaca: Cornell University Press, 1980), 108–13.
113. Suzanne Desan, *The Family on Trial in the French Revolution* (Berkeley: University of California Press, 2004), 94–96.
114. *Ibid.*, 94.
115. Quoted in Traer, 122–23.
116. Quoted in Dominique Godineau, *Women of Paris and Their French Revolution*, 18.
117. *Ibid.*, 14.
118. Andrew Hussey, *Paris: The Secret History* (New York: Bloomsbury, 2006), 201.
119. Susan P. Conner, "Politics, Prostitution, and the Pox in Revolutionary Paris, 1789–1799," *Journal of Social History* 22, no. 4 (1989): 713–34.
120. Michael David Siobalis, "The Regulation of Hale Homosexuality in Revolutionary and Napoleonic France, 1789–1815," in *Homosexuality in Modern France*, eds. Jeffrey Merrick and Bryan T. Ragan, Jr. (Oxford: Oxford University Press, 1996), 80–96.
121. *Ibid.*, 95.
122. Quoted in *Ibid.*, 93.
123. For details of the case, see *Ibid.*, 88–92.
124. Desan, 137–40.

Chapter X

1. Frederic Morton, *A Nervous Splendor, Vienna 1888/1889* (Boston: Little, Brown, 1979), 313–14.
2. Peter Gay, *Pleasure Wars: The Bourgeois Experience from Victoria to Freud* (New York: W.W. Norton, 1998), 28–32.
3. Jesus Cruz, *The Rise of Middle-Class Culture in Nineteenth-Century Spain* (Baton Rouge: Louisiana State University Press, 2011), 58–59.
4. Gay, 56.
5. Jennifer Phegley, *Courtship and Marriage in Victorian England* (Santa Barbara: ABC-CLIO, 2011), 3–5.
6. Queen Victoria, *Journal*, February 11, 1840.
7. James F. McMillan, *Housewife or Harlot* (Sussex: Harvester Press, 1981), 185.
8. Quoted in Lucy Bland, *Banishing the Beast: Feminism, Sex, and Morality* (New York: Tauris Park, 2002), 55.
9. William Alcott, *The Physiology of Marriage* (Boston: Jewett, 1856), 167.
10. Neville Kirk, *The Growth of Working Class Reformism in Mid-Victorian England* (New York: Taylor & Francis, 1985), 185.
11. Alain Corbin, *Women for Hire*, trans. Alan Sheridan (Cambridge: Harvard University Press, 1990), 145–46.
12. Fraser Harrison, *The Dark Angel: Aspects of Victorian Sexuality* (New York: Universe Books, 1978), 167–68.
13. Michael B. Miller, *The Bon Marché: Bourgeois Culture and the Department Store, 1869–1920* (Princeton, NJ: Princeton University Press, 1981), 220.
14. Michael Mason, *The Making of Victorian Sexual Attitudes* (Oxford: Oxford University Press, 1994), 120.
15. Kon, 43–4.
16. Edward Ross Dickinson, "The Men's Christian Morality Movement in Germany, 1880–1914: Some Reflections on Politics, Sex, and Sexual Politics," *Journal of Modern History* 75, no. 1 (2003): 85.
17. Rosario, 38.
18. Jane Jordan, *Josephine Butler* (London: Continuum, 2007); Corbin, 214–20.
19. Dickson, 59–110.
20. David Biale, *Eros and the Jews: From Biblical Israel to Contemporary America* (New York: Basic Books, 1992), 150–61.
21. Ze'evi, 2006, 70–76.
22. Ze'evi, 2006, 96–98; Ze'evi, 2002, 34–53.
23. Quoted in Ze'evi, 2002, 48.
24. Celâl Nuri, *Kadınlarımız* (Istanbul, 1913), 139, translated in Davis, 94.
25. Davis, 92–95.
26. Cruz, 46–9.
27. Quoted and translated in Abrams, 72.
28. Quoted in Gay, 71.
29. Lynn Abrams, *The Making of Modern Woman* (London: Routledge, 2002), 72.
30. Gay, 175–77.
31. David I. Kertzer and Marzio Barbigli, *The History of the European Family: Family Life in the Long Nineteenth Century* (New Haven: Yale University Press, 2002), 285–87.
32. Abrams, 85–89; Colin Heywood, *Growing up in France: From the Ancien Régime to the Third Republic* (Cambridge: Cambridge University Press, 2007), 144.
33. Angus McLaren, *A History of Contraception: From Antiquity to the Present Day* (London: Basil Blackwell, 1990), 184–87.
34. Dagmar Herzog, *Sexuality in Europe: A Twentieth-Century History* (Cambridge: Cambridge University Press, 2011), 19.
35. *Ibid.*, 10.
36. Angus McLaren, "Sex and Socialism: The Opposition of the French Left to Birth Control in the Nineteenth Century," *Journal of the History of Ideas* 37, no. 3 (1976), 475–92.
37. Herzog, 2011, 20.
38. *Ibid.*
39. McLaren, 1990, 190.
40. Mary Wollstonecraft, *A Vindication of the Rights of Woman*, Chapter 8.
41. McLaren, 1990, 191.
42. Herzog, 2011, 23.
43. Bernstein, 32.
44. Maria Luddy, *Prostitution and Irish Society, 1800–1940* (Cambridge: University of Cambridge Press, 2007), 102–14; Abrams, 157.
45. Quoted in Rosario, 39.
46. Richard Krafft-Ebing, *Psychopathia Sexualis* (1886), 286.

47. Herzog, 2011, 29.
48. Karl Heinrich-Ulrichs, *The Riddle of Man-Manly Love,* trans. Michael Lombardi-Nash (New York: Prometheus Books, 1994), 2.3.12.
49. *Ibid.*, 1.2.31.
50. *Ibid.*, 1.3.12.
51. *Ibid.*, 1.4.49.
52. *Ibid.*, 1.2.23.
53. *Ibid.*, 2.9.4.
54. Krafft-Ebing, 285.
55. Rosario, 83–89.
56. "An Editorial on the Publication of Havelock Ellis' Sexual Inversion," *Lancet*, 1896.
57. Sigmund Freud, *Three Essays on the Theory of Sexuality,* ed. and trans. James Strachey (New York: Basic Books, 2000), 4–5.
58. Magnus Hirschfeld, *The Homosexuality of Men and Women,* trans. Michael Lombardi-Nash (New York: Prometheus Books, 2000), 369.
59. Rosario, 89–93.
60. Herzog, 2011, 36–37.
61. *Ibid.*, 57.
62. H. Montgomery Hyde, *The Cleveland Street Scandal* (New York: Coward, McCann & Geoghagen, 1976).
63. Neil McKenna, *The Secret Life of Oscar Wilde* (New York: Basic Books, 2005), 57–59.
64. For a description of the criminal trials and sentencing, see Michael S. Foldy, *The Trials of Oscar Wilde* (New Haven: Yale University Press, 1997), 31–47.
65. Quoted in Jeffrey Weeks, *Sex, Politics, and Society: The Regulation of Sexuality since 1880* (New York: Longman, 1989), 103.
66. Herzog, 2011, 38–41.
67. Patricia Anderson, *When Passion Reigned: Sex and the Victorians* (New York: Basic Books, 1995), 101–4.
68. Steven Marcus, *The Other Victorians* (New York: Basic Books, 1964), 197–216.
69. Henry Spencer Ashbee, *Index Librorum Prohibitorum* (London, 1877), xxvii.
70. Sarah Leonard, "Wanderers, Entertainers, and Seducers: Making Sense of the Obscenity Law in the German States, 1830–1851," in Lisa Z. Sigel, *International Exposure: Perspectives on Modern European Pornography, 1800–2000* (New Brunswick: Rutgers University Press, 2005), 37–42.
71. *Ibid.*, 28, 37.
72. Lisa Z. Sigel, *Governing Pleasures : Pornography and Social Change in England, 1815–1914* (New Brunswick: Rutgers University Press, 2007), 27.
73. Herzog, 2011, 25.
74. Ian R. Dowbiggin, *Inheriting Madness* (Berkeley: University of California Press), 119–25.
75. Matt T. Reed, "From Aliéné to Dégénéré: Moral Agency and the Psychiatric Imagination in Nineteenth-Century France," in *Confronting Modernity in Fin-de-Siècle France: Bodies, Minds and Gender*, eds. Christopher E. Forth and Elinor Accampo (New York: Palgrave Macmillan, 2010), 73–74.
76. Sir Francis Golton, *Essays in Eugenics* (London, 1909), 20.
77. Herzog, 2011, 26.
78. Quoted in Rosario, 152–53.
79. Freud, 26.
80. William Thompson and Anna Wheeler, *An Appeal...* (1825), 79.
81. Keith Taylor, *The Political Ideas of the Utopian Socialists* (London: Frank Cass, 1982), 120–21.
82. Abrams, 161.
83. Anna Clark, *The Struggle for the Breeches: Gender and the Making of the British Working Class* (Berkeley: University of California Press, 1997), 185–87.
84. Quoted in Kon, 53.
85. Alexandra Kollontai, *Theses on Communist Morality in the Sphere of Marital Relations* (1921), no. 8.
86. Quoted in Kon, 59.

Epilogue

1. BBC, http://news.bbc.co.uk/2/hi/europe/4309012.stm, accessed January 15, 2013.
2. Quoted in Dan Healey, *Homosexual Desire in Revolutionary Russia* (Chicago: University of Chicago Press, 2011), 191–92.
3. Kon, 70–74.
4. Quoted in Herzog, 2011, 66.
5. Jonathan C. Friedman, *Speaking the Unspeakable: Essays on Sexuality, Gender, and Holocaust Survivor Memory* (Lanham, MD: University Press of America, 2002), 15–18.
6. *Ibid.*, 24.
7. Richard Plant, *The Pink Triangle: The Nazi War against Homosexuals* (New York: New Republic, 1986), 154.
8. For examples regarding Weimar Berlin, see Mel Gordon, *Voluptuous Panic: The Erotic World of Weimar Berlin* (Los Angeles: Feral House, 2006).
9. John London, *Theatre under the Nazis* (Manchester: Manchester University Press, 2000), 8.
10. Quoted in Florence Tamagne, *A History of Homosexuality in Europe. Vol. II: Berlin, London, Paris, 1919–1939* (New York: Algora, 2004), 18.

Bibliography

Abrams, Lynn. *The Making of Modern Woman*. London: Routledge, 2002.

Aeschylus, trans. Alan H. Sommerstein. Cambridge: Harvard University Press, 2008.

Agapitos, Panagiotis A. "The Erotic Bath in the Byzantine Vernacular Romance Kallimachos and Chysorrhoe." *Classica et mediaevalia* 41 (1990): 257–73.

Alcott, William. *The Physiology of Marriage*. Boston: Jewett, 1856.

Allen, Robert. *Classical Origins of Modern Homophobia*. Jefferson, NC: McFarland, 2006.

Amussen, Susan Dwyer. *An Ordered Society: Gender and Class in Early Modern England*. London: Basil Blackwell, 1988.

Anderson, Karen. *Chain Her by One Foot*. London: Routledge, 1991.

Anderson, Patricia. *When Passion Reigned: Sex and the Victorians*. New York: Basic Books, 1995.

Aretino. *Dialogues,* Trans. Raymond Rosenthal. New York: Ballantine, 1973.

Ariès, Philippe, and Duby, George. *History of Private Life, vol. 2: Revelations of the Medieval World*, trans. Arthur Goldhammer. Cambridge, MA: Belknap Press, 1993.

Ariès, Philippe. *Centuries of Childhood: A Social History of Family Life*, trans. Robert Baldick. New York: Alfred A. Knopf, 1962.

Aristophanes, trans. Jeffrey Henderson. Cambridge: Harvard University Press, 1999–2000.

Arjivi, Antii. *Women and Law in Late Antiquity*. New York: Oxford University Press, 1996.

Ashbee, Henry Spencer. *Index Librorum Prohibitorum*. London, 1877.

Aucassin et Nicolette, trans. Eugene Mason. Cambridge, Ontario: In Paranthesis, 2001.

Augustine, *The Fathers of the Church: Augustine*, trans. Vernon J. Bourke. Washington, D.C.: Catholic University of America Press, 2010.

Bailey, Derrick Sherwin. *Homosexuality and the Western Christian Tradition*. London: Longmans, 1955.

Balich, David L. "1 Corinthians 7:32–5 and Stoic Debates about Marriage Anxiety and Distraction." *Journal of Biblical Literature,* 102, 3 (Sept., 1983): 429–39.

Bardsley, Sandy. *Women's Roles in the Middle Ages*. Westport, CT: Greenwood Press, 2007.

Barrett, Anthony A. *Livia*. New Haven: Yale University Press, 2002.

Barrett, Anthony A. *Agrippina: Sex, Power, and Politics in the Early Empire*. New Haven: Yale University Press, 1998.

Barstow, Anne Llewylyn. *Married Priests and the Reforming Papacy*. Lewiston, NY: E. Mellen Press, 1983.

Beaucamp, Jöelle. *Le Statut de la femme á Byzance (4e-7e siècle)*. Paris: De Boccard, 1990.

Beck, Hans Georg. *Byzantinishes Erotikon*. n.p., 1986.

Bede, *The Ecclesiastical History of the English People,* trans. Bertram Colgrave. New York: Oxford University Press, 1999.

Bennett, Judith. "'Lesbian-Like' and the Social History of Lesbianisms." *Journal of the History of Sexuality* 9:1/2 (2000): 1–24.

Bernstein, Alan. *The Formation of Hell*. Ithaca: Cornell University Press, 1993.

Bernstein, Laurie. *Sonia's Daughters: Prostitutes and Their Regulation in Imperial Russia*. Berkeley: University of California Press, 1995.

Bettridge, Tom. *Sodomy in Early Modern Europe*. Manchester: Manchester University Press, 2002.

Biale, David. *Eros and the Jews*. Berkeley: University of California Press, 1997.

Biale, David. *Eros and the Jews: From Biblical Israel to Contemporary America*. New York: Basic Books, 1992.

Bickerman, Elias J. *The Jews in the Greek World*. Cambridge: Harvard University Press, 1988.

Bird, Phyllis A. *Missing Persons and Mistaken Identities: Women and Gender in Ancient Israel*. Minneapolis: Fortress Press, 1997.

Bitel, Lisa. *Women in Early Medieval Europe, 400–1000*. Cambridge: Cambridge University Press, 2002.

Bland, Lucy. *Banishing the Beast: Feminism, Sex, and Morality*. New York: Tauris Park, 2002.

Bogin, Magda. *Women Troubadours*. New York: Norton, 1980.

Boser, C.R. *The Christian Century in Japan, 1549–1650*. Berkeley: University of California Press, 1967.

Boswell, John. *Christianity, Social Tolerance and Homosexuality: Gay People in Western Europe from the Beginning of the Christian Era to the Fourteenth Century*. Chicago: Chicago University Press, 1980.

Boswell, John. *Marriage of Likeness: Same-Sex Unions in Pre-Modern Europe.* London, 1995.

Boutière, Jean and Schutz, Alexander. *Biographes des troubadours.* Paris: Nizet, 1964.

Boyce, Mary. *A History of Zoroastrianism*, vol. 2. Leiden: E.J. Brill, 1982.

Boyd, David Lorenzo and Karras, Ruth. "The Interrogation of a Male Transvestite Prostitute in Fourteenth Century London." *GLQ: A Journal of Lesbian and Gay Studies* 1 (1995): 459–65.

Brenz, Johannes. *Godly Magistrates and Church Order,* trans. and ed. James Estes. Toronto: University of Toronto Press, 2001.

Bristow, Edward J. *Vice and Vigilance: Purity Movements in Britain Since 1700.* Lanham, MD: Rowman and Littlefield, 1977.

Brown, Peter. *The Body and Society: Men, Women, and Sexual Renunciation in Early Christianity.* New York: Columbia University Press, 1988.

Brundage, James A. *Law, Sex, and Christian Society in Medieval Europe.* Chicago: University of Chicago Press, 1987.

Brundage, James. "The Church Judges Sexual Crimes." In *The Medieval World.* London: Routledge, 2002.

Brundage, James. "Sin, Crime, and the Pleasures of the Flesh." In *The Medieval World,* eds. Janet Nelson and Peter Linehan. London: Routledge, 2004.

Brundage, James. *Medieval Canon Law.* London: Longman, 1995.

Buck, Anne. *Dress in Eighteenth-Century England.* New York: Holmes & Meier, 1979.

Bugocka, Maria. *Women in Early Modern Polish Society.* London: Ashgate, 2004.

Bullough, Vern. *The History of Prostitution.* New Hyde Park, NY: University Books, 1964.

Bullough, Vern. *Sexual Variance in Society and History.* New York: John Wiley, 1976.

Bullough, Vern, and Bonnie. *Prostitution: An Illustrated Social History.* New York: Crown, 1978.

Burkhart, Louise M. *The Slippery Earth: Nahua-Christian Moral Dialogue in Sixteenth-Century Mexico.* Tuscon: University of Arizona Press, 1989.

Burns, R.I. "Socio-economic Structure and Continuity: Medieval Spanish Islam in the Tax Records of Crusader Valencia." In *The Islamic Middle East, 700–1900, Studies in Economic and Social History.* Princeton: Darwin Press, 1981.

Bushkovitch, Paul. *Religion and Society in Russia: The Sixteenth and Seventeenth Centuries.* New York: Oxford University Press, 1992.

Butrica, James L. "Some Myths and Anomalies in the Study of Roman Homosexuality." In *Same-Sex Desire and Love in Greco-Roman Antiquity,* eds. Beert C. Verstraete and Vernon Provencal. New York: Routledge, 2006.

Çakici, Aytu. "Immoral Earnings: Portraying Prostitutes in Ottoman Turkey." In *Illuminating the Dark Side: Evil, Women and the Feminine,* eds. Andrea Ruthven and Gabriela Mádlo. Witney: Interdisciplinary Press, 2010.

Calame, Claude. "Sappho's Group: An Initiation Into Womanhood." In *Reading Sappho: Classics and Contemporary Thought,* ed. Ellen Greene. Berkeley: University of California, 1995.

Cañizares-Esguerra, Jorge. *Puritan Conquistadors: Iberianizing the Atlantic, 1550–1700.* Stanford: Stanford University Press, 2006.

Cantarella, Eva. *Pandora's Daughters: The Role and Status of Women in Greek and Roman Antiquity.* Baltimore: Johns Hopkins University, 1987.

Cape, Robert W. "Roman Women in the History of Rhetoric and Oratory." In *Listening to their Voices: The Rhetorical Activities of Historical Women,* ed. Molly Meijer Wertheimer. Columbia: University of South Carolina Press, 1997.

Carter, Angela. *The Sadeian Woman and the Ideology of Pornography,* rev. ed. New York: Penguin, 2001.

Carvajal, Garza. *Butterflies Will Burn: Persecuting Sodomites in Early Modern Spain and Mexico.* Austin: University of Texas Press, 2010.

Celsus, *On the True Doctrine: A Discourse Against the Christians,* trans. R. Joseph Hoffmann. New York: Oxford University Press, 1987.

Charlemagne and Louis the Pious: The Lives by Einhard, Notker, Ermoldus, Thegan, and the Astronomer, trans. Thomas F.X. Noble. University Park, PA: University of Pennsylvania Press, 2009.

Chevallier, Pierre. *Henri III, Roi Shakespearien.* Paris: Fayard, 1985.

Chidester, D. *Christianity: A Global History.* San Francisco: Harper, 2000.

Childs, Margaret. "*Cigo Monogatari*: Love Stories or Buddhist Sermons?" *Monumenta Nipponica: Studies in Japanese Culture* 35 (1980): 127–151.

Choksy, Jamsheed K. *Purity and Pollution in Zoroastrianism, Triumph Over Evil.* Austin: University of Texas Press, 1989.

Christine de Pizan, *The Writings of Christine de Pizan,* ed. and trans. Charity Cannon Willard. New York: Persea Books, 1994.

Chrysostom, *Complete Works,* trans. Henry Lamar Crosby. Cambridge: Harvard University Press, 1946–51.

Cippola, Carlo. *Before the Industrial Revolution,* 2nd ed. New York: Norton, 1980.

Clancy, Joseph, ed. and trans. *Medieval Welsh Poems.* Dublin: Four Courts, 2002.

Clark, Anna. *Scandal: The Sexual Politics of the British Constitution.* Princeton, NJ: Princeton University Press, 2004.

Clark, Anna. *The Struggle for the Breeches: Gender and the Making of the British Working Class.* Berkeley: University of California Press, 1997.

Clarke, John. *Roman Sex.* London: Harry N. Abrams, 2003.

Cohen, Daniel. *Law, Sexuality, and Morality: The Enforcement of Morals in Classical Athens.* Cambridge: Cambridge University Press, 1991.

Cohen, Daniel. "Law, Society, and Homosexuality in Classical Athens." *Past & Present* 117 (1993): 3–21.

Cohen, Daniel. "Sexuality, Violence, and The Law of Hybris." *Greece & Rome* 38 (1991): 171–88.

Cohen, Mark R. *Under Crescent and Cross: Jews in the Middle Ages.* Princeton, NJ: Princeton University Press, 1995.

Cohen, Rip, ed. and trans. *500 Cantigas d'amigo: A Critical Edition.* Porto: Campo das Letras, 2003.

Collins, John Joseph. *The Bible After Babel: Historical Criticism in a*

Postmodern Age. Grand Rapids: Eerdmans, 2005.

Conner, Susan P. "Politics, Prostitution, and the Pox in Revolutionary Paris, 1789–1799." *Journal of Social History* 22.4 (1989): 713–34.

Connor, Carolyn. *Women of Byzantium*. New Haven: Yale University Press, 2004.

Constantelos, Demetrios J. *Byzantine Philanthropy and Social Welfare*. New Brunswick, 1968.

Cooper, Michael, ed. *They Came to Japan: An Anthology of European Reports on Japan, 1543–1640*. Berkeley: University of California Press, 1965.

Corbin, Alain. *Women For Hire*, trans. Alan Sheridan. Cambridge: Harvard University Press, 1990.

Crawford, Katherine. *European Sexualities, 1400–1800*. Cambridge: Cambridge University Press, 2007.

Crawford, Katherine. "Love, Sodomy, and Scandal: Controlling the Sexual Reputation of Henri III." *Journal of the History of Sexuality*, 12.4 (2003): 513–542.

Crompton, Louis. *Homosexuality & Civilization*. Cambridge: Harvard University Press, 2003.

Croutier, Alev Lytle. *The Harem: The World Behind the Veil*. New York: Abbeville Press, 1989.

Cruickshank, Dan. *London's Sinful Secrets*. New York: St. Martin's Press, 2009.

Cruz, Jesus. *The Rise of Middle-Class Culture in Nineteenth-Century Spain*. Louisiana State University Press, 2011.

Dainville, Oudot de. "La Consistoire de Ganges a la fin du XVIe Siecle," *Revue de L'Eglise de France* 18 (1932): 464–85.

Damian, Peter, trans. Pierre J. Payer, *Book of Gomorrah*. Wilfrid Laurier University Press, 1982),

Darnton, Robert. *The Devil in the Holy Water, or the Art of Slander from Louis XIV to Napoleon*. University of Pennsylvania Press, 2010.

Darnton, Robert. *The Forbidden Best-Sellers of Pre-Revolutionary France*. New York: W.W. Norton & Co., 1996.

Darnton, Robert. *The Great Cat Massacre and Other Episodes in French Cultural History*. New York: Basic Books, 1984.

Davidson, Nicholas. "Atheism in Italy, 1500–1700." In Michael Hunter and David Wootton, *Atheism from the Reformation to the Enlightenment*. Oxford: Clarendon Press, 1992.

Davies, Christie. "Sexual Taboos and Social Boundaries." *The American Journal of Sociology* 87.5 (March, 1982.

Davies, Norman. *God's Playground: A History of Poland*, vol. 1. New York: Columbia University Press, 1982.

Davis, Fanny. *The Ottoman Lady*. Westport, CT: Greenwood Press, 1986.

Davis, N.S. "Sodomy in Early Modern Venice." In *The Pursuit of Sodomy: Male Homosexuality in Renaissance and Enlightenment Europe*, eds. Kent Gerard and Gert Hekma. New York: Harrington Park Press, 1989.

de Brantôme, Pierre de Bourdeille. *Lives of Fair and Gallant Ladies*, trans. A.R. Allinson. New York: Liveright Publishing Corp., 1933.

de Busbecq, Ogier Ghislain. *Turkish Letters*, trans. E.M. Forster. New York: Oxford University Press, 1968.

de Jean, Joan. *The Reinvention of Obscenity*. Chicago: University of Chicago Press, 2002.

de la Barre, François. "On the Equality of the Two Sexes." In *Three Cartesian Feminist Treatises*, trans. Vivian Bosley. Chicago University Press, 2002.

de L'Éstoile, Pierre. *Mémoires-Journaux*, ed. G. Bruner et al. Paris, 1888.

D'Emilio, John, and Freedman, Estelle B. *Intimate Matters*, 2nd ed. Chicago: University of Chicago Press, 1997.

Deming, Will. *Paul On Marriage and Celibacy*. Cambridge: Cambridge University Press, 1995.

Desan, Suzanne. *The Family on Trial in the French Revolution*. Berkeley: University of California Press, 2004.

Dickinson, Edward Ross. "The Men's Christian Morality Movement in Germany, 1880–1914: Some Reflections on Politics, Sex, and Sexual Politics." *Journal of Modern History* 75.1 (2003): 59–110.

Divan, ed. Dov Jaren. Jerusalem, 1966.

Długosz, Jan. "Annals of the Kingdom of Poland," trans. Martha A. Brozyna in *Gender and Sexuality in the Middle Ages,* ed. Martha A. Brozyna. New York: McFarland, 2005.

Dowbiggin, Ian R. *Inheriting Madness*. Berkeley: University of California Press, 1991.

Downing, F. Gerald. *The Cynics and Christian Origins*. Edinburgh: T&T Clark, 1992.

Downing, F. Gerald. *Cynics, Paul, and the Pauline Churches*. London: Routledge, 1998.

Duff, Tim. *Plutarch's Lives: Exploring Virtue and Vice*. Oxford: Clarendon University Press, 1999.

Durnston, Christopher. *The Family in the English Revolution*. New York: Basil Blackwell, 1989.

Durnston, Christopher. "Puritan Rule and the Failure of Cultural Revolution, 1645–1660." In *The Culture of English Puritanism, 1560–1700*, eds. Christopher Durston and Jacqueline Eales. New York: Macmillan, 1996.

Eichmann, Raymond, ed. and trans. *Cuckolds, Clerics, & Countrymen: Medieval French Fabliaux,* eds. and trans. John DuVall and Raymond Eichmann. Fayetteville: University of Arkansas Press, 1982.

Elias, Norbert. *The Civilizing Process,* rev. ed. London: Blackwell Publishing, 2000.

Elison, George. *Deus Destroyed: The Image of Christianity in Early Modern Japan*. Cambridge: Harvard University Press, 1973.

Ellis, Robert Richard. "'The Best Thus Far Discovered': The Japanese in the Letters of Francisco Xavier." *Hispanic Review*, 71.2 (2003): 155–69.

El-Rouayheb, Khaled. *Before Homosexuality in the Arab-Islamic World 1500–1800*. Chicago: University of Chicago Press, 2005.

Encyclopedia of Homosexuality, ed. Wayne R. Dynes. New York: Garland, 1990.

Engel, Barbara Alpern. *Women in Russia, 1700 -2000*. Cambridge: Cambridge University Press, 2000.

Epicurus, *The Philosophy of Epicurus: Letters, Doctrines, and Parallel Passages from Lucretius,* trans. George Kleppinger Strodach. Evanston, IL: Northwestern University Press, 1963.

Erasmus, *Complete Works*, ed. and trans. J.K. Sowards. Toronto: University of Toronto Press, 1985.

Erdoğan, Sema Nilgün. "The Love of Boys in Arabic Poetry of the Early Ottoman Period, 1500-1800." *Middle Eastern Literatures* 8.1 (2005): 3–23.

Erdoğan, Sema Nilgün. *Sexual Life in Ottoman Society*. Istanbul: Dönence, 1996.

Evans-Grubbs, Judith. *Law and Family in Late Antiquity: The Emperor Constantine's Marriage Legislation*. Oxford: Clarendon Press, 1995.

Faderman, Lillian. *Surpassing the Love of Men: Romantic Friendship and Love Between Women from the Renaissance to the Present*. New York: Harper, 2001.

Fairchilds, Cissie. *Women in Early Modern Europe*. London: Longman, 2007.

Farr, James F. *Authority and Sexuality in Early Modern Burgundy (1550–1730)*. New York: Oxford University Press, 1995.

Foldy, Michael S. *The Trials of Oscar Wilde*. New Haven: Yale University Press, 1997.

Fone, Bryne. *Homophobia: A History*. New York: Metropolitan Press, 2000.

Foucault, Michel. *Abnormal: Lectures at the College de France, 1974–1975*, eds. Valerio Marchetti and Antonella Salomoni and trans. Graham Burchell. London: Picador, 2004.

Foucault, Michel. *History of Sexuality, vol. 1: An Introduction*, trans. Robert Hurley. New York: Pantheon Books, 1978.

Frantz, David O. *Festum Voluptatis: A Study of Renaissance Erotica*. Columbus: Ohio State University Press, 1989.

Freud, Sigmund. *Three Essays on the Theory of Sexuality*, ed. and trans. James Strachey. New York: Basic Books, 2000.

Friedman, David M. *A Mind of Its Own: A Cultural History of the Penis*. New York: Simon & Schuster, 2008.

Friedman, Jonathan C. *Speaking the Unspeakable: Essays on Sexuality, Gender, and Holocaust Survivor Memory*. Lanham, MD: University Press of America, 2002.

Friedman, Richard Elliot. *Commentary on the Torah*, vol. 2. San Francisco: HarperCollins, 2001.

Frye, Richard N., ed., *Rivayat-i Hemit-i Ašawahistan, A Study in Zoroastrian Law*, trans. Nezhat Safa-Isfehani. Cambridge: Harvard University Press, 1980.

Frymer-Kensky, Tikva. "Law and Philosophy: The Case of Sex in the Bible." In *Women in the Hebrew Bible*, ed. Alice Bach. New York: Routledge, 1999.

Gagarin, Michael. "Women's Voices in Attic Oratory." In *Making Silence Speak: Women's Voices in Greek Literature and Society*, eds. A.P.M.H. Lardinois and Laura McClure. Princeton, NJ: Princeton University Press, 2001.

Gardner, Jane. *Women in Roman Law and Society*. Bloomington: Indiana University Press, 1989.

Garland, Robert. *Daily Life in Ancient Greece*. New York: Greenwood Press, 2008.

Gay, Peter. *Pleasure Wars: The Bourgeois Experience from Victoria to Freud*. New York: W.W. Norton and Company, 1998.

Gerard, Kurt and Hekma, Gert. *The Pursuit of Sodomy: Male Homosexuality in Renaissance and Enlightenment Europe*. New York: Routledge, 1989.

Gerig, Bruce. "The Levitical Ban: The Final Verdict." http://epistle.us/hbarticles/leviticus6.html.

Gerli, Michael. *Medieval Iberia: An Encyclopaedia*. New York: Routledge, 2003.

Gernet, Jacques. *China and the Christian Impact*. Cambridge: Cambridge University Press, 1985.

Gerson, Jean. *Early Works*, ed. and trans. Brian Patrick McGuire. New York: Paulist Press, 1998.

Gilbert of Nogent, *Self and Society in Medieval France*, ed. John F. Benton. Toronto: University of Toronto Press, 1994.

Godbeer, Richard. *Sexual Revolution in Early America*. Baltimore: Johns Hopkins University Press, 2002.

Godineau, Dominique. *Women of Paris and their French Revolution*, trans. Katherine Streip. Berkeley: University of California Press, 1998.

Goldsmith, Netta Murray. *The Worst of Crimes*. Aldershot: Ashgate, 1998.

Goodlich, Michael. *The Unmentionable Vice*. Santa Barbara, CA: ABC-CLIO.

Gordon, Bruce. *The Swiss Reformation*. Manchester: Manchester University Press, 2002.

Gordon, Mel. *Voluptuous Panic: The Erotic World of Weimar Berlin*. Los Angeles, CA: Feral House, 2006.

Gorski, Philip S. *The Disciplinary Revolution: Calvinism and the Rise of the State in Early Modern Europe*. Chicago: University of Chicago Press, 2003.

Graham, Michael. *The Uses of Reform: "Godly Discipline" and Popular Behavior in Scotland and Beyond*. New York: E.J. Brill, 1996.

Greenberg, Steven. *Wrestling with God and Men: Homosexuality in the Jewish Tradition*. Madison: University of Wisconsin Press, 2005.

Gregory, Tullio. "Charron's 'Scandalous Book.'" In M. Hunter and D. Wooton, *Atheism from the Reformation to the Enlightenment*. New York: Oxford University Press, 1992.

Gregory of Nyssa, *On Virginity* in *The Fathers of the Church: Gregory of Nyssa*, trans. Virginia Woods Callahan. Washington, D.C.: Catholic University Press, 2010.

Gregory of Tours, *History of the Franks*, trans. Lewis Thrope. New York: Penguin, 1976.

Gregory the Great. *The Letters of Gregory the Great*, trans. John R.C. Martin. Toronto: Pontifical Institute of Medieval Studies, 2004.

Grendler, Paul F. "Printing and Censorship." In *The Cambridge History of Renaissance Philosophy*, eds. Charles Schmitt and Quentin Skinner. Cambridge: Cambridge University Press, 1988.

Griffen, Lois. *Theory of Profane Love among the Arabs: The Development of the Genre*. New York: New York University Press, 1971.

Hallett, Judith P. "Sappho and Her Social Context: Sense and Sensuality." *Signs* 4 (1979): 447–64.

Hanawalt, Barbara. *The Ties That Bound: Peasant Families in Medieval England*. New York: Oxford University Press, 1986.

Harrison, Fraser. *The Dark Angel: Aspects of Victorian Sexuality*. New York: Universe Books, 1978.

Hattox, Ralph S. *Coffee and Coffeehouses: The Origins of a Social Beverage in the Near Middle East*. Seattle: University of Washington Press, 1985.

Haynes, Alan. *Sex in Elizabethan England*. Sutton: The History Press, 1999.

Healey, Dan. *Homosexual Desire in*

Revolutionary Russia. Chicago: University of Chicago Press, 2011.

Heinrich-Ulrichs, Karl. *The Riddle of Man-Manly Love,* trans. Michael Lombardi-Nash. New York: Prometheus Books, 1994.

Henriques, Fernando. *Prostitution in Europe and the New World*. London: MacGibbon and Kee, 1968.

Herlihy, David. *Medieval Households*. Cambridge: Harvard University Press, 1985.

Herzog, Dagmar. *Sexuality in Europe: A Twentieth-Century History*. Cambridge: Cambridge University Press, 2011.

Hesiod. *Theogony,* trans. Hugh Evelyn-White. Mineola, NY: Dover, 2006.

Hesiod. *Works and Days,* trans. Hugh Evelyn-White. Mineola, NY: Dover, 2006.

Heyd, Uriel. *Studies in Old Ottoman Criminal Law*. New York: Oxford University Press, 1973.

Heywood, Colin. *Growing Up in France: From the Ancien Régime to the Third Republic*. Cambridge: Cambridge University Press, 2007.

Higgs, David. "The Portuguese church." In *Church and Society in Catholic Europe of the Eighteenth Century,* eds. William J. Callahan and David Higgs. Cambridge: Cambridge University Press, 1979.

Hildegard of Bingen, *Scivias,* trans. Columba Hart and Jane Bishop. Mahwah, NJ: Paulist Press, 1990.

Hill, Christopher. *Milton and the English Revolution*. New York: Penguin, 1979.

Hill, Christopher. *The World Turned Upside Down: Radical Ideas during the English Revolution*. London: Penguin, 1972.

Hinsch, Bret. *Passions of the Cut Sleeve: The Male Homosexual Tradition in China*. Berkeley: University of California Press, 1990.

Hirschfeld, Magnus. *The Homosexuality of Men and Women,* trans. Michael Lombardi-Nash. New York: Prometheus Books, 2000.

Hobhouse, John Cam. *A Journey Through Albania and Other Provinces of Turkey in Europe and Asia, to Constantinople*. London, 1817.

Hodkinson, Stephen. "Female Property Ownership and Empowerment in Classical and Hellenistic Sparta." In *Spartan Society,* ed. Thomas Figuiera. Swansea: Classical Press of Wales, 2002.

Hodkinson, Stephen. *Religion and the Greeks*. Boston: Duckworth Publishers, 2001.

Homer. *Homeric Hymns,* trans. Diane J. Rayor. Berkeley: University of California Press, 2004.

Homer. *Odyssey,* trans. Rodney Merrill. Ann Arbor: University of Michigan Press, 2002.

Hope, Valerie M. *Roman Death: Death and Dying in Ancient Rome*. London: Continuum, 2009.

Hope, Valerie M., ed. *Death in Ancient Rome: A Sourcebook,* ed. Valerie Hope. New York: Routledge, 2007.

Hopkins, Keith. "A Textual Emendation in a Fragment of Musonius Rufus." *Classical Quarterly* 15 (1965): 72–74.

Horner, Tom. *Jonathan Loved David: Homosexuality in Biblical Times*. Philadelphia: Westminster Press, 1978.

Hubbard, Thomas, ed. and trans. *Homosexuality in Greece and Rome: A Sourcebook*. Berkeley: University of California Press, 2003.

Hughes, Lindsey. "From Caftans into Corsets: The Sartorial Transformation of Women during the Reign of Peter the Great." *Gender and Sexuality in Russian Civilization* 5 (2001): 17–23.

Hull, Isabel. *Sex and Law in Early Modern Germany*. Ithaca: Cornell University Press, 1997.

Hunt, Lynn. *The Family Romance of the French Revolution*. Berkeley: University of California Press, 1992.

Hussey, Andrew. *Paris: The Secret History*. New York: Bloomsbury, 2006.

Huttunen, Niko. *Paul and Epictetus on Law: A Comparison*. London: T&T Clark, 2009.

Hyde, H. Montgomery *The Cleveland Street Scandal*. New York: Coward, McCann & Geoghagen, 1976.

Ibn Hazm. *The Ring of the Dove: A Treatise on the Art and Practice of Arab Love,* trans. A.J. Arberry. London: Luzac, 1953.

Israel, Jonathan I. *Radical Enlightenment*. New York: Oxford University Press, 2001.

Iston, George Cyprian. "Double Monasteries." *The Catholic Encyclopedia,* vol. 10. New York: Robert Appleton Company, 1911.

Jacob, Benjamin. "Whore, Court, Church, and the Origins of Modern Obscenity." In *Papers Presented at the Third Global Conference on Sex and Sexuality*.

Jacob, P.L. *Curiosites de l'Histoire de France: IIe Serie: Proces Celebres*. Paris: Paul Lacroix, 1848.

Jacquart, Danielle and Thomasset, Claude Alexandre. *Sexuality and Medicine in the Middle Ages*. New York: Polity Press, 1988.

Jochens, Jenny. *Women in Old Norse Society*. Ithaca: Cornell University Press, 1998.

Jordan, Jane. *Josephine Butler*. London: Continuum, 2007.

Jordan, Mark. *The Invention of Sodomy in Christian Theology*. Chicago: University of Chicago Press, 1998.

Kafadar, Cemal. *Between Two Worlds: The Construction of the Ottoman State*. Berkeley: University of California Press, 1995.

Karras, Ruth Mazo. *Common Women: Prostitution and Sexuality in Medieval England*. New York: Oxford University Press, 1996.

Karras, Ruth Mazo. "Prostitution." In *Handbook to Medieval Sexuality,* eds. Vern L. Bullough and James Brundage. New York: Routledge, 1999.

Karras, Ruth Mazo. *Sexuality in Medieval Europe: Do Onto Others*. London: Routledge, 2005.

Kates, Gary. *Monsieur d'Eon is a Woman,* rev. ed. Baltimore: Johns Hopkins University Press, 2001.

Kelly, Henry Ansgar. "Bishop, Prioress, and Bawd in the Stews of Southwark." *Speculum* 75 (2000): 344.

Kendrick, Walter. *The Secret Museum: Pornography in Modern Culture*. Berkeley: University of California Press, 1987.

Kertzer, David I. and Barbigli, Marzio. *The History of the European Family: Family Life in the Long Nineteenth Century*. New Haven: Yale University Press, 2002.

Khadduri, Majid. *Law in the Middle East,* vol. 1. Washington, D.C.: Middle East Institute, 1955.

King, P.D. *Law and Society in the Visigothic Kingdom*. Cambridge: Cambridge University Press, 1972.

Kingdom, Robert M. *Adultery and Divorce in Calvin's Geneva*. Cambridge: Harvard University Press, 1995.

Kingdom, Robert M. "The Control of Morals in Calvin's Geneva." In

The Social History of the Reformation, eds. Lawrence P. Buck and Jonathan W. Zophy. Columbus: Ohio State University Press, 1972.

Kirk, Neville. *The Growth of Working Class Reformism in Mid-Victorian England.* New York: Taylor & Francis, 1985.

Knust, Jennifer. *Abandoned to Lust: Sexual Slander and Ancient Christianity.* New York: Columbia University Press, 2006.

Kon, Igor S. *The Sexual Revolution in Russia,* trans. James Riordan. New York: The Free Press, 1995.

Kristeller, Paul Oskar. *Greek Philosophers of the Hellenistic Age,* trans. Gregory Woods. New York: Columbia University Press, 1991.

Lactantius, *Divine Institutes,* trans. Mary F. McDonald. Washington, D.C.: Catholic University of America, 1964.

Laiou, A.E. *Mariage, Amour et Parenté à Byzance aux Xie-XIII3 Siècles,* Travaux et Mémoires Monographies 7. Paris, 1992.

Lambert, Michael. *Medieval Heresy.* New York: Holmes and Meier, 1977.

Lambert, Royston. *Beloved and God: The Story of Hadrian and Antinous.* New York: Viking, 1984.

Langlands, Rebecca. *Sexual Morality in Ancient Rome.* Cambridge: Cambridge University Press, 2006.

Laqueur, Thomas. *Solitary Sex: A Cultural History of Masturbation.* New York: Zone Books, 2003.

Lauxtermann, Marc. "The Erotic Muse." In *Desire and Denial in Byzantium,* ed. Liz James. London: Ashgate, 1999.

Lawrence, C.H. *Medieval Monasticism.* London: Longman, 1984.

Le Bras, Gabriel. "Canon Law." In *The Legacy of the Middle Ages,* eds. G.C. Crump and E.F. Jacob. New York: Oxford University Press, 1959.

Lemay, Helen Rodnite. "Human Sexuality in 12th to 15th Century Scientific Writings." In *Sexual Practices and the Medieval Church.* New York: Prometheus Books, 1982.

Leupp, Gary. *Male Colors: The Construction of Homosexuality in Tokugawa Japan.* Berkeley: University of California Press, 1997.

Levey, Martin and Souryal, Safwat S. "Galen's On The Secrets of Women and On the Secrets of Men: A Contribution to the History of Arabic Pharmacology." *Janus* 55 (1968): 210–1.

Levin, Eve. *Sex and Society in the World of the Orthodox Slavs.* Ithaca: Cornell University Press, 1989.

Levy, L.W. "Accusatorial and Inquisitorial Systems of Criminal Procedure: The Beginnings." In *Freedom and Reform,* eds. H. Hyman and L. Levy. New York: Harper and Row, 1967.

Lieu, Samuel N.C. *Manicheanism in the Later Roman Empire and Medieval China.* Tübingen: Gulde-Druck, 1992.

Liliequist, Jonas. "State Policy, Popular Discourse, and the Silence on Homosexual Acts in Early Modern Sweden." In *Scandinavian Homosexualities: Essays on Gay and Lesbian Studies,* ed. Jan Löfström. New York: Haworth Press, 1998.

Lilja, Saara. *Homosexuality in Republican and Augustan Rome.* Helsinki: Societas Scientiarum Fennica, 1983.

Liu, Benjamin. *Medieval Joke Poetry.* Cambridge: Harvard University Press, 2004.

Livy. *The History of Rome, Books 1–5,* trans. Valerie M. Hope. Indianapolis: Hackett, 2004.

Löfström, Jan. *Scandinavian Homosexualities: Essays on Gay and Lesbian Studies.* New York: Psychology Press, 1998.

London, John. *Theatre Under the Nazis.* Manchester: Manchester University Press, 2000.

Lord, Evelyn. *The Hell-Fire Clubs.* New Haven: Yale University Press, 2008.

Luddy, Maria. *Prostitution and Irish Society, 1800–1940.* Cambridge: Cambridge University Press, 2007.

Luther, Martin. *What Luther Says,* ed. and trans. Ewald M. Plass. St. Louis: Concordia Press, 1959.

Luther, Martin. *Works,* ed. and trans. Jaroslav Pelikan. St. Louis: Concordia, 1955–86.

Maccoby, Hyam. *Ritual and Morality.* Cambridge: Cambridge University Press, 1999.

MacCulloch, Diarmaid. *The Reformation: A History.* New York: Penguin, 2005.

Macdonald, Margaret Y. "Early Christian Women Married To Non-Believers." *Sciences religieuses* 19 (1990): 221–34.

MacMullen, Ramsey. *Christianizing the Roman Empire.* New Haven: Yale University Press, 1986.

Macnama, Ellen. *Everyday Life of the Etruscans.* New York: Putnam's Sons, 1973.

Mandeville, Bernard. *The Fable of the Bees: Or, Private Vices, Publick Benefits,* 2. vols. Oxford: Clarendon Press, 1924.

Manning, Patricia. *Voicing Dissent in Seventeenth-Century Spain: Inquisition, Social Criticism and Theology in the Case of El Criticón.* London: Brill, 2009.

Marcus, Steven. *The Other Victorians.* New York: Basic Books, 1964.

Marquardt, Patricia. "Hesiod's Ambiguous View of Woman." *Classical Philology* 77.4 (1982): 283–91.

Martens, John W. *One God, One Law: Philo of Alexandria and Greco-Roman Law.* Boston: Brill Academic, 2003.

Martial, *Epigrams,* trans. James Michie. New York: Random House, 1978.

Mason, Michael. *The Making of Victorian Sexual Attitudes.* New York: Oxford University Press, 1994.

Masson, Georgia. *Queen Christina.* New York: Farrar, Straus, and Giroux, 1968.

Matheron, Alexandre. "Spinoza and Sexuality." In *Feminist Interpretations of Spinoza,* ed. Moira Gatens. University Park: Penn State University Press, 2009.

McCall, Andrew. *The Medieval Underworld,* 2nd ed. New York: Barnes & Noble, 1993),

McElvaine, Robert S. *Grand Theft Jesus: The Hijacking of Religion in America,* 2nd ed. New York: Three Rivers Press, 2009.

McGinn, Thomas A.J. *Prostitution, Sexuality, and The Law in Ancient Rome.* New York: Oxford University Press, 1998.

McKenna, Neil. *The Secret Life of Oscar Wilde.* New York: Basic Books, 2005.

McLaren, Angus. *A History of Contraception: From Antiquity to the Present Day.* London: Basil Blackwell, 1990.

McLaren, Angus. "Sex and Socialism: The Opposition of the French Left to Birth Control in the Nineteenth Century." *Journal of the History of Ideas* 37. 3 (Jul.–Sep., 1976): 475–92.

McMahon, Darrin M. *Enemies of the*

Enlightenment. New York: Oxford University Press, 2001.

McMillan, James F. *Housewife or Harlot*. Sussex: Harvester Press, 1981.

McNamara, Jo Ann. *Sisters in Arms*. Cambridge: Harvard University Press, 1996.

Mendell, Clarence W. *Tacitus: The Man and His Work*. New Haven: Yale University Press, 1957.

Merrick, Jeffrey, and Regan, Bryant T., eds. *Homosexuality in Early Modern France: A Documentary Collection*. New York: Oxford University Press, 2001.

Merrick, Jeffrey, and Regan, Bryant T., eds. *Homosexuality in Modern France*. New York: Oxford University Press, 1996.

Meyerson, Mark D. *The Muslims of Valencia in the age of Fernando and Isabel: Between Coexistence and Crusade*. Berkeley: University of California Press, 1991.

Mikelson, Jon D. *Athenian Popular Religion*. Chapel Hill: University of North Carolina Press, 1983.

Miller, James E. "The Practices of Romans 1:26: Homosexual or Heterosexual?" *Novum Testamentum* 37, 1 (Jan. 1997): 1–11.

Miller, James Maxwell. *A History of Ancient Israel and Judah*. Philadelphia: Westminster Press, 1986.

Miller, Michael B. *The Bon Marché: Bourgeois Culture and the Department Store, 1869–1920*. Princeton, NJ: Princeton University Press, 1981.

Miller, Patricia Cox, ed. *Women in Early Christianity: Translations from Greek Texts*. Washington, D.C.: Catholic University of America Press, 2005.

Molvaer, Raedulf K. "St. Paul's views on Sex According to 1 Corinthians 7:9 & 36–39." *Studia Theologica* 58 (2004): 45–59.

Montagu, Lady Mary. *Turkish Embassy Letters*. Athens, GA: Broadview Press, 1993.

Monter, E. William. *Frontiers of Heresy: The Spanish Inquisition from the Basque Lands to Sicily*. Cambridge: Cambridge University Press, 1990.

Monter, E. William. "Sodomy and Heresy in Early Modern Switzerland." In *The Gay Past*, eds. Salvatore J. Licata and Robert P. Peterson. Binghamton, NY: Harrington Park Press, 1985.

Morton, Frederic. *A Nervous Splendor, Vienna 1888/1889*. Boston: Little, Brown, 1979.

Mott, Luiz. "Crypto-Sodomites in Seventeenth Century Brazil." In *Infamous Desire: Male Homosexuality in Colonial Latin America*, ed. Pete Sigal. Chicago: University of Chicago Press, 2003.

Mott, Luiz, and Assunção, Aroldo. "Love's Labors Lost: Five Letters from a Seventeenth-Century Portuguese Sodomite." In *The Pursuit of Sodomy: Male Homosexuality in Renaissance and Enlightenment Europe*, eds. Kent Gerard and Gert Hekma. New York: Harrington Park Press, 1989.

Moulton, Ian Frederick. *Before Pornography: Erotic Writing in Early Modern England*. Oxford University Press, 2005.

Mungello, D.E. *The Great Encounter of China and the West, 1500–1800*. Lanham, MD: Rowman & Littlefield, 1999.

Mungello, David E. "Leibniz's Interpretation of Neo-Confucianism." *Philosophy East and West* 20:1 (1971): 3–22.

Murray, Jacqueline, and Eisenbacher, Konred, eds. *Desire and Discipline*. Toronto: University of Toronto Press, 1996.

Murray, Stephen O. and Roscoe, Will. *Islamic Homosexualities: Culture, History, and Literature*. New York: New York University Press, 1997.

Mussallam, B.F. *Sex and Society in Islam: Birth Control Before the Nineteenth Century*. Cambridge: Cambridge University Press, 1983.

Namias, June. *White Captives: Gender and Ethnicity on the American Frontier*. Chapel Hill: University of North Carolina Press, 1993.

Nash, Gary B. "The Hidden History of Mestizo America." In *Sex, Love, Race: Crossing Boundaries in North American History*, ed. Martha Hodes. New York: New York University Press, 1999.

Nissinen, Martii. *Homoeroticism in the Biblical World: A Historical Perspective*. Minneapolis: Fortress Press, 1998.

Noel, Charles C. "Missionary Preachers in Spain: Teaching Social Virtue in the Eighteenth Century." *The American Historical Review* 90.4 (1985): 866–892.

Noonan, John Thomas. *Contraception: A History of Its Treatment by the Catholic Theologians and Canonists*. Cambridge: Belknap Press, 1986.

Norton, Rictor. *Mother Clap's Molly House*. London: Gay Men's Press, 1992.

Norton, Rictor, and Louis Crompton. "Gay Genocide from Leviticus to Hitler." *The Gay Academic* 7 (1978): 73–91.

Nykl, Alois Richard. *Hispano-Arabic Poetry and Its Relations with the Old Provençal Troubadours*. New York: Hispanic Society of America, 1970.

O'Callaghan, Joseph F. "Mudejars of Castile and Portugal." In *Muslims Under Christian Rule, 1100–1500*, ed. James M. Powell. Princeton, NJ: Princeton University Press, 1990.

O'Corráin, Donnchadh. *Marriage in Early Ireland*. Dublin: A. Cosgrove, 1985.

Offen, Karen. *European Feminisms, 1700—2000*. Stanford: Stanford University Press, 2000.

Ogden, Daniel. *Polygamy, Prostitutes, and Death*. Aberystwyth: Classical Press of Wales, 2000.

Olwyn, Saul M. "'And with a Male You Shall Not Lie the Lying down of a Woman': On the Meaning and Significance of Leviticus 18:22 and 20:13." *Journal of the History of Sexuality* 5 (1994).

Otis, Leah Lydia. *Prostitution in Medieval Society*. Chicago: University of Chicago Press, 1985, 2009.

Ozment, Steven. *When Fathers Ruled: Family Life in Reformation Europe*. Cambridge: Harvard University Press, 1983.

Parker, Holt N. "Sappho Schoolmistress." *Transactions of the American Philological Foundation* 123 (1993): 309–10.

Payer, Pierre. *Bridling Desire: Views of Sex in the Later Middle Ages*. Toronto: University of Toronto Press, 1993.

Payer, Pierre. *Sex and the Penitentials: The Development of a Sexual Code, 550—1150*. Toronto: University of Toronto Press, 1984.

Peakman, Julie. *Lascivious Bodies: A Sexual History of the Eighteenth Century*. London: Atlantis Books, 2004.

Pequigney, Joseph. "Sodomy in Dante's Inferno and Purgatorio." *Representations*, 36 (1991): 22–42.

Percy, William Armstrong. *Pederasty and Pedagogy in Archaic Greece*.

Urbana: University of Illinois Press, 1995.

Percy, William Armstrong. "Reconsiderations About Greek Homosexualities." In *Same-Sex Desire and Love in Greco-Roman Antiquity and in the Classical Tradition of the West,* eds. Beert C. Verstraete, Vernon Provenca, et al. New York: Harrington Park Press, 2005.

Perry, Mary Elizabeth. *Gender and Disorder in Early Modern Seville.* Princeton, NJ: Princeton University Press, 1990.

Perry, Mary Elizabeth. "The Nefarious Sin in Early Modern Seville." In *The Pursuit of Sodomy: Male Homosexuality in Renaissance and Enlightenment Europe,* eds. Kent Gerard and Gert Hekma. New York: Harrington Park Press, 1989.

Phegley, Jennifer. *Courtship and Marriage in Victorian England.* Santa Barbara: ABC-CLIO, 2011.

Phipps, William E. *Clerical Celibacy: The Heritage.* New York: Continuum, 2004.

Pierce, Leslie. *The Imperial Harem: Women and Sovereignty in the Ottoman Empire.* New York: Oxford University Press, 1993.

Pierce, Leslie. *Morality Tales: Law and Gender in the Ottoman Court of Aintab.* Berkeley: University of California Press, 1995.

Plant, Richard. *The Pink Triangle: The Nazi War Against Homosexuals.* New York: New Republic, 1986.

Plotinus, *Enneads,* trans. Stephen A. McKenna and B.S. Page. London: Faber, 1957.

Plummer, Charles. *Historia Ecclesiastica gentis Anglorum.* Oxford, 1896.

Polizzoto, Lorenzo. *The Elect Nation: The Savonarolan Movement in Florence, 1494–1545.* Oxford: Clarendon, 1994.

Pomeroy, Sarah. *Goddesses, Whores, Wives, and Slaves: Women in Classical Antiquity,* 2nd ed. New York: Schocken, 1995.

Porter, Roy. "Mixed Feelings: The Enlightenment And Sexuality In Eighteenth-Century Britain." In *Sexuality in Eighteenth-Century Britain,* ed. Paul-Gabriel Boucé. Manchester: Manchester University Press, 1982.

Porter, Roy, and Lesley Hall. *The Facts of Life: The Creation of Sexual Knowledge in Britain, 1650–1950.* New Haven: Yale University Press, 1995.

Poska, Allyson M. *Regulating the People: The Catholic Reformation in Seventeenth Century Spain.* Leiden: Brill, 1998.

Powers, D. "Women and Divorce in the Islamic West: Three Cases." *Hawwa* 1 (2003): 29–45.

Price, Huw. *Native Law and the Church in Medieval Wales.* London: Clarendon Press, 1993.

Procopius, *The Anecdota or Secret History,* trans. H.B. Dewing. Cambridge: Harvard University Press, 1935.

Psellus, Michael. *Chronographia,* trans. E.R.A. Sewter. New Haven: Yale University Press, 1953.

Pseudo-Lucian, *Affairs of the Heart,* trans. M.D. McLeod. Cambridge: Harvard University Press, 1967.

Puff, Helmut. "Female Sodomy: The Trial of Katherina Herzeldorfer (1477)." *Journal of Medieval and Early Modern Studies* 30 (2000): 41–61

Puff, Helmut. *Sodomy in Reformation Germany and Switzerland, 1400–1600.* Chicago: University of Chicago Press, 2003.

Pushkareva, Natalia. *Women in Russian History,* trans. Eve Levin. Armonk, NY: M.E. Sharpe, 1997.

Rabelais, François. *Complete Works,* trans. Donald M. Frame. Berkeley: University of California Press, 1999.

Rapaport, Chaim. *Judaism and Homosexuality, An Authentic Orthodox View.* Portland, OR: Valentine Mitchell, 2004.

Rapoport, Yosef. *Marriage, Money, and Divorce in Medieval Islamic Society.* Cambridge: Cambridge University Press, 2005.

Reed, Matt T. "From Aliéné To Dégénéré: Moral Agency and the Psychiatric Imagination in Nineteenth-Century France." In *Confronting Modernity in Fin-de-Siècle France: Bodies, Minds and Gender,* eds. Christopher E. Forth and Elinor Accampo. New York: Palgrave Macmillan, 2010.

Ricaut, Paul *The Present State of the Ottoman Empire.* New York: Arno Press, 1971.

Richard, Charles-Louis. *Exposition de la doctrine des philosophes modernes.* Lille, 1785.

Richards, Jeffrey. *Sex, Dissidence, and Damnation: Minority Groups in the Middle Ages.* London: Psychology Press, 1994.

Richelieu, Duc de, Armand de Vignerot du Plessis. *Mémoires,* ed. J.L. Giraud Solaire. Paris: Joseph de Boffe et al., 1790.

Richlin, Amy. "Not Before Homosexuality: The Material Reality of the Cinaedus and the Roman Law against Love between Men." *Journal of the History of Sexuality,* 3.4 (1993): 528–71.

Riddle, John M. *Contraception and Abortion from the Ancient World to the Renaissance.* Cambridge: Harvard University Press, 1992.

Riddle, John M. "Contraception and Early Abortion in the Middle Ages." In *A Handbook to Medieval Sexuality,* eds. James Brundage and Vern Bullough. New York: Garland, 1996.

Riddle, John M. *Eve's Herbs: A History of Contraception and Abortion in the West.* Cambridge: Harvard University Press, 1997.

Ringdal, Nils Johan. *Love for Sale: A World History of Prostitution.* New York: Grove Press, 1985.

Rix, Robert. "William Blake and the Radical Swedenborgians." http://www.esoteric.msu.edu/VolumeV/Blake.htm.

Rocke, Michael. *Forbidden Friendships.* New York: Oxford University Press, 1996.

Roper, Lyndal. "Discipline and Responsibility: Prostitution and the Reformation in Augsburg." *History Workshop* 19 (1985): 3–28.

Roper, Lyndal. "Sexual Utopianism in the German Reformation." *Journal of Ecclesiastical History* 42.3 (1991): 399–403.

Rosario, Vernon A. *The Erotic Imagination: French Histories of Perversity.* New York: Oxford University Press, 1997.

Rosemary Rader, *Breaking the Boundaries: Male/Female Friendship in Early Christian Communities.* Mahwah, NJ: Paulist Press, 1983.

Rossiaud, Jacques. *Medieval Prostitution.* London: Blackwell, 1988.

Roswitha. *The Plays of Roswitha,* ed. and trans. Israel Gollancz. London: Chatto & Windus, 1923.

Rousseau, G.S. "The Sorrows of Priapus." In *Sexual Underworlds of the Enlightenment,* eds. G.S. Rousseau and Roy Porter. Chapel

Hill: University of North Carolina Press, 1988.

Rousseau, Jean-Jacques. *Politics and the Arts: Letter to M. d'Alembert on the Theatre*, trans. Allan Bloom. Ithaca: Cornell University Press, 1968.

Rowson, Everett K. "The Categorization of Gender and Sexual Irregularity in Medieval Arabic Vice Lists." In *Body Guards: The Cultural Politics of Ambiguity*, eds. Julia Epstein and Kristina Straub. New York and London: Routledge, 1991.

Ruiz, Juan. *Book of Good Love*, trans. Elisha Kent Kane. Chapel Hill: University of North Carolina Press, 1968.

Rupp, Leila J. *Sapphistries: A Global History of Love Between Women*. New York: New York University Press, 1999.

Ryan, F.X. "The Lex Scantinia and the Prosecution of Censors and Aediles." *Classical Philology* 89.2 (1994): 159–62.

Saint-Saëns, Alain. "'It is Not A Sin!': Making Love according to the Spaniards in Early Modern Spain." In *Sex and Love in Golden Age Spain*. New York: University Press of the South, 1996.

Sappho, *A Garland: The Poems and Fragments of Sappho*, trans. Jim Powell. New York: Ferrar, Straus, Giroux, 1993.

Sargent, Bernard. *Homosexuality in Greek Myth*. Boston: Beacon Press, 1984.

Sariyannis, Marinos. "Prostitution in Ottoman Istanbul Late Sixteenth-Early Eighteenth Century." *Turcica*, 40 (2008): 37–65.

Savonarola, Girolamo. *Selected Writings*, trans. Anne Borelli. New Haven: Yale University Press, 2006.

Sawyer, Birgit and B.T. *Medieval Scandinavia: From Conversion to Reformation, 800–1500*. Minneapolis: University of Minnesota Press, 1993.

Scarr, Ruth. *Fatal Purity: Robespierre and the French Revolution*. New York: Henry Holt and Company, 2006.

Schama, Simon. *Citizens: A Chronicle of the French Revolution*. New York: Vintage, 1989.

Schlesinger, Roger. *The Impact of the New World, 1492–1650*. Wheeling, IL: Harlan Davidson Inc., 1996.

Scott, Roger D. "Malalas, The Secret History, and Justinian's Propaganda." *Dumbarton Oaks Papers* 39 (1985): 104.

Segal, Alan. *Life After Death: A History of the Afterlife*. New York: Doubleday, 2004.

Semerdjian, Elsye. "Sinful Professions: Illegal Occupations of Women in Ottoman Aleppo, Syria." *Hawwa* 1 (2003): 60–85.

Shapiro, Norman R., Vadsworth, James B., and Bowden, Betsy., eds. *The Comedy of Eros: Medieval French Guides to the Art of Love*. Urbana-Champaign: University of Illinois Press, 1971.

Sigal, Pete. *Infamous Desire*. Chicago: University of Chicago Press, 2003.

Sigel, Lisa Z. *Governing Pleasures: Pornography and Social Change in England, 1815—1914*. New Brunswick, NJ: Rutgers University Press, 2007.

Sigel, Lisa Z., ed. *International Exposure: Perspectives On Modern European Pornography, 1800–2000*. New Brunswick, NJ: Rutgers University Press, 2005.

Singer, Irving. *The Nature of Love*. Cambridge, MA: MIT Press, 1980.

Sison, Lydia. *Doctor of Love: James Graham and his Celestial Bed*. London: Alma Books, 2008.

Skinner, Patricia. *Women in Medieval Italian Society*. Upper Saddle River, NJ: Prentice Hall, 1998.

Smith, Nathaniel. "Games Troubadours Play." In *Poetics of Love in the Middle Ages*, eds. Moshé Lazar and Norris J. Lacy. Fairfax, VA: George Mason University Press, 1989.

Smythe, Dion C. "Same-Sex Desire." In *Desire and Denial in Byzantium*, ed. Liz James. Aldershot, 1999.

Socolow, Susan Migden. *The Women of Colonial Latin America*. Cambridge: Cambridge University Press, 2000.

Sørenson, Aage B. "On Kings, Pietism, and Rent-Seeking in Scandinavian Welfare States." *Arts Sociologica* 41.4 (1998.

Spence, Jonathan. *The Memory Palace of Matteo Ricci*. New York: Viking, 1984.

Steakley, James D. "Sodomy in Enlightenment Prussia: From Execution to Suicide." In *The Pursuit of Sodomy: Male Homosexuality in Renaissance and Enlightenment Europe*, eds. Kent Gerard and Gert Hekma. New York: Harrington Park Press, 1989.

Stehle, Eva. "Emotional Sensuality, Poetic Sense: A Response To Hallett On Sappho." *Signs* 4 (1979): 464–71.

Stehling, Thomas. *Medieval Latin Poems of Love and Friendship*. New York: Garland, 1984.

Stein, Claudia. "The Birth of Biopower in Eighteenth-Century Germany." *Medical History* 55.3 (2011): 331–7.

Stengers, Jean. *Masturbation: History of a Great Terror*, trans. Kathryn A. Hoffman. New York: Palgrave, 2001.

Stern, Samuel Miklos. *Hispano-Arabic Strophic Poetry*. New York: Oxford University Press, 1974.

Stewart, Desmond. *The Burning of the Vanities: Savonarola and the Borgia Pope*. Stroud: Sutton, 2006.

Stollhens, Cynthia. "Michelangelo's Nude Saint Catherine of Alexandria." *Women's Art Journal* 19.1 (1998): 26–30.

Stow, Kenneth. *Alienated Minority: The Jews of Medieval Latin Europe*. Cambridge: Harvard University Press, 1998.

Strabo, trans. Horace Leonard Jones. Cambridge: Harvard University Press, 1966–70.

Strother, Darci L. *Family Matters: A Study of On- and Off-Stage Marriage and Family Relations in Seventeenth-Century Spain*. New York: Peter Lang, 1999.

Szesnet, Holger. "Philo and Female Homoeroticism: Philo's Use of Gunandros and Recent Work On Tribades." *Journal for the Study of Judaism* 30.2 (1999): 140–7.

Talvacchia, Bette. *Taking Positions: On the Erotic in Renaissance Culture*. Princeton, NJ: Princeton University Press, 1999.

Tamagne, Florence. *A History of Homosexuality in Europe, Volume II, Berlin, London, Paris, 1919–1939*. New York: Algora Publishing, 2004.

Taylor, Keith. *The Political Ideas of the Utopian Socialists*. London: Frank Cass, 1982.

Taylor, Scott K. *Honor and Violence in Golden Age Spain*. New Haven: Yale University Press, 2008.

Taylor, Timothy. *The Prehistory of Sexuality: Four Million Years of Human Sexual Culture*. New York: Bantam, 1997.

The Anti-Nicene Fathers, vol. 3, eds. Alexander Roberts and James Donaldson. Edinburgh: T&T Clarke, 1873.

The Apocryphal New Testament, ed. and trans. M.R. James. Oxford: Clarendon Press, 1924.

The Civil Law, Including the Twelve Tables, trans. Samuel Parsons Scott. New York: AMS Press, 1973.

The Gnostic Scriptures, ed. Bentley Layton. New York: Anchor Bible Reference Library, 1995.

Theocritus, trans. Anna Rist. Chapel Hill: University of North Carolina Press, 1978.

Thomas Aquinas. *Summa theologiae,* trans. Thomas Gilby et al. New York: McGraw-Hill, 1964–73.

Thompson, E.P. *Customs in Common.* London: New Press, 1993.

Todd, Margo. *Christian Humanism and the Puritan Social Order.* Cambridge: Cambridge University Press, 1987.

Tomkins, Stephen. *William Wilberforce: A Biography.* Oxford: Lion, 2007.

Topsfield, L.T. *Troubadours and Love.* Cambridge: Cambridge University Press, 1975.

Traer, James F. *Marriage and the Family in Eighteenth-Century France.* Ithaca: Cornell University Press, 1980.

Trexler, Richard C. *Sex and Conquest.* Ithaca: Cornell University Press, 1995.

Turner, David. "Adultery: Comparative History." In *The Oxford Encyclopedia of Women in World History.* New York: Oxford University Press, 2008.

Turner, James. *Schooling Sex.* New York: Oxford University Press, 2003.

Ulrich von Lichtenstein, *Service of Ladies,* trans. J.W. Thomas. Chapel Hill, NC: University of North Carolina Press, 1969.

Uluçay, M. Çağatay. "The Harem in the XVIIIth Century." *Akten des Vierundzwanzigsten Internationalen Orientalisten-Kongress, München, 28 August Bis 4. September 1957.*

Valantasis, Richard, ed. *Religions in Late Antiquity in Practice.* Princeton, NJ: Princeton University Press, 2000.

Vollendorf, Lisa. *The Lives of Women: A New History of Inquisitional Spain.* Vanderbilt University Press, 2005.

von Rosen, Wilhelm. "Sodomy in Early Modern Denmark: A Crime Without Victims." In *The Pursuit of Sodomy: Male Homosexuality in Renaissance and Enlightenment Europe,* eds. Kent Gerard and Gert Hekma. New York: Harrington Park Press, 1989.

von Rossen, Wilhelm. "Denmark." In *Queer Masculinities, 1550–1800.* New York: Palgrave Macmillan, 2006.

Ward, Roy B. "Why Unnatural? The Traditions Behind Romans 1:26–7." *Harvard Theological Review* 90.3 (1997): 263–84.

Watanabe, Tsuneo and Iwata, Jun'ichi. *The Love of the Samurai: A Thousand Years of Japanese Homosexuality,* trans. D.R. Roberts. London: GMP Publishers, 1990.

Weeks, Jeffrey. *Sex, Politics, and Society: The Regulation of Sexuality Since 1880.* New York: Longman, 1989.

Weisner-Hanks, Merry. *Christianity and Sexuality in the Early Modern World: Regulating Desire, Reforming Practice.* New York: Routledge, 2010.

Wemple, Suzanne. *Women in Frankish Society: Marriage and the Cloister.* Philadelphia: University of Pennsylvania Press, 1981.

West, David. *Reason and Sexuality in Western Thought.* Cambridge: Polity Press, 2005.

William IX, , trans. James H. Donalson, "I Set Myself to Love." colecizj.easyvserver.com/virbooks.htm.

Williams, George Huntston. *The Radical Reformation.* Kirksville, MO: Sixteenth Century Journal Publishers, 1992.

Williams, Stephen. *Diocletian and the Roman Recovery.* Boston: Belknap Press, 1985.

Williams, Walter L. *Sexual Diversity in Native American Culture.* Boston: Beacon Press, 1986.

Wohl, Victoria. *Love Among the Ruins: The Erotics of Democracy in Classical Athens.* Princeton, NJ: Princeton University Press, 2002.

Wood, Neal. *Cicero's Social and Political Thought.* Berkeley: University of California Press, 1988.

Yuzgan, Arsian. "Homosexuality and Police Terror in Turkey." *Journal of Homosexuality* 24.3–4 (1993): 159–70.

Ze'evi, Dr'or. "Hiding Sexuality: The Disappearance of Sexual Discourse in the Late Ottoman Middle East." *Social Analysis*, 49.2 (2005): 42–53.

Ze'Vi, Dror. *Producing Desire: Changing Sexual Discourse in the Ottoman Middle East, 1500–1900.* Berkeley: University of California Press, 2006.

Zilfi, Madeline C., ed. *Woman in the Ottoman Empire.* Leiden: Brill, 1997.

Index

abortion 53, 83, 85, 98, 166, 231–232
Adam and Eve 13–14, 65, 76, 154, 176
adultery 15–16, 21–2, 31, 32, 42, 43, 58, 67, 71, 75, 98, 102, 103, 110, 140, 151, 157, 159, 160, *passim*; double standard 9, 60, 67, 68, 71, 74, 102, 135, 153
afterlife 53–55, 67–68, 132, 136
Americas 175–180
Aquinas, Thomas 116–117
Aristophanes 26–27, 31
Aristotle 29, 30
Augustine of Hippo 39, 51–2, 63, 76–77, 79, 80, 94, 97, 109, 116, 127
Augustus 42, 43, 44–45, 69

Behn, Aphra 175, 187
Bentham, Jeremy 196
bigamy *see* polygamy
birth control pill 245

Calvin, Jean 152, 159–161
Cartesianism *see* Descartes, René
celibacy 52–53, 66, 75–76, 77–79, 89–92, 112–113, 152, 194
Christianity 56–79, 89–101, 109–117, *passim*; Catholicism 163–170; Orthodox 109, 120–121, 162–163; Protestantism 150–162, 170–171
Clement of Alexandria 36, 66, 67, 69, 75, 116
Communism 241–242, 243–244, 245
Constantine I 56, 69, 70–71, 81
contraception 230–231; *see also* birth control pill
Cynicism 35, 36, 53

Dante 132
Descartes, René 184–185, 186–187
Diderot, Denis 193–194, 215
divorce 9, 15, 30, 31, 32, 37, 41, 67, 71–72, 75, 85–86, 88, 118, 121, 141, 155, 156, 160, *passim*

East Asia 180–184
Epicureanism 35–6
eros 20–21
eugenics 239–240
Eve *see* Adam and Eve

Foucault, Michel 3–4, 18, 45, 190, 191, 209
French Revolution 218–220

Graham, James 206–207

Halperin, David 5, 45
harem (Ottoman Empire) 144–147
Hebrew Bible 7–17, 67
Hell *see* afterlife
Hesiod 22–23
HIV/AIDS 246
Homer 20–22, 58
homosexuality, sodomy 10–13, 24–30, 35, 45–50, 59, 72–73, 87, 94, 98–99, 100–101, 103–104, 105–106, 119, 129–134, 142–144, 151, 157–158, 160–161, 192–193, 194, 200, 212–215, 228, 230–237, *passim*
hybris 30–31

illicit sex *see* nonmarital sex
incest 29, 32, 42, 58, 88, 99, 110, 114, 117, 141, 218
Islam 101–106, 117, 140, 192

Jesus Christ 60–61, 63, 64, 65–66, 67, 68, 81, 98, 137, 183, 205
Judaism 7–17, 57–60, 117–119, 227
Justinian I 81–84

Kant, Immanuel 189, 196, 198

Lateran Council (1215) 111
lesbianism *see* homosexuality
lex Julia 44–45, 48, 70
literature: medical and advice 205–208, 229; romantic and erotic 8–9, 96, 104–105, 121–126, 172–175, 187–188, 215–218, 237–239
Lucretia 38–39
Luther, Martin 149, 151–152

marriage 9–10, 32, 41, 65–66, 70–71, 74, 75–77, 88, 111, 118, 140–142, 153–154, 156, 192, *passim*; *see also* divorce
masturbation 98–99, 207–208, 232–233
Montesquieu, Baron de, Charles Louis de Secondat 192–193

Napoleon Bonaparte 218–221
Nazism 244–245
New Testament 60–64
nonmarital sex 15, 30–31, 32, 40, 70, 87–88, 93–94, 98, 102, 103, 110, 120, 151, 159, *passim*

Old Testament *see* Hebrew Bible
Origen 65, 68

Paul 14, 57, 61–64, 67, 68, 72, 102, 110
pederasty 24–30, 35, 59, 142–143; *see also* homosexuality
penitentials 95, 97–99
Philo 58–60
Pizan, Christine de 115–116

Plato 24, 26; *Laws* 28–9, 32, 36; *Republic* 19, 32
polygamy 41–2, 85, 95–96, 102, 154–155, 170–171, 228
pornography *see* literature, romantic and erotic
promiscuity *see* nonmarital sex
prostitution 14, 31–32, 35, 50–51, 89, 99–100, 102–103, 126–129, 147–148, 156, 199, 200–201, 226–227, *passim*
Puff, Helmut 5
Pythagoreanism 20

rape 15, 38–39, 151
Rochester, Duke of, John Wilmot 187–188
Rousseau, Jean-Jacques 4

Sade, Marquis de, Donatien-Alphonse-François 196–199
Sappho 23
Savonarola 137–138
Society for the Reformation of Manners 204–205
Socrates 24, 26, 28, 32, 58
Sodom and Gomorrah 11, 15, 59–60, 61, 64, 75, 82, 101, 104, 129, 130, 132
sodomy *see* homosexuality
Song of Solomon 8–9
Spinoza, Baruch 185–186
Stoicism 35, 49–50, 52, 58–9
syphilis 154

Tertullian 65, 66, 67, 70, 75
Torah *see* Hebrew Bible

Trent, Council of (1545–1563) 163–164

Vestal Virgins 51–52
Victoria 225
virginity 9, 15, 85; *see also* celibacy
Voltaire 131, 192, 194

Xenophon 24, 26, 28, 31